ISBN 978-1-5279-9019-7
PIBN 10167565

ABRAHAM LINCOLN

AND

THE MEN OF HIS TIME

HIS CAUSE, HIS CHARACTER, AND
TRUE PLACE IN HISTORY

AND

THE MEN, STATESMEN, HEROES, PATRIOTS, WHO
FORMED THE ILLUSTRIOUS LEAGUE
ABOUT HIM

BY

ROBERT H. BROWNE

———

REVISED SECOND EDITION. ILLUSTRATED

———

IN TWO VOLUMES
VOLUME II

———

CHICAGO:
THE BLAKELY-OSWALD PRINTING COMPANY
1907

CONTENTS OF VOLUME II.

3

CONTENTS.

CHAPTER XXIX.

CHAPTER XXX.

CHAPTER XXXI.

CHAPTER XXXII.

CHAPTER XXXIII.

CHAPTER XXXIV.

CHAPTER XXXV.

CHAPTER XXXVI.

CHAPTER XXXVII.

CHAPTER XXXVIII.

CHAPTER XXXIX.

CHAPTER XL.

CHAPTER XLI.

CHAPTER XLII.

CHAPTER XLIII.

CHAPTER XLIV.

8 CONTENTS.

CONTENTS.

CHAPTER LII.

CHAPTER LIII.

CHAPTER LIV.

CHAPTER LV.

CHAPTER LVI.

ABRAHAM LINCOLN

AND

THE MEN OF HIS TIME.

CHAPTER XXVI.

SHORTLY after Wilson Shannon's arrival in the Territory of Kansas in September, 1855, the contest was carried on vigorously on both sides, and civil war existed in every inhabited part of it. Lawrence was held in a state of siege for several days. The inhabitants, knowing that they were vastly outnumbered, submitted to the search for arms, ammunition, and other plundering and pillaging, rather than attempt resistance at such unequal advantages. They did so, too, on Shannon's promises of protection. Shannon was entertained on his arrival in their best and most uproarious style by Atchison and his followers. They had denounced Reeder out of office, as they believed, and had not been backward in giving their opinions as to the kind of man to be sent as his successor, if one was sent. The truth was, they would have been entirely satisfied with no successor, but to continue with Secretary Woodson as acting governor, who was one of them, and as certain to execute their most devilish plans, as Atchison and Jefferson Davis were to make them.

The Administration would have been altogether willing for this, but public indignation was wrought up over
Reeder's removal and the deviltry of the border war. So
a reputable Democrat, who could be influenced and molded
to the liking of the slave extenders, was a necessity. Shannon was selected, after careful consideration of his disposition and qualifications, as the most willing and service-
able man they could get. This he proved to be for a time.
He was plastic, soft clay in their hands, pliable and un-
complaining, until he realized, in the spring of 1856, that
he was not expected to interfere with the operation of their
plans, and that if he did, they would soon be rid of him.
Finding that Atchison was really governor, no difference
who held the title, he resigned, and attempted to leave the
Territory, thoroughly disgusted, while Atchison, Woodson,
and their hordes were assembling for another raid against
the free State settlement of Lawrence. Before leaving, they
compelled him to assent to the mustering in, as Kansas
militia, all the armed Southern immigrants brought in, as
heretofore related, which Woodson took up at once and
completed. He had gained authority again, where he could
for a brief season play the willing agent and petty tyrant,
and, as he hoped, provoke the free State people to open
resistance of the authority of the United States. This, of
all things, these slavery leaders most desired, so that the
regular army might be used against them to their utter
and complete destruction.

The free State movement had been broken up, as much
as it could be by threats, writs issued, arrests made, and
the dispersion and scattering of the members wherever it
was possible. What was left of the free State Legislature
had, among other dispositions, adjourned in March to meet
again on the 4th of July, 1856, to receive the action of
Congress on their application for Statehood. In this situation, with Shannon fleeing and glad to be free of them,

Atchison and Woodson thought the time was opportune to provoke the free State people to resistance.

With a chance that they regarded almost a certainty, Woodson recited President Pierce's Proclamation. He issued his own proclamation, forbidding all persons claiming to have legislative power and authority, as aforesaid, from assembling, organizing, or acting in any legislative capacity whatever. Colonel Sumner, who had been assigned to duty by direction of General Scott, was a fair, impartial officer, and, so far, the friend of the free State people, and so desirous of peace that he determined to aid in a peaceful dispersion of the free State Legislature; but with these intentions, he was so limited by his instructions that there was nothing left for him to do but to disperse the unoffending body of men by armed force if they attempted any resistance. In this way Jefferson Davis used the army for the suppression of liberty and the dispersing of a peaceful body of "Squatter Sovereigns," exercising their rights to assemble, organize, and, as has been done over and over in our progress, petition Congress for admission as a State.

In this move, as in many others, Atchison and Woodson were playing against a man much better informed and with more than double their combined wisdom. The free State people gathered, but not in any public place. Robinson explained the situation, and disclosed the trap set for their destruction. Colonel Sumner fully understood it. The free State Legislature did not assemble at their regular place of meeting, but quietly separated. At noon, July 4th, Colonel Sumner lined up his dragoons in front of the free State Hall; but there was no free State Legislature there to disperse or disband, and nobody present for the dragoons to kill. Atchison, Woodson, and Jones were chagrined and humiliated again by Robinson.

Early in May, 1856, United States Marshal Donaldson took Buford's Southern men and several others, amount-

ing to five hundred, into his service as deputies. These
and Jones's posse, and a lot of the Missouri invaders, in
armed movement, laid siege to Lawrence the second time,
about May 1, 1856, under promise of protection of life
and property. The citizens, not being in condition to contend against such unequal forces, not having more than
two or three hundred men capable of making any kind
of defense, surrendered their arms and offered no resistance. Atchison arrived before the capitulation. As soon
as the arms were surrendered, the town was entered, pil-
laged, and almost destroyed. The Free State Hotel, Governor
Robinson's house, and two printing establishments were
burned, with many other buildings. The stores, shops,
mills, and many dwellings were robbed, and everything of
value taken that this invading, vandal horde desired to
take or destroy.

From this an aggravated stage of the war developed. Men
were called together in all the settlements to organize and
get into fighting shape in the shortest possible time, to
save their homes and help as they could to repel this Missouri and Federal office-holders' invasion. Money, arms,
and many other supplies were sent by the friends of the
oppressed and war-plundered people from all over the free
States. In a few weeks Lane and others had gathered together and armed a very determined force of several hundred, who, from that time forward, were the hope and
security of the free State people.

John Brown was attacked at Pottawatomie on May
26th. Five of the assailants were killed against his loss
of two or three. He was attacked again at Black Jack,
where he repulsed them again. This hostile condition lasted
until late in August. A marauding, pillaging, and destroying war was kept up as long as Woodson was acting governor, and the management of affairs in the Territory was
under the control of Atchison. His policy was the same

in this as against the free State Legislature. He expected
to carry on his invasion and outrages until the people became incensed and began armed resistance, when he would
call on the President to declare the Territory in a state
of rebellion. Woodson had done so in June. Under the
President's order they fully expected and intended to declare martial law, take military possession, and drive out
all the free State people under some pretext or other.

Shannon was awaiting removal, and in June tired of
his work. His negligence in trusting too much to Woodson resulted in civil war, which was in full and dreadful
progress before July. When he saw this fearful harvest
of the pillagers and marauders, with Lawrence smoking
in its ruins, although ready and anxious to leave, he sum-
moned courage to call on Colonel Sumner for United States
troops at Lawrence, Lecompton, and Topeka, to insure
"the safety of the citizens in both person and property."
The next day the outraged people of Lawrence, from out
the ruins and desolation of their helpless town, saw the
relief for which hitherto they had prayed in vain. Notwithstanding that the sacking of Lawrence had aroused
the passions of men, although peacefully inclined, the free
State people believed that the crime invited and would
bring the swift punishment it deserved. They began the
most active preparations for peace by driving out the worst
disturbers of it, those who had prevailed so long in the
war on the border. It was a game of house-burning,
guerilla-killing, and marauding of the free State people on
the part of the invaders; and guerilla hunting, destroying,
capturing, killing, and driving home the bandits on the part
of the settlers who had risen, in their wrath, to drive out
their murdering oppressors.

On June 4th, Shannon issued his proclamation "direct-
ing military organizations to disperse, without regard to
party names or distinctions," and called on Colonel Sumner

to enforce it. Sumner was a good man and a good soldier to the end, and wanted, just what all of pro-slaverydom did not want, peace; hence he went to work immediately and earnestly to enforce Shannon's orders. He at once disarmed the free State improvised militia, Brown, of Ossawatomie's companies, among the first, and liberated the prisoners of both sides. He drove Delegate Whitfield, militia General Coffee, Atchison, and his Westport clubs, and all the Missouri companies, bag, baggage, and plunder, back over the border peacefully, without firing a gun or wounding a man.

He stationed five companies along the border, and reported to Jefferson Davis, on June 23d, just what the Secretary did not want to hear, as follows: "I do not think there is an armed body of either party now in the Territory, with the exception, perhaps, of a few freebooters. My measures have necessarily borne hard against both parties, for both have, in many instances, been more or less wrong. The Missourians were perfectly satisfied so long as the troops were employed against the free State party, but when they found that I would be strictly impartial, that lawless mobs could no longer come from Missouri, and that their interference with the affairs of Kansas was brought to an end, then they immediately raised a hue and cry that they were oppressed by the United States troops."

The hue and cry, however, reached the War Department first, where it was much more heeded than Colonel Sumner's report of how he had dispersed and disarmed the contending forces, and brought peace where the worst form of pillaging and desultory war had been in unmolested progress. If further proof had been needed of the desire and purpose of the Pierce-Davis Administration, it was fully given in the action of the War Department in removing Colonel Sumner at once.

On June 23d, Sumner dated his report, and on June 27th he was relieved. The order was issued, and General P. F. Smith, an officer with well-known pro-slavery proclivities, was appointed his successor. It was a long, tedious route in those days from Washington to the border. Shannon had left the Territory disheartened and disgusted with the slave-leaders' designs, a resigned, removed Democrat, who could not serve the Administration and be an honest man at the same time. Woodson had succeeded him, and had proclaimed the free State Legislature out of existence. Colonel Sumner had peacefully dispersed it before he was aware of his supersedure for not violating the rights of the free State people and provoking them to armed resistance, as he was expected to do under his orders.

When General Smith was selected, General Scott knew very well that, although he was a pro-slavery man, he was, above all, an honest, courageous officer, and in no sense a border bandit. He knew him to be a man that would in no way cover up lawlessness or rascality, and Davis would find out again, as he had found out before, when he and Scott agreed on an officer to take command in this border war, that he was the very man whom Davis did not want. When all the men and officers get due credit for their peaceful, if not valiant work, in this border war against the pioneer settlers, General Scott will hold his high place among the friends of freedom for his ceaseless efforts to save the oppressed free settlers in Kansas.

The army had grown up, under his observation, like a child to manhood and age. He knew almost every officer in it, and knew them much better than any other; better than Davis did. Scott understood strategy and the craftiness that Davis so often mistook for it. Scott was immovably at the head of the army. Nothing less than death or disability could remove him, which Davis knew very well. Davis, as Secretary, could remove any officer, or as the President would have done at his bidding; but the general of the army, by the regulations and all precedents, must consent to the appointment, and could nominate successors until the Executive was satisfied.

Hence Davis played, through the four years, against Scott, to get a supple servant of the slave-power in Kansas in chief military command; but the old hero outwitted the artful Secretary every time. It will ever remain an example of party strength, discipline, and training, that such an unfit, weak, and shallow-minded man as Franklin Pierce defeated Scott in 1852, who was a citizen, soldier, and patriot, without a blot or scratch on his noble escutcheon, for almost two generations. The Higher Wisdom, that led men in that day, allowed the slave-leaders to work out the plan that wrought the destruction of their system a few years later.

The strength of a partly-free Democracy was tested in the corruption, faithlessness, and treason-breeding of two such Presidencies as those of Pierce and Buchanan. However, their plannings, plottings, and wretched derelictions of duty did not enable them to remove the old veteran. If they did defeat him for President in the madness of manufactured party strife in 1852, he was unbeatable in all their plans to force slavery on an unwilling. people. Scott kept an honest man in command, and in that way defeated all their schemes. He was in many ways a great man, and, although living through a period of great leaders and statesmen, he was, without doubt, one of the ablest and most reliable among our distinguished men.

When the plans were made to extend slavery into the Western Territories, which were no doubt begun as early as 1820, the slave-extenders had no intention of observing the limitations of the Missouri Compromise further than they were compelled to do as their interests changed.

The plans for slavery extension were always a generation ahead of the general information given to the public. For at least that length of time the skilled engineers and pioneers of the army, and an intelligent, well-trained body of men in and about the departments at Washington, knew very well that the "Plains," as they were called, west and southwest of the Missouri River, were fertile and productive far beyond any report ever made concerning them. They had annual production of plants, roots, and grasses that supported buffalo, elk, deer, and numberless· other animals, as well as birds by the millions. Also, unnumbered thousands of Indians, as healthy and strongly-developed as any of their race, lived and thrived all over the almost boundless region.

It was in this way the slave-leaders contrived, not for a system based on contingencies, unexpected happenings, or emergencies, but in a steady, determined progress, with plans that were all that the wits, knowledge, and ingenuity of their best-informed and most capable men could make them. During this time freedom and free institutions for this great expanse were quieted to sleep under the fascinating delusion that free labor would drive out slave labor in a competition for supremacy.

In the plans of making Missouri a slave State, it was as much a part of them to gain and keep control of the Missouri River as it had been to acquire and maintain control of the Lower Mississippi. At that time there was no thought of carrying on any considerable commerce or travel other than by means of water transportation. The slave-leaders in the earlier days of the Republic had full confidence of retaining complete control of the entire valley, its products, commerce, and industries, by reason of their control of the lower river, in which they were fully justified in the history of the migrations, business settlements, and progress of our race.

Their plans were never small or hedged in by any kind

of avoidable obstacles. They had no doubt of being able to control the entire valley of both rivers from the day that Missouri was made a slave State. They were still full of this belief in 1854, when they inaugurated their movement to extend slavery into Kansas. They held possession of most of the western rivers, and entire control of all the traffic and commerce on the Missouri River. The order went forth, and was obeyed, that no free State emigration was to be permitted through the State by land or up the river. Although railroads were being built in the West, and a line had been finished from Chicago to St. Louis in 1853-54, the work of building them was slow and tedious. It was a new process of industry to the people, and the slave-leaders had no thought that a railroad could be built in time to affect their plans.

They were fully satisfied that, in closing the Missouri River to free State emigration, they would approximately stop it, for the only other route open to these people was an overland journey, through Iowa and Nebraska, of at least four hundred miles, twice as far, while there were lands of better repute open to settlers on this northern route. They planned that shutting off "Yankee emigration" would leave the Territory fully under their control as soon as they could drive "the Emigrant Aid Society people" out, which they fully expected to do. Atchison repeatedly informed their junta at Washington that he could do all this in a few weeks' time if they would put the force of the army under command of one of their friends. He named several such men that he had become acquainted with in his long residence at Washington; and wanted them to keep away these "half-Abolitionist Democratic governors, and let Woodson act and bear the responsibility."

They tried very hard to do all this for Atchison at Washington, and carried it into execution to the extent of their ability. Again and again they went to General

Scott and pleaded for the appointment of some favorite of Atchison or Davis to take military command in Kansas; but the old general would say, "When 'Blank' is relieved, I will consider with you the matter of appointing his successor. Until then I do not care to take it up. 'Blank' suits me very well, and I will do nothing now about selections for the future, or removals." But, in the making and unmaking of governors, they kept the road thronged from Washington to Leavenworth, as we learn in counting all of the five, from Reeder to Sam Medary, in order that Atchison and his man Woodson might be free from "Yankee Democratic governors" as much of the time as possible.

They greatly mistook and underrated the grit and determination of the industrious free State people to open and build some other line for commercial use besides the Missouri River. Indeed, they did not know that they had started a new era and lasting benefit to commerce when they shut off "Yankee emigration" and travel on that river; for, though it is true that the "Yankees" were 'cute and knew a great deal in those days, they did not know the bottom "aggravatin's" of that stream; for, whatever might have been generally known of the science and art of commerce and navigation of that time, what there was of the Missouri, and what there was of trade and barter on it, was entirely confined to the hardy river men, who went up and down, through its soft mud and sandbars, about once a year if they had good luck; and the patient inhabitants living along it were old men, at an average of twenty-five years, by reason of their repeated disappointments and original belief that it was a navigable stream.

Great contentions and disputes were breaking out somewhere along its course almost every day about this. One man, for instance, contended that it was a navigable stream, and that for freighting merchandise as far as twenty miles

it was preferable and more speedy than the other man's ox-
teams or "gravel-line" of freighters. This provoked the
man with the oxen to a trial, so that when the *Merchant's
Express*, a new steamboat, got off the bar at Booneville at
four o'clock one day, the owner, with his wagon-load of
freight drawn by two yoke of oxen, started up the river to
Lexington, about seventy miles, on a race with the boat.
The steamboat turned the bend in an hour, and was out
of sight, with the oxen only three miles on the way, when
there were cheers for the swift boat, and the poor fellow,
poking up his oxen along the sandy road, harassed by
swarms of flies, was declared out of the race; but he plodded
on, and "poked and hollered up his cattle." In five days
the tired freighter and his more tired oxen did n't fly into
Lexington. No, but just slowly "pulled into town." He
drove up to the post-office, where he inquired, "Hev' you
hear'n tell anything uv the *Merchant's Express?* Has she
gone up the river?" The postmaster replied: "Not that
I know of, Jim. If the boat has gone, she passed up in
the night without landing, which would be singular. Yesterday she was stuck on the bar between Soakum's Bend
and Floating Island. They are worried over her. She 's
loaded down four feet, a foot and a half too much for
the water. They had forty men at work all day yesterday
building a dam and a two hundred yard chute to run in
the water and float her off. Tom Pulloff is there with
his men, and I expect he 'll get her off to-day. When are
you going with your sugar?"

When Jim disposed of his load, he headed down the
river, keeping a close watch for the *Merchant's Express*,
the fast new steamer. He found her hanging in the sand
at the foot of Floating Island, as he expected, almost ten
miles from Lexington. As he drew up to the shore, he
called for the captain, as the boat was not over fifty yards
from the shore. "I am not the captain. He left us, sick,

at Jefferson City. I am part owner of the boat. This is her first trip up the river, and I have never been above Jefferson City before. I live in St. Louis, where a few of us have undertaken the work of building some strong, light draught-steamers for the Missouri River trade. The clerk has charge of the work. He will be down shortly and see you."

During this parley Jim sat crosslegged on a plank across the middle of his wagon-box, with his long ox-whip in his hand, "chawing" his long-green "tobacker" vigorously, and expectorating loosely, muttering to himself, "He's a tender-foot, sure, and mor 'n half Yankee." The clerk, an average river man, soon arrived, saying, "Are you Jim Totem, one of the Totem river and plain freighters?"

"Yes, I 'm Jim. Me an' Ben 's in the bizness. Ben 's on the way up with two loads from Booneville. I 'm lookin' fur him ev'ry minit. He 's got two uv our best wagons an' four-yoke teams, uv the 'Gravel Road Express.' That beats steamboatin' on this river all holler. Yes, thar he comes roundin' the hill on this side uv the crick. We 'd be glad to akommodate you. Yer not likely to git off soon. What kin we do fur you? Our charges is reasonable."

The clerk replied: "Yes, we 're stuck hard. I hardly expect we can get off this week without unloading; and then to reload takes time, so I am inclined to believe that we had best unload and get down stream as soon as possible, before the water gives out. How much will you take the load into Lexington for, and two or three tons each to Liberty and the mouth of the Kaw?" Jim replied: "You 're right, only it 's a 'tarnal sight wus than you 're sayin'. The June rise is mighty nigh over, and she 's goin' down mor 'n an inch a day, and if your boat sticks thar two days longer she 'll winter right thar, and not git away till next April onless a high river kums along kind uv accidental."

Ben arriving, terms were concluded, the boat was unloaded, at once floated into the current, and ready to get
down stream, but without any load of consequence. Before leaving, the Totems went aboard, where they enjoyed
a good dinner and refreshments with the owner and clerk.
While on board the owner had an interchange of opinions
with the Totems. · Turning to Ben, he said: "I knew something of the Missouri River, but nothing in comparison
with what I have learned on this first trip. It do n't look
much like a river here now; it appears like no more than
a string of muddy ponds or little lakes, with a shallow
center stream connecting them, where, some places, there
is not now over two feet of water. It is all nonsense to
talk about carrying much commerce on it, as it runs so
low and is frozen up for so many months that there can
be no certainty about such business. What is it good
for, anyway?" "Well, well," replied Ben, "good fur, sure
enough; why it's the best thing in Ameriky fur the boat-
builders, fur no un ever seed it the fust time that he
did n't b'lieve it wuz a river; them and the bilermakers
jinin' to git new fellers like you to build boats and bilers
and hev 'em repaired arter ev'ry trip, whar they've bin
bulgin' thru the sand, reg'lar like, and thumpin' up agin
the bars fur a day and nite at a time, and a biler busted.
A'most ev'ry trip makes 'em mity tired uv the boat-buildin'
and navigatin' business; so down on it that they frekintly
sell 'em out fer ferry-boats.

"Ez yer a new man, yer orter know that the main holt
iz to git a propriashun frum Congris; fur this the Mizouri
iz a long ways ahed uv enything hearn tell uv in these
parts, even the big corn-craps, when they're not drownded
out. Ez to onsartanty, there's nothin' ekal to thet thar
river. Thar's Jim Tompson, over thar on the line 'tween
Cooper an' Saline Counties, one uv the likeliest men all about
heer, who mite a bin sheriff uv Cooper, and maybe Saline,

ef he hed node a year ahed which county his farm would
be in arter the June rise; en' it makes him look pale en'
old like; fer thar 's nuthin' more disconsolatin' than to be
that nigh onto an office en' not git it. Speakin' uv the
river, ef they 'd quit wastin' money on dredgin's thet fill
up over nite, en' build a strong, high levy, en' narrer down
the stream ez fer ez they cud, en' do it well, ef it war only
five mile a year, they 'd git a river, or a peece uv one, in
a few years, thet hed water in it, ez fer ez they banked
it up, enyway; but it would be hard on some fellers thet
depend reg'lar on 'propriashuns fer a thousand miles up en'
down the Big Muddy."

If the patient reader believes that these outlines may
be overdrawn, or that farms do not grow larger or smaller
or wash away altogether, and change people's property, or
wash it out of existence every year, he can examine for
himself, for all there ever was of the river is there yet,
where he will find the shifting Missouri, doing all or more
than has been written, where the appropriations of Congress flow into the sand and float downstream as regularly
as farms, towns, and cities, or islands change boundaries
and are obliterated in the June rise of the Big Muddy.

CHAPTER XXVII.

THE closure of the river and driving back several bodies of emigrants somewhat delayed their movements; for the river, shallow, shifting, and uncertain as it was, had to be used as much as possible. Its traffic was then conducted by as enterprising and persevering a force of river-men as ever pushed commerce along any stream; but it was as idle a piece of folly as ever men attempted, to think that western travel and emigration could be checked by excluding them from three hundred miles of so "sorry" a route, or that it would stop a single determined Yankee from going to Kansas.

Railroad building was going on rapidly all over the West. This piece of Atchison's wretched work was not only a part of his scheming that delayed emigration to Kansas for a few months, but it was a setback for Missouri and her western river towns for a full generation, and lost them the first transcontinental line terminus, which was taken two hundred miles north.

Two lines of railway were then in course of construction across the State, which would soon have been completed, and as certainly secured the benefit designed by building "the highway to India," of Benton, whose ideas and ambition prompted the first undertaking of it. However, Missouri, under her Atchisons, Polks, Claibornes, Jacksons, Greens, and Prices, was "mired down" in their pro-slavery madness, and eschewed statemanship for fellows "who could run a nigger tobacco plantation and make it pay." They overthrew Benton, Phelps, Gratz Brown,

26

the Halls, the Glovers, Henderson and Frank Blair, throwing aside men of good sense and knowledge of public affairs for pro-slavery zealots "who could lick a nigger and drive the Yanks out of Kansas."

They also threw aside their only opportunity for getting the main thoroughfare of the Nation across the rich and fertile State, with such inviting resources. Among other advantages, it would have held its part of the main line from the Atlantic to the Pacific. But they turned the first main railroad across the continent north into Iowa and Nebraska, among a people friendly to immigration, railroads, bridges, schools, colleges, free institutions, and modern progress.

In the spring of 1856 the Missouri mobs, having closed what part of a navigable stream they had, the more enterprising people of the free States began to open railroads across the State of Iowa. This was no less than disaster, deep and irremediable, well understood from Washington to Westport. In addition, "Jim Lane," who had gone North the fall before to avoid imprisonment, returned with a few organized companies from the free States, emigrating to Kansas, to take their chances in the fight for freedom.

Of all the free State leaders, Lane was the boldest and most daring. For good reasons his forces, being the best organized and equipped, were respected and feared by the "raiders." Lane would not only fight his way out and defend himself and his party anywhere, but would follow up his advantage, pursue his assailants, and punish them with all his power, with superior tact and skill above all the border leaders on both sides. When the Iowa route was opened, and the facility of getting free State emigrants that way became known, the consternation was increased by reports that Lane was coming with an "Emigrant Aid Society" army of thousands. This was partly true; only it was four or five times overcounted; but a real terror to the bandits, considering the kind of guns they carried.

Lane sent forward and brought with him, all arriving in small squads, five or six hundred well-prepared and armed men for the conflict. Although not the five or six thousand reported, nevertheless it was a formidable force, that gave hope and encouragement to the hunted and looted settlers. In addition to their numbers and that they were equipped with "the dreaded Sharpe's rifles," it was well known that they had a leader who would fight and knew how to do it, who would pound away and take advantage of every chance, and pursue the raiders until there were driven back into Missouri, where he intended to follow whenever his force was strong enough.

The free State party, thus re-enforced, began a vigorous warfare on all the pro-slavery bands, and, being much better armed, dispersed a number of them and drove them to their hiding. This led to recruiting and preparations for another invasion. Atchison's paper sounded the assembling as follows: "So sudden and unexpected has been this new attack by the Abolitionists, that the law and order party was unprepared effectually to resist them. To-day the bogus State Government is to assemble at Topeka. The issue is distinctly made up. Either the free State or pro-slavery party is to have Kansas. Citizens of Platte County, the war is upon you, and at your very doors. Arouse yourselves to speedy vengeance, and rub out the bloody traitors."

This was in August. Shannon had not left, though he had turned over the direction of affairs to Woodson. For some weeks he was expecting to be relieved; but the renewal of energy on the part of the free State men alarmed him. He dreaded the renewed conflict which seemed imminent. General Smith, having newly arrived, partook of his fears. All the Kansas militia, which was composed of the armed pro-slavery bands of Missouri and the other Southern States, were placed under his command. He was also authorized by the President to call on Illinois and Kentucky for two regiments each. In a few days he satisfied himself that he had no need of troops from anywhere, and that the very best way to bring peace was to dismiss from service and pay these border bands under the name of Kansas militia. He instructed Colonel Cooke accordingly, who was in command in the field by reason of Smith's poor health.

General Smith had reliance and full confidence in Colonel Cooke, who was another of Scott's selections. In a day or two after his arrival, August 28th, he wrote Colonel Cooke as follows: "It has been rumored for several days that large numbers of persons from the State of Missouri have entered Kansas at various points, armed, with the intention of attacking the opposite party and driving them from the Territory, the latter being also represented to be in considerable force. If it should come to your knowledge that either side is moving upon the other with a view to attack, it will become your duty to observe their movements and prevent such hostile collisions." This was sure evidence that Scott had trusted in the right man, no matter what might be his personal beliefs about slavery.

This was gall and wormwood to Atchison and his followers. What to do with Smith they did not know; however, there was no relaxation in their zeal or determination, for they were aware that the Administration and powers at Washington would do all they could to keep as many armed men on the Kansas border as it was possible, in every sort of Government service, in courts, militia companies, and deputies, all of which were paid by the United States.

Woodson had declared the Territory in a state of rebellion and had called on General Smith for its suppression;

but Smith at once became inquisitive, and determined to ascertain who were the insurgents. Very soon after General Smith's arrival, he made a preliminary report to the Secretary of War, in which he related the condition and the attitude of the contending parties as well as he could do in the short time, and wrote especially of the prevailing alarm and the immediate danger of more desperate conflict between them.

Secretary Davis replied almost immediately, as follows: "The position of the insurgents, as shown by your letter and inclosures, is open rebellion against the laws and Constitutional authorities, with such manifestations of a purpose to spread devastation over the land as no longer justifies hesitation or indulgence. To you, as to every soldier whose habitual feeling is to protect the citizens of his own country, and only to use his arms against a public enemy, it can not be otherwise than deeply painful to be brought into conflict with any portion of his fellow-countrymen; but patriotism and humanity alike require that rebellion should be promptly crushed, and the perpetration of the crimes which now disturb the peace and security of the good people of the Territory of Kansas should be effectually checked. You will, therefore, energetically employ all the means within your reach to restore the supremacy of the law, always endeavoring to carry out your present purpose to prevent the unnecessary effusion of blood."

Under these instructions General Smith was expected to disperse all the free State forces, who were by this Davis order denounced as insurgents; but the general had learned much concerning the border war, and the purposes underlying it, and the motives of the contending factions. Under the direction of Smith, Cooke placed his small force of only four companies between Lawrence and Lecompton, a central location, where he could observe the movements of both parties, exercise a salutary effect by reason of it, and prevent a collision by anticipating and preventing it. Shortly after doing this, Acting Governor Woodson was notified that some of his irregular militia bands were pillaging and burning the houses of the free State people in every direction.

This was known to Woodson beforehand. He, of course, paid no attention to the report, and without heeding it in any way, as it was what he desired, he sent Colonel Cooke a demand to take military possession of Topeka by whatever force he needed, that if help was necessary, to take command of all his (Woodson's) militia, destroy any and all fortifications or protecting barricades, etc., disarm all persons, and hold them as prisoners, and to arrest all of Lane's men, armed or not.

Colonel Cooke promptly replied that he was present with his force to keep the peace and to aid the legal authorities to preserve it, and serve legal processes, but not to levy war nor commit violence against peacefully-disposed people anywhere. Colonel Cooke gathered the information desired by General Smith, who very soon understood the situation, and learned how it was maintained, just as Colonel Sumner had. Being an honest and capable man, able to tell what he knew, and not believing that the War Department desired to be deceived, he, in the plainest sort of way, reported the conditions existing in his command on the border, as follows:

"In explanation of the position of affairs lately and now, I may remark that there are more than two opposing parties in the Territory. The citizens of the Territory, who formed the majority in the organization of the Territorial Government and in the election for its Legislature and inferior officers, form one party; the persons who organized a State Government, and attempted to put it in operation against the authority of that established by Congress, form another;

a party at the head of which is a former senator from Missouri, and which is composed in a great part of citizens from that State who have come into the Territory armed, under the excitement produced by reports, exaggerated in all cases and in many absolutely false, form the third. There is a fourth composed of idle men congregated from various parts, who assume to arrest, punish, and even kill all those whom they assume to be bad citizens; that is, those who will not join them or contribute to their maintenance. Every one of these in its own peculiar way (except some few of the first party) have thrown aside all regard to law, and even honesty, and the Territory under their sway is ravaged from one end to the other. Until the day before yesterday I was deficient in force to operate against all of these at once, and the acting governor of the Territory did not seem to take a right view of affairs. If Mr. Atchison and his party had had the direction of affairs, they could not have ordered them more to suit his purpose."

This last clause was the information desired by Secretary Davis, and just what Atchison desired to continue, instead of dispersing insurgents and all violators of the law, as their orders proclaimed. The matter contained in General Smith's and Colonel Cooke's reports were quite distasteful to Secretary Davis, who really desired that the ravaging policy should be continued. But he was chagrined and angered beyond means of expressing it, that the whole plot and situation had been laid bare by these pro-slavery inclined officers, who in the beginning were deceived by the pretense that the Administration desired peace; whereas, the strongest purpose of all the pro-slavery powers and factions was to provoke revolt and a state of rebellion, as Woodson had already characterized it.

Their plan was to proceed under a merciless use of the regular troops and all the bands of militia, to kill, destroy, capture, and drive the Free State settlers out of the Terri-

STEPHEN A. DOUGLAS

plunder and pillage their towns and settlements, and burn up or take possession of their homes; but the inval-id old soldier was an honest American, and stood heroically in the ° of any such policy. How to get him out of the way was ... ous and perplexing, and how to do better with "Old Scott," if they removed Smith, was more so.

The Secretary's indorsement on Smith and Cooke's reports shows plain enough the anger of the plotting dictator, who wanted a war of extermination waged against the free settlers, who had been hunted and driven like beasts where it was possible to do so. When they were able to turn on their murderers and pursuers they were denounced as "insurgents, and proper subjects on which to employ the military force." He who was then plotting his slave empire as a contingency, and using all the powers of the Government to force his system into free territory, indorsed these reports as follows:

"The only distinction of parties, which in a military point of view it is necessary to note, is that which distinguishes those who respect and maintain the laws and organized Government from those who combine for revolutionary resistance to the constitutional authorities and laws of the land. The armed combinations of the latter class come within the denunciation of the President's proclamation, and are proper subjects upon which to employ the military force."

In the latter part of August, and up to September 8, 1856, when Governor John W. Geary arrived, the border war was at its most furious progress. Sumner had been retired, Smith his successor was not fully informed, but was proceeding cautiously to keep the peace. On August 14th, a free State company attacked Titus, and captured him with twenty pro-slavery militia. On the 17th, Governor Shannon before leaving brought about a compromise, by which Titus and his men were exchanged for some free State prisoners taken at the burning of Lawrence, and the cannon were also returned to the free State company. In a day or so Shannon was notified of his removal, when, as Atchison most desired, Woodson again became acting governor.

They very soon learned that General Smith would not be a party to their hellish, killing work. In the time quite a number of Lane's men had gathered, who were in good fix for the strife. Atchison and Woodson carried on the hideous work with all their strength and resources for three dreadful weeks against the settlers. August 25th, Woodson issued another proclamation, declaring the Territory in a state of rebellion. About the same time Atchison entered the Territory with a newly-armed and equipped force of eleven hundred and fifty invaders, which, added to the others, made a pro-slavery force of five thousand. On August 29th, a force of five hundred attacked John Brown at Ossawatomie, where he fought them all day with thirty men, with a loss of two killed, inflicting a loss of five; but being heavily outnumbered he was compelled to fall back on Lawrence.

Here he was joined by heavy re-enforcements. With this force he drove Atchison's force back into Missouri in almost a stampede. They were driven out, but not until they had committed frightful outrages and desolated the region on their line of march. The plundering, devastation, and burning of this marauding, murdering expedition amounted to more than half a million dollars' loss. Thirty houses were destroyed in Ossawatomie alone, and several small settlements, houses, and improvements were burned up and obliterated. Leavenworth was attacked on September 1st, but not taken. Several free State men were killed and wounded, two hundred of whom were driven from the State. This was done by one of Atchison's raider bands, with which he was supposed to be present.

Governor Geary on his way heard of the horrible state

of affairs. Making all possible haste, he arrived several days before Atchison was looking for him. In doing so, he undoubtedly prevented a more desperate conflict near Lawrence. This interposition probably delayed the slavery war with all its changed conditions for five years, for both sides were ready for a battle that would have been serious enough, from all that any one could see at the time. With these two forces of armed Americans of five thousand each ready to fight, and both determined to win, it would have aroused the Nation to war.

On his way he met Shannon, glad to get away, alarmed for his own safety. He told Geary the truth about the situation, which was that Atchison, the despot and ruler behind every movement, was levying war against the free State people, and fully intended to drive them out. He predicted Geary's failure as certain to come as his own, because Atchison was and would be sustained by the Administration. On his last part of the journey, up the Missouri, Geary was on a boat carrying a full company of Missourians going to the war in Kansas. He reached the landing at Leavenworth September 8th. Hastening to the fort, he held hurried counsel with General Smith. He immediately proceeded over the fifty miles with all possible speed. He located himself at Lecompton in the midst and between the contending forces, with a few companies of United States troops under Colonel Cooke.

He issued a proclamation at once, assuming control and direction of affairs. He revoked all of Woodson's orders and proclamations declaring "the Territory in a state of rebellion." He ordered that all bodies of armed men in the Territory, except two hundred to be selected by himself, and the forces under General Smith be at once disarmed and returned to their homes. He promised protection to the free State people, if they would lay down their arms. This was all they desired, and, being assured of his sincerity and the attitude of General Smith, they complied. He as firmly determined that he would measure strength with Atchison in the beginning, as he would have to do it in the end, and the longer delayed, the harder to accomplish. He insisted that his order to disarm and disband should be obeyed, and that Atchison and his Missourians and all others should comply with it. Instead of compliance, they assembled and concentrated a force of twenty-five hundred, divided into three commands with artillery, all within striking distance of Lawrence or Topeka, the main free State towns.

This force was directly under one of Atchison's lieutenants, one Colonel Reed, then a member of the Missouri Legislature, with Atchison's company forming another force of equal or greater strength on the river and near, to re-enforce in case of a heavy conflict. The assembling and threatening was pushed to intimidate Geary, Smith, and Cooke. Neither of them faltered or wavered a moment, and Atchison, who believed himself in sight of victory, was balked, and finally beaten, not by fault or failure on his part; for his men were surely ready to fight, and a battle would have ensued but for the pending Presidential election and the force of loyal Democratic opinion in the free States. It was this that forced the appointment of an honest, fearless man like Geary, who halted Jefferson Davis and his coadjutor, Atchison, on the border, when the borderers were ready to strike.

In three or four free State towns, and in the camps along the Kansas River for twenty miles, there was every indication of approaching battle. It all hinged on the conclusions of the slavery leaders. Their force was ready, or getting ready, to fight a decisive battle. Colonel Cooke put his five companies and one battery into camp within call for action any moment. There were over two thousand free State men who had laid down their arms; but if Atchison had been allowed, or had made the hazard, every one of these would have had his arms restored, and been back into line at the signal of the first hostile gun flashing in the red September sun.

A hand somewhere held back and compelled the fiery, unwilling, outgeneraled senator, who was ready for the pro-slavery war. His force of Missourians returned to their border homes as sullenly and unforgivingly as they had plundered and burned the homes of thousands of helpless people in the Territory. This was a great victory for Geary, Smith, Cooke, and the brave men who were firm and faithful in the moment of danger. Governor Geary was a man of courage and high executive capacity. This he developed in less than two days after his first landing, when an hour's delay would have precipitated the Nation's catastrophe. One of our country's strongest resources is, that the moment the land or our liberties are in peril, a man of the Joshua kind springs like Geary into the conflict, so fully equipped and ready for the work that we know that God fitted him in mind and strength for the emergency.

Geary liberated Robinson and all the free State prisoners. There was rejoicing everywhere, and Geary's grit and unflinching courage, that saved us from civil war, and unwittingly made Buchanan's election possible, was instantly recognized and appreciated. On the retreat of the Missouri invaders, Buffum, a free State settler, was shot down without provocation, within hearing of Geary, who forthwith ordered the arrest of his slayer, one Haines. The notorious Judge Lecompte, who was convenient, and a supple servant of Atchison's, at once liberated the murderer on bail, and shortly afterwards practically discharged him on a writ of habeas corpus. Geary now developed his strength. He wrote out a truthful account of the crime, and demanded the removal of Lecompte. This was done, reluctantly however; but they were well aware that a man of Geary's mettle had to be sustained. He was then forcing back the suppressed wrath and indignation of the Administration, that removed him later.

The removal of Geary was in store for him from the time of the suppression of Atchison; but to have made it then would have cost Buchanan the State of Pennsylvania and his election. Thus Davis and his junta, so unquestionably and decisively beaten, could do no better than bide their time. Atchison was smothered. His defeat was rank, and left him no more than a wreck, who could deceive no one nor serve his bad cause to further advantage. Poor, little, thin-faced Lecompte, the supple-minded top of a court, that was never a judge in any sense save form, was removed, and J. C. Harrison, of Kentucky, was appointed in his place; but the murderer of the free State settler, Buffum, was never tried.

While negotiations were in progress, an attack was made on a Missouri company at Hickory Point. They were taken and sent home. There were two or three casualties on both sides. Several of the free State men were afterwards tried and sentenced by one Judge Cato, who had participated in that and similar assaults. Governor Geary released them.

In a short time after Geary's arrival he gathered a full knowledge of the state of affairs prevailing under Atchison and Woodson, who were in full sweep of their own and Davis's policy to drive out the free State people. His report to the Secretary of State corroborated all that had been disclosed, and left no room for doubt or dispute as to conditions in the Territory. He said: "I have not simply to contend against bands of armed ruffians and brigands, whose sole end and aim are assassination and robbing, infatuated adherents and advocates of conflicting political sentiment and local institutions, and evil-disposed persons actuated by a desire to secure elevated positions; but the worst of all, against the influence of men who have been placed in authority, and have employed all the destructive agents around them to promote their own personal interests at the sacrifice of every just and honorable consideration. Such is the condition of Kansas, faintly pictured. In making the foregoing statement I have endeavored to give the truth, and nothing but the truth. I deem it important that you should be apprised of the actual state of the case; and whatever may be the effect of such revelations, they will be given from time to time, without extenuation."

It was a dire necessity that such a man as Geary should be appointed; but not even his remarkable promptitude and success could keep thousands from deserting the Democratic party. Their going became an alarming condition, and betokened, as clearly as events could, that unless some man was sustained there as governor who could bring peace and civil order out of the horrible disorder and murderous border war, the party was as good as defeated. So in the pending catastrophe Atchison's power had to be broken, faithful and Satanic as he had proven himself. Some man that would temporarily serve the purpose, preferably from Pennsylvania, where Buchanan lived, had to be found, or he could not be elected. Geary, an able, true, and patriotic Democrat, whom all parties in his State were satisfied with, was selected. He was appointed, and unanimously confirmed by the Senate the same day.

He won distinction in the Mexican War, where he was a volunteer in a regiment from his State. He was promoted, finally to be its colonel, for gallant and conspicuous service, when by reason of this and his legal and business qualifications, he was made a funding commissioner by the California Legislature. He had also been, in the government of that Territory, alcalde or mayor of San Francisco. Such Geary was, a man whose knowledge, capacity, and experience made him a leader of high character and well-merited distinction.

It was one of the mockeries of that period that such a

man was used as a foil to distract, and for a time conceal,
the real designs of the slave-power, just as Secretary Marcy
was, who demanded and wrote up Geary's instructions. He
was one of the wisest and ablest statesmen of his day. Other
hundreds were being used and cast away as ungratefully and
unmercifully, when they could serve the monster sin no
longer. Marcy was probably the only man in Pierce's Administration strong enough to comprehend that unless the
conditions in Kansas were mended at once, rightly and honestly, Buchanan could not be elected. This was grateful
party service, as he did not owe the Democratic party anything at the time. He had been unceremoniously cast aside,
notwithstanding his eminent ability in that weak Administration, which, like Buchanan's succeeding one, did not
reach mediocrity, in which all the talents and work of both
ran to the most menial subserviency.

Marcy instructed Geary to use his untiring efforts "to
tranquillize Kansas by your energy, impartiality, and discretion," which Geary earnestly set about. He succeeded
so well, that by the close of September, in less than one
month's sincere and courageous work, he reported "that
peace had been restored and reigned supreme in Kansas."

With the enthusiasm of one who succeeded where others
had failed, and without the light of subsequent events, Geary
believed what so many tireless workers do in similar places,
that he could bring about harmony and reorganize all the
factions of the Democratic party in the Territory. He was
still a zealous Democrat. He discovered, too, what so many
others had neglected, that more than half of the free State
settlers were Democrats, who went to the Territory fully
convinced of the good faith and promises of the party, that
at the proper time slavery would be settled according to the
will of the majority fairly given and expressed.

In this attempt he found himself thwarted and beaten
at every point. He learned, to his sorrow, that there was

to be no relief from pro-slavery control and dictation, except in overwhelming defeat of the party. This was a hard and biting conclusion to him and to the great heart of the Northern anti-slavery Democracy. He learned before he had been there many days what was the true state of affairs; that Atchison was the real leader on the border, that as soon as the election was over the pro-slavery power would be asserted, and that he would be compelled to submit or be relieved, just as his predecessors were, all the more certainly because of his success in doing just what the slave-leaders did not want.

In calling for help, one of Atchison's newspapers, fully in his confidence, said: "We have asked opportunity for the appointment of a successor to Shannon, who was acquainted with our condition, with the capacity to appreciate and the boldness and integrity requisite faithfully to discharge his duty, regardless of the possible effect it might have upon the election of some petty politician in a distant State. In his stead we have one appointed who is ignorant of our condition, a stranger to our people, who, we have too much cause to fear, will, if no worse, prove no more efficient to protect us than his predecessors. . . . We can not await the convenience in coming of our newly-appointed governor. We can not hazard a second edition of imbecility or corruption. Let Woodson continue and be appointed to the governorship, as he should be at once."

Although all of Geary's efforts in the direction of political harmony were fruitless, his restoration of civil order was as complete as it well could be after two years of such guerrilla warfare and marauding. He was honest and impartial in the administration of his office. He brought the border warfare to an end, and further accomplished lasting good in establishing a precedent for his successors, which all of them were compelled, willingly or not, to follow; and although removed for not carrying out the pro-slavery plans, his successful career and restoration of peace and its salutary example ruined forever the business of Atchison and his followers, the lesser conspirators who waited anxiously for any villainy within reach.

He was prompt in the suppression of all kinds of outlawry, and fair enough in the organization of the small force of two militia companies which he mustered and kept in his service, to take one of them from the free State and the other from the pro-slavery inhabitants. It has often been said that the pro-slavery leaders then gave up the plan of forcing slavery by force of arms into Kansas, and decided to accomplish that, and retain control through fraudulent voting and elections. At all events it was true that henceforward in their elections fraudulent ballots fell into the boxes like the leaves in autumn, and the ballot-boxes were padded as full as the trunks of a returning American from Europe. From this time forward intimidation and skillful counting were more relied upon than any other means at hand. This and the Supreme Court's decision were sufficient, in their opinion, to force slavery into Kansas without awaiting the result of any election.

It was told for political effect that the South had given up all idea of taking slavery into Kansas; but it was an idle tale. They had served too long and too hard. They had suffered too much and had been beaten too often to give up the forcible plan if it had been possible to continue it; but the effect of the border war on the public mind, the rending and tearing to pieces that was in steady progress in the Democratic party, and the courageous work of Geary, sustained so well by General Smith and Colonel Cooke, compelled the Southern leaders to change their plan of action.

The border war was over. It had ruined thousands of free State people. Many were killed and many more lost their homes and all they had. Many of these were Demo-

crats to begin with; but they became Abolitionists before
the conflict was over. Thousands of the border pro-slavery
men perished, and went down in' this first onset of the
"lost cause." But the most cruel effect of it after the
wretched and unprovoked slaying of innocent people, was
its lasting effect on many of the men on both sides, whom it
brutalized for their lifetime and cast its baneful shadow on
the coming generation.

Atchison was completely "used up" by the border war.
He had been zealous in the public work, and had risen to
power where he helped to overthrow Benton a few years
before. After this he seemed to wax stronger, and became
the leader of his party in the West, so much so that he felt
himself leader, subject only to Jefferson Davis, where he
had, as he believed, reached the point of being able to dictate
a policy to the United States Senate, and to remove such a
leader as Douglas at his pleasure. He reached the high
honor of being second in office in the Republic, where he felt
himself clothed with arbitrary power, the acting Vice-President from the death of King, and President of the United
States for a Sunday, technically, perhaps, between a retiring and incoming President.

All this Atchison had been. He was a capable and indomitable leader, who went down in character and standing
in proportion to his zeal and unscrupulous service, in the
debauchery and sin of slavery, and the plunging of a peaceful people into horrid civil war. He earned, to begin with,
the condemnation of his honest political associates, as well
as his antagonists, not because of partisan differences, but
by his dastardly ravaging, maraudings, and killings of helpless people. Soon all fair-minded men united in condemning
him. His conscience convicted him. He felt its shadow on
himself, and remained absent for periods, from an honored
place in the Senate, to wage war and rapine against the free
State people. When his term expired he had not failed.

No man living could have done the bloody work better to the slaveholders' liking. The propaganda sustained him, and boldly declared that he would succeed and be re-elected. But Missouri would not and did not re-elect him; whereas, without the blast of the slavery curse upon him, no man could have been his competitor. Hence every change was one notch further down for the border leader.

When the border war was over, and Geary had so effectually circumvented and defeated him, he went down to the bottom in a plunging lurch, and Woodson, Calhoun, Reid, Stringfellow, Sheriff Jones, and a host of smaller fellows, went rattling into obscurity like the deadened forest in the winter wind. Soon Geary declared a peace. Atchison was out of office, and his occupation was gone. He could not further serve the bad cause, and to be true to their unvarying ingratitude to a wornout servant, or broken leader, they were as unmindful of him as they were of Pierce, Marcy, or Benton. Oblivion came to him almost before he died, and thousands of pretty well-informed people know little of the great border leader, and there are thousands of his own Missourians who do not know that such a man as Atchison ever lived. Some people believed during their time that he and Jim Lane "were well matched antagonists;" but wild, uncouth, and vicious as Lane no doubt became in a hand-to-hand conflict for years, it stands to his credit that he always fought for the rights of his fellow-men.

The war made Lane and many such the wild, daring, reckless, and adventurous partisans of the border, who took up the business of hunting and killing men, because they were hunted and killed themselves. Atchison, on the other hand, was a capable man, ruined and obliterated by the consequences of the murderous warfare he planned and executed. He remains the undisputed leader of a war against helpless men, women, and children, that he might sell other men, women, and children, and in the progress of it pillage, devastation, and murder were not only common, but the most of it.

Following this, the Legislature elected under the Topeka Constitution met at that place on the 6th of January, 1857, and organized next day. The United States marshal arrested the President of the Senate, the Speaker of their Assembly, and several prominent members, who were taken to Tecumseh, charged with "having taken upon themselves the office and trust of the Legislators for the State of Kansas, without lawful deputation or appointment." The Houses, thus left without a quorum for business, met next day, and adjourned to meet in June following. Shortly afterwards a Territorial Legislature, made up altogether of pro-slavery men, chosen in an election by pro-slavery men, in which free State men did not participate because of illegality, assembled at Lecompton.

They here began the celebrated contest of the Lecompton Constitution. They passed the act providing for the election of delegates to a Convention which was to frame and submit a State Constitution.

About the same time, in January, 1857, the House of Representatives at Washington passed an act declaring all laws, resolutions, and enactments of the Lecompton Assembly, as they were denominated, null and void, by reason that they were cruel and oppressive, and that the said Legislature was not elected by the legal voters of Kansas, but forced upon them by non-residents, as declared upon the testimony of hundreds of witnesses.

This act clearly set forth the feeling and force of public sentiment in the free States; but it failed to pass the Senate, which was still strongly pro-slavery. The Senate, too, failed to confirm Judge Harrison, of Kentucky, who had been appointed successor of the thin-headed and narrow-minded Lecompte, who, by reason of this failure to confirm his successor, remained the chief judge of the

Kansas Territorial Court. This was in accord with the desire of Buchanan's Administration, learning which, Governor Geary resigned and left the Territory, not only disgusted, but wrought up to all his powers, ready for work elsewhere. He had great influence in his home in Pennsylvania, where the next year Buchanan's Administration got a much better knowledge of the man. He and Thad. Stevens and a few other such leaders brought on the revolution that almost obliterated the long-time powerful Democratic party in that State, where, as far as men know, the party has not recovered to this day.

JAMES BUCHANAN

WINFIELD SCOTT

JOHN C. FREMONT

CHAPTER XXVIII.

ON Buchanan's inauguration he formed a Cabinet and instituted an Administration as fully committed to the service of the slave-power, led and managed, as Pierce's outgoing one had been, by the daring cabal of the Southern pro-slavery leaders. Buchanan and his chief man of affairs and reliance, Jere Black, were surely not as zealous pro-slavery men as Jefferson Davis and Alex. Stephens, if they had been untrammeled; but while in office, in every visible way they seemed, as far as their capacities and willingness permitted to be, as docile and bidable servants of slavery as the latter. When elected, Buchanan was a soured, disappointed old man, who had been neglected and forgotten so long, and sent away so much, that, when he gained his ambitious desire, the channels of his blood ran low. As a statesman, metaphorically, he was cold even in July. Black, on the other hand, could fire up to fever heat on an "Abolitionist" any time, even in January.

Thad. Stevens made them his prey, under whose hands they were as green cheese beneath the paring-knife of the German Burghers, whose horror of slavery was next to their hope of a better future. The story of what Geary saw and did on the border, and how those bandits were sustained by their own citizen, Buchanan, told in any town or village, and retold to the President, as imprudent persons were constantly doing, would throw the poor, shivering old man into a chill and paroxysm any day, and Abolitionist-hating Jere into a wrath and fever that consumed his senses for a week. Nevertheless, the story told turned Pennsylvania, with fifty thousand votes, against Jefferson Davis Democracy; and it is still a wonder in the Pennsylvania hills that such things happened, that a State that should hold the treasured memory of William Penn and Benjamin Franklin must shiver and roast and argue over the descent of man, from those to Buchanan and Jere Black.

The civil war in Kansas was a bloody sacrifice. Hundreds had been slain, and thousands were to suffer on under as bad or worse inflictions of the power of human greed; for it is one of the truths of our being and tenure of life that tyrants and oppressors will usurp all available power, and grind men down as long as men will bear it. Hence God favors the nations and the men who fight and die, when need be, for their liberties; but he wants true, devoted, heroic men, and never a hypocrite. The fattened ones, sluggards in wealth and ease, nations as men, whether in one year or a thousand, all perish.

The Kansas Legislature, in 1859, when the excitement was over and the passions of men had subsided as much as could be in the ante-bellum period, created and empowered a non-partisan board to collect testimony concerning the ravages of their civil war. The board, after a careful investigation of all that was left to guide them, made an official report of all the facts and information available. These facts are accurate and reliable, most of which were given by present witnesses and the participants on both sides. They fixed the beginning of the war about November 1, 1855, and its termination about December 1, 1856. The entire loss and destruction of property, at a gross estimate, was over two million dollars. Half of this or more was taken from or expended by the people of Kansas. They reported four hundred and seventeen cases for payment in full or in part. Among the items are: Crops destroyed, over $37,000; buildings burned and destroyed, $78,000; horses taken or destroyed, $368,000; cattle taken or destroyed, $533,000; property destroyed or taken, owned by pro-slavery men, over $77,000; the same owned by free State men, over $355,000; property taken or destroyed by pro-slavery men, over $318,000; the same by free State men, over $94,000. Concerning the loss of life the board reported: "Although not within our province, we may be excused for stating that, from the most reliable information we have been able to gather, the number of lives sacrificed in Kansas, during the period mentioned, probably exceeded, rather than fell short of two hundred."

The Congressional Committee reported "that the excitement in the Eastern and Southern States in 1856, instigated by garbled and exaggerated accounts of Kansas affairs published in the Eastern and Southern newspapers is true, most true; but the half that was done by either party was never chronicled." (House Reports 2, Session 36, Congress.)

In the matter of property lost, taken, or destroyed the above items are probably correct; but the loss of life in the smaller encounters, on both sides, was scarcely half reported. Men frequently disappeared, and were never again heard of, in over five hundred reported cases.

In 1856 the slavery question entered its second trial by bloody contest. Through their sagacity the slave-leaders led the Nation through a victorious war with Mexico, by which they added an empire in area, which they expected to become slave territory. Although California had been wrested from them, they yet doubled the region that men generally agreed would be nothing but slave territory in the expected progress of events. The victory and extension brought neither moderation in their desire nor the disposition to submit to peaceful adjustment in our Western Territories. On the contrary, it stimulated and maddened the ambition of the men who planned and plotted for empire for more than one generation.

In this turn of events the people were roused from their stupefaction in the belief that the slavery question was permanently settled by the agreements of 1850, to the truly appalling situation that another war was being waged in our own land. The people were awakened, like one from a frightful dream. There was a prospect that slavery might be fastened deep and strong in the vitals of the great and growing West, so full of resources, so vast and unmeasured for the coming millions, and that in such a fall human liberty would lurch backward five centuries.

The agitation burst into a fury. The discussion of what had been done and what might be done to keep a peaceful solution a possibility passed away, and the story of the border war burst open the floodgates of anger, passion, and determined resistance to the slave-power that rolled over the land in a swelling, resistless tide. It had come to be a quarrel that could not be composed or adjusted in the debates of Congress, courts, or councils. It was a changing period; a new era in the progress of advancing civilization. It was an awakened people threatened with the loss of their liberties, aroused from the siren's luring song of Constitutionalism. It was a turning, like all movements ahead, to better life and living. God was stirring up the dull consciences of the people to the virtue of recognizing the rights of men, so defiantly written in the Declaration of Independence, "that all men were created free and equal," and the working out in completeness the charter law of our existence.

Society, and all that were known as the established institutions among men, were rocking to and fro like ships in tropic storms. Families differed and doubted; Churches divided, and many of their fraternal relations were dissolved; long business dealings between men were broken up; commercial undertakings of many kinds were limited, changed, or altogether discontinued; political parties were breaking

asunder and wrecking on the reefs, or bending and writh-
ing under the conscience-lashing truths that Christian men,
in party form, were tolerating and sustaining this sum of
human misery.

The Whig party, with as distinguished, powerful, and
patriotic a leader as Winfield Scott, rang its last tattoo and
sounded its last battle-call. The chronicles of its brave
and valiant deeds, its broadened conceptions, its wisdom
in war and peace, up to its stop-off on human slavery, were
laid away in the scrolls, among the papyri and mummies,
in moldering tombs, with forgotten war-cries. The Democratic party, that was born in the storm of the revolution
for human rights, was treason-belted and treacherously led.
It was running ashore on narrow inlets and sunken rocks,
where, bold and faithful as it had been, it must turn or
perish, or divide in the honest wrath that was winnowing
men out of it by the hundred thousand.

The artful, scheming, lifetime servitors and projectors
of the slave-system, in shrewdness, perseverance, and cunning far beyond any political leaders of their time, had
loosed the old party of human liberty and the equality of
all men from its moorings, from the teachings of Jefferson, Madison, Monroe, Jackson, Benton, and Douglas, to
where Calhoun, Stephens, Benjamin, and Jefferson Davis
were sailing on the shoreless seas of tyranny, slavery, oppression, and death.

It was not men alone, nor any nor all of their best-wrought
plans that saved it from utter ruin through the ante-bellum
campaigns and war-breeding Administrations of Pierce and
Buchanan. It was God's assurance, with hope to men
planted deep in their hearts, that this old friend of human
rights, however misdirected or misled, would be shriven,
and come back to its soundings true and steadfast in the
faith of the fathers of the Republic.

This chronicle is not to be in any sense a partisan one.

Parties are good for what they do and lead men to, and should be so far credited, and no more. The constant object is to show what they and their leaders did, regardless of promises or what they held as beliefs or assumed to believe. The Democratic party was taken far from its true principles and its higher than sworn duty by plotting, faithless, and treacherous leaders.

At the same time, the body of men who held to its primary and fundamental truths through all its trials, wreckings, disasters, and sorrows have been and are as true and patriotic Americans as ever uncovered their heads on sea or land. Enthusiasts, rash and inconsiderate men, partisans who "go with their party," and newspapers, pamphleteers, and book-writers in thousands, have attempted and written and retold the narrow belief that all parties except theirs were lacking and destitute of fealty, devotion, and loyalty to our truly great and exalted Republic. But when a man grows old he will learn that there are more loyal men in all parties, a thousand times, than the partisans and scribblers who denounce them.

Besides these, there was Fillmore's party, the "Know-nothings," or, more descriptively, the "Tell-nothings." They were so, perhaps, in good part for the significant reason that they had next to nothing to tell. They were more truly a native American party, brought together at that juncture because of many awkward ventures in public improvements, corrupt city and municipal schemes, where crafty party tyrants, or "bosses," could lead and manipulate the newly-arrived, untrained, and ignorant immigrants to their own selfish ends in office.

But nativism would scarcely be the foundation for any national party. The movement of the political bosses and foreign interfering Churches was only local, and could not be enlarged to national grievances for causes justifying the organization of a national party. There was the valid objection to this party attempt, that its proceedings were all secret. This made it distasteful at once; for no secret political society can safely exist in a land of freedom, where every measure proposed, entertained, or adopted should be as freely and publicly discussed as any one desires, with no concealment of plan or purpose whatever. There was little to be claimed for nativism in a land where, at best, not more than one-fourth of the inhabitants could trace their Americanism further back than the birth of their grandparents. Fillmoreism, or the party beliefs of the projectors of this segment of the breaking-up Whig party, had no distinct feature except its professed Americanism.

Its relation to the slavery question, the principal topic of the time, was the same as that of the Democratic party as declared by the Cincinnati Convention. In addition, Fillmore had a more unsavory and subservient reputation on slavery than Buchanan. He had favored and aided in the passage of the slave-extending Compromise Measures of 1850, including the infamous Fugitive-catching Law, which President Taylor, a slaveholder, did not sanction, but positively rejected. This segment of the broken-up Whig party, headless and aimless, was drifting, without a leader, whither they knew not, for Fillmore was neither statesman nor leader, nor even a successful trimmer. He used all the patronage at his command for his renomination. At his best he could do no more than defeat Webster, his party's ablest and wisest man, and a statesman beyond cavil or controversy. Failing himself, his party control was sufficient to bring about the nomination of General Scott, who did not desire it.

Webster was defeated, whose life's ambition to attain the Presidency led him into the verge of the camp of the slave-worshipers, which, by the same means, brought his own and his party's downfall. He was a leader and statesman, one always to be remembered as among his Nation's wisest, most capable, and eminent men. Fillmore, when remembered, will be as one of the New York "accidents" in our politics. Thousands of the Americans, the remnant of the Whig party, though agreeing with the Democratic party's declaration on slavery, would not unite with them because most of them were taught and learned, as their course of political action, to oppose Democracy and everything known as Democratic. Party divisions were clear, distinct, and tenaciously held under such leaders as Jackson and Benton against Webster and Clay. Especially was this true of the parties in the time of Jackson and Clay, who held to their leaders as zealously as an anchorite holds to his faith. Clay's followers held to him through three defeats for President.

The vote given to this American party in 1856 was a severe condemnation of the faithless pro-slavery leaders of the falling-to-pieces Whig party. In order to serve two masters they evaded slavery, and in endeavoring to serve two they served neither, but fell in fragments without leaders. This heavy body of voters, of almost a million, could easily have made the strong basis for a reorganized Whig party; but for want of leaders with bold and definite declarations on living issues, it fell by the wayside, and continued its ten years' disintegration, from 1850 to 1860, when a man who declared himself a Whig was held to be in his dotage.

Amid the deafening roar and storm of slavery-assaulted liberty, the wrecking, sundering and severing, the political concussion came that stunned; the convulsion followed that shattered the aforetime strongest associations of a free people, and buried some of their political parties. Amid this eruption that was no less than a political Vesuvius, when God in his wrath was running red-hot currents against slavery through every party in the land, the Republican party sprang into life without any one's preparation for

it, or reasonable knowledge of its coming, or why it should
be, or what it should be; and what of it, and what was it?
It was a revolt as widespread as the freedom of speech,
carried wherever human tongue and the public press could
take it. There were in every township, town, village, and
city throughout the free States, and the towns and cities
along the border, meetings, where all the opponents of
the slave-power met and discussed, and usually organized
a club, society, or town-meeting to resist and denounce the
arrogant pretension and encroachments of slavery.

There was no common qualification required at these
meetings, more than that all persons opposed to the extension of slavery were invited to participate. This became the basis of the new party's creed, but in no way
excluded those who believed in a more vigorous contention
with slavery. These meetings were held in many States
in the winter of 1854-55, and took tangible form of organization in several of them. In Illinois, as noted, and about
the same time in Wisconsin, Michigan, New York, and
Massachusetts, at least, the party took the name Republican, and was so organized as early as 1855. In 1856, in
all the States where this anti-slavery party had any kind
of organization it took that name, since which it has been
known and dealt with as the Republican party. The
heterogeneous elements out of which it grew were so in-
congruous in many ways at its beginning that it seemed
a doubtful matter for years whether they could be harmonized into one organization.

There were men, leaders, newspapers, and other pub-
lications, supporting the party directly, indirectly, and incidentally, of every shade of diverging beliefs on the slavery question, from Phillips, Garrison, Giddings, Wade,
Chase, Lovejoy, and Sumner, Greeley and his *Tribune*,
Seward, Weed and his Albany *Journal*, who all avowed open
hostility to slavery in every form; to the more conserva-

tive Western and border State leaders, such as the Blairs,
Lane of Indiana, Bates of Missouri, and many other such
who united in the belief that no more than opposition
to slavery extension should be undertaken. In addition
to these, there were a few leaders, with about the same
number of followers of the dissolved Whig party, who
were scarcely anti-slavery, but strongly democratic, and
who would not support any one for office whom they chose
to designate "an Abolitionist." Of such there were a number in Illinois, whom Mr. Lincoln had to pacify and deal
with from time to time, who remained in the party more
because of his leadership than any particular belief. Conspicuous among them were his law partner, Herndon, Judge
Logan, of Springfield, Browning, of Quincy, David Davis,
of Bloomington, and others.

The parties thus held and divided went into the vigorous and excited Presidential campaign of 1856, when, for
the first time in our country, the system of slavery and
its extension or restriction were the stubbornly-contested
issues. The rising, giant-like new organization, the Republican party, had daring and energy to force the contest. It had been brought into existence as the power of
the people against the audacities of the slave-leaders, and
was growing strong on their delinquencies; but the storm
of indignant resistance not only made this new party and
gave it unexampled strength in a few months, but gave
new energy to men in all parties in the free States, and
aroused them as they had not been, to the fast approaching conflict.

Not every man by any means who was ready to resist
slavery at some stage of its aggression, was ready to leave
his party to do so. Thousands did, and there was endeavor
then and since to exaggerate their number, and to de-
nominate all who remained in the Democratic and American parties as pro-slavery inclined people, which was not

even an approximation of the real condition of public sentiment and party divisions.

To illustrate this, the Republican party, with all its enthusiastic vigor and accumulating strength, polled only a little more than one-third of the vote at the November election, while it was as well known as such matter could be, that two-thirds of the people of the free States were positively set and determined against further extension of slavery.

Another important condition of the political divisions in that election has not received proper recognition, and has not been conceded by the opponents and denouncers of Judge Douglas. This was that, so far as the vote had significance, it was an approval of his dogma of "Squatter Sovereignty" as the way in which to settle slavery in the Territories, for the aggregate Democratic and American party vote, both of which indorsed it, was 2,712,000 against the Republican vote of 1,341,000.

This approval was limited to the requirement of a free discussion and vote, and an honest counting of the result. This is noted here to show that, notwithstanding the furious denunciation of Judge Douglas in 1854, the people settled down in two years, satisfied with his proposed form of settlement. It was developed that, with a fair vote, honestly declared, Kansas would be a free State as surely as California. This was Douglas's belief before the passing of the Kansas-Nebraska Act. It was no less the opinion of Jefferson Davis and his party that the Territory could not be made a slave State in a fairly-conducted election, as their conduct better than their words disclosed. Hence, it was through Administrative influences, the courts, and direct force of arms that they intended making it such.

This seems like taking a low average of public opinion on slavery, yet it was the true one, for, with the teaching

that had prevailed in all parties and among the people
every way concerning the black man's freedom or slavery,
it was an advance, a real progress of sentiment indeed,
to reach the solution, by a majority vote of the Nation,
that the people of a Territory could exclude slavery from
it in organizing a State, by a fair vote, and be sustained.
To this settlement the slave-power instantly objected, and
proceded to the most effective propaganda of their system.

Slavery ought to have been excluded from the Territories because it was a system of wrong and injustice, just
as it should have been excluded from the Nation at once,
or at the farthest, in a definite period, as the slave-trade
was in a completed Nation under the Constitution. This
was not done, but the reverse was done. In this neglect,
indifference, and the indirect recognition of it, concessions
were made, whether we liked or disliked it. Through the
small negligences of the men who framed the best Government on the earth, slavery became a threatening monster before it was realized as such, and was so thoroughly knotted,
twisted, and ground into our system that nothing but the
rending and tearing process of war, that usually divides
or destroys nations, could tear it out of our free system.

It had prestige. It had precedent. It had been suffered to grow up from the very beginning of the settlements of the builded Nation. It was fastened on men and
parties, by law, concessions, and traditions, in so many
ways for centuries, that it was certainly a great achievement, in 1856, to have discovered and determined that
it could be voted out of a Territory; and if this could be,
it certainly could be voted out of the States as well, and
organized resistance was possible and a recognized necessity.

The border war in August threatened and almost certainly foretold Democratic defeat; but the restoration of
peace under Geary's determined measures saved Buchanan
from the defeat that seemed, a few months before, a cer-

tainty. The political events of the year began at the American party's Convention, which was held at Philadelphia, in February, 1856. Millard Fillmore, of Buffalo, New York, was made their candidate for President, and Andrew Jackson Donelson, of Tennessee, was nominated for Vice-President. Donelson was brought up in the Jackson household and named for the old hero, but with that the relation ceased. He was as inconspicuous and as rapidly forgotten as the brave soldier of New Orleans was eminent and kindly remembered.

The Democratic party met in Cincinnati on the 2d of June. It was a large, anxiously-expected, and fully-attended Convention. President Pierce, like many Presidents before and since his day, was anxious for renomination; but the border war was rank and obnoxious to thousands of Northern Democrats. His Administration, his policy, and his Cabinet were wholly devoted to the interests of slavery. The South would have accepted Pierce. The Northern Democracy had not only become tired of him, but would not take up Marcy, of New York, who, with Douglas, were the only Northern leaders left in the party who had any real strength.

Marcy was blamed for his service and acquiescence in the work of Pierce's slave-serving Administration. He had remained silent when he should have bravely spoken out. He had saved his party from defeat in the work of sending and sustaining Geary in Kansas, which very few of them saw or appreciated as well as he did; but with the silence that he did not have courage or disposition to break, he was no more than one of the servitors of Jefferson Davis. In addition, Marcy, one of the most capable statesmen of his day, who went down of too much silence on slavery and the border war, helped along, very much as several have done since, by dividing New York at the very worst point of emergency.

General Lewis Cass, though an old man, was strong
and vigorous in mind as he had ever been, but his defeat
for President in 1848 and the later defeat of his party
in Michigan wore heavily upon them. The contest narrowed to three, Pierce, Douglas, and Buchanan, and as
Douglas had no real chance in that Southern-controlled
Convention, the contest from the beginning was between
Pierce and Buchanan, whenever the latter gentleman should
be discovered to the Convention.

Buchanan had been minister to England during the
four years of Pierce's Administration, where, for the purposes of political advancement, no absence ever served
this venerable figure that looked like a man so well. Mr.
Blaine put it very forcibly in saying that "an alibi never
served any politician so well." In fact, he was nominated
because he had waited long enough, and was absent at
the right time to get the help of a Cabinet full of fossils
as antiquated as the country contained, that he would serve
the slave-power as willingly as any Northern figure of a
man, and that he was absent while Jefferson Davis and his
cortege were riding the party to the plains of civil war.

Buchanan was nominated on the sixteenth ballot, on
the fifth day, when Pierce's patronage-held delegates
were worn out. Buchanan received 168 votes, of which
121 were from the free States, 47 from the slave States.
Douglas received 122 votes, 49 from free States, 73 from
slave States. Cass had only 6 votes. Pierce never reached
a hundred votes, and was dropped on the fifteenth ballot.
After the sixteenth ballot, Buchanan's nomination was
unanimously agreed to. There was little or no significance
in the way the votes were given or what part of the country
they were from, for manipulation as an art was never
more successfully carried on than the slavery leaders had
the means and capacity for; consequently, there was never
an accident sprung on them in any Convention. It was

always fixed to suit their finest taste long before the idea
was announced or the man was turned loose in such a roaring crowd of disorderly Americans as a Democratic Convention. John C. Breckinridge, one of the most talented
Southern leaders, was nominated, without contention, for
Vice-President.

The platform was a lot of declarations, so skillfully
and ambiguously drawn out that only the designers could
understand or interpret. They were run out in such pliable
phraseology that, from the tyro, in his first written address in his club, to the roaring giant in the back timber,
they could be curved and inclined to fit the party beliefs
anywhere. All others, doubters, had no choice but to follow or leave the party in disgrace for insubordination.
The main issue was the relation of slavery to the Territories, on which the Northern Democracy demanded a
plainly-written avowal of the Squatter Sovereignty dogma,
so generally taught as the national panacea for its settlement.

The anxiety of the people of that day for a definite
form of law, together with the stronger desire for a peaceful method of settlement were so all-prevailing that, if
the Southern leaders had abided honestly by it as agreed
in Convention, it would have become the accepted plan.
This would have been submitted to on the part of the
Northern people, even with the addition of more slave
States, if the making of them were honestly conducted
when the Territory had the qualification for Statehood.

The free State people were earnestly opposed to further
extension, because of the inherent wrong of the system,
and because of the increasing power and domination of
the slave-kings, the threatening danger to free labor and
free institutions; but, notwithstanding these evil features
of slavery and the monopolistic control of parties growing
out of them, the desire for peace was so general that, with

faithful observance on the part of the South, it would have become the accepted solution. Their course of action disclosed the truth without comment, that the Southern leaders never intended to submit to it, but, on the contrary, intended to maintain control of the National Administration, when, by deception, intimidation, and force, they would fasten and sustain slavery where they wished. These facts, which were revealed to the light of all men beyond dispute, in the Kansas procedure, fastened on the slave-leaders the guilt and responsibility of plunging the Nation into the four years of Civil War.

The agreed declaration ran as follows: "*Resolved,* That we recognize the right of all the people of the Territories, including Kansas and Nebraska, acting through the legally and fairly expressed will of a majority of actual residents, and whenever their number justifies it, to form a Constitution, with or without slavery, and be admitted into the Union upon terms of perfect equality with the other States."

CHAPTER XXIX.

LIKE as in many similar gatherings all over the free States, some twenty persons met at Decatur, Illinois, on February 22, 1856. More than half of them were newspaper men conducting and publishing their papers with as much or little opposition to the spread of slavery as the people in their localities sustained them in doing, or going beyond that in some instances. They were not all Republicans, nor "Knownothings," nor Whigs without a party, nor Anti-Nebraska Democrats, nor Abolitionists; but they were all "forninst" the Democratic party and the further spread of slavery. They were gathered together in the excited state of public feeling, as American citizens, to do their part in making a new party with as strong anti-slavery declarations and leanings as the fact and the halting and drifting of unassimilated elements would permit them.

Mr. Lincoln was at the meeting, showing, as usual, his high capacity for entertaining others pleasantly and agreeably. His unequaled sagacity in shaping public or political movements, his good-humored way of unraveling tangles and harmonizing heterogeneous factions and elements into a strong and united body, rose, on this occasion, just as the exuberant hopes of the little assembly did, to the harmonious mixing of these lately contending partisans. This made him the most conspicuous "event of the meeting," as related by one of them. According to another: "Any man who could settle twenty men down peacefully in two hours' running talk, who had been jawing each other all at once all the forenoon, could make a political party if

63

any man could." Another of them said: "In his address
and work of two hours he brought us all to our senses, and
told us what we were there for, and how to do it.   He
set the whole of us to laughing and rolling over the benches,
so that when we regained our equilibrium we were ashamed
to differ any further in his presence.   We finished up our
business at once, and came home satisfied that we had
organized a harmonious party.   In the tangle and diverging
opinions there represented it seemed that no other man
could have accomplished it."   Another said: "Abe Lincoln
did it easier than I can tell it.   I tell you now that I verily
believe he could take any one of us into any party he
wanted to.   Men may say what they please about Lincoln,
but if he is not the strongest man in the country to lead
other men I am very much mistaken, and I do n't know
anything else very well.   I said that no other man could
have settled the differences that came up and kept coming
up until he got to his plans and solutions, which were accepted by all of us as soon as we came to understand them.
I do not believe that all of the rest of us put together
could have done it.   We know how difficult it is to get
even two editors to agree on any disputed question.   Then
think what we had in mind.   Over a dozen were contending,
and every one thoroughly convinced that he was right.
You may know what I think of a man who did this.   I
am for Lincoln all the time."

In this meeting the first Republican State Convention
in Illinois was called.   The Convention assembled May 29,
1856, at Bloomington, in the midst of exciting events and
more rising wrath on the part of the people than any one
of that day had ever known.   Alarms were spreading and
sounding all over the land where there had been nothing
but peaceful progress in happy and contented homes.   The
people were assembling in all their party organizations,
anxious to devise the ways and means to bring moderation

and peace rather than the war that was then in progress and spreading under the baleful influence of the slave-leaders. Atchison and his border gangs were deep in bloody war where wickedness reached its limit, where armed marauders were invading and destroying the homes and killing the free State people of Kansas. Only a few days before their most thriving town was sacked and burned, where the helpless and homeless citizens were driven from it, or bowed down in its ashes, suffering amidst its smoking ruins, wrought out with the consent, if not by direction, of the Pierce-Davis Administration.

The operations of this maddened and war-levying slave-power were reported over the land with every morning's sorrow-laden news. The discussions in Congress had risen to the rhetoric and impulse of war. Then, too, some men from the free States had got there who were not to be intimidated by the bluster and bravado of plantation society or the inhuman swagger of Atchison's marauders. There were a dozen or more like "old Ben Wade," of Ohio, and Potter, of Wisconsin, strong and determined men, who could loosen and use their tongues like flashing blades, and who were as determined to have a fair and free discussion of public affairs as men of their heroic character could.

These men in Congress, who were really the vanguard of the Union army in resisting the assaults of the slave-power, determined that, if needful in defense of their persons or the rights of the people they represented, they would use their fists, cutting weapons, and guns whenever the prize-ring methods were added to the achievements of the propaganda and Atchison's law-breaking bandits. In this tide of threatening danger, angry disputes, and pro-slavery war, another cowardly bully of a man, a Representative from South Carolina, one Brooks, crept up behind Senator Sumner and struck him down in his seat, beat him over his head and shoulders until he was insensible and almost killed. This, happening only a few days before the meeting at Bloomington, spread further alarm, and brought the most quiet and conservative men to the determination that these assaults and crimes must end, or if those hot-headed, devil-spirited slave-extenders would have war, assault, and bloodshed, they should have war in earnest, and enough of it to settle their caste-breeding system for all time.

It was this positive sentiment in the men of all loyal parties that forced the Davis propaganda and Pierce's reluctant Administration to arrest at once the infamous Atchison border law, and restore law and order under Geary.

In the blazing light of these events, such as no people could submit to and live in without the loss of self-respect, the Bloomington Convention was assembled. Ex-Governor Reeder addressed the arriving delegates the evening before. He was then fully aroused to the dangerous situation, from which he had barely escaped with his life; for, although he had faithfully served them, when out of office, he was a dangerous witness against them, and a hundred knives were drawn to slay him. This design was arrested, not out of respect of care for him, but from fear of the effect his murder might arouse. He had passed through Atchison's primary plans and crimes like a half-choked and stupefied man; but he was then out, and laid bare the wickedness of the marauders, led by the Vice-President, with consent of the Pierce-Davis Administration, so truthfully as to carry conviction wherever it was told.

When the Convention was assembled, it was a conglomerate political body; but in the enthusiasm produced by the slave-leaders' daring and audacity, all became willing to harmonize and concede something of former party beliefs, to join in common cause against partisans who had grown to be criminals.

Among those assembled were Judd, Cooke, and Palmer, who would not support Lincoln against Trumbull, now coming forward as a rebuke to their late party associates. Lincoln was perfectly willing to condone and do all he could for these and numbers of others like them, who met and harmonized against the more formidable enemy. "Dick Yates," who never lowered his standards nor lost a friend, who was an able leader all his life in the prairie kingdom, was there. Dick Oglesby, scarcely less than the others mentioned, was there in the front ranks, to stand and fight until he went down stricken almost to death. There were many others, a long list of able men, among whom were Swett and Arnold, that held character and position in any assemblage.

Trumbull was there. He had pardoned Lincoln for opposing him for the Senate, when he had three against Lincoln's forty-seven supporters. Owen Lovejoy, the brother of Elijah, who was murdered at Alton, Jesse Fell, some two or three Abolitionists, and the writer had an inconspicuous corner, where we had freedom of speech, but were cautioned to be careful, and not precipitate the Convention into a dispute over the relation of the forming Republican party to the various anti-slavery factions, which were then called Abolitionist. Lovejoy had been nominated for Congress in the Bloomington District by the consent or inaction of all the opposition to the Democratic party. Nevertheless, it was the general opinion that Judge Norton, the sitting Democratic member, would be re-elected. Lovejoy was let alone very seriously by many of the old-line Whigs and a few others in the Convention. These were supporting Norton against Lovejoy, because they would not support "an out-and-out Abolitionist" such as he was and declared himself to be. Lovejoy was nominated, not because of the favor toward him personally, nor yet in recognition of the Abolition element of the new party, but mainly because of his zeal and strength as a leader against the system that had slain his brother. Although not supported harmoniously, as many Abolitionists were not, nevertheless, as was the case all over the free States, these shunned Abolitionists were always present, helping, in every possible way, in the organization of the new party, because they believed in right against such a hideous and glaring wrong.

Our small corner of anti-slavery delegates, "Abolitionists" as we were then called, were content. We knew well that all the frowns of this new party against us would cease, and in the future we would be advised with because many thousands of quiet voters were with us. We could not escape the denunciation of the Democracy as it was then controlled; indeed, we rather desired it, as their denunciations, more rapidly than their professions, were driving the pro-slavery-inclined Democrats more and more every day in the direction of a distinct pro-slavery party. It was our constant object to make this plain; for there were thousands on thousands of anti-slavery Democrats who, the moment we convinced them of the fact that their party was sustaining the work of extending slavery, then and there would leave the party and act with us.

There were five hundred anxious, determined men in that memorable Convention with the sentiments, party beliefs, and leanings we have mentioned. In addition, there were a dozen or more, perhaps, of the David Davis type of followers. There were thousands of Whigs who soon became zealous anti-slavery men, among whom were Dubois and Hatch, John Wood, of Quincy, Oliver Davis, of Danville, Hurlbut, of Belvedere, and hundreds who attested their faith in the most zealous party work ever accomplished in the State, which turned the strong Democratic State to one that is yet as positively Republican as Pennsylvania, in less than two Presidential campaigns.

David Davis, Browning, and a few old Whigs, with pro-slavery leanings, loitered through the Convention, as they did through the years of intense application, labor, and sacrifice for the principles that regenerated the Republic, without a word in their favor, who were never satisfied in that or any other party when they were outside of the highest positions it had to give. There were not many of these, but in the crucial test of the Nation's peril even these few were needed. It comes now as indubitable proof of Mr. Lincoln's wisdom and far-seeing capacity that he worked and managed and crawled along as best he could, and kept a few thousand of these half-hearted men in the service and help of the party, and later of the Nation, because of the peril of our free institutions, that needed the help of every hand that could help to save, even those founded on the "recompense of the reward."

Other leaders not so wise would have broken with them; but this would have brought new and unseen dangers; while he, with unexampled strength and careful, wise management, although hampered and embarrassed beyond the point of most men's endurance, kept these half-baked Ephraims and office-fed mercenaries in useful service in the party and on the side of the Union. While he was using the strongest reasons for unity and harmony, and holding every faction or division in line for the most determined and united efforts, there were others, called prominent leaders, who were busy creating divisions and dissensions. His capacity to unite men was as clearly shown at Bloomington as it had been among the newspaper men at Decatur.

The ordinary work of the Convention was soon completed. A declaration that they were unalterably opposed to the extension of slavery was the main plank of their platform. This was agreed to without opposition or division, the only one unanimously accepted. A ticket composed of as true and patriotic men as ever led in any cause was unanimously nominated. Colonel W. H. Bissell, anti-

Nebraska Democrat, who had led a gallant regiment of Illinois volunteers at Buena Vista, was made candidate for governor.

When the nominations were over, at about three or four o'clock, the noise and confusion of the day quieted down. There were a full hundred of the five hundred delegates, who were apt, ready, gifted men, leaders and orators in the great, growing State, in all its divisions. These really able leaders were not given to silence, but prone to fervid and earnest speech. Ordinarily they could and did hold their hearers under their trained logic and reasoning, in all the regions round about. Here, with unexampled opportunity and the most enthusiastic body of men ever gathered in the State as auditors, every one of these leaders sat dumb and speechless, as much as if they had lost the gracious gift, until the single name of Lincoln broke the silence.

That Lincoln had reached high leadership was fully attested. Not one of the hundred or more distinguished leaders and speakers could be heard until he had spoken and led the way. There were Washburne, Trumbull, Lovejoy, Yates, Oglesby, Arnold, Swett, and Hurlbut, perhaps others we did not know so well, who had few equals; yet no one of them could have been prevailed on to speak, and, highly as they were respected and honored, no one of the Convention expected it.

Lincoln was the uncontested leader of his party in the State. Every one present, delegates and listeners, fully believed that he had a great duty before him, that he was the man for the time, and that he was God's leader or prophet, which was more firmly established in men's minds than it had ever been.

It was a pleasant May day. The hall was filled. Two thousand people or more were there besides the delegates. The windows were open and filled with anxious listeners.

The aisles were full of people, with chairs, boxes, and boards turned to their best use for seats. The stage, or platform, was raised some two feet, upon which most of the delegates took seats.

When Mr. Lincoln stepped to the front an expression of satisfaction ran through the assemblage, like the warm greetings to a returning friend. There was no distinct applause, but hearty consent and approval ran over every face. Above all, quiet prevailed, for all were intent on hearing the opening address, and all of it to the close, on the living topic that so completely filled the minds of men.

He was in the full vigor of his strongest manhood. In observing him there was a conscious feeling of the welladapted physical to his mental strength in his appearance. He stood a moment before the densely-crowded hall. In response, his attitude commanded attention. Standing erect in an easy attitude, calm, with a thoughtful cast shadowing his kind and mobile, but expressive face, he arrested every man's profound attention before he spoke a word. He was not pallid, nor melancholy, as he was at times, but careful, deliberate, and earnest as man ever was. His manner, position, and movement, as he stood before his anxious, expectant hearers, confirmed him in our minds as mighty and majestic a leader as God ever called to labor on the earth.

The thousands before him and the hosts they came out of believed in him. All this passed before us. He was as conscious, too, as leader ever was, of the load and the duty that came, not unexpected, but unsought. He was ambitious to be the leader, or whatever his people made him, but as wholly devoted to his work and cause in following as in leading, as he did that year for Fremont and Bissell, when there appeared to be nothing for himself but hard work and devotion. His address was a plain, candid story of the slavery question, its history in the Colonial times, at the forming of the Constitution, and the agreements then made, and the hope of the patriot fathers who made it; of its extinction in half the States; of its continued growth and expansion in the Southern part of the Nation; of the slave-trade; of its spread and encroachments into free territory, and the iniquity of fugitive-remanding laws.

He discussed the compromises the South had always demanded and so constantly violated; the war with Mexico, and the great extension accomplished by it. He analyzed the compromises or settlements of 1820 and 1850, and how the former had been disregarded and set aside; and the war for slavery, and nothing else, then raging on the border. All these were told intelligently, and truthfully explained, showing careful, patient study of the subject, with knowledge of the whole of it, and capacity to lay the whole matter plainly before them, illustrate its wrongs and diabolical horrors, including the war, where sons and brothers of some of the men before him had fallen.

This was the foundation of his address and appeal to the people. His pleading was that peace might be restored, that the evil might be restricted, and the Union, for which so much in blood and treasure had been freely given, might be saved. In this fervent appeal he was inspired; from the solid basis of an unassailable foundation, he rose to the realm of such startling grandeur and awe-inspiring thought that a conviction came and spread throughout the hall that the fire which touched his soul was more than human.

He was there, in that tragic rendering, leader, lawgiver, and prophet of the Most High. He was lost to all else save following the pathway God opened for him; where he reached commanding heights, and was pleading for justice, righteousness, and mercy, he appeared lost in the intensity of his theme, and brought hundreds involuntarily to their feet. An old man with his two sons sat near us, the father in front, who rose instinctively, his eyes fixed

on the speaker as if transfixed by the words poured forth,
and the whole three thousand were as children in the hands
of this master mind. His son spoke softly: "Father, you
are standing so that some of us can not see Lincoln's face.
We do n't want to miss a word or a look." The father
replied: "Well, John, I did n't know it; I felt as if something raised me. I do n't believe in spirits or supernatural
sights these days, but the light that flashed into my heart
was more than any man alone can diffuse. Did you see it,
John?" John replied: "Yes, I saw it and feel it, and I
believe everybody does. If you watch a minute, you will
see half the crowd leaning away forward or rising as you
did. They all seem to be held by the spirit, or something
else, that Lincoln has more of than any other man."

He had reached the hearts and consciences of the people.
They were swayed to and fro by the fire that burned in his
great soul. It was no mere happening. It was not in any
sense spontaneous or unexpected to him. There was no
part of his careful review, the legal summary or the merciful pleadings for right, justice, and mercy, but had been as
thoughtfully and laboriously framed and wrought out as
the achievements of architects, artists, or sculptors in their
highest designs, in either the Sistine Chapel, the Dome of
the Capitol, or St. Peter's. It had all been brought to
symmetry, beauty, and strength in as severe and skillful
work as any of these had ever been.

He thought out and told from his heart the plain, burning truths that defend and sustain the rights of men. He
stirred thousands more, and then the people of the land,
who followed him as Israel did Moses, to the foot of another Sinai, where they communed with God.

He aroused the people, not on Constitutions, laws, and
a Nation's boundaries, which of themselves are topics of
absorbing interest, but out of the stupor and confusion of
usurped law and authority that were plunging the Nation

into desperate war. He could and did reach the reason and judgment of men. His analytical and reasoning powers were not surpassed by any of the able men with whom he lived, discussed, and contended in friendly, busy labor for so many years.

This well-prepared address was not only his argument, but the fiery consummation of justice against the evil that threatened the peace and well-being of the people on every hand. In its delivery he gave himself to the subject so freely and completely that men, strong men, wept over the cruelties of human oppression and the assaulted liberties that had been baptized so often in patriot blood. He appealed to them in the truest eloquence of the human soul, arousing them to the truth, that "when the black man's slavery is complete and spreads all over the land, the white man's freedom will perish in the grinding of the white man's tyranny and oppression."

His address was that of a strong man, confident in right and justice in the work that has given poet, statesman, leader, and soldier their highest theme, that of manhood or the rights of man. Better or more powerful reasoning made in that high cause can only be found in the gospel of the Divine Master. In nearing the close of his triumph, for it was no less, he placed man "along the shining pathway in God's image, and only less than his Creator, where he would be and could be but for the misuse and abuse of those Divinely-given powers of his soul." There was nothing of malice or malediction in this beautiful, highly-wrought appeal, to help the weak and downtrodden, and more than appeal, almost command, "to preserve intact the best there is of human government on the earth, our blessed, glorious Union."

When he finished this wonderful address there was no hatred against the slaveholder, as such, in the hearts of his audience, but rather pity. Neither were there any

Anti-Nebraska Democrats, Whigs, Knownothings, or Free-
soilers, nor were there any Abolitionists, the despised sect;
for all had been harmonized into one body, to contend manfully for liberty and against slavery. All were Republicans,
according to the definition he had given.

He was made one of the electors-at-large for the State
for the fifth time. He gave this public service his attention without remuneration or expectation of reward, in
office, or emolument of any kind. He canvassed the State
more vigorously, if possible, than he had ever done. In
this campaign the interest was great, and the earnestness
of the people so intense that he gave more time to the
work than he had ever done before. The population had
rapidly increased, railroads had been built across the State,
so that he could get over it and see and address more
people, several times over, than he had ever done. In the
three months devoted to the work, from early August to
the election, he spoke about every day and night, frequently as often as three times. He visited over two hundred towns and villages in the State. The people were
deeply absorbed in the agitation, so much so that the whole
country for miles in every direction "turned out to hear
Abe Lincoln."

It was a common occurrence for ten to twenty thousand
people, farmers and their families, to attend the county
mass-meetings. Judge Douglas was in the same canvass
for the Democratic party. In two or three places they met
and held joint discussions, as they had before done in several campaigns. That year the State was quite evenly
divided between the two parties.

It was an unusual occurrence for any State to have
two such leaders. The spirit which these two men gave
to their followers, the ambition and energy it stirred up,
stimulated all to their highest performance of party service
or public duty. Although differing widely in capacity, in-

clination, and character, they were, nevertheless, just what they were held to be by the people, two of the strongest, most capable leaders and statesmen of their time or country; and, judged by the contests of a lifetime, they were more evenly matched than either side would concede to the other.

One of the main charges against the Republican party was that it was a sectional and disunion organization. This charge was taken up and replied to by Mr. Lincoln in his clear and direct reasoning as follows: "You further charge us with being disunionists. If you mean that it is our aim to dissolve the Union, I, for myself, answer that it is untrue; for those who act with us I answer that it is untrue.. Have you heard us assert that as our aim? Do you really believe that such is our aim? Do you find it in our platform, our speeches, or anywhere? If not, withdraw the charge. But you may say, that though it is not our aim, this will be the result, if we succeed, and that therefore we are disunionists in fact. This is a grave charge you make against us, and we certainly have a right to demand that you specify in what way we are to dissolve the Union. How are we to effect this?

"The only specification offered is volunteered by Mr. Fillmore in his Albany speech. His charge is that if we elect a President and Vice-President both from the free States it will dissolve the Union. This is open folly. The Constitution provides that the President and Vice-President of the United States shall be of different States, but says nothing as to the latitude and longitude of those States.

"In 1828, Andrew Jackson, of Tennessee, and John C. Calhoun, of South Carolina, were elected President and Vice-President, both from slave States; but no one thought of dissolving the Union then on that account. In 1840, Harrison, of Ohio, and Tyler, of Virginia, were elected. In 1841, Harrison died, and John Tyler succeeded to the

Presidency, and King, of Alabama, was elected acting Vice-President of the Senate; but no one supposed that the Union was in danger. In fact, at the very time Mr. Fillmore uttered this charge, the state of things in the United States disproved it. Mr. Pierce, of New Hampshire, and Mr. Bright, of Indiana, both from free States, are President and Vice-President, and the Union stands and will stand.

"You do not pretend that it ought to dissolve the Union, and the facts show that it won't; therefore, the charge may be dismissed without further consideration.

"No other specification is made, and the only one that could be made is, that the restoration of the restriction of 1820, making the United States territory free territory, would dissolve the Union. Gentlemen, it will require a decided majority to pass such an act. We the majority, being able Constitutionally to do all that we purpose, would have no desire to dissolve the Union. Do you say that such restriction of slavery would be unconstitutional, and that some States would not submit to its enforcement? I grant you that an unconstitutional act is not a law; but I do not ask and will not take your construction of the Constitution. The Supreme Court of the United States is the tribunal to decide such a question, and we will submit to its decisions; and if you do also, there will be an end of the matter. Will you? If not, who are the disunionists, you or we? We, the majority, would not strive to dissolve the Union; and if any attempt is made, it must be by you, who so loudly stigmatize us as disunionists.

"But the Union, in any event, will not be dissolved. We don't want to dissolve it, and if you attempt it we won't let you. With the purse and sword, the army and navy and treasury in our hands and at our command, you could not do it. This Government would be very weak indeed if a majority, with a disciplined army and navy and a well-filled treasury, could not preserve itself when attacked by an unarmed, undisciplined, unorganized minority. All this talk about the dissolution of the Union is humbug, nothing but folly. We do not want to dissolve the Union; you shall not."

It was foreseen, that if peace was not restored in Kansas, Buchanan's defeat would be a certainty. Mr. Marcy, Secretary of State, through the efficient and courageous work of Governor Geary, turned public sentiment, and made Buchanan President, without the help of Jefferson Davis and his associates and in spite of them. The Republican party, however, developed decisive strength, and was not a bit discouraged with the result, but ready to take up and carry on the contest with more vigor and energy and with better organization.

The campaign resulted in Buchanan's election by the following vote: Buchanan, 174 electoral votes; Fremont, 114 electoral votes; Fillmore, 8 electoral votes. The popular vote was over 1,800,000 for Buchanan, over 1,300,000 for Fremont, and almost 900,000 for Fillmore. Buchanan received the vote of the following States: fourteen slave States, Alabama, 9; Arkansas, 4; Delaware, 3; Florida, 3; Georgia, 10; Kentucky, 12; Louisiana, 6; Mississippi, 7; Missouri, 9; North Carolina, 10; South Carolina, 8; Tennessee, 12; Texas, 4; and Virginia, 15; and of free States: California, 4; Illinois, 11; Indiana, 13; New Jersey, 7; and Pennsylvania, 27. Fremont received the vote of the following eleven free States: Connecticut, 6; Iowa, 4; Maine, 8; Massachusetts, 13; Michigan, 6; New Hampshire, 5; New York, 35; Ohio, 23; Rhode Island, 4; Vermont, 5; and Wisconsin, 5. Fillmore received the vote of one slave State: Maryland, 8.

In the Illinois State election, Bissell, Republican, received 111,372 votes; Richardson, Democrat, 106,643 votes; and Morris, American, 19,241 votes. Buchanan's plurality was 9,164, while Bissell's, for governor, was 4,729.

This result came because of Colonel Bissell's gallant
service in the Mexican War, and because of an acceptance
to fight a duel with Jefferson Davis over a dispute concerning the battle of Buena Vista. Bissell, being the challenged party, chose muskets, with ball and buckshot, at
thirty paces. When Davis's friends found that Bissell was
in earnest, they declared that the acceptance was barbarous, to which Bissell readily assented, replying that, as
he understood it, that was just what dueling was, except
in cases where it was all braggadocio. When Davis's friends
discovered that if Bissell fought he intended to hurt somebody, they soon found means of explanation and peaceful
adjustment.

In that time when the swaggering bullies were threatening, not only the peace of the Nation, its States, and Territories, but orderly-inclined men in Congress and elsewhere,
free State people were pleased at the courage of Bissell
and Potter. The latter was a strong, resolute man, "a six-
footer" from the pineries of Wisconsin, who offered to
fight "one of the blue-blooded from one of the first families" with bowie-knives. His antagonist also believed that
such cool, deliberate carving as that would be barbarous,
to which Potter, as Bissell, agreed, with the reply, that if
they did not want to be "barbarous," the best way was to
settle their differences like civilized people.

This gave Bissell a decided advantage, but the underlying facts were that the Western people were strongly
attached to the Democratic party, and Douglas's great
power as a leader held them from a serious breakdown
that year.

Fremont was a gallant leader and organizer, but he did
not seem to develop the qualities of mind and statesmanship the people desired against antagonists prepared by
the slave-system for every encounter.

At the December session of Congress in 1856, President

Pierce, who was very much in the file-gnawing mood over his defeat for renomination, the rebuke of his party, and especially the policy of his Administration and the restoration of peace under Geary, wrote, in his Annual Message, the strongest denunciation of the "disunion Republican, sectional party," as his Secretary and master, Davis, dictated.

The campaign fully aroused Mr. Lincoln. Seeing the opportunity, he soon afterward made an address in Chicago, in which he very resolutely replied to the strictures and misrepresentations of Pierce's message, as follows: "We have another Annual Presidential Message. Like a rejected lover making merry at the wedding of his rival, the President felicitates himself hugely over the late Presidential election. He considers the result a signal triumph of good principles and good men, and a very pointed rebuke of bad ones. He says the people did it. He forgets that the people, as he complacently calls only those who voted for Buchanan, are in a minority of the whole people by about four hundred thousand votes, one full tenth of all the votes. Remembering this, he might perceive that the rebuke may not be quite as durable as he seems to think; that the majority may not choose to remain permanently rebuked by that minority. The President thinks the great body of us Fremonters, being ardently attached to liberty in the abstract, were duped by a few wicked and designing men.

"There is a slight difference of opinion on this. We think he, being ardently attached to the hope of a second term, in the concrete, was duped by men who had liberty every way. He is the cat's-paw. By much dragging of chestnuts from the fire, for others to eat, his claws are burnt off to the gristle, and he is thrown aside as unfit for further use. As the fool said of King Lear, 'He's a shelled peascod.'

"So far as the President charges us with 'a desire to change the domestic institutions of existing States,' and of 'doing everything to deprive the Constitution and the laws of moral authority,' for the whole party on belief, and for myself on knowledge, I pronounce the charge an unmixed and unmitigated falsehood.

"Our Government rests in public opinion. Whoever can change public opinion can change the Government just so much. Public opinion on any subject always has a central idea, from which all its minor thoughts radiate. That central idea in our political public opinion at the beginning was, and until recently has continued to be, the equality of men. And, although it has always submitted patiently to whatever of inequality there seemed to be as matter of actual necessity, its constant working has been a steady progress towards the practical equality of all men.

"The late Presidential election was a struggle by one party to discard that central idea, and to submit for it the opposite idea, that slavery is right in the abstract, the workings of which as a central idea may be the perpetuity of human slavery and its extension to all countries and colors. Less than a year ago the *Richmond Enquirer,* an avowed advocate of slavery regardless of color, in order to favor his views, invented the phrase 'State Equality,' and now the President, in his message, adopts the *Enquirer's* catch-phrase, telling us the people 'have asserted the constitutional equality of each and all of the States of the Union as States.'

"The President flatters himself that the new central idea is inaugurated; and so, indeed, it is, so far as the mere fact of a Presidential election can inaugurate it. To us it is left to know that the majority of the people have not yet declared for it, and to hope that they never will. All of us who did not vote for Mr. Buchanan, taken together, are a majority of four hundred thousand. But in

the late contest we were divided between Fremont and
Fillmore. Can we not come together for the future?

"Let every one who really believes, and is resolved that
free society is not and shall not be a failure, and who can
conscientiously declare that in the past contest he has
done only what he thought best, have charity to believe
that every one else can say as much. Thus let bygones
be bygones: let past differences as nothing be: and with
steady eye on the real issue, let us reinaugurate the good
old central ideas of the Republic. We can do it. The
human heart is with us; and better, God is with us. We
shall again be able, not to declare that 'all States as States
are equal,' nor yet that 'all citizens as citizens are equal,'
but to renew the broader, better declaration, including both
these and much more, that 'all men are created free and
equal.'"

This was the true Lincoln, in mind, purpose, and character, as he revealed himself in his plain and expressive
forms of language. He proceeded directly to his subject,
and, in well-rounded periods, hammered out the ground-
ings of his faith, in such forcible and unmistakable speech
that no prevarication nor misconstruction could fairly becloud or darken it. He was able to contend and differ in
the consideration of the theories, logic, and polemics of
systems and the details of government; but this was the
higher subject, the rights of man, in which every tendency
and inclination of his noble nature was wrought up to its
highest purpose and action.

It was so congenial and all-engaging to him that, with
his untiring strength, his means of research, and his unflagging devotion to the cause, he became the great master of humanity to man and the ablest defender, liberator,
and prophet of the century. He was a powerful, wise,
and discerning man in any undertaking, who would have
succeeded in many; but it was in behalf of oppressed and

struggling men he exerted himself to his highest capacities, and became God's leader among the people.

Whether it was in chopping wood for the widows and helpless about New Salem in the severe winters, helping many a hard-working settler save his homestead, helping many poor and distressed people in the courts through entanglements beyond their means or knowledge, teaching honesty, justice, and righteousness in his laborious campaigns, or in the use of the resources of our mighty Nation in saving the Union and liberating the darker men of our race, he was ever and always the same constant and determined friend and defender of the rights of his fellow-men. He was so true in this work that those who knew him best knew beforehand what would be his relation to any cause or individual in time of need.

Mr. Lincoln could have achieved and won success in many directions, especially in fortune-making, and have reached more than ordinary success among so many willing and helping friends. However, he steadily declined anything of the kind, chiefly because it would have taken his attention from the main purpose of his life. His success in his profession, when established, gave him the means of comfortable living. He could have won a fortune, as many did about him. He was frequently advised by friends to do so, but he always found more pressing duty, and declined.

He was a reformer; not one of those who grew angry and filled their minds with sharp criticism, severe denunciation, or malice toward those who differed with him. He was full of the idea that most men, when properly approached, were fair-minded and reasonable. Hence he was of all men the kindest natured, most considerate, and respectful with all who were anxious to learn, no matter how prejudiced they were. If they were sincere, his patience and good humor never failed him. But to the mere captious critic or noisy disturber he seldom gave attention, unless it provoked him to reply in some withering humor that would leave the poor fellow helpless, though generally benefited.

One of these asked him, at the close of an address, "Mr. Lincoln, how would you like to have your daughter marry a nigger?" Without apparent disturbance, he immediately replied: "My dear sir, it so happens that I have not been blessed with a daughter; but under such condition as you state, I would expect her to use as much discretion in the matter as yourself, and that she would find a great many white men that it would be best to avoid. She might, too, if you insisted in pressing your suit, ask you, 'Was your grandfather a monkey?'"

On one occasion, some time in 1856, he came into the private room in the rear of Mr. Gridley's bank. He laid about one thousand dollars on the table. Taking up a part of it, he handed the remainder, about nine hundred and forty dollars, to Mr. Gridley, saying: "I have collected more than I expected to-day. I would take it home with me if I was going there; but I am going to Chicago, and will leave it with you for the present." Mr. Gridley was a true friend of Lincoln's, and one of the most anxious that he should be "making more money." So taking the money, very pleasantly he said: "I know of a very good quarter section of land in the southwest part of the county. It belongs to a non-resident, who is anxious to sell it. It can be had for about $1,200, and is worth fully $1,600. It will sell for double that price within a year. I will, if you like, invest your sum here mentioned, and take care of it for you. I think you will double your money on it in a year, or perhaps less. Indeed, I will guarantee that much, if you desire, as you know I have several times wished to do as much as this. It will not bother me, and I will be glad to do it."

Mr. Lincoln turned uneasily in his chair, and facing Mr. Gridley with a pleasant but thoughtful look, replied about as follows: "Mr. Gridley, you know that I am deeply grateful for your disposition to favor me, and for the many kind and considerate evidences of it, which do not let me forget it, were I disposed to do so. I am thankful to you, for I appreciate what you do and continue to do for me in so many unselfish ways that no one knows of save myself. Nevertheless, I must decline this kind offer of yours that would, no doubt, profit me, and harm no one directly, as I view it. I have no maledictions or even criticisms on those who honestly buy, sell, and speculate in lands; but I do not believe in it, and I feel, for myself, that I should not do it. If I made the investment, it would constantly turn my attention to that kind of business, and so far disqualify me for what seems to be my calling, and success in it, and interfere with the public, or half-public service, which I neither seek nor avoid. So, with a feeling of increased friendship for you, I feel that I must be firm in purpose, and not engage in anything that will turn my mind from my present and increasing duties in the work I have chosen.

"In my early career I was unfortunate in business, as you know, which I now attribute to lack of experience and insufficient needs. I am satisfied of that in my own mind, and believe that very men have failed in business in our new, developing country because our ambition is so apt to outrun our judgment; but, notwithstanding these mishaps, I am confident enough of my own capacity to believe that, with the present need and opportunites, especially through the help of a man like yourself, whose business sagacity is beyond question, I could very well conduct some kinds of business and save money. But for the present I am wholly devoted to my work, and do not feel that I could divide the time so much needed in it with anything else. My work, too, I must say, presents itself to me now, which I have no right to avoid."

Although Mr. Gridley had known Mr. Lincoln well for at least fifteen years, and intimately for six or seven, he was completely upset and amazed at Lincoln's remarks. He was usually quick-tempered, excitable, and impulsive, and he would not have listened contentedly a minute to such statement as Lincoln's from any other man; but Lincoln's influence over him was so complete that he sat still. He said nothing until Mr. Lincoln finished, when he looked calmly across the table at Lincoln's earnest face, and thus addressed him: "Mr. Lincoln, you astonish me, indeed you do. I have been keeping along with a great many of your advanced ideas and foolish philanthropies, but this surpasses all. I don't take your design nor your work as foolish, mind you; it is good, better than people deserve. They are about all worshiping some stone or wooden god. A great many of them are content with these rich prairie lands of Illinois that I've been trying to point out to you as a real Canaan. You'll work and strive with the people, and some politician will get the turn on you as Trumbull did, and secure the senatorship, and leave you the applause. Really, Mr. Lincoln, I believe that you had better be conservative, like me, keep out of politics, go into the land business, and make a competency out of corn, cattle, and hogs. Let those who will sweat over governorships, senatorships, and judgeships. But, besides this, you have more than surprised me about land ownership. Are you turning, just at the age when men should be getting wise, to the French 'Fourierism'—I believe it is—or to Emerson's school of air and thin soups, a cosmogony or theories attenuated through and beyond the gases to a something beyond nothing? For neither Frenchman nor Yankee has seen enough of it to give it a name or tangibility.

"Do not let me annoy or disturb you. I am going to

take care of that piece of land myself, and some of these days, when we abolish slavery, and you are old and worn-out in public service, you shall have that identical piece of rich Illinois land to live on, while Emerson and Fourier are getting ready to live on unsubstantial things, on an exact, correct theory, while we will be living on the fat of these fertile prairies."

Mr. Lincoln replied: "You are challenging my judgment as to which to admire or which to do; whether I must admire your sarcastic humor and unsparing analysis, and contend for my side, or forget my own convictions and accept your conclusions. You are aware, however, that I can not avoid my duty, and whether I succeed or meet frequent disappointments as I have done, there is no man in the State who would require of me a more unflinching devotion to that duty than you would. I grant you, that if I should fail to render that dutiful service, your friendship is so sincere that you would let it burn in your heart and scarcely mention it; but you would know, as few men can, deep in your conscience, how Lincoln had failed, while you expected so much better of him, and had good reasons for it; and if I accepted this generous offer you would not be entirely guiltless."

Mr. Gridley replied: "You are correct, no doubt, in what seems to be a necessity, that no matter what may be the recognition you receive, or what remuneration may come to you for all your years of faithful public service, if any; nevertheless, I see it just as you say. You can have no divided duty, but must diligently pursue the work you have undertaken or give it up altogether. It seems strange, after two thousand years of the spread of Christian belief, that so little of it is put into practical operation. Men are, as I understand, constantly blaming me as greedy and over-reaching in my business, most of which is, I think, no more than envy. Some of these who have made these unfriendly remarks have been in undertakings of such doubtful morality that I would not, under any circumstances, engage in them. These are often very loud in their profession of the Master's belief; but money divides their duty, as it does the rest of us, and Pluto's gods possess them all or a good part of the time afterwards.

"You have chosen the life of a reformer. You have, as human affairs go, a self-denying, sacrificing career before you. I, as one who desires your highest good, would like to see a more peaceful and comfortable life ahead for you than that can be; but knowing that your course has been determined, no one will be more sincere in your cause as it needs time or the best means at my command.

"I am given to hasty, and sometimes inconsiderate expressions, rash outbreaks, or eruptions, as you might call them, which friends have misunderstood and taken offense at occasionally; but when men know me as well as you do they know it is a harmless idiosyncracy. So do not take any note of what I think you should or should not believe. I think that every one who can, should think, and be earnest about it, and do all he can. There are many things to reform before they are settled right. God put us on the earth to work, and to work out improvement and better living. It seems his plan that man should get only what he earns, for either his mind or body, and hence the struggle of centuries will, in some distant future, come to an honest, developed manhood, in which there will be neither tyranny, oppression, murder, slavery, nor extortion, but where men will be brethren as God designed them. How it will be with those who will not come to this belief I wot not."

Mr. Lincoln said: "I have enjoyed your kind interest. Your eruptions are not unpleasant. In an ordinary sense I have not sought the relation I hold in public affairs. I often come to a point where I feel I have done all the going and talking I can consistently attend to for awhile,

and settle down more determined to follow my law business; then I find a condition like the present, where I can
not decline going into a political campaign without dis-
appointing good friends, which no sensible man would do
without much better reason than I have. Besides all that,
and above it, the cause to which I have promised my best
efforts needs help. It seems more needy of it as the years
roll by. I feel that I can not abandon it, no matter whether
it brings success or defeat, as it has so often brought in
the past.

"Christ knew better than we that 'No man having put
his hand to the plow and looking back is fit for the kingdom
of God;' nor is any man doing his duty who shrinks and is
faithless to his fellow-men. Now, a word more about Abolitionists and new ideas in Government, whatever they may
be: We are all called Abolitionists now who desire any restriction of slavery or believe that the system is wrong, as
I have declared for years. We are called so, not to help out
a peaceful solution, but in derision, to abase us, and enable
the defamers to make successful combinations against us.
I never was much annoyed by these, less now than ever. I
favor the best plan to restrict the extension of slavery peacefully, and fully believe that we must reach some plan that
will do it, and provide for some method of final extinction
of the evil, before we can have permanent peace on the subject. On other questions there is ample room for reform
when the time comes; but now it would be folly to think
that we could undertake more than we have on hand. But
when slavery is over with and settled, men should never rest
content while oppressions, wrongs, and iniquities are in force
against them.

"The land, the earth that God gave to man for his home,
his sustenance, and support, should never be the possession of
any man, corporation, society, or unfriendly Government,
any more than the air or the water, if as much. An indi-

vidual company or enterprise requiring land should hold no
more in their own right than is needed for their home and
sustenance, and never more than they have in actual use
in the prudent management of their legitimate business, and
this much should not be permitted when it creates an exclusive monopoly. All that is not so used should be held for
the free use of every family to make homesteads, and to hold
them as long as they are so occupied.

"A reform like this will be worked out some time in the
future. The idle talk of foolish men, that is so common
now, on 'Abolitionists, agitators, and disturbers of the peace,'
will find its way against it, with whatever force it may possess,
and as strongly promoted and carried on as it can be by
land monopolists, grasping landlords, and the titled and un-
titled senseless enemies of mankind everywhere."

If all that Mr. Lincoln did in his busy twenty years
or more, to help people get or keep their homesteads or claims,
were told, it would throw a clear light on the work and real
character of the man. As it is, enough is known to establish beyond doubt that it took much of his time, and that
he never gave up the cause of any settler or distressed lit:-
gant while there was hope of saving it, and that most of
this was done for people who had scanty means of payment,
quite often none. Many were not able to pay anything at
the time. None of them paid more than very moderate
fees. The work was congenial to him, and no earnest man
ever came that he did not set to work at once, with all his
ability, influence, and untiring perseverance. He seldom
failed, and few doubted his success who saw the energy and
determination he had about it.

A number of friends talked this over at Bloomington
about the time of his inauguration. There were several of
us there at court, from the seven or eight counties where he
had been so actively employed for years, and a few from more
distant counties. All of us knew of some cases, some more,

some less, some for two or three years, and some as long
as ten years. One man had knowledge of a hundred or more
instances. Thus talking and estimating, we reckoned up
near one thousand homes and farms which he had saved
or helped to save for our people. His work was so complete
that no one knew of an entire failure; none that were even
partly so could be charged to him. Some of the claimants
had emigrated while he was contending for them. He saved
several of these after the parties had left, and only a few
were lost to them, and those because of abandonment.

It is well to think of such a record, especially those
who would and can do something for their fellow-men. During all this time many lawyers were making more out of
foreclosures and forced bankruptcies than he was making in
saving men's homes. In all this his law and court proceedings were only a small part of the labor. He hesitated at
no amount of outside service, as it was called, and carried
it on with all the patience required to bring final success.

We have related how he helped one settler, giving him
his own horse to get to the land office at Springfield. After
getting there himself, he rendered still further service that
aided the settler in securing his homestead. In a claim
against the Illinois Central Railroad, the writer became interested and helped in one case, which was about as follows:
A farmer in Champaign County contracted, through the
railroad agent, for a half-section of land, three hundred and
twenty acres. A few days after the farmer's last payment
the agent of the company absconded. The company refused
to complete title to the purchaser, averring that they were
not liable for some neglect of the purchaser, which, however,
was only technical.

The farmer had paid the company several thousand dollars. The tract had rapidly increased in value, and it appeared as necessitating a very serious loss or the doubtful
contingency of a lawsuit with a moneyed corporation. He

took counsel from lawyers in his vicinity and several friends, who gave him little or no encouragement, telling him that if he did succeed it would be after long litigation, which would probably cost him more than the repurchase of the land at double the former price. This double price was the best compromise offered him.

In this condition the claim came to the writer's knowledge. The farmer was an honest, hard-working man who had earned all he had by his own persevering labor. At his age, over fifty years, the loss would have been a crushing one. I wrote a letter to Mr. Lincoln, giving him the principal facts and asking his advice. In the return mail he replied, "Send me the papers, and I will give it attention." The papers were sent at once, and Mr. Lincoln started to Chicago the same day, where he laid the claim before the manager of the company, saying he would be in the city a day or two and await their reply to his plain demand for a complete conveyance of title.

The business took a full half-day, in which he was very earnestly engaged with the railway officials, including their counsel. His argument was clear and distinct. He demonstrated the company's liability beyond legal doubt. They wanted time, they said; but he insisted. So next day, without considering the liability, the manager informed him that they would not make the title as applied for; that the precedent would be injurious in several ways, and would likely encourage other agents to default and abscond.

The conclusion of the negotiations was related by Mr. Lincoln as follows: "When they rejected the honest and lawful settlement I was as near being angry as I ever permit myself to be. I stood a minute to think, so as not to make any faulty statement or propose anything which I could not carry out. My wits came to me in good time, however, and satisfied me at once. So, after fully recovering my equanimity, I replied: 'Gentlemen, Mr. Manager, and Counsel, I will be at the —— Hotel until four o'clock to-morrow afternoon, within which time I shall expect a deed as prayed for. This is something out of my present law work. It is a case I have taken up mainly on behalf of good friends. My client is justly, and by every fair consideration of the facts and equities, entitled to his deed. It is in my judgment a claim which any court of honorable men will concede on presentation; one such as your company can not afford to deny. Unless the conveyance is forthcoming, or your agreement for it in my hands before leaving the city, I will engage with our people to take every claim or suit against your company, where there is apparent liability, with or without compensation;' on which I left the office."

The next day the deed, with a very courteous letter, was sent him. Thus, through this determined sort of work, our friend and client saved his land, worth fifteen thousand dollars at the time. Mr. Lincoln was satisfied with a fee of fifty dollars and expenses, less than one hundred dollars all told.

Such acts as these were of common occurrence, and establish the truth, wherever they are learned and told, that his highest ambition was to be faithful and true in the service of his fellow-men, taking fees so moderate, or none at all, as to place his unequaled services within the reach of all who were under the hand of the oppressor, in whatever form or kind of distress.

CHAPTER XXX.

LATE in August, 1856, the writer met Judge Douglas in Bloomington. We had a pleasant evening together. Although I had met him occasionally, this was the first extended conversation since we lived in Springfield several years before, when I was a boy. He was worn and tired with the hard work of his canvass and the irregular traveling required to get to so many places, many of which were off the railway or steamboat lines. He had aged very perceptibly since we had known him so well in Springfield. He had a careworn, anxious look, that betokened mental worry, and without hesitation he said that he was greatly distressed by the strained and threatening relation of the North and South on the slavery question.

He received me graciously, and our conversation ran freely. His friendship for my father put us at ease at once. As he encouraged the conversation on public affairs, I was pleased to let it take that direction, and listen to what he had to say. I asked him questions which brought him at once to a full declaration of his beliefs and opinions. He said, "I suppose you are an ardent Abolitionist, and are following your father in a much more rapid development of his ideas than he ever expected?"

I said: "I have been counted an Abolitionist until recently. This year we are all Republicans, who seem to be going as far on slavery as it is prudent, or possible, at least; but I am really an Abolitionist, with no desire to shift the responsibility. After a few such campaigns, which are getting to be as much war as politics, I believe you and your

94

Northern Democrats will be as much Abolitionists as any of us." I reminded him then that I heard Nimmo Browne tell him that the slave-leaders were getting ready to extend their system by force, civil and military, if need be, since 1845, when they waged war against Mexico.

Douglas replied: "I see you people do not have the respect for the Constitution and the agreements made in consonance therewith and under its authoritative protection. You assail slavery as a moral wrong, and end there, forgetting that if it is wrong, it still has for right of existence the protection of our Constitution and over sixty-five years of continuous, friendly legislation and settlements to sustain it. Further, the Southern people are more excitable and hot-tempered than we are, and, regardless of our opinions, they look upon interference with slavery as an attack on their vested rights under the Constitution and these long years of uninterrupted protection.

"This is their contention, and no matter how much you are opposed to their system, their rights should be fairly considered and recognized. Your party seems to hang its entire belief on opposition to the extension of slavery. The Democratic party, after the most careful consideration of the question, and demanding concessions from both its Northern and Southern factions, has agreed that the best way to settle the dispute whether slavery shall be extended into any forming State is to let the people, who are to be the real State, settle that for themselves, as they do all other domestic questions. This they practically did in California in 1850, and I hope they may do the same in Kansas. I assure you that, to accomplish a fair settlement and an honestly-conducted election by the qualified voters, I will do all that is in my power."

I replied that I was pleased to hear this statement, but that it was very apparent that the slave-leaders, who were leading the Democratic party, neither desired nor expected

a fair and honest settlement, and were then forcing slavery
into Kansas and killing its people in armed invasions. I
said that, like my father, I did not believe that any man
possessed the right to vote another man, red, white, black,
or yellow, into slavery, even with his consent, as it was a
wrong against society, bringing their labor unjustly into
competition with that of free men, and a sin against men
and against God, who made men equal in law.

"If you will stand firmly by your determination," I continued, "that slavery shall not be established in Kansas, however, until it is done and ratified by a majority, the people
will agree to this as a settlement. Indeed, it is the best
they can hope for; but the slave-leaders will not submit.
They know as well as we do that slavery is doomed to certain exclusion, whenever it is honestly submitted. They are
in full possession of all the powers of Government, and are
forcing slavery into the Territory. Neither are they deceived
about you, as it appears even now. They will turn against
you as mercilessly as they have turned against Benton the
moment they feel certain you will serve them no longer.
You are a Democrat; but no slave-leader is, or ever was one.
Without being presumptuous, I am full of my father's belief, that the party is now preparing for your overthrow.
It is indeed true, as you fear, that this is a perilous time,
and we believe that the cause of it is away deeper than
political parties, their organization, or supremacy. It is the
slave-leaders' determination to make this a slave Republic
by force of arms. Failing in that, they will attempt to
separate and divide the Union."

The meeting was a pleasant one, where the conversation was
unrestrained, conducted in running friendly talk that made it
an agreeable private chat. He said: "The Southern leaders
have always mistrusted me, for since I have been in Congress I have always sustained Jackson and his ideas, as against
Calhoun's. Without any evidence beyond my own apprecia-

tion of what is going on, I am certain that Davis, Benjamin, and Mason are plotting against me personally, envious because of my hold on the Northern Democracy. I could not say so in so many words that overtures were made to me before the Cincinnati Convention, for I turned them aside to begin with; but I was well aware than any concessions on my part would be met at once. In place of making any concessions, I stated, in the presence of Benjamin and Mason, their leaders in the Senate, that I would go no further than the 'squatter sovereignty' principle for the settlement of slavery in the Territories, and that it must be honestly and fairly voted upon, without armed interference or molestation of any kind.

"At the same time I most unequivocally denounced Atchison's invasions and the whole border imbroglio from beginning to end. I would not have changed my position in the least to receive the nomination for President. This much the Southern leaders know very well. They would like very well to set me aside, as they did Benton, Cass, Marcy, Ewing, and others; or, better still, they would prefer provoking me to leave the party. I think I understand my duty. It seems very plain. I will neither retire nor be driven. I have been in the party all my life. I may be mistaken, and make errors, as men are so liable to do, but I fully intend to be faithful to its principles as long as I live.

"I am constantly annoyed by the men and newspapers that have such sudden convictions, and leave their party all at once. Upon their leaving, before there has been the change of a word or line in any party belief, they set to work, with unspeakable venom, to denounce the party, and myself, more positively, as a scheming politician, faithless to my duties. It has been one of the continuing labors of my life to help and try to help this graceless sort of men."

This danger was imminent and threatening. President Pierce's Administration was wholly devoted to the pro-slavery cause, checked only that they might elect another President who was fully pledged to the slave-leaders before his nomination. Intimidation, bluster, and assault were not only raging on the border, but the swagger of the "bully," and the cowardly, creeping assault of the assassin had reached the halls of Congress.

Senator Sumner, of Massachusetts, was stricken by Preston Brooks in his seat, while helpless, in the presence of two other conspirators aiding the cowardly wretch, all three of them members of the House of Representatives. The petext for this attack on a senator was an alleged punishment for a speech delivered by him upon the "Crime in Kansas." His disclosure was so fearlessly done that they determined to kill him for it. Brooks, of South Carolina, vile enough for the work, was found, and the others, Edmonson and Keitt, of the same State, were the cowardly conspirators in the venture.

Sumner's speech could not be replied to. It was the truth, and it revealed the planned and premeditated murder of helpless people in Kansas. These were some of the villains of the propaganda rising to the bloody spirit of the border, in endeavor to kill the witness that was telling the world of their border atrocities. It was true that Sumner knew how to tell such a tale as the killing at the behest of the slave-power. In it, too, he put Butler, a senator from South Carolina at the time, the uncle of the "Bully" Brooks, into the crucible of his fusing rhetoric, that left the maligner of the Western people no more than a little dross, burned out and useless.

Sumner said: "With regret, I come again upon the senator from South Carolina, Mr. Butler, who, omnipresent in this debate, overflowed with rage at the simple suggestion that Kansas had applied for admission as a State, and, with incoherent phrases, discharged the loose expectoration of his speech, now upon her representative, and then upon her people. There was no extravagance of the ancient parliamentary debate which he did not repeat; nor was there any possible deviation from the truth which he did not make, with so much of passion, I am glad to add, as to save him from the suspicion of intentional aberration. But the senator touches nothing that he does not disfigure with error, sometimes of principle, sometimes of fact. He shows an incapacity of accuracy, whether in stating the Constitution or in stating the law, whether in detail of statistics or the diversions of scholarship. He can not open his mouth but out there flies a blunder."

This gun-scaring, strike-and-run terrorism against helpless people in and about Congress and the Capitol was the same in spirit and character as that of the more courageous outlaws on the border; but it ended when our side got out their guns and brickbats. The speech for which Senator Sumner was so feloniously assaulted was delivered in an open session of the Senate, to which no objection was made by any Southern senator nor the presiding officer. Mr. Sumner, although a peacefully-inclined man, was in no sense cowardly or evasive. He was strong-framed, muscular, and active, and could have overpowered Brooks in an equal contest.

About the same time a violent member of the House made an assault on Mr. Greeley, of the New York *Tribune*, on the streets of Washington. Another, from Virginia, attacked a Washington publisher, and still another, from California, shot and severely wounded a Negro waiter at Willard's Hotel. The Capital was full of the swaggering "bullyism" of the plantations until some two or three hundred Northern people thereabout armed themselves and informed these braggadocios that they were ready to protect themselves. When this was done, the cane-and-pistol war subsided; for much as they blustered, they were not seeking an equal encounter. They were only the small desperadoes set on by the more cowardly and cunning to terrorize the people and their representatives from the free States.

Several challenges to fight duels were made. The principal one was sent by Brooks to Anson Burlingame, from Massachusetts, who had unmercifully scored and denounced Brooks in the House. Burlingame accepted, and chose rifles at thirty paces, and some place in Canada for the meeting, to which Brooks objected that his life would be in danger in passing through such a hostile country. Senator Wilson, of Massachusetts, was also challenged by the same red-handed Brooks, to which Wilson replied, saying, "I never fight duels; but I religiously believe in the right of self-defense." Rather than meet an investigation, this same Brooks was permitted to resign, when he was immediately re-elected.

Senator Sumner went abroad, where he was treated through a long and painful illness of some two years. His injuries resulted in permanent affection of the brain. He was re-elected, and held his senatorship during his life. He did not return for participation in public affairs until June, 1860, when the heated discussions foretold the coming conflict. Brooks died in 1857, as also did the aged Butler, the senator, so that when Sumner returned both the senator and the man who waylaid and struck him had passed into eternity.

Sumner came back to his service without passion or desire for revenge, but more determined against slavery and better informed than most men on the terrible nature of the coming conflict. His strong words corroborated the belief that many had reached, some as far back as 1845. After his return, in his first address in the Senate he said in part: "Time has passed, but the question remains. Slavery must be resisted, not only on political grounds, but on all other grounds, whether social, economical, or moral. Ours is no holiday contest; nor is it any strife of rival factions, of white or red roses, of theatric Neri and Bianchi; but it is a solemn battle between right and wrong, between capital good and capital evil. Grander debate has not occurred in our history, rarely in any history; nor can this debate close or subside except with the triumph of freedom."

He returned to a Senate that had greatly increased its anti-slavery membership, so largely that the opprobrious name of "Abolitionist" was not applied to him, and, for company,. more than half the Senate were determined that Kansas should have a fair vote on slavery.

The election of Buchanan, with a pro-slavery Congress in both branches, and full control of the Government, marked the final and supreme triumph of the slave-power, as held and declared, if not believed by the slave-leaders. The strongest facts against this final settlement of slavery were that, although Buchanan and a pro-slavery Congress had been elected, it was the result of breaking up parties into divisions, with an imperfect understanding of the one great question, and that he and those elected with him did not represent anything like a majority of the people, but fell short of it almost half a million votes.

The Fillmore vote of over eight hundred thousand was the uncertain quantity; but the grip on the Government by this baleful dictatorship was strong, almost to death, against freedom. In addition to the control of the Executive and Legislative branches, they prepared for and held as certain control of the Supreme Court as they did over a pro-slavery caucus in South Carolina. The court consisted of nine members. Five of them were from slave States, and were indebted to Calhoun and his successors, Jefferson Davis and his coterie of control, for their positions. They were as fully subservient to the political control and desire of these leaders as the corporation lawyers, advanced to that high tribunal in later times, have been and are to the combinations which gave them breath and existence. It was then, as it is perhaps now, no more nor less than a partisan political body, as much so as the Senate and House of Repre-sentatives. In the ante-bellum court such eminent jurists and statesmen as Crittenden, of Kentucky, and Badger, of North Carolina, were rejected by the Senate for political causes. The five members from the South were so devoted to the behests of slavery that Davis, Benjamin, or Stephens could not have served slavery better. These five from the South were the Chief Justice Taney, Catron, Wayne, Daniel, and Campbell. The four from the Free States were Asso-ciate Justices McLean, Nelson, Grier, and Curtis.

This partisan court rendered a decision in the case of "Dred Scott" and his wife, and took opportunity to declare a usurping, extra-judicial opinion, which would have left little more of usurpation to be done to give authority to hold slaves in any State of the Union permanently. The decision did declare that the slave Scott and his family were slaves after two years residence in the free State of Illinois, and what was supposed, up to the date of this infamous de-cision, to be the free Territory of Minnesota.

The case had been hanging in the court for years, all made up, biding the time when the slave-leaders thought that the opportune moment to fasten slavery on the Nation had arrived; but they went too far. They were no more then than conspirators provoking the wrath that was to work out and compass their downfall. President Pierce had knowledge of the case. President Buchanan had more positive knowledge of it, and the Administration had con-trol of it, as a forthcoming settlement of the slavery ques-tion, referring to it in his Inaugural Address.

He had no more right to private knowledge of what would be the future action of the court in any case before it than any other citizen. The effect of the unrighteous decision was that, notwithstanding the domicile of the slaves by voluntary act of their master in the free State of Illinois for more than two years, and in a Territory of the United

ROGER B. TANEY

BENJAMIN R. CURTIS

JOHN M'LEAN

SAMUEL NELSON

States, Minnesota, then under the operation of the Missouri Compromise, these people, made free by the State of Illinois and this act of Congress, were remanded back to slavery.

In addition, the decision proceeded to declare that the Missouri Compromise was unconstitutional, and that slavery existed, by right of law under the Constitution, in all of the Territories of the United States, and that Congress did not have power in any of said territory. This much for the Territories, which, with the other part of the dark, inhuman decision, that the laws of Illinois, although assuming to prohibit slavery, could not do it, left very little or nothing, if not stubbornly resisted, to make the United States a slave Empire under the mask of a Republic.

The decision was not the settled belief of the court, such as it should have been, on a subject of vital and commanding importance, but an overreaching act of a partisan court. We have related the effect and the act of the court remanding these people into slavery; but in this dishonored body there were two brave, clear-headed members whose wisdom, learning, and fitness for their high place could not be questioned, whose reasoning, courage, and integrity could not be shaken. These were Associate Justices McLean and Curtis. McLean's dissenting opinion, which held to the spirit as well as to the letter of our institutions, was better law and much better policy and sense than the majority decision. It is as follows: "It involves a right claimed under an act of Congress and the Constitution of Illinois, which can not be decided without the consideration and construction of those laws. Rights sanctioned for twenty-eight years ought not and can not be repudiated, with any semblance of justice, by one or two decisions, influenced, as declared, by a determination to counteract the excitement against slavery in free States. Having the same rights of sovereignty as the State of Missouri in adopting a Constitution, I can perceive no reason why the institutions of Illinois should not receive the same consideration as those of Missouri. The Missouri court disregards the expressed provisions of an act of Congress and the Constitution of a sovereign State, both of which laws for twenty-eight years it has not only regarded, but carried into effect. If a State court may do this, on a question involving the liberty of a human being, what protection do the laws afford?"

The dissenting opinion of Justice Curtis was more elaborate and fully as determined as the above extracts from McLean's. It was more specific, but threw no clearer light on the law and rights involved. Curtis had been appointed on the recommendation of Daniel Webster. McLean, who had been Postmaster-General under Adams, was appointed by President Jackson.

The opinion of Judge Curtis in part is: "Congress has complete control of the Territories, under the Constitution, to pass all needful legislation for their government and control. All persons and property for the time are subject to its authority and legislation. It has authority in law and precedent to abolish slavery in the Territories, and in the District of Columbia." The two judges also sustained the good old English law that slavery was an unjust, iniquitous system, so vile and inharmonious to all human law that it could not exist anywhere except under positive legal enactment, with power to enforce it. Hence, inferentially, it was such an evil that force alone could sustain it under wicked and inhuman legislation.

Taney was a man of learning and ability, appointed by Jackson. He was a venerable old man, who had held many public offices for a lifetime, and was a man of many private virtues. He was charged with the chief responsibility of this outrageous decision and the more obnoxious extrajudicial opinion, which decision and opinion, taken together, were equivalent to the declaration that the Negro was no more than an animal, a property possession, "who had no rights which a white man was bound to respect." The law, as construed by the Supreme Court, established slavery in the Territories, and, by inference, it would and could extend it into the free States.

There was small wonder that the heavens were aflame with the maledictions and emphatic resistance of all kinds of people in the free States. Men by thousands were astonished, and were brought to their most busy preparation for ways and means to contend against this defiant aggression of slavery. Democrats, Republicans, and men of all beliefs and creeds were outraged with this pusillanimous betrayal of the court. Taney passed under an unmerciful castigation by freedom-believing people everywhere, such as no high civil officer of our Government ever did; and he deserved it, as far as he had the sense and courage to be responsible; but the truth was that the weak old man, in his dotage perhaps, was no more than untempered mortar in the hands of a builder.

Taney was always counted the chief sinner in the work of making this devil-dictated decision; but he was hardly more responsible, even if he was in full possession of his senses, than Davis, Benjamin, Buchanan, Mason, and Jere Black, who at the time controlled every utterance of the court. The history of this should remind the people that the frequent and convenient prevarication of law and sense, against a hundred years of accepted Constitutional laws, and several half-leaning decisions sustaining property rights against the rights of men, should lead to an entire reform in the manner of constituting our highest court. No civil officer can be safely trusted with the prerogatives and power now asserted by that court without direct responsibility to the people. No man in the Republic should hold civil authority or power for more than four years without re-election.

This decision was bad; nothing less than a cruel and diabolical distortion of law from the beginning to the end of its two hundred and forty pages. It was an insolent defiance of the laws of God, as well as utter disregard of the merciful enactments of man, under English and American law. Taney said: "In the opinion of the court, the legislation and histories of the times, and the language used in the Declaration of Independence, show that neither the class of persons who had been imported as slaves, nor their descendants, whether they had become free or not, were then acknowledged as a part of the people, nor intended to be included in the general words used in that memorable instrument. It is difficult at this day to realize the state of public opinion in relation to that unfortunate race which prevailed in the civilized and enlightened portions of the world at the time of the Declaration of Independence and when the Constitution of the United States was framed and adopted. But the public history of every European nation displays it in a manner too plain to be mistaken. They had for more than a century been regarded as beings of an inferior order, and altogether unfit to associate with the white race, either in social or political relations; and so far inferior that they had no rights which a white man was bound to respect; and that the Negro might justly and lawfully be reduced to slavery for his benefit. He was bought and sold, and treated as an ordinary article of merchandise and traffic whenever a profit could be made by it."

This false, distorted, and heartless consideration of human rights was argued, in painful particularity, from the false basis to the more false structure. It was a Nation-enslaving decision, and so intended. It was poured out in columns and pages in as dull a stream of besmearing justice as ever befouled the record of any court, all terminating in the foregone and foreordered declaration that a Negro was not a man, but property, and no better than a chattel. To those who are curious to know the arrogance and tyrannical heartlessness of slavery as it existed here before its overthrow, this decision throws a full light on the subject that so brutalized men and dulled the wits of senators, judges, and Presidents that it hardened their hearts, who, like tyrants of all times and history, in greedy gain justified the bondage of men in defiance of God's law.

Taney further declared: "The only two provisions of the Constitution which point to them include them as property, and make it the duty of the Government to protect it. No other power in relation to this race is to be found in the Constitution." It seems incredible now to think that any court in Christendom, since the Spanish Inquisition or the murdering one of Jeffreys, could be found so trained and bound that its humanity had so withered and its wisdom so turned backward, that all it had of "justice tempered with mercy" had fled. To this diabolism of misconstructed law and falsified history Justice Curtis asserted and replied in part:

"In five of the thirteen orginal States at the adoption of the Constitution colored persons then possessed the elective franchise, and were among those by whom the Constitution was ordained and established. It is not true in point of fact that the Constitution was made exclusively by the white race; and that it was made exclusively for the white race is, in my opinion, not only an assumption not warranted by anything in the Constitution, but contradicted by its open declaration that it was ordained and established by the people of the United States for themselves and their posterity; and as free colored persons were then citizens of at least five States, and so in every sense a part of the people of the United States, they were among those for whom and whose posterity the Constitution was ordained and established."

In another paragraph he rent asunder still further the wretched opinion, saying: "I shall not enter into an examination of the existing opinions of that period respecting the

African race, nor into any discussion concerning the meaning of those who asserted in the Declaration of Independence that 'all men are created equal; that they are endowed by their Creator with certain inalienable rights; that among these are life, liberty, and the pursuit of happiness.' My own opinion is, that a calm comparison of these assertions of universal abstract truths, and of their own individual opinions and acts, would not leave these men under any reproach of inconsistency; that the great truths they asserted on that solemn occasion they were ready and anxious to make effectual, whenever a necessary regard to circumstances, which no statesman can disregard without producing more evil than good, would allow; and that it would not be just to allege that they had intended to say that the Creator of all men had endowed the white race exclusively with the great natural rights which the Declaration of Independence asserts."

On the authority of Congress over the Territories his reasoning overwhelmed Taney, both in fact and the unopposed construction of law for sixty years; in theory, practice, and precedents. On this point Judge Curtis says: "There are eight distinct instances, beginning with the first Congress and coming down to the year 1848, in which Congress has excluded slavery from the territory of the United States, and six distinct instances in which Congress organized Governments of Territories by which slavery was recognized and continued, beginning also with the first Congress and coming down to the year 1822.

· "These acts were severally signed by seven Presidents of the United States, beginning with General Washington and coming down regularly as far as President J. Q. Adams, thus including all who were in public life when the Constitution was adopted. If the practical construction on the Constitution, contemporaneously with its going into effect, by men intimately acquainted with its history from their personal participation in framing and adopting it, and continued by them through a long series of acts of the gravest importance, be entitled to weight in the judicial mind on a question of construction, it would seem to be difficult to resist the force of the acts above adverted to."

On the history of our fundamental law and the declared purposes in the establishment of the new Nation and its relation to slavery, no logic or reasoning was clearer than that of Judge McLean, who said: "I prefer the lights of Madison, Hamilton, and Jay as a means of construing the Constitution in all its bearings, rather than to look behind that period into a traffic which is now declared to be piracy and punished with death by Christian nations. I do not like to draw the sources of our domestic relations from so dark a ground. Our independence was a great epoch in the history of freedom, and while I admit that the Government was not made especially for the colored race, yet many of them were citizens of the New England States, and exercised the rights of suffrage when the Constitution was adopted, and it was not doubted by any intelligent person that its tendencies would greatly ameliorate their condition.

"Many of the States, on the adoption of the Constitution, or shortly afterwards, took measures to abolish slavery within their specific jurisdiction, and it is a well-known fact that a belief was cherished by the leading men, South as well as North, that the institution of slavery would gradually decline until it became extinct. The increased value of slave-labor in the culture of cotton and sugar prevented a realization of this expectation. Like all other communities and States, the South were influenced by what they considered to be their best interests. But if we are to turn our attention to the dark ages of the world, why confine our views to colored slavery? On the same principle white men were made slaves."

Of the authority of Congress he said: "The judicial mind

of this country has agreed on no subject within its legitimate action with equal unanimity as on the power of Congress to establish Territorial Governments. No court, State or Federal, no judge or statesman, is known to have had any doubt on this question for nearly sixty years after the power was exercised."

This famous Dred Scott decision was one of the culminating events of the slave-power's ascendency in the Nation. It had been conveniently held back a year or more so as not to interfere with the election of Buchanan. If it had been delivered before, he would have been defeated; but after his and the party's apparently decisive triumph, the slave-power felt sure of their continuing supremacy. They thought that nothing stood in the way of their unlimited control; hence this barbarous decision and their attempted overthrow of Douglas. But human events are controlled by a higher power, and God, in his beneficent wisdom, makes the wrath of men to praise him. Dred Scott, his wife, and two daughters were liberated at St. Louis, Missouri, May 26, 1857. During the progress of the case in court they became the property of Mr. Chaffee, a Republican member of Congress from Massachusetts, who emancipated them.

This decision, instead of being appropriate and the thing needed for complete and effectual settlement under the supremacy of the slave-power, was the one thing apparently needed to arouse the people from their lethargy to the most resolute defense of their liberties. The public press, the Christian denominational papers and periodicals, men in all kinds of callings, took time out of their busiest days unsparingly to denounce it. It seemed that almost everybody was wrought up as never before on any public concern.

Much as had already been said on the slavery question, and terrible as had been the invading warfare of the border, thinking men by the thousands were now suddenly con-

vinced that all that had been charged against the advancing
slavery despotism was true. Their tongues were loosed at
once, and they came to the rugged determination to take
up this defiant assumption of the slave-power and fight it
out to the bitter end.

The result was that the Supreme Court was properly
adjudged to be a political body, fully in the service of the
slaveholding element. The people have since that time lost
confidence and respect for it as a high judicial tribunal, and
have held it to strict accountability for its several acts as
a political body. Lamentable as this history may appear,
the court has, nevertheless, been more noted for its judicial
acts in the restriction than in protecting or enlarging our
democracy or the rights of men.

No other man in the Nation was placed under the torture, jeopardy, and political tribulation that Judge Douglas
was by this overreaching decision and party declaration; for
it was no less. The slave-power, in long years of management and manipulation, had gained complete control of the
Government. They had overcome and overthrown every
prominent leader in all parties, North or South, except
Douglas, who resisted their dictatorship. He stood so much
in their way as to be their principal obstacle, and of all they
encountered he had the most stubborn will and lion-hearted
courage.

He acted to the lasting benefit of free Government and
his own unimpeachable honor, regardless of the bitter and
unjust denunciation against him, serving faithfully and proving true to his country, whether misguided for a time or not.
Of all the men the party then had outside of the slave
States, no one was in their way like him. They prepared,
in their unquestioned progress of iniquity, this travesty of
law, their decision. In general, it was to carry on their
remorseless spread of slavery, to overturn the obnoxious
"Squatter Sovereignty" plan, which they never intended to

follow, and to eliminate from party control all such fearless and independent leaders.

There were thousands of Democratic leaders of minor importance who could exercise their independence and leave or neglect to act with the party at their discretion. But Douglas had an entirely different relation with it. The slave-leaders desired nothing better than that he would repudiate the decision and leave the party. In this the party would have been torn into at least two angry, contending factions; but the slave-leaders would have held control of the Administration and the strongest faction, wholly subservient to their plans. By this Douglas would have been a discarded leader as helpless as they could have made him, with Breckinridge or some such man as the leader of all that was left of free State Democracy.

Hence Douglas, for policy's sake, yielded to the decision, and held his place as the unquestioned leader of the Democracy of the free States and as many of the border slave States as were not suffocated by the suppression of free speech and a free press. He knew better than any of his defamers what the decision meant and what it was made for. He was a statesman of learning and ability, and possessed rare knowledge of our history and the men and events in it from the beginning. He was fully cognizant of all the planning and plotting of the leaders, and could have compounded with them any time before the Cincinnati Convention.

Not yielding then, after Buchanan's election, when they believed their power was equal to it, they determined to crush him. Some people thought he had hope of nomination for President by an undivided party as late as the time of his public discussion with Mr. Lincoln in 1858. Some are still inclined to that belief, but the truth here given is corroborated, not only by his own conversation, but by many collateral proofs that, as early as the Atchison invasion, in 1856, and at the Convention of that year, when he would not lend himself to the forcible introduction of slavery into Kansas, he was marked for destruction.

Mr. Lincoln was fully aware of Douglas's situation, and did not take any unfair advantage of him; but he took opportunity to tear the wretched thing called a decision into such fragments, with the other frazzlings in progress, that it never rose to respectful existence in law.

Douglas, on the contrary, held an altogether different relation to it. He was the leader of the Northern Democracy, which was more than half pro-slavery, so far as to let the system alone and protect it in the slave States; willing, too, that the system should have an even chance with freedom in the Territories, and have as many slave, as the North had free States, added to the Union, provided these slave-extensions were fairly and legally transacted. Nevertheless, they were a resolute body of loyal men, that neither slavery nor any other system could lead one step toward dissolution of the Union.

That Douglas maintained his high leadership through those terrible years, and held the Northern Democracy loyal and intact, in spite of the slave-leaders' determination to destroy him, and at the same time held himself the contender and political antagonist of Lincoln, the ablest leader of men that the Nation ever had, is at once the strongest and most conclusive proof that he was one of the wisest and most patriotic statesmen of his era. Douglas with Lincoln in the stress and strain of public affairs confronted forming treason, and led the American people to the exalted striving and preparation that saved the Nation and enlarged the liberties of men everywhere.

The writer, by reason of our friendly relations, had several opportunities when meeting him of knowing the situation, that the "Dred Scott" mistrial put Douglas into his party, and that the above is a fair statement of it. He could not say much of it, and was too high-spirited to apologize, even to a friend, for his political beliefs or conduct; but he said after a talk over it: "You are aware of the relation I hold to the party. I know those Southern leaders and their purposes as well as I know anything, and I assure you that under no circumstances shall they use or drive me. I have fought them for years. I am entitled to leadership, or I would not hold or desire it, and they shall not deprive me of it."

This was true of Douglas, if ever it was of any man or party leader who contended with those Southern aristocrats. No one ever held leadership in our country against such overwhelming odds as he did, measured with leaders in his own party. He was offered the temptation of power, influence, and money; but rather served and led his part of his party against all, a powerful Democratic Administration under Buchanan, and a more powerful organizing party under Lincoln. He was re-elected senator, defied the slave-power and its scheming leaders, and defeated them in their determination to make Kansas a slave State. He kept every one of his followers in the line of patriotic duty who faithfully heeded his advice, without whom, leader or men, it did not appear that the Union could have been saved. In proof of his patriotism and integrity, with abundant opportunities for a lifetime to enrich himself, he died an honest poor man.

On the promulgation of the decision, hundreds of thousands of copies were printed by Congress at the public expense, and thousands on private account of the pro-slavery members of Congress. In addition to this, the press of the free and border States published extracts from the decision and opinion, showing their meaning, character, and purposes. These resulted in the most widespread distribution that had ever been given any such proceeding.

In the light afforded by this new wickedness, added to the border war and ceaseless work of these slave-extenders, the resolution of the people went deeper, that the time had arrived to restrict and restrain the slave-system, and not to extend its influence and power. However, the slave-leaders seemed altogether content and satisfied. They expected that the trouble and agitation would prove no more than a political excitement, and that they would go on in their plan to overthrow Douglas, and make Kansas a slave State.

They were in war anyway, and had only restrained themselves under the pressure of a Presidential election. They had control of all the powers and resources of the Government. They expected opposition from the rising Republican party, and it was making rapid and unprecedented. growth, demonstrated at every election in the free States. They rather desired the opposition of the Republican party and all anti-slavery people, even to the point of producing an insurrection. This they intended to suppress with United States troops, restore civil order, and retain their supremacy.

But things did not happen or come that way. Douglas, whether wisely or sincerely, supported the court's decision, and again they were nonplused in their attempt to overthrow or limit his political leadership. His wisdom and foresight surprised and chagrined them, and led them to more active and desperate plans for his defeat. If he was not altogether sincere, he was at least a thousand times more so than they were.

Douglas, informed as he was, an able lawyer which he certainly was, knew the intent and meaning of the decision; but like a capable soldier or strategist, took advantage of the slaveholders' movement to overthrow him, without resigning or surrendering his command. They were sorely disappointed in the action of Douglas, who by his acquiescence in the decision still remained the undisputed leader of his division or faction of the party.

CHAPTER XXXI.

ALTHOUGH the free State people, men leaders, and newspapers emphatically denounced the decision, not a hand was raised nor a movement taken in the courts or Congress to set aside or resist it. It was choked down all it could be, when its flatness was discovered, and kicked under the benches as a sterile hatching. Without being enforced or resisted, it was let alone to perish as an unobserved political scheme of the slave-power, remembered chiefly as one of their disastrous failures and disclosed designs, that aroused the people to a sense of the slaveholding iniquity. Douglas's submission to it was in a measure compulsory. He characterized it "as a legal construction which of necessity had to be obeyed;" but if any slaveholders were venturesome enough to take their slaves into the Territories, they would do so at the risk of losing them.

In proof that the decision was never more than a political device, the slaveholders would not trust it as any sort of settlement in law by which they could take their slaves into the Territories. The Republicans and the anti-slavery people all over the land treated it as a political design that gave them unexampled opportunity for denouncing slavery and all that were concerned in it, but made no preparation to resist it, nor to reverse or set it aside in any court of the land.

It was shattered and shorn at once of all its wickedness, even as a provocative in one political campaign. After the war was over and slavery was finally disposed of, Congress forgave the weak old judge who rendered it, without ever having obeyed his scheme of slavery proselyting as it was

116

designed, called by courtesy "A decision." When this was done his bust was planted among the other distinguished and antiquated gentlemen of the Supreme Court who have construed, decided, and confused our laws and Constitution for almost a century.

Douglas said in discussing it: "The material and controlling points in the case, those which have been made the subject of unmeasured abuse and denunciation may thus be stated: First. The court decided that under the Constitution of the United States a Negro descended from slave parents is not and can not be a citizen of the United States. Second. That the Act of. March 6, 1820, commonly called 'The Missouri Compromise Act,' was unconstitutional and void before it was repealed by the Kansas-Nebraska Act, and consequently did not and could not have the. legal effect of extinguishing a master's right to his slave in either of those Territories. While the right continues in full force under the guarantees of the Constitution, and can not be diverted or alienated by Act of Congress, it necessarily remains a barren and worthless right, unless sustained, protected, and enforced by appropriate police regulations and legal legislation, prescribing adequate remedies for its violation. These regulations and remedies must necessarily depend entirely upon the will and wishes of the people of the Territory, as they can only be prescribed by the local Legislatures. Hence the great principle of popular sovereignty and self-government is sustained and firmly established by the authority of this decision."

This decision, with its pronged, reaching-out opinion cure-all and save-all for slavery under the Constitution, was made up and held ready to spread slavery all over the land; but it became a stumbling-block to the leaders who framed and so rashly and inconsiderately announced it. It gave Mr. Lincoln the best chance of his life up to that time, such an opportunity as had not been before within reach, to get at the real wickedness of slavery and what it required of its defenders. With the most incisive penetration, the keenest and most searching analysis, without restraint of any sort, and the high qualifications of a judicial reasoner, he tore the flimsy fabric to pieces, and laid the motive bare, and uncovered it to the gaze and judgment of mankind.

He said in one of his speeches in the summer of 1857: "And now as to the 'Dred Scott decision:' First, that a Negro can not sue in United States courts; and, secondly, that Congress can not prohibit slavery in the Territories. It was made by a divided court, dividing differently on the different points. Judge Douglas does not discuss the merits of the decision, and in that respect I shall follow his example, believing I could no more improve on McLean and Curtis than he could on Taney. He denounces all who question the correctness of that as offering violent resistance to it. But who resists it? Who has, in spite of the decision, declared Dred Scott free, and resisted the authority of his master over him? Judicial decisions have two uses—first, to determine absolutely the case decided; and, secondly, to indicate to the public how other similar cases will be decided when they arise. For the latter use they are called precedents and authorities. We believe as much as Judge Douglas in obedience to and respect for the judicial department of the Government.

"We think its decisions on Constitutional questions, when fully settled, should control, not only the particular cases decided, but the general policy of the country, subject only to be disturbed by amendments of the Constitution as provided in that instrument itself. More than this would be revolution. But we think the 'Dred Scott decision' is erroneous. We know that the court that made it has often overruled its own decisions, and we shall do what we can to have it overrule this. We offer no resistance to it. Judicial decisions are of greater or less authority as precedents according to circumstances. That this should be so, accords both

DRED SCOTT

HARRIET, WIFE OF DRED SCOTT

with common sense and the customary understanding of the legal profession.

"If this important decision had been made by the unanimous concurrence of the judges, and without any apparent partisan bias, and in accordance with legal public expectation, and with the steady practice of the department throughout our history, and had been in no part based on assumed historical facts which are not really true; or, if wanting in some of these, it had been before the court more than once, and had there been affirmed and reaffirmed through a course of years; it then might be, perhaps would be, factious, nay, even revolutionary, not to acquiesce in it as a precedent. But when, as is true, we find it wanting in all these claims to the public confidence, it is not resistance, it is not factious, it is not even disrespectful, to treat it as not having yet quite established a settled doctrine for the country."

In a more general review of slavery in a later speech, he demonstrated that the court had distorted and misstated the well-known events in our history, as follows:

"The Chief-Justice does not distinctly assert, but plainly assumes as a fact, that the public estimate of the black man is more favorable now than it was in the days of the Revolution. This assumption is a mistake; in some trifling particulars the condition of that race has been ameliorated; but as a whole, in this country the change between then and now is decidedly the other way; and their ultimate destiny has never appeared so hopeless as in the last three or four years. In two of the five States, New Jersey and North Carolina, that then gave the free Negro the right of voting, the right has since been taken away; and in a third, New York, it has been greatly abridged; while it has not been extended, so far as I know, to a single additional State, though the number of States has more than doubled.

"In those days, as I understand, masters could at their own pleasure emancipate their slaves; but since then such legal restraints have been made upon emancipation as to amount almost to prohibition. In those days Legislatures held the unquestioned power to abolish slavery in their respective States; but now it is becoming quite fashionable for State Constitutions to withhold that power from the Legislatures.

"In those days, by common consent, the spread of the black man's bondage to the new countries was prohibited; but now Congress decides that it will not continue the prohibition, and the Supreme Court decides that it could not if it would. In those days our Declaration of Independence was held sacred by all, and thought to include all; but now, to aid in making the bondage of the Negro universal and eternal, it is assailed and sneered at, and construed and hawked at, and torn till, if its framers could rise from their graves, they would not at all recognize it.

"All the powers of earth seem rapidly combining against him. Mammon is after him, ambition follows, philosophy follows, and the theology of the day is fast joining the cry. They have put him in his prison-house; they have searched his person, and left no prying instrument with him. One after another they have closed the heavy iron doors upon him; and now they have him, as it were, bolted in with a lock of a hundred keys, which can never be unlocked without the concurrence of every key; the keys in the hands of a hundred different men, and they scattered through a hundred different and distinct places; and they stand musing as to what invention, in all the different dominions of mind and matter, can be produced to make the impossibility of his escape more complete than it is.

"There is a natural disgust in the minds of nearly all white people at the idea of an indiscriminate amalgamation of the white and black races; and Judge Douglas evidently is basing his chief hope upon the chances of his being able to appropriate the benefit of this disgust to himself. If he can, by much drumming and repeating, fasten the odium of that idea upon his adversaries, he thinks he can struggle through the storm. He therefore clings to this hope as a drowning man to the last plank. He makes an occasion for lugging it in, from the opposition to the 'Dred Scott decision.'

"He finds the Republicans insisting that the Declaration of Independence includes all men, black as well as white, and forthwith he boldly denies that it includes Negroes at all, and proceeds to argue gravely that all who contend that it does, do so only because they want to vote, and eat, and sleep, and marry with Negroes. He will have it that they can not be consistent else. Now I protest against the counterfeit logic which concludes that because I do not want a black woman for a slave, I must necessarily want her for a wife. I need not have her for either. I can just leave her alone. In some respects she certainly is not my equal; but in her natural right to eat the bread she earns with her own hands, without asking leave of any one else, she is my equal, and the equal of all others."

In one of his aptly-applied illustrations of the decision, charging that it was no more nor less than a partisan scheme, he stated what was true, that the Kansas-Nebraska Act assumed to leave the people of these Territories "perfectly free to settle slavery questions for themselves, subject only to the Constitution of the United States." This limiting proviso was, he said, "the exactly fitted niche for the 'Dred Scott decision' to come in and declare the perfect freedom to be no freedom at all."

In his good-humored way of illustration he fastened this political scheme and its designs on the Administration so clearly, that in a few short sentences the planning was laid bare, more plainly and positively than it could have been in labored arguments. In one assumption of his illustration he was mistaken; in naming "Stephen," which was Douglas, as one of the framers. This was, however, pardonable, for almost everybody then believed that Douglas was in full accord with the slave-leaders. He was too much of a strategist, as we have reasoned before, to deny his previous knowledge of the decision, which would have opened his party dispute with them, and led to the party break that the slave-leaders ardently desired. The truth is, that Douglas was unaware of the nature of the decision until it was published. If the name of Douglas had been omitted and Jefferson Davis substituted, the si$_m$i$_l$e would have been complete. This defect, so far as including the name of Douglas is concerned, was not the fault of Mr. Lincoln, but Douglas, who bore the responsibility silently, rather than make the break with them, for which neither he nor the country was ready.

He swallowed the decision as Benton said he "swallowed the Cincinnati platform, just as a sick man does a dose of ipecac," with the difference, that Douglas swallowed the "Dred Scott decision," and said he liked it. This, however, does not take anything from Mr. Lincoln's philosophic humor nor his quaint and homely manner of getting at the design and the men who made it, for it was a political scheme from beginning to end.

Mr. Lincoln said: "If we saw a lot of framed timbers gotten out at different times and places by different workmen, Franklin and Stephen and Roger and James, and if we saw these timbers joined together and exactly make the frame of a house, with tenons and mortises all fitting, what is the conclusion? We find it impossible not to conclude and believe that Franklin and Stephen and Roger and James all understood one another from the beginning, and all worked on a common plan before a blow was struck."

In his closing remarks, in one of his able speeches in this series of several good plain and easily understood ones, he held the court and the pro-slavery leaders to an account for their narrow-minded construction of the Declaration of Independence, the Constitution, and the foundations upon which our Government and our liberties were builded, saying:

"Chief-Justice Taney in his opinion on the 'Dred Scott decision' admits that the language of the Declaration is broad enough to include the whole human family; but he and Judge Douglas argue that the authors of that instrument did not intend to include Negroes, by the fact that they did not at once actually place them on an equality with the whites. Now this grave argument comes to just nothing at all by the other fact that they did not at once or forever afterwards actually place all white people on an equality with one another. And this is the staple argument of both the Chief-Justice and the senator, for doing this obvious violence to the plain, unmistakable language of the Declaration.

"I think the authors of that noble instrument intended to include all men; but they did not intend to declare all men equal in all respects. They did not mean to say all men were equal in color, size, intellect, moral development, or social capacity. They defined with tolerable distinctness in what respect they did consider all men created equal; equal with 'certain inalienable rights, among which are life, liberty, and the pursuit of happiness.' This they said, and this they meant. They did not mean to assert the obvious untruth that all men were actually enjoying that equality, nor yet that they were about to confer it immediately upon them. In fact, they had no power to confer such a boon. They meant simply to declare the right, so that the enforcement of it might follow as fast as circumstances should permit.

"They meant to set up a standard maxim for free society, which should be familiar to all and revered by all; constantly looked to; constantly labored for, and, even though never perfectly attained, constantly approximated, and then, by constantly spreading and deepening its influence, augmenting the happiness and value of light to all people and all colors everywhere.

"The assertion that all men are created equal was of no practical use in effecting our separation from Britain; and it was placed in the Declaration, not for that, but for future use. Its authors meant it to be, as, thank God! it is proving itself, a stumbling-block to all those who in after times might seek to turn a free people back into the hateful paths of despotism. They knew the proneness of prosperity to breed tyrants, and they meant, when such would reappear in this fair land and commence their vocation, they should find left for them one hard nut to crack."

CHAPTER XXXII.

EARLY in the year 1857, Robert J. Walker, of Mississippi, was appointed governor of Kansas, with the hope that the slave party would have full opportunity to take their system into the Territory. Walker, the fourth in line of Democratic governors, was from a slave State, though born and educated in Pennsylvania, where he had something of an acquaintance with President Buchanan. Walker was an able, learned, fair-minded man, who had been prominent in public life for several years prior to this. Under equal conditions, he would have favored the pro-slavery people of the South. He had lived in the Southern States a number of years, and whether originally a slave advocate, he had identified himself with the section, and was what they believed him to be when appointed, a zealous supporter of the slave system. Nevertheless he was an honest man. He grew to his position with the knowledge and capacity for public business, and though a pro-slavery man, something like General P. F. Smith, he was there honestly to enforce the law.

If slavery was to be taken into the Territory with his consent, it would not be by three or four thousand invading Missourians voting for and sustaining it. Out of some ten to twelve thousand legally-qualified voters of the Territory, there were seventy-six hundred free State against thirty-seven hundred pro-slavery. Walker did not believe that with more than two to one, for a free State, the pro-slavery voters could adopt slavery, and fasten it on the Territory at a fair election. This was precisely what Buchanan's pro-slavery Administration desired and expected Walker to do. When they learned

125

that they had appointed a fourth governor for Kansas, whose integrity disappointed and surprised them, they set about means for his embarrassment or overthrow.

Atchison had failed ignominiously, and his man Woodson, secretary of the Territory, the supple pro-slavery "acting governor" in so many notorious ways, in the absence of the rapidly-moving governors, was so universally bad by repute, that Buchanan's Administration, puerile or bad, or both, could carry the load of their iniquity no longer. Pennsylvania exhibited almost certain signs of party revolt; and the poor old dupe of Jefferson Davis, his man Friday, Jere Black, saw almost certain evidences that if they saved Kansas to Davis for his slave propaganda, they were without a show of honesty in doing it, and sure to lose Pennsylvania. So, whether willing or not—for Pennsylvania's vote was a vital as well as a critical quantity—Atchison, Woodson, Stringfellow, and the disappearing, lesser Calhoun and their ilk, ruffians, rascals, invaders, and all, to the last awkward recruit, had to be discarded and abandoned, not because of principle or change of heart, but because of Pennsylvania.

Frederick P. Stanton, a reputable man, who had been a member of Congress from Tennessee, was appointed secretary of the Territory, where he arrived in the early part of 1857 with General Walker. What was known as "the Bogus," or more definitely, the Missouri-elected Legislature, held a session at Lecompton in January, at which they passed an Act authorizing the formation of a State Constitution, and fixed the date for the election of delegates on June 15th to the Convention, which should frame and submit it to the people.

This invaders' Legislature was a hostile body to the actual settlers in every respect; but was so sustained in the camps and border settlements that the free State men would have had no chance for a fair election. The pro-slavery delegates would have been "counted in" as the members of the Legislature there; so the free State men wisely, to prevent a conflict, refrained from voting for delegates to the Constitutional Convention, as they had previously done in the election of the Legislature. Hence the election held on June 15th resulted in the unopposed return of the pro-slavery delegates. There were polled two thousand votes, about fourteen hundred of the voters being invading Missourians, when, as stated above, there were about twelve thousand legal voters in the Territory.

On the assurance of a fair election some weeks later, the free State voters elected Marcus J. Parrott delegate to Congress by 7,600, against 3,700, votes, nine out of seventeen of their council, and twenty-seven of their thirty-nine representatives, giving the free State people thirty-six members of the two Houses of their Legislature, against twenty pro-slavery members. In this election the qualified legal voters of both parties generally voted.

There was an attempt to change the result by some of the expiring border gangs. Oxford, a small place with a few houses, reported as ten or a dozen small cabins, with not over twenty-five inhabitants, reported that 1,624 qualified voters had eight representatives and three members of the council, which, if admitted, would have made the Legislature pro-slavery. This attempt proved Governor Walker's courage and integrity. He investigated the election at once, honestly, and with the purpose of ascertaining the truth. The names of about 1,600 of the voters were copied without a break from a Cincinnati Directory. He found it as stated, and repudiated the whole of it. This lost him friends among the pro-slavery leaders and in the Administration; but he had the satisfaction of an honest duty well done.

This prevented another desperate struggle in Kansas, and held it free from slavery, notwithstanding that under the Dred Scott decision slaves in any number could have been taken and held under protection of the law. Singular as it may seem, regardless of the alarm in the free States and the excited determination of the South to extend slavery under it, of the few slaves held in the Territory along the Missouri border many of them were taken back into Missouri and the other slave States, and the remainder were watched more closely than ever and kept within a few minutes walk of the slave State of Missouri, so that under its unresisted supremacy slavery was not only not extended, but diminished and restricted, at the culminating point where the obstinate contest between slavery and freedom was in progress.

This developed the caution and sense of slaveholders in general, as against the pro-slavery leaders. The decision gave them no confidence; it rather created distrust. If there had been general confidence, they could have made Kansas a slave State by taking their slaves there in great numbers under the protection of the court and Buchanan's Administration. But judged by the best test of confidence and sincerity, they dreaded the encounter of a fair settlement. It had been made free territory, and notwithstanding all that had been achieved in support of slavery as claimed, the watchful owners of the human chattels had more respect for the dissenting opinions of Curtis and McLean, than for the law-establishing edict of the court.

Another feature of the slavery agitation seldom mentioned was, that slaves declined in value in proportion to the organized strength of parties opposed to it. In 1849 to 1852, after the discovery of gold in such abundance, a healthy strong man or woman sold in St. Louis at from $800 to $1,600. In 1853-54, when Congress took it up as the leading topic of discussion, their values constantly declined until in 1858 they became almost unsalable. Thus slavery was perishing in the denunciation of it as an evil, when one man on God's side was putting "a thousand to flight." The slaveholders realized this shrinkage, and in some instances destruction of values, far more than their opponents; but instead of inclining them to remunerated emancipation, it all the more determined them to fight and hold their supremacy.

Late in June the delegates elected by the pro-slavery voters and the invaders assembled at Lecompton to frame a State Constitution. This they did, and made provision for its submission, December 21, 1857. Four sections of the proposed Constitution related to and established slavery permanently, another recognized that slavery existed by right of law under the Supreme Court decision.

The only question submitted to the voters was to be printed on ballots, "Constitution with slavery," or "Constitution without slavery." So the Constitution was to be adopted anyway, regardless of the voter's desire, for there was no way provided in law to vote against it. The ballots, so far as they indicated anything, assumed that the voters had the choice of voting for or against slavery; but when the juggling trick was disclosed, it was found that there was no plan provided for in the submission, other than the adoption of the Constitution, for all the ballots provided for, were to be, "For the Constitution with slavery," or, "For the Constitution without slavery;" but there were other sections of this disfigured proposed act which provided that no amendments could be made to it until 1864—seven years ahead. As the Constitution recognized the existence of slavery under law, the effect of the votes against slavery would have been the adoption of a Constitution which would have made Kansas a slave State for seven years.

It was an outrageous presumption against the intelligence and honesty of sensible people to offer to submit any proposition to them in such an iniquitous disfranchising method. But the border gang, who had practiced so much deviltry in the previous months, could do no better than risk everything on this culminating Constitution-making scheme, which was an affront to the ingenuity of Satan. If it had been tolerated, it would have been all that these

coarse butchers of liberty desired, to whom liberty **meant**
no more than gratified'passions, the wassail, the drink; and
riot in looted meat-houses.   There was small wonder that
marauding mercenaries like these aroused antagonists who
deliberately hunted them as they did vicious animals.   They
fully matched their assailants in the killing work along the
border that came so near making Kansas a slave State; but
in the providence of God, never quite did it.

At the election held in December, the declared vote was
6,226 for the Constitution, or strictly, for the Constitution
with slavery, with 559 against it; but as the free State men
did not participate in the election, the opposition votes were
like most of those in its favor, either cast by the invading
Missourians, or fraudulently counted, as those referred to
at Oxford had been.   The election was never carefully investigated, because Governor Walker and all fair-minded
men were so fully satisfied of the fraudulent character of
the entire proceeding that an examination was not necessary to establish the well-known and flagrant violations of
all honest means of conducting any election.

Over half the votes reported cast at the election were in
counties along the Missouri border, whose entire voting population was less than one thousand, all told.   The opposition
to this high-handed usurpation was strong, bitter, and determined in the Territory, and included men of all parties.
The opposition would soon have taken definite shape in some
kind of movement against it in the Territory, had it not
been that Governor Walker, being an honest man, held the
people in check.

He assured them, and was earnest in doing so, that he
did not believe that Buchanan's Administration, pro-slavery
as it was known to be, would countenance or tolerate such
a usurpation of law and all decent processes of government,
and that he would proceed personally to Washington, where,
after laying the whole mess of wickedness before the Presi-

dent and his advisers, he fully believed they would denounce it, as he had done. This quieted the intense feeling for a time. He started; but his mission had been anticipated. The slave propaganda still dominated the weak old man. Walker learned, to his astonishment and disgust, on reaching the Capital, that President Buchanan had indorsed and approved the vile, dishonest, and flagrant violation of law, known as the Lecompton Constitution, had submitted it to Congress, and urgently recommended the admission of Kansas as a slave State under it at once. Thus he committed his Administration and his party, which held a majority of both Houses of Congress, as far as such acts and influence could, to the most nefarious scheme ever attempted under our government: to rob a Territory and its people of their rights and liberties. This plan of making a slave State by force and knavery was so thoroughly bad that the Democratic party, then in power, turned away from the high-wrought wickedness, and from which six Democratic governors revolted, and left the Territory in sorrow, disgust, and shame.

On learning what Buchanan's Administration had done, Governor Walker resigned, that he might not be held, in any way, responsible for accumulating sins which he could neither arrest nor moderate. J. W. Denver, who had seen some military service on the border during the Mexican war, was appointed as Walker's successor; but the scene of the chief point of the struggle for freedom in Kansas shifted to Washington, leaving the governors less to do in Kansas.

The Territorial Legislature, elected mainly by the free State people under the promise of protection of Governor Walker, passed an act submitting the wretched Lecompton Constitution the same day with the election provided to elect officers under the Lecompton Constitution, which the pro-slavery invaders' Legislature had declared to be adopted. This election, in which no intimidation was permitted, was

generally participated in all over the Territory, and freely
discussed; but the pro-slavery men would not vote, claiming that the Constitution was already adopted. The majority against the Constitution.was 10,226 votes, with very few
in favor of it.

Following this matter,.to the neglect of other events, it
is plain that this attempt to force slavery into Kansas was
planned by Buchanan's Administration. The President asserted in his Message that the Constitution was a fair expression of the will of the people, that "slavery existed there
as much as it did in Georgia or South Carolina," and that
"the factious opposition to it was rebellion." This brought
on the angry discussion in Congress that widened the break
in the Democratic party to separation, and continued with
increasing division and disintegration up to the election
of Mr. Lincoln.

With only a few exceptions, the American people, although energetic and often enthusiastic partisans through
our ordinary Presidential campaigns, are usually as energetic and persevering in their ordinary pursuits, in the intervals between them, as they have been earnest and zealous
while they lasted. So these intervals in our history have
been marked as periods of peace, quiet living, and substantial progress.

From 1856 to 1860, and on to the close of the war, there
was a period of uninterrupted, ceaseless strife, struggle, and
combat. During the discussion, disputes, and the getting
ready for the eventual conflict there was so much evasion,
so many untiring and continued attempts to mislead and deceive the people concerning the real purposes of the slaveholders, that the charlatans of statecraft all over the free
States fed and fattened, held high place and power, on the
favor and promise of the slave-leaders. They were rewarded
according to their leadings and confoundings in the work
that took men into the unrighteous and ungodly progress

of plundering the earnings and usurping the rights of their fellow-men. As early as 1856 the lines were so strongly and distinctly drawn that the ultimate division was obvious to considerate people looking at the unmistakable drift of parties and divisions. They were not and could not be misled by party promises, pretensions, names, or disintegrations.

These political movements raised up a class of men— pseudo-statesmen—as destitute of the knowledge that makes men fit representatives in a Republic as they were of the most common notions of integrity or the means of earning an honest living. The deadening effect on morals of this abominable curse and the means of discussing, approaching, or disposing of it, were evident, too, beyond any sort of concealment, in that the organizing Republican party, with all the anti-slavery factions in it, still palavered and doubted, rather than openly denounced slavery in every form. It would have done this if public men had taught the truth concerning it instead of palliating, compounding with, and concealing it for more than a century.

This realistic anti-slavery party, in the minds of many of its timid, lame, and half-halting leaders, could then do no more than resist the spread of slavery into new territory. These timid, half-hearted leaders so embarrassed Mr. Lincoln that he had to limit himself to this beggarly beginning against the defiant monster evil. This consideration will show more clearly than arguments the strength and prevalence of the pro-slavery dogma. The organizing anti-slavery party and its faithful, honest leader could make no record or protest against the Fugitive-slave Law and the traffic between the States, nor any attempt to abolish it in the District of Columbia, but had to remain content with simple opposition to its extension.

The slavery question, the disputes, debates, and the political parties and their relations to it, the war and its dreadful consequences, have been treated and considered as under the control, made, and determined by a few leaders; but the truth is, that the causes lay deeper down, in the greed and the hearts and consciences of the people. On one side the heartless purpose was power and aggrandizement, on the other the conviction that, under all definitions, slavery was an unmixed and inexcusable evil. As far as leaders were concerned, unless they were men of distinct character or principle, their relations to it were no more than contingencies—men whose places were taken, changed, and re-filled as readily as party details were carried on in other public affairs.

There were, however, beginning with the compromises of 1820, as many as four pro-slavery, one compromising, and four anti-slavery leaders, whose capacity and character were so prominent that a narration of one is that of the other. We have referred to all of them, and have given them place and consideration in the progress of the dominating sin that destroyed leaders and victims alike.

As we approach the culminating struggle and the consummation of God's wrath for its destruction, it becomes, more than ever, necessary to keep correctly in mind and understanding the true relation of the people of the section, the parties, as they represented or served them, and as surely and distinctly of the principal leaders, who served them, shaped, guided, or controlled opinion and action for the time.

The Southern people, in time, like all apparently prosperous people, lost all respect or desire for a democracy in the profits of unpaid slave-labor. This they did as early as the beginning of the century. There were contentions and divisions among them; for not all of them by any means believed in tolerating the system, but enough of them did in every slave State to continue it and make the early Republic, for which they sacrificed so much in valor and patriotic blood, as thorough and servile a despotism for black men and poor white men as Poland or Hungary.

Calhoun, whose eminent ability and capacity were never questioned, formed a faction of power, control, and conduct of public affairs superior to and regardless of parties, nor subject to their control. Over this he held absolute supremacy from the time of his attempted nullification, when Jackson temporarily unhorsed him. From about 1842 until 1850, when he died in action, he was so feeble and infirm of body, yet so determined in spirit and grasp of power, that a listening Senate and anxious millions of followers and antagonists waited and stood patiently for the declarations and edicts of the passing leader. Through frailty of body he could utter them no better than through the voice of the next in line, as Mason, of Virginia, then expected to be. This, however, was not to be; for after a short consideration, the mantle and succession to Calhoun fell logically and by general consent upon Jefferson Davis. He was a man of marked ability and determination, daring, and audacity far beyond Calhoun, but far below that organizer in scheming policy, statecraft, and the finesse of a great political chieftain. He was more venturesome and despotic many times over, and held his power to the end of the great struggle. He accepted counsel of those he selected and raised to power and preferment about him; but he conceded nothing to any one as leader, save to General Lee, who, as the Confederacy was dissolving into fragments, came, by wise, soldier-like capacities, to be the father of his army as well as its commander.

To Lee, in this contingency, Davis, in his straits, conceded something, but never willingly, nor when it was not dire necessity. Hence Davis came to power and led the Southern people, from the death of Calhoun to the bitter and consuming end of slavery, in as firm and determined purpose and absolute mastership as any dictator from Tamer-

lane to Philip of Spain. He had Benjamin,. Stephens, Breckinridge, Mason, and Lee, *in extremis*, as coadjutors, but no
one of them nor all of them as recognized counselors, with
whom to share or divide his power and authority. Under
Calhoun, Davis, and their irresponsible partisans, the Southern people were rushed and hurried into war with Mexico,
into slavery extension, against Benton, Houston, Clay, Crittenden, and Taylor, and into the War of the Rebellion, with
as little heed or concern for their rights, their opinions, or
their comfort as they had for the slave-gangs working like
beasts on the sugar-cane and cotton plantations.

This aggrandizing, slave-extending *régime*, in party form
and through and by its hold on men of all parties, held
power that ruled the Nation through combinations and in-
trigue for the greater part of the time from 1820 to 1860.
They actually represented the Southern people of the slave
States, whose voting strength in 1860, when war became the
means of settlement, approximated 1,450,000. The voting
strength of the people of the free States at the time was
about 3,250,000. These together made a voting population
of 4,700,000, in the aggregate an enormous body of strong,
stalwart men, a formidable, visible force indeed from which
to levy and mobilize armies.

At the first thought the difference between the sections
was so disproportionate that there seemed no basis for anything like equality in the inevitable contest at arms; but
the difference was more apparent than real. -In addition,
the South had about four million slaves. These, by nature
of the conflict, the Southern leaders would not arm, equip,
or muster into military service; but they were so strong,
well-grown, and capable for toil that, in a country where
the whole population was practically in war, they served as
useful a purpose in daily labor as the men at arms.

Out of the four million slaves as many as half of them
were filling men's places in the various producing and in-

dustrial pursuits that gave the South the labor or producing
basis on which to carry on war. In farm labor, stock-rais-
ing, milling, and all manner of food and clothing production, uot only half the slaves, but all from ten to sixty years
of age were constantly engaged in the work of providing
subsistence, clothing, and shelter, and a great deal of the
work of the camp and field, for men and armies. In the
work of transportation, bridging, and fortifications, Negro
labor was the best. Thus, when the Negro was duly considered, the South had the advantage of the service of about
two millions of the hardiest and best-trained laborers as
auxiliaries to subsist and support armies in the field, in
which they were as useful and indispensable to them as the
armed men in the ranks.

Hence the force of the slave States for war, in men capable for military service and the auxiliary force for subsistence and support, was equal to that obtainable from a population of a little less than fifteen millions—formidable
enough, as time and events disclosed, to conduct one of
the most determined and desperate contests between men
since the beginnings of history.

Against this powerful force of men and their supporting bondmen, under the unquestioned control and direction of a single leader and dictator, favored by natural productions, climate, and means of transportation that were
equal to the best on the earth, the arms-bearing and producing
people of the free States were organized, led, and eventually
brought to and through the conflict that settled and obliterated slavery and some of its collateral sins, we hope, for all
time.

In the free Democracy of the North it took the full fifteen years of the latter part of the bitter slavery dispute,
from 1845 to 1861, to unite the differing factions against
slavery, and the most laborious and persevering application
of widely differing and diverging leaders and divisions of

society to effect the party union. There were leaders of differing influence and capacity by thousands, arousing the people to the impending danger and almost certain conflict; but of the great leaders who were capable, faithful, and who fought out their part of it, or to the end, there were not many.

Of the eminent and conspicuous there was Garrison, never to be forgotten. There was Clay, who should be remembered for his good intentions and lifetime pursuit for the success of some plan of gradual emancipation, for his indirect help, through compromise and postponement of the conflict, when unorganized Democracy was unequal to the contest with the better-disciplined, firmly-held, and more firmly-led slave *régime* and ascendency.

There was Seward, with high capacity, fearlessness, and perseverance to lead among hundreds, who were all wise and able statesmen. There were Sumner, Greeley, Chase, Thaddeus Stevens, and Lovejoy, who were only a shadow less; and there was Brown, of Ossawatomie, full of the Spirit of God, ready and anxious for the fight with Satan on his own terms and premises, who won a patriot's name through humiliation and sacrifice for the rights of men that will last when his treasonable executioners, who were then plotting their country's ruin, are long forgotten.

In his way, President Jackson was a strong anti-slavery leader, but more certainly an impassable obstructor of the plans and purposes of the slaveholders. He was in no sense an anti-slavery man personally, nor from sympathy with an oppressed race, nor antipathy to the system. On the contrary, he was a slave-owner; and, though in no way a harsh or severe master, he was no more or less, personally, than a pro-slavery believer, who, under the circumstances, justified the system as it existed. He was, however, a man of such positive determination, unfaltering integrity, and love of his native land, "The Union," that he soon detected the disloyal, plotting schemes of Calhoun and his followers. Abhorring dishonesty and disloyalty as kindred sins, when President he laid heavy hand on them and their nullification schemes and defiance of the laws, with such force and celerity of action that he smothered the forming insurrection and intended separation for one whole generation.

His instant suppression of their intended secession taught them caution, but in no way changed their purpose to sustain, protect, and extend their system by separation whenever they deemed it necessary. From this time forward, however, they made and perfected their plans more cautiously. When the actual struggle began, it was Jackson's honest resolve, his party teaching and high purpose, running through the party and raising up other leaders in succession, like Benton, Cass, Marcy, and Douglas, that saved Kansas from slavery.

Thus considered, Andrew Jackson was an anti-slavery leader, because he held firmly and truly to the teachings and principles of an honest Democracy, which, when rightly administered, makes slavery an impossibility, as it does the other kindred evils of wealth and aggrandized power. When freemen in a true Democracy are left untrammeled by the influences of these selfish and grasping powers, as they should be, however much they may be deceived and blunder for a time, they will recover under the operation of free speech, free discussion, and free exercise of their franchises, and will destroy prerogatives, the wealth that usurps human rights, caste, and unnatural distinction of whatever kind or character.

These overturnings and upheavals may come where men are oppressed and misled in a peaceful discussion, a revolution, or a holocaust of sacrifice and suffering, as it did in the destruction of slavery; but come it will as sure as God rules and nations live and men are left free to combat evil. In the same way Benton, although living in and representing a slave State in the Senate, became a prominent anti-slavery leader. Being an honest man, to begin with, he held to the principles of a true Democracy, and had the ability, in the distempered condition of his State, for thirty years, to contend for honest government, direct accountability of all public servants to the people, economy in public affairs, and the equality of all men before the law.

These ideas were all hostile and antagonistic to slavery; and when the *régime* of the slave-power gained ascendency in the party and the Nation, Benton was left out of his party's councils, and his State was compelled to send more supple-minded and submissive senators. In the same way Lewis Cass and W. L. Marcy—honest Democrats and, there-fore, anti-slavery men, like Benton—were overthrown and cast aside. In the same way that leadership came to these eminent and distinguished men, it came to Judge Douglas, friend and fellow-citizen of the people of Illinois, and, nec-essarily, one of the principal subjects of our work. He was, from his election to the United States Senate in 1843, one of its senators during his life, who, with Lincoln, was one of its most distinguished citizens. These two led the forces that grappled with the rapacious sin and crushed it in its hell of horrors, one taking up chief leadership as the other laid it down, making it possible for the disenthralled Nation to advance and more stubbornly contend for man-hood and freedom.

Douglas was not *per se* an anti-slavery man, nor was he the leader of an anti-slavery party, but indirectly became such a leader, because he was an honest, patriotic man. He became the leader of his part of the party that followed him loyally, and believed in the true principle of a free Democracy. He and his section of the party became all this because they were, first of all and beyond all, men who loved our country, with its free institutions, and were ready to serve and die for it.

In the early '40's, when Douglas entered the House of Representatives at Washington, 'he embraced the first opportunity to defend General Jackson against the impositions, fines, censure, and various inflictions of law that had been heaped upon him by envious rivals and incapables of differing degrees. None of them were more competent for public service than to cavil over the achievements of the grand old hero, who saved our Nation from Britain's second invasion in 1812-14.

In narrow, misdirected consideration of affairs, the State of Louisiana and the United States courts in that State censured and fined Jackson for the use of their cotton-bales and some other available property that he used in saving all there was of the city of New Orleans, or of the State, perhaps the Nation, from capture by the British. Nevertheless he had violated local laws in taking the cotton; and the State and the courts were small enough to inflict the penalties. The State and the courts were shamed into a rectification of it, so far as it could be done or the General would permit; for he never would accept reimbursement for the fine of one thousand dollars imposed for using the cotton-bales and other loose property, which he used in making barricades in a hurry, as the best fortifications available for the defense of the city and his little army.

The influence of Calhoun against Jackson prevented correction of the record of Congress, until Douglas entered the House of Representatives, where the censuring record sustaining the local authorities of the State of Louisiana against Jackson stood unrepealed and unexplained. Douglas introduced resolutions to expunge the unfriendly record against the great soldier, approving, at the same time, Jackson's seizure and use of property for defense in battle. His masterly reconsideration and revision of the entire subject, his patient and concise statement of the details, the knowledge and power of the man, his familiarity with the most

profound questions on statecraft, his easy and abundant references to international law, the conduct and articles of war,
belligerent rights, and the rights of property, and that of
cities, States, and individuals and kingdoms, as held and
observed in modern times—in fine, his complete and comprehensive knowledge of the subject—surprised and delighted
the House of Representatives, which, without further contention, passed the expunging resolutions, discovering at the
same time that Douglas was a statesman of learning, decided
force of character, and high capacity. This was at the time
when Webster, Clay, Calhoun, Benton, Crittenden, and Cass
were in one or the other House of Congress or in the Cabinet.

In his argument Douglas took high ground on one or
two very important points in law and procedures in peace
and in war. His first was that the House of Representatives,
or other representative legislative bodies, could, in the
exercise of the power of the people, expunge, rescind, or
obliterate any unfriendly, objectionable, or blundering record of its predecessors, regardless of how unrepealably certain its supporters had attempted to fix the record, and that
the power of the people, exercised through their properly-
chosen representatives, was above and superior to all forms
of parliamentary law and usage, and that under its operation there was power in the people to dissolve a disobedient
court, State Government, or, in extremity, a Parliament, as
Cromwell did.

On the subject of the use of any kind of property in war
his references and illustrations went far beyond anything
ever before attempted or thought necessary in Congress.
The strongest single provision, however, was that the Nation, to preserve its existence, can use, and, in the exercise
of prudent authority, should use, the property of any of
its citizens or inhabitants with impunity; that, in the exercise of this high power to preserve the life and entirety of
the Nation, it can and should call on any of its citizens for

its defense, at the peril of their lives, if need be, which is a higher exercise of power than the sequestration and use of any property belonging to any citizen or inhabitant.

This relieved the name and memory of Jackson. It was done, too, in the sense and spirit of our laws and free institutions, with such copious attestations and references as to leave it a precedent in the conduct of war and public affairs. It relieved the Government from the envious strictures and vicious tangles of Calhoun and his saturnalia, that justified any reach of power "to nullify or secede," but not the use of a pound of cotton to save a Nation without a fine. Besides this, it left a precedent in the conduct of war and public affairs, affording President Lincoln one of the most justifiable precedents for his emancipation of the Negro people.

The opposition to this legal, judicial, and forensic achievement of Douglas came from the believers in the dogma of "States' rights," who held any form or variation of opposition that suited their convenience. It was a doctrine prescribing a limit of National power, good when a slave State desired its observance, and of no good when it did not. Under it the Nation could enforce no law in any State without that State's approval. In the contention of Calhoun, the Nation could not levy nor collect revenue in the State's limits without its assent; but *vice versa* any slave State or its citizens could pursue and capture any fugitive slave from within the limit of any free State or Territory, or take their slaves with them to or through any of the States or Territories.

It was one of the palavering foils used in the slaveholders' dilemma of how to avail themselves of the power and protection of both State and National authority for slavery. It was a condition of supposed National existence, under which a Nation could be dissolved and parted into fragmentary dependencies or half-helpless States at the pleasure of one or more of the States, under this absurdity of law called State Rights, or the rights they had not parted with, in the formation and foundation of the Nation under the Constitution.

That it was incoherent law and logic, destitute of sensible form for any Government and practical utility, as measured in the powers and prerogatives of Governments among men for all time, was of little consequence to the slave-leaders. They held to it as a doctrine of convenience, from which they were able to gain all the advantages they desired, but which was never to be enforced against themselves. When their unnatural system required the exercise of National authority in their behalf, it should be enforced without limit, regardless of State or municipal law.

It was one of the sophistries of law, National existence, or the form of it, that the great Webster took up, unraveled, and tore into strings and tatters, as, piece by piece and item by item, he cleared, to the common understanding of men, the subject and substance of fundamental and Constitutional law and settlements, as the fixtures, foundations, and necessities of all National existence. This he expounded, while he unraveled like strings the fallacy of a State within a State holding reserve or other power or authority that was greater, or assumed to be greater, than the sovereignty of a whole people, as made and represented in the builded. and completed Nation, which can have no limit to its authority that they do not consent to under the laws of God and men.

Webster's great and decisive argument, definitely settling our foundations of law, was not delivered directly against Calhoun, who was then in the Cabinet, but who was virtually in the debate as dictator of the form and facts on his side of the discussion. His spokesman, Hayne, was no more than the miniature reflection of the great slave-leader. Hayne was, at the time, a senator from South Carolina, fully under his impulse and direction. It was one of the practices of Calhoun to make his pleas and arguments for slavery through another, where he avoided the defense of false law and logic as much as possible, which he considered a shrewd avoidance of responsibility.

In this way of conducting his schemes and plans he held certain advantages over the open one of avowing his responsibility, which he reserved until he had time to observe its effects, and for consideration and revision.

From the time that Douglas took up the defense of Jackson and the work of "expunging" the unjust and unfriendly record, and declared himself a Democrat of the Jackson school, strictly adhering and conforming to honest government, with no misuse or usurpation of delegated power, direct responsibility to the people, and faithful service on their behalf, he gained, like Jackson, Benton, and Cass before him, the ill-will and concealed enmity of the slaveholders' faction, then in control of the Democratic organization. As they had discarded and overthrown these and others, they attempted to do with Douglas from the time of his appearance in Congress as a leader.

One of the principal and prevailing mistakes in the career and work of Douglas, affecting Lincoln as one of the principals concerned, is that in the eventful Douglas-Lincoln debate of 1858. Douglas made declarations of political belief which rendered him useless and unacceptable to the Southern faction of the party as a candidate for President. This was true enough, but only a part of the truth, and therefore quite misleading. The party, under the rule of the slave-leaders, was the most undemocratic organization that ever existed in the country, and had nothing left of it but the name. Nevertheless, Douglas, in his sturdy vigor, with a million and a half true and devoted Democrats in the free and border States, held firmly to the party with the resolute determination to reform it and remain with it.

Of course, Douglas, as such a leader, was in no way acceptable to the slavery faction as a Presidential candidate; but he was no more so in 1856 to 1860 than in his early career. He was never taken into, nor ever held, the confidence of Calhoun or Davis and the slave-conspirators. It stands to his credit and integrity as a leader, while so many were faithless, that he was the most forceful man in any party, from Jackson to Buchanan, who would not make the concessions to the Southern leaders for a Presidential nomination.

Of the able and distinguished leaders of both parties for twenty years up to 1860, about all the principal party leaders made all the concessions that the slave-leaders demanded and expected. Among these were Clay, Webster, Fillmore, and Everett, of the Whig, and Van Buren, Dallas, Pierce, and Buchanan, of the Democratic parties. In this review we can see the position and real character of Douglas as a party leader. He was, through all of this period, much the strongest man in his party, the one whom the Southern leaders ardently desired, if he would submit, like those named, to their domination.

On the contrary, he not only would not submit to them, nor any other hierarchy in the party, but began an honest contention, as early as it was prudent for him, for the principles of the party, the ones, in his belief, that were best fitted for a free people. This was well known to the slavery faction and all well-informed men of the time, as well in 1845 as it ever was.

His sturdy Scotch ancestry, his early education and training, his entire dependence and reliance upon himself in his beginnings, made him resolute and determined as a party leader. With Lincoln he grew up side by side. Both were party leaders who believed in the people, and, as far as they could throughout their lives, faithfully represented them. The great mistakes in giving the relations of these two leaders have always been in representing them as antagonists and contending combatants, and nothing else. They differed as partisans, but no further than the political parties they represented required and expected from such competent and thoroughly-informed men; but in all that affected the well-being of the country and its entirety as one great people, their differences were trivial compared with those of other contending leaders of their time.

The difference that led to the division of the Democratic party began with Andrew Jackson, who boldly pronounced Calhoun a traitor and his nullification scheme a treasonable plot, which he, as a patriot, promptly suppressed. Strange as it may seem, Calhoun was stronger with the slaveholding faction ever after, and organized them into a body that soon obtained control of the party.

Douglas, by his espousal of Jackson and his cause against Calhoun, incurred their active and unceasing hostility, and entered into a contest with them that ceased only when, worn and overwrought, he passed away twenty years before his time. The Southern leaders, under Calhoun and his successor, Jefferson Davis, planned for and fully expected to compass the downfall of Douglas.

Thus surrounded, Douglas was constantly in jeopardy by the divisions and factions in his own party. Under strong and active opposition by the strong and forming Republican party he was driven, by policy's sake, to make concessions to slavery; but these were never personal, but always made as concessions to his party as a party and the slaveholders in it who were a large part of it, but never a single concession to the slave *régime* that dictated terms and conditions to candidates. He took counsel of nothing less than his party, and submitted to no other authority or dictation.

A great many estimable people and some very well-informed men affected to believe, during the angry discussion and approaching conflict, that Douglas should denounce slavery and oppose the system definitely in every way. This would have been inconsiderate and thoughtless beyond any present calculation or understanding. If he had done so, as he was the leader of a party more than half of which were in some degree pro-slavery, and in which were very few opposed to it, he would have lost his leadership at once.

This was what the leaders of the South were anxious he should do; and they did all in their power to provoke him to it. He understood their designs and purposes, and, not desiring to be another Benton for their inquisition and torture, he conceded all that he could to the party, but not to them, and remained in defiance of their schemes and party tests, where he held leadership of the free Democracy, knowing and appreciating that this strong body of men were not many of them anti-slavery, but loyal and patriotic. In the paramount issue then approaching they would be on the right side of it, against disunion, and as fully determined to save the Union, with or without slavery.

Douglas should be credited as one of the wisest and most far-seeing statesmen of the period. His mind had the grasp of the whole subject to better knowledge and purpose than any other principal leader who passed through the fiery fifteen years' dispute and trial with him. Some man, either he or some one else in his place, had to lead the free State Democracy eventually to a loyal support of the Union for the conflict; otherwise it could not have been saved. Who but Douglas could have done it? There was surely no other man in sight to the men of that day who could have done it as well, if indeed any other man could have done it at all. He was wise and cautious, eager, competent, and so apt to unravel their designs, that at once he became the confounder of the whole slavery *régime*, far superior in skill and management, as we have seen, to Atchison, Davis, Benjamin, Stephens, Mason, and Breckinridge. He became the leader, uncontested, of the loyal Democrats of both Houses of Congress. He defeated the slave-leaders so decisively that they gave up the struggle for slave extension into free territory under law, and sought their only alternative of saving their slave-system in levying war against the Union, which had long been their last resort in extremity.

It remains true that Lincoln was incomparable as a leader, and that he and many able men did lead the anti-slavery elements that coalesced into the Republican party, with several thousand halting, apologizing, slavery-minded Whigs and others, to a loyal support of the Union; but how could he, able and godlike as we believe he and his purpose was, have led the party that Douglas did to a loyal and fighting support of the Nation?

No men of that day in their sober senses believed that Lincoln or any other man than Douglas could have done this. Lincoln was not in Congress to lead and help to shape public affairs for seventeen years, as Douglas was. He was not in favor with the Democratic party of the free States as a leader, and in various other ways did not have the facilities or opportunities to prove himself, as Douglas did. It was, as Lincoln once said, "God's own cause to save the Union;" and without doubt he raised up Douglas, as he surely did Lincoln later.

CHAPTER XXXIII.

DOUGLAS, in succession as a great leader, believed in an honest Democracy, true to the principles and beliefs of its founder, Thomas Jefferson, the most eminent partisan and organizer of his day. He formed into a working body his following against Hamilton and as able a body of men as ever contended for the vestiges of monarchy and prerogative. In Jefferson's party logic, he understood well that slavery was an antagonism, an alien and unnatural relation of men, a cross purpose and flat contradiction of the definite declaration "that all men are created free and equal." He not only squared and accommodated himself to this slavery obstacle personally by manumitting all his slaves, but labored and succeeded with others to limit the cession of the "Northwest Territory" to the United States by the provision "that neither slavery nor involuntary servitude should exist within it" in the boundaries of a domain that equaled a kingdom in breadth and resources.

Andrew Jackson, though less forceful in logic and as a reasoner, had other capacities and qualities of character that made him scarcely less than the party's founder. He had the indomitable will, fitness, and courage of a hero leader, and, although not anti-slavery from sympathy or the thoughtful reasoning of Jefferson, he adhered to and taught a pure, unblemished Democracy so rigidly and faithfully as to broaden the foundation of free government among men. From his time forward the slave-leaders realized that a corrupted Democracy was a necessity in their achievement of pro-slavery domination.

To this single purpose and determination they set themselves, with their influences so earnestly and assiduously used that, to their own minds, they were within reach of undisputed power from 1850 to the revolt of Douglas in 1857. How near they came to final success will never be known. Douglas for a time seemed the only obstacle that filled the narrow margin. Their power was tremendous, and Douglas was only a man—of leaders all were beaten and overthrown but him. If he had failed or faltered or fallen in the work, who was the next in line? Or, was there one? There were Logan, McClernand, Broderick, and Cass, young and old and infirm—good men, true patriots—but no one of them filled the measure of the unbeaten Douglas, resolute and determined, who could and did resist their wiles and temptations.

Before Governor Walker accepted his appointment as governor of Kansas, he wrote his inaugural address to the Legislature and people of the Territory while in the city of Washington, where it was submitted to President Buchanan, and received his approval. In it Walker said, "I repeat it as my clear conviction that, unless the Convention submits the Constitution to the vote of all the actual resident settlers, and the election be fairly and justly conducted, the Constitution will be, and ought to be, rejected by Congress."

After Walker and his secretary, F. P. Stanton, who had been a member of Congress from Tennessee, while Walker had been United States senator from Mississippi, had passed through the experience related, and had taken the side of the free State settlers, as the former governors, military officers, and fair-minded people generally had done when the "pro-slavery crowd" in the Territory had given up the contest as being beaten and outvoted more than three to one of the actual settlers, they learned to their astonishment that the Southern leaders and the Administration had ordered the forcing through Congress of what was known as the

"Lecompton Constitution" without submission to the vote of the people of Kansas in any form.

Walker, still believing in the honor and integrity of President Buchanan, hurried to Washington to sustain his own promises and to disillusionize the weak old man, where, by his power and influence, he could help to arrest and prevent the passage of the flagrant outrage against Democracy as well as common decency. He and his faithful secretary did much. The detailed story would fill volumes. The contest was an exciting, perilous one. In the one Walker learned, to his sorrow and that of thousands of honest Democrats, that the leadership and control, including Buchanan and his Administration, were completely in the hands of Davis and his conspirators, and that it had been fully determined to defy every opposition and admit Kansas as a slave State under this rotten Constitution, without reference to or any vote of the people.

This was the turning point in the legal battle for and against slavery. The fate of the Nation, no less of human liberty, hung trembling, lashed to and fro in the perilous, pitiless storm against freedom. A Democratic Administration was faithless to the people. It had fallen prostrate before the Moloch of slavery and human greed. Every principie of Democracy and honest government had been violated and outraged to carry out this long-conceived subjugation of the Republic.

If by any means, fair or treacherous, as the work had been on the border, the crime, in the form of this repudiated Constitution, could have been driven through Congress, then indeed the slave empire of Calhoun would have been a reality, and another divided Poland or subjugated Ireland would have closed the glorious but unequal struggle for freedom on the American Continent. When Walker reached Washington, he learned definitely of the changed policy and conduct of the President. The Supreme Court had fallen.

Buchanan and his Administration had cut loose from the patriotic moorings of liberty. The gaps were down and breaking almost everywhere; and the streams of man's impudent authority were rushing in aristocracy, power, and prerogative, unmasking in the strength of clutched and almost certain victory. Men and leaders had fallen by the thousand, distress and sorrow prevailed all over the land of freedom, and the lovers of liberty were in sackcloth and ashes, mourning over the Nation's threatened downfall.

But they were indeed mistaken. It was saved, saved by a margin so narrow that slavery set its fangs deep in the heart of liberty, and darkened its hope through ten years of war and humiliation—five of dreadful strife and approaching conflict and five of desperate battle and settlement. Walker sat in the Senate, where he heard Bigler, the faithless senator and the President's spokesman, from Pennsylvania, announce: "It was held by those most intelligent on the subject that, in view of all the difficulties surrounding that Territory, the danger of any experiment at that time of a popular vote, it would be better that there should be no such provision in the Toombs Bill; and it was my understanding in all the intercourse I had that the Convention would make a Constitution and send it here, without submitting it to the popular vote."

This was the speech of the oracle who was speaking and representing the President in the Senate. Douglas's remark was this: "If this conclusion is true, that the usurpation of making a Constitution did not need the assent of the people, nor approval by the popular vote, why was there need of further pretense, and why not state the truth, that the whole outrage was managed at Washington, regardless of right or the commonest forms of law? This is conclusive, that this Lecompton Constitution, with all its distressing items in the progress of thus making a slave State, has been planned and provided for here."

Walker was convinced of this truth, and, after all, could do no better than resign his governorship, or be removed, as his predecessors had been, in disgust and shame. While he was in Washington, in December 1857, the secretary, Acting Governor Stanton, convened the legally-elected Legislature, which greatly disturbed the composure of the Administration, not without ample cause for it; for this body was fairly elected, and did not intend peacefully to submit to the pro-slavery outrage planned against them.

This aroused the slaveholders immediately to action. The result was disclosed in a letter of the Secretary of State to J. W. Denver, which ran as follows, "You have already been informed that Mr. Stanton has been removed from the office of secretary of the Territory of Kansas, and that you have been appointed in his place." Secretary Cass further informed this new victim for the dead-house of Kansas governors and secretaries with an occasional captain, colonel, or general, "that President Buchanan was surprised that the secretary and acting governor had on the first of December issued his proclamation for a special session of the Territorial Legislature on the 7th instant, only a few weeks in advance of the regular session, and only fourteen days before the decision was to be made on the question submitted by the Convention. This course of Stanton, the President seriously believes, has thrown a new element of discord among the excited people of Kansas, and is directly at war, therefore, with the peaceful policy of the Administration. For this reason he has felt it his duty to remove him."

Outrage and treachery to the rights of the people could go no farther. There was nothing left in the prosecution of the crime but for Congress to consummate it and turn the Republic over full and complete to the government of the slave conspirators. Governor Walker had gone to Washington, not only as a faithful public servant to help the President avert such direful calamity, but also to counsel him from such conspiring treason, as an old friend and acquaint-ance. Finding his best intentions spurned and arrogantly resented, and himself made a victim of the old man's im-becility or alienated mind, with treacherous counselors guid-ing him, in humiliation he joined the procession of disap-pearing Kansas governors, whom the Administration could not corrupt.

On December 15, 1857, in a letter to Secretary Cass, Governor Walker wrote: "I learn, from the events occurring in Kansas as well as here, that the question is passing from theories into practice, and that as governor of Kansas I should be compelled to carry out new instructions, differing on a vital question from those received at the date of my appoint-ment. Such instructions I could not execute consistently with my views of the Federal Constitution, of the Kansas-Nebraska Bill, or with my pledge to the people of Kansas. The idea entertained by some that I should see the Federal Constitution and the Kansas-Nebraska Bill overthrown and disregarded, and that playing the part of a mute in a panto-mime of ruin I should acquiesce by my silence in such a re-sult, especially when such acquiescence involved, as an im-mediate consequence, a disastrous and sanguinary civil war, seems to me to be most preposterous."

Before the legislative struggle over the admission of Kan-sas under this outrageous Constitution had begun in Congress, Judge Douglas visited President Buchanan and protested against the scheme in his usual positive and forcible lan-guage, which no man of his day could use in more cutting irony and bitter condemnation. He did this so emphatically that it became at once a reproof and punishment, under which the cowardly, vacillating old man winced and shivered, more, as we suppose, than David did under the terrible castigation of Nathan, but to much less purpose; for Buchanon was then bound hand and foot in the grasp of the slave-leaders, and as helpless as any old political trimmer in his dotage. His last remark to Douglas was to "beware of the fate of Democratic leaders who have defied and resisted the President and his policy." To which Douglas replied more emphatically and ironically than before: "Sir, I will take care of myself, and it will be well with you if you take the same concern of yourself, in this project of a violation of plighted faith and outraged Democracy; and this will perhaps recall the fact to your mind, that General Jackson is dead."

Notwithstanding the facts that Buchanan had been elected on the faith of the free State Democracy, that slavery in Kansas would be fairly settled by an election of the qualified voters, and that the party had lost its hundreds of thousands by reason of its pro-slavery leanings, the blustering aristocrats, without a leader like Calhoun, who had learned caution from experience, plunged heedlessly and madly into the contest, regardless of all consequences, and took Buchanan, Jere Black, and whatever else was left of the pliable Pennsylvania Democracy into hopeless and lasting ruin.

Of the slave-leaders the most daring and capable were Davis, Benjamin, Toombs, Mason, and Slidell. When the plot was fully developed, these men belonged to the "win or fight faction." Against them Stephens, Joe Brown, Clingman, and others were of the more conservative faction; but all of them were forced into the contest with all their vigor and energy, because of the danger of delay, and because in the gathering storm they would need to fight for what they could get. They perceived the truth, that was hardly realized by others, that their power was slipping away, that this was their last chance to sustain a failing system, and that they would fare much better in a bold adventure than to trust the uncertainty of the next Administration or the next Congress; hence they began their vigorous and desperate contest to make Kansas a slave State; failing in that, to get all they could from the willing pro-slavery Administration, and prepare for separation and war. This war faction, under

Davis and his followers, took complete control and management of their party, and forced it into this contest for the passage of the obnoxious and unadopted Constitution.

. ... Douglas accepted the challenge for the contest, doing so regardless of any knowledge, save what was public information, of how many Democrats would stand with and sustain him. He was then something over forty years of age, in the full development of his intellectual strength, with powers that were not equaled by any parliamentary debater of his time. In his ordinary work and duties in the Senate he had long held position among the most eminent lawyers, statesmen, and leaders. He met and contended with almost all of the ablest and strongest men of that remarkable period, when he held himself an equal or more than that in many encounters. It surely needs no further affirmation than then, in this desperate dispute, he was the foremost leader against slavery aggression, and that when he defied these slave-conspirators and a servile Democratic Administration under their paralyzing and blasting leadership, they realized that they were in his grasp and in the presence of defeat.

He was tireless and energetic, and, with those members of Congress who would undertake the struggle with him, he counseled and planned for the most persevering, determined, and effectual resistance in their power. His work in that eventful session, 1857-58, was accounted to have been the most stubborn, carefully-arranged, and the best-managed legislative combat that his associates had ever seen. This was fully corroborated in the tireless forcing of his fearless opposition against the whole power and leadership of the forming slave confederation and a faithless Democratic Administration.

As it was carried on, it became the one absorbing topic of that highly-excited and wrought-up fevered session of Congress. He made it so, and planned that it should become the one of such vital interest as to engage the attention and serious consideration of the people, and bring the whole scheme and treasonable plan before the public as a court of last resort for judgment and righteous settlement. This public campaign against the slave-conspirators and their daring and audacious plans was an absolute necessity. Douglas, seeing this, properly inaugurated it against them, as he knew very well, as all well-informed people did besides, that in the desperate struggle it would require the effect of public condemnation to arrest the work of forcing this Lecompton villainy through Congress. The Administration made every possible use of party caucuses, party organization, and patronage, favor, and money, such as men had not heard of till that day. One of the strongest instruments used against this influence, was this publicity before the country, before the court of the people; and no one could cut them deeper than Douglas.

It was, of course, the plan of Douglas to arouse Congress to a full realization and decisive action against the Constitution that was to be forced upon an unwilling people, and it was no less a part of his farseeing and comprehensive plan to make it the most vigorous and determined campaign of resistance, both in Congress and before the people.

When the contest was over, and the iniquitous proposition of organic law that was full of undemocratic provisions lay before him and his victors, it was a dismembered and broken instrument of the conspiracy. There was then no doubt in Congress, nor in the public mind anywhere, that the slave-power had been encountered and defeated by a leader who was more than their equal. Seward, Chase, Thad. Stevens, Logan, and a host of loyal men in all parties stood by him in the long contest, where all of them had increased respect and honor for him as the greatest anti-slavery antagonist in that famous Congress. But the great slave-leader verified his leadership more distinctly, and realized that the overthrow of Douglas was a necessity, and that their only alternative was secession.

It is true that Douglas had the help and co-operation of
all the loyal factions, but in the peculiar situation he was the
only leader where so many had failed and fallen, who could
compass the slaveholders' crushing defeat. He had "stooped
to conquer," and had accomplished his work so well that he
bore to the end of his days the grudge and lasting enmity of
the cabal he had so decisively defeated. He had seen leaders
great and small go down by ones, twos, and hundreds before
them, so that it appeared that the cause of true Democracy
and human liberty was going down in hopeless defeat. But
it was only the destruction of the weak and faithless when
human power was failing and God's leaders were coming in,
and Douglas in that Congress was one of them.

It is true that at the time he was a candidate for his third
term in the Senate from the great State that was then honored with two such leaders as Lincoln and Douglas. When
considered, it seems fair enough that it was no more objectionable for Douglas to desire re-election than for Lincoln to
contend against him. It seems true, too, that the people of
Illinois were so nearly divided on the merits of the men, that
it was difficult to determine which had the stronger hold
upon them.

The story of Lincoln has often been attempted by those
who sought to prove his elevation and superiority in narrow-
minded abuse and detraction of Douglas, whom they often
wrote of as a "double-dealing, adroit politician." These
essays, like their framers, are being worn-out and forgotten.

On the break with Buchanan, Douglas planted himself
at once for the struggle, and in distinctness and boldness of
speech that could not be mistaken or doubted, he began the
furious debate that ended in the utter defeat of their odious
Constitution, saying: "I will stand by the Democratic doctrine that leaves the people perfectly free to form and regulate
their institutions for themselves, in their own way; do this,
and your party will be united and irresistible in power. Aban-

don that great principle, and the party is not worth saving,
and can not be saved after it shall be violated. I trust we.
are not to be rushed on this question. Why shall it be done?
Who is to be benefited? Is the South to be the gainer? Is
the North to be the gainer? Neither the North nor the South
has the right to gain a sectional advantage by trickery or
fraud. . . .

· "I am told on all sides, 'O, just wait; the pro-slavery clause
will be voted down.' That does not obviate any of my objections; it does not diminish any of them. You have no more
right to force a free State Constitution on Kansas than a slave
State Constitution. If she wants a free State Constitution,
she has the undoubted right to it, and to make it. It is none
of my business which way the slavery question is decided. I
care not whether it is voted down or voted up. Do you suppose, after the pledges of my honor, that I would go for that
principle, and leave the people free to vote as they choose;
that I would now degrade myself by voting one way if the
slavery clause be voted down, and another way if it be voted
up? I care not how that vote may stand. . . . Ignore Lecompton; ignore Topeka; treat both those party movements
as irregular and void; pass a fair bill, the one that we framed
ourselves when we were acting as a unit; have a fair election,
and you will have peace in the Democratic. party, and peace
throughout the country in ninety days. The people want a
fair vote. They will never be satisfied without it. But if
this Constitution is to be forced down our throats in violation
of the fundamental principles of free government, under a
mode of submission that is a mockery, fraud, and insult, I
will resist it to the last."

Douglas made his first argument against the admission
under the Lecompton Constitution, December 9, 1857. Early
in the following February, President Buchanan transmitted
the famous document to Congress, asserting in his special
message that it was a fairly-adopted organic law of the people,

that the opposition of the free State people was factious, and that by often and repeated neglect to vote, and willful acts at sundry times and places, they had lost all right to objections, and that they were then in a state of chronic insurrection and revolution. All this, as he represented, was by reason that the free State people had given up all thought of voting at elections where they were regularly outvoted or outcounted by non-resident invaders.

He urged the acceptance of the Constitution as a final settlement of the question. In reference to the break between himself and Governor Walker over the violated promise to submit the law to the people, he passed lightly in a clumsy evasion of the vital part of it, saying: "For my own part when I instructed Governor Walker in general terms, in favor of submitting the Constitution to the people, I had no object in view except the all-absorbing question of slavery. I then believed, and still believe, that under the organic act the Kansas Convention were bound to submit this all-important question of slavery to the people. It was never, however, my opinion that, independently of this act, they would have been bound to submit any portion of the Constitution to a popular vote, in order to give it validity."

To a President, Cabinet, and slave hierarchy, that had forced the slave-expanding opinion of the Supreme Court, it seemed to be no serious offense to arrogate to themselves or to usurp any right or franchise of the people. There could be no sufficient explanation of the outrage and violation of law and all honorable conduct of affairs in the Territory as reported by Governor Walker; hence the slave-leaders, realizing that no advantage would accrue to them by further defense of the border invasion or its deplorable consequences to the party, forced the weak-minded, slavery-poisoned President to declare as follows:

"It has been solemnly adjudged by the highest judicial tribunal known to our laws, that slavery exists in Kansas by virtue of the Constitution of the United States. Kansas is, therefore, at this moment as much a slave State as Georgia or South Carolina. Without this, equality of the sovereign States composing the Union would be violated, and the use and enjoyment of a Territory acquired by the common treasure of all the States, would be closed against the people and the property of nearly half the members of the Confederacy. Slavery can therefore never be prohibited in Kansas except by means of a constitutional provision, and in no other manner can this be obtained so promptly, if a majority of the people desire it, as by admitting it into the Union under its present Constitution."

If Congress had accepted this definition of constitutional law, and approved this Lecompton atrocity, as it was plainly and abruptly ordered to do, there would have remained little more to do to nationalize slavery, when liberty would have been crushed out, how far and how long, no man can tell. It was well, then, for the Nation that Douglas and his stalwart few in Congress rose to the conflict, resisted and fought this monstrous aggression to the death. They were brave and heroic to a man. The persecutions, tormenting and dictatorial interference, the odium and villainous slanders that were cast upon them, were more than men had ever borne in such a cause or in such a body, vastly more than ever was or will be told. Regardless of every assault or temptation, the four Democratic senators—Douglas, Broderick, Stuart, and Pugh—and twenty-two representatives remained true and faithful, who followed and fought with Douglas leading, until the conspirators' scheme of a slavery Constitution for Kansas lay strangled and dead at their feet.

Broderick of California, Stuart of Michigan, Pugh of Ohio, and twenty-two of the fifty-three free State Democrats remained faithful for the two months' contest. The House of Representatives, by the narrow margin of five votes, on April

1, 1858, defeated the Lecompton Constitution, when it was amended so as to refer it back to the legal voters of Kansas, where it was defeated by a vote of ten thousand against it, with only a few hundred in its favor, as previously given.

Of the free State Democrats in the House of Representatives who stood so manfully in this contest against slavery, there were from California one, Illinois five, Indiana three, New Jersey one, New York two, Ohio six, Pennsylvania four; in all twenty-two. Of the free State Democrats in the House who voted for Lecompton, there were from California one, Connecticut two, Indiana three, New Jersey two, New York ten, Ohio two, Pennsylvania eleven; in all thirty-one. It will be seen that the slavery-extending conspiracy had been planned for, and that it held its stronghold, outside of the slave States, in New York and Pennsylvania. Having those States and their representatives in their grasp, the conspirators felt almost sure of success; but the independent men, who had the courage and conscience to defeat their scheme under the lead of Douglas, were, like him, of the Middle West and the heart of the Republic.

There was a compromise agreed to called the "English Bill," by which the Lecompton Constitution was submitted to the resident voters August 3, 1858, with a large land-grant added as a temptation. This the slave-leaders hoped would be a sufficient inducement to accept the ungodly thing, the bad features of which would have filled a volume. Every effort of the Administration was made to persuade the people of the Territory to accept it. Fraudulent work of every kind had been so thoroughly exposed and invasions had been made until they had to be abandoned, because of their outrageous character as related. Every one of these turned some formerly Democratic State over to the Republicans. Nevertheless the odious Constitution, with its unheard-of land-grant temptation, was swept under by a majority of ten thousand votes, and the slavery question was settled in Kansas, and the slave-holders knew as well that the only hope of slave-extension was in war.

Their enmity against Douglas increased, when with the full power of the Administration they set themselves at the most vigorous means to compass his defeat for re-election to the Senate. This fight should be kept in mind, for the detractors and enemies of Douglas made their strongest accusation in that he was constantly aiding and abetting and using all his powers in breaking down the barriers to freedom, and helping as best he could the extension of slavery. But the exact reverse was true all the time, when, in place of having the slaveholders' aid and support, he had their opposition and enmity to desperation in such defamatory and defiling language as no public man had ever endured.

This was their course and method of contest and retaliation. There seemed abundant and ample cause for it, in seeing how he defeated them, and how they estimated him; for under his skillful and unceasing campaign against them they had never in all their thirty years of propagandism suffered such unexpected and disastrous defeat. We have related that he did not have their favor in the Conventions of 1852 nor 1856. After the well-known defeat of Lecompton under his commanding leadership, they held him no less an enemy than Sumner or Greeley, and would have supported either one of them for President as readily as Douglas.

In speaking of his detractors, and their assaults upon him in the Senate, in referring to a Washington newspaper stricture, he said: "It has read me out of the Democratic party every other day at least for two or three months, and keeps reading me out; and as if it had not succeeded, still continues to read me out, using such terms as traitor, renegade, deserter, and other kind and polite expressions. I know this maligner as a hireling of the Administration, who is so profusely pro-slavery that he denounced emancipation acts of New England, ·

New York, and Pennsylvania as violations of the rights of property and the Constitution of the United States, who further arrogates to himself such profound knowledge of constitutional law that any slaveholder has a right to move from South Carolina with his Negroes into Illinois, to settle there and hold them as slaves, anything in the Constitution and laws of Illinois to the contrary notwithstanding."

Every pro-slavery newspaper in the South, and every one in the free States under control of the Administration, and many envious Republican newspapers, were full of this malicious abuse of Douglas, who seldom sought correction, or made explanation or apology for his course as a public man.

He boldly charged that "this abusive stuff is poured upon me by the Administration and the Cabinet. Of this particular Washington editor, who is so vituperative, it is probably partly owing to the fact that I had the pleasure of voting against his confirmation for Public Printer; but as all know, it is mainly caused by my determined opposition to the manner in which they have attempted to force the Lecompton Constitution on an unwilling people with his odious property doctrine. I have only this much further to say, that if my protest against this interpretation into the policy of this country or the creed of the Democratic party is to bring me under ban, I am ready to meet the issue."

It was one of the best features in the excited condition of the people and the desperately-angered relations of parties, that in the time when one strong leading faction was preparing for war, all loyal divisions of all parties were gathering in opposition for defense. Douglas and the patriotic Democrats who contended with him against the encroachments of slavery, and fought side by side, were of the bravest, who after his death followed such leaders as Logan, Hancock, Rosecrans, McClernand, and a host of others, who deserved all the Nation has to give.

In measuring the capacity and work of such men, parties,

and their relations to them, should long since have been laid aside and forgotten. If Douglas was a partisan, and contended so strongly with Lincoln, he was no less a patriot. When the time came for the highest sacrifice any great leader of this country had ever made as a partisan, he bore his personal defeat as a true hero, and in submission to Lincoln as duly elected, he and his party proved themselves what they had declared, patriots for the Union and against its enemies.

No one can estimate what would have been the disastrous results upon the Nation, if Douglas had failed or faltered, as almost every other distinguished party leader of anything like equal capacity and opportunity had done. Benton alone had about the same record; but he had been overthrown and left as helpless as a child by his surroundings for any service to freedom or his country. This was the era before Lincoln, when he could do little to stem the frightful stream of slavery, secession, and ruin that was pouring down in pitiless floods upon the land. If this lion-hearted Douglas, not misnamed "The Little Giant," had not filled the breach with his cohorts of loyal men and stemmed the furious tide, who and where was the man living or the leader who could have done it?

God alone could and did provide such a leader as Douglas, such as was absolutely needed at the time, and so he remained to the end. When he had done his great work the Master took him. Lincoln was then coming, rising in strength, and was soon recognized as the great leader and President. Logan and the Democratic leaders we have named were in appearance raising their standards and unfurling their colors for war and duty.

What has been said of Douglas and his course through this threatening and alarming period of the Nation's history was well known to those best informed. Much of this information was gained from the personal and family acquaintance we have spoken of with Judge Douglas, and a large personal acquaintance with the leaders of all parties in the State. Not a little of it came from my own independent ideas on slavery, which grew stronger on a nearer acquaintance and active support of Owen Lovejoy, who was for years and until his death our Representative in Congress, where he became one of the strongest Abolition and Republican leaders of the Nation years before and through the war.

He was a man of such fealty and unswerving integrity in the anti-slavery cause, of fitness, capacity, and information, that his opinion and estimate of the conduct and value of the services of Judge Douglas through the Lecompton crisis were as good and of as much weight as those of any member of Congress. Lovejoy's opinion was that, without the determined, heroic, and persevering work of Douglas, no other power or available means within his knowledge was equal to prevent the consummation of the slave-leaders' crime for the admission of Kansas as a slave State. Lovejoy was familiar with the work of Douglas, and co-operated so incessantly from beginning to end that he knew the relation of every one to it in Congress or the Administration in the desperate struggle. He said, in substance, that without it the consummation of the slaveholders' grasp on the Territory by the admission of Kansas, the project of a slave empire, could have been prevented only by a revolution of the people against the intrenched slave-power.

With these ideas prevailing, it was natural enough that leading men in Congress and thousands of grateful anti-slavery people all over the land were kindly disposed toward Judge Douglas, and looked upon his return to the Senate by Illinois as a common and necessary act of approval. Mr. Lovejoy, with almost every Republican member outside of Illinois, held this common view and estimate as a recognition of the invaluable service and leadership of Judge Douglas, and so acted until contrary action was reached in Illinois. He did so until the Illinois Republicans, regardless of any outside belief or interference, as they came to look at it, made Mr. Lincoln the candidate of the party against Douglas. When this was done, regardless of personal knowledge or personal leanings, Mr. Lovejoy entered into the campaign in support of Lincoln zealously and effectively. He was the brother of the murdered Elijah, whose three anti-slavery printing presses had been thrown into the Mississippi River before his cowardly assassination by a pro-slavery mob of Illinois ruffians, as dastardly as any that subsequently infested the Missouri border in the same sin-breeding cause.

Owen Lovejoy, like his brother, was for many years an acceptable and earnest minister of the gospel. He had a powerful and well-rounded physique, weighing about two hundred pounds. He was over six feet in stature, as fearless as he was strong and majestic, with such force of speech and distinct utterance that he could be easily heard by twenty thousand people in the outdoor meetings, so common in the excited interest of the people. Mr. Lincoln, although having a clear, ringing voice, like a clear-toned bell, could not comfortably talk at the same meetings to half that number; nor could Judge Douglas talk to more than half as many; hence Lovejoy was perhaps the most noted and commanding stump-speaker and pathetic orator of his time. Those who knew, said he resembled Tom Corwin, of Ohio, who had few, if any, equals in holding or addressing crowds, and that Lovejoy could talk to and be heard by a third more people.

Lovejoy was a member of the Legislature and one of the most faithful supporters of Lincoln, who finally united on Trumbull at Lincoln's urgent desire. He was elected to Congress, not only without the support of Judge David Davis and a coterie of Old-line Whigs, but against their strongest and "bolting" opposition. Their support of another candidate was, however, a harmless pastime, except as showing the political leanings and animus of Davis and his little body of Whigs. These demanded the very best the party could give; but they were only partisans enough to fill Cabinet positions, to be judges, marshals, and attorneys or general managers, while the common people were expected to sustain them in any service required for the good of the cause. This was not unusual service, but it should have been reciprocated by this little knot of Whigs, who would not make speeches or support an "Abolitionist" for office.

We have run through this explanation that it may be shown that Mr. Lovejoy was as careful an observer of the services of Douglas and as fully capable and qualified to estimate the effect as any man in Congress. As we proceed, we shall learn how these Whigs would not support Owen Lovejoy.

From these events and concurrent ones happening in the opening of the memorable and exciting Douglas-Lincoln campaign of 1858, the writer had relation to them where he obtained a knowledge of the men, before unknown, and inner knowledge of the true character and greatness of Lincoln that is ineffaceable. I was busily engaged in professional work requiring such constant labor and attention that I had no desire for political place or employment. In the fall of 1857 I attended a county Convention in Champaign County, where I then resided, for party organization and other political purposes, where, without thought or appreciation of what it was to be, I was made secretary of the County Committee, which place I held until the opening of the war in 1861. Champaign County was then an extremely important community in the strongly-contested campaigns in the State, principally because the Republican majority ran from 800 to 1,000; but it had a larger body than any one suspected, before it was developed, of independents and Abolitionists, who often varied it 400 or 500 votes, and in some cases elected a favorite Democrat rather than an unsatisfactory or apologizing Republican. This position, held uninterruptedly for five years, gave me personal knowledge and acquaintance with prominent party leaders in the State and a knowledge of public affairs in all the movements of that period.

In the beginning of 1858, Judge J. O. Cunningham, then and still a prominent and highly-respected citizen of Champaign County, with myself, attended the Republican Congressional Convention at Bloomington as delegates. The Judge was chairman of the County Committee. As it happened, no other of the eight delegates to which we were entitled attended, and, as usual, we were given the full vote of the county. We found, on arrival, that the contest between Lovejoy and his opponents was so close that our votes would nominate or defeat him, as we determined. Judge Cunningham being a discreet and prudent man in such an emergency, we kept silent. Keeping our own counsel and gathering all the information that was possible in the early morning gave us a clear understanding of the situation before the assembling at eleven o'clock. Before the noon recess, after the Convention was organized, we ascertained that four of our eight votes would renominate Mr. Lovejoy, and that we could vote for him and compliment some other gentlemen with the other four votes as we liked. After full deliberation, our conclusion was that Lovejoy deserved the approval and indorsement for faithful and courageous service in Congress, where he had made a manly defense of the cause and our people, then the most populous district in the United States.

This conclusion we reached on consideration of all the information at hand concerning the wishes of the people of the county whom we represented; and though it accorded with our inclinations, it was not for these that we concluded to vote for him, but because it was the desire of our people, who believed, as we did, that because of his faithful service he deserved it. The contest against him was conducted with vigor and vehement denouncement of his abolition belief, as far as it was prudent to venture it.

JOHN SHERMAN

JOHN B. HENDERSON

DAVID DAVIS

STEPHEN T. LOGAN

We determined not to disclose our intentions, unless there was some necessity for it, and so save ourselves from the bitter disputes of the almost furious leaders prevailing and raging all about us. We were called on and visited and argued with in the zeal and earnestness of the leaders of the opposing factions, but without any declaration on our part until a few minutes before the time of the reassembling at one o'clock.

By this time the contention had reached such intense interest on the part of Lovejoy's opponents that Judge Davis approached me in an austere, authoritative sort of manner, and demanded why I was not in sympathy and why I had not been in counsel with those "who desired the nomination of some Republican who could be elected rather than training with the Abolitionist, Lovejoy, who could not be." Presuming on my former relation, when a student at college, he assumed a patronizing air, which was very unpleasant, if no more.

Maintaining my composure as well as I could under the prevailing excitement, I replied that Judge Cunningham and myself were representing our county, and that we did not recognize his or any one's authority in it, except that of our own people, to catechise or arrogate the right to dictate to us what we should do; that, while we were there to carry into effect our people's and our own wishes as well as we could, I would be glad to have him understand that Mr. Lovejoy was no more an Abolitionist than I was, and had been such for years, as he well knew, and that was the belief of thousands of like-minded voters in our district.

At this he took it for granted that we intended to give the vote of Champaign to Lovejoy, when he swelled up and roared out his condemnation of Lovejoy and his agitating Abolition supporters, including me, of course, like one of the bulls of Bashan. Pointing his finger menacingly at me, he declared: "You had better training than this. Mr. Lincoln's advice and prudent interest should have left a deeper impression on you." Saying this, he stormed away, and strode off in anger.

In this passionate episode, walking along, we had reached one of the office rooms in the court-house. The Convention was assembling. Several eager contestants of both factions followed us in. When Davis made the accusation that Lovejoy was an Abolitionist, and I had retorted as stated, it was taken for granted that we of Champaign were for Lovejoy, and, being so, his nomination was certain. This was taken up by the hundred or more Lovejoy delegates and friends with so much noise, shouting, and enthusiasm for him as to smother all remonstrance of Davis and his little crowd, who had gathered about him. They left at once, chagrined, outwitted, and beaten in their determined effort against one noted Abolitionist, for the time at least. The Convention soon reassembled, when Lovejoy was renominated, as he deserved to be, for faithful service and manly conduct in perilous times and against blusterers and braggarts in Congress.

Judge Davis having accused me of disregard and want of respect of Mr. Lincoln, concerning whom of all men I held and entertained the highest opinion, I determined it was a duty to see him and make an explanation, and have some kind of understanding and settlement, if it were possible, because it was a situation that seriously concerned others, and consequently it was more than a personal difference between us. When I called on the judge, I introduced the subject, saying: "Notwithstanding your open declaration that you would not support Lovejoy, and would absolve me from all need of seeking any kind of explanation, my concern for the welfare of others involved has led me to ask you why you asserted so emphatically that I have disregarded the teaching and interest Mr. Lincoln has shown and continued in me, and how I have crossed it by a preference for Mr. Lovejoy?"

He was still in bad humor, but mellowed down from the higher pitch of the morning. To my question he muttered something, and said: "Mr. Lincoln is opposed to the nomination of all such Abolitionists as Lovejoy, and you ought to know it, with the knowledge you have of him, as well as any one else." I replied that I did not believe what he said of Mr. Lincoln, and that if he would agree to it, we would submit it to him, with the understanding that we would abide by the settlement. He did not like this; but as I told him I intended to see Mr. Lincoln and submit the facts about it, seeing it could not be avoided, he yielded reluctant consent.

We agreed to turn it over to Mr. Lincoln, who, as we knew, would be in Bloomington shortly. In the interval, Davis and the "bolting delegates" offered the dissenting nomination, with the promise of Democratic support, and no other candidate in the way, to Mr. Leonard Swett, one of the ablest lawyers of the Bloomington bar and a strong supporter and a warm personal friend of Mr. Lincoln. As Davis understood it, Swett had it under serious consideration for reply on the day that we submitted the subject.

It was a delightful summer day when we met in Bloomington to lay the whole proceeding before Mr. Lincoln. It came about in the form of a friendly conversation, in which Davis and myself answered Mr. Lincoln's questions, which were brief and strongly in the direction of the facts, especially those not published. After this, to the surprise of both of us, he reviewed the case impartially, with the relations of the contestants fairly stated and the strained conditions before us at home and in the whole country, with knowledge and grasp of the delicate political situation so complete that the contest was decided in his general remarks before he reached it in form or detail. By this Davis became aware intuitively that the case was going against him, that Lincoln was on Lovejoy's side, and had been, even before the meeting, in all probability. This angered him at once. Being a stout man, the bloodrush filled his face and throat to the point of choking his free utterance; but, stammering it out as best he could, he remarked, rising and pacing the floor in a state of suppressed agitation, because it was Lincoln, bringing his heavy fist down on a table of books that shook and rattled every one of them, he said in his deciding sort of emphasis, "We will not support such an Abolitionist, such an outspoken one as Lovejoy; and we are sure that Swett can defeat him," and, pointing his finger almost in Mr. Lincoln's face, inquired, "Do n't you believe it?"

Mr. Lincoln turned about in his chair, with his face breaking into a smile, and said: "Judge, I understand it all. As I was crossing over to the court-house, I met Mr. Swett, who told me that you had offered him a sort of nomination for Congress, but that he would under no circumstances accept it, and asked me whether he was right. I told him, as I tell you, that he was wise in having nothing to do with it, and that the very best thing for all of us is to unite, and not to divide, and elect Mr. Lovejoy to Congress; for he has fairly earned and deserves re-election." Lincoln was evidently much affected by the remarkable fervor of Davis's opposition and the excitement he had worked himself into. They had been intimate friends for years, which no doubt restrained him; but his statements, although pleasantly spoken, had no lack of firm and positive expression. He sat for awhile thoughtful and motionless, save the penetrating cast of his rolling brown eyes. Finally, in minutes or moments—none of us remembered which—his humor came; and with a great broad smile he turned to Davis, who was still striding the floor in a sort of growl. He said: "Judge, Lovejoy is only a little ahead of us. We will soon catch up. And, by the way, did you know that they say Seward is ahead of him now, and that he has taken a notion to Lovejoy, and is giving him his full sympathy and countenance as he can? You know it is not wise to antagonize him. He is one of the prophets. And, by the way, Judge, did you ever hear Lovejoy? He fills the benches with new converts every night, as the Methodist brethren say. He is one of the most powerful and convincing speakers in the country, and, without doubt, the ablest we have in our State. He can talk to twice as many people as I can; and I tell you, Judge, it won't do for us to be selfish and try to turn him out; and, further, we might not succeed if we tried."

In reply, Davis sounded out a kind of guttural, smothered, "No, I never have, and I do n't know that I ever will." The temper and tone were away down and softened. Lincoln's reference to Seward had developed Davis's predominating caution; for above all other things, his desire was to be a National figure in public affairs. Although he would not tolerate such an Abolitionist as Lovejoy at home, he could bear them just as well as not in New York or Massachusetts, or even as near as Chase in Ohio, if he regarded them as prominent and influential leaders.

The distinct result of this transaction was the suppression of Davis in the most skillful and effectual way. Lincoln calmed the domineering judge in his fit of rage, or the appearance of it. Realizing this at once, and that his plan was working, he continued saying: "Judge, Lovejoy will be here on a date near at hand. He is an entertaining speaker, and what I like so much about him is that he is always so much in earnest that you know he believes what he says. You will be delighted. I am going to be here to meet him. He has sustained Douglas, and says that his opposition to Lecompton was the greatest defeat slavery ever had in Congress. I do n't want him to follow Douglas too far. We will all go and hear him; and the first one of us that do n't support him, seeing that his nomination was regular and fair every way, we will have to discipline in some way; but we won't turn anybody out of the church, for just now we are weak, and we want all of the converts we can get. Our good-natured friend here—Robert—is young and ambitious. He will get over it and forgive everybody and vote for the first Old-line Whig we put up."

Davis yielded in silence, although there was small probability that he supported Lovejoy. At the best, his candidate declined his "sort of nomination," and his opposition to Lovejoy was shorn of all its power, save his own vote; for at that day no one acting with the party would have undertaken the serious task of opposing Mr. Lincoln, least of all conservatives like Davis, who stood waiting, "ready for a better office."

CHAPTER XXXIV.

THIS unpleasant episode that amused and provoked me for several days was what drew Mr. Lincoln, in his great, sympathetic nature, nearer to me than anything that had happened between the kind-hearted man and the boy and growing man, who trusted Lincoln as a father. After leaving the court-house he remarked: "Robert, it is past noon. We will go and get our dinner. Then we will go out to the grove, and hear Judge Douglas this afternoon. As you are to return by the way of Clinton, we can go that far together. I am to speak there to-morrow. We will leave here on the late train, after my speech to-night, when I intend something of a reply to Douglas, after hearing him."

This plan of something to do changed my gloomy reflections on the harassing episode. The invitation was so open and cordial that the disagreeable things passed from mind, and I was pleased at the thought of passing the day and evening with the great leader of the common people. I had not had such an opportunity for something like three years. It was in the time when the correspondence was about completed that resulted in the joint debate of that year. When the day was gone, and we parted, long after midnight, the pleasure and the hopes of the morning had been far more than realized. I had been all day with God's prophet-leader of the people, and in a conscious but inexpressible way I knew and felt the full power of the man and his leadership. I had seen his power in the morning, how exerted, and how easily he turned and smoothed and

managed the wrathful and, to other men, unmanageable
judge. In the evening I had seen so much that was beautiful and charming in character, sympathy, and integrity as
to make me feel the effect of it all my days.

When I saw him at night, and knew the man better
whom I had known 'so' well .for years, and yet had never
known, I left him, amazed and astonished at his inspiration,
his exaltation, which I never had doubts of afterward. As
we passed along to the hotel, he recognized and greeted
almost everybody, and was as warmly received in return;
for although the town was full of the thousands who were
there to hear Douglas in the daytime and Lincoln at night,
he knew almost every man at sight, and most of them by
name, besides a great many of their wives and children. He
spent a full hour on our way to dinner, going two or three
hundred yards. In illustration he was so genial, kind, and
attentive to all of them, that no one man, woman, or child,
was passed by who desired his friendly recognition. His
stature, his unequaled strength, remarkable and apparent
as he mingled in that multitude of strong, rugged farmers,
his majestic presence and bearing that gave him the strength
of a lion and the gentleness of a child, proved him at once
a leader among men without an equal, and still one of them
whose virtues and power were growing and gaining ascendency the more they met and the better they knew him.

He had worked hard in travel and what we have related
all the morning, and was a big, hungry man as we sat down
to a well-cooked Illinois dinner. He told the waiter, "Bring
us a plain, well-cooked dinner, and plenty of it, with corn-
bread, a good, big slice of fat corned-beef, and, if you can
get it, a quart of fresh buttermilk." This was his dinner,
and it made a hearty one, which he fully enjoyed.

In the afternoon we walked out half a mile to a grove
to the Douglas meeting. The trees were thick enough to
give good shade and a pleasant grassy sward, as convenient

and suitable a location as could have been found. A small platform for the speakers had been built, and there were rough board seats for a few hundred; but most of the six or eight thousand people stood around the platform, sat down, and spread all over the soft grass within hearing.

The people were, most of them, farmers and their families, all intent and anxious to hear one of the most prominent leaders of the time discuss the topics that so fully engaged and absorbed their minds. More than half of them were Democrats; but Douglas, in the past session, had been far more than a partisan leader. This was shown in the meeting of the people of all parties by thousands, who were anxious to hear him and so far encourage him in his manly and patriotic service as a distinguished citizen of our State. There was enthusiasm for the great party leader; but the bitterness of 1856 had perceptibly moderated, so that those of all parties gave the senator careful and patient hearing.

We sat down on the grass at the root of a tree as near to the speaker as we could locate ourselves. Mr. Lincoln took his well-used silk hat, that was always full of letters, references, and memorandums tucked in behind the band, put it over one knee, and made a desk of it, on which he laid his scraps of paper, torn-up envelopes, and ends of letters, which he wrote full. In this way he took a fairly good synopsis of the important parts of Douglas's speech, with his arguments.

Douglas was well aware of Lincoln's presence. He was all the more cautious in consequence, and measured, shaped, and shaded his address to protect himself; for no man knew Mr. Lincoln's capacities better, if as well. He was there before the people as a candidate for re-election; and in compliance with a well-observed custom, he was giving his ideas and opinions on the questions of the day and his and their relation to them. He had been the subject of unlimited abuse and detraction. At the time every newspaper supporting Buchanan's policy and Administration and every office-holder having place or power under it, to the smallest post-offices, were instructed and compelled to compass his defeat. They were not only instructed, but a set of supernumeraries scattered all over the State as inquisitors reported every Douglas Democrat for lack of fealty or delinquency in the slavery cause or any inclination to support Douglas for sena-tor, for either of which reasons they were promptly removed.

Removals were frequent and made in the reckless man-ner in which spiteful personal campaigns are usually con-ducted. There were many neighborhoods in the State where all the Democrats were for Douglas, and the little post-office had to be given to some Republican. This proscrip-tion ended, as it mostly does, in uniting his followers all the more zealously in support of their chosen leader.

His address on this occasion was nearly two hours long, in which he reviewed the slavery question, the relation of parties and his own relation to it, the history of the long and bitter struggle over the Lecompton Constitution in the session of Congress just then over. He arraigned the Re-publican party for its narrow-minded policy on the slavery question and its want of courage to declare itself what it was in reality, an Abolition organization, an agitators' party, and confined to one section of the Union—the Northern—and by its policy of interference with domestic institutions could never be other than a sectional party. He also ar-raigned the party for its denunciation of the other "twin relic of barbarism"—polygamy—declaring that "it was all sound, and that Mormonism would not be seriously disturbed if the Republican party came into power."

This he thought was not improbable, rather an event to be expected, as the Democratic party was then dividing, and all the more certain if the slaveholders controlled one party and the Abolitionists the other. He closed his long and able address with a defense of his own conduct and an appeal to the people to sustain him and a loyal Democracy that would save the Union.

When he finished his address, I went to the platform and congratulated him on his stubborn and successful contest with the slave-leaders, assuring him that it was a patriotic and praiseworthy service from an out-and-out Abolitionist, as he knew us, father and son, and that if he continued as faithful I would be willing to bear his strictures on the "Abolitionists." He was glad to meet me and pleased with my reference to his contest.

He replied: "I recognized you in the audience with Mr. Lincoln, and you both seemed interested in my statements. I suppose you are logically a supporter of Lincoln." To this I replied: "I am, so far as to belong to the most advanced section on the slavery issue; and I believe if you remain steadfast, as I fully expect, in your opposition, as we always expect a Scotchman to do, you will be 'logically' with us in a few years."

During this chat a strongly-inclined pro-slavery Democrat, an opinionated man in whatever he did, finding a chance, broke into the talk, saying: "Then I was not mistaken: that really was Abe Lincoln who sat in front of the stand with you, leaning agin' a tree, and he was a-takin' notes. I have always heerd that he looked like a nigger; and he never knowed much anyway." I was indeed much surprised that the man should make the very impolite remark when he did, not any more at his remarks than his temper; for stupid-minded and stubborn fanatics were as ignorant then as now, for party divisions were strong and bitter.

In catching Judge Douglas's face I saw that he was wrought up and angry, as well as provoked. Turning suddenly on the man, he gave him a sort of double penetrating look that shook him all over, saying: "You are a fool. Mr.

Lincoln is one among the ablest lawyers and public men in
this country. He is fit and competent in every way to be
a leader, and, in my opinion, as much so as any man in
his party, in which he has the same right to act and contend for what he believes as we have. It is often just such
hot-tempered bigots, as you seem by your remarks to be,
that bring the bitter personal and party disputes of our time,
of which I believe I have endured more than any other
dozen whom I know; and I am only grieved at such insolent
references as you have made on Mr. Lincoln."

When parting, I said, "I feel very sure you are
making progress, and we will soon have you on the front
benches." He smiled out of his grim remembrance of the
ugly incident, saying: "Do n't mention anything about this
unpleasant occurrence to Mr. Lincoln. What an incorrigible
Abolitionist your father was! and I have always missed him.
I would be very glad indeed to have him with us, unreasonable as he was on slavery; but I see he has impressed you
to follow in his footsteps, and you seem to be improving
the opportunity."

I went back to the hotel with Mr. Lincoln. After a very
light meal he spoke to an outdoor meeting, a street full of
enthusiastic thousands, for more than an hour, from the
upper floor of the hotel porch. A great many farmer people
had remained to hear, and the city was ablaze with coal-oil
lamps and party-shouting and enthusiasm. He was as much
at home there as anywhere in the State out of Springfield.
The people never tired of greeting him and turning out
in thousands to hear him. This was as true of those who
heard him frequently as of those who did for the first time.
It was what was called a rousing political rally, and the light
that flashed from the torches reflected another light from
the faces of enthusiastic men. This was the beginning of the
blazing torch and street parade of hundreds of men marching in line—"Wide-awakes," as they were named. They grew

to permanent organization as marching clubs, and became a prominent feature in political campaigns from that time in all parties.

Douglas returned to Illinois from the long contest in Congress, and entered the public discussion for re-election with the favor and earnest sympathy of many prominent Republicans, independents, and loyalists in the East, with Senator Crittenden, of Kentucky, and a few prominent Whigs like him, who were isolated and independent of all parties. Of the general desire for his return to Congress, Crittenden's indorsement in a public letter was conclusive. Besides being a lifelong opponent of Douglas in their long service in the Senate, his support was full corroboration of the high estimate that had been placed on the patriotic service of Douglas. It was a high recognition that conservative men like him—Badger, of North Carolina; John Minor Botts, of Virginia, and others—sustained Douglas as they did. It was all the stronger in the case of Crittenden, who had been for years, and remained, a personal friend of Lincoln.

Notwithstanding this strong outside influence in favor of Douglas, it was an impossible realization, though seriously entertained by many worthy and distinguished men, that the Republican party of that day could consent to it without contesting his re-election. The Democratic and Republican parties in the State were two strong, hopeful, powerful, and nearly equally-divided parties. They agreed in enough to make them both faithful, patriotic Americans, but still differing enough to make them distinct and determined contestants.

With this view of it, if all the leaders of both of them, big and little, or any one of them, had failed and left them, there were enough talented young men to select from, with every qualification for leadership, except the experience. This would soon have been gained by these ambitious young men, like all our people, who can soon fit themselves for any necessary occupation or employment. Under such consideration we can understand that an earnest political contest in Illinois in 1858 was a certainty, with Douglas and Lincoln as leaders, or even without them.

At the time we write of, Mr. Lincoln had been selected by the Republican party of the State, by the desire of many of the Republicans and by many independents, as the party's candidate for senator; and the correspondence was about completed which provided for the joint debate with Douglas. Mr. Lincoln was ambitious, more for the cause than for his own personal distinction. He was never in better physical health and the enjoyment of ripened and matured manhood, making him easily the best-fitted and strongest man for such an encounter that could have been found in the land. He was then a wise, experienced leader, with popular qualities, the wit, the humor, and, far above these, the genius that made him the distinct character that he was. He was the equal of Douglas, who was, as we have written, then in his full prime as a great leader, which had been proven by his long struggle with the slave-leaders.

With this common belief and confidence prevailing in both parties and their respective leaders, with the alternative thought among many that, next to their own leader, the other leader—whether Douglas or Lincoln—was the best man in the country, the coming debate between these distinguished and incomparable leaders was a pleasure and high expectation to the whole population, such as they had not anticipated. As public dangers multiplied and widened in the gravity, the overturnings, and the growl of the approaching storm, the people in Illinois first, and then all over the loyal States, gathered around and drew closer to these wise and trusted men, and hung more confidingly on their words of wisdom and counsel as the conflict ripened into dreadful war.

Mr. Lincoln's speech at night and the one of Judge Douglas in the afternoon were made in anticipation of the earnest and exhaustive dispute that both, like athletes, were

measuring and stripping themselves in readiness for. Mr.
Lincoln spoke for more than an hour in his earnest and sincere way, with interludes of wit and humor that kept the
multitude as much interested as he was, eager and enthusiastic to the close.

Late at night we took a train for Clinton, twenty miles
south. It was a slow train, besides being late, so that we
were on it two hours or more, arriving at our destination
about midnight. There were crowds, noise, and confusion
about the station where we took the train. A lot of the
people were getting home who had attended the meeting,
and delayed it with the getting on and the frequent stops to
get off at their homes. We sat down about the middle of a
smoky, crowded car. As we did, we saw a few interested and
excited people had gathered together about a very noisy
talker in the front end, who derisively mentioned Mr. Lincoln's name several times.

Not knowing the man, I turned to Mr. Lincoln and inquired, "Who is he?" He smiled, and, raising his voice to
one of its high-sounding keys that rang through the car,
replied: "That's Long Jim Davis, of ——. There are two
of them, both small politicians in the same town; and the
'Short Jim' Davis is very much the best man. He has
something in him like integrity and gratitude; but this
one hasn't a bit of either in his make-up, and is only a
man because he looks like one. Through my recommendation he was given an appointment under the Harrison Administration in 1841, and returned to the same place under
Taylor in 1849, with a relative or two crowded into office
employment with him. He not only has not recognized my
help in a grateful way, but has been busy ever since the
Democrats turned him out in abusing me. He claimed to
be a Whig, but kept blaming me for not keeping him in
office, as he insisted I was able to do, against all parties
and what was common practice of the Democrats in making

removals. Now I understand he has turned Democrat, with
all the zeal of a new convert, and is set on me like a little
fice, to provoke and annoy me. I am to speak in the afternoon; and he will raise his lofty voice in his lost-office sort
of disappointment that will be chiefly personal strictures of
myself. He has been running very loosely for some time
that way, as I learn. For myself, I am glad to be rid of
him, even on his terms; but before I take up the subject of
my speech I am going to take him up first, and peel him
as clean as you can strip a hickory sprout when the sap
rises in the spring."

From this cutting, humorous disposition of "Long Jim"
I was at once interested in him and went to the end of the
car to hear what I could. It was the bitterest personal denunciation I had ever heard him utter against any one. When
I reached the crowd, I found that Mr. Lincoln had effectually silenced him and all the rest of them. I could not get
any replies or satisfaction from him or the rest of them
as to what he had said. Jim himself curled up in his seat,
and was too sleepy to talk. At Clinton he was sound asleep
in his seat, and went on with the train south; and that ended
his following and replying to Lincoln.

When the talk quieted down, Mr. Lincoln doubled himself down on two seats turned together, where he took a
good hour's sleep. When he was comfortably at his ease,
he could lie down and take an hour's sound refreshing sleep
almost anywhere, rise up from it rested, invigorated, and
ready for the irregular and laborious work of his campaigns,
for which no man had the health, strength, and endurance
he then had.

It was almost twelve o'clock when we left the deserted
railway station at Clinton. He was strong, vigorous, and
active, and had something like the speed of a race horse,
as I then thought, after the run to the hotel. I was about
a foot under his height and not near his weight, but young

and vigorous. He took my arm as we stepped from the platform, saying, "Come, Robert, now for our hotel and a roost, and a late one for me, as I have nothing much to do before noon, seeing that Long Jim has run away." He almost lifted me from the ground in his strong, firm grasp, that filled me besides with a sense of the wonderful energy of the man.

We made the half-mile trot and run to the hotel in a few minutes, where a sleepy watchman took us upstairs to the end rooms of a narrow hall, giving us two little boxes on either side of it, with the doors opening and facing each other. He took us there because these were farthest removed from the noisy part of the house, where Mr. Lincoln could take an undisturbed sleep in the morning. The speed from the train had stirred up our blood, so that neither of us was ready for the sleep we were anxious for.

In this mood, with our doors wide open, as the outside windows were also, Mr. Lincoln called me into his room, where, in it and the narrow hall, we sat over two hours, one of us on the side of our beds, changing at intervals, or on the only chair in either of our rooms, with the other standing or sitting on the bed. The air was soft and warm, and everything was quiet and still about us, with no sound but our own voices, which, as far as we knew, in that remote corner, would not disturb any one. In his pleasing and entertaining talk, that was sure to interest any one to whom he gave his confidence, he reviewed the exciting passages of the day in humor and pathos that would have held a houseful in close attention. He made it so real that it seemed that we had passed them all over again in full campaign style, in the way he led and recited the events, item by item, man for man, and feature for feature.

As we went over the incidents of that day and the campaign just then opening, he became entirely absorbed, serious, and thoughtful. He would sit at his ease, attentive for a few minutes, then arouse suddenly, as if to take out the burdensome task that was always present and deeply impressed him. Although we were alone, with no helps to raise his spirit or lighten it up, like the presence of a crowd, I never heard stronger nor more pathetic appeals for the liberties of men nor sympathetic outbursts of hopeful expectation that our land and its free institutions might be saved, that the Union, at once God's promise and fulfillment of free goveernment on the earth, might be preserved, and much as earnestly delivered that has been forgotten.

What he said of himself, his beliefs, his duty, or mission, or what he felt he must do and could not evade, can not be forgotten. To me he opened his great heart as he appeared and stood, the anointed of God, as much in mind as I had Moses, David, Cromwell, or Washington. He seemed in his line of duty and succession with these, with the care and weight developing in his soul, under the load of a greater undertaking and responsibility than any one of them. He said: "I have not sought nor wanted leadership, such as this, that comes like this Lovejoy contention; but I am conscious that I must do as I have done, and sustain our cause with whatever strength or power I have, if it sacrifices opinions and men by the score to do it. I have never sought position, and dislike very much to exercise the power I have; but whenever it becomes my duty, I will carry it out with as much celerity and determination as Jackson ever did.

"I have not desired to be in the strife of contending parties. I like the discussion of any question of right or justice for my own and the general good that comes from these; but since my settled success in the profession and my defeat by Trumbull I have felt all the more certain that I should abandon general politics or national issues as much as possible, and positively give up all thought of being a candidate for any political office.

"After I saw that I had to give way to Trumbull, when I had practically done all the work, had united all the factions and followers of the variously-named candidates, all that were united, several of whom, besides myself, had a better following than Trumbull, and I had forty-eight to his three, I was more tired of and disgusted with the office-seeking, office-getting, and distributing business than I have ever been. I gave it up without reserve in my own mind, and have been earnest and persistent as it is possible in avoiding even the appearance of the evil of office-seeking. Our friends are making me the candidate against Douglas, honestly enough, no doubt. This is easier to do than to get the senatorship; but with the probable contingency that, if we succeed, some unheard-of person, with no more following than Trumbull, will get it. He shall have it, too, as I willingly gave it then.

"I am not at all unwilling to contend for the senatorship with Douglas, especially so as I have not sought it; but I am much more willing to discuss the threatening condition of things, and help arouse the people to the impending danger, that they may rise in their might and save our country and its liberties, which are actually the one and only hope of free government on the earth. In that duty I feel that, to the eextent of my abilities, no one shall surpass me, and that I have as high a purpose before me as any man can have."

I said: "The people of the State have a high appreciation of you as a lawyer, a wise man of sound judgment, and a learned counselor. Were it not for the conspicuous and patriotic service of Judge Douglas, your defeat would be impossible. As it is, from all we can learn—and we have been anxious and inquisitive about this—we believe that your chances are as good as his. It is certainly a great opportunity for you, whether you win or not. With your masterly ability and the affectionate hold you have on the people, to meet on equal terms and contend with a statesman and leader of such unquestionable eminence and distinction as Judge Douglas firmly holds, is a necessity in your present situation and party relations that you can not decline.

"In your kindness, though a young man, you have made me a personal friend, and, against my strong Democratic inclinations, an earnest follower. I have mingled lately with a lot of your best friends, all of them, as far as I could see them. After all the talk, with Mr. Gridley leading, perhaps we are all united and all anxious that you should strip yourself for this political battle as you never have done, and make it the most earnest and noted contest of your life. It seems to me that your whole career—all there is of you as a leader—is wrapped up in this honorable contention against Douglas, whom we should not misunderstand. He is a great man, an untiring and capable leader, and now in the best favor he has reached for years, because of his recent patriotic and able contention against the slave-power.

"If men follow destiny, it is surely yours to contend with Douglas as you have done from the time of your beginnings. There is no doubt of his ability and learning; but he has fallen into the common error of nearly all our prominent statesmen since the foundation of the Government, and deals with slavery, not as a wrong, but as a question of policy and expediency. Whereas I am satisfied, confirmed by your independent and resolute action to-day, and your beliefs sustaining, that you will take it up on the basis of principle and high public morality, according to God's law that all men are equal before him. There are thousands of young men in the State who share my views, who, if they had gained your confidence, as you have favored me, would be as zealous as I am, or perhaps more so, and among your earnest and stalwart supporters.

"If you had given way to Davis in his suppression of Lovejoy, or in his attempt to suppress him, I would have been sorely disappointed. As it stands, Davis has no just reason to complain. I had full confidence that you would decide it as you have. Nevertheless I feel that you have rendered a great service to the men so deeply concerned, and greater, if possible, to the cause you so manfully upheld. As it is, I am delighted and believe in you as our chief leader, if not in this, then in some future campaign; for I am sure that God's cause of right is growing rapidly among the people, and no one appears anything like so outspoken in its presentment and defense.

"I saw Mr. Gridley this afternoon, and talked to him of our trial and arbitration of the Lovejoy dispute before you to-day. He replied, as you can easily appreciate, but as those who do not know him never can, saying: 'Why, Robert, you are all a pack of Abolitionists, and it will be all that Judge Davis and the Springfield crowd of Old-line Whigs, Browning, of Quincy, and such reliable and conservative men as myself, can do to hold you impulsive young men back and save the Union and a good many offices for these experienced old-liners; but, seriously, I am glad to see you so well pleased. Lincoln is growing, and the best thing about him is that he is always big enough for the question when it comes.'"

When I paused, I saw that my remarks pleased and the facts and recital sustained him, as he believed he should be, in what was public and friendly employment. He was thoughtful a few moments; the melancholy cast ran down slowly over his clear-lined face. In a few moments it had passed, when he raised his hand and rushed it through his coarse, tangled, dark hair, that lighted up his pale face in reflection, when he continued.

He said: "Robert, if you are not an Abolitionist, since the Bloomington meeting, you are an enthusiast. I concede what you say of Douglas. I could do no less; for so many men in all parties have done so, that it would seem small and spiteful in me not to agree with them. Your father was

a man of learning and ability, an avowed Abolitionist, twenty
years ago, when it was a disadvantage and a perilous venture
to many. His opinion running that way with others, helped
me to respect the man, while I disapproved the politician.
He said that Douglas was an able, indefatigable man, serving the slave-power for policy's sake. He was right. His
judgment was correct, and he discerned then, in the time
of the Mexican War, what Douglas did not and would not
believe, that the slave-mongers would cast him aside as mercilessly as they do others. They cast Benton aside, ripe in
age, experience, and stored-up wisdom, throwing him off
like an old shoe, as they are now trying to do to Douglas.

"But do you believe that a plain, common man, as I am,
of the back-river, if not 'backwoods' country, is or can be
what you so ardently wish I should be, a real leader of the
people? You surely do not believe that I am a great man,
but rather that I am an earnest and sincere one."

I looked directly into his soul-expressive face, and the
words of my reply seemed to come to me without thought
as I said: "I do not know whether you are a great man or
not; but I do know that you have the strongest power over men
—whether a houseful, or a streetful, or over me here alone—
in effect and speech of any one I ever saw. You know that
we Scotch people are determined and stoutly held, faithful
in our beliefs, and slow to change. We are called hardheaded,
cautious, even superstitious, never ahead, but commonly
behind the drift of popular opinion. We all believe in Robert Bruce, William Wallace, John Knox, Robert Burns, and
sympathize with the persecuted and unfortunate Mary Stuart.
Now, by the faith and sympathy I have in these, one of them
and all of them together, and as I believe in Moses, Joshua,
David, Luther, Cromwell, and Washington, I firmly believe
that you are a great leader, and more than that, and for
good reasons, much more, to my mind, in the approaching
crisis; for responsibility increases in the world's and man's

development. You are one of God's leaders of the people. I have faith—growing faith—that you, plain man of the people, are all this, and that you will be faithful to the end.

"You know me well, and have from schoolboy to the present beginning manhood. You can put the value of all I know on my knowledge or opinions. If I am wrong in this, I am in all else of thought or reasoning. I have contrasted you with men I know; and more, I have studied hard to understand; with those like Davis, Trumbull, Logan, Browning, and many such. They are changing, doubting, half-going, half-coming, temporizing all the time. I have put you alongside Douglas, the untiring student, so alert and full of energy that he never seems to rest. He has more of the statesman and statecraft about him than the others, but he is yielding in principle, too often giving way to the false and fading lights of expediency, as my father held.

"I have likened and compared you with each other. I like Douglas; my father loved the man, and believed that he would outlive his frailties, which he hoped were more of caution than settled disposition. There can be no comparison between you. Illinois is big enough with its two parties for both. Douglas is without any doubt a great leader, and as surely as he is, you are. It seems his duty to lead a great party on the lines of policy and expediency. Is it not yours to lead another on the broader grounds of God's eternal truth, justice, and law, against evil and wrong of whatever kind or character?"

Mr. Lincoln replied: "All the reforms in human history come under active and independent leadership and bitter contest. In free government, to keep the doctrine of human liberty alive it must have progress. War for increased liberty is better than acquiescence and submission to wealth, and arrogated power in any form that always accompanies it in eras of increasing wealth and apparent prosperity. Under these all the increase drifts into the hands of a few, whether of

wealth or power. Hence now, as in all past time, if freedom
is to live on this continent, a heroic body of men, party, or
army must fight its battles on principle, against the greater
evil of avowed prerogative of every kind, and the lesser ones
lurking under conservatism, policy, and expediency."

After this he seemed lost in thought again, and the deep
melancholy shade again overspread his features. His face was
loosely held and the lines were more deeply drawn; the in-
tegument almost folded over itself as it rolled down on his
neck. He had a mobile, quick-answering face, with the most
prominent features; and notwithstanding the loosely-held
muscles and soft parts he had it under perfect control, so
much so, that for the purposes of explaining his thoughts
and illustrating his ideas his expressive eyes and easily-con-
trolled face and countenance were trained and skilled to his
use, just as his tongue and voice were. His voice rang out his
emphasis, his desires, his facts, and his pathos in tones, tuned
in high melodious chords, like skilled performers, under his
liking and bidding. He could soften his voice down to the
movement of a bird floating at ease in the soft summer air,
or he could raise it up in all its tones to a bugle-call that
rolled over multitudes, as an imperative summons to duty, an
assertion of power and expression that God alone could give.
The inspiration of such a soul and this melodious, or bugle-
noted, voice became the precious memory of the thousands
who heard him and caught his spirit.

He continued: "Robert, you have been candid. You are
young and enthusiastic, and so excusable for your friendly
estimate. It is something that no man has ever talked to me
about so freely. My own experience and heart in the work are,
what you say, an important part. I feel that I have a duty
before me, not in any sense a general idea of such a thing,
as I have about ordinary business, but an ever-present sense of
labor. That comes along in invitations and requests, almost
without number. When I set my mind at work to find some

way of evading or declining a journey, a speech, or service, instead of my own spirit a something stronger says, You must go. You must not disappoint these people, who have given you their confidence, as they have no other man.

"I am a full believer that God knows what he wants men to do, that which pleases him. It is never well with the man who heeds it not. I talk to God. My mind seems relieved when I do, and a way is suggested, that if it is not a supernatural one, it is always one that comes at the time, and accords with a common-sense view of the work. I take up the common one of making a speech somewhere or other. These come almost every day. I get ready for them as occasion seems to require. I arrange the facts, make a few notes, some little memorandums, like those you have seen so often and are so familiar with. I take them, and as far as facts are concerned confine myself to them, and rarely make any particular preparation for feeling, sympathy, or purely sentimental thoughts.

"When my plans for the discussion are made, and the foundations are laid, I find that I am done and all at sea unless I arouse myself to the spirit and merits of my cause. With my mind directed to the necessity, I catch the fire of it, the spirit, or the inspiration. I see it reflected in the open faces and throbbing hearts before me. This impulse comes and goes, and again returns and seems to take possession of me. The influence, whatever it is, has taken effect. It is contagious; the people fall into the stream and follow me in the inspiration, or what is beyond my understanding. This seems evidence to me, a weak man, that God himself is leading my way."

This was the faith of Abraham Lincoln. To him it had imperative meaning, and carried with it direct responsibility which he neither sought nor tried to evade. Under his strict rules of honor and integrity as applied to himself, no believer, devotee, reformer, or martyr ever served more faithfully or heroically to the end. Time and events proved that he was all these. Our pleasant review closed after two o'clock in the morning, when the tallow-candle burned out in the socket of the old brass candlestick. I rose early to take my road home across the country, leaving him to the rest he needed, where he slept until nearly noon, as he afterwards told me. To me it was a revelation, always remembered as the day and night when we made the election of Lovejoy a certainty, preventing serious party division, and I had looked into the soul of Lincoln.

On the 16th of June, 1858, the Republican State Convention at Springfield declared Mr. Lincoln their first and only choice for United States senator. This was done to forestall a result like that which defeated him in 1854, when Trumbull maneuvered into the senatorship that the party and thousands of other people would gladly have given to Lincoln. After the adjournment of the Convention he delivered one of the most carefully-prepared addresses and startling announcements he had ever made, in which he verified Mr. Gridley's remarks that "Mr. Lincoln was growing."

He boldly took advanced ground on slavery, far in advance of his party declaration, limited as we have stated. He clearly and emphatically declared, in the strength of the prophet he had grown to be, without qualification that "a house divided against itself can not stand," and applied it directly to slavery in this country. Many a weak conservative trembled and predicted defeat, and shifted their responsibility for such advanced opinions. He paid no attention to them, but increased in earnestness and vigor, denounced slavery as an "over-all evil," and for every conservative that faltered and fell by the wayside two or more robust anti-slavery believers were added.

His meetings increased in interest, and larger multitudes came to hear the leader of the common people, who honestly and fearlessly discussed slavery as an evil, regardless of legal enactments or constitutional intrenchment. Douglas was lead-ing patriotic Democrats. He had rendered valiant service and stopped where he would make no further concession to slavery. These leaders in this sort of a campaign marked a new era in public controversy, when they carried on a dis-cussion of slavery under conditions that would not have been tolerated five years before that time. The people of both par-ties realized it, with the result that everybody in the State in these almost equally-divided parties went into the business of discussing slavery, one way or the other, under these great leaders.

In his Springfield address, Lincoln made his celebrated and world-spreading announcement, as follows: "If we could first know where we are and whither we are tending, we could better judge what to do, and how to do it. We are now far into the fifth year since a policy was initiated with the avowed object and confident promise of putting an end to slavery agitation. Under the operation of that policy that agitation has not only not ceased, but constantly augmented.

"In my opinion it will not cease until a crisis shall have been reached and passed. 'A house divided against itself can not stand.' I believe that this Government can not endure permanently half-slave and half-free. I do not expect the Union to be dissolved—I do not expect the house to fall; but I do expect that it will cease to be divided. It will become all one thing or all the other. Either the opponents of slavery will arrest the further spread of it, and place it where the public mind will rest in the belief that it is in course of ulti-mate extinction; or its advocates will push it forward until it shall become alike lawful in all the States, old as well as new, North as well as South.

"We have had almost complete preparation for the latter result in the events that have given us the repeal of the Mis-souri Compromise, the Dred Scott decision, which declared that, subject to the Constitution, neither Congress nor a Territorial Legislature could exclude slavery from a Territory. Putting all these together, with the dominant slavery faction in full control of the Nation, leaves another little niche, which we may see erelong filled with another Supreme Court decision, declaring that the Constitution of the United States does not permit a State to exclude slavery from its limits. It has come to this indeed, that such a decision is all that slavery now lacks of being alike lawful in all the States. In the present drift of things we will lie down, pleasantly dreaming that the people of Missouri are on the eve of making their State free; and we will awake to the reality instead that the Supreme Court has made Illinois a slave State."

In closing this remarkable address, in which he advanced to the strongest position against slavery as a destroying evil, one that could not exist in a free Government, in which one or the other must perish, he had reached and achieved leadership beyond dispute. This took firm hold and went deeper into the hearts of the people day by day, when the character and capacity of the coming leader strengthened and sustained his unassailable pronouncement against slavery.

He brought it directly under the malediction of God's eternal laws of truth, righteousness, and justice, when in the language of the Master he demonstrated its antagonism and incompatibility with free government and the rights of men. He braved every danger and planted himself on the rock on which the battle must be fought. He had "talked with God," taken up the contest in his name, and was armed, belted, and buckled for the combat with aggressive despotism, that lacked only another decision of the Supreme Court to obliterate the great Republic, bring in the Empire with the pageantry of prerogative and aristocracy, and crown Jefferson Davis king or dictator.

In the struggle against this culminating and frightful assault against human liberty Lincoln was God's leader, who knew and learned it day by day as the truth dawned and

never departed from him. With the confidence that the right
and justice of the cause inspired him he closed: "Our cause,
then, must be intrusted to and conducted by its own undoubted friends, those whose hands are true, whose hearts
are in the work, who do care for the result. Two years ago
the Republicans of the Nation mustered over thirteen hundred
thousand strong. We did this under the single impulse of
resistance to a common danger. With every external circumstance against us, of strange, discordant, and even hostile
elements, we gathered from the four winds, and formed and
fought the battle through under the constant hot fire of the
disciplined, proud, and pampered enemy. Did we brave all
then to falter now—now, when that same enemy is wavering,
dissevered, and belligerent? We shall not fail. If we stand
firm, we shall not fail. Wise counsels may accelerate or mistakes delay it, but sooner or later the victory is sure to come."

The outside interference of many prominent Republicans
did not seriously disturb or disconcert him, as it did many
timid and weak-spirited followers in the party. Some of them
held and believed that the success of the anti-slavery cause
and Lincoln's leadership depended upon the issue of the contest of these almost evenly circumstanced men for the senatorship. This was true of the purely political followers who
doubted and wavered by the thousand, for the contest was
a close one, and known to be so from the beginning; but the
anti-slavery people were in the work heart and soul, because
it was right. They expected no offices or personal gains, and
brought determined thousands where we were losing wavering
hundreds.

In Lovejoy's district we gained several thousand. He was
leading the conflict, and in no uncertain way he struck directly at the dominating evil of slavery, whose leaders he denounced as undemocratic despots, plotting and planning for
their country's ruin. He had stood on the floor of the House
of Representatives at Washington through tempests of their

furious bravado and bluster, reasoned with them, or tried to, met them in their blustering roar as they came, stood his ground against them; and, minister of the gospel as he had been, he took his position, delivered what he had to say, and defied them. This work he explained to the people, the condition of things at the Capital, the perils that threatened us and our liberties under these slave aristocrats.

He went into the work earnestly, and laboriously supported Lincoln, regardless of the spite and defection of Davis and the few whom he could influence. The result of this bold and fearless campaign was encouraging. The increased majority for Lovejoy over his vote of 1856 would have assured Lincoln's election, if it could have been distributed over the State, or if the same gains had been made in the other districts. Every member of the Legislature in our district supported Lincoln. This clearly developed to our minds the foresight, wisdom, and integrity of the leader against the attempted dictation of David Davis.

Mr. Lincoln knew as well as any one that the outside leading Republicans favored Douglas, because of his patriotic service and the lasting defeat of the slaveholders; nevertheless he bore the defection, whatever it was, patiently, without complaint. Though defeated because of their work, the contest was so close that a few votes determined the result.

While considering this campaign, it must be mentioned that it was "an off year;" but we were plunged into one of the most hotly-contested elections of the forming war period in Illinois. It was comparatively a time of rest in the Nation. This was distinctly favorable to Douglas. Another item in his favor was that the impotent rage of the Buchanan Administration and plottings against Douglas stimulated Douglas's friends to redoubled energy and persevering labor, to muster every possible vote for him; so their wrath in this roundabout way was a great help to Douglas.

In the narrow margin and close vote, where a few votes

here and there scattered over the State so effectually changed
the result, no other dozen men of all these anti-slavery outsiders contributed so much toward Mr. Douglas's re-election
as Horace Greeley and his New York *Tribune*, and of conservatives none approached the work of Senator Crittenden
of Kentucky. Without the active work and co-operation of
these, he would have been decisivley beaten. The *Tribune*
was more generally read by the anti-slavery people and Repub-
lï.cans than any other newspaper. Mr. Greeley, in his assump-
tive, know-all, friendly, dictatorial way, substantially advised
the people of Illinois to make little or no opposition to the
return of Douglas. This of itself influenced enough votes
throughout the counties where his paper circulated to change
the result.

Senator Crittenden, of Kentucky, became so anxious for
the success of Douglas—forgetting his anti-Democratic beliefs and affiliations of a lifetime and long and faithful service
of Lincoln with him in the Whig party, whom he knew and
highly respected—that he published a letter strongly urging
the return of Douglas as a necessary rebuke to the faltering,
fraud-hatching, slavery-forcing Administration. This letter
was widely circulated in Central and Southern Illinois among
thousands of Kentucky Whigs, who had come to the State
in an early day to avail themselves of its convenient, fertile
lands.

To most of these Crittenden, next to Clay, had been a lifetime Whig leader, whom all respected for his wise and patriotic service. Many of the Whigs were changing; they were
trained to "despise Abolitionists." The slave-leaders adroitly
stimulated all their leanings and prejudices in that direction.
Many of them were not much opposed to slavery, but decidedly
opposed to any interference with it where it existed. They
were generally loyal, and strongly inclined to follow Clay and
the Kentucky leadership; hence there was little doubt that
Crittenden's letter favoring Douglas took several thousand

of them, not only to his support for senator, but permanently into the Democratic party.

Mr. Lincoln understood the situation well. He carried on the unequal contest against him, regardless of disappointments, defections, sacrifices, and heavy personal expenses, and like the great generous-hearted man he was under all circumstances, never changed his mind nor held any sort of grudge against the prominent leaders whose meddlesome interference led to his defeat.

He said about it: "I have never said or thought more as to the inclination of some of our Eastern Republican friends to favor Douglas, than I expressed in your hearing on April 21st at the State Library here. I have believed, and believe now, that Greeley, for instance, would rather be pleased to see Douglas re-elected over me or any other Republican; and yet I do not believe that he prefers Douglas by reason of any secret arrangement with him. It is because he thinks Douglas's superior position, reputation, experience, and ability, if you please, would more than compensate for his lack of a pure Republican position, and therefore his re-election would do the general cause of Republicanism more good than would the election of any one of our better undistinguished pure Republicans.

"I do not know how you estimate Greeley; but I consider him incapable of corruption or falsehood. He denies that he directly is taking part in favor of Douglas, and I believe him. Still his feeling constantly manifests itself in his paper, which, being so extensively read in Illinois, is and will continue to be a drag upon us. I have also thought that Governor Seward, too, feels about as Greeley does; but not being a newspaper editor, his feeling in the canvass is not so much manifested. I have no idea that he is, by conversation or by letter, urging Illinois Republicans to vote for Douglas.

"As for myself, let me pledge you my word that neither I nor any friend, so far as I know, has been setting stake against Governor Seward. No combination has been made with me or proposed to me, in relation to the next Presidential candidate.

"The same thing is true in regard to the next governor of our State. I am not, directly or indirectly, committed to any one; nor has any one made any advance to me on the subject. I have had many free conversations with John Wentworth; but he has never dropped a remark to lead me to suspect that he wishes to be governor. Indeed, it is due to truth to say that while he has uniformly expressed himself for me, he has never hinted at any condition. The signs are that we will have a good Convention on the 16th of June. I think our prospects generally are improving every day. I believe that we need nothing so much as to get rid of unjust suspicions of one another." (Letter to Wilson, June 1, 1858.)

In the beginning of this senatorial contest he had a full realization of the capacity, strength, reputation, and leadership of Douglas. The party following Douglas was chiefly in the free States; but while loyal, it was strongly tinctured with pro-slavery sentiments. Douglas could do no more nor less than keep along with them and maintain his leadership. Lincoln realized, before the contest began, that he was bound in honor and the confidence of his followers to make it, no difference who might win the senatorship. No one knew the capacity and standing of Douglas better than he did, and he knew as well that if his contest with him was defective or disclosed any want of information, ability, or power on his part, it meant his certain retirement.

Douglas could have failed in the memorable debate or in the election, and have made some satisfactory apology or explanation. He had stood the equal of any man in debate and discussion of the gravest public affairs in the Senate for fifteen years, from Calhoun, Clay, and Webster, to Seward, Chase, Benjamin, and Davis. Lincoln was to him only a beginner. From the first, Douglas had no doubt of his advantage in training and experience for the contest. As firmly he believed that these would make him an easy victor, and that he would entangle Mr. Lincoln in the mazes of detailed party discriminations, personal debates, and leave him an unhorsed, confounded, and deserted leader.

He reckoned this on the ground that Lincoln would take and confine himself to the Republican policy, that was in principle and fact little different from his own doctrine of "Squatter Sovereignty." It was a plan of advanced expediency against slavery extension, as results proved, while the Republican party opposed the extension of slavery by excluding it by some Act of Congress. This was no more than Douglas had done, and he came home to make his contest for re-election with the authoritative proof of prominent Republican leaders that he had done so. With this understanding it was small wonder that he believed Mr. Lincoln would fail for want of an issue, if no more.

Mr. Lincoln gave the subject deep and profound study. He realized all that Douglas had anticipated. He knew, as well as any one, that if he followed the usual routinism of party defense with no better contention against Douglas than opposition to the extension of slavery, which was the Republican creed, he would fail, and be the victim. But with deeper thought and wisdom he developed himself a statesman and leader beyond controversy, and confounded Douglas, his friends, and the Republican outsiders. He boldly took God's side of the question, going to the root of the evil when he arraigned slavery as a system that could not exist in a free democracy.

On this plane of fearless assertion of the truth, and with equal or surpassing strength, voice, capacity, and argument, he proved himself a master. He did it so decisively and emphatically that it was soon realized throughout the land what a great achievement he had won, and that no other living American could have done it. He took a position in which he did not plead for an issue, but made it. Continuing in his Springfield speech, he said: "How can Douglas oppose the advances of slavery? He do n't care anything about it. His avowed mission is impressing the public heart to care nothing about it. For years he has labored to prove it a sacred right of white men to take Negro slaves into the new territory. Can he possibly show that it is a less sacred right to buy them where they can be bought the cheapest? Unquestionably they can be bought cheaper in Africa than in Virginia. He has done all in his power to reduce the whole question of slavery to one of a mere right of property. Now as ever I wish not to misrepresent Judge Douglas's position, question his motives, or do aught that can be personally offensive to him. Whenever, if ever, he and we can come together on principle, so that our great cause may have assistance from his great ability, I hope to have interposed no adventitious obstacle; but clearly he is not now with us, he does not pretend to be, he does not promise ever to be."

In his humorous way he sketched some of the difficulties. No audience ever tired of his drollery and wit, in which his dramatic performance always better illustrated the humor, the argument, or the strength of his story. In his close at Springfield, he said: "Senator Douglas is of world-wide renown. All the politicians of his party, or who have been of his party for years past, have been looking upon him as certainly at no distant day to be President of the United States. They have seen in his jolly, fruitful face, post-offices, marshalships, land-offices, and Cabinet appointments, charge-ships and foreign missions, bursting and sprouting out in wonderful exuberance, ready to be laid hold of by their greedy hands. And as they have been gazing upon this attractive picture so long, they can not in the little distraction that has taken place bring themselves to give up the charming hope; but with greedier anxiety they rush about him, and give him the marches, triumphal entries, and receptions, beyond even what in the days of his highest prosperity they could have brought about in his favor. On the contrary, nobody has ever expected me to be President. In my lean, poor, lank face no one has ever seen that any cabbages were sprouting out. These are the disadvantages all taken together that the Republicans labor under. We have to fight this battle upon principle, and upon principle alone."

CHAPTER XXXV.

THE Republicans of Illinois were aware that the peculiar nature of the contest over the election of a senator involved national issues, with defection at home and outside interference in favor of Douglas. They knew that they must make as strong and determined opposition to the return of Douglas as lay in their power, otherwise the State would probably be carried by the Democracy at the Presidential election. Without division or discussion all had full confidence in Lincoln, and believed that if any man could meet and contend with Douglas he was the man. In this consideration a joint discussion was arranged for at Ottawa, Freeport, Jonesborough, Charleston, Galesburg, Quincy, and Alton, seven smaller cities of the State, so selected as to give the people in all parts of it the opportunity to meet and hear these prominent leaders.

By the agreement in detail Douglas had the advantage of the opening and closing at four places, while Lincoln had three. The meetings were so largely attended that the average ran above twenty thousand. Douglas, in his conditon of voice and strength, could not be heard by more than five thousand out-doors; while Lincoln, in his full vigor and strength and perfect voice, could be heard by most of them. Hence the advantage of one opening and one closing was more than compensated for by Douglas's inability to be heard by these outdoor multitudes.

A reporter who was with them, talking of it afterward, said, making an estimate: "The meetings averaged twenty thousand. Douglas could only be well heard by about five thousand, and many times he spoke under a continual strain, with a failing voice. This would give him at the seven meetings thirty-five thousand who heard him; whereas, Lincoln talked to all of them, with no sign of flagging, but rather increasing strength. This gave him an audience, all told, of one hundred and forty thousand, or four times as many." In the meetings held this was no exaggeration, as it appeared, at all, and gave Mr. Lincoln a very decided advantage.

Douglas and his friends throughout the State were wrought up to their best energies, and a very excited condition of things prevailed in many localities, inflamed and aggravated by the meddlesome interference of Buchanan's Administration, so that receptions, processions, street displays, brass bands, awkward men on untrained, galloping horses in hundreds, were common where the country boys were turning out in thousands.

Before the opening up of the contest between them, Lincoln made his Springfield address, which, from the bold assertion that slavery and freedom were incompatible conditions that would divide or destroy the Nation, or that one would prevail, attracted general and widespread attention. Douglas at once recognized this, and saw the gravity of the assertion. He knew that it would eventually reduce the slavery debate to two contending parties, one for and the other as positively against slavery, removing altogether the middle position, on which so many statesmen and others had hammered, trimmed, pounded, and compromised over for some fifty years. Notwithstanding all the contests and the threatening conditions at the time, great progress had been made. Free speech had been restored in the free States, when, in 1858, Mr. Lincoln triumphantly announced that "The battle had to be fought on principle, and principle alone." This obvious principle was that slavery was wrong, and that as such it could be discussed and debated in every part of the State as it could not have been ten years previously.

The pro-slavery party, however, wherever it could, suppressed opposition, and one of the beneficial results of its intolerance was that it had raised up Douglas and his free State Democracy to contest this pretension with it. At this time parties had grown to the strength to contend directly with it, meet men with their pro-slavery dogmas, and when necessary defy them. This foreshadowed the mingling of all parties into two contending bodies, and the elimination of all intermediate ones. The signs of the times foretold this, and as wise a man as Lincoln anticipated it, hoping for a peaceful solution that might be realized within the space of one hundred years.

Douglas was as fully aware as any man then living that the real issue, when stripped of maneuvering and dissembling, was a battle to the death between slavery and freedom, the same that had been demonstrated and waged in the bloody victory of the free State men in Kansas. But, as we have related, he was peculiarly situated. He was then the rising, but the recently-persecuted, leader of a pro-slavery sympathizing and partly-believing pro-slavery faction, but a loyal and patriotic party. He knew well that he could only avoid a fate like Benton's, by maintaining his leadership of this partly pro-slavery free State Democracy. To do this, and meet the direct contention of Lincoln, he could do no better than dodge the inevitable consequences of a direct issue for and against slavery, like Clay, Webster, Cass, and the entire school of compromisers, who had so well succeeded, from as early a time as 1820.

To maintain himself against the direct and open charge of Lincoln, the strongest diverting sophistry became his most available means for defense. Mr. Seward's statement that "there is an irrepressible conflict between freedom and slavery" he interpreted as indubitable proof that the Republican party was an Abolitionist organization, and, consequently, a disunion and disloyal one. Slavery had existed in accord and harmony with freedom, and experience proved beyond question that it could do so in the future, and Lincoln's assertion to the contrary, which he wrongfully maintained by quotations from Scripture, meant only the disruption and dissolution of the Union, as far as it had any meaning or effect. He contended that opposition to the decision of the Supreme Court in the Dred Scott case and the masked opinion that slavery already existed in all the Territories, meant a desire on the part of the Republicans for amalgamation of the races and absolute Negro equality. The truth was that the contest was desperate, and the day of the compromiser was over. Douglas learned in this canvass that, if he was to fight on the side of freedom, he must do more than defeat the slave-power in Kansas. The battle was on between freedom and slavery, and, misguided, loyal leader as he was, for a time he strove hard to evade the truth of Lincoln's declaration and his harder blows, sustaining it in the fallacies of such popular delusions as "Negro equality."

Lincoln's high capacity for leadership was never more positive and independently shown than in the direction of this senatorial contest. He was making it, not for a day, nor the present success, but for all time, on the basis of principle, right, and justice, regardless of the close-lapping struggle that so completely filled the minds of men.

The advance he had taken and bravely declared was against the advice of every political friend to whom he submitted it, except two or three Abolitionists, who were pleased and delighted with his courage and independence in making it. Mr. Gridley said: "It shows his high, independent character. It is his own act. No man advised it, and no man can change it. . . . He is like Paul, speaking again before idolatrous Greeks. He declares the justice and right of the unrespected and, in practice, then unknown law of God against the beastly sin of slavery. Some time he will win, if he does not this year, when the minds of men are open to the truth."

David Davis said: "No man can carry the State of Illinois on the 'higher-law creed.' Seward may succeed with his doctrine of an irrepressible conflict in New York, but it would defeat him in Illinois. I consider it rashness on the part of both of them; but Lincoln's strong personal influence may save him."

Lovejoy said: "It sounds like God's truth from the mouth of his prophet. Do good? Yes, and shatter the doubtings of thousands of weak and timorous souls who are under the ban of pro-slavery sympathizing and small despots all about us. They can now defy these in the strength of Lincoln's leadership. To the faithful it is a new hope, and we will buckle on our armor for a harder battle with slavery and its myrmidons, such as we never have had with it in its long greedy and bloody career."

Mr. Leonard Swett, who was an able lawyer, a close reasoner, and a very conservative Republican, who admired Mr. Lincoln's courage and independent action, said: "It leaves no doubt in the public mind as to his capacities for great leadership. I believe it will stimulate and consolidate his followers, who need a strongly-developed issue to counteract and hold his party against an able and popular leader, as Douglas is in his well-disciplined party, which has held supremacy in this State since the time of Jackson. The contest would have been a close one any way. The Republicans might have broken down under a contest, depending on which had done the most to keep slavery out of Kansas; but Lincoln's assault on slavery itself is the thought and act of a wise, capable, and heroic leader. It will command attention and harmonize his followers, whose strongest common ground of belief will be opposition to slavery. It will perhaps drive away some of the older and more timid, such as the Old-line pro-slavery Whigs, but it will bring in their place the young and the enthusiastic from all quarters. With the increased energy that a fight for principle will throw into the canvass, I believe that he will be justified; but it is a movement ahead of time in Illinois, and only under the indomitable energy and genius of Lincoln can the surprising result of carrying the State be possible. With the unquestioned valuable and patriotic services of Douglas, everywhere conceded, the probabilities were strong against the Republicans, to begin with. Lincoln's bold and aggressive departure and fight against slavery may change it; but the State has been Democratic so long that the result is in great doubt."

With the exception of a few voters held against Douglas by the Buchanan Administration, which was only five thousand in a vote of two hundred and fifty thousand, the Democratic party was united and heartily supporting him with perfect harmony and earnestness prevailing all over the State. Popular and reputable men were selected as candidates for the Legislature. The Democrats gained strength as the contest continued, and became more and more confident of success. It was a distinct advantage to the Democrats that they had the most experienced and best-known local leaders in over two-thirds of the State, which the forming party did not have.

These various opinions afforded a basis for as careful estimate of parties and probable results as could have been made in the State. The topic of the senatorship was an all-absorbing one. People of all parties were heartily engaged in it. The Democrats were hopeful, and became more confident of success. The Republicans, Independents, and all the anti-slavery elements were fighting under Lincoln for principle for the first time they had ever had such opportunity, and, though determined and courageous as the leaders had to be, the result was involved in doubt and uncertainty to the close.

Mr. Lincoln's addresses were always skillfully laid, deliberately and effectively delivered; and in no one of them did he neglect to bring in the real issue, usually in some positive way or in striking comparison and logical illustration that left a lasting impression on his hearers. Replying to Douglas's endeavor to make the Republican party and its Abolition doctrine the issue, and evade the already accomplished work of the pro-slavery Democracy, in his unanswerable logic he said that "it is merely for the Supreme Court to decide that no State, under the Constitution, can exclude it, just as they have already decided that, under the Constitution, neither Congress nor the Territorial Legislature can do it. When that is decided and acquiesced in, the whole thing is done. This being true, and this being the way, as I think, that slavery is to be made national, let us consider what Judge Douglas is doing every day to that end. In the first place, let us see what influence he is exerting on public sentiment. In this and like communities, public sentiment is everything. With public sentiment, nothing can fail; without it, nothing can succeed. Consequently, he who molds public sentiment goes deeper than he who enacts statutes or pronounces decisions. He makes statutes and decisions possible or impossible to be executed.

"The Democratic policy in regard to that institution will not tolerate the merest breath, the slightest hint of the least degree of wrong about it. Try it by some of Judge Douglas's arguments. He says, 'I do n't care whether it is voted up or whether it is voted down in the Territories.' I do not care myself, in dealing with that expression, whether it is intended to be expressive of his individual sentiments on the subject, or only of the National policy he desires to have established. It is alike valuable for my purpose. Any man can say that who does not see any wrong in slavery; but no man can logically say it who does see a wrong in it, because no man can logically say he do n't care whether a wrong thing is voted up or voted down. He may say he do n't care whether an indifferent thing is voted up or voted down, but he must logically have a choice between a right thing and a wrong thing. He contends that whatever community wants slaves has a right to have them. So they have, if it is not a wrong. But if it is a wrong, he can not say people have a right to do wrong. He says that, upon the score of equality, slaves should be allowed to go into a new Territory like other property. This is strictly logical if there is no difference between them and other property. If it and other property are equal, his argument is entirely logical; but if he insists that one is wrong and the other right, there is no use to institute comparison between right and wrong.

"You may turn over everything in the Democratic policy, from beginning to end, whether in the shape it takes on the statute-book, in the shape it takes in the Dred Scott decision, in the shape it takes in conversation, or the shape it takes in short-maxim-like arguments, it everywhere carefully excludes the idea that there is anything wrong in it. That is the real issue. That is the issue that will continue in this country when these poor tongues of Judge Douglas and myself shall be silent.

"It is the eternal struggle between these two principles—right and wrong—throughout the world. They are the two principles that have stood face to face from the beginning of time, and will ever continue to struggle. The one is the common right of humanity and the other 'the divine right of kings.' It is the same principle in whatever shape it develops itself. It is the same spirit that says, 'You work and toil and earn bread, and I will eat it.' No matter in what shape it comes; whether from the mouth of a king who seeks to describe the people of his own nation and live by the fruit of their labor, or from one race of men as an apology for enslaving another race, it is the same tyrannical principle."

Douglas's doctrine of "Squatter Sovereignty" having been constructively overruled and set aside by the Dred Scott decision, Lincoln drove Douglas into a corner on it. that was apparent, almost distressing. Douglas's only reply was that "local police regulations adopted by any Legislature of a free Territory would exclude slavery." And Kansas was given as an example of it. The facts were that the decision was so repugnant to the independent American people of that day that no single attempt was ever made to enforce it, and its beneficiaries—the slaveholders—never ventured with their slaves where its power could be tried.

Lincoln said: "This settlers'-right or 'Squatter Sovereignty' doctrine is the most arrant quixotism that was ever enacted before any community. Does he mean to say that he has been devoting his life to securing to the people of the Territories the right to exclude slavery from them? If he means so to say, he means to deceive, because he and every one knows that the decision of the Supreme Court, which he approves and makes especial ground of attack upon me for disapproving, forbids the people of a Territory to exclude slavery.

"This covers the whole ground from the settlement of a Territory until it reaches the degree of maturity entitling it to make a State Constitution. So far as all that ground is concerned, the Judge is not sustaining 'Squatter Sovereignty,' but absolutely opposing it. He sustains the decision which declares that the popular will of the Territories has no Constitutional power to exclude slavery during their Territorial existence."

The slavery leaders and their followers of every description were presumptuous and arrogant, as oppressors and usurpers always are, holding it to be their right and prerogative to declare, not only their belief, but to exercise the same privilege for their opponents. Hence they not only sustained slavery wherever and in whatever way they desired, but defined and denounced the belief of all opponents at will, calling them "Disuninoists" if they disagreed to the slavery code and their construction of it.

Douglas was in sore distress, being confronted with the gaunt and greedy specter of slavery; and he yielded to the slaveholders' distracting cry. He charged Mr. Lincoln and all anti-slaveery believers as Disunionists, and declared that they were in favor of the amalgamation of the races and Negro equality. He did not disclose the facts, or was, perhaps, not then aware that racial amalgamation was rife and common in many slave communities, as we have elsewhere related; that many social leaders were fed, nourished, and brought up, suckled and cared for by strong, lusty, black-skinned nurses. This was sufficient approach to amalgamation, and always existed alongside the real mixing of races, where itself was real Negro equality, the most pronounced anywhere to be found in the land; but this fact seemed to be ignored by the small as the great defenders of slavery.

Douglas yielded to the slaveholders' infirmity and coarse-mouthed methods of accusation, of abusing every one who did not agree with them, calling them "names," as they had inveterately done with him very recently in Congress. His by-pleading and attempted distraction did not disconcert Mr. Lincoln, or prevent him from giving slavery a square front-blow at every opportunity.

Replying to these Negro-equality "fandangles," as he once called them, he said: "There is a physical difference between the two, which, in my judgment, will probably forever forbid their living together upon the footing of perfect equality; and inasmuch as there must be a difference, I, as well as Judge Douglas, am in favor of the race I belong to having the superior position. I have never said anything to the contrary; but I hold that, notwithstanding all this, there is no reason in the world why the Negro is not entitled to all the natural rights enumerated in the Declaration of Independence: the right to life, liberty, and the pursuit of happiness. I hold that he is as much entitled to these as the white man. I agree with Judge Douglas, he is not my equal in many respects—certainly not in color, perhaps not in morals or intellectual endowment—but in the right to eat the bread, without the leave of anybody else, which his own hand earns, he is my equal and the equal of Judge Douglas and the equal of every living man."

In support of the rights and privileges of anti-slavery people and parties of all shades and opinions, and the right of free speech, he said: "Now, at this day in the history of the world we can no more foretell where the end of this slavery agitation will be than we can see the end of the world. The Kansas-Nebraska Bill was introduced four years and a half ago; and if the agitation is ever to come to an end, we may say we are four years and a half nearer to the end. The Kansas settlement did not conclude it. If Kansas should sink to-day, and leave a great vacant space in the earth's surface, this vexed question would still be among us. I say there is no way of putting an end to the slavery agitation amongst us but to put it back upon the basis where our fathers placed it; no way but to keep it out of our new Territories—to restrict it forever to the old States where it now exists. Then the public mind will rest in the belief that it is in the course of ultimate extinction: This is one way of putting an end to the slavery agitation. The other way is for us to surrender, and let Judge Douglas and his friends have their way, and plant slavery all over the States. Cease speaking of it as in any way a wrong. Regard slavery as one of the common matters of property, and speak of Negroes as we do of horses and cattle.

"But while it drives on in the state of progress as it is now driving, and as it has driven for the last five years,

we will have no end to the slavery agitation until it takes
one turn or the other. I do not suppose that in the most
peaceful way ultimate extinction would occur in less than
a hundred years at least, but that it will occur in the best
way for both races, in God's own good time, I have no doubt."

One never-failing element of Mr. Lincoln's addresses,
speeches, letters, and public communications of every kind
was the robust and living patriotism, genuine love of country and our people, and his unfaltering respect and honor
for the fathers who laid the principles of free government
on such firm and lasting foundations. Instead of being
bothered or confused over the narrow constructions and
contracted definitions of the class-breeding judges of the
Supreme Court and like-minded aristocrats of smaller degree, he opened the great charters of liberty to the common
mind and understanding, as you would spread out a nour-
ishing, substantial feast to a hungry, famishing man.

He confounded the confounders, and broadened the work
of the patriotic heroes of the Revolution, in the light of
God's wisdom, raising him in the spirit that enabled them
to plant the abutments of the Declaration of Independence
and the American Constitution on the eternal rocks of justice, humanity, and the equal rights of men, beyond their
power to loose, shake, or unfasten them by the puny strength
of monarchs, slaveholders, wealth-grinders, usurpers, or the
smaller selfish and despotic men of every race and creed.
The great rights, these firmly established, might be wrested
from careless and cowardly, indolent men; but the truths
of these charters of liberty will remain the light and hope
of men.

Mr. Lincoln's finely-developed body, with mind symmetrical, desiring the best natural growth, gave him strength,
endurance, and the confidence in his own powers that fitted
him for any undertaking. This helped very much in making
up his fearless and independent character; but the striking

feature, and the one most respected in remembrance, after knowing that God had given him genius and capacity, was his rocklike integrity on the side of right, because it was right based on God's immutable laws. So he lived, and so he taught that, as far as he could determine for himself, or influence men by his knowledge, belief, or conduct, these should prevail. In his progress in meeting men, ideas, and events, he was kind, impartial, and fearless; hence in his contest with Judge Douglas and in his dispute with the Supreme Court, he was as plain and well understood in the discussion as if he had held it with a neighbor, or his determined disagreement had been with a justice of the peace.

Coming back, in his rounding-up argument, against all those who would limit the meaning and the all-embracing principles of the Declaration of Independence in the force and power of his way of settling things, one had to see and hear him before realizing his enormous strength and corresponding wisdom.

To these he replied: "At Galesburg I said the other day, in answer to Judge Douglas, that three years ago there had never been a man, so far as I knew or believed, in the whole world who had said that the Declaration of Independence did not include Negroes in the term, 'All men.' I assert it to-day. I assert that Judge Douglas and all his friends may search the whole records of the country, and it will be a matter of great astonishment to me if they shall find that one human being three years ago had ever uttered the astounding sentiment that the term 'all men' in the Declaration did not include the Negro.

"Do not let me be misunderstood. I know that more than three years ago there were men who, finding this assertion constantly in the way of their schemes to bring about the ascendency and perpetuation of slavery, denied the truth of it. I know that Mr. Calhoun and all the politicians of his school denied the truth of the declaration. I know that

it ran along in the mouth of some Southern men for a period of some years, ending at last in the shameful, though
rather forcible declaration of Pettit, of Indiana, upon the
floor of the United States Senate, that the Declaration of
Independence was, in that respect, 'a self-evident lie,' rather
than a self-evident truth. But I say, with a perfect knowledge of all this hawking at the Declaration, without directly
attacking it, that three years ago there never had lived a
man who had ventured to assail it in the sneaking way of
pretending to believe it, and then asserting that it did not
include the Negro.

"I believe the first man who ever said it was Chief-
Justice Taney, in the Dred Scott case, and next to him was
our friend, Judge Douglas. And now it has become the
catchword of the entire party. I would like to call upon
his friends everywhere to consider how they have come in
so short a time to view this matter in a way so entirely different from their former belief, to ask whether they are
not being borne along by an irresistible current, whither
they know not?"

Afterwards, when not limited to the one hour and a half
of the joint debates, he demonstrated beyond any kind of
doubt his knowledge and complete understanding of the
designs of the framers of the Declaration and the Constitution. When they made and founded the Nation, they made
the defiant, fearless declaration of principles, and built our
fundamental laws upon them, under which it was never intended that the rights or liberties of any person should be
abridged or wrested from them. He said: "The Declaration
of Independence was formed by the representatives of
American liberty from thirteen States and the Confederacy,
twelve of which were slaveholding communities. We need
not discuss the way or the reason of their becoming slaveholding communities. It is sufficient for our purpose that
all of them greatly deplored the evil, and that they placed

a provision in the Constitution, which they supposed would gradually remove the disease by cutting off its source. This was the abolition of the slave-trade. So general was the conviction, the public determination to abolish the African slave-trade, that the provision which I have referred to as being placed in the Constitution declared that it should not be abolished prior to 1808. A Constitutional provision was necessary to prevent the people, through Congress, from putting a stop to the traffic immediately at the close of the war.

"Now, if slavery had been a good thing, would the fathers of the Republic have taken a step calculated to diminish its beneficent influence among themselves, and snatch the boon wholly from posterity? These communities, by their representatives, in old Independence Hall, said to the whole race of men, 'We hold these truths to be self-evident: that all men are created equal; that they are endowed by their Creator with certain inalienable rights; that among these are life, liberty, and the pursuit of happiness.' This was their majestic interpretation of the economy of the universe. This was their lofty and wise and noble understanding of the justice of the Creator to his creatures—yes, gentlemen, to all his creatures, to the whole great family of man. In their enlightened belief, nothing stamped with the Divine image and likeness was sent into the world to be trodden on and degraded and imbruted by its fellows. They grasped not only the whole race of man then living, but they reached forward and seized upon the farthest posterity. They erected a beacon to guide their children and their children's children and the countless myriads who should inhabit the earth in other ages.

"Wise statesmen, as they were, they knew the tendencies of prosperity to breed tyrants; and so they established these great self-evident truths, that when, in the distant future, some man, some faction, some interest, should set up the doc-

trine that none but rich men, or none but white men, **or**
none but Anglo-Saxon white men, were entitled to life, liberty, and the pursuit of happiness, their posterity might look
up again to the Declaration of Independence, and take courage to renew the battle which their fathers began, so that
truth and justice and mercy and all the humane and Christian virtues might not be extinguished from the land, so
that no man would hereafter dare to limit and circumscribe
the great principle on which the temple of liberty was being
built.

"Now, my countrymen, if you have been taught doctrines
conflicting with the great landmarks of the Declaration of
Independence; if you have listened to suggestions that would
take away from its grandeur and mutilate the fair symmetry
of its proportions; if you have been inclined to believe that
all men are not created equal in those inalienable rights
enumerated by our chart of liberty, let me entreat you to
come back, return to the fountain whose waters spring close
by the blood of the Revolution.

"Think nothing of me; take no thought for the political
fate of any man whomsoever, but come back to the truths
that are in the Declaration of Independence. You may do
anything with me you choose, if you will but heed these
sacred principles. You may not only defeat me for the Senate, but you may take me and put me to death. While pretending no indifference to earthly honors, I do claim to be
actuated in this contest by something higher than an anxiety
for office. I charge you to drop every paltry and insignifi-
cant thought for any man's success. It is nothing; I am nothing; Judge Douglas is nothing. But do not destroy that immortal emblem of humanity—the Declaration of American
Independence!"

At the close of the Ottawa debate, in Northern Illinois,
Douglas read a series of anti-slavery resolutions which had
been adopted at some convention in the State, charging

Mr. Lincoln with having written them and being responsible for them. Mr. Lincoln replied that he had nothing whatever to do with the resolutions, and that in the current debates he represented the Republican party at the request and by direction of the State Committee; that he stood committed to the declaration and beliefs of the party, and no further, unless he saw fit to do so for himself; and that Judge Douglas, as he understood his relation, was alike responsible for his party beliefs and his own public record and declarations, and no more, unless he, too, assumed some extraneous belief or opinion.

Douglas felt that he had somewhat entangled Mr. Lincoln at this first meeting, and showed that by his persistence and in the line of his policy he had beaten and defeated the ultra pro-slavery party in Kansas. He said that the Abolitionist party was equally dangerous, and that "Mr. Lincoln belongs to it, and he would here state: My object in reading these resolutions is to put the question to Mr. Lincoln to-day, whether he now stands by each article in that creed, and will carry it out. I ask Mr. Lincoln these questions, in order that, when I trot him down to Lower Egypt, I may put the same questions to him."

If Douglas had well-grounded hopes of preserving the entirety and harmony of the Democratic party, North and South, and of reuniting the contending factions on slavery, he never made anything like so serious a blunder as to open the opportunity and set such a far-seeing and deeply-discerning man, as Mr. Lincoln was, to the business and work of asking questions. It was generally understood, and Mr. Douglas was supposed to know it as well as any one, that in his kind, all-embracing sort of ease and composure, Lincoln could draw out of any witness all the facts in his knowledge, whether willing or not. So it seemed that, if Douglas started the questioning, it would scarcely terminate without a complete disclosure of the differences and divisions between the Democratic factions in the slavery dispute and the extent and gravity there was in the division.

Thus, somewhat provoked into the plan of asking and replying to exact and direct questions by Mr. Douglas, Mr. Lincoln framed a series of questions to be propounded to Mr. Douglas, which, if he answered, as the facts established the alarming condition, it would accentuate the division, and open wider the breach between the Northern and Southern ern factions of the party in the next Presidential election, then only two years ahead. Instead of being the strong, consolidated, thoroughly-disciplined organization it had been for most men's lifetime, and particularly through the two previous elections of Pierce and Buchanan, it would be broken, dismembered, and unable to elect a President or either branch of Congress.

The most vital one in these questions and answers was contained in Mr. Lincoln's question number two, which asked, "Can the people of a Territory exclude slavery at any time before making a State Constitution?" This involved all the contention then pending between the Democratic factions. The Supreme Court decision held that neither Congress nor the people could exclude slavery from any Territory; that it was a property right of the slaveholder, protected under the Constitution.

Douglas's "Squatter-rights" doctrine, under which the slavery question was determined in Kansas, although through civil war and the serious difficulties we have related, held that squatters—the people of the Territory—had supreme power to exclude slavery under our law and procedure, the Kansas-Nebraska law and, in principle, under the old English law decisions; that slavery could only exist under positive local law.

If Douglas and his faction adhered to their avowed belief, it would raise the whole dispute between freedom and slavery, as it had done in Kansas. It was fairly understood that Douglas could take no other course than to sustain the people's right, as he had so faithfully done in the Senate. However, the Supreme Court had set aside the squatters' or the people's rights in doctrine; and, though, there never was an attempt to enforce it anywhere, it still was the declared law of the land.

One of the contrarieties of the situation was that Douglas assumed to accept this decision as law, but declared it an inoperative one against the power of "police regulations," which became the convenient resource of the people to set aside the repugnant decision or law. The truth was that his submission to the outrageous decision was an act of self-defense and necessity for the occasion. By it he postponed his revolt against the pro-slavery leaders, and put off the division of the party until he was at home among his people, where he knew no other Democrat could make headway against him. Mr. Lincoln understood every feature of the contest and the threatened party disruption, which was then —in 1858—only a question as to the time when the Democratic party would divide.

Mr. Lincoln's capacity, comprehensive grasp of public affairs and sagacity were never more positively shown and distinctly proven than in forcing the issue and precipitating the irreconcilable break in the Democratic party. It should have been Douglas's certain and settled policy to delay the division until after the senatorial contest; but he was incited to the slavery discussion by the intolerant interference of the Administration, and further stimulated in it by the active help of outside Republicans and Old-line Whigs. If it had been made a personal contest, with no outside interference, and without the conspicuous battle of Douglas, Mr. Lincoln would have had more than equal chances in a purely personal and ordinary party contest, so far as the senatorship was an issue; for he had remarkable power of persuasiveness, with aptitude to make friends everywhere.

But the campaign rose to National issues and proportions in the preparation and announcement for it, and to considerations of vastly greater moment as it progressed, to the spread or restriction of slavery, unsettled still in the Kansas dispute or border war. The Republican party, of which Mr. Lincoln was a conspicuous leader, was forming and contending for every foot of free territory possible or available. The Democratic party was inharmonious and dividing, with a Presidential election only two years off. If Douglas could have held the free State Democracy intact, and the Southern leaders had been quiet and submitted, the party would probably have elected another President in 1860. At least, as a National leader, it was his manifest duty to put forth his best and untiring efforts to that end.

However, the situation was, that if Mr. Lincoln, like a great soldier, in masterly maneuvering and movement, under his own plan and direction, could divide the strongly-organized party, or sensibly help, two years before the coming election, he would make his party's success a probability, and, better, make the success of the great cause he held above all other considerations a certainty; for the spread of slavery was an impossible achievement with a divided Democracy, as had been shown in the Kansas struggle.

Douglas submitted his questions to several friends and party leaders, all of whom advised him against making them. He was a resolute, determined leader, if anything, who had never divided authority or responsibility with any one in the State; so he held firmly to his plan to force Mr. Lincoln to an acknowledgment that he and his party, one or both, were "Abolitionists," and would, if possible, interfere with slavery in the slave States.   ·

It became known also among the leading Republicans of the State that Mr. Lincoln's principal question would involve Mr. Douglas and his party's position on the right of the people of a Territory to exclude slavery before forming a

State Constitution. A number of the weak and faint-hearted among them caught up with him in a sort of chase to be wise, at Mendota, the night before the debate at Free-port, and wrestled the most of the night with him. They endeavored, in their strongest arguments, to dissuade him from asking his main question, which would renew, as they greatly feared, the slavery agitation that had raged so furiously over the Kansas struggle.

He knew very well how to deal with these, and could have settled the difference at once; but in his good-natured way he listened patiently, and spent most of the night going over the details, when he very much needed rest. He finally answered them that, agitation or no agitation, the spread of slavery was the main question of public interest and discussion, and that, if they and all the people in the State refrained, it would still be the same; that the best way to tackle the subject was to do it in an open, positive manner, without doubt or hesitation, tell the truth about it, and lay the whole of it before the people, and trust their judgment, as he had always done, and firmly intended to do.

Mr. Judd, of Chicago, and Judge Cook, who were nearer the town, were the first to arrive. They were two of the three who defeated him for senator in 1854. Judge Davis was there, who said in substance: "If you ask Douglas this question, it will arouse an entirely unnecessary slavery discussion and agitation, and will lose us a great many conservative votes. We ought to have relief from this pro-slavery discussion on one side and the demands and exciting work of the Abolitionists on the other, and save the Republican party from being known as the ally of the Abolitionists at least, by which it is sure to be broken up, as all of them, the Liberty, Free Soil, and Abolition parties, have been."

Others, to the number of a full dozen, were there, and had their say without in any apparent way affecting Mr. Lin-

coln. In the early morning, several of them, as if by one
accord, met him, and when they felt that all that could be
had been said, one of them closed, saying, "Well, Mr. Lincoln,
if you do ask the question, and bring on the angry discussion,
you can not be elected senator."

Mr. Lincoln replied to this, in substance, that "the real
question involved in this contest so deeply is the spread and
nationalization of slavery. The restriction of it is of so much
greater importance than personal success, senatorships, or
other positions, as to be far beyond any sort of comparison.
If I am defeated for senator, the Democratic party will be
hopelessly divided. It will be impossible for Mr. Douglas
or any other Democrat to be elected President, and, much
better for the free people of America, the extension of slavery will be a greater impossibility. So it might be truthfully said of us that we have bigger game on hand than a
senatorship."

Of the number then present, most of them were so
much disconcerted by the result, after a long night of unheeded appeals, that their accounts of it were given in a
reckless or careless vein, very much below the sober earnestness and comprehending thoughtfulness of Mr. Lincoln, who,
in his wise and broader statesmanship, planned a victory for
principles as well as present success, which he as conspicuously and wisely helped to win and make possible in 1860.

At the Mendota meeting, none of our Abolition section
were expected, and seats were not provided; however, Lovejoy sent Lincoln a message the same day: "The cause is
prospering. I believe a Lincoln man will be elected from
every legislative district in my Congressional district. Stand
firm on the Springfield speech." But Lincoln's auditors and
comforters did not want to hear anything from Lovejoy,
and made grimaces at the mention of his name.

The remarks they made on and about Mr. Lincoln's statements in the meeting are scarcely worth mentioning; but

some of them left the meeting, making one misleading statement that has long obtained credence, and needs correction; namely, "that Douglas's answer to the second question was the determining result that made his nomination or election as President impossible by a united Democracy."

The truth is, that Douglas had no hope of nomination by a united party, nor support of the pro-slavery faction, certainly never after their terrible defeat and discomfiture at his hands; nor did any man understand all this better than Mr. Lincoln. Hence his remark above was "that neither Douglas nor any other Democrat could be elected President if this movement widened, and permanently divided the Democratic party on the subject of slavery. If Douglas answered the question as he would have to do to be in accord with the Democracy of Illinois and be elected senator, this would be the result."

The division came, as Mr. Lincoln expected and planned. The free State faction followed and sustained Douglas, but so divided with all the outside helps, that he was barely elected senator; and the party was more hopelessly divided because of his success. The pro-slavery faction in the slave States opened wider the breach, denounced Douglas and his followers as distinctly and positively as Mr. Lincoln, and made this division in the party that was never closed, and sent the powerful organization into retirement for more than thirty years.

Mr. Leonard Swett, of Bloomington, who was there, gave the following account of it, and Mr. Lincoln corroborated it when I saw him later, shortly before the Charleston debate, when he went over the question in particular, and described the kind of meeting and the men in it at Mendota. There was an amusing incident concerning Mr. Swett's presence at the meeting and Lincoln's inquiry concerning his opinion. Swett was a quiet sort of man, and Judge Davis fully believed him to be a very submissive conservative, so obedient that he offered him the conservative nomination for Congress against Lovejoy. On the evening of the meeting, Davis invited Swett, and insisted so much that he went with them.

Swett was silent, but sat with them until midnight, then went to bed, and very sensibly rested until morning. Lincoln met him early next morning, and, not remembering to have heard him say anything, but believing him to be in sympathy with Davis, asked him: "Mr. Swett, I do n't remember hearing you express yourself. It would please me to know what as still a man as you were in such a talking crowd thought of the council." Mr. Swett replied: "I did not participate in the talk, and came without knowing much about what it would be, at the request of Judge Davis. We have had a pleasant evening together. I went to bed at midnight. I do n't know as much of it as the others do, who were so earnestly engaged, but I believe, considering it as it ran, you have settled the matter as well as I could have done it myself; but I think it complicates the situation, and will not add to your strength for the senatorship."

The debate filled the minds of the people for months. What was preserved makes a volume that was a political "Vade Mecum," and remains an abundant reservoir of forensic, polemical, and political facts and arguments for students. It will remain an indispensable source of information to every American who desires to get full and comprehensive knowledge as to the rise, progress, and spread of slavery up to the period of its arrest and downfall. Mr. Lincoln maintained his power and strength to the end, seriously engaging the people, who admired his candor and truthfulness the more they heard and saw him.

Mr. Douglas's strength and voice almost gave way under the severe labor, outdoor exposure, and the mental strain that his sanguine, more excitable make-up could in no wise endure like the unflagging energy and fiber of Lincoln. Both of them came out of the contest with honorable distinction as the great leaders of their parties. Lincoln had risen to National distinction before this; but he came out of the discussion without a rival on the anti-slavery side, except Mr. Seward, whose political strength was more that of his unrivaled State, sustained by the anti-slavery people of New England, than his own.

Douglas came out of the debate unimpaired and unsmirched and free from the dragnet of the slave-leaders. He had contended and maintained his high capacity as leader of the free Democracy of the Nation. He could not lead the pro-slavery faction, nor overthrow the usurping leaders, who had emasculated the principles of Jefferson, Jackson, Benton, and the founders and great leaders of the party. He had fought a great battle, not only with an antagonist like Lincoln, but also against the full power of the Southern leaders. He had won the senatorship, but more the right to remain the faithful leader of free Democracy in a contest that raised him to uncontested leadership.

At the Ottawa meeting, Mr. Lincoln said: "I now propose to answer any of the interrogatories, upon condition that Judge Douglas will answer questions from me not exceeding the same number. I give him opportunity to respond. The Judge remains silent. I now say that I will answer his interrogatories, whether he does mine or not, and that after I have done so, I shall propound mine to him."

At the Freeport meeting, Mr. Lincoln having had the written questions a sufficient time, they were propounded by Mr. Douglas and answered by Mr. Lincoln, as follows:

Question 1. "I desire to know whether Lincoln stands, as he did in 1854, in favor of the unconditional repeal of the Fugitive-slave Law?"

Answer. "I do not now, nor ever did, stand in favor of the unconditional repeal of the Slave Law."

Q. 2. "I desire him to answer whether he stands pledged

to-day, as in 1854, against the admission of any more slave States into the Union, even if the people want them?"

A. "I do not now, nor ever did, stand pledged against the admission of any more slave States into the Union."

Q. 3. "I want to know whether he stands pledged against the admission of a new State into the Union with such a Constitution as the people of that State may see fit to make?"

A. "I do not stand pledged against the admission of a new State into the Union with such a Constitution as the people of that State may see fit to make."

Q. 4. "I want to know whether he stands to-day pledged to the abolition of slavery in the District of Columbia?"

A. "I don't stand to-day pledged to the abolition of slavery in the District of Columbia."

Q. 5. "I desire him to answer whether he stands pledged to the prohibition of the slave-trade between the different States?"

A. "I do not stand pledged to the prohibition of the slave-trade between the different States."

Q. 6. "I desire to know whether he stands pledged to prohibit slavery in all the Territories of the United States, north as well as south of the Missouri Compromise line?"

A. "I am impliedly pledged, if not expressly pledged, to a belief in the right and duty of Congress to prohibit slavery in all the Territories."

Q. 7. "I desire him to answer whether he is opposed to the acquisition of any new territory unless slavery is first prohibited therein?"

A. "I am not generally opposed to honest acquisition of territory; and in a given case I would or would not oppose such acquisition accordingly as I might think such acquisition would or would not aggravate the slavery question among ourselves."

These answers disclosed Mr. Lincoln's evasion and his determination not to discuss his personal beliefs or sympathies, but to represent his party, and maintain his leadership in it, while contending with Judge Douglas as a similarly-situated party leader; that he would take the common ground of belief in his party, confine himself to it, and, through it, hope for getter government than was attainable through any defense of his individual beliefs or opinions.

Douglas very shrewdly contrived to connect Mr. Lincoln with some of the aggressive movements against slavery which were growing fast in the face of slavery's violent propagandism; but Lincoln was then a leader of the Republican party and various anti-slavery factions. In his contention he was partaking something of these various elements and their different shades of belief, but carrying along the combined parties of the people prudently, as far as such movements could be made in such a delicate situation.

After replying to these, he asked Judge Douglas, who had previously been furnished a copy, the following:

Question 1. "If the people of Kansas shall, by means entirely unobjectionable in all other respects, adopt a State Constitution, and ask admission into the Union under it, before they have the requisite number of inhabitants, according to the English bill—some ninety-three thousand—will you vote to admit them?"

Q. 2. "Can the people of a United States Territory, in any lawful way, against the wish of any citizen of the United States, exclude slavery from its limits prior to the formation of a State Constitution?"

Q. 3. "If the Supreme Court of the United States shall decide that States can not exclude slavery from their limits, are you in favor of acquiescing in, adopting, and following such decision as a rule of political action?"

Q. 4. "Are you in favor of acquiring additional territory in disregard of how such acquisition may affect the Nation on the slave question?"

When Mr. Douglas had taken up and considered Mr. Lincoln's second question, he replied: "I answer emphatically, as Mr. Lincoln has heard me answer a hundred times from every stump in Illinois, that in my opinion the people of a Territory can, by lawful means, exclude slavery from their limits prior to the formation of a State Constitution. Mr. Lincoln knew that I had answered that question over and over again. He heard me argue the Nebraska Bill on that principle all over the State in 1854-5-6; and he has no excuse for pretending to be in doubt as to my position on that question. It matters not what way the Supreme Court may hereafter decide as to the abstract question, whether slavery may or may not go into a Territory under the Constitution, the people have the lawful means to introduce or exclude it, as they please, for the reason that slavery can not exist for a day or an hour anywhere unless it is supported by local police regulations.

"Those local police regulations can only be established by the local Legislature; and if the people are opposed to slavery, they will elect representatives to that body who will, by unfriendly legislation, effectually prevent the introduction of it into their midst. If, on the contrary, they are for it, their legislation will favor its extension. Hence, no matter what the decision of the Supreme Court may be on that abstract question, still the right of the people to make a slave Territory or a free Territory is perfect and complete under the Nebraska Bill. I hope Mr. Lincoln deems my answer satisfactory on that point."

The vigor, strength, and clearness in which he made his declaration was a surprise to all, none more than Mr. Lincoln. It was a flat, open denial and defiance of the doctrine of the Dred Scott decision, and left no common ground for amelioration, compromise, or settlement of the slavery division between the Northern and Southern factions of the Democratic party. The division on this deplorable question that had separated individuals, societies, Churches, and parties throughout the land, had reached the alarming place in public affairs that divided the strongly-organized and best-disciplined party, the only organization, if the slaveholders had correctly interpreted the signs of the times, that could have saved their system from restriction and eventual over-throw.

Douglas had done what other leaders, thousands of them, had done before—he had served faithfully, patiently, and well; but now, in the midst of the people who had so long trusted and honored him, he, in effect, deliberately declared that the encroachment of the slave power could be tolerated no further, and led his party—the free Democracy—against the slavery-extending *régime* and governing faction of the party. It was true that, in his dilemma, before he could get among his own people into his campaign for re-election, he had submitted to what was a repugnant, unnatural, and illogical decision.

The Southern leaders knew him well. Jefferson Davis and Benjamin, a more cunning and crafty man, had him under watch from the days of his defense of Jackson, and under their ban and condemnation from their defeat over Lecompton, from which time they would have submitted to the leadership of Mr. Lincoln as readily as to Douglas. In this long contest with them he had erred, as many believed, but whether certainly and seriously we know not. If so, he surely made amends when he defied them, and led one and a half million voters—about eight millions of people—from under the control and domination of the slave-extending conspiracy, when a word of concession would have made him President.

Under merciless review and castigation from so many quarters he stood firm as a rock on his original proposition or doctrine of Squatter Sovereignty, or the right of the people of the Territories to settle slavery as they did other matters.

It may have been wrong in principle, as we verily believed at the time; but we had proof beyond doubt from time to time that it was a successful anti-slavery measure in its practical operation. Under it the people of California had made a free State; and, hampered, hindered, and killed, as hundreds were in Kansas, the settlers there prevailed. Against pro-slavery Legislatures, Territorial Conventions, the United States Senate and House of Representatives, one or both part of the time, and a servile Supreme Court, and two pro-slavery Administrations all the time, the free State people again prevailed with the grit and determination of Americans, in spite of forces that would have won a kingdom. This settlers' right saved Kansas to freedom, and, in God's own way, slavery halted forever.

Whether right or wrong in policy, in principle Mr. Lincoln held undisputed advantage when, by Judge Douglas's very defective reasoning, he set aside and repudiated the Supreme Court decision, wherein it conflicted with the rights guaranteed in the Kansas act. To emphasize this meant the disruption and tearing asunder the already separating factions of the Democratic party, and victory, in consequence, for the cause of human liberty and the principles for which Mr. Lincoln so manfully contended. To emphasize the widening division, and hold Judge Douglas to his virtual repudiation of the decision, he held up Douglas's position in clearness, argument, and reasoning that could not be misunderstood.

When done, if it was well done, it would be a splitting open and irreparable separation of the Democratic party and fulfillment of the hope that liberty would not perish. Realizing all this, without personal animosity for Judge Douglas, and anxious for such an opportunity, Mr. Lincoln, in clear, earnest words, said: "As I have a few minutes left, I will employ them in saying something about this argument Judge Douglas uses, while he sustains the Dred Scott decision, that the people of the Territories can somehow exclude slavery.

"The first thing I ask attention to is the fact that Judge Douglas constantly said, before the decision, that whether they could or could not was a question for the Supreme Court; but after the court has made the decision, he virtually says it is not a question for the Supreme Court, but for the people. And how is it he tells us they can exclude it? He says it means 'police regulations,' and that it admits of 'unfriendly legislation.'

"Although it is a right, established by the Constitution of the United States, to take slaves into a Territory, and hold them as property, yet, unless the Territorial Legislature will give friendly legislation, and, more especially, if they adopt unfriendly legislation, they can exclude them.

"Now, without meeting this proposition as a matter of fact, I pass to consider the real Constitutional obligation. Let me take the gentleman who looks me in the face before me, and let us suppose that he is a member of the Territorial Legislature. The first thing he will do will be to swear that he will support the Constitution of the United States. His neighbor by his side in the Territory has slaves, and needs Territorial legislation to enable him to enjoy that Constitutional right.

"Can he withhold the legislation which his neighbor needs for the enjoyment of a right which is fixed in his favor in the Constitution of the United States, which he has sworn to support? Can he withhold it without violating his oath? And, more especially, can he pass unfriendly legislation to violate his oath? Why, this is a monstrous sort of talk about the Constitution of the United States! There has never been so outlandish or lawless a doctrine from the mouth of any respectable man on earth. I do not believe it is a Constitutional right to hold slaves in a Territory of the United States. I believe the decision was improperly made, and I go for reversing it. Judge Douglas is furious against those who go for reversing a decision; but he is for legislating it out of all force while the law itself stands. I repeat, there has never been so monstrous a doctrine uttered from the mouth of a respectable man."

After a vigorously-contested campaign of some three months, the result was close. Enough members of the Legislature were elected to return Mr. Douglas to the Senate. The numerical strength of parties on the State tickets were: Republican, 125,430; Douglas Democrats, 121,609; Buchanan Democrats, 5,071. In the Legislature 54 voted for Douglas, 46 for Lincoln. The population of the northern and central portions of the State had increased so rapidly that the legislative apportionment was four or five votes in Douglas's favor. This was, however, no more than ordinary political advantage, held then and to this day by all parties. These should be avoided, not only by the election of senators, but in the election of all public servants, the judges of the United States Supreme Court included, by the direct vote of the people.

CHAPTER XXXVI.

MR. LINCOLN acquiesced in the result of the senatorial campaign as cheerfully as any one. Though coming out of his splendid canvass with all the vigor and as much as he expected in the beginning, as fully aware of the political benefits to the party and the success of many friends and supporters, his mind took one of its melancholy, thoughtful turns, so that, in all personal references to the result, he held that he was permanently retired from public life, and seemed entirely satisfied that it should be so.

Among others, he expressed himself to me in that way a short time after the election. I said to him: "The Republican party was never so strong nor confident. Your splendid campaign and movement and the splitting wider open process you inaugurated, makes you our most conspicuous leader. Seward is no more than your equal, if as much. You will soon have all the West and Northwest in your following. The people have taken to you as to no other man; and to thousands of them you are not only a political leader, but a recognized prophet. Not claiming unusual or wide information for myself, but accurate and correct as far as it goes, I know that you never had so strong a hold as you have on party and people to-day.

"In my estimation, your future is to be the best that the party and your unfaltering friends can make it. Although defeated for the senatorship by a scratch, you have won a conspicuous personal triumph. To show you something of public feeling, I asked our friend C——, who is a zealous

Democrat, yesterday, how he was pleased at the success of Douglas. He replied: 'Yes, I am pleased; but it would please me now almost as much to have Abe Lincoln a United States senator too. Both of them deserve to be; and if you folks can put Abe in the next time in place of Trumbull, there are a whole lot of us Democrats all over the State who won't fight it very hard. We could n't desert Douglas this time, after his manly fight with those Southern fire-eaters.'

"This, I am certain, is the feeling of thousands of the strongest and most sensible men in both parties. As I understand affairs to-day, you can no more relinquish your leadership and retire than it would be right and sensible for us to give up our cause. No one can forecast results in such rapidly-moving events; but, with so many believing it, we can surely elect you senator on the expiration of Trumbull's term. The majority of the people are with you, and a plurality voted for you as it is. We know that you are not desirous of opposing Trumbull; but the senatorship was yours by right when he was elected. And whether you feel so inclined, you will have to oppose him in the canvass for his re-election."

My remarks seemed to cheer him somewhat; but I soon realized, as I had seen him do before, that such talk would do a great deal more good when his reflective period of a few weeks was over. We always knew that these would come to him after any such exhilarating event as that canvass had been, whether successful or not.

He replied: "Robert, you surprise me, indeed, in this personal talk; and to show you how my mind has been running, I have written two or three letters to friends, saying that I have retired from politics, as though people would n't know it as well as I do. Your assurances are encouraging, and you are always enthusiastic. It is true that our party is gaining, and never had so much cause to be hopeful, but to me, I feel that, by some kind of happening, inscrutable to me, they are always putting me in the place where somebody has to be beaten and sacrificed for the welfare of the party or the common good; and you know there are few men who can be beaten very often whose party success is a possibility. So I have been thinking, and no one knows better than you do that I have never desired office for the sake of holding it, because it has always been unprofitable to me, if for no better reason. As an example, I have paid and am to pay over five hundred dollars of personal and campaign expenses, besides giving three months' time, in which I have done little besides. You are young and ambitious and quite partial to me. I appreciate the good wishes of young men, independent enough to have stood the slang against Abolitionists, as you have for years, and I admire your courageous work for Mr. Lovejoy. I am glad that your judgment has been sustained.

"The name of Abolitionist will not bother us much in the future. They are the men who have been thinking the most seriously for years on slavery, that, in one way or the other, engages the attention of all intelligent people. I am going to think it over further, and I will make a little address, as you suggest, in Bloomington and, perhaps, Urbana; and we will have an 'experience-meeting' the first time I can make it convenient all around, which will be very soon."

About this time, in a letter to a friend, he said: "For the future, my view is, that the fight must go on. . . . We have some one hundred and twenty thousand Republican votes. That pile is worth keeping together. It will elect our State ticket two years hence. In that day I shall fight in the ranks, but I shall be in no one's way for the places. I am especially for Trumbull's re-election; and, by the way, this brings me to the principal object of this letter. Can you not make your draft of an Apportionment Law, and revise it till it shall be strictly and obviously just in all

particulars, and then, by an early and persistent effort, get
enough of the enemy's men to enable you to pass it?
. . . Unless something be done, Trumbull is inevitably
beaten two years hence. Take this into serious consideration."

In a candid letter to Mr. Judd, of Chicago, chairman of
the State Committee, he wrote one of his characteristic letters on his personal finances as follows: "Yours of the 15th
is just received. I wrote you the same day. As to pecuniary
matters, I am willing to pay according to my ability, but I
am the poorest hand living to get others to pay. I have
been on expenses so long, without earning anything, that I
am absolutely without money now, even for household expenses. Still, if you can put in two hundred and fifty dollars for me towards discharging the debt of the committee,
I will settle it when you and I settle the private matter between us. This, with what I have already paid, with an
outstanding note of mine, will exceed my subscription of
five hundred dollars. This, too, is exclusive of my ordinary expenses during the campaign, all of which, being
added to my loss of time and business, bears pretty heavily
upon one no better off in world's goods than I; but as I
had the post of honor, it is not for me to be over-nice. You
are feeling badly, and this, too, shall pass away. Never fear."

Extracts from two private letters emphasize what was
apparent in his look and manner when I met him a short
time after the election—that he was in one of his deep,
thoughtful, or melancholy moods. That he felt deep disappointment when it was all over, there is no shadow of
doubt. It had long been his cherished ambition to be a
United States senator, if he ever held office again. In any
important matter, public or private, especially in important law cases, he invariably passed through these reflective,
sometimes gloomy, "spells." It was just as the old colored
woman said of him when a seven-year-old boy in Kentucky,

"Abe allus had them mopin' spells, but they never 'peared to 'fect his mind."

To one he wrote: "You doubtless have seen. ere this the result of the election here. Of course I wished, but did not much expect, a better result. I am glad, however, that I made the late race. It gave me a hearing on the great and durable question of the age, which I could have had in no other way; and though now I sink out of view, and shall be forgotten, I believe I have made some marks which will tell for the cause of liberty long after I am gone."

And to another he wrote: "Yours of the 13th was received some days ago. The fight must go on. The cause of civil liberty must not be surrendered at the end of one or even one hundred defeats. Douglas had the ingenuity to be supported in the late contest, both as the best means to break down and to uphold the slave interests. No ingenuity can keep these antagonistic elements in harmony long. Another explosion will soon come."

After the election the breach that had been widening between the pro-slavery and free State factions of the Democratic party was more emphasized and deeply cut between them as the matter and form of the Lincoln-Douglas debates were known and published throughout the Southern States. The slave-leaders held absolute control of the Southern press, every member of which, without reference to former party belongings, came out in unmeasured condemnation of Douglas.

Lincoln's statesmanship, operating on Douglas, the leader of the free State Democracy, had torn the factions wider apart, and placed them on irreconcilable ground. He had, unconsciously to thousands, even in his own party, delivered a tremendous blow against the institution of slavery, his first noted one as a national leader. More than this, in wisdom that surpassed friendly expectation, and in prudence, and with the master hand of a great strategist, he sustained himself in every future emergency all over the free States. He persevered delivering blow on blow in increasing power as easily and obtrusively as his sphere of action increased, becoming the Nation's leader by reason of his high capacity and unequaled fitness. He had the full confidence of the masses because he lived in their hearts, held their full, unbroken trust, never for a moment forgetting or forsaking them, remaining just the same after he had risen to the most exalted station, as he was in his beginning, when he became the plain leader of the people of our great State.

I met Judge Douglas, and had a pleasant evening with him shortly after the election. Although he was much pleased by his re-election, which he believed he had earned at the hands of his followers, he was none the less silent, but perplexed and seriously broken in health, vigor, and strength, as I distinctly learned for the first time. He said, recalling Nimmo Browne: "What would I, or rather, what would n't I give for an hour with your Abolitionist father! I know I could not agree with him living, as I could not now, if he were here; but his knowledge and penetration of hidden purposes and his being so fearless a man made his friendship a comfort to a degree that has never been filled.

"I see very well that the designs of the pro-slavery leaders are culminating more rapidly than Browne thought possible, although he held that their only limit or delay was for preparation and from expediency. I have been lately informed from trustworthy sources that they are planning for reopening the African slave-trade. I fully believe that they are conspirators, and that they are getting ready for a conflict at arms. Jefferson Davis is as much a despot as Nicholas of Russia, and of narrower mold. He is leading to civil war; while Benjamin, Mason, Toombs, and Slidell are denouncing all the world that is not rank pro-slavery, and myself, with the fiendish malice that is born of desperate defeat. Some zealous friends, untrusted by the slave-power, in several Southern cities, have invited me to visit them and make a series of political addresses in the direction of harmony before the assembling of Congress.

"I have accepted the invitation, not with assurance that it° will bring personal benefit or vindication, but to see and make up my mind as to the real state of feeling in the South. I have conceded much, and would concede more to save the Union. I think the situation is threatening and ominous. If they consummate their plot, it will take the strength of every Union man to save our country. Both sections are now underestimating the strength of the other. If the struggle comes to war, it will be desperate; for no men in the world will fight with more daring and reckless courage than Americans, and in this there is no difference in the sections, North or South.

"I have been accused only recently of yielding submission to the pro-slavery ideas and leadings of these Southern hotspurs to gain a Presidential nomination; but every well-informed man knows they would not support me since their Lecompton defeat, nor since before the Cincinnati Convention in 1856. These same Southern leaders know as well as I do that on their terms I would have declined. My friends did the same for me in 1852, when Mr. Pierce was nominated. When so many men in all parties know these facts, it seems cruel, and, in many newspapers, a determined, malicious purpose, to continue accusing me of the unbridled ambition to be President.

"I am growing more and more of opinion that the charge is stimulated by Davis and his conspirators, in order to provoke me to a disclosure of my plans while he is conspiring. I am now to be more wickedly denounced for a few months than ever, to give some pretense whereby I may be removed from the chairmanship of the Committee on Territories, the place I have held for years, and which, by reason of my re-election, I should retain with better right. But I am to be punished; and the conspiracy to force slavery somewhere, regardless of right or the will of the people, is to be pursued. When the division comes that seems almost inevitable, it will be your duty and mine, and every patriot's, North or South, to stand by the Union and the Constitution."

He said during the pleasant evening's talk that the debates had in no way estranged him from Mr. Lincoln, and that he respected and esteemed his friendship, and that he had capacity for anything that came his way. We talked freely on every phase of the exciting situation, except the Dred Scott decision, which he seemed purposely to avoid when I referred to it. I asserted my strong anti-slavery opinions, and called them Abolitionist ideas without any qualification. In parting I said that, in the ordinary progress of events, Abolitionists will soon be taken back into the house of the faithful, and be as good Democrats as ever.

He said, very good-naturedly: "Your father's anti-slavery ideas were strong enough to last two generations, as I see. I wonder every day at the clearness of his foreseeing and penetrating mind, telling us years ago what we have lived to prove, and erring only in giving thirty years for what has happened in fifteen. He once said to me that if I lived out my days I would be an Abolitionist. I am nearer one now than I ever thought possible until recently; and if those conspirators do not quiet down some way, I have not reached my limit in dealing with them and their plans, which they are forcing upon us."

I was pleased and saddened by the pleasant meeting. He had shown a warm appreciation of my father, which was manly and kind to me, who had so earnestly opposed him. He said I had done right with the beliefs I held. His appreciation of my father seemed a satisfaction to him; and I then felt that my father's courageous Abolitionism had not been in vain, and was ever present in the minds of his friends. I parted with him, full of sorrow that the two hours' pleasant talk—some of it quite earnest—tired him out so much that he had to lie down. He was then not much over forty-five years old. His work was almost done, and the Master was winnowing his sheaves, when the dauntless leader was nearer the harvest than we knew.

In a short time he made his visit to several Southern cities, and made addresses in Memphis, New Orleans, Charleston, Savannah, and Richmond. He conceded all he could, hopeful for what seemed to be impossible; but he found no reason, and was barely tolerated enough to be permitted to speak and maintain his position and political integrity. He endeavored to satisfy those who did not desire nor deserve the effort he made; but he got no thanks for the service in which he strove to reason with and reconcile them. They neither respected him nor his desire for a peaceful solution, but mocked him in their newspapers, and were barely civil where hospitality was held in high pretension.

When he reached Washington, he was informed that he had been removed from the position as chairman of his committee, and that Senator Benjamin, of Louisiana, had denounced him personally on the floor of the Senate. A copy of the uncivil speech of this servile conspirator was handed Douglas, with the statement that it was the author's own corrected copy, kept so that Judge Douglas could use it in his reply.

To this Douglas, stung deeper by the ungracious removal in his absence, more than by anything a subordinate Southern leader could say, said, laying the copy down: "No, it is not serious enough for that. I will wait, and, as Benton once said, 'I will take him and all the underbrush up, and dispose of them all at once.' Then I will take up the real leader and head conspirator, Calhoun's successor, Jefferson Davis." In this malicious piece of work Benjamin became highly incensed, and several times afterward endeavored to provoke a personal dispute; but Douglas did not notice him, nor make reply, and the wrath of the apostate Hebrew waxed warmer, but hurt no one so much as himself.

In the winter of 1858-9 the debates in the Senate were stronger, more acrimonious, and tending more to open conflict and division of the Democratic party, but reduced in length of statements, arguments, and conclusions. They became more positive and to the point as the issue narrowed down. Senator Brown, of Mississippi, for the slave-leaders, put the whole relation of their contention in plain statements and questions, asserting "that he neither desired to cheat nor be cheated, but that the South would positively demand protection for their slaves under the Constitution, as declared by the Supreme Court."

As Douglas was understood to deny this right, they desired to know the position of other Northern Democratic senators and representatives on the subject, asking: "'If a Territorial Legislature refuses to act, will you act? If it passes unfriendly acts, will you pass friendly ones? If it passes laws hostile to slavery, you will annul them, and substitute laws favoring slavery in their stead? I would rather see the Democratic party sunk, never to be resurrected, than to see it successful only that one portion of it might practice a fraud upon the other." To his mind and purpose the party would be acceptable only as long as it protected and extended slavery.

Douglas met the issue squarely and positively, as he had done in his debates with Lincoln. Most alarming, too, to the Southern leaders then deep in the conspiracy was the accumulating proof that the free State Democracy, regardless of the faithless Buchanan Administration and some recreant free State senators and representatives, sustained and stood by Douglas, and were ready to stand with him in whatever conflict they made against him. . Pennsylvania had repudiated Buchanan, and the slavery-ridden party was narrowing down to the section of the slave States and not more than half of the people in the border slave States. Douglas's position, that he would not abandon the principle or doctrine laid down in the Kansas-Nebraska Act, under any circumstances, not even by the indirect method of the Supreme Court decision, seemed clear enough. He adhered to it through every debate and in every political campaign from the time of its passage. It was no new thing to these Southern Democrats; but, as we have before remarked, no matter what its merits or its defects were, it proved to be the plan of action under which none but free States could be admitted, and they determined to annul it in some way or other.

So great was the slaveholders' dread of it that, if they had carried out their first intention of making four new States out of Texas, they would not have submitted to their being admitted, since the actual residents would have a vote for and against slavery. They were asked to do so, but ascertained that in all probability two or more of them would vote against slavery, and make two more free States.

This the slave-leaders knew, and, knowing the fate of their institution, if left to a fair vote, there is little wonder about their opposition, hatred, and malice toward Judge Douglas, the fearless leader of the free State Democracy. They realized, too, that, if they could not outwit, remove from power, and crush him altogether, their days of power were limited to those of the Buchanan Administration; hence they kept up their assaults upon him.

His reply to the renewed attack led by Senator Brown, of Mississippi, was clear, concise, and not subject to misconstruction or double-dealing, of which they made common practice of accusing him. Douglas said—about February, 1859—in the Senate: "I tell you, gentlemen of the South, in all candor, I do n't believe a Democratic candidate can ever carry any one Democratic State of the North on the platform that it is the duty of the Federal Government to force the people of a Territory to have slavery when they do not want it. If you repudiate the doctrine of non-intervention and the rights of the people, residents or squatters, and force a slave-code by act of Congress on an unwilling people, the days of your power are numbered, and more, you are not Democrats, and must step off the Democratic platform."

This declaration was clear and distinct. Still there were men and newspapers all over the South, including those of the border and a few malicious ones in the free States, that constantly maligned Douglas with the charge that he was yielding and pandering to the pro-slavery leaders for the Presidential nomination.

Not long afterward he wrote a friend, authorizing the statement, or, rather, a re-statement of his position, for publication, if it was desired, writing, at length, that, if the Democracy adhered to its former principles, his friends might support him for the nomination; on the contrary, "If it shall become the policy of the Democratic party to abandon or repudiate their time-honored principles, on which we had received so many patriotic triumphs, and, in lieu of these, the Convention shall interpolate into the creed of the party such new issues as the revival of the African slave-trade, or a Congressional slave-code for the Territories, or the doctrine that the Constitution of the United States either establishes or prohibits slavery in the Territories, beyond the power of the people legally to control it as other property, it is due to candor to say that, in such an event, I could not accept the nomination if it were tendered to me."

In this memorable contest with the Southern leaders, who had then become actual conspirators against their country, there is no doubt that the scheme and plan of secession and the creation of a slave empire had long been in the minds of Davis and Calhoun and his followers, and many others.

It would be difficult to fix the time when the idea took definite form in their minds for this reason, if no other, that its progress was always delayed and held in abeyance so long as the propaganda were in control of the Government, as they had been in the later Democratic Administrations.

However this may have been held on contingencies, there is no doubt, in the winter of 1858-9, when they saw the power slipping out of their hands, and felt the effect of the free State uprising, that Davis and his cabal of conspirators who followed him hastened every preparation for separation and war to sustain the secession of every slave State, if they were resisted.

During this intensely exciting prelude to the conspirators' tragedy, while Douglas was firm and strong as any patriotic leader ever was, he was as resolutely sustained in the Senate by Broderick, of California; Pugh, of Ohio, and Stuart, of Michigan, of the free States, and twenty-five as brave members of the House of Representatives. And above, and greater than all, the uncorrupted free State Democracy had so firmly planted themselves in his support that not all the domineering, swaggering arrogance nor faithless and cowardly Administration, nor treasonable senators and representatives, could turn them from Douglas.

The hearts of the people in the free States and also in the border and other slave States, wherever they could be heard, were right. They had caught the sound and divined the purpose of the conspirators' destroying scheme, and, whether Democrat, Republican, or Independent, they flocked to the support of Douglas in unbroken faith, and did their best to save the dissolving Union.

In a few short weeks, Mr. Lincoln passed out of his reverie, his period of thoughtful and deep reflection. We called them "spells" of melancholy. His strongest and most earnest supporters and friends were more or less uneasy during their continuance, and were always delighted as the clouds lifted. As these passed, we could see the returning joyous and courageous spirit that filled his soul to running over, and spread everywhere to the remotest corners, and lightened the hearts of men as no other could.

He came to the Urbana court, and was there a day or two. He congratulated us on our thousand majority for Lovejoy. We had a pleasant day with him, and he was in the best of humor. His wit and striking illustrations rolled along unconsciously, like a bubbling, dashing stream down the hillside. He was quietly approached by a very prudent, but a faint-hearted old man, who dreaded disunion and the name of a Disunionist, who, in the dangerous emergency, believed that men of all parties should unite. He was a sober, well-ordered citizen in ordinary times; but the condition of public affairs very much alarmed him, as it did many, even less timid. He knew Mr. Lincoln very well, and managed to get with him in a back corner of the court-room, when he was disengaged. Speaking very low, but earnestly, Mr. B—— said, addressing Mr. Lincoln: "The Abolitionists are growing so fast that we old-timers, Old-line Whigs and conservatives, are really alarmed. You are about a great deal, and know better than we do whether the present alarm is justifiable; but do n't you believe that such agitators as these Abolitionists will alienate a great many old Whigs and conservative Union men, and drive them over to the secessionists?" He felt what he said, and was serious about it. In his answer, Mr. Lincoln wanted to encourage him; for he was a very reputable man, only dangerously timid, as many were in those days. The question, and Mr. Lincoln's attention to it, removed all secrecy, and, a crowd gathering around, Mr. Lincoln had to mount a chair to reply. This he did in such an unspeakably droll and humorous way that very few could control their risibilities enough to hear what he said.

His reply had to be in the nature of a talk to the whole

assemblage in the court-room, and was about as follows:
"No, Brother B——, I am not afraid of the Abolitionists
driving the loyal Old-line Whigs and conservatives over
to secession. I used to think the Abolitionists and their detractors were a little noisy, but I got along so that the agitation never hurt me. But you can't drive a real Union man
of any party into disunion, unless you have him down
South, and do it as they drive the 'Niggers.' I used to be
more afraid that we Old-line Whigs would drive the Abolitionists out of our party, but I found out later that it was
useless uneasiness, and that there was n't a bit of danger;
for there were n't enough of us, all told, to scare anybody."

Lincoln lost the senatorship; but no man ever won more
conspicuous distinction and widespread reputation in his
party. He rose, in the West, to relative position against
Douglas in the Democratic party. Douglas recognized Lincoln's leadership by contending with him as the true leader
and exponent of the Republican and anti-slavery organizations. Lincoln gained strength in the hearts of the people,
mainly, it seemed, because he reached the common mind,
and made the slavery question one of right and morals, as
well as one of political economy. He did this in the most
pleasing manner, sympathizing with the suffering and downtrodden everywhere. He aroused the deepest and most lasting sentiments of their hearts as he revealed the sin and
infamy of the whole slave system and the corresponding
oppression of wealth. He tore open the whole contention,
and laid the horrid carcass of slavery in its naked vileness
before the most thoughtful for fair and impartial judgment.
Nor was it in any sort of accident that he came to this great
work. He had improved the talents God had given him, and
stood before the people, pleading for right and for more of
human kindness.

In God's own way he had been trained to become the
prophet, leader, and reformer in his ceaseless struggle for

the rights of men against the powers of evil. With due credit to all others, he was the only leader who developed the high capacity and fitness to deal prudently and appropriately with slavery. There were many worthy and capable men who could and did deal with one or more features of it among the insufficiently-organized elements in opposition to it. Lincoln could and did successfully deal with all and every feature of it in patience, careful consideration, without rashness, hasty judgment, or precipitation. He had seen the folly and failure of the two compromises of 1820 and 1850, which were yielded to by the wisest and ablest statesmen of the periods, managed in chief by Henry Clay, whom he respected and believed in as in no other man of his time. In contrast, after showing that slavery was an incessant, continuing evil, and that "a house divided against itself can not stand," he took positive grounds for its restriction and ultimate extinction, to which he adhered with unvarying purpose and integrity. He would not lead a forcible, harsh, and aggressive movement against slavery, such as the pro-slavery leaders, in their folly and madness, were leading against freedom, but a carefully-considered, just, and reasonable, though positive and certain policy against it, "that would place it in the public mind, where it could rest in the belief of its ultimate extinction," as the founders of the Nation did.

This was Lincoln's belief and position, on which rests his fame as the wise and great leader of a free people. At the same time, as we have gathered from the facts, Douglas was an able and, in many ways, an incomparable leader, who, in appropriate relation with Lincoln, was the man and leader, without whose valiant, heroic, and capable leadership neither Mr. Lincoln nor any other leader could have succeeded.

Douglas, brave leader, as he must be placed and held, grew up, was trained in, and fully believed in the plans and policies of the statesmen of all parties for over two generations, which were those of expediency and toleration of slav-

ery, as illustrated by the two noted slavery-conceding compromises. He was so vigorous and successful in the defense
of the modified Compromise of 1850 through the years to
1856-9, that little doubt remained of their continuance by
concession under his leadership. But the slave-leaders
had been so surfeited with power that they positively rejected the odious pro-slavery compromise, severed the Democratic party, and provoked the conflict.

. As a chief Democratic leader, Douglas could not have
been an out-and-out anti-slavery leader such as Lincoln.
His party faction was mostly loyal, but not half of it was
anti-slavery in belief. Well-informed men in all parties
knew this; still many untempered reasoners expected him
to take advanced ground against slavery. If he had done
so, he would have lost his leadership as certainly as his
vantage position against the leaders, and hence had to submit, by a quasi-obedience, to the decision of the Supreme
Court, which he knew was bad law as soon as it was announced. He held on in this half-forced submission until
his defeat of Lecompton and his contest with Lincoln cost
him his leadership under the pro-slavery Administration,
when he took his true position in open revolt.

Lincoln had taken strong ground against him, as related;
but Douglas had so far succeeded before his debate with Lincoln, that, under his leadership, it seemed a possible conclusion that, with his re-election, Congress would agree
upon some further patching compromise on slavery. The
first serious obstacle in the way of this new compromise was
the slave-leaders, who remained too greedy to announce the
conditions on which they would agree. In this condition
of affairs several prominent Republican leaders took about
the same position in hope of settlement without war or conflict, as Douglas. That Douglas had succeeded to the point
of the probable adoption of some compromise, if the Southern leaders would consent, has been related.

Mr. Seward was then in high position, and favored with distinct capacity, aptitude, and apparent strength of mind for chief leadership. In earnest devotion to principle he could easily have taken and held leadership for years in advance of Lincoln, as he had every opportunity of position, influence, and long exercise of power; while Lincoln had few of these helps. He was defeated with his party in his State about nineteen times out of twenty in the twenty years from 1840 to 1860, and held leading positions only, as he hewed it out of the rocks of debate and his persevering, candid presentation of the truth to the people.

The truth is that Seward did not have the intellectual strength and comprehensive grasp of Lincoln to see and seize the position that would certainly divide and defeat his opponents. Anti-slavery leader, governor, and senator as he was, for years he tacitly consented to the fusion, compromising position of Douglas, and with about all the Eastern Republicans, favored the re-election of Douglas, and so far entered into approval for combination or co-operative action as to desire the return, and of course the ascendency of Douglas.

This at the very best, however, would have been no more than a new compromise with slavery. Senator Chase of Ohio, Representative Colfax of Indiana, and most of the prominent Republicans in Congress were committed to this policy, so far as to agree to the return of Douglas, which would almost of itself have been sufficient for a determined effort in the direction of another compromise. The co-operation of Crittenden of Kentucky, Badger of North Carolina, Botts of Virginia, Edward Everett, and several Union men of experience and ability, strongly foreshadowed the success of this movement. Strange as it may seem, the impulsive and irascible Greeley, with his widely-circulated *Tribune,* united in this purely Eastern scheme.

Against this, almost alone among the men whose minds

and talents shaped a Nation's destiny, Abraham Lincoln took
up the cause of human rights. He opposed all such compromises or composition with slavery, on the grounds of justice
and the equality of men. He struck the evil at its roots,
heedless of doubting friends and the most powerful combination against his ideas, conducted his campaign in his own
way, and passed on to commanding leadership and the exercise of wise statesmanship, unsurpassed and seldom if ever
equaled in the history of men.

In a few weeks after the State election, about the Christ-
mas-time of 1858, Lincoln had fully passed his period of
gloom or melancholy. It should be noted that these were
common in all the important events of his life, so much so as
to create little uneasiness on the part of those who knew him
best, but often quite the reverse to those who did not so well
understand them. He had not been elected senator, but he
had fought a great battle, with ten times more than ordinary
forces against him, including the outside and a whole lot of
the inside of his own party, with no shadow of patronage or
office to sustain him. Even so hampered, he was in one sense
victor with the people of the State, a plurality of four thousand having voted for him.

More than this, he had fought manfully for our cause
on principle, and stood on the high and independent ground
against one of the most eminent men of his time, who had
no superior in the highest debating and sifting council-house
of the Nation. He had made an issue, divided an enemy, and
more than equally contended with a truly great man and his
party. He sustained himself, and won not only local success
and the undisputed right to lead the Republicans and anti-
slavery elements of Illinois; but in the logic of a statesman
among a host of doubters, trimmers, and conceders, he had
won, not only without help, but against more than half of
the prominent leaders of his own party. In this he had
reached the commanding position of the most fearless, con-

sistent, plain leadership among the people, and became the strongest defender and expounder of the doctrines of all anti-slavery people first, and parties afterward.

After this the thinking and reading people of the Republic first, and the world later, rediscovered Mr. Lincoln, the distinguished leader who leaped into favor and distinction everywhere, almost at once. They had not been without knowledge of him before, as far into the cradle-land of liberty and learning as Boston, where in that and other places he had talked earnestly and convincingly to the people of New York and New England. This he did in the early fifties, when the great Webster was flinching and going down in defeat and death, under the reach and reverberating crack of the slave-driver's lash, while the young representative, Lincoln, was gaining knowledge and forming character, laying the foundations of his career, climbing up against odds to positive and unhesitating opposition to the aggressive ascendency of the Southern leaders. He talked to the people of the East effectively in that earlier day; and again in 1858, when he had taken the stronger and more immovable stand against slavery, all who had ever heard, and thousands who had not were anxious to see the fearless Western leader.

He was soon in receipt of invitations, letters of approval, and commendation. Among them were many personal requests to visit towns, cities, and States in all parts of the country, to make addresses to all sorts and kinds of people. They wanted to see and hear this wonderful new leader, the plain, common-talking sort of a man whom everybody could understand, and to have him lay before them in easy and sensible explanation the intricate, important, and all-absorbing topic then so earnestly and deeply fastened in the public mind. Mr. Colfax, of Indiana, who had been deep in the plan for the return of Douglas, but had come back "into the Church," as Lincoln said, wrote to him: "Your counsel carries great weight with it. There's no political letter that falls from your pen which is not copied throughout the Union," and closed by asking him to make some addresses in Indiana.

Replying to an invitation from Massachusetts, he wrote on the proposition to form a coalition with the "American party" and others believing in the doctrine of "Native Americanism" as follows: "I am against its adoption in Illinois or any other place where I have the right to oppose it. Understanding the spirit of our institutions to be for the purpose of elevating men, I am opposed to whatever tends to degrade them. I have some little notoriety for commiserating the oppressed condition of the Negro; and I should be strangely inconsistent if I could favor any project for curtailing the existing rights of white men, even though born in different lands and speaking different languages from myself. As to the matter of fusion, I am for it if it can be had on Republican grounds; and I am not for it on any other terms. On any other, it would be as foolish as unprincipled. It would lose the whole North, while the South would remain under control of the common enemy."

There was remarkable consistency in all his speeches, addresses, letters, messages, documents, and important papers, in that he invariably made a clear and explicit statement of his belief in the rights, privileges, and equality of men. He did this still more emphatically, if there can be difference, in his reply to an invitation to celebrate Jefferson's birthday in Boston: "But soberly now, it is no child's play to save the principles of Jefferson from total overthrow in this Nation. One would state with great confidence that he could convince any sane child that the simpler propositions of Euclid are true; but nevertheless he would fail utterly with one who should deny the definitions and axioms. The principles of Jefferson are the definitions and axioms of free society. And yet they are denied and evaded, with no small show of success. One dashingly calls them 'glittering generalities.'

Another calls them 'self-evident lies.' These expressions, differing in form, are identical in object and effect, the supplanting of the principles of free government and restoring those of classification, caste, and legitimacy.

"They would delight a convocation of crowned heads plotting against a people. They are the vanguard, the miners and sappers of returning despotism. We must repulse them, or they will subjugate us. This is a world of compensation; and he who would be no slave, must consent to have no slave. Those who deny freedom to others, deserve it not for themselves; and under a just God can not long retain it.

"All honor to Jefferson, to the man who, in the concrete pressure of a struggle for national independence by a single people, had the coolness, forecast, and capacity to introduce into a merely revolutionary document an abstract truth, applicable to all men and all time, and so to embalm it there, that to-day and in all coming days it shall be a rebuke and a stumbling-block to the very harbingers of reapproaching tyranny and oppression."

This is as clear as the catechism of the martyrs of all ages for human liberty, and is and should be sounding as the bugle-call to every freeman throughout the land to gird on his armor, and while life lasts never cease contending for human liberty. If there is in the record of what men have said and written, outside of Holy Writ, any clearer or more distinct definition of the rights of men under law and before their Maker than Jefferson's immortal declaration, these are to be found in the words and maxims of Lincoln.

The slave-leaders' faction openly declared that the Supreme Court decision firmly established the right of the slaveholder to take and hold his slaves in any Territory. Buchanan's Administration asserted this to be the law, and the super-serviceable Jere Black, his attorney in fact and his Attorney-General, wrote and declared that it was the law under the Constitution; but no slaveholder would trust such flimsy protection for his "niggers." It all ended in "declared opinions" of the smaller sort, announcing and repeating the will and pleasure of Jefferson Davis.

Douglas and Lincoln, as recognized national leaders of their respective parties, took part in the Ohio campaign in 1859, both maintaining themselves on the grounds of difference so earnestly held the previous year in Illinois. Mr. Douglas found the Ohio Democracy in full sympathy, sustaining the squatters' rights in the Territories, decision or no decision, and that it would not make further concessions to slavery; that none could be made or expected until the National Convention made a different declaration of party creed.

Ohio had become a Republican State, and so voted that year; but Douglas's participation was well received, and a cordial support of its Democracy was significant in the terrible crisis then threatening the party, and the Nation no less. This support was proof beyond dispute, that in spite of the faithlessness and perfidy of Buchanan's Administration and its malicious purpose to overthrow Douglas, he still remained the unremoved leader of free Democracy, as well as leader and defender of the national doctrines of the party announced and declared at the Cincinnati Convention, when Buchanan was nominated, on which platform and declaration of principles he had been elected in 1856.

Both Lincoln and Douglas made speeches at Columbus and Cincinnati. They held very much the same answer-and-reply sort of discussions they had in Illinois, but not in joint debate. The book of speeches, as made in the Illlnois debate, with no other matter, was published and sold by the thousands. It was then, and for two years afterwards, accepted as a political handbook by both parties. In 1860 one Ohio publishing-house sold over thirty thousand copies, mainly for circulation in that State, as large editions of it had been published in Illinois.

Nothing in our history to that time so aroused the people

as the continuing and dangerous encroachments of slavery on our free institutions, and the usurpation of power growing out of it, and the almost certain loss of liberty, unless the people arose in masses against it. The interest of both parties on the subject was well shown in the widespread circulation of these printed debates; and the acknowledged leadership of these two able leaders, who both practically determined to arrest the spread of slavery, was as fully shown, in that the book was bought, sold, and relied upon so much by all parties. The loyalty, capacity, and patriotism of both leaders went without question. In those years the pith of the whole dividing dispute with the free State people of all parties as between these eminent leaders was substantially, How far can we submit to the domination and aggression of slavery? and, Shall we as a people intrusted with the preservation of free government among men, bow down any longer to the liberty-destroying and free-labor-crushing iniquity? These were the questions uppermost in the minds of all our people.

The published discussions and addresses of these men laid the whole of it plainly before the common understanding. It was one of the strange conditions of the time, but a striking coincidence that these two grew up together, with about the same following, in numbers, intelligence, and patriotism, always contending in honorable, anxious rivalry, and sometimes the keenest antagonism of political opposition. As they progressed, the strange relation passed away in the widening field of action, when it was known to both of them and their friends that either of them was better because of the other, and that in the end they were leading to the same result.

Some passages in Mr. Lincoln's Columbus and Cincinnati speeches were the clearest, most conclusive, and unanswerable reasons of his lifetime, as the following extracts show: In Columbus, September 16, 1859, he said: "They say if this principle is established, that there is no wrong in slavery, and whoever wants it has a right to have it; that it is a matter of dollars and cents, a sort of question how they shall deal with brutes; that between us and the Negro there is no sort of question, but that at the South it is between the Negro and the crocodile; that it is a mere matter of policy; that there is a perfect right, according to interest, to do just as you please. When this is done, where this doctrine prevails, the miners and sappers will have formed public opinion for the slave-trade.

"You need but one or two turns further until your minds, now ripening under these teachings, will be ready for all these things; and you will receive and support, or submit to, the slave-trade revived with all its horrors, a slave-code enforced in our Territories, and a new Dred Scott decision to bring slavery up into the heart of the free North."

At Cincinnati, September 17th, he said: "This Government is expressely charged with the duty of providing for the general welfare. We believe that the spreading out and perpetuity of the institution of slavery impairs the general welfare. We believe, nay, we know, that this is the only thing that has ever threatened the perpetuity of the Union itself."

In the following, although taking the strongest ground against slavery, his position was something like that of Douglas, but limited by prudential, more properly prejudicial, reasons, and his party's timid belief and declarations. He said: "I say we must not interfere with slavery in the States where it exists, because the Constitution forbids it, and the general welfare does not require us to do so. We must not withhold an efficient fugitive-slave law, because the Constitution requires us, as I understand it, not to withhold such a law. But we must prevent the outspreading of such an institution, because neither the Constitution nor the general welfare requires us to extend it. We must prevent the revival of the African slave-trade and the enacting by Congress of a Territorial slave-code. We must prevent each of these things being done either by Congress or courts. The people of the United States are the rightful masters of both Congress and courts, not to overthrow the Constitution, but to overthrow the men who pervert the Constitution."

CHAPTER XXXVII.

A FTER Mr. Lincoln's progress to high leadership, his successful contention with Douglas, his growing strength as shown in the Ohio canvass, and his rise to undisputed leadership in the West and Northwest, there was an unusual interest springing up everywhere, East as well as North, and to the farther West, to see and hear this rising, plain man of the Western prairies. Of the thousands who were in and about New York City, many wise, prudent, and well-informed men were earnest in the desire to see and hear the man who astonished so many so far away from the Atlantic. There were, besides these, a smaller number who did not especially care to see Lincoln, for fear he would make his coming a success, as he was likely to do if given the opportunity to talk directly to the people.

These were the statesmen, wise in their day but narrow and cunning as foxes, who had fled in many a chase, men of influence, men of power and position, men of wealth and standing, men of imports and exports, men who had been governors, senators, and occasionally a President or Vice-President, and had held other places of trust and profit, who were still hankering for the fleshpots; and occasionally a mayor or an alderman, when the hordes of Tammany could be composed; all in unison against any such leader, but as well agreed to conceal their desires. These men had done almost everything in the buying and selling line, successfully and profitably in all that they had undertaken. Their success had been so pronounced, and their confidence in themselves so strong, that it was a difficult thing for them to believe

265

that anything, or any man, from no matter where, could at all compare with anything or any man of the great State and city óf New York, and especially that an awkward, ungainly "country lawyer" from the raw Western prairies could rise to such pretentious leadership.

They had succeéded so well in the management of commerce and the public affairs of their great State that they determined to make Governor Seward the Republican candidate, and probably President of the United States. They arranged their plans, working under Thurlow Weed for their own man, and endeavoring the best way they knew to tangle or suppress Lincoln. There was never a doubt that Lincoln's progress would not escape his master hand in the grasp he held on public affairs. He was a very useful man in his way, and a faithful writer in sustaining such things as New York ascendency, regencies, and commercial enterprises that taxed the people of the whole land. He was at the time considered a fair exponent of his party and its general conduct of affairs, who in craftiness and skill had no ascertained rival. This astute manager-in-chief for Mr. Seward had taken charge, under designated committees and smaller auxiliaries, of the ways and means of getting Lincoln's proposed address before the people of New York in the most round-about way, "hiding him under a bushel," in Brooklyn, or keeping him away altogether.

As it came about, there was an invitation and correspondence over it for some weeks. The first plans were suggestions from the corresponding committees. They were not for a political address to the public in New York City, such as had often been made by eminent and distinguished men like Clay, Webster, Benton, Tom Corwin, and Douglas, but for a paid lecture to a select crowd; and while reputed to be in New York City, it was arranged to be in Brooklyn, then much smaller and holding more inferior relation to New York than at present.

In brief, Mr. Lincoln was advertised everywhere as going to New York to make an address to the public, while in fact the plan arranged for was for him to deliver a pay-address to a select few in Brooklyn, not as a chief party leader, but as Wendell Phillips, Theodore Parker, Bayard Taylor, Henry Ward Beecher, or other platform speakers of the day might do. They had suggested, too, that a lecture on some general topic, such as "Western Development" or the "Waterways of the Continent," would be acceptable, and had "fixed an early day for his lecture."

Mr. Lincoln saw through the project at once. He remarked of it: "I will accept the invitation on such terms as we can agree upon. I will trust going there and getting out without difficulty. I have several invitations to speak in the East, and will fill as many of them as I can conveniently. I understand this thing pretty well; the people of New York want Mr. Seward nominated as the next Republican candidate for President. It is a laudable and honorable ambition, on which I have no remarks to offer. He is probably the widest known leader in our party, and entitled to the nomination about as much as two or three others, but hardly more.

"If he is nominated, which seems a probable event, I will earnestly and sincerely support him, as I did Fremont, and I will persuade every one whom I can to do likewise. But I don't like this petty interference of Weed about a speech I may or may not deliver in New York. I understand that Governor Seward is to deliver an address in Chicago erelong. I hope that every means will be afforded him to meet his friends and speak to the people in as public, free, and unrestrained manner as possible. When I get down to New York I am certain that I will have a chance to talk to the people in some way; but as to going, I must have my time; and as to the subject, I will determine it for myself.

"Speaking now to you as friends, I have no hesitation in laying before you the grounds on which I would be willing to be a candidate for any office. I have no desire that will lead to any effort or solicitation on my part. I accepted your nomination for senator because it appeared to be the unanimous wish of the Republicans and Independents of the State that I should. Some very zealous friends have talked of me for President. I have not entertained the thought, because I do not believe I have reached the place in the public mind as one among the people that would justify my selection as a wise and prudent one.

"That is, I do not possess the wide acquaintance and confidence of the people in a sufficient degree for the party to unite on me as the most available and acceptable man. Understand me, I am not without the desire and the ambition, if you please, to be the Republican candidate, if it could come to me after mature consideration and due deliberation of the people; but in no other way. And let me assure you that I do not have the thought in my mind in any reasonable way that I will be considered eligible. I would not have it any other way if I could. I would not be a 'Jack in a pinch' candidate for any office."

This was the substance of his remarks on the subject about December, 1859. I met him several times at Bloomington, Champaign, and Springfield, and although Oglesby, Davis, Gridley, and several others were beginning seriously to undertake some preparatory work for him, he did not believe himself an available man, such as his own ideas required. He talked it all over among us with freedom and candor, and in a more impartial and disinterested way than any of us.

Mr. Gridley was "never in politics." He seldom took part in conventions or meetings of any kind; but when the plan to nominate Lincoln took shape in December, he said: "I want you to understand that I am in this undertaking, to advance Lincoln and nominate him if we can, with all my might, and I do n't want any blundering accidents or mishaps. I know Thurlow Weed and his way of pushing things along better than all the rest of the men of this State. I knew him well in New York State years ago. I do not expect any dishonorable work on his part in the interests of Mr. Seward; but it will be selfish and for Seward first, and so on to the end, with energy and zeal far beyond the imagination of untrained politicians elsewhere."

Thus the proposal of the New York address stood in a correspondence which Mr. Lincoln never made public, but about as related here. The usual result was reached in time. He went to New York as invited by a letter from "the Secretary of The Young Men's Central Republican Club of New York City," February 9, 1860, as follows: "The Young Men's Republican Club of this city very earnestly desires that you should deliver what I may term a political lecture. The peculiarities of the case are these: A series of lectures has been determined upon. The first was delivered by Mr. Blair, of St. Louis, a short time ago. The second will be in a few days by Mr. Cassius M. Clay, of Kentucky; and the third, we would prefer to have from you, rather than any other person. Of the audience, I should add that it is not that of an ordinary political meeting. These lectures have been contrived to call out our better but busier citizens, who never attend political meetings. A large part of the audience will consist of ladies."

This somewhat remarkable letter, from that remarkable club, which among other singular things classed the citizens who "never attend political meetings" as "our better, but busier citizens," was one of the agencies of the Seward-Weed "upper air" organizations, that were contrived to hold Conkling's "solar walk" people to the support of their favorite. Therefore this "better and busier" people's club that "ladies attended," afforded the very best means to isolate Mr. Lincoln, surprise him with the dazzling splendor of beauty, gay attire, and jewels commensurate with the city's commercial supremacy. He was to go and be confronted and entangled with an array of fair women, judges, governors, editors, and a host of such as were thrifty, and could mingle thought, sentiment, literature, and the higher gifts of men with commerce, or in our plainer phraseology, with the dicker and profit of trade.

He went in time, and met many of the fair women and learned and wise men with respect and satisfaction. His great discourse reached not only the crowded thousands in the hall of Cooper Institute, but it sounded as a tocsin of freedom to every American, from the rugged rocks of Maine and the pines of the Androscoggin to the mellowed, unwintered slope of the Sierras, the mammoth pines of Calaveras, and the softened swell of the placid waters of our western ocean.

We do not exaggerate the effect of Mr. Lincoln's Cooper Institute address. It would be beyond any one's power to do it; for without doubt, of our millions of reading and thinking people throughout the free States and many thousand in the border ones, there were not ten in a hundred who did not read or learn of the master arguments of the genius who unlocked the treasures of liberty, and laid them before a waiting, patient, and patriotic people.

This was not done without an important change of the plan of the Seward-Weed "better class" "Union Club." When Mr. Lincoln reached New York a day or two before his proposed address, he still fully expected that the paid-for and advertised one was to be held in Brooklyn, which would afford him opportunity to announce another meeting under his own management for the next evening at some convenient place in the larger city; but he found sufficient confusion and misunderstanding about the Brooklyn meeting, and the manner and plan of having it and paying for it, to enable him to take hold of it himself, and announce it for the next evening at the large hall of Cooper Institute.

He was not without suspicion as to whether the confusion over the Brooklyn plan was real. At all events, he found and made opportunity to speak to the people in the greater city, and a whole multitude of them. The work and preparation of making these changes stirred him up as he had never been on such a subject. The exciting interest was good for him, bracing him up and stimulating him to the use of all his powers as he had never been on any single occasion. In the multiplicity of seeming obstacles, he ran on to a happen-so, or a Providence that was entirely unexpected.

As we have related, Horace Greeley had been friendly to and had favored the re-election of Douglas. This Lincoln knew very well, and concluded to be courteous, and so called early on "the man of the *Tribune*." Greeley was delighted at this, and congratulated him on his astonishing rise in the confidence and hearts of the people. He had been afraid that Lincoln had come East unaware of the power and meddling ways of the Seward-Weed combination; but not feeling warranted by past relations, he did not feel like writing or interfering before Lincoln's arrival. However, when he had made the cordial overture, Greeley was entirely relieved, and found an easy way of telling what he desired from the beginning.

Mr. Lincoln said on his return that "Mr. Greeley made his story short and plain as a pikestaff, saying: 'I have made a hard fight for Seward. He could hardly be where he is if I had not done it. The work was all new, and the party had to be made out of fragments before anybody could hold office or place under it. Weed came in and worked manfully, and with his long experience and prominence did well; but the result was, that as the party got strong enough to have something to give as well as to beg for, which had been its principal business with me, the gains all went to the two first members of the political firm of Seward, Weed, and Greeley, or as they wanted them to go; and now I am at your service, with the announcement that the firm is dissolved by the retirement of the junior partner. You may have heard of it, or you may not. Be that as it may, we will get ready for your speech. We shall engage the Cooper hall. I 'll do that much on my own account. We will fill it too, from the upper tiers to the pit and the aisles of the lower stories, when the seats are full. Your meeting shall have notice and advertisement of one or as many columns of to-morrow's *Tribune* as may be necessary to give it wide circulation all over the city and the surrounding towns. I predict such a meeting for you as has not been held here for many a day, and such as Weed's stripling Club did not intend to have.' "

From this time forward Greeley and his friends took charge of all necessary preparations, and did so well as to fulfill and overdo his predictions. The hall was packed from top to bottom, wherever there was sitting or standing room. There was a mysterious abundance of admission tickets. Some of these had been provided for by the "better class" club before Mr. Greeley came into the management. A number had been sold, and the paid admission plan could not be dropped altogether, as Mr. Lincoln wished; but as long as there was room to sit or stand in the hall, tickets were within reach of all who came.

It was a large American audience, with perhaps a quarter of foreign-born people, estimated at twelve thousand. These had about the same appearance and intelligence, but no more than others whom he had frequently addressed in his own State and elsewhere. There was much said in some Eastern papers about the "high character and standing of many distinguished people in the audience;" but with the exception of Mr. Bryant, the poet, who was then publishing a newspaper, and who presided at the meeting, he had frequently addressed other meetings where there were as many or more prominent and noted people present. It was common for representatives in Congress, senators, governors, and other officials in high places, as well as the oppressed and overburdened men and women everywhere, to go and hear Abraham Lincoln.

Our own family lived in the great city some fourteen to twenty years. There the writer was born and reared to a certain age of importance, leaving the knowledge and remembrance full in mind, how the newspapers of the great seaport could sound "their own horns," exalt, inflate, and distinguish their citizens at will. Accordingly, we knew that a very "common crowd out West" would be described as "a distinguished, talented, and highly-cultured audience of the better class," if held in New York, and two or more of their newspapers thought it "the newest thing on earth to blow it."

However, Mr. Lincoln's audience at Cooper Hall was a large and respectable one, with several prominent people in attendance, of whom Mr. Greeley and Mr. Bryant were the most conspicuous. But in the great throng, as far as known, there was neither Seward nor Weed, nor were there other prominent persons of their faction, leaving in mind the unavoidable conclusion that the "immense crowd and distinguished audience" were mainly the followers of the junior partner of the recently dissolved political firm.

Those who were there heard in the two hours' earnest argument one of the strongest political addresses ever delivered by man. The local opposition had nerved Mr. Lincoln to the use of his highest powers, and in something of the same way that the American people took up and read Mrs. Stowe's plaintive tale of Uncle Tom's Cabin, in almost a day the Cooper Institute speech was carried everywhere in the North; and in two or three days in the weeklies and monthlies it spread as if "on the wings of the wind" all over the land.

This wide circulation made Mr. Lincoln in a few months to the whole people what he had been so many years in our State, a man rising in wisdom and integrity, equal to the use, without misuse or usurpation, of any power the people gave him.

This speech, printed and reprinted in whole and in part hundreds of times, and in as many languages as there were a thousand in the land anywhere to read it, was one of the factors that made him in so short a time a qualified and available candidate for the office of President, as he was already capable to fill it.

At the Cooper Institute meeting, presided over by the poet-editor Bryant, February 27, 1860, David Dudley Field, "the biggest lawyer in New York," escorted Mr. Lincoln to the rostrum, and introduced him to that great audience, where he stood one of God's strongest men on earth. He opened the memorable address with a quotation from Douglas's speech at Cincinnati the previous September, "Our fathers when they formed the Government under which we live, understood this question just as well as we do now, and even better." Following this he said: "Does the proper division of local from Federal authority, or anything in the Constitution, forbid our Federal Government to control as to slavery in the Territories? Upon this Senator Douglas holds the affirmative, and the Republicans the negative. This affirmation and denial form our issue, and this issue—this question—is precisely what the text declares our fathers understood 'better than we.' "

He then proceeded to state the historical facts concerning the men, their beliefs, what they did, and the spirit that held and animated them, who agreed to adopt, and did adopt, the Declaration of Independence, the Constitution, and the twelve amendments to it shortly afterwards. He showed how they provided for the earliest extinction of the African slave-trade in 1808; how they almost universally agreed, with the people of the State of Virginia, that slavery should not exist in any of the territory of the newly-formed Nation, and endowed Congress and the Executive with full legislative authority over the said territory under our system until such time as it should be made and become new States of the Union.

His recital of historical facts, with his knowledge of the men and the prevailing ideas of the time, was not only entertaining, but full of instruction. It showed to the most scholarly and learned men before him that his work was carefully and well done, that his research had been complete into all the available records bearing upon the subject of slavery and Congressional authority over it in the Territories, and the power of Congress to legislate for the Territories, over mails, transportation, commerce, and civil order. He seemed familiar with Madison's "Notes on the Adoption of the Constitution;" with the Jersey Presbyterian Witherspoon's Essays; and Franklin's common-sense writings. He availed himself of Hamilton's fund of learning, and the combined knowledge of what these able men and compilers of our fundamental law had gone over in tedious labor. He was a reasoner without an equal, and disclosed the inclination and tendency of Hamilton and two or three others to the side of prerogative and regal right, as well as Jefferson's contention against it. He spoke in reverence, how Washington was moderate, even-minded, calm, and impartial where there was equal right, but providing that the liberties of the people and the independence of the Nation should never be abridged, nor its standards of right and justice ever be polluted in the mire of greed or despotism.

There before an audience of as capable and intelligent people as could be gathered on the earth stood the gifted Lincoln, reciting, explaining, and discussing the meaning of the provisions of the Constitution and their relations to each other, and the rights and duties of Congress, courts, and Presidents and the people under them. His information was so accurate and comprehensive, that one might almost suppose that he had been a prominent member of the Convention, and had helped make the Constitution for the best purposes in civil government.

He said: "The sum of the whole is, that of our thirty-nine fathers who framed the original Constitution, twenty-one, a clear majority of the whole, certainly understood that no proper division of the local from the Federal authority, nor any part of the Constitution, forbade the Federal Government to control as to slavery in the Territories; while all the rest probably had the same understanding. Such unquestionably was the understanding of our fathers who framed the original Constitution; and the text affirms that they understood the question 'better than we.'

"It is surely safe to affirm that the thirty-nine framers of the original Constitution, and the seventy-six members of the Congress which framed the amendments thereto, taken together, do certainly include those who may be fairly called our fathers who framed the Government under which we live. And so assuming, I defy any man to show that any one of them ever in his whole life declared in his understanding any proper division of local from Federal authority, or any part of the Constitution forbade the General Government to control as to slavery in the Federal Territories.

"I go a step further. I defy any one to show that any living man in the whole world ever did, prior to the beginning of the present century, or even prior to the beginning of the last half of the present century, declare that in his understanding any proper division of local from Federal authority, or any part of the Constitution, forbade the Federal Government to control as to slavery in the Federal Territories. To those who now so declare I give, not only our fathers who formed the Government under which we live, but with them all other living men within the century in which it was framed, among whom to search, and they shall not be able to find the evidence of a single man agreeing with them.

"Now and here, let me guard a little against being misunderstood. I do not mean to say we are bound to follow implicitly in whatever our fathers did. To do so would be to discard all the lights of current experience—to reject all progress, all improvement. What I do say is, that if we would supplant the opinions and policy of our fathers in any case, we should do so upon evidence so conclusive and arguments so clear that even their great authority, fairly considered and weighed, can not stand; and most surely not in a case where we ourselves declare they understood the question better than we."

He found himself in the commercial metropolis let alone and unrecognized by the office-holding faction of Weed. There was enough in the neglect to arouse and stimulate him to the exercise of power and independence that was all unusual where commercialism was bending its suppliant knees to the behest and favor of the slave-power. The coincidences that brought him into cordial sympathy with Greeley and his independent *Tribune* could have been no less than the hand of God's providence. The *Tribune* of those days was the great light of freedom that found its way into the homes of the reading millions of freemen, who were then organizing against the deceptions, intrigues, and conspiracies of the Southern leaders.

The *Tribune* and its founder took to Lincoln, and gave him the audience of the widely-circulating newspaper; and the readers, countless as the leaves of the forest, took to Lincoln more firmly and graciously, in perfect content with the plain way of saying what he intended. They could understand the direct assault he made on slavery and its ceaseless infringements and the spread of its blasting power. They saw and heard his blows like sounding hammers, that fastened the shafts of truth like bolts of polished steel into the heart of yielding Senates, a faithless and disintegrating Administration, and the apologizing and twisting Supreme Court. He tore the flimsy sophistry from the scheming decision of the Court to nationalize slavery by the rank betrayal and reversal of law and precedent; that slavery existed everywhere under the Constitution, where not prohibited by State law;

that Congress was so restricted that it could not exclude it from the Territories, but could pass laws to sustain, enforce, and spread it.

That he could be plain and emphatic was clear enough in his address to the blustering, conspiring leaders. He said: "You say that you will not abide by the election of a Republican President; in that supposed event you say, you will destroy the Union; and then you say the great crime of having destroyed it will be upon us. That is cool. A highwayman holds a pistol to my ears, and mutters through his teeth, 'Stand and deliver, or I shall kill you, and then you will be a murderer.' To be sure, what the robber demanded of me, my money, was my own; and I had a clear right to keep it; but it was no more my own than my vote is my own; and the threat of death to me to extort my money, and the threat of destruction to the Union to extort my vote, can scarcely be distinguished in principle.

"It is exceedingly desirable that all parts of this great Confederacy shall be at peace and in harmony one with another. Let us Republicans do our part to have it so. Even though much provoked, let us do nothing through passion and ill-temper. Even though the Southern people will not so much as listen to us, let us calmly consider their demands, and yield to them if, in our deliberate view of our duty, we possibly can. Judging by all they say and do, and by the subject and nature of their controversy with us, let us determine, if we can, what will satisfy them.

"Will they be satisfied if the Territories be unconditionally surrendered to them? We know they will not. In all their present complaints against us the Territories are scarcely mentioned. Invasions and insurrections are the rage now. Will it satsify them if in the future we have nothing to do with invasions and insurrections? We know it will not. We so know, because we know we never had anything to do with invasions and insurrections; and yet this total abstaining does not exempt us from the charge and the denunciation.

"The question recurs, What will satisfy them? Simply this: We must not only let them alone, but we must somehow convince them that we do let them alone. This we know by experience is no easy task. We have been so trying to convince them from the very beginning of our organization, but with no success. In all our platforms and speeches we have constantly protested our purpose to let them alone; but this has had no tendency to convince them. Alike unavailing to convince them is the fact that they never have detected a man of us in any attempt to disturb them.

"These natural and apparently adequate means all failing, what will convince them? This, and this only—cease to call slavery wrong, and join them in calling it right. And this must be done thoroughly, done in acts as well as words. Silence will not be tolerated; we must place ourselves avowedly with them; the proposed new sedition law must be enacted and enforced, suppressing all declarations that slavery is wrong, whether made in politics, in presses, in pulpits, or in private. We must arrest and return their fugitive slaves with greedy pleasure. We must pull down our free State constitutions. The whole atmosphere must be disinfected from all taint of opposition to slavery before they will cease to believe that all their trouble proceeds from us.

"I am quite aware they do not state their case precisely in this way. Most of them would probably say to us, 'Let us alone, do nothing to us, and say what you please about slavery.' But we do let them alone, never disturb them; so that, after all, it is what we say which dissatisfies them. They will continue to accuse us of doing until we cease saying.

"I am aware, also, they have not, as yet, in terms demanded the repeal of our free State constitutions. Yet those constitutions declare the wrong of slavery, with more solemn emphasis than do all other sayings against it, and when all these other sayings shall have been silenced, the overthrow of these constitutions will be demanded, and nothing left to resist the demand. It is nothing to the contrary that they do not demand the whole of this just now. Demanding what they do, and for the reason they do, they can stop nowhere short of this consummation. Holding, as they do, that slavery is morally right and socially elevating, they can not cease to demand a full national recognition of it as a legal right and social blessing.

"Nor can we justifiably withhold on any ground, save on our conviction that slavery is wrong. If slavery is right, all words, acts, laws, and constitutions against it are themselves wrong, and should be silenced and swept away. If it is right, we can not object to its nationality—its universality. If it is wrong, they can not justly insist upon its extension or enlargement. All they ask we could readily grant, if we thought slavery right; all we ask they could as readily grant, if they thought it wrong.

"Their thinking it right and our thinking it wrong is the precise fact upon which depends the whole controversy. Thinking it right as they do, they are not to blame for desiring its full recognition, as being right; but thinking it wrong as we do, can we yield to them? Can we cast our votes with their view and against our own? In view of our moral, social, and political responsibilities, can we do this?

"Wrong as we think slavery is, we can yet afford to let it alone where it is, because that much is due to the necessity arising from its actual presence in the Nation; but can we, while our votes will prevent it, allow it to spread into the national Territories, and to overrun us here in the free States?

"If our sense of duty forbids this, let us stand by our duty fearlessly and effectively. Let us be divided by none of those sophistical contrivances wherewith we are so indus-

triously plied and belabored, contrivances such as grasping
for some middle ground between, vain as the search for a man
who should be neither a living man nor a dead man, such a
policy of 'do n't care,' on a question about which all true men
do care, such as Union appeals beseeching true Union men
to yield to Disunionists; reversing the Divine rule, and calling, not the sinners, but the righteous to repentance; such as
invocations to Washington imploring men to unsay what
Washington said, and undo what Washington did.

"Neither let us be slandered from our duty by false accusations against us, nor frightened from it by menaces of destruction to the Government, nor of dungeons to ourselves.
Let us have faith that right makes might, and in that faith
let us to the end dare to do our duty as we understand it."

Thus he closed. He had talked with such fervor, earnestness, and power to the great multitude for two hours that
they caught his inspiration, and rising at the close in one
movement with unrestrained joy, gladness, and overflowing
hearts, they rang out a welcome to the great American in
human voice mightier than the roar of the incoming sea.

He had done more than Cæsar when he had conquered
Gaul, and the nation lay bleeding and helpless at his feet,
trembling and suing for mercy, because of the strength of
the mailed and fleet-limbed Roman legions. He had done
more than win a kingdom on fields where the slain were piled
in heaps of uncounted thousands. He had won the hearts
of a free people.

He had done wonderful things in speech and labor from
a boy; but so far, never more than in this. He had taken
thousands of the people of the metropolis and adjoining cities
into his heart, as he had done so many in his own State. He
had done much more, not only convinced these thousands
and turned them into enthusiasts for liberty, but through
fortunate opportunity he had opened a speaking, listening,
and reading acquaintance with the millions who read and be-

lieved in the *Tribune,* then accepted as the "Shorter Catechism" on the doctrines of liberty and the rights of men. On such subjects it was under its fearless and independent printer, publisher, and editor, "the defender of the faith."

Its pages from this time gave a new tongue to his logic and reasonings, where he was able to commingle in friendly confidence, not only in the little town meetings like those of Springfield and Bloomington, but with the most multitudinous audience any political leader had ever essayed to address. To the whole thirty-one millions of people he was, with this iron and inky tongue of the *Tribune,* to talk to and interest more than half of them henceforward, in some congenial, interesting way every week; and to the opposition in a form of speech and utterance giving due notice that the loyal people of the Nation could not longer be deceived, and that they had made their last concession to the slavers' greed. In this way the schism of Greeley leavened and wrought wonders, when by it Lincoln was able to talk to the people of the Nation.

Mr. Greeley was one of the best-informed writers and men of affairs, with ample knowledge of the current topics, then in the fever-heat of angry discussion. He was one of the men who had worked his way from the type-cases, and persevered in making an independent newspaper, with power for himself and his journal that was not equaled, because the people had faith in his honesty, capability, and his fearless declaration of right. In his rise, progress, and success, he had always, like Lincoln, stood true and steadfast in any cause of the people. He was sanguine, impulsive, industrious, and persevering to a fault. He was, with his *Tribune,* one of the strongest powers in the land; and he made the paper such a weapon against slavery that the labor and effects were far beyond calculation. In most of the slave States the *Tribune* was declared to be "an incendiary publication," and was rigidly excluded from the mails; but this did not stop its dis-

tribution even in those States. The dissolution of the part-
nership before mentioned, as Mr. Greeley told him, had far-
reaching consequences. It helped to make Mr. Seward's
nomination an impossibility; but, being in control of the
State organization, Weed and Seward paid little attention
to Greeley. Lincoln became the beneficiary of the dispute,
not as the result of any plans, but by the incident coming at
the right time, which Mr. Lincoln, with foreseeing capacity,
used to his advantage.

While he had done nothing to foment or prolong this factional division, he was aggravated, as he had not been elsewhere, in any preparations for making an address. Being
in this mood, he let the advantage come his way, in which
his sagacity and foresight were never better shown. Without doing anything to antagonize Seward and his experienced
leader, he received the full benefit of Greeley's cordial and
earnest support and, much better, the unrivaled opportunity
of talking to the people through his *Tribune*.

From this time forward he fully realized his "availability"
as a candidate. It made no difference in his conduct. His
mind seemed perfectly at ease, without anxiety; but we
knew that the whole subject had undergone a great change
in his thoughts from the time of the success of this Eastern
campaign. He was calm and apparently as unconcerned about
it as ever. To the few men who had been anxious before,
who had seen the new light, it was the turning-point. Haste,
zeal, perseverance, and determination were called into exercise and operation at once by these earnest few who had to
learn, as they pushed along, what to do. The most certain
fact that came just then was that we had the capable supervision of one who knew how, but had "never been a politician," and was never one afterward.

On the morning after the delivery of his great speech,
the notoriety of it kept spreading until it reached a
sensation such as the city never had on such a subject. "The

unlettered Western lawyer" had delivered an address that challenged lawyers, scholars, logicians, polemical professors, or statesmen, as to form, style, substance, impartial reasoning, clearness, and directness of expression. The newspapers, one and all, Whig, Democrat, and Republican, published the speech in full, and columns of particulars about the meeting and the overflow that would have filled another such hall, if as many more could have heard him.

The *Tribune* said: "We present herewith a very full and accurate report of this speech; yet the tones, the gestures, the kindling eye and the mirth-provoking look defy the reporter's skill. The vast assemblage frequently rang with cheers and shouts of applause, which were prolonged and intensified to the close. No man ever before made such an impression on his first appeal to a New York audience."

Very soon the *Tribune* printed this remarkable speech in a pamphlet, which was sold and distributed all over the country. This was followed by many subsequent reprints and editions, showing it to be one of the plainest and most widely-read arguments ever published in the hotly-contested period of discussion preceding the war. It was also published and widely circulated in the campaign of 1860, when, of the many able and patriotic addresses of that year, this Cooper Institute speech held its place as the one most extensively read and circulated.

Before returning home, Mr. Lincoln made a tour of two or three days in New England. He delivered an address in Boston, and some shorter ones on the route. The people were delighted with him wherever they could meet and listen to his plain, earnest words. His homely ways, the direct . and artless manner of telling his stories and anecdotes, and the exact way he had of emphasizing important facts, the strength of principle, and his pleasing way of reasoning out things plain enough for the most common understanding, made him, not only political, but personal friends by thousands, who always wanted to see and hear more of this wise as well as entertaining man.

It was on his trip through New England at this time that Mr. Gulliver, a minister, had a pleasant chat with him in a railway car, which he wrote for a New York paper in 1864, as follows: "When I spoke to him, he said, 'You remind me of a most extraordinary circumstance which occurred in New Haven the other day. They told me that the professor of Rhetoric in Yale College—a very learned man, is n't he?' I replied, 'Yes, sir; and a very fine critic too.' He continued: 'Well, I suppose so; he ought to be, at any rate. They told me that he came to hear me, and took notes of my speech, and gave a lecture on it to his class next day, and, not satisfied with that, he followed me up to Meriden the same evening, and heard me again for the same purpose. Now, if this is so, it is, to my mind, very extraordinary. I have been sufficiently astonished at my success in the West. It has been most unexpected. But I had no thought of any marked success at the East, and, least of all, that I should draw out such commendations from literary and learned men.'

"Mr. G. replied: 'That suggests an inquiry which has several times been upon my lips during this conversation. I want to know very much how you got this unusual power of putting things. It must have been a matter of education. No man has it by nature alone. What has your education been?'

"Mr. Lincoln replied: 'Well, as to education, the newspapers are nearly correct. I never went to school more than a few months at a time in my life. But, as you say, this must be a product of culture in some form. I have been putting the same question you asked me to myself while you have been talking. I say this, that, among my earliest recollections, I remember how, when a mere child, I used to get irritated when anybody talked to me in a way I could not understand. I do n't think I ever got so angry at anything else in my life. But that always disturbed my temper, and has done so ever since. I can remember going to my little bedroom after hearing the neighbors talk of an evening with my father, and spending no small part of the night walking up and down, and trying to make out what was. the exact meaning of some of their, to me, dark sayings. I could not sleep, though I often tried to, when I got on such a hunt after an idea, until I had caught it; and when I thought I had got it, I was not satisfied until I had repeated it over and over, until I had put it in language plain enough, as I thought, for any boy I knew to comprehend. This was a kind of fashion with me, and it has stuck by me; for I am never easy now, when I am handling a thought, till I have bounded it north and bounded it south, and bounded it east and bounded it west. Perhaps that accounts for the characteristic you observe in my speeches, though I never put the two things together before.'

"Mr. G. said: 'I thank you for this. It is the most splendid educational fact I ever happened upon. This is genius, with all its impulsive, inspiring, dominating power over the minds of its possessors, developed by education into talent, with its uniformity, its permanence, and its disciplined strength always ready, always available, never capricious— the highest possession of the human intellect. But let me ask you, did you not have a law education? How did you prepare for your profession?'

"He replied: 'O yes, I read law. But your question reminds me of a bit of education I had, which I am bound in honesty to mention. In the course of my law reading I constantly came upon the word *demonstrate*. I thought at first that I understood its meaning, but soon became satisfied that I did not. I said to myself, What do I do when I *demonstrate*, more than when I reason or prove? How does demonstration differ from any other proof? I consulted

Webster's Dictionary. That told of certain proofs, "proofs beyond the possibility of doubt;" but I could form no idea of what sort of proof that was. I thought a great many things were true beyond the possibility of doubt, without recourse to any such extraordinary process of reasoning as I understood demonstration to be. I consulted all the dictionaries and books of reference I could find, but with no better results. You might as well have defined blue to a blind man. At last I said to myself, I can never make a lawyer if I do not understand what *demonstrate* means; and I left my office in Springfield, went home, and staid there till I could give any proposition in the six books of Euclid at sight. I then found out what *demonstrate* means, and went back to my law office.'

"Mr. G. replied: 'Your success is no longer a marvel. It is the legitimate result of adequate causes.'"

This conversation was written as much as four years after its occurrence, when much of speech and manner was forgotten. It misrepresents Mr. Lincoln in some degree; still it has enough of fact to render it interesting and enough of Lincoln in the incidents mentioned to reveal to a very common understanding that he was a student and scholar, no matter whether or not he dug up his knowledge in the discipline of academical rules and courses.

The whole academic or collegiate business is, to one who becomes a scholar, about this: Some discipline, rigid or not, with whatever training and learning of facts may be obtained in the course. This is only a start on the road for an education. He who follows the discipline and digs it out, in or out of scholastic limits, does what Mr. Lincoln did. He mastered the art of expression, delivery, and rhetoric until a college tutor followed him to gain better and further knowledge of his own branch of study, as the preacher relates above. Mr. Lincoln did not believe himself an ignorant, nor even an unlettered man, nor did he say or believe or lead others to presume that his learning and knowledge came through collegiate rules or forms.

The men who contended with him most, many of whom were collegiates of good standing—bright ones, too—never complained of any want of or defective education on his part; but some teachers and formalists down East always did, who will not give up the habit, no matter what the proof or the "demonstration" may be. This is no grumbling complaint from one who disbelieves in colleges and institutions of learning. On the contrary, it is in full accord with family history for generations, to believe in them, go to them, and get the knowledge they have to give, work through them, and as constantly support and sustain them.

John Brown

JOHN BROWN

CHAPTER XXXVIII.

IN a short time after these Cooper Institute and other Eastern speeches I met Mr. Gridley in Bloomington, where we were having some preliminary meetings, relating to Lincoln as a candidate for President. Mr. Gridley was more sanguine than I had ever known him to be, although he was well known to be excitable, quick, and nervous. His sagacity and perfect control of himself was so strong that, in reaching a conclusion on any important undertaking, he was one of the most careful, cautious, and conservative of men; but when conclusions were reached, the process of work or the enterprise under his direction fairly flew into shape under his skilled hands, ample means, and the management that embraced every movement and detail. In the work of the Chicago Convention occasion will require frequent reference to his sincere devotion and most efficient labor.

On meeting me, he said: "Robert, do you believe that we realize the advance Lincoln has made and is making? He has taken the Eastern people along with him, the same that he does with us here at home. I have never doubted his ability to do so, when I come to think about it; for they are the same people, and no better than we are. He is the most finished political debater and reasoner in our politics. He has the courage and integrity to face a cannon, and would not hesitate, if he were called upon for any sacrifice to serve the people. We must stand by him to a man. There is no such statesman living, or I am so prejudiced that I see no equal anywhere. His movements are astonishing, not

only in idea, but in performance, and, whether he is assisted
or not, he sustains himself like a great soldier in forming
and executing them.

"He led Douglas, who is, by all odds, the ablest statesman in his party, to statement, and repeated assertion of it,
that has permanently divided the Democratic party, North
and South, for and against slavery. Without intrusion he
went to New York, where he shook off the little cobwebs
with which they expected to tangle him, upset him, and send
him home a broken Western lawyer. He tore these away
as easily as he could 'shuck an ear of corn.' He has divided
Seward's support in his own State, without himself having
done anything to antagonize Weed or Seward, and has gained
the stronger support of Greeley and his *Tribune,* the anti-
slavery text-book, and the most powerful political newspaper in the world. Call it genius, sagacity, good management, or what you will,—it is astonishing success beyond
any man's expectations, even beyond his own, as I saw when
I talked to him yesterday. He has moved in at the right time,
made one of the most profound and unanswerable arguments ever delivered on any subject. The general result is
that Greeley and his millions of *Tribune* Republicans have
come over to Lincoln, and left Seward as smoothly as a
little minnow slips out of your net into the water.

"He has divided or deepened and emphasized the division so that Mr. Seward can not be nominated, and, for the
first time, I fully believe that Mr. Lincoln can be, if no
mishaps turn us the wrong way and we do our whole duty.
You remember, I was a resident of New York long enough
to be fairly conversant with their politics and party factions.
There seems to be something in the make-up of their people
and their differing nationalities, that makes them a peculiar
community. They are always disputing, with two or three
factions in their State politics, as a rule, or among themselves, as the old Dutch governor, Peter Stuyvesant, did

when he had no one else to quarrel with. They enjoy a faction in politics as a cow does fresh grass and a cool drink in summer.

"They began with Whigs, Republican, and Tory, and have never had less than that number since; usually more. When only two of the regular parties of the State are in the field, some one of them, in the most cunning way possible, starts a faction on some local issue. Their divisions have been so constant and frequent that one side or the other is always able to make a faction or diversion of some kind in any campaign before it is over.

"Mr. Weed is undoubtedly an able and experienced party man, as such things go in that State. He leads and manages all the politicians, while Greeley, as everybody knows, is no politician, and will not work with them, and will be independent of all such uncertain connections as Mr. Weed dearly likes to manage. Greeley's strength is mainly with the farmers and busy traders and agricultural people, who will not exactly antagonize Seward; but they will take to Lincoln in towns and townships by the thousand when Greeley indorses him, which I understand he has done.

"Hence you see, I think Mr. Lincoln has at least even chances for the nomination. I know Mr. Weed and his ways quite well. He does not recognize me as in any way interested in politics, which is true in general, but not in particular, as in this case, and all the better. Here among ourselves the political and outside work is in good hands, and I have no desire or need to take any part in that:

"Dick Oglesby and others can lead and manage that if any set of men in the State can. But I know Mr. Weed's ways of managing Conventions far better than any one here. I will keep even with him, and I intend to do so. I will do my part, and will help to win. I am not going to blame anybody with my mistakes either. I want so to manage

what I do that, if we fail, it will not be the result of mistakes or misconduct on our part; and when it appears that
any one can look after the business details of the coming
Convention better than I can, I shall welcome him as heartily
as any one of you.

"The Convention is to be in Chicago, and, while there
are many good people there who are identified with and
feel a common interest with us in the rest of the State,
still a great many more than half of them are from the
East, and, while they will take no active part against Lincoln, they are really for Seward, and will tacitly let things
go his way if we neglect our work. Mr. Weed's plan will
be to fill the town with thousands of Seward men for the
three days, and take his candidate through on a bulge.

"You are well acquainted there. While I am there quite
often, and feel that I have the run of the town as well as
any outside citizen of the State, I want several of you to
go there, and, by capable, discreet, and careful observation
and the poking-about kind of inquiry, ascertain the actual
conditions existing, see what are the tendencies, and what,
if any, outside movements are being made, so that I will
have the facts to support and help me in my work.

"We do n't want to do a dishonorable act, nor countenance one, for Mr. Lincoln is not to be helped that way;
but we do n't want to let this experienced New Yorker, sly
and cunning as a fox, with his helpers, sleepless as owls,
beat us on our own ground. Mr. Swett will go. He has
keen wits, and will do well; but he is too good-natured,
and takes too much to lawyers as a class. He believes them
often when they are planning against him, and takes too
much on hearsay. I want all the facts you can gather
around the courts, hotels, the railroad offices, and among
the Churches. Gather all you can, and let me know whether
what you get are facts or surmises. Mr. Jesse Fell is going,
and a more careful observer can not be found. All I fear

of him is his polite timidity. You are young and active, and can get in many places and do better and be more exact and particular than if you were older. What I want you to do, more than usual, is to be inquisitive."

I went several different times, and spent a few days in each in making the most careful investigation possible, as the others mentioned did, and reported accordingly to Mr. Gridley. We gave the work particular care and attention, because every one of us knew that the situation in Chicago was a matter of great concern, and that, without the management of some capable man to prevent it, it could easily be turned in the interest of Seward, which Mr. Weed intended to do, knowing the situation as well as any of us.

During this time Mr. Gridley made careful investigations for himself as well. The work for Lincoln went on in the most persevering way, with horse and man strapped and mounted for action, and ready, without a string loose or a bridle down. Before the Republican Convention met and marked the dial of our swift-speeding little planet in its progress, and before all were counted and named to lead, ours, too, had entered the conflict of the century with the force of a new battle for freedom in all our hearts.

There was a crashing and sundering in the breaking-up and dissolving of the old parties that had led in so many famous triumphs, in which young men had grown gray and worn and feeble, and had died in its service. Peace had departed from the great Democratic party. It was separating in arming factions, while sorrow and alarm prevailed throughout the land. There was little hope of returning peace without war; and the people of the Nation were entering the greatest distress that had come upon us since the days of the Revolution.

On October 16, 1859, John Brown, of Ossawatomie, one of the suffering victims of the pro-slavery invasion of Kansas, made a furious assault on the United States arsenal and small military station at Harper's Ferry, Va. His force, white and colored, all counted, without the promise of a single auxiliary, was twenty-two men, armed with pikes.

It was a revolt or persecuted people's insurrection of such limited numbers and powers, and so destitute of support, that it could have been suppressed and ended without spreading further alarm in any one day in any ordinary county or town of five thousand people in any of the free States. It was promptly suppressed with much more noise and parade than if it had been a real approaching danger. Colonel Robert E. Lee had a detachment of United States troops and marines stationed at Washington, to which Governor Wise added "the whole power of the State of Virginia," then some twelve hundred militia in imposing array. This combined force of fifteen hundred captured the four times wounded old man and his three wounded followers.

This misguided man's assault raised all of pro-slaverydom in terror and alarm, in dread of the spread of this suppressed outbreak of an old man's wrath, whose property had been burned or stolen and his children hunted and slain. If slavery had been what they claimed it, right and just, forty such invasions and foolish adventures would have created no more than local alarm; but their hearts proved the falsity of their pretensions. The entire South, slaveholding or not, was stricken with terror—needlessly so; for the blacks were never a bloodthirsty people, but bore their burdens in servitude, and suffering patiently, returning faithful service and kindness under the hands that smote them.

The widespread terror proved that the system was a dangerous one, and tottering to decay, as well as unjust, as all humane-minded men had for centuries declared it to be. In place, however, of taking a temperate and sensible view of it, and settling on some means for the gradual extinction of so bad a system as their conduct and suggestive fears abundantly established, the slave-leaders at once, although they knew better, accused every anti-slavery person in the country of complicity or willingness to aid in and undertake such rash and mad-minded insurrections. In truth, there were no other twenty-two people anywhere known who could have been persuaded or driven into such a foolhardy performance.

.The sum of all their philosophies was like saying to us: You anti-slavery people are responsible. You are Abolitionists, therefore insurrectionists, disunionists, and invaders, because we know it and say so. You are in favor of slave insurrections and the murder of our families. We know it because you are opposed to slavery, and we will not in the future trust Douglas Democrats more than black Republicans, for you are all alike. This was the substance of their reasoning after this raid, in which no slave was liberated, and no slaveholder or his family injured. This folly of speech was thundered against all of the free State people, even those who had been mild and timid enough to do no more than believe that the spread of slavery should be restricted. These and all of us were accused of guilt and connivance in all manner of crime, with no better reasons for it than their unsupported accusations.

The conspiring leaders wrought the Southern people into a whirlwind of fury, rashness, inconsiderate action, and persecution of all anti-slavery people over this poor man's maddened retaliation. They made it one of their strongest pleas for war, and used it as the occasion to drive countless thousands of poor, impoverished, and degraded white men, made so by their caste-breeding system, into it. These filled the ranks, the rifle-pits, the trenches, the ditches, and the graves of these free Americans fighting for slavery and a king. The old man and his two survivors were executed. The law was satisfied. He paid a terrible penalty for doing what had been done to him and his. When the test of

loyalty to the Government came, of the two prominent leaders, who enforced the law without mercy or delay, and executed the three survivors, the remnant of the twenty-two
men, who were fighting back as they had been fought, one
of them, who had been the Nation's protégé—Robert E.
Lee—joined his country's enemies, while the other—Governor Wise—delayed his going for "a convenient season."

As time rolled on, through the winter of 1859 and the
spring of 1860, when the National Democratic Convention
was to assemble to nominate candidates for President and
Vice-President, the Northern and Southern factions of the
already broken party were wrought up to their most positive
and unshaken antagonism short of blows. The free Democracy, following Douglas, was strong and inflexible, and
would not yield another inch to slavery. They had conceded many and many times, until certain defeat threatened them and the contest seemed close and doubtful. The
party was going to pieces, although it held in its ranks thousands of capable, brave men and patriots, true and unflinching, who had faced and fought in many a contest, and
weathered many a political storm, but it had never met
any crisis like this. States that had been reliably Democratic for more than a generation were lost or losing themselves to the rising new party. All of New England had
gone. Pennsylvania, too, one of the stanch and most reliable, while its faithless Democratic son was President had
gone by so many thousands that it was irrevocable. Illinois, which had never been shaken before, and Indiana, almost as reliable, were even then in doubt, gone, perhaps,
where, with a single additional move to advance or extend
slavery, other thousands were ready to leave the party.
They had grown up in it and believed in it all their lives.

While in this condition of things, the South seemed more
clamorous and demanding than ever. Thousands of patriotic Democrats, reared in the principles of the party, stood

ready to leave it, not because of its Democracy, as some cried, but for the lack of it. The Southern leaders had long and persistently denounced all kinds of anti-slavery people as Abolitionists and, therefore, disunionists. This embraced all, from those like the independent Democrat, David Wilmot, whose desire was only to exclude slavery north of "thirty-six thirty," to Brown and his men, who were willing to destroy and divide the Nation. This was no more than the ordinary scheme of men in disreputable and wicked plans making a loud noise in order to distract attention while they executed them. The strange part of it was that it deluded many otherwise well-meaning people, and formed the foundation for the abusive policy of many newspapers in the free States. The entire Democratic press, what was left of the old Whig newspapers, and many of the slavery-poisoned leaders in both of these parties, denounced the Republican as a disunion party for no better reason than its opposition to the extension of slavery.

This was done for no better reason than the determined and successful opposition of Douglas Democrats to the forcible extension of slavery attempted against an unwilling people. But the unjustly-accused faction of Douglas Democrats of 1860, for supposed party advantages, had repeatedly made the same charge against the Republican party; but it did n't go down that time without a fight. Hence the disputes long before the assembling of the Charleston Convention presaged a phenomenal tumult, with a settlement of cartels for the conflict, rather than a harmonious patriotic body of Americans agreeing on men and measures for success.

It was the plan of Jefferson Davis to put some stalwart advocate of the advancing despotism ahead, when changes or increased activity appeared necessary, as related in the debate, where the extreme ground was taken by Senators Brown, Mason, and Benjamin. In addition to the debate carried on incessantly in the Congress of 1859-60, one of the most hot-headed and fiery-tempered of all these Southern conspirators—W. L. Yancey, of Alabama—was thrust forward like a thunderstorm by Davis, to arouse the Southern people for war. Yancey was a strong, vigorous man physically, popular among the Southern people, had pleasant address, and the furious temper to win the applause of a maddened crowd. He had a good voice, and was tireless, persevering, and ambitious, so ardent in the cause of the South that he declared that "the slave States should have the power to reopen the African slave-trade as they desire."

This strong-limbed enthusiast traveled all over the South, especially the cotton States, during the winter and spring prior to the Convention, teaching and arousing the people with the most inflammable sort of talk in the work of Southern independence, separation, and a new nation, founded on the asserted right of slave-labor. With scarcely an attempt at concealment, he industriously taught this organizing treason for months. Thus, for the first time in the history and progress of their system of slavery, he openly and candidly declared it their settled and determined purpose to separate in the event of their defeat at Charleston, which they expected and were getting ready for. He attended Conventions, Legislatures, councils, conferences, and meetings all over their States, and was so successful in the propaganda that it became the settled purpose of the Southern people. Persuasion, reason, and argument were as useless against it as the king's order to stop the incoming tide. He helped with all his energy, fiery zeal, and intemperate madness the chief conspirators in council, and Davis as chief plotter and despot, when, in this furious hatching of treason, they lashed the excitable and courageous Southern people into war.

In his speech before the Alabama Convention, in January, 1860, this tongue-fighting Yancey said: "If we are to get the benefit of the Democratic party in this contest, it is necessary to make the contention in its Charleston Convention. In that Convention Douglas and his adherents will press his doctrines to a conclusion. If the States' Rights men keep out of that Convention, that decision must evidently be against the South, and either in direct favor of the Douglas doctrine or an indorsement of the Cincinnati platform, under which Douglas claims shelter for his principles.

"The States' Rights men should present, in that Convention, their demands for a decision, and they will obtain indorsement of their demands or a denial of these demands. If indorsed, we shall have a greater hope of triumph within the Union. If denied, in my opinion, the States' Rights wing should secede from the Convention and appeal to the whole people of the South, without distinction of parties, and organize another Convention on the basis of their principles, and go into the election with a candidate nominated by it, as a grand Constitutional party.

"But in the Presidential contest a black Republican may be elected. If this dire event should happen, in my opinion, the only hope of safety for the South is in a withdrawal from the Union before he shall be inaugurated—before the sword and the treasury of the Federal Government shall be placed in the keeping of that party. I would suggest that the several State Legislatures should, by law, require the governors, when it shall be made manifest that the 'black Republican' candidate for the Presidency shall receive a majority of the Electoral vote, to call a Convention of the people of the States to assemble in time to provide for their safety before the 4th of March, 1861.

"If, however, a black Republican should not be elected, then, in pursuance of making this contest within the Union. we should initiate measures in Congress which should lead to the repeal of all the unconstitutional acts against slavery. If we should fail to obtain so just a system of legislation, then the South should seek her independence out of the Union."

This was the culminating declaration and test of fealty to the Constitution, according to the statesmanship of the men who had made such pretentious devotion and undeviating professions of loyalty in its support. It meant obedience just so long as they could remain in power and control the Government; but if the Republicans should legally elect the President, their treason was prepared for and complete even as to the time when the governors should call Conventions and launch their States into rebellion. Of this infamous, bloody purpose and its progress and daily acts of plotting insurrectionists for more than twelve months, Buchanan's Administration had no end of guilty knowledge.

In October, 1859, Senator Douglas, in a reply to Jere Black, Buchanan's Attorney-General and general apologist for slavery, very clearly stated the belief of the free Democracy as against the above Southern States' Rights faction and their purposes of treason and disunion, saying: "We will suppose it true that I am a Presidential aspirant. Does that justify a combination by a host of other Presidential aspirants, each of whom may imagine that his success depends upon my destruction, and the preaching a crusade against me for boldly avowing now the same principles to which they and I were pledged at the last Presidential election? Is this a sufficient excuse for devising a new test of political orthodoxy? I prefer the position of senator or that of a private citizen, where I would be at liberty to defend and maintain the well-defined principles of the Democratic party, to accepting a Presidential nomination upon a platform incompatible with the principle of self-government in the Territories or the reserved rights of the States, or the perpetuity of the Union under the Constitution."

On Monday, April 25, 1860, the irreconcilable assemblage of Democratic delegates met in Charleston, South

Carolina, to make effort in some way to reach an adjustment of the contentions between the factions, but they were no more than representatives with limited powers as to future agreement on slavery; and the free State delegates were regarded as being only messengers from their States, to declare that no further encroachments of slavery upon free territory would be permitted.

Since 1820 the slaveholding States had been demanding more drastic legislation for the extension and protection of their system, claiming, at the same time, the possession of an indefinable resource of power—that of States' rights. They held it to be the reserved right of any State to secede from the Union at its discretion, and in any disagreement with the Federal Government the aggrieved State could retire. This false and pernicious doctrine was equivalent to a declaration of State supremacy. It was an incompatible and practically impossible relation of National and State Government; still it had been so continuously and persistently taught and held to by Calhoun, Davis, and hundreds of their leaders, that the Southern people, almost to a man, affected and affirmed their belief in it.

However, the falsity and incongruity of the doctrine must have been known to informed men; for, when brought to the practical test of a State law in conflict with the Fugitive-slave Law, these same States' Rights projectors held that the State law was void. Hence, when forced to conclusions, the pro-slavery States' Rights doctrine in the support and protection of slavery was sound and Constitutional; but in all disputes or contentions on the subject of slavery or the rendition of fugitives a State law would not be considered and had no binding force whatever.

From the beginning of the century no restriction or obstacle had been put in the way of slavery or its extension by Congress or any President's Administration, or any court of the United States, unless the so-called "Missouri Compromise" should be so held. Under it Congressional interference made Missouri a slave State, without which and the bullying threats of the slave-leaders it would have been a free State as certainly as Illinois. In proof of this there never was a time afterward that the State would not have abolished slavery at an honest election.

In the work of shaping and preparing beforehand what should and what should not be done, the conspirators had everything in their own hands. The Democratic organization, officers, committees, secretaries, clerks, and servants were all of their own appointing and ready at call to do their will. There were seventeen free and fifteen slave States. By the liberal use and distribution of patronage a few pro-slavery or anti-Douglas delegates had been elected in some of the free States. In addition to these, Ex-Senator Gwin, of California, spent time and liberal sums of money, whereby, in his zealous work, he manipulated the party organizations of California and Oregon, and held them under personal control in the pro-slavery interests. This included committees and delegates, who were under his bidding and direction and as faithful to•slavery as though from Virginia, which State was Gwin's actual residence.

This gave the pro-slavery faction entire control of seventeen States, against fifteen for the Douglas Democrats. Under party precedents and usages the Southern faction secured control of the assembling Convention, its temporary and permanent organization, and all the committees. The rule of forming these in all such bodies is to take one from each State for all the important committees, and follow in the same ratio throughout. This gave them the naming of all the officers of the Convention, as this was agreed to by committees. The only means available to the Douglas Democrats against this plan would have been to make a contest against the committee nominees on the floor of the Convention, for which they had a majority of delegates, had they so determined; but they more wisely concluded to let the plan and personnel of organization prevail, and to make their contest openly, without evasion or concealment, on the principles involved and in the nomination of candidates for President and Vice-President.

This they well understood had many disadvantages for them; but, on the other hand, a contest over the organization might bring in personal matters, or confuse the real issue in some kind of misconstruction, and give the slave-leaders a pretext other than the real one for carrying out their long-threatened separation and the willful division of the party. A fair discussion, consideration, and vote on the principles would give no such opportunity.

Caleb Cushing, who, by the favor and patronage of the Buchanan Administration, had been slipped in as a pro-slavery delegate from Massachusetts—a State where it was understood that the only men holding such belief were in present or prospective employment of the Administration, was elected presiding officer of the Convention. Ordinarily this would have been an important advantage to the Southern leaders, and would have been so then, if the questions in controversy could have been settled by partial rulings, the work and creation of committees, and personal influences; but the real dispute, after some tedious delays, turned into a stubborn fight on irreconcilable ideas, in which the presiding officer had as little to do as several prominent delegates.

After seven weary days' constant wrangle, Cushing realized that he had less power or reputation than the able leaders of the free Democracy. However, he used all the advantages of his place and position in the interest of those that elected him; and he did it as well as if he had been one of them. This accomplished nothing more than delay, and the result was not different from what it would have been if the Douglas Democrats had been given control of the Convention from the beginning. They were entitled to it, having a majority of twenty-seven on every test vote.

Mr. Cushing was then in the zenith of his kaleidoscopic career, one of the most mixed, vacillating, and changeable of all his class of prominent actors in our history. He was Attorney-General under President Pierce, when he served the slavery extensionists as well and as much to the detriment and loss of his own section as Jere Black was doing at the time in President Buchanan's Administration for his and the President's State.

The principal dispute was in the Committee on Platform and Resolutions until Thursday, when, late at night, the four days and nights disputing committeemen reached the desperate party-splitting conclusion to disagree and report separately their disagreements to the Convention. Thus the great party of Jefferson, Jackson, Benton, Marcy, Cass, and Douglas was wrecked under the dictatorship of Jefferson Davis and his followers, Benjamin, Stephens, Mason, Breckinridge, and others.

This was done before interference of any kind had been made with their domestic institutions, or a hand had been raised against it under law, and the party that had favored and tolerated their exactions so long, to the detriment and lasting injury of its most powerful element, its free State Democracy, was smitten almost to death in the house of its pretended friends and certainly its beneficiaries. It had been bravado, bluster, and threat for many years before this; but then, with no sufficient cause except their maddened love of power, those Southern leaders destroyed the power as far as their plotting heads and bloody hands could compass it.

In the discussion some of the more hopeful free State delegates pleaded with them not to enforce the undemocratic doctrine of slavery upon them. Through Mr. Yancey, the slave-drivers' orator, the free State delegates were inundated with a gushing and outpouring flood of sugar-and-cotton-plantation eloquence, reasoning, and logic for the subjugation of all inferior races. He declared to them in substance: "You have failed because you have not had the courage to defend and sustain slavery. You must no longer be making excuses or apologizing for its existence. You must defend it everywhere, not be conceding that it is wrong and unjust, but take up the defense of it, and be as zealous in it as you are in support of your own local institutions.

"When you do so, and have the boldness and courage to sustain your arguments as you should, you will regain your lost ground, and the States will return to the party when the beneficial and benign results of slavery will be conceded all over the land, as they are now from the Potomac and the Ohio to the Gulf, where scarcely a voice is raised against slavery where once there were thousands. This has been done through the wisdom, persevering courage, and ceaseless attention of our people, who have thus built up and sustained by general approval the best, most humane labor system possible for the Negro race."

This was the ultimatum of slavery in 1860, far ahead of what any one had expected ten years before. It was twenty years ahead of Nimmo Browne's expectations, who told Judge Douglas in 1845 "that they would overthrow him, drive him from the party in disgrace, if they could, and inaugurate war, as he believed and gathered from the progress of similar events in history;" or that the country "would be all slave or all free," as Lincoln verily believed and announced in 1858, when he hoped a peaceful fulfillment of his prediction in perhaps a hundred years; but in war or tumult he ventured no opinion.

These beliefs had been entertained by prudent men for several years; but in 1860 the slave conspirators were disrupting parties ahead of all calculations, and were getting ready for war in more furious progress every day, until they passed beyond even the leaders' control. The contest on the part of the free State Democracy was intelligently and manfully conducted. There were many capable and distinguished men who made the memorable fight for freedom at Charleston. There was no sulking; and not a delegate shirked or shunned 'his duty by missing a single vote. Senator Pugh and Representative Payne, of Ohio, replied, among others, to the demands of the Southern leaders. They had stood firm and unfaltering with Douglas in the work of disclosing and defeating the Lecompton atrocity.

Pugh replied to the turgid bombast of Yancey, in substance, as follows: "We spurn with honest indignation your degrading proposition that we are to teach the rightfulness of slavery to a free and independent Democracy, or that they shall cease to believe it an evil competing system of labor. We have done too much for it against our interests and the welfare of our people already. We will let it alone as an unavoidable and perhaps an incurable evil where it exists; but ask us no more. For one thing we thank God: that you are candid and outspoken and honest enough to make an open declaration of your belief, which should have been made, in honest dealing, ten, or even twenty years ago. You have now told the whole truth, and have boldly announced to the country the rapacious and increasing demand of your dominating slave system. You have led us, year by year and step by step, to defeat and disaster, and now, by more obnoxious demands, to certain and irretrievable ruin. Now, when your system has weakened and threatened us with destruction, you irritate us with new accusasations, with unfaithfulness in teaching the beauties and benefits of slavery, and mock us, saying that, if we will not do it, we must put our hands on our mouths, and bow down in the dust before you. I tell you, Southern gentlemen, as firmly and positively as you are trying to project your offensive doctrine into the creed of the Democratic party, that we will not do it. Come what may, we will be free to declare our principles."

In such fervid impulses and independent moods the Convention worked and labored earnestly seven days and almost as many nights to be sure, on the part of the Douglas Democrats, that every honorable hope and means of settlement might be exhausted before making public declaration of the deplorable division of the party, that was really broken asunder on the defeat of the Lecompton Constitution, over two years before this.

On Friday, the 27th, the fifth day, the Committee on Resolutions reported that they could agree on formal recognition of the Cincinnati platform, and they advised: 1. The faithful execution of the Fugitive-slave Law; 2. The protection of naturalized citizens; 3. The construction of a Pacific Railroad; 4. The acquisition of the island of Cuba; but they regretted that upon the important topic of slavery in the Territories they could not agree.

The majority report, which was made so by the action of the California and Oregon delegates uniting with those of the slave States, was:

"*Resolved*, That the platform adopted at Cincinnati be affirmed, with the following additions:

"*Resolved*, That the Democracy of the United States hold these cardinal principles on the subject of slavery in the Territories: 1. That Congress has no power to abolish slavery in the Territories; 2. That the Territorial Legislature has no power to abolish slavery in any Territory, nor to prohibit the introduction of slaves therein, nor any power to exclude slavery therefrom, nor any power to destroy or impair the right of property in slaves by any legislation whatever.

"*Resolved*, That it is the duty of the Federal Government to protect, when necessary, the rights of persons and property on the high seas, in the Territories, or wherever else its Constitutional authority extends."

The minority report was:

"*Resolved*, That the Democracy of the Union, in Convention assembled, declare our affirmance of the resolutions unanimously adopted and declared as a platform of principles by the Democratic Convention at Cincinnati in the year 1856, believing that Democratic principles are unchangeable in their nature when applied to the same subject-matter; and we recommend as the only further resolution the following:

"*Resolved*, That all questions in regard to rights of property in States or Territories arising under the Constitution of the United States are judicial in their character, and the Democratic party is pledged to abide by and faithfully carry out such determination of these questions as has been, or may be, made by the Supreme Court of the United States."

The stormy debate continued throughout Friday and Saturday, the sixth day, when there were as many as fifty of these six hundred delegates and alternates talking at once, many times, and late at night. It ran along in this way regardless of Chairman Cushing's efforts to check or control it. When exhausted, tired, and worn out, he let the debate run about as the Convention liked, and listened, or shut it off by so much noise that no one could be heard. Cushing reached the stage where the honor and dignity and his desire to preside had all vanished, when he sought in vain for some Douglas Democrat to take his place. Finally late on Saturday both reports were recommitted. This was done in the last effort to calm the turbulent storm, and to give the slavery, or war, boasters the quiet of a few hours for rest and composure.

When the Convention reassembled on Monday, the 30th of April, its seventh working day, the noisy ones had recovered their voices, and the babel of tongues was renewed. At this stage of the angry dispute, when all hope of an agreement

had passed and the Southern leaders under Yancey were pro-
longing the sessions only to confuse the free State delegates,
Payne of Ohio made the motion to substitute the minority
report for the majority one. He. held the floor, and refused
further delay. The Southern men fought against it for
awhile; but the delegates were all tired out, the presiding
officer more than any of them. Payne kept the floor, and contended resolutely against all delays until his demand was
sustained; and the minority report, the one of the Douglas
Democracy, was adopted by the clear and distinct vote of
165 to 138, a majority of twenty-seven for it, with every
delegate voting in a Convention where they had wrangled
continuously night and day for a week, and so many were
ailing and sick.

This vote, rejecting the majority report, brought the
event which Yancey and his fiery hotspurs had repeatedly
declared, would cause them to leave the Convention. But
to the astonishment of every one, after its passage quiet prevailed as it had not done since the first roll-call. Yancey and
his contingent that sat together and acted as a unit under
him, appeared as if stunned and confounded. Nobody wanted
them to go at that stage, and all except themselves wondered
why they did not go, as they had so often threatened they
would.

At this moment in the dead calm of the stormtossed
assemblage, Benjamin F. Butler, of Massachusetts, the same
who was on more sides of every political question and party
than any other American citizen ever was, except Cushing,
took advantage of the moment's calm before the approaching
storm to move the adoption of the Cincinnati platform without change. This was done without debate. The effect of
this did not change anything, as the platform of the minority
report included it, and nothing of the minority report was
changed or rescinded by the adoption of Butler's resolution,
which in effect readopted it.

This move of Butler's was made by the Northern pro-slavery delegates, in the interest of sustaining Buchanan's Administration, and as a sort of peace offering on their part. They were there, some twenty or more of them, under the direction of Butler and Cushing, and while they were super-serviceable in the cause of slavery, as far as they could be, they were not going to walk out with Yancey and his mad-caps of the Gulf States.

Hence they concluded to take the time and the opportunity by the forelock, readopt the old platform, nominate some one, any one, for they could not miss it much on any-body, as a weaker character than Buchanan could not have been found again; perhaps they might even have renominated and repainted the old figure of a man, so that he could last through another campaign as he had lasted so unexpectedly in 1856.

Butler was full of resources, and shifty in the worst turmoil and confusion of men. Cushing was as cunning as Butler was adroit, and always ready. They conjured but never disclosed its object in that mêlée and uproar of men. They evidently believed that the bringing out of "Old Buck" for another four years might take as a diversion; at least they thought the effort was worth trying, and they tried it, with no perceptible result.

Butler's resolution carried without debate, having two hundred and thirty-seven against sixty-five votes. Instead of pacifying and stilling the angry tempest that had lashed and kept them in the seven days' fury, Yancey and his men took this at once as their long-threatened opportunity, raised the red flag of rebellion, and with the delegates from Alabama, Mississippi, Louisiana, South Carolina, Florida, Texas, and Arkansas, walked out of the Convention, divided the party that had done nothing but favor and protect them for over thirty years, and now, when it would not, and could not, serve them and their cursed system any longer, they turned in their wrath, and gnashing their teeth in defiance, divided it. Henceforward they planned the Nation's destruction.

After the delegates of the seven cotton States seceded, Mr. Douglas could have been almost unanimously nominated by the remaining two-thirds or more of the delegates. At least he could have been by a two-thirds' vote, but the long-standing traditional rule requiring this was generously held to include two-thirds of all the delegates elected, even those who voluntarily surrendered their rights. This would have required two hundred and two of the three hundred and three votes. The Convention continued in session until the third of May. Douglas's vote was 152.

Cushing held his place as chairman, and with the Administration Democrats he still held control of all the offices and committees, and kept up uninterrupted, friendly relations with Yancey and his seceders. Although the Douglas Democrats had a large working majority, Cushing's control kept them at a decided disadvantage. They cast several hundred ballots with no progress and no result, except to emphasize the determined revolt against the Southern leaders. On the third of May, the tenth day, they adjourned to meet in Baltimore, June 18th.

CHAPTER XXXIX.

THE withdrawal of Yancey and his excited delegates did not remove them from participation and effect upon the doings of the Convention, as much as their changed relation required. They were still counted as members on every roll-call and on all the vital concerns, in the nomination of candidates and the conduct of business. They remained in the town, and were in full consultation with Cushing, Buchanan's postmasters, and other favored officeholders. By Cushing's ruling and counting absent members, the seceders were still in the way as much as ever; and, to the full extent of their opportunities, they delayed action by this maneuvering as effectually as before the secession. They had not gone out on an honest separation and disagreement, to leave the regular body free to reach harmonious conclusions, but retired with their faction on a threat. They remained on the field, in full sympathy and collusion with those in control of the Convention. They expected to compass the complete overthrow of Douglas, disperse his delegates, and proceed to the suppression of his free State Democracy.

On leaving, the seceders made some temporary kind of organization, and adjourned to meet in Richmond the following month; but remained in Charleston, to be near Mr. Cushing and to advise with him. Both were within easy reach and under the chief control of Jefferson Davis at Washington. In the emergency the Douglas Democrats should have reorganized the Convention at once; but like most of the fairminded free State people, they yielded everything of that kind, in hope of possible settlement, rather than believe in or resort to warlike preparations, as these seceders were busy doing at the time. Following their withdrawal, so as to harass the regular Convention in every possible way, when they met in Richmond they adjourned again to meet in Baltimore, on the 18th of June, the time and place to which the regular Convention adjourned.

On this bursting up at Charleston the contest was transferred to the United States Senate for the time, where Jefferson Davis and his supporting conspirators renewed the dispute in the form of resolutions for discussion. The two principal ones declared "That neither Congress nor a Territorial Legislature, whether by direct legislation or that of indirect and unfriendly character, possesses power to annul or impair the constitutional right of any citizen to take his slave property into the common Territories, and there hold and enjoy the same while the Territorial conditions remain." And "That if experience should at any time prove that the Judiciary and Executive authority do not possess means to insure adequate protection to constitutional rights in a Territory, and if the Territorial Government shall fail or refuse to provide the necessary remedies for that purpose, it will be the duty of Congress to supply such deficiency."

These declaratory resolutions had been introduced the previous February, where they were at hand in the event that the Convention at Charleston should not adopt the slave-leaders' creed. They were resuscitated soon afterward, declared the doctrine of the Democratic party as stated by the Senate, passed and promulgated, ex-cathedra, as the edict, rule, and inviolable doctrine of the Southern conspiracy.

Senator Douglas promptly objected to their passage, both as to the matters contained as virtually the same as the resolutions so recently rejected by the National Convention of the party; and because of the impropriety and reversal of the usages and precedents of the Democratic party, and so far of all our parties, holding it to be usurpation and arrogant assumption of power for the Senate, the House of Representatives, or an Administration, to formulate or declare what should, or should not, be the doctrines and creed of any body or organization of the people.

Douglas held that under our free system these bodies were the agencies, and for the time the servants of the people, who should be in spirit and act representative, and nothing else; that especially they should not return to the policy of the asserted prerogative of tyrants, kings, and despots, to declare what should be the social, religious, or political beliefs of the people. Proceeding, he disclosed the disunionist and treasonable plot of the Southern leaders, as shown in the management and conduct of public business in the Senate by the Administration, over which they held complete control, and in their desperate attempt to force their creed upon the National Democracy; the disruption and secession of Yancey and his fellow-seceders, who were in full accord with the rule or ruin policy of the conspirators and these Senate resolutions. He showed that this cabal and governing body in the slavery propaganda had failed, after uninterrupted opportunities, to force their belief on the party. They then pronounced and declared, through the medium of an act or resolutions of the Senate, their intention to put in force and continue this usurpation, where they would, if possible, divide or destroy any party, or the Union itself, whenever their success made it necessary.

Douglas was then in full exercise of all his intellectual powers. The severe labors of his campaigns had seriously exhausted him and reduced the energy of his younger days; but he was still the great leader and the full equal in debate of any man in the Senate. The dragon of the slave-power had been fierce on his path for years. Now after his re-election to the Senate, and their crushing defeat at Charleston, the arch-conspirator Davis renewed the contest against him in the Senate, that he might formally lay down the law

of the slave-code to his followers, time-servers, and mercenaries, engage and, if possible, entangle Douglas to his detriment, and achieve his possible overthrow before the meeting
at Baltimore.

This must not be regarded as less than a very serious
assault on Douglas, for they had been invariably successful
in their overthrow of Northern and anti-slavery Democratic
leaders, even those of the mildest and most moderate inclinations against slavery. They had successively overthrown
every leader in the Democratic party who would not do their
bidding from the time of Jackson, whom they left alone
and unnoticed from his retirement to the hermitage in 1837
to his death in 1845. This they did, for the good reason that
he was a patriot who loved the Union, whose enemies they
were, and they realized his power to strike and save.

They threw Van Buren aside, and stood willing and impartial observers when he reaped his revenge and compassed
the defeat of Cass, for neither of these could serve them further. They would never take up Clay, for they never fully
trusted him. His long life was full of the ambition to be
President, and his compromising measures were always full
up to the limit that the free States would bear; but he was
never a plotter, and of better mold than to serve slavery more
than his country, or to nourish treason and help build a slave
empire, as the alternative of passing power and the progress
of free institutions.

Webster was never seriously entertained by them as a
candidate for the Presidency. His insatiable ambition to be
President lured him to destruction, and he tarnished the fame
of one who had earned a place among the loved and honored
few whom you can run over in memory and count on your
fingers. They cast Franklin Pierce aside indifferently, and
that elegant and sprightly gentleman went immediately from
the Presidency into oblivion. William L. Marcy, who saved
them from the obloquy of continuing the border war and

forcing slavery into Kansas, who had qualifications for statesmanship in a real Democracy, was never so much as inquired
for after the exit and obscuration of Pierce. Fillmore, who
had willingly done what Zachary Taylor, President and slaveholder, would not do for them—approved the whole mess of
slavery-saving, slavery-protecting, and slavery-catching measures, known as the compromises of 1850—was laughed down
as a harmless diversion, and used as a foil to save Buchanan
and defeat Fremont; after which Fillmore was never heard of.

Of Benton, we have written so fully that short mention
of the great leader and the utter degradation they attempted
to put on him, will suffice. He was a man who would not
serve the slave-power to the injury and ruin of his country.
With much of the character and integrity of Jackson, with
his strong, rugged sense and courage, he neither flinched nor
shook before them, from Calhoun to Davis. After thirty
years of service in the Senate, and two in the House of Representatives, he was beaten and cast into the mire of defeat.

"Old Sam Houston" was another patriot whom they
would not trust. He was a captain and true soldier, who
defeated Santa Ana with a few Americans at San Jacinto;
won a nation in war and made it a Republic; fashioned it
in full harmony, and brought it to us the richest gift of land
and treasure of the century. He had been citizen, soldier,
general, and President of Texas, and after its cession a senator
of the United States. In his ripened age and experience he
was made governor of his State, that had been a nation.
He was always a plain man of the people. He was kind,
simple, gracious, and considerate to the weak and helpless,
and no less a hero, with the strength and courage of an
American, to every foeman and oppressor.

He was a wise man and a statesman. He had led men in
the conduct of public affairs, and was able to be again, what
he had been, a President, who would seek the welfare of
his people. With him as candidate of the undivided party in

1860, the Democracy would have been sure of victory; but slaveholder as he was, though never an unkind one, they cast him off, and would have none of him. He braved the conspiracy in their highest purpose, and witnessed their crushing defeat. He stood by and sustained Douglas, and voted with him against Lecompton. He believed in the strongest union of States and the greater, stronger Republic, which he labored, served, and fought for. In matured experience and satisfied ambition, he was earnestly, outspokenly against its dismemberment. The old man, although he had brought their greatest achievement, was cast aside like all before him.

The gallant, brave, and generous-hearted David Broderick, of California, got in their way, and was very deliberately slain. He was talented, and a promising leader in the great and enterprising State. He was the hope of a better Democracy and a higher manhood in our vast and newest region of untold and unmeasured resources. He had the strength of a leader who could not be beaten. He was in the way of the policy of the cabal to hold the Pacific States for the balance of power, as far as such could be, as we have seen in the Charleston Convention. To hold these, Broderick had to be got rid of and overthrown, for Gwin and his shallow, perishable imitations were no more in the way of a leader like Broderick, than the white frost is in the way of the melting sunshine. With Broderick there successful, as he was sure to be without unforeseen happenings, the Pacific States' and slave States' coalition would snap asunder like a rotten hawser in a storm at sea; hence an inferior scullion and a lower menial than we have ever written of, hounded, followed, and challenged him until he fought, as he thought, a duel with one Terry, who had been practicing and preparing for it for months. But it was not a fair fight, and Broderick was slain, the victim of the conspirators' demoniac wrath and wicked ambition. Their responsibility for it was, of course, denied, and who and how many were implicated none but

God and this later Cain ever knew or told. But the blood-stained Terry was and remained a member in full sympathy and unimpaired standing with the slavery faction of his party. Every one of them sustained this human wretch, favored and upheld him to the day of his own killing by a deputy marshal, who was compelled to do it or be killed himself in making his arrest. The motive for the removal of Broderick was political power, of which the Southern leaders of the slave conspiracy were the beneficiaries.

We have traced some of the leaders of the Democratic party whom the slavery leaders deposed, laid aside, overthrew, degraded, and killed. There were hundreds of intelligent strong men who shared the same fate as these. · With all the powers of the Nation, except the House of Representatives, at their call and under complete control, they lost the forensic battle at Charleston. Victory came not to them as they desired. They were chagrined at their defeat, and unsatisfied with it; hence in continuation, the chief conspirator, Davis, reopened the ugly dispute in the Senate.

The defeat of the Southern leaders at Charleston was an event in our history, in its consequences upon the Nation, our institutions, and its relations to the rapidly-approaching conflict, that has been underestimated and too often considered a mere party defeat or a factional division. On the contrary, it was the turning of the tide. It was the battle of dispute, in which the slavery cause met irrecoverable defeat. The pro-slavery forces were under absolute control. The fight for the extension of slavery had been made and lost, under an Administration that was lenient and able to serve their system more than ever could be expected again, unless the National Democracy could be committed to the doctrine that slavery existed in the Territories by constitutional right.

In this condition their contention for slavery occupation and protection under the Constitution, as they put it, was a vital one. If slavery extension was to depend on its submission to the people of the Territories at honest elections under the squatter-sovereignty doctrine of the Cincinnati platform of 1856, it meant certain defeat of extension, and exclusion from most, if not all, of the Territories; the restriction of political power by reason of the rapid increase in Western population and increase in the number of free States to be admitted; the restriction of power that would soon be followed by free State control of the Nation; the curtailing, modifying, and repealing of obnoxious slave-codes, and the institution of more humane rules and administration; under all of which slavery would be made subject and under control of law.

At Charleston the Southern leaders set the limit of their future action and observance of the principles and policy of the party, in presenting their unqualified demand to hold slaves by right of constitutional law in any Territory. On this demand the aggressive, overshadowing slave-power of the party hung their fate, well-being, and existence. To sober men of that day it came as the slave-leaders' declaration of independence, on the result of which depended peace or war. In truth they laid it down as their ultimatum, and expected concession of some kind, as the past history of parties and their dealings with them justified them in doing. No party with which they had acted up to this time ever made unqualified denial of their demands. Some concession or compromise had always been reached; but in this ultimatum they asked a pronouncement of belief so repugnant to the people of the free States, in the surrender of all the Territories to slavery, that submission to it would have resulted in the creation of an unrestricted slave Nation, or the certain defeat of the Democratic party in every free State.

In this consideration of their demands, denial meant no less than a divided country as well as a divided party, for they could have no hope of success without the power to enforce their slave-code in one or both of them. Hence their defeat and withdrawal from the Convention was no less than a conditional declaration of war. Certainly it was a sufficiently public and declared danger, to have put any patriotic Administration in condition, where ample means were at hand, to protect and defend all public property, and instantly to suppress any effort of these leaders to arouse or encourage disorder or insurrection, which they were engaged in by their own acts and declarations. Instead of this, not a hand was raised nor a single preparation made to save the threatened Nation. On the contrary, these insurrectionists were given unmolested opportunity to take as they desired, arms, ammunition, navy-yards, ships and shipping, and the forts belonging to the Nation in almost every harbor in the Southern States.

The pending and momentous consideration at Charleston was, "Would the loyal Democrats of the free States yield, and give up or disorganize in the face of the demands of these men who were threatening the life of the country and its free institutions?" There were misgivings all over the land, because so many had yielded and so much had been done before for conciliation. But these Democrats of the free States stood together without a break, enough of them, who could not be intimidated, threatened, or bullied, who stood firmly where they would concede no more. They stood there, firm as the everlasting rocks, for their principles and their leader, whom they held the equal of any man in capacity and love of country.

These delegates did not yield. Being brave and patriotic as any equal body of men ever assembled in our land, they reaffirmed the "Squatter-sovereignty" doctrine by the re-adoption of the Cincinnati platform. They defeated the slavery-spreading conspirators, with so many disadavantages against them, by a majority of twenty-seven, with every delegate present and voting. This was equivalent notice to the rash conspirators, there plotting and attempting their treason, that the people of the free States had reached their limit, and that their treasonable plot to destroy their party and the Union would be met by a more stubborn and determined purpose to save it.

In that body of delegates from the free States there were many brave men and coming leaders in the great struggle and conflict for freedom, who led in the thickest of every combat, as they did in this parliamentary defeat. Among them were Senator Pugh, Representatives Payne and Cox of Ohio, McDonald and Hendricks from Indiana, Stuart from Michigan; Dodge, Samuels, and Jones from Iowa; John B. Henderson, W. P. Hall, James Craig, and Barton Able from Missouri; John A. Logan, William Richardson, John A. McClernand, Robinson, Morrison, and Moulton from Illinois; with over a hundred more as brave and capable and as heroic men as ever sat in any Convention or labored in any contest for the people.

Much is due those men for the saving of the Union and the arrest of slavery; but we can only mention the event and the high character of their services. They were men of courage, with sensible and moral fitness for the supreme duty of the hour. They soberly and firmly declared to the Southern conspirators, and their highly-wrought-up, half-informed, and infuriated followers, that if they were in earnest in what they said, that they would either extend slavery peaceably or go to war for it, they would get all the war they sought, and until they were utterly defeated; for there were enough independent Union men, who sustained them, to save it in peace, or in the dreadful alternative of war, if they forced it.

Not any single party deserved all the credit, counting all their zealous and faithful work in the cause of the Union, nor did any one Convention so deserve; for there were thousands of country-loving, devoted people in all our parties doing all they could in service and sacrifice to save the Union.

Among them all there was no single Convention anywhere that stood so strong in the right, at the right time, or made a better defense in their effective work, than the free State Democrats did at Charleston. It took the help of every one who would lend his voice or his hand, where every one was necessary. These delegates were often censured and berated for not doing more, because they did not make a sufficiently definite platform of principles; but in truth they did all that was possible under the circumstances. When the angry dispute sagged down to its bottom, there were just two sides to it. On one side were those who were against the Union and for slavery; on the other side were those who were for the Union and more free territory and more and stronger free men. These same men who were sometimes blamed for incompleteness were those who squarely took and held their ground on the first open division for and against the Union. They were faithful then, and so remained in its service to the end.

When Senator Davis called up the Senate resolutions as declaratory of the Southern slave-power, and what was to be accepted as the same for the party or Nation, if the South was to remain in the Union, he knew that his faction had full control over a majority in the Senate, and could pass whatever their slavery *régime* dictated. He confidently assumed direction of the discussion and progress of the resolutions with the impudent bravado, domineering pretension, and the lordly slave-leaders' style that prevailed all over the South and in Congress, known as "plantation manners." In his arrogance he did not appear to realize that Senator Douglas would accept his contest, and lead him to such an overwhelming defeat in the debate as he and his conspirators had not so far encountered or expected. Davis, with the air of the dictator he really was in his coterie, laid down his commands in these resolutions, that they might be adopted at the Baltimore reassembling. In support of the resolutions Davis said: "And, sir, when we declare our tenacious adherence to the Union, it is the Union of the Constitution. If the compact between the States is to be trampled into the dust; if anarchy is to be substituted for the usurpation which threatened the Government at an earlier period; if the Union is to become powerless for the purposes for which it was established, and we are vainly to appeal to it for protection—then, sir, conscious of our course and self-reliant within ourselves, we look beyond the confines of the Union for the maintenance of our rights."

This was all there ever was of the secession doctrine, boldly declared, without limit or qualification. If those slaveholding barons and aristocrats could not get what they wanted in the Union, and have full control of it, they were going to leave.

As related, Senator Douglas was in full command of his intellectual and reasoning powers. His high capacities and long experience, that made him a formidable antagonist on any subject, kept him ready at hand in this life battle of patriotism for a coherent and undivided Union. He was a foeman that a stronger and better-equipped man than Davis would have shrunk from and evaded, if it could have been. But Yancey, having executed the threat of the dictator, with the same ambition rising in himself, and the whole Southern country aroused and answering for war, Davis had to place himself in the lead of the pro-slavery revolt if he was to continue the real leader, which he had assumed to be. This much, of necessity; he was compelled to launch the dispute again in the Senate, regardless of whom he should meet, or its consequences.

He had, too, a personal reason of great significance for forcing the contest at the time. Although he was dictator by consent, his position was held by a slight tenure, that any untoward difficulty or unseen breaker might have capsized in a moment. There were three or four as evil and

ambitious spirits serving with him in the Senate who would
have been glad enough for opportunity to overthrow him
any day, which they would have done, if the four could
have agreed on which one of them should be his successor.
There were Benjamin, Mason, Breckinridge, Slidell, Soule,
and Stephens, all of whom considered themselves fitted
for the place, with the daring and reckless Toombs,
who wanted to be so consideed. All these were prying in
and watching to see what Davis was going to do after his
unquestioned defeat at Charleston, when, in the midst of
these dilemmas, here came the shooting star, the plunger
Yancey, the advance slavery crusader at Charleston, who,
without some authoritative exercise of leadership, being
more ambitious and daring than any of them, stood ready
to take control and command of secession and all there
was in it, unless Davis sprang to the issue.

With these complications and the defeated and deplorable conditions of the movement, that required constant
progress, like any conspiracy, on seeing the defeat at Charleston, both to hold his leadership and sustain his desperate
cause, he forced the issue, and kept it moving for the
time in the Senate resolutions. They were not then ready
for the open work of the conspiracy that this hotspur Yancey
forced upon them; hence they assumed something of loyalty "to the Constitution." "The Union of the Constitution," or, to be plain, such an observance of a Constitution
as they and their pro-slavery court would construe.

Senator Douglas took up "the Constitution" and the contention, going over it in detail, deliberately, in a two-days'
argument against their resolutions. He took up the whole
subject in patient, careful detail and legal construction,
with such definiteness and exact knowledge of their plot
and all that was in it as to confound them. He charged
the conspiracy to secede, overthrow the power of the Nation, and divide it, to Davis and his followers, giving par-

ticulars in items and events, going back to 1856, when the governors of the slave States entered into collusion and correspondence with each other and their senators and representatives in Congress as to their best means of arming themselves and carrying out their plans in concert with each other. This correspondence revealed how they were to be prepared for timely and simultaneous action, how to get the best arms, have their old muskets remodeled into modern guns, with as many new and remodeled rifles placed in the forts and arsenals and other military stations in their States as possible, to be within reach of those conspiring governors, so that they would get a full equipment of arms in case of sudden need to arm their forming militia, and to have arms, accouterments, and equipments at the Government's disposal within reach at these various stations.

This treason was carried on to a concluding agreement forcibly to resist the inauguration of Fremont, if he had been elected; but as Buchanan was, fortunately for them, elected, and served the slave power as faithfully as any one of themselves could have done, the correspondence and agreements were held to be in abeyance, affording valuable preparations and experience as to the groundwork necessary in their movement, and the more practical result, that the Buchanan Administration remodeled the arms and distributed them and other supplies of the army and navy as the Southern governors' combination had agreed.

Douglas stated that, in 1858, after his re-election, the alarm was again sounded, as in 1856, and the South was again ordered to prepare for secession and ultimate war, as in their conduct at Charleston in the secession of Yancey. Also, in obedience to the orders of Davis, the chief leader of the conspiracy, Yancey, although leaving the Convention, remained in collusion with its chairman and officers, making every possible effort for its further division and disorganization. In the interim they were making preparations to reassemble with the regular Convention at Baltimore, where they would continue their work of disruption and dismemberment of the party. Their scheme and plot for secession and the division of the Union was then in progress, sustained by the Administration and the majority in the Senate in all its destroying power, to the utter neglect of public business. Important and necessary legislation for the welfare and protection of public property and the various wants in any well-conducted administration of government were all carelessly disregarded in the determined purpose to control or break up the Union.

All this Douglas recited, for which he arraigned them in strength of argument that was convincing and irresistible. He laid open before the American people the wicked and iniquitous plot to dissolve the Union long before most men would believe that such purpose was in existence. He directly charged Davis and his cabal in the Senate as the chief conspirators. These, he said, were the same plotters and caucus managers who have "read me out of the party so often as to show that it is an ineffectual dictum properly resented and exposed by the party to the Nation and people."

The disclosure and argument of Douglas, Davis did not attempt to contradict. He was outwitted, circumvented, and unmasked, and although he and his conspirators continued and pushed forward, even with increased zeal, all their schemes and plans that were possible because of the guilt or heedless connivance, or both, of Buchanan's do-nothing, treason-breeding Administration, it was never done afterward without the full knowledge of all men who cared to know their doings, as other current events.

Douglas, in the strength of his unanswerable charges against Davis and his coadjutors as chief conspirator in the gigantic crime against their country, brought Davis down from his lordly plantation style to that of a plain, pleading hypocrite when 'he reiterated the hollow professions of respect and confidence in the Union, which no one believed, and which his conduct and whole life belied. Davis said: "I have great confidence in the strength of the Union. Every now and then I hear that it is about to tumble to pieces, that somebody is going to introduce a new plank into the platform, and, if he does, the Union must tumble down, until at last I begin to think it is such a rickety old platform that it is impossible to prop it up. But when I bring my own judgment to bear, instead of relying on witnesses, I come to the conclusion that the Union is strong and safe, strong in its power as well as in the affections of the people."

He closed the debate with pretended fealty for the Constitution, which, if he and his few hundred active traitors had sincerely believed and as faithfully adhered to, there would have been another history of the extinguishment of slavery under free institutions.

The resolutions, as one of the desperate emergencies of the pro-slavery faction, were hurried forward, and passed the Senate by nearly a full vote of the Southern senators and several hypocritical ones serving the traitors at the time from the free States, who flagrantly misrepresented their States. They were passed and declared by the Senate caucus to be the binding Democratic doctrine, May 25th, about three weeks after the breakdown at Charleston.

About this time some independent Whigs of the free States, the remnant that was left as a reminiscence of the party, together with what was left of the party in the slave States who did not desire to associate with the conspiring pro-slavery faction of Davis, held a national Convention. This remnant of the broken Whig party, with an aversion to Davis and his côterie of control that was never mended in the lifetime of any of the leaders, met at Baltimore on the 9th of May, 1860, and organized what they were pleased to name "the Constitutional Union party," with no creed or belief other than the Constitution of the United States. With a united Democracy, like that of 1856, this movement would have had little or no significance; but with the breakdown at Charleston and the gap widening every day, with the Southern faction under complete control of the most excitable, domineering, and dictatorial leaders so unpopular to the former Whigs of the South, the movement became at once a formidable and threatening one to Davis and his Southern faction. Their platform was agreed to without much discussion. It was broad enough for any party in the country at the time, except that of Davis and his faction, who would have demanded an explanatory declaration that it was to be the Constitution as construed by the Taney decision of the Supreme Court. John J. Crittenden, of Kentucky; John Bell, of Tennessee; Edward Everett, of Massachusetts, and Washington Hunt, of New York, were the leaders of this party that seemed to be without any definite political object other than a refuge or sheltering organization for all who were indifferent or inattentive on the subject of slavery when it was the main topic of dispute in all other parties and of the people.

Bell and Crittenden, following in the line of Clay and his compromisers, were opposed to the repeal of the settlement of 1820, known so long as the Missouri Compromise. Both had been opposed to the forcible extension of slavery into the Territories, and positively so to the odious Lecompton iniquity; and both were, after long public service, resolutely and firmly opposed to the disunion leadership of Davis and his conspirators, whom they understood better than most of the public men of that day. Crittenden was so firm in his belief that he remained true and steadfast to the end through the war. Bell resisted awhile, but finally yielded, accepted Davis's lead, and went with his State into rebellion.

After a two-days' meeting at Baltimore, where some twenty-two States were partly or fully represented, mostly by half-filled delegations, this "Constitutional Union Convention" nominated John Bell, of Tennessee, and Edward Everett, of Massachusetts, for President and Vice-President. It was a movement of small importance in the free States. Crittenden would have been more acceptable than Bell; but he more wisely, having much less confidence in the movement, declined. Everett was without political following or support, an orator without a party, a man of letters out of joint, like Winthrop, Cushing, and B. F. Butler at the time, out with the people of his section—a man who was losing something in literature and scholastics, with little, if any, prospect of success in politics.

Although this was the relation of the "Constitutional" party in the free States, where the nominations were not much more than mentioned, they had a very different and vastly more important meaning, an overhanging dread and threatening danger, to the Davis supremacy, if it could be supported by a majority in the slave States.

The first effect of these Bell and Everett nominations aroused a more determined and unremitting opposition to Douglas in the South. He was not acceptable to any party among them, more positively by his successful opposition to the spread of slavery. Whatever might be the pretense, this was the real cause of his waning support in the South. He was then as objectionable to the South as Seward, Chase, Thad. Stevens, or Fremont; for whatever others had said, Douglas stood in the front line, and delivered the actual blows which restricted the spread of their favorite institution.

In this situation, with Bell and Douglas as the opposing candidates in the slave States, it was almost a certainty that Bell would get the electoral vote of every one of them. In that case Bell and his supporters would gain power and ascendency in the slave States, with Davis beaten and as certainly removed from power and influence.

Before submitting to this threatened and unexpected defection and following catastrophe, to prevent it, Davis would have risked himself as the candidate of the seceding faction. Although far from being a popular man among the Southern people, he was always considered one of their most capable men in personal character. He was a venturesome, persevering leader, resourceful in contrivance and combination all over the South—a man who was far ahead of his fellows in being prepared and ready at any time to put his plans into execution. At the time of the Conventions he was in such complete control of his faction that a word to Yancey and a few others would have made him their candidate.

Things were drifting that way at Charleston plain enough for Benjamin F. Butler, of Massachusetts, one of the longest-headed, shrewdest Northern men then serving the slave power, to see just where the tide was setting when he cast every ballot for Davis. The Southern leaders would have turned that way with little exertion, if Douglas could have been overthrown. Events were running and so firmly set in that direction that no one but Davis himself could have hindered it, if his faction had succeeded.

The nomination of John Bell upset the Davis scheme at once, not by any counseling or agreed-to plan, nor by any belief of the delegates who nominated Bell that there was a reasonable hope of his election, but because it was well known that Bell was one of the most popular leaders in the Southern States. With all the organized strength, diligence, and discipline of what was known as the slave-power to contend against, the tide of popular favor was likely to turn to Bell in a strain of approval that would have been irresistible.

Indeed, it became plain to Davis that the Southern

people were almost certain to turn to Bell, whom they liked. One strong reason to thousands of them was that he was a Union man, and would earnestly try to save it, as against Davis. He knew of his own knowledge that his own people still loved the Union, and that most of them would vote that way. If Bell had won against Davis even half the slave States, it would still have left Davis, not a dangerous plotter against his country, but a defeated factionist, with no following that would have justified any attempt at insurrection.

With this full knowledge of what would be the result of the divided Democracy and Bell's candidacy and the imminent danger of the slavery conspirators' overthrow, Davis was retired at once. John C. Breckinridge, then Vice-President, the most popular man in the South, was selected. He was a brave, generous-hearted man among his associates. He was a man more commonly respected among the people and far more genial and kindhearted in his dealings with them than the ordinary, rough, blustering Southern leaders of the time.

His selection saved the conspirators' faction from the unexpected danger of the Bell movement. It was planned at Washington, and was one of the acts of the leaders that was popular and approved by the Southern people. Breckinridge was a capable, fine-appearing and talented leader, whom the pro-slavery people supported as heartily and zealously as the free State people did either Lincoln or Douglas. At Baltimore, after the complete division, Breckinridge's selection seemed to be a spontaneous movement, having been so well planned and carried out that it appeared to be reached in the ordinary course of business on the floor of the Convention.

CHAPTER XL.

WHEN the factions of the Democratic party reassembled at Baltimore on the 18th of June, there was no sign of amelioration or amendment. When the body was called to order, there was doubt whether order or confusion prevailed. Chairman Cushing was considered the ablest parliamentary lawyer and presiding officer of that day, yet for ten days at Charleston and then five days at Baltimore he presided over the most disorderly meetings ever gathered for any kind of business on the continent. The furious Yancey, still the agent of the conspirators, returned with his irreconcilables, when he claimed, on reflection, they were anxious for harmony, and sought readmission, to avoid disruption of the party. A number of delegates claiming appointment from several States after the Charleston break-up were there also, asking admission in place of those who had voluntarily walked out.

They met in the Front Street Theater, the inside of which resembled a Babel of noise, confusion, and disorder. In the street outside, where open meetings were in progress, it was hardly less than a five days' and nights' riot. Confusion reigned above all. There was no man among the thousand capable ones there who could calm the turbulent slavery powers, who were then driving the Nation to conflict.

Neither the five days' whirling, zigzagging, overwhelmed, and overhammered threats, nor all the scullionism of the unchecked rioting of the pro-slavery town could shake the free State delegates from the determination in which they

332

were more firmly rooted and grounded than ever on their reassembling. Regardless of all the vocal thunders and mimic war so obnoxiously carried on around them, they had only to repeat what they had said a hundred times, that no further concession would be made to slavery, that if the conspirators carried out their dreadful threats, there would be no parties in the free States until the Union was saved.

Judge Douglas was in Washington, where he received intelligence as to their progress, or, rather, the want of it. He sent three messages, in order to restore harmony and save the party and the Nation, withdrawing his name, and promising his unqualified support to any one they could, in their combined wisdom, agree upon. If further proof of his unselfish devotion to his country and his cause had been needed, these messages surely gave it. The true and faithful delegates were more firmly set in his support as the contest went on. They well knew that he had risen far above personal ambition long before this in his contest with the slave-leaders, that it had been one of principle on his part, and that these same leaders would as readily combine against and destroy, if they could, any equally honest and capable leader of true Democracy. These delegates formed one of the strongest and most resolute bodies of Americans that ever attended any Convention; hence, when Mr. Douglas's messages were received, with better knowledge of the situation than he, they tore them up, and continued their fighting.

It was said of these faithful Douglas Democrats that they were a mere handful, and could not carry a single State for their candidate. It came true that, though they could not secure many Electoral votes, they were indorsed by sixty-five per cent of the whole Democratic vote. Under all the embarrassments and besetments of a divided party and growing antagonism to their former leaders, they lacked less than half a million of as many votes as Mr. Lincoln received.

After five days' desperate work, the Douglas delegates were as firm and unyielding as on the first. Then the second disruption of the Convention occurred. The delegates from the slave States of Virginia, North Carolina, Tennessee, Delaware, Maryland, and Kentucky joined the seceders, under full control of Yancey. There were also some apostate delegates from the free States who joined the seceders, and were admitted. There were, of course, Gwin and Jo. Lane of Oregon, who represented their States in like manner as Cushing and the Northern postmasters, who were there and admitted because "Old Buck" had ordered the office-holders of those States to send delegates, as he had done in the Illinois campaign in 1858 against Douglas.

Thus, in the close, most of the delegates of the slave States, except Missouri, and some scattering loyalists, seceded from the regular Democratic Convention because the majority would not submit to the pro-slavery doctrine and conspiracy of the minority. These joined the disunionist conspirators under Davis, with Breckinridge as their candidate.

In the furious tearing and sundering the strong Democratic State of Missouri stood firmly and faithfully for Douglas, and so remained, giving him its electoral vote, showing conclusively that the Democracy of the great central State was made up of men of heroic character, integrity, and patriotism, of far better stuff in every way than Atchison's marauding gang of the border.

When all the disrupting, seceding delegations and the accredited allies from the various post-offices were assembled, Cushing was retained as chairman of the seceders immediately, very much because of his previous neglect and want of desire to enforce order and to conduct the business in a sensible, expeditious way. He had sat apparently listless, helpless, and certainly doless in the riotous confusion he suffered to grow and prosper all about him to the point that he could not control his own subordinates. By reason of his skill as an embarrasser and cunning leader he was made the chairman and chief contriver of the bolting Convention.

After this their work was soon completed. The Senate resolutions platform was hurried through with no objection. Breckinridge was selected, as previously determined on and as the emergency required. The only delay was a short consultation as to which of several pro-slavery favorites in the free States, who had been slaveholders, should be selected for Vice-President. The nomination was finally given to Jo. Lane, of Oregon, one of the most unlettered and unfitted, but one of the most willing and obedient men to be found in such emergency, who was ever mentioned or suggested for such an honorable position. This, however, had little, if anything, to do with his selection one way or the other; for no election was expected. They cared only to know that he had been faithful to every behest in the interest of slavery. He had been, and probably was then, a slaveholder in Kentucky, residing at the time in the new State of Oregon, where he was under the political leading of Gwin, both of whom were believers in divine authority for slavery. Gwin also believed, as related, in wearing by "divine" right the title of "duke" as he pleased in Virginia or California. Jo. Lane would have believed in it, too, without reserve if Gwin had so wished, and Jo. could have been brought to understand what a harmless thing the dukedom was that Gwin had bought in some forgotten Italian duchy.

The strength and diabolism of the conspiracy was that they had carried out their plan and threat, and planted the seed for the destruction of the Union. They had strangled and suppressed free speech and a free press all over the South, and had raised the hand that was, in a few short months, to fall reeking with blood. In this way Breckin-ridge and Lane were nominated May 23, 1860.

When the seceders left the regular Convention with their noisy people and their uproar-breeding chairman, who knew so well how to cultivate disorder, how not to enforce ordinary parliamentary rules and procedure, or to preserve order and decorum, or what was left of it, there remained full delega-tions from all the free States, from Missouri, and some oc-casional ones from several slave States—over two hundred in all—who settled down to work at once without noise, dis-agreement, or disturbance of any kind in the regular dis-patch of business. One of the vice-presidents took the place of the departing Cushing; and the work in hand was con-cluded without delay. Senator Douglas was nominated by unanimous vote on the first ballot as the nominee of the regular Democratic Convention for President. Herschel V. Johnson, of Georgia, who had been a member of Congress, was nominated for Vice-President. He was a loyal, com-petent man, who left the honorable record of not participat-ing in secession, directly or indirectly, nor in the war against the Union.

No further attempt was made in the adoption of the platform after the defeat of the Yancey report at Charles-ton and the reaffirmation of the Cincinnati platform, with its Squatter Sovereignty doctrine, together with a resolution that, without mentioning opinions, they agreed to abide by the decisions of the Supreme Court.

The nomination and platform sustained Douglas's deter-mined and effective opposition to the Lecompton measure and other schemes to force slavery on an unwilling people. In full knowledge of all this he was, without division, made the chief leader of the free Democracy. These facts all taken together had more significance and made a more com-plete declaration of principles than any or all the platforms.

Mr. Douglas had not sought the nomination. He had

·repeatedly asked to withdraw, hoping that some one acceptable to all the factions might be found; but it must not
be understood by this that he ever offered to concede an
inch that his sturdy, loyal Democrats did not go with him
and believe him to be right. He was not going to be limited
in his leadership by any usurping or outside interference.
It had been his high ambition to lead his party and, in the
fullness of time, be its candidate and the Nation's President. This was to him the most honorable and highest
responsibility on the earth. To this idea he was true
through his life; for it he labored with all his fervency
and zeal in the light and experience of all that he had and
held dear. · He had qualifications, fitness, and capacity that
no one serving with him surpassed; yet for all these he had
never been willing to surrender his integrity; and he
never did.

This pleasant ambition, with all its hoped-for powers,
benefits, and consummation was shattered and sundered,
while the hand of God was laid heavy on the land because
of our transgressions, and the once powerful party lay
broken from top to bottom, wounded to the heart, but
still living and defying the wrath of defeated and frenzied
usurpers. After this, with cleaner hands and more resolute
purpose, it stood firm against attempted disunion and war.
It asked him to lead, not with the hope of victory, nor
Fame's approving favor, but to a stubborn, unyielding, and
hopeless contest—in the contention of a forlorn hope, with
certainty of defeat that year, but still to be made one of
the most noted and memorable combats in the cause of human rights and true Democracy. He accepted the charge
for the unpromising contest in as cheerful spirit and as
willing acquiescence and fidelity as he had when his party
had generously promoted him and confirmed its choice, with
the most responsible distinctions at its disposal.

In this way Douglas began and made the great campaign

of 1860, addressing the people to the full extent of his·
strength, with the free Democracy earnestly supporting
him. It was really a co-operating force for the inauguration of Abraham Lincoln, the strong support of his Presidency, and the salvation of the Union. Without this sustaining power, Mr. Lincoln's Administration would have
been the shadow of the passing and expiring Nation.

When I met Judge Douglas, in the summer of 1860,
at Bloomington, he was more seriously broken in health than
the previous year. He was still a young man, only forty-
seven years of age; but every line in his strong, positive cast
of face and features told too plainly of the incessant struggle, the worry, trying and wearing-out debates, the loss of
Broderick (who had been killed the previous September), the
apostasy of one after another of those who should have remained true to him and more to the cause they so easily
deserted. He was then a wearied, wornout man, burning his
life's light at both ends. The spirit of the dauntless and
stricken, but not overthrown leader was buoyant and hopeful
as ever, and remains a pleasant memory to me, as to every
one who loves our country and the courage and integrity
that never quailed in the face of danger.

He had been delicate in his youth, but care and discretion developed a stronger body than his parents expected,
but it was not symmetrical or well-balanced growth. He
had the head, the shoulders, the breast, and the heart and
lungs of a strong, robust man, and in proportion he should
have been six feet in stature, with proportionate strength;
but he was barely five feet, with weak, half-developed limbs,
and defective alimentary and digestive systems. This contrast of growth and development was striking and so no-
ticeable that, when quite a young man, with his strong head,
face, and shoulders only visible, he was conspicuous in any
assemblage, apparently one of the strongest and most robust-
looking when seated. His intelligence sustained the impres-

sion, out of which came the expressive sobriquet of "Little Giant," that stuck to him as those of "Expounder," "Compromiser," and "Pathfinder" did to Webster, Clay, and Fremont, respectively.

To thousands of people he was then no more than a politician, the candidate of his part of the party, because he held office and position. Many Republican newspapers and speakers denounced him as severely and thoughtlessly as they had ever done, not recognizing in any public expression that his break with the Southern leaders was final and complete, that thousands of his faithful followers, who had been with the majority party for a generation, had accepted defeat voluntarily rather than bend their necks in the service of a slave propaganda that would subjugate and enslave the people, regardless of race or color, as fast as they were safe and secure in their power to do so.

To the thoughtful it became a season of infinite peril. To the timid every threat of the Southern leaders spread the alarm. To the bravest hearts it was a crisis that was trying men as they never had been tried before. To Douglas, gallant leader of this strong body of patriotic citizens, it came with a crushing stroke, because for years he had been the most prominent of those who had exhausted the means of fair and honorable settlement, and at the same time neither shunned nor evaded their assaults.

The nomination of Douglas and Lincoln by the Democratic and Republican parties, respectively, in 1860, brings us again to the parallels and coincidences of these two strong men in their almost equally-divided parties. They grew to manhood in the same State, at the same bar, their homes were mainly in the same town, and they were the uncontested head men of their parties, as well as in their profession, for almost twenty years, before the break-up in 1860. They were earnest contestants with each other in the courts and in their respective parties, made up, as they were in those days, of robust, independent men, whose political differences were often more apparent than real.

These Western men liked a strong, vigorous contest, a close one; and the closer it became, the more zealously they "pitched in" and fought it out against each other, with all the energy and strength of strong-willed men. They took sides and made "things rattle" from the beginning to the end of their political battles. Their captains and men of affairs had to be men of sense and courage, men of "gumption," fearless, with spunk and mettle that would make them and keep them ready for a bridge-building, a house-raising, a deer chase, a coon hunt, or a political campaign. Those who led them had to be "mighty smart men," or these Western stalwarts would "light on" and find the flaw or weakness about them, when "that fellow would be done for." Many a misguided, unseasoned man realized his mistaken calling, who imagined he had talent to be up at the head among these strong, rugged men, who, though lacking in "book larnin'" and polish, had no defect in sound sense, mother wit, and the faith and deep conviction that their votes were the strongest force in the land.

Thousands of capable and intelligent men worked their way to the front, who were strong and maintained their position because of the strength and resolute zeal of the men who subdued the forests, streams, and prairies, and turned them into civilized homes. They fought their political battles with the same earnestness and vigor that characterized them in so many other undertakings. Opinions and policies were stubbornly contested, but never on the question who loved our State or country best. The jewel of human liberty was the priceless possession of one party, just as it was the others, and of no one more than his fellow-men.

Douglas and Lincoln began their rise among and as part of the two millions of independent Americans then

settling and making homes in our great State. Each soon
reached distinguished party favor for his side, and they ran
close along together in qualification, ability, and following
to such wise management that no one seriously or to better
purpose contended with them.

They were not alike, but lived in and passed through
close coincidences. They successfully contended, in periods
closely following, with the slave-power, when each, in his
time, was the chief leader of the free State people against
it, so for a long series of years. After Douglas's long years
of devotion, toil, and contest, he and his followers almost
to a man gracefully merged into the same host following
the great Lincoln, when the longer-contending Douglas laid
his weary burden down. They were chieftains among the
same people, in about the same relation, who, in succession,
made the final grapple and wager of contest with slavery.
Lincoln could not reach a senatorship, Douglas did, and
held without a break for three terms, but could not reach
the Presidency, which Lincoln did for two terms.

They fought and contended with each other in courts,
Legislatures, councils, and before the people, as few men
ever did, for the long period of about twenty years, never
in unfriendly contest, but always striving and anxious that
it should not be so. They were contestants to the close,
who prospered only as their parties and people did in their
well-conducted discussions and debates. They disseminated
useful information and public instruction, then so urgently
required, concerning slavery and the plainest relation about
the approaching crisis, making these a school for the people
on public affairs, indispensable in any free country.

They were both great men and great leaders in the full
meaning of these overworn phrases, often misused. Douglas
had instinct and conspicuous talent, capacity, and perseverance that could not be surpassed in getting knowledge and
knowing all that man could know in his line of pursuit.

Lincoln had distinct and positive genius, and learned with more ease what Douglas labored so hard to get. Douglas dug the jewels he had out of the earth; Lincoln gathered his as the harvester gathers the sheaves and shocks the grain; but when the work of the digging and harvesting were over, one of them knew all that the other did. Knowing these facts so well of both men, as years gave time and opportunity, it seemed folly to believe that these learned and eminent men were ever written of as "backwoods lawyers."

In the two or three meetings I had with Senator Douglas in the summer and fall of 1860 he talked freely about the dangerous situation, without passion or excitement. He passed over the facts and course of events like a judge going over a complicated, tedious, and impressive cause in review, carefully noting everything before giving judgment. He was then leading a larger body of independent voters than any man ever had in personal contest in our country up to the time, as many as 1,500,000 voters. It is true that 1,866,000 voted for Lincoln that year, but of these he was only one of several who had large following in the Republican party. Senator Seward's was so large that he lacked only the vote of some eight delegates, with the followers of several others combined against him for Mr. Lincoln; while the free State Democracy were so unanimously for Douglas that it was conceded that they were all for him, Missouri included, without opposition. These and other border State Democrats, who were independent, were as zealously for him as his own State of Illinois.

He spoke freely of the prospects of the different candidates, and was among the first Democrats I heard who conceded Lincoln's election as a strong probability. He said of the event that Lincoln's election would not be justifiable cause for breaking up the Government, as many Southern leaders and newspapers—some North, and all of the South—

were then boldly declaring. In one of these talks he said
in substance: "From the beginning I have not desired the
nomination of a divided party; but the movement passed entirely out of my hands in the crisis. I was supported unanimously after the Convention had been purged of its conspirators and bolters, by all who remained. They were
independent Democrats, whose integrity can not be im-
pugned; for they have no superiors anywhere. These were
united as one man and without interference, when, against
my judgment, they made their nominations. It was a body
of men that honored every one who belonged to them and
the Nation in their resolute integrity. With such men and
such devotion, would I, or would any man they sought, decline any service they had to ask? Not I; and I assure you
that, regardless of results, I am at their service."

On another occasion he said: "I had sent two or more
messages declining the nomination, asking that my name
be withdrawn. If any concession or sacrifice, save that of
principle, could be made, I urged them to make every possible effort to that end. Besides, I saw and talked with a
hundred or more of those brave men, to whom I explained
my opinions more at length, making the same request. In
the excited state of things I urged upon them my opinion
that some other Northern Democrat would likely receive
more votes. The only reply I received was notice of my
unanimous nomination. Senator Pugh, of Ohio, told me, 'If
you had been in the Convention, nothing but your open refusal would have changed the result; and if you had been
there, you would not have entertained the thought a minute.'
So I have accepted the nomination as an unqualified personal indorsement, which I hardly expected; but more and
far above that, it is independence and high devotion to patriotic duty that should honor these men as long as men
honor and fight for Democratic principles. They yielded
and gave all that men could for peace and a united party,

save a surrender that would have left us nothing but the name of our once honest Democracy; and, sooner than accept such humiliation, we have invited defeat rather than the hope of victory at the price of dishonor."

He was a delightful talker as well as public speaker. His gathered knowledge was stored in memory that was remarkable. His grasp of the underlying principles of government, science, sociology, and commerce made him one of the most entertaining conversationalists I have ever had the pleasure of meeting. In these chats his voice had a low, mellow tone, smoother than the strained effort in his public speaking. This, with his earnest, self-forgetting manner, led one along with him as you follow the details of a pleasing, well-told story. Unlike his ancestry, unlike other men of such definite professional training, ability, and general knowledge, he seemed almost without inclination to art, literature, poetry, or sentiment in nature; and yet his heart was full of human sympathy.

Nimmo Browne once asked him which he admired and believed in most of Scotland's great poets, Burns or Scott, and what he thought of the reputed traditional story of Ossian. He said: "I like Burns's beautiful poems. Who does not? They are never long, and any man can understand them. Scott is perhaps just as good; but I have never had time to read them carefully, so I could understand any of his stories or longer poems; but by hearsay I know they are excellent. Some day I hope to find time to read some of the best of these and all our literature. So far I have been a bookworm in law, logic, and polemics. Ossian I had forgotten. I have not seen it since I was a boy. I think I never read it. My mother often told me that my father admired it, and urged me to read it."

At another time he said to me: "Your father's premonitions, both as to the Southern leaders' intention to overthrow me whenever I or any one got in their way of extending slavery, and their more wicked intention to levy war to extend it, were right. I have lived to see them fulfilled; but I still think his judgment was wrong when, about 1845, he urged me to make an open contest against them and their system, as in the end it would be a necessity for every party leader and patriot in the free States. I have held to my first ideas through storms of denunciation and vile abuse, such as no other man, to my knowledge, in this country ever endured. I have been determined, not obstinately, but mainly because I believed it to be prudent and right, and because I had the unwavering and friendly support of so many loyal Democrats, first in our own State, and now of all that is left of the party in the country, I might well say; for these Southern people are no longer Democrats. I feel now that, with the help of these brave men, who made a most effectual and telling contest against disunionists and conspirators, I must persevere with all my remaining strength, even to the point of certain defeat by the election of a Republican.

"Whatever this may be to others, I feel justified. The party's undivided approval, when rid of these disturbers, has more value than a bitterly-contested nomination. Their simple indorsement is satisfaction for all I have done and endured. I have, too, the further satisfaction that, in spite of all the abuse I have received from some ignorant Republicans and a very bitter Republican press, while their party has had two years' control of the House of Representatives, no change has been made for the admission of new States into the Union. Thus it has indirectly approved and left unchanged the much-derided Kansas-Nebraska law under the settlers' right as the law and policy of the Nation.

"Your father came here at a very opportune moment for me. He was a man of intelligence and learning, trained in a school and university as good as the world has. Besides, he was an enthusiastic young man fresh from the earnest

discussion that ended in the abolition of slavery in all the
colonies of Britain. He was himself so zealous and earnest
about the matter, and so well informed, that he sustained
himself in all his arguments. He believed that Christian
civilization had made wonderful progress, and was then demanding the abolition, amelioration, or restriction of slavery
everywhere, and that the settled policy of the best, most
prosperous, and humane civilizations on the earth were in
favor of its extinction or restriction. He also believed that
it would be a narrow-minded, even a suicidal policy for the
great American Republic, resting on human rights, to attempt any arrest of this beneficent reform, and fly in the
face of the world's progress.

"He taught Abolitionism from its highest vantage-
ground, and so sensibly and well that his neighbor slaveholders in the city of St. Louis always hearkened and gave
him respectful attention. Most men of his belief made the
subject so personally disagreeable that they would not listen
or give it consideration. He steadily declined office or public position outside of his regular work as an architect and
engineer, when his capacities afforded him unusual opportunity. It was his professional employment that brought
him here at my request. I was immediately impressed with
him at our first meeting in St. Louis, after which we remained friends.

"He was one of the most thoroughly-grounded men in
the principles of Democracy I ever met. To him slavery and
usurped or aggrandized power, that brought vast sums of
money and control into the hands of a few, were the deadly
foes of democracy, and, if unchecked, they would work its
certain ruin and destruction, as had been the case over and
over in the rotted-out republics and democracies of former
centuries.

"He wisely believed that the prosperity that gave a
few thousand men the control of commerce, products, and

the property of a nation, such as slavery had done in the Southern States, would very soon destroy any democracy. He was firmly of the belief that Christian education and civilization were the safest and almost the only bulwarks of the people against the domination of wealth and the sequestration, little by little, or in great jumps at opportune seasons, of the rights of the people; that liberty had no foe more formidable than the slaveholder or capitalist who had gathered his wealth from the unpaid earnings of his fellow-men. He was my friend and one to be remembered while I live.

"Only last year the brave and gallant Broderick fell a victim, through mistaken sensitiveness on the exhibition of his personal courage, to the same kind of men who would enjoy my taking off as much as his, from all I know. He was too brave and too useful to be so needlessly sacrificed. Some day men will learn that none but cowards will practice with arms for weeks in order to kill some unsuspecting and unprepared hero, such as Broderick was, in a duel.

"I will not fight with them that way, and not at all, unless I must; but when compelled to fight, as we soon may be, from appearances, we must have the same practice and preparations and the very best guns we can make. When war comes with these maddened zealots, as they so flippantly threaten, it will be merciful to make it as swift, unerring, and destructive as possible. In this way free and independent men who will fight and die for their rights must teach tyrants and usurpers forgotten lessons that can be taught no other way."

In the progress of years I kept up the family friendship, and enjoyed besides the pleasure of meeting the indomitable man, then one of the wisest statesmen of his period. I came to know how faithfully and zealously he was leading the free Democracy to the patriotic defense of our country, as no other man could have done, a party that, at the begin-

ning of his leadership, was, more than half of it, committed
to slavery, one that held any Abolitionist as a disunionist,
to be shunned and dreaded, no matter how mild his anti-
slavery opinions were.

From this sort of beginning, about the Mexican War
period, from 1845 to 1860, this party in the free States
was brought under the common accusation of Abolitionists
in 1860, and more vehemently denounced by the Southern
leaders as time and opportunity divided the party than the
Republicans. Through all this, from the beginning of the
Lecompton contest, I fully believed that Douglas was in
more effective work to prevent the extension of slavery,
and practically to bring about a united body of free State
people against an earlier united pro-slavery party in the
slave States. This was plain and apparent to me long before most of our anti-slavery people and Republicans would
concede it. Many of them continued to class Douglas as an
ally of the slave-power or whatever else their political necessities seemed to require.

By reason of our personal friendship I did as much and
went farther than was prudent, to sustain the true relation
of Douglas and his followers. Owing to our pronounced
anti-slavery opinions I was able to set his party relations
right with some very good anti-slavery people and Republicans. But party prejudice ran so high those days that I
was badly misrepresented in some instances, because of my
desire that Douglas and his party should be fairly represented before the people.

Aside from many politicians and newspaper publishers,
who used such accusations against Douglas for purely partisan reasons, there were many who were called level-headed
men in our State and other free States who believed that
Douglas was one of the strongest and most zealous pro-
slavery men in Congress. So industriously had this charge
been circulated against him that for years after the South-

ern leaders had broken with him in the Lecompton contest, hundreds of credulous and easily-beguiled people were led to believe it. The designers and fabricators of these outrageous falsehoods were so constant and untiring in their ignorance or malice that there are people professing to believe them unto this day.

Of the many with whom I talked over these subjects, none took more interest or expressed so much satisfaction about it as Mr. Gridley. After I had related the substance of Mr. Douglas's remarks, about 1860, he replied: "I am gratified indeed to hear it, and I fully believe it. Mr. Douglas, when he was young and beginning and could do no better, carried too much mud and untempered mortar for those cotton and sugar lords and the commoner border State slave-breeders, who raised and shipped niggers as we do cattle and hogs.

"He has been a master. They tampered with and ied Clay into slavery-extending compromises all his life. They overthrew Benton, and have tied down Houston, their very best men since Jackson. They tangled Marcy, and have Lewis Cass still in the net; and now they have poor, simpering old Buchanan overloaded and overdaubing everything with their unmixed mud.

"Douglas—our own Scotch-Yankee Douglas—who left Vermont to get more room, tipped the last cartload of their pro-slavery mud back in their faces, and has driven his unloaded cart on to free soil, lightened of the terrible load, leaving Davis, Benjamin, Breckinridge, Mason, and Stephens and a smaller assortment of little lords tearing and clawing the vile mixture that was to mire Douglas out of their eyes and hair ever since.

"Of course, they feel somewhat unpleasant toward Mr. Douglas just now. He has struck the system that is as much degrading to white as black men a terrific blow, and they are staggering under it more than we will ever know. If it would put as much patriotism and sense of duty into the white-faced, leg-shaking Buchanan Administration as to save the smallest village on the Canada frontier, slavery could be managed and brought under the rule of law and civilization, where the public mind would rest in the belief of its ultimate extinction, as Mr. Lincoln put it.

"It seems strange that General Cass, Jere Black, and poor, old, putty-faced Buchanan can not see and feel the load of cowardice and obloquy that is firmly settling upon them. If war comes after this warning of Douglas, Buchanan and his aspen-shaking Administration can read their fate in that of Belshazzar's, which happened several years ago.

"As the situation now stands, this mutinous disorder and threatened insurrection all over the South could be quieted and suppressed by a President like Jackson, in a few weeks. If Buchanan is going to parley with treason until the Capitol comes tumbling down upon them, Black, Cass, and Cushing, if they are loyal, as they firmly assert, had better come out in the open with Douglas, and not be buried, Samson-like, in the falling ruins—not that they at all resemble Samson, but they are too weak to get away from the tottering temple of liberty before its fall.

"Seriously, it is a glory, and no common one, that our Douglas has the sense, the true courage and determination to come out boldly on the side of our country and its liberties at the very time he could have tempered his defense with the partly slavery-poisoned party he is leading. He is a giant in mind, if not in stature, and not all the slavery devils together can shake him from his leadership, as they have so often tried.

"Now he marches his legions equipped and complete, with their cannon shotted, into the lines of liberty. He has thus made a solid North for the Union, with Missouri on our side, against a solid South, if that is their desperate determination. In this way we can surely save the Union and

keep it within the bounds of decent civilization, and not
fall into a sea of barbarism. There is fame and honor for
Douglas and the party that has made him great and strong.
This should be conceded here in his home State without
grudging and without notice from Horace Greeley that we
ought to do it.

"It is a great achievement for our State, even if we
did n't all help do it, because we 've been busy, some of us,
raising up another leader, perhaps the greatest, who knows?
Would n't it be glory indeed and in truth when we elect
Abraham Lincoln President, to have Douglas the leader of
an unpolluted and unslaved Senate, and to have the foul-
smelling carcass of slavery removed?

"If this were done, and slavery were extinguished under
the force and impetus of his civilizing triumph, they should
build monuments of bronze and granite and iron in Richmond
to our Illinois leaders, Douglas and Lincoln; for he or they,
whoever may rid the South of its horrid, dragging-down slavery system, will be the Southern States' greatest benefactors.
This will be so recognized in one or two hundred years—
perhaps a little sooner—when sense takes the place of the
usurping madness of the time."

Mr. Gridley said more. There was a sense, not unpleasant, like the ringing rattle of metal striking metal, in his
clear-cut sentences. He understood and used the emphatic
eloquence of keen words and phrases that never missed their
meaning or object. He made no effort to be rhetorical, but
to be earnest, speaking in a style that embraced and took
in all his intellectual powers. He was exact and positive
and clear, so that he never missed the distinctness of his
illustration or the object of his delivery. He never needed
further explanation of what he had said when he had made an
assault. We will need to tell more of him soon in the trying crisis that tested all there was in his highly-strung,
energetic temperament. It would exhaust the strongest

words and their clearest force of description to lay before the reader in plain, intelligible shape the marvelous achievements of this tireless spirit, who never hesitated in any undertaking. He was light and lithe of limb and build, in form and appearance almost running to a shadow. He had clear perceptions, with an open expression of countenance and a clear bluish-gray eye that can scarcely be described. Although light, his muscles were strong, and withal there was a sense and presence of matured manhood about him that missed nothing. One said of him that "he was graceful and easy in all his movements, so wiry and active a man, that you never ceased liking him. He had a few pounds of bones and muscles, and the rest of him was all motion and strung-up nerves." He was always full of business, and seldom by his own fault missed his reckonings. He made a fortune, and lost it by the failure of others in the wild, greedy, and moneyless panic of 1837. He entirely recovered from this, and accumulated another of ten times what any other man then controlled in our part of the country, and saved it when most men were losing all they had in the repeated panic of 1857. He loved Lincoln until his sentiment for him seemed to be his highest ambition, if not a passion. He had the best of practical sense and adaptable means and powers of doing business. He surely had capacity in trading, dealing, or speculating far ahead of any one in our Central Illinois region, where these were then waiting stronger use and development.

He had means beyond limit for any undertaking in our new and unimproved condition of the country. His neverneglected ambition was to prosper Mr. Lincoln. In 1859-60 he grasped the opportunity in the most persevering and tireless way to help make him President. To this end he brought the full measure of his talents and means, honorably and diligently pursued. We will need to take up the story in its course, unwind the tale of our modern Warwick, who, in what he did, acted full as well as the first "king-maker."

Mr. Gridley was not a bit like him in much of his career, but came into the plan to make Mr. Lincoln President in its crucial, most critical beginning, where he helped and followed it to a successful ending, with sleepless and never-flagging energy. This was certain to all those who fully understood the inner workings of that personal movement. That he did all of it is not the story, but that he did much of it, and what no other man was able, or appeared to be able and ready to do, is the strength of the tale.

In the preceding there is much that recalls the belief and opinions of the best-informed men of the time, that the concentration and power of wealth in the hands of a few thousand, as represented in the slaveholding system, was an alarming and threatening danger to free institutions, and so to free or democratic government, and necessarily as much against the freedom, personal and civil rights under our system of law, based on the rights of the people.

On these ideas there were no differences between Douglas and Lincoln, nor in their parties. All agreed that the vast concentration of wealth in the hands of a few was a formidable danger, whether it was accumulated and held in the hands of a few slaveholders or greedy men in other labor-oppressing and grasping systems. The effect was always the same and directly against the rights of the people. Continuing so, what would those good men think of our situation, if living to-day, when the accumulation of vast and unheard-of sums of the few has more than quadrupled the increase of all Europe put together in the past thirty years?

Vol. II.—23.

CHAPTER XLI.

THE closely-contested Presidential campaign in Illinois of 1856 and the senatorial campaign of 1858 were both characterized by their strenuous disputes on slavery. It was a subject that involved the life and perpetuity of the Republic; and the State became the center of the anti-slavery agitation from the campaign of 1858 to the inauguration of Mr. Lincoln in 1861 and the opening of the Civil War. Something of the interest and magnitude of the work may be gathered when we understand that both parties in 1858 held about one hundred and fifty day-meetings each, with an attendance averaging ten thousand, or an aggregate attendance of one and a half millions for each party. This was when the population of the State was a little less than two millions. This estimate is exclusive of the joint debates in 1858 heretofore considered.

These facts give evidence of healthy and well stirred-up public sentiment on the serious condition that aroused such general interest that the people went almost unanimously to hear the strong discussion, not only of one, but of both parties. During the campaign of 1858 it was common to have meetings where the attendance was over twenty thousand. In many of them the people were too numerous to be counted by any means at hand, arriving and going in so many ways. At Bloomington, Springfield, Urbana, and Danville there were Republican mass-meetings so large that there were four speakers addressing multitudes at the same time, where Lincoln, Lovejoy, Trumbull, and others were the speakers.

About the same time, Douglas, Logan, and others addressed two of the largest outdoor mass-meetings ever held at Champaign and Decatur. There were lawyers in almost every county-seat, and others who were able and inclined to carry on these interesting public discussions. Men of both parties, as their capacity ran, drew their thousands; and from this there were smaller meetings held in every town and in almost every schoolhouse in the State.

In something of this manner the people of the free States in every community discussed and came to a general understanding of the differences between the North and South on slavery and correlative public questions. The nature and effects of the slave system, its extent and relation to labor and property values, both in the North and South, were thoroughly considered. In this way public discussion became a school of civil government, including commerce, revenue, and various systems of taxation, suggesting the means and arousing the people to renewed energy in the conduct of every industrial pursuit, positively so in the urgent need of more and better means of transportation.

These meetings, general talks, and intercourse led to progress and improvement in every branch of living, in every society or community, so that, although the cause that brought them together and the progress of the discussion was full of alarm and danger, their mingling together and planning for the public good stimulated them to renewed energy and better knowledge of what could and what should be done to save the country and civilization in every proper way. These were all necessary. The general acquaintance, the common understanding, the expectation, and the preparation, as well as increased knowledge, were everywhere apparent when the crisis came that plunged us into war. Then every one realized that the five or ten-years' better acquaintance with these subjects was of incalculable value to millions. Without it they would have been helpless; but in this preparation they were schooled and ready to work at once in whatever came to be their duty. Neither must it be understood that this political activity and excited interest in public affairs caused or suggested neglect or in any way retarded our work and progress, but it increased the zeal and energy of every one in his life work, kindling courage and patriotism as the fields and valleys responded with increasing yield to the husbandman's increasing strength, skilled labor, and enlightened methods of industry.

Our people were masters in labor, as well as eager and multitudinous in politics. They had the thrift and energy that got them up and in the field, shops, and business places at sunrise, where, in honest toil and hammering blows, they pounded out success and prosperity so real as to have the produce, the grain, the cattle and hogs to feed millions.

While they were attending mass-meetings by counties, and ripening their minds in civil affairs as the grain matures and yellows for the sickle, they were making material progress beyond comparison. No one had ever seen an invasion like it, where husbandry, the arts, sciences, and social facilities were developing a basin as fertile as the Nile and as large as Europe. This increase in three States of the Central Mississippi region is shown as follows:

	Population 1850.	Population 1860.	Increase.
Illinois	851,410	1,719,951	860,541
Iowa	192,214	614,913	482,699
Missouri	682,044	1,182,012	499,968
Totals	1,725,668	3,507,876	1,843,208

	Property Value 1850.	Property Value 1860.	Increase.
Illinois	156,260,008	871,860,282	715,595,276
Iowa	23,714,638	247,338,265	223,623,627
Missouri	137,247,707	501,214,398	363,966,691
Totals	317,257,351	1,620,412,945	1,303,185,594

This extraordinary increase was made from 1850 to 1860, when our political contentions were at their highest tension, and we were approaching the great struggle. From 1857 to 1860 our State and all the Western States suffered one of the worst financial panics and revulsions in all business enterprises in our history. A moneyless, bank-breaking period prevailed, as destructive of values and much worse in the West than that of 1837, twenty years before. With all these drawbacks the increase was marvelous.

The population of the three States named was more than doubled, and the increase in values had more than quadrupled during these years of angry political disputes. The population was twofold in 1860 what it was in 1850, with an excess of 117,000, almost as much as the population of Chicago, where the Republican Convention assembled in 1860. More remarkable than the rapid increase in population was the fourfold increase of the value of property in those ten memorable years of strife and growing sectional antagonism. Yet the people fully believed that they had never seen such "hard times," and that they were growing poorer every day.

Other Western States were developing in about the same ratio. It was sometimes said of the Western people that they had "taken to politics" and were becoming thriftless and neglectful of their ordinary pursuits, and that their farms, agricultural implements, and stock were wasting or perishing. The above facts, which could be amplified and extended to every Western State in detail are sufficient refutation, if any were ever needed, that Western people did not let political or other extraneous subjects interfere with their industrial and material progress.

The defenders of aristocracy and prerogative in every degree and the money squeezers have always bewailed political agitation as inimical to progress and prosperity. The reverse is the truth of history. Cromwell agitated and tore a dynasty down, leveled and buried most of it. This became the foundation of Britain's ascendency, freeing men and advancing manufactures, commerce, and navigation to all the world. Luther had agitated before him, and Washington since. Then Douglas and Lincoln further agitated, and, as the result, slavery fell, and human rights prospered. In all of them the people, their trade, and industry prospered.

What the world needs is more, not less, agitation. Every rotting or festering iniquity should be laid open, disclosed, and talked about. No blameless business needs concealment, and no bad one should be permitted to have it. The agitators and reformers who have unshackled and unslaved the bodies and minds of men, have always been clear and outspoken about it; while tyrants and aristocrats have invariably corrupted governments, usurped and exercised unlawful powers in secret schemes and by the aid of secret councils. In these they have wasted the people's substance, which could not have been done if public affairs and public policies had been agitated and open to them.

It should be the continuing purpose and determination of the people of every Government, big and little, to know all there is to know of public acts, the record and the policy, before they are adopted. There is peril and hidden danger in being ignorant or uninformed concerning all these; and the people who consent to hidden conduct in government, in whole or in part, by commissions, agents, or treaty-builders, without direct responsibility to themselves, have in so far parted with the dearest rights of free men. More dangerous yet, they have laid the foundation and set the example by which all that is left of liberty may be taken.

Agitation, free speech, and a free press are the anchors of hope and the means of preserving free government for a free people. Besides all else learned from the struggle of the past, we should know there is no danger, but much good, in stirring up and agitating every public question or movement, and, instead of being a detriment, it continues an incentive, a stimulant to real progress and prosperity. Our State of Illinois had wonderful growth and development of every product of intelligence and industry. From 1850 to 1860 we had, among many other advantages and facilities, real statesmen to lead and guide our people in the planting of real and substantial improvements that made the best things of their kind in its possession.

Chicago had grown to over two hundred thousand. It was the commercial metropolis and great Western town for the accumulation, barter, sale, and disposal of farm and manufactured products, with many other attractive advantages. It had unsurpassed waterways—the lakes and canals—to the seaboard. It had railways built or building in every direction, that made it what it continues, the wonder of the Western world. All this the inhabitants mentioned to visitors and new settlers, until they, too, could tell the story as well.

It did not have all the place has to-day, and was nothing near so big nor so bad; but along with its commanding position and highways for hauling products to market and returning manufactured supplies in variety, it was the same town in miniature. Everybody hurried, and their faces sharpened, like their wits. The people generally think more of how to do business and make lots of money than of any problem of life or living; and no reputable man, woman, or child ever strikes any other than a rapid gait, with sound limbs and understanding.

In the early fifties a well-planned and complete system of railroads was undertaken. These were about all built from 1852 to 1856, when they were in successful operation. This was the industry that most generally benefited the city in fixing it as the grain, cattle, and hog-shipping center, as much as for all other exported products. It became also the receiving and distributing port for imports and merchandise for the West and Northwest.

The lines in operation of that day were one or two up the west shore of the lake to Milwaukee and north and northwestward. The Northwestern extended to the Galena lead-mine region and the Mississippi River north and westward. The Burlington and Quincy, from which latter point it connected with the Hannibal and St. Joseph across the State of Missouri, made connections at its terminus, St. Joseph, with the freight and stage routes across the plains. The other branch of the same line to Burlington, Iowa, made connection there with the first line built across that State to the Missouri River. The Chicago, Alton and St. Louis Line went southwest through the towns of Joliet, Bloomington, Springfield, and Alton to East St. Louis. The Wabash began at Meredosia on the Illinois River, going east through Jacksonville, Springfield, Decatur, and Danville to Logansport, Indiana, where it connected with lines east. It was very soon extended to Toledo, on Lake Erie. The Ohio and Mississippi went westward from Cincinnati through Ohio, Indiana, and Illinois to East St. Louis. This line, the Terre Haute and St. Louis, and the Wabash were the only lines of any importance not making Chicago a terminus.

In addition to these, which made a very complete railway system in its day, Judge Douglas, with the help of his co-laborers in Congress and the consent of the people, secured a land grant for the building of the Illinois Central Railway, which extended, beginning at Galena, south and easterly, through Freeport, Dixon, Mendota, Ottawa, Bloomington, Decatur, and Centralia, to Cairo, at the junction of the Mississippi and the Ohio Rivers, its southern terminus—a distance of over four hundred miles. It had also a branch, more important, from Chicago almost due south through Kankakee, Champaign, Effingham, then fifty miles southwesterly to Centralia, on the main line, about three hundred miles south of Chicago and fifty miles east of St. Louis.

This gave the State a north-and-south line of railroad, traversing the State in two lines, with an aggregate of over seven hundred miles. The corporation that built the lines received a valuable land-grant of several million acres. The lands were sold out rapidly to actual settlers during this period of remarkable progress referred to.

The proceeds of the sale of these lands would have built two such railways. It was among the first of what have been called "land-grant railroads." The question is still one of earnest doubt whether it was wise policy to build so many Western roads under the land-grant policy. While we have no intention to discuss the wisdom of the plan, it remains true that, as the railroad was desirable and it was universally agreed that it should be built, Judge Douglas, the State Legislature and the people in approval, made the best terms in building this line of any land-grant railroad that has ever been made.

The company, by its charter, was obliged and required in perpetuity to pay into the State treasury annually seven per cent of its gross earnings in lieu of all taxes for the State. counties, cities, and schools. This has proven satisfactory, and remains a permanent income that more than supports the State Government. The road and its owners have prospered under the plan and payment. It would have been a wise settlement of the railway and transportation problems if the people of the States and Territories had made the same charter requirement from all land-grant or aided railroads.

The building of these lines and other like improvements, the rapid influx of population and wealth, and the increase in property was one of the most remarkable advances and increase in values ever made by any one of our great States in the ten years. This rapid advance in the material and industrial conditions of the State had built and equipped a system of over five thousand miles of railroads that were built when farming and all commercial enterprises made like progress. By it Chicago became one of the greatest modern cities, mainly through the building of this unequaled extension and grasp of the highways of commerce, centering them in the Illinois town on the sands and marshes at the mouth of the malodorous little stream, or "Polecat" River, translated straight from the plain Indian to the plain Western Yankee dialect. The name became that of the town as well as the river.

The wisdom of those "ancient builders" of the city by the lake from 1830 to 1860 was phenomenal. They were wiser than they knew. Besides building a trading town, they made it the termini of the whole Western, Northwestern, and Southwestern railway systems, and kept their place, developing rapidly in all material and intellectual progress. They laid the foundation for an industrial and commercial metropolis, and no less of art, literature, and science, that has so often doubled and quadrupled its population and its business in steady growth, that it remains the marvel of the century.

What has been done there, the immensity of trade, traffic, and commerce that can only be counted in billions annually, and the enlightened means of trade that crosses, recrosses, and girdles the continent, is realized only by a few people. What it can be, and what in reason we should expect it to be, in the progress of Christian civilization, is perhaps as marvelous as how Joshua's knowledge of astronomy helped him to be the successor of Moses and the bravest leader in Israel.

In 1860—the year of the memorable Convention—Chicago had more than three times the people and business it had in 1850. This of itself would appear sufficient proof of the energy and industry of the people of the city and the

State, and surrounding States as well. This was done and accomplished through the period of the most earnest and impassioned political discussion held by our people since the days of the Revolution.

The rapid improvement, advancement, and prospering civilization were not exceptional in the State of Illinois or Chicago; for the whole country, from its earliest settlement had never made such progress. Manufacturing, shipbuilding, and commerce had made rapid strides all over the Atlantic States as far south as New Jersey, where the people became interested in such enterprises. The acquisition of California and the Pacific domain of over one thousand miles coast-line, with a belt as wide of fertile and rich mineral lands running eastward, in a few years more than quadrupled our production of the precious metals, and made current money in such abundance and general distribution as to inaugurate an era of improvement such as we had never expected or thought possible.

Our population increased from over twenty-three millions in 1850 to over thirty-one millions in 1860, an increase of eight and a quarter millions of people. During the same time the property values, by the best attainable estimates, were from seven billion dollars to sixteen billions of dollars—an increase that was two billions above twice as much in ten years. This gave, in the aggregate, an average of a little less than eleven hundred dollars for every man, woman, and child in 1860.

Slave-labor had been very profitable. The production of cotton had risen from 2,400,000 bales of 400 pounds each to 5,300,000 bales in 1860, which alone amounted to about three hundred millions of dollars. This was the largest single crop produced. Slave-labor, however, in the production of corn, tobacco, hemp, sugar, and rice, amounted to an equal value, reaching an aggregate of more than five hundred million dollars annually. Over one-half of this was net increase and profit to not more than four hundred thousand slaveholders from the labor of four million slaves.

The enormous profits of slave-labor by all ordinary estimates exceeded this sum annually. Most of this vast wealth was monopolized in the hands of a few grasping men. This greed and desire for wealth and power and distinction has existed in all ages. It has always been the same in intention and purpose. It had then, and has never had other restrictions than God's moral laws, enforced against wickedness by intelligent, God-fearing men, who, in courage, in success or disaster, have fought it in all forms throughout the centuries, that the rights and liberties of men might not perish from the earth. When the brave are not fighting and contending against the consumers of men's toil, the lordly Cains are in some way dragging men down, usurping their rights, and deceiving or robbing them of their labor or its products.

Mr. Lincoln sincerely believed that in and with slavery the thirst for money was a potential danger that stood with uplifted arm, threatening the perpetuity of our free institutions. In a speech he made about September, 1858, he said, in substance: "I have no wrought-up prejudices against slaveholders, rich men, or large owners of property as such. Any one of them may have come into use, control, or possession of these innocently enough and without a harmful thought or desire in doing so. It is the use men make of wealth, property, or power, and their purpose, as it is with those who succeed to official place and authority, that determines whether it is rightfully or wrongfully held.

"All property and all that has existence in or upon the earth belongs of right to its Maker. You are for the time the custodian of what you have or get control over, as you are over your talents or your mental endowment. Your purpose, as it is God's in investing you with these—money, property, power, or mind—should be to make as many men happy and comfortable as the means at hand will suffice you to do. You brought nothing into the world with you. You will take nothing with you when you go out of it.

"When you enslave or take men's earnings, or oppress them, you are not doing what your Maker intended with the means confided to your care for the benefit and welfare of your fellow-men, for which purpose he supplied you the ways to do so. In that he has done so to you, in like manner you should do to all mankind as your brethren. All else is wrong and leads straightway to evil, as misuse of God's wealth, property, talents, and blessings, of which he has given you much or little, not alone for your own selfish use and enjoyment, but that, as he has been bountiful and provident with you, so should you be with your fellow-men.

"I am well aware that no man can arrest mankind in the maddened race for wealth, position, and power until God's own time to do it; but I am quite as sure that, if one earnestly undertakes it and honestly and courageously adheres to it to the end, he will make some men better and himself what he could not have been without it, and more of what God intended men should be, and more in the line and make-up of our immortal Declaration of Independence, which starts all men out in life or being as equal under law.

"As God never makes men less in right nor worse in life or character, but always makes them more merciful, more humane, better and stronger in all that is good and wise, as they observe and follow him, why should not we do all within our limited means that we can to elevate men, and neither sell, degrade, oppress, nor filch the products of their toil? The Master never intended we should. I do not know or even believe that it is always true; but it is true enough to be a rule for the opinion and government of human affairs that, whenever you see a man with a million dollars of his own accumulation in his possession, he has a lot of other people's money, property, or earnings that he has in some way extorted from and oppressed or ruined a whole lot of people in the getting of it. The men who have millions accumulated otherwise are the beneficiaries of some person that did all these, and oppressed perhaps a million people for every million dollars so accumulated.

"One million dollars is such a sum that no man can honestly earn it, or anything like it in a lifetime. When it is conceded that it is lawful and morally right for a few men to control such vast sums, we have in so far parted with our liberties, our franchises, and privileges, or by force they have been taken from us in measures, such as the recognition of slavery or the slave-trade, which should never be granted, because in the operation of this same surrendering policy all our rights, franchises, wealth, property, and power will slip away from the people and be eventually concentrated in the hands of a few.

"When this comes, and the wealth or power of the land is in the control of a few, as it exists now in many of the slave States, or in Europe, our liberties will perish, the Republic will die, and, whether in name or not, we will have a monarchy in fact. This, should it come, will surely destroy the Republic, the best and wisest Government God ever gave to men."

This was Mr. Lincoln's opinion on the subject of vast accumulations of wealth and power in the hands of a few men, as it was suggested and brought to his mind by slavery and the iron hold and exercise of power by a few in the slave States and the Nation, as far as their clutching grasp went unrestricted.

As Mr. Lincoln held and believed on these subjects, so did Judge Douglas. No man of his time, or before it, in our country was more firmly grounded and immovably determined in favor of an actual and real democracy than he was; and no one before or since ever believed in or carried out his belief of the direct responsibility of every officer and representative to the people who gave or assented to his official term. In short, he was honest, and believed in the rights of the people, and not in assumed or arrogated power as against them. He was a democrat who not only held office and represented the people who sent him, but lived in public and private life, a democrat; who, when he could have amassed a large fortune, was happy and contented in plain, simple living; who, like Lincoln, left the lasting example of honorable service, and believed that there are better things than wealth or usurped authority that always oppresses some one.

I had several talks on occasions with these men—true-hearted patriots, as they were—on the subject of vast accumulations of wealth and property. They both held the belief that the vast accumulations of those days and the granting of almost unlimited franchises were threatening dangers, and that, as soon as the slavery issue was settled, the people should set about the work in earnest to restrict them. All in office or authority should be held to a strict accountability to the people. Especially railways and public carriers of all kinds should be brought under unqualified obedience to law, and should render good service at reasonable rates, and bear a pro rata tax similar to that required by the charter of the Central Railroad Company. The plan of this tax on the gross earnings of this road was approved by both of them. No plan so fair and just to all concerned has been made since. It was made as the result of combined wisdom and experience, and approved by all in the State as the best plan under which to grant valuable franchises.

In conversation concerning the reckless granting of franchises, lands, and public privileges, Judge Douglas said: "The British people, in order to relieve themselves of the oppressive rule of the Stuarts, invited William III to the throne, that they might have peace, protection, and civil liberty, as kings of that day doled out rights and favors to their subjects when they were so minded. William came, and with him came a host of Hollanders, Lower Rhinelanders, Belgian, and Swiss mercenaries. For a time many Britons feared that they had chased out a fox with the help of a wolf. Nevertheless William was there and, with the people divided, had brought force enough with him to stay and maintain himself. He restored civil order with the grip and strength of a hand of iron, where it could be done no other way. Peace soon prevailed throughout the kingdom, enforced on the Russian plan by the sturdy burghers of the Lower Rhine wherever there was opposition.

"With the settlement, oppressive as it was to many, the Nation soon reached better conditions. Industries, commerce, and prosperity predominated that were impossible under the corrupt and tyrannical rule of the Stuarts. One of the worst evils of his reign, and a glaring bad one in precedent and example, became its lasting means of corruption. This was the profuse generosity, if it can be so called, by which he distributed favors, offices, lands, properties, and franchises to his kindred. He gave lavishly and abundantly to a few hard-hitting and hardheaded Hollanders—Mynheer van Rysdycks, Orange, and Bentinck families—what belonged to others, taken by confiscation. With it he conveyed the right of power, in greater wealth, substance, and franchises than all of the province of Orange, in which his ancestors contended with the Germans, French, Spanish, and the waters of their rough seas for their lives and something of human liberty.

"This scion of a brave and heroic line was elected to the British crown in the contingency, and, by the tyranny and the corruptions of the Stuarts, fell to giving away Englishmen's possessions in quantities that would have been realms to him or his ancestors in their little Duchy of

Orange. In this way, probably, the pernicious example of giving away the rights, franchises, and properties of the public to a few was fixed and settled on this continent, as well as in Britain. New Holland, later New York, was parceled out in lands, freeholds, and privileges to the few who had the strength and courage to maintain their gifts. Britain held to and extended this plan of giving away the lands and belongings of the people to a favored few, who were granted the authority to tax and govern them. In this way African slavery was brought over and established in every colony before our ancestors had or could have settled and established systems of government.· These evils and others that are the legacies of tyrant kings and aristocrats in less or greater degree, are with us, and will remain until they can be peacefully legislated out of existence, or go down piecemeal in a war of sections, or in a general revolution."

The aggregation and concentration of wealth, as we have recited, filled the hearts of these wise and eminent men with anxiety and alarm for the safety of our Government and the perpetuity of our free institutions one short generation since. If they were living to-day, with the lessons and experience of the flying years to their enlightened wisdom, what would they think when, in all sorts of questionable ways, the concentration of wealth in the hands of fewer men and the power it carries have been many times quadrupled?

In the time of William III and his Holland families a few thousand controlled Britain; but here in our own country, as boastingly declared by a railroad lawyer recently, "we have reached a point in development and enterprise where less than fifty men control every wheel and every industry in the United States, and can stop every one of them within twenty-four hours whenever they may wish." Reflecting on

the words of Lincoln and Douglas, it is high time to think
over and consider this unexampled piling up of wealth that
belongs of right to all men, now in the hands of a very few,
and what the others of our more than seventy-five millions
will or can be doing when these "less than fifty" stop or
say they can stop all our carrying and industrial operations.

CHAPTER XLII.

THE men of the great States of the West were descended from the stalwart, most rugged, and strongest nations of the earth. They should be known intimately and well; for these sturdy, lithe-limbed, full-breasted, and hard-headed millions were the most overwhelming and irresistible military and industrial actors in one of the most notable nations of all history, who, near the period of which we write, were to pass through the most desperate war of modern times. They were victors in an advancing revolution and development of freedom in which God planned the destruction of slavery.

All of them—farmers, artisans, men of commerce, and the liberal professions—were trained and skilled to labor, and in the toil of a faithful day's work earned an honest man's bread. They were brought up in useful occupations and grounded in the belief that the best in life required steady and constant performance of duty. With only an occasional exception they were not rich, not powerful, nor were they disposed in any way to oppress or distress their fellow-men. There were none who were industrious, temperate, and worthy, and who had health and strength for it, that did not have opportunity to earn an honest living.

It was rare indeed that any worthy person ever lacked a comfortable habitation or needful subsistence. The few unworthy ones could live, if they worked as others did; but even these, when needy and helpless, were not neglected. Schools, colleges, and institutions of learning were established wherever there were pupils and the shadow of coming necessity.

Communities, counties, towns, and then cities and States, filled up with teeming millions, separate and isolated perhaps in commerce and the goings to and fro, were striving, struggling, pushing ahead under the inspiring impulse of liberty. They were happy and contented under the severest trials and endurance, fully decided in mind that a man's life was worth no more than freedom and free institutions; and they were as fully determined to maintain both upon the earth as the men of the older Revolution had been. Their marvelous progress is accounted for in their steady toil and unflinching endurance. They resolutely and peacefully set themselves down for the severest labor that men and women could endure, determined to hold on and fight out the industrial battle to the end.

Thus they continued in effort and exhausting application that often made men old and broken down at forty years. The world-had not seen such a body of immigrants, subduing wastes, reducing to tillage so large an area with the simplest implements of agriculture and careful husbandry in shorter period. They were raising up, by the majesty of labor, art, and commerce, in a few decades, communities, cities, and States. They founded a Christian civilization, too, in which the schoolhouse and the meeting-house were in sight of almost every human habitation. It was a great migration that put three million Hebrews into Canaan in forty years; but here were over eight millions of the strongest races of men who came into our upper valley in no more, perhaps a little less time—twenty to thirty years—mainly from 1830 to 1860.

In the early days of the century they came West by the chain of the Great Lakes as far as Illinois and Wisconsin. Another route was the great National turnpike, from Philadelphia west, across the Alleghanies to Pittsburg thence down the Ohio and up the Mississippi River to any one of a half dozen Western States. In March and

April, 1841, the writer's little family of four came over this route from New York City by rail and stage-coach and freight wagons to Pittsburg, down the Ohio, and up the Mississippi to St. Louis in three weeks—the same journey that is made every twenty-four hours by swift-fleeting trains at forty miles an hour.

There was also the water route to New Orleans, up the Mississippi River, and over numerous connecting rivers. This was a good route for travel up the river as far as Galena, Dubuque, and Fort Snelling in an early day; but it was a long, tedious voyage from Europe, and almost as long from the Atlantic Coast, so that it was nothing nearly so generally used as the other routes. However, a large number of settlements were made along the main river and several of its tributaries during the French and Spanish occupation of the lower basin. These settlements were widely separated, and usually consisted of a few adventurous pioneer hunters and trappers, who made the earliest trading-points and formed the nucleus for the coming settlement. There were military and missionary stations all along the big river and its network of tributaries far into the wilderness and on the frontier.

In addition to these mixed and more lengthy routes were the numerous shorter overland, mud, sandy, and rocky ones, some with and some without bridges and ferries over the larger streams, but often with none of these except those temporarily made by the hardy emigrants pushing and wading along these rough and rugged roads of destiny. These open, all foot or horse and wagon routes began in the States of Virginia, Maryland, Pennsylvania, and New York, all leading westward to the fertile and inviting fields, out of which eleven States were then growing.

These were in sight and open on our eastern boundaries, with areas known and understood. Then there were unknown ones on our western slopes, with less-understood resources large enough to make as many, or twice as many, States in the progress of time, about which they marveled much in those days. They knew there was a great waste of plain, of rocks and rivers, and an almost boundless area, of which they knew little or nothing beyond its immensity. There were stirring tales related of sandy deserts, alkaline and barren sweeps of treeless plains, where they once thought that neither man nor beast nor fish nor fleeting bird could live and thrive.

These stories and legends ran that, far across the continent, bordering the soft, mellow-zoned Pacific, there was a wide-belted country skirting the placid ocean, studded with gold and silver and gems that would outweigh those of Ophir and the Ind of ancient story. If you had told the veteran of 1849 that in his overland journey thither he had passed over fertile plains, with proof of animals and herbage for them in sight, mountain lodes laden with precious and useful metals beyond all he could see on the ore-creased sides of the Sierras, or beyond his calculation, he would have declared you stark mad, and proven you so by every overland "Forty-niner" who had crossed and seen the two thousand weary miles of sandy desert, saleratus valleys and endless rocky wastes, in which human occupation or habitation was then impossible.

Still those "Forty-niners" were wise and brilliant men in their day, who philosophized not much, but went after things, and got them. They did much in founding commonwealths by the tides of the boundless ocean, as well as inland. These have made homes and habitations, with churches, schools, and colleges, and many other better things than the tantalizing gold. The alluring vision that sharpened their wisdom to the venture for wealth brought to light almost a new continent to the coming American.

The mid-continent migration that lined the roads and thoroughfares, and made and built them and their bridges for twenty years, to 1860, across the States of Ohio, Indiana, Illinois, and into other Western States, was the most remarkable passage, among many, of humanity's sweeping westward marches in history. In number they were multitudes, millions past any enumeration. Long before permanent settlements began, thousands of men, with horse-and-wagon trains, crossed the Mississippi and the Missouri, without being counted, who were pushing on to mold and build States, open mines that pour out streams of wealth, boundless and inexhaustible still.

They moved west in streams, in single families, in one or more wagons, up to neighborhoods, pulling up and taking with them all of their belongings that could be transported, making long caravans of from five to one hundred wagons each, all directed to some previously-selected localities, where they, too, were to found or add to a colony, a town, or county. In some instances all of these moving people, in their trains of covered wagons, crossed several States, and traveled a full thousand miles to begin their new settlements. In these caravans the women and children took the wagons with the older men, while the younger followed on foot, mule or horse-back, to drive along the milk cows and other live stock, which they took with them in great number.

For years, when I was a lad in Central Illinois, part of our boyish occupation was to count the "movers' wagons" and men on horse-back. For many years, in the seasonable months, from May to December, on our one line through Danville, Bloomington, and Peoria, the stream would often reach one hundred wagons a day and two hundred men on horseback. The summer and fall of 1854-5, counting and estimating, we put the total at one quarter million people who passed westward over this famous wagon-route. There were several others south and north of us.

Ours was the central route, where the business brought

conveniences **not** available to others; hence ours was full for several years in the fall season. The white covered wagons, with their cheerful, happy loads were never out of sight, and their bright camp-fires were so generally lined out along the roads through the timber belts, that their blazing fires lighted the roadways from border to border of the timber. Often, in the course of a mile or two, a thousand tired-out people, and as many or more animals, were soundly sleeping and resting themselves for the next day's march.

They went in every conceivable sort of vehicle of the time. The most common was the two-horse farm-wagon, covered with white muslin, still in use all over the West. These often had double teams of four horses or mules, with enough loose ones in the drive to put fresh teams to the haul every day. There were boys in carts and riding horses by the thousand. They had, in some cases, larger and heavier wagons, with as many as four, and even eight horses, with the long-topped "prairie schooners" and flaring ends, that could hold two tons of goods and provisions, and shelter ten to twenty people.

They made them pioneering campaigns, with enough hardship, labor, and endurance to bring healthy appetites and refreshing rest and sleep, with new developments of nature's wealth and resources in unrealized new regions to keep their minds and reasoning powers keyed up to their highest activities. The long overland journey was an enjoyable epoch in every one's mind who made it. It was often the means of restored and invigorated health that nothing could have secured so well, inspiring all with energy and others with regenerated zeal and spirit that made them leaders in their day.

In all it enlarged and more firmly fastened the love of country and free institutions in their hearts. In widening areas and endless regions beyond their anxious, intensified

vision they realized something of the great valley that
God had given to free men and for the best and highest
growth of our race, who have and will keep it in their
memories forever. There was a migration, a settling-up
of new lands and growth, improvements, and resulting bet-
terments such as men have never surpassed. Of the movement of population the following table is readily understood:

Population of eight Upper Mississippi Valley States,
1840 to 1860, and increase:

STATES.	Population 1860.	Population 1840.	Increase.
Indiana	1,350,428	685,866	664,562
Illinois	1,711,951	476,185	1,235,768
Iowa	674,913	44,112	629,801
Michigan	749,113	212,267	536,846
Minnesota	172,023	6,077	165,946
Missouri	1,182,012	383,702	798,310
Ohio	1,980,329	1,510,467	469,862
Wisconsin	775,881	309,450	744,936
Totals	8,596,650	3,350,619	5,246,031

These tables are partial records of the movement where
three and one-third millions grew to eight and one-half
millions in twenty years, with about another half million
who came West in the same migration and pushed. on to
the farther Western frontier and Northwest Territories,
making a population of nine millions 'in the States and
Territory of the Revolutionary and eighteenth-century
dates—three times as many as achieved our independence.

There was, in the eight States, an increase of five and
one quarter millions of people in the time, doubling the
population, with as many above as the State of Ohio, the
most densely populated of any of the eight States in 1860.
This moving multitude came into the Upper Mississippi
and in the Lower Missouri basins, and rested there to
build up and give strength to the half-throttled Nation that

would need every one of them and every fiber of their strength in their conflict that the God of nations alone comprehended.

They could have gone further, as well as where they were, to seek for hidden wealth and habitations so alluring to brave, venturesome men; but a mightier hand stayed them and held them, not to scatter, but gather together to support the tottering Republic, and to grow and prosper and save the increase of the richest inhabited valley of the earth for war, then almost upon them.

It was not, perhaps, through any miracle, but it was prescience, prudence, and high capacity in the best use of every facility far above human wisdom that led them, verifying what Mr. Lincoln said, that "God was leading our Republic in his own time and way to its high destiny, and would deal with it and fulfill every promise to men if the men of our day would but do our duty."

In the time when there had gathered and grown these nine millions of people in one division of our great country, two millions of them could bear arms. Leaders rose who were the complement and the necessity as well of such men. One chief leader came for the stronger lash and measure of man against man, and another of steel with steel in the battle on open fields, tempered and hardened for every blow. The chief, the great prophet-leader, fitted for the strife as the days dawned upon him, entered the conflict alone. He felt all earthly holdings and human weakness passing when, with firmer grasp, he said: "I have talked with God. It is his cause, and the Union is his. As he willeth, so it will be. We can but follow and pray for its integrity and for mercy to the fallen."

There was a strong, resolute population in the mighty Western States, and it is no disparagement to our brother millions of the Atlantic States that we had more of flocks and herds and the products of farms and fields and the substantial possessions that come from the continued, well-directed labor and prudent saving, than any had ever earned, produced, and held for a Nation's need in so short a time.

The struggle was coming. It was inevitable, and danger was threatening every day. We had nine millions in the great Northwest, such as were never surpassed in labor, industry, or mental achievement. Besides we had the products of human toil in their richest abundance, horses, mules, neat cattle, hogs, sheep, fowl—animals for use, comfort, and subsistence in such numbers and quality that no other people, equal in number, held or owned half so many. We had, too, products of the soil, corn, wheat, oats, barley, rye, hay, and forage in the same relation and abundance. These products, hitherto unequaled, were with the men and the leaders, the bounties and saving resources of the people.

What these men were and what they had of that day, and how it was used, should be known and accounted to them; and all concerning them should be told and treasured in the minds of to-day and succeeding time. They were daring and brave, although it had been said of them that they were not; and some very foolish Americans in the slave States affected to believe the story until they were brought a terrible awakening to the contrary.

We have written of them more in detail, because of the crisis that was heavy on them in 1860. A Convention was to be assembled in the chief city of the Northwest at the most critical moment of the rising struggle—the most anxious and strained situation of the country since its founding under Constitutional law. One great Convention of a long powerful party had been stricken by a confusion and clash of policies and principles, as declared in irreconcilable resolutions, and distractions were widening the gap every day.

The wrath of men had fallen heavily on the party of

Jefferson and Jackson. It was parting in twain, with certain prospect of defeat if the wisdom of men did not bring a settlement at once. That God's wisdom did not guide them seemed clear in that one faction would not leave off its oppressions and despotic party control, but seemed full of the wrath of men when sense and wise judgment were never more needed, but for the time had parted with all it had.

The men of the Northwest—the first time in the history of our country—were going to have a National party Convention of a party mostly confined to the northern section of the country for necessitous reasons. It was to hold its second Convention to nominate candidates for President and Vice-President in Chicago. Our Western people, of whom we have written something, were getting ready to attend, not only the few hundreds who would be delegates and the wiser and more experienced, but the masses by thousands. They were getting ready to go by rail and river and lake, in such streams and hosts of stirred-up enthusiasts as had never gathered in or graced any city on the continent.

There was fevered interest and intensity of feeling all over the free States and along the border for the Union— a sentiment that had no corresponding or equal hold on the hearts of the people. The times were portentous. Every day added some mischief to the swelling current that was drifting and carrying the South in the wake of passionate and impulsive leaders, who had declared for separation on the basis of "State sovereignty," which was no less than war, or the alternative of submission to slavery without restriction or interference.

The agitation over slavery grew to be, first, the determination that the Union must be saved, no matter what came in the way, while the fury was rising all over the South. The Southern press was full of passionate appeals and extravagant boastings, the madness and ambition of thoughtless men, who should have been their careful and experienced advisers. Governors, courts, and Legislatures, from Washington to the Rio Grande, boastfully declared that the Northern people were a pusillanimous set, who would neither stand nor fight, but would hide and flee from the semblance of danger, "that one well-armed Southern man could lick five blue-bellied Yankees any day."

According to Senator Hammond, of South Carolina, an accredited authority, "the Northern people, the greasy laboring men and mechanics, were the mudsills of society." They were, in fact and in the ordinary progress of our affairs, the slaves of the Northern capitalists, who controlled the industrial and commercial enterprises; consequently they could neither manfully contend for their rights "on field of honor or war," nor dare to meet in hostile combat the sword of the cotton States' "hero, so gallant in war." Perhaps the most blustering bully of them all was Senator Robert Toombs, of Georgia, who declared that he would some day "call the roll of his slaves under the shadow of Bunker Hill Monument."

Their fury ran in senseless braggadocio and empty swagger. Their ferocious threats ruled men all over the slave States, where ministers in almost every Southern pulpit and many Northern ones were justifying and sustaining slavery. It was a storm-blast against the threatened destruction of our Government and the stranglers of human liberty, when parties were dissolving, when cowardly, shivering Presidents and Cabinets were in another Assyrian feast, falling, with their knees knocking like broken staves, and bending like willows in a blast, serving and cringing before the advancing Moloch.

In the early months of the year, while agitation and tumult prevailed in the South, the more independent free people of the country, wherever they could do so, were making arrangements to send delegates to the Chicago Convention. They were stinging with resentment against the false accusations denouncing their courage, and the impudent assaults on their domestic, industrial, and social relations made by the furious Southern leaders.

The purpose of the slave propaganda then was to fire the Southern heart and arouse the animosities of their people against "Northern menials and greasy mechanics." This plan of the slave-leaders prevailed, until it brought to hundreds of thousands of misled and misinformed brave Southern men boundless experience and positive knowledge of the deadly effect of well-made Yankee guns, and that these "menials," whom they were to chase off, one to five, had the habit of staying and using their weapons all the more vigorously the closer these brave Southrons got and remained in range.

Some of them, it appeared, could not have missed the merciless conscription; but all who got into their real fighting lines were always satisfied with "one Yankee agin' him," and as much less as circumstances permitted. The slave roll-call was not only not sounded on Bunker Hill, but the slave-owners were backward about being very near or calling any roll-call even in the vicinity of any Yankee camp. They verified the saying that the loudest and most pretentious "are never the bravest and truest in war."

In this time of dispute, circulating slanders, wrangling differences, and irreconcilable systems, the free State people were anxious to have a courageous body of men of any and all shades of loyal and anti-slavery beliefs meet and emphatically declare themselves on the common ground of the integrity and perpetuity of the Union and the restriction of slavery to the States where it existed. This was the hope of the Chicago Convention.

These people of the free States, in the face of weak Administrations, plotting Cabinets, and bold, outspoken disunionists, wanted a common, definite assertion of principles on which all loyal men could agree. In addition, brave men all over the North, with a million or more of them in the Northwest, wanted a definite refutation of the wanton and wicked slanders propagated and spread all over the South by these blustering, bullying disunionists, that the Northern people were unlawfully interfering with their domestic institutions, and that they were all cowards and would not contend manfully and fight for their rights, as Americans had always done.

The Convention was coming. These Northwesterners knew full well that no reputable body of men would take its time replying to these Southern threats and slanders, but they were going to attend the Convention and be numerous and expressive enough to notify the whole tribe of Southern hotheaded leaders that, if fighting was what they wanted, they could have all of it they liked. When the Chicago illuminated, blazing, torch-bearing, fifteen miles of marching double columns, and all that could be carried there on every route, met in session, they had plump and positive proof of it. Of this history-making body of Americans much has been said and much more perhaps will be said. Much could have been said heretofore but for the personal sensitiveness of some of the chief actors. The actors and relators have passed away over the silent river with much knowledge of value in this heroic event, known only to a few.

Of the Convention record there is a book—a huge volume—of what the delegates and those from every State made as their daily minutes of transactions. Pamphlets and voluminous reports that spread all over the country were in abundance at the time. It was a turning-point in the career of the Nation. It was so in the lives of many distinguished men, besides the one whose life became the beacon-light of humanity because of its favor. In writing of it, it is not all a question of how much or how little of its proceedings to consider, but how to get at the truth of the main subjects and the transactions of interest that concern the people.

There were no less than three distinct factions in the commingling that came to be the Republican party. There were the Abolitionists, of whom we have written sufficiently. Time had softened the asperities against this faction. Douglas and many of his more zealous followers had derisively called them Abolitionists. The Old-line Whigs enjoyed this more than anything the Democrats had said; for they had said as much, or more, themselves. Besides, Douglas had been a tireless and keen-cutting satirist of the Whigs, and had said many things of them for which he had not been forgiven; but when he denounced our faction as Abolitionists, these old Whig fossils enjoyed it, and, elevating their noses, they gave us second seats only in the formation of the new party. We accepted these restrictions uncomplainingly, fully believing Lincoln's prophecy in more ways than one, that our new party would soon be "all slave or all free," as well as the Nation, and that we would quietly endure the transformation that was going our way. As time passed, the Southern leaders, in 1858, still high authority to many on mongrel slang and party epithets, kept on denouncing Mr. Seward and Mr. Lincoln and the old Whig part of the forming black Republican party. After this they openly denounced Judge Douglas as having surrendered to the Abolitionists. Where men were not throttled or restrained in speech, this "Abolitionist" slang and epithet-making fell like a broken kite. But a few of the most silvered of the antediluvians in all parties were reconciled to us, and we took front benches in all the Republican meetings of 1860.

The Whigs claimed to be first in succession in the work of construction. Their party had so generally and

completely fallen to pieces in 1852 that there could be no
doubt that they were the first ready for some kind of re-
organization, as they had been without any two years before the Republican party had any kind of existence. This
put them in the most favorable condition in the free States
to be the first body of recruits in the new formation. This
was the case, as a rule, in all the States east of Indiana,
where Mr. Seward, Mr. Greeley, and the New England contingent, following and succeeding Mr. Webster, Mr. Choate,
and others, became the leaders.

These Eastern Whigs took kindly to all anti-slavery
societies, Free Soilers, and others, readily uniting on the
basis of Seward's "higher law" on the most advanced anti-
slavery ground then held, short of actual interference with
slavery where it existed. They recognized Mr. Seward's
position that there was "an irrepressible conflict" between
freedom and slavery.

Mr. Seward's "higher-law" interpretation was, in substance, that God's righteous laws would sooner or later
prevail against slavery and all other forms of human oppression. On these findings, Seward, Weed, Greeley, and
the whole Eastern and New England section were denounced
as Abolitionists by the slave-leaders, and held to be more
dangerous than the older Free Soil party, because of the
boldness of Seward's "unconstitutional" "higher-law" doctrine. So the accession of these leaders and their followers
to the new forming party was from purely Abolition
sources in the slave-leaders' definitions.

They were mainly Whigs, however, with anti-slavery
beliefs, who came into the new party after having zealously
supported General Scott in 1852. Scott was too good a
man, too faithfully and sincerely devoted to our country
and its institutions and a stalwart patriot, and chiefly because of this he was deliberately defeated by the pro-
slavery faction of his own party, who gained nothing bet-

ter than extinction in the defeat of the patriot of Chippewa, Lundy's Lane, and Chapultepec.

The subdivision of the Whigs in Ohio, Indiana, Illinois, and States westward, were mostly of the Henry Clay faction. Thousands of these were from the slave States— mainly Virginia, Kentucky, and Tennessee—in which and in all the West, Mr. Clay was the lifetime leader, without a rival, for almost fifty years. This was the exact reverse of the situation in the New England and North Atlantic States, where Mr. Webster was the most prominent leader and advocate of any party during the last thirty years of Clay's lead and ascendency in the South and West.

The main body of these Southern people who emigrated to the fertile lands of the Northwest were hard working and industrious. They were from the rocky, mountainous, unproductive, and, in some parts, the almost barren regions of the States mentioned. They were descendants of the Scotch-Irish, Irish, English, and Welsh peoples, generally the most independent and determined of our race to begin with. Two or three generations of growth and development in the mountainous limestone regions of the Alleghanies had taken nothing from their self-reliance, but strengthened their independence of character.

This mountainous Alleghany region, though lacking the productive qualities of richer, wider alluvial valleys, was full of the elements that grow massive, large-boned, strong-framed, iron-sinewed men, whose stature averaged six feet in many localities. These people heartily disliked slavery in any form, not because of much sympathy with the Negro, but that their beliefs were that all, without exception, should work and follow some industrious occupation for themselves. They did their own work, and wanted neither slaves, dependents, nor supernumeraries about them, in the way, or in competition with them. Their mountain elevation gave them abundant oxygen and uncontaminated air.

Their waters were filtered and cleansed through sand and limestone beds, with finely-blended iron and soluble phosphates. The hills, the mountains, the varying landscape, were magnificent in nature's splendor, inspiring to this thoughtful commingled race, who had all these and the expanse, bounded only by their highest peaks, from earth to sky, to grow and mature tribes of as clear-headed men as have ever been produced in our marvelous civilization. With the strong aversion of this Southern mountain people to slavery, they were nevertheless, by kindred ties, association, the few Negroes among them, and neighborly considerations, so tinctured by the influences of slavery that they were firmly opposed to all kinds of interference with it or speech against it. They looked upon Abolitionists as meddlesome agitators who would stir up needless strife and perhaps bloody insurrection.

Mr. Lincoln was one of this race of people. His family had made several migrations westward. He had been in two of them. He had grown to manhood and political leadership alongside such men; but, leader as he always was to them, and much as they honored and respected him for his integrity and high capacities, there was no faction or part of one in the forming new party so hard to reconcile to any declaration against or interference with slavery or its extension as this same free State body of emigrating Clay Whigs, with whom Mr. Lincoln had no end of trouble.

He labored with them so patiently and so long that many of them grew to think that they alone were the men who should guide him or who could save the new party, or, in the greater emergency, the Nation, but that they would render that service only on condition of getting all they wanted in favor or office-holding. They were an inconsiderable part in the forming party, of which ninety per cent were stoutly opposed to further spread of slavery and the least aggressive policy of the slaveholders. Still this little faction domineered as far and as long as they could. That Mr. Lincoln succeeded and had no open rupture with this faction, out of which he grew, was proof of his surpassing capacity and abilities; for they would not and did not submit to any other leadership, nor could any other man then living have conducted the war and the ordinary affairs of state and kept so many antiquated statesmen from destroying each other, as himself. It must be remembered also that this small faction had to be kept on the side of the Union, if it was to be saved.

Out of these two East and West factions of Whigs, and all the factions of anti-slavery people indiscriminately, with the larger faction coming from the dissolving Democratic party, the Republican organization was formed and sprang into strong and actual existence as a great party.

The people of the Northwest, in large majorities, had been Democrats from the time of the admission of several of the Territories as States, firmly and almost unchangeably so from the time of Jackson. They were well informed, as intelligent a mass of men as ever tilled the soil, who fully employed themselves in the kindred pursuits of opening up and building into civilization a new country. Most of them were Democrats because of the principles and traditions of the party.

Those of them who were foreign born, and, in some instances, the second generation, were Democrats because of the oppressions in the lands from which they had emigrated. All had groaned under the heaviest loads they could bear, imposed on them by the oppressive exactions of tyrants, until they were distrustful of even representative government, and wanted in its stead self-government. With this influx added to the strong Puritanism of the North Atlantic colonies, the great Northwest had been zealously and reliably Democratic as the Nation had been.

When the Charleston Convention was assembled, the

Democracy could look back over a period of more than thirty years of almost unbroken supremacy. They could have continued so under a wise and just administration, but the spirit of Pharaoh was rampant and ascendant. A great popular leader was to be stricken because he would not bend his neck to the broken faith. They marshaled their hosts against him; and their best Democratic statesman and best-followed leader was beaten in the sundered, dissolving party.

God laid the finger of his wrath upon them, and not Rameses and all his godless Egyptians suffered greater privations, plagues, and slayings than the designing propagandists and the deluded, suffering, and dying Southern people. Poor, old, shaking Buchanan, the wretched specter of a man, late an honored citizen, willingly obeyed them and piteously pleaded for peace after he had faithlessly thrown away his opportunity to command and enforce it. He vainly endeavored to arrest the dreadful, war-rising destruction his neglect had done so much to precipitate, but his prayer and his power were mocked, and he stood before the unmasked treason of his own Cabinet and the ruin of his once powerful party, a broken, palsied, chattering President, parleying for peace, when the conspiracy that had thrived and grown under his want of observance and exercise of force to suppress it was taking the field for war.

God weighed him and, though he was not bad in everything of himself, he proved lighter than the chaff of the threshing-floor. Nebuchadnezzar was not more completely driven from power and authority. Nor was his seven years' grass-living more distinct or impressive than Buchanan's life-ending solitude, which never for a day lifted from or left him.

The breaking-up of the Democratic party brought recruits to the Republicans by hundreds of thousands. It was because of their independent character that two millions of them, sure of political power, willingly broke in fragments the party they held next to Church and family altar, rather than have continued power at the cost of sacrificed principles. Out of these elements which have passed before us was made the powerful, victorious Republican party. The dissolution of the Democratic party was an illustration, oft-repeated, of the downfall of conceited, self-glorious men, parties, kingdoms, and dynasties.

CHAPTER XLIII.

IN the latter months of 1859, in the central counties of
Illinois, the main subject of interest was what would be
done in the way of getting ready and presenting Mr. Lincoln as our choice for nomination at Chicago. He was our
home man, and almost every one in those eight counties
knew him and held him as a friendly adviser in all matters
of trouble and distress. To those who knew him well—
and there were many who shared his confidence—he was
very much the same as a father, a brother, or a dutiful son;
and these people had taken him into their hearts as they
could take no other man.

With this plain understanding it will be clear to the
minds of men that, when he was being considered and looked
over as a contingent availability for President, the question in our home counties was not, "Will you support him?"
but "What can we do to help?" It was in the air, and it
was the spirit of the people that they were for him as far
as they could be, including thousands of Democrats. Many
Democrats whom I knew said something like this: "If you
Republicans would do so sensible a thing as to nominate Abe
Lincoln, I will vote for him. I am a Democrat, and I have
not deserted my principles nor our leader, Judge Douglas,
whom we would support more earnestly than ever if he had
any chance; but those Southern fire-eaters, who are no better than traitors, have made his election impossible ever
since he stood firm for fair elections in Kansas, and I would
like to give them a lesson in electing Abe Lincoln that they
will be sure to remember. He is as smart as any one of

them. He is as loyal as any man that lives. He is always for the poor man and always on the side of any one in distress. He's always just plain Abe Lincoln, as friendly to a poor boy as he was to me when I had no vote and was n't thinking of such a thing, as he was to the big men, the politicians, judges, or governors, who could influence a hundred to my one any time. I tell you, I like Abe Lincoln, and sure as he is nominated, I 'm going to vote for him straight; and if you let me know how I can help to hurry up things and help nominate him, I 'll do it."

In the winter, as time sped along, it came to be the important subject that required some kind of settlement. There were several able men, decided favorites in their States or localities, who were being written of as capable and worthy the high distinction by reason of their devotion and service in the cause of human rights. In that direful time, without need for sensational or actual alarm, our Nation, and all it held, seemed plunging like a vessel on the shifting sand and sunken rocks of a treacherous shore.

In the preliminary work of the Convention, in the first meetings, and henceforward, my opportunities for accurate knowledge of every political movement were as full and complete in every way as our location, my personal acquaintance, and other ordinary facilities could make them. I was continued secretary of the Champaign County Committee until the opening of the war, in 1861. It was one of the heavy Republican counties, held and relied on as one of the best-organized in the State. It was centrally located, and was a Lovejoy-Lincoln county out and out. It was a great factor in a close State. It became the political campaigning ground of great importance for all parties.

This gave me unusual means of becoming well acquainted with every prominent political leader and speaker in our own State, and others from Missouri, Iowa, and a great many from Indiana. Being young and ambitious and anxious to keep such business as came in order, and never being a candidate for office, I had the full confidence of all our side in political affairs, and was always welcome in all conferences, committee work, or Conventions wherever I had occasion or necessity of attending. In addition, our personal intercourse with Douglas and other Democrats gave me reliable information on political matters.

I still kept up my personal relations with Mr. Lincoln, who stood to me very much in the place of a father. Political work came to me as an incident and without desire to do more than to advance and defend my father's and my own belief on the all-absorbing topic of human slavery. In beginning my political work I became the pupil and protégé of Mr. Gridley, under the fatherly supervision of Mr. Lincoln. These I followed with the zeal and aptitude of a new recruit. Gridley was one of the brightest and best-informed men I ever knew. He was a style-cutter and parer-down to the point where he got the clearest meaning out of words and sentences that seldom missed the brilliant and exact expression he wanted. He joined words into phrases that ran like 'shears cutting steel, with the brilliancy and brightness that fastened them as he went along in his direct, incisive, and frequently amusing descriptions, that gave his talk a pertinence and power that were all his own.

My place up to the opening of hostilities seemed commonplace enough, and was no more than what a great many were doing elsewhere in ordinary party work and progress at the time; and not until later in life did it come to me in all its force that I had the best of opportunities to gain a full knowledge of Mr. Lincoln and the men who made his career possible. This party service of mine, and the facilities I had, opened the doors for seeing and gathering the knowledge and fathoming the motives of the chief actor and leader through the preparation and struggle of war.

In the fall of 1859 and January of 1860, and from that time on, our people took a much-increased interest in the candidacy of Mr. Lincoln. He was spoken to quite often about it. Newspaper men in several localities were ready to take up his candidacy, in order to unite the friendly Republican and other newspapers in his favor. Numerous friends wrote to him urging him to give his consent. As frequently happens in the rise of a man in the people's confidence, there were several who were ambitious to be the very first man or newspaper to discover him and his ability, and at that time to make him President.

His constant and unvarying reply to the few intimate friends with whom he talked about it after his surprising campaign of 1858, was, in substance: "I do not feel that I have reached the place in public estimation, nor do I feel that I possess the fitness and qualifications to be nominated for and possibly be elected President. Much as I esteem the favor and generosity of friends who are kind and partial enough to overlook my want of these, my ambitiou has been, and still is, to serve the cause with whatever of ability I have, to do so faithfully, without public office or position, until, in fulfillment of expectation, I may be elected a senator from Illinois. This would satisfy all the ambition I have for office or public service. With a full appreciation of the struggle, I do not feel any desire to undertake the responsibility of the Presidential office."

This was the substance of his remarks as late as a few days before Christmas 1859, when a few of us met him and talked over the public interest in the subject in all our central counties and over the State, and in some other Western States as well as we could learn. At the time several States were naming candidates. Ohio and Missouri were doing so conspicuously. We knew that Mr. Lincoln's qualifications were certainly equal to any of the others mentioned, and that Illinois was an essential and very important State,

as parties then stood, for the Republicans to win. In any
contingency it was a close and doubtful one, and almost
sure to vote for Douglas as against any Eastern Republican.
His friends in our home counties were zealously for him,
and esteemed it an honor to name him in form and in season
to the Republicans of Illinois and as many as could be led
in other States to believe in our candidate.

He took it all in his candid, open-hearted way, thanking his friends for their generous interest and kind expressions in his favor. We met him again the next day
when, taking a more serious look, he invited the half dozen
or more to be seated, when he said: "One thing you have
mentioned has all the importance, or even more than you
give it; that is, that the nominee should be one who will
be the most acceptable to the party in the three doubtful
States of Pennsylvania, Indiana, and Illinois, as without
two of these States for our man we can not succeed.

"For myself, I can cheerfully support any one of the
able and distinguished men named so far, and I will go
into the canvass for any one of them with all my might;
but as you make it, it is too delicate a subject for me to say
who can, or who can not, carry enough of these doubtful
States to be elected. You, friends, have very kindly suggested the use of my name as a candidate from this, one of
the doubtful States. I can not, so far, see that it is the
best thing to do; but you are all, as I am, aware and duly
appreciate that our party and many others in the State
have sustained me with such unhesitating and lasting favor
that no well-considered request from you and them can be
declined, no matter whether it suits or serves my personal
convenience.

"As there are several candidates anyway, and only one out
of the six or seven is to be chosen, the mention of another
name should not seriously affect those already in the race.
The presentation, which will be perhaps no more than a per-

sonal compliment, may have the beneficial effect in our own doubtful State that, as it has presented one of its citizens, it may—at least, it should—more zealously support whoever is nominated by the Convention.

"In conclusion, after thanking you, gentlemen, as good friends as any man ever had or deserved, we will do this. As it has been stated, the State Committee will assemble in a few weeks to call a State Convention for whatever may be considered appropriate business. It will have an attendance from every part of the State. If you will serve me further by letting the subject rest until then, without agitation, the committee may settle and determine this, as they did in 1858, and, I hope, with as satisfactory results; for, although I was defeated, it was close running. I was not badly hurt, and, as you see, I am well and as ready for the next race as the rest of you.

"In your remarks you were sensible in believing that it is going to be a hard pull indeed to defeat Judge Douglas in this closely-balanced State. I came as near doing it as any one ever did, and I know just what kind of a job it is. With those fiery hotspurs of the South attempting to punish and overthrow him, he is growing stronger with our people and the entire Northern faction of his party every day.

"We can hardly foretell the situation two weeks ahead in the feverish and excited condition in the South, and at Washington as well. So it is mostly speculation what may happen to one or both parties by Convention or election time. But of one thing we are quite certain: if Judge Douglas receives the nomination of his party and we can carry this State against him, it will be a campaign where several thousand of you will earn the victory by as hard labor and perseverance as he who gets his living out of his every-day's toil. I have tried it, and know a little better

perhaps than any one of you what sort of an undertak-
·ing it .is."

With cordial handshakings the little meeting dispersed.
It was satisfactorily settled. Little was said or talked of
concerning it; for all desired that his wishes should be fully
complied with. As the result came about, Mr. Lincoln was
as much a candidate henceforward as either Seward, Chase,
or Bates; and Richard J. Oglesby, his neighbor, of Decatur,
was made the marshal militant of the hosts in the field in
our State and, incidentally, anywhere else, to lead in a
campaign where, for the first time in twenty years, Mr.
Lincoln was not the field-leader himself.

In the Christmas-times, not many days after the Springfield conference with Mr. Lincoln, I went to Bloomington
to talk over the Chicago Convention situation with Mr.
Gridley, as, by Weed's consent, it was as good as settled
that the National Convention would be held there. In the
two or three intervening days he had been apprised of the
result of the conference, so when I met him, he seemed
full of spirit, more brightened up and sharpened for re-
partee and pungent wit than I had ever seen him.

I can only give a brief account of our two-hours' pleasant conversation here. Much of it was, in comparison, like
zigzagged, forked lightning, in blazing splendor, that would
have held any audience content and eager in his earnest,
fascinating delivery. Not much of such direct or energetic
speech can be written; for without the trained facial expression and the vigor of the arm and other bodily movements
that in themselves were flashes of wit, humor, or tragedy, we
can not put his thoughts into dull, plodding words.

He said in part: "You have nominated Mr. Lincoln. I
hope you may consummate it fully and elect him; but, Robert; I thought that you personally were not going into politics. While I have been so easily beguiled, I hear that you

and some very worthy gentlemen have ventured the highest
performance of the art, and have already made a President."

I replied to this that I had faithfully observed his advice as to myself, that I desired no place or position, not
even the one that was all work on my part, that I would give
that up any day there appeared an agreeable way of doing
it. "But," I said, "from what I see of you now, I fully expect to see you make a greater departure, and be, very
soon, one of the busiest men in politics in the State, because no power on earth can hold Illinois from going into
this work like fire in dry stubble.

"I know you to be one of the most faithful and capable
friends of Mr. Lincoln, which he knows as well as I do;
and nothing I can think of can keep you out of the work
in which you will soon be fully absorbed. If you had been
at Springfield, you would have been one of the chieftains.
For myself, I said very little; but, as you know, by general
favor I am always admitted wherever there are prospects
for hard work, in which our county, and all of us in it, are
expected to do our full share. I enjoyed the meeting, and
know that all present would have heartily welcomed you."

He replied: "I would have enjoyed being there and
talking to them if they would hearken and heed my advice and keep still about it. I feel that no one more earnestly desires Mr. Lincoln's nomination and election, or
would do more of what I am able to do, and I feel somehow that he is to be God's man in spite of all our blundering. But what supreme folly and two-year-old innocence
it is for a few men, or the whole State, to make a hurrah
nomination of Mr. Lincoln! The whole thing, if not
planned and exactly executed, and fought out inch by inch
and man against man and State, will be no more than a mess
of parsley and mutton-chops for Mr. Weed's breakfast.

"I tell you that your crowd and our State and its Conventions, without positive, earnest work at every point, will

leave us 'babes in the woods' in the hands of this trained master, New York's leader. Everything in his plan is provided for months ahead as well as any one of Cæsar's campaigns ever was; and we can have no reasonable hope of success without a counter-plan at every point in skilled movement and competent hands that he wots not of.

"As an illustration of what this political Cæsar can do, you are well aware that Mr. Weed's political supremacy, is so complete that Mr. Greeley, with all the influence that a clean, independent newspaper, so largely read, with all the healthy influence it possesses, can not secure the appointment of a single delegate to any Convention in any county in his State. Weed controls; hence Greeley will not be able to be appointed a delegate or control the appointment of any one to the Chicago Convention. Weed can send the most notorious ward politician in New York or Albany, who never voted a Republican ticket in his life, and never will.

"I know and admire the man, and have seen and known of his work for years. He is as tireless as Satan or any of his kind. He has as much scheming sense as a dozen or two like Seward, or any one I know in any party in the country. I do n't look on it as a possible thing to beat him, if he discovers our plan, or even that we have one. His plan is to girdle Chicago as an axman does his tree, and, in season, when it dries out, he will come along, cut it down, and take it away. I have it from reliable sources that he has plans ahead to get to the Convention with about two hundred of the two hundred and thirty votes it will take to nominate.

"He has selected Chicago to deceive us, a comparatively small city for the gathering; but, left alone, as it is now, it is a more thoroughly New-York-influenced town than any place near its size outside of his State. He has matured plans for and will almost surely get the delegations from Michigan, Wisconsin, Iowa, and Minnesota. Surrounding us with all these States against us, only Illinois and Indiana are not yet in his scheme; but they are held off now to avoid a contest with Mr. Lincoln, and are yet to play for.

"The Convention will be held in June, with the lakes full of every kind of steam and sailing craft. The railroads, boats, and everything that can haul a Seward man to Chicago will be in crowded operation; and such a crowd of Seward-Weed men as no one anticipates will overrun Chicago, make it another Albany, shout themselves hoarse, and nominate Mr. Seward in a skyrocketing performance. Then they will go home full of the story of their triumph over some 'Western backwoodsmen, who imagined they had a candidate for President, but who could not control their own city of Chicago.' "

When he paused a moment, as if to expect approval, I took opportunity to say: "It would ill beseem me, whom you have always favored and befriended, to say to you, whom I have respected and honored since boyhood as a man of wisdom and experience, what you should do or not do; still it is no ordinary undertaking that calls for and demands the best any of us can do. You know my relation to the work. I have been allowed to be present, and know what our strongest and ablest men intend to do. I was not called in to dispute, but to listen, be obedient, take the place of a young man, and, in whatever comes of duty, to do it well. I expect to do no more than suggest to any one. The suggestion I have to make now is that you do not want the whole procedure to end so that the keenest observation you could make of it when it is all over would be, 'I saw all the blunders, was surprised that our people did not manage Mr. Lincoln's candidacy better, or keep out of it altogether; and I am not a bit surprised at his defeat.' "

I continued: "The men in this movement, with Oglesby now leading, seem to me as able, determined, and capable men as ever espoused any cause. They are in it in such numbers, earnest purpose, and unbounded courage, that, like our Western people, they will never let go what they undertake. They are just what you are. They want Mr. Lincoln nominated, and want no blunders committed anywhere. They will not have any if they can be avoided or prevented. They know you well and how strong and purposeful your friendship for Mr. Lincoln is.

"They have seen and admired your almost marvelous career, how, as a business man, in the face of repeated adversity, you have achieved success. With every duty of a good citizen fulfilled, you grasped the resources of this new and promising country, and you have laid the foundation and built a fortune—not once, but twice—and in doing so none of it rested on your neighbors' ruin or oppression. On the contrary, our people, your neighbors, have enjoyed the benefit of your enterprise, and it has never missed your purpose or the energy that very often got you out twenty miles through mud and water on a railroad dump at seven o'clock in the morning. The number who have shared your success and bounty are an unknown multitude. Therefore they are aware of your capacities, your managing ability, your tireless devotion and application to all you undertake. They know what you can do and what is sorely needed in this critical juncture of Mr. Lincoln's career, with all the possibilities that would follow the work of a mind and capacity like yours. It is their combined judgment that spontaneous enthusiasm will not suffice to nominate Mr. Lincoln.

"In your place to-day you can do for Mr. Lincoln what appears impossible for any other friend, or a dozen of friends, to do. Since I saw you last, I have had a strong verification of your opinion of Mr. Weed. Mr. Crandall, now publishing a newspaper in Champaign,.was in the same business for many years in a Central New York county, where he became well acquainted with Mr. Weed, and has been familiar with his wonderful success for years. He is recently from there, and is well aware of all there is in the Greeley disruption. Crandall is sincere in his support of Mr. Lincoln. Just before going to Springfield, he said to me: 'No matter how anxious we all feel for the success of Mr. Lincoln, knowing what I do, I can hardly have any hope that we can defeat Weed's well-laid plan to nominate Seward. I am not saying this in discouragement of the present general desire of our people; for I am supporting and will support Mr. Lincoln one way or another.' "

Continuing, I said to Mr. Gridley: "These men know your outspoken directness, but are not all as well-informed about it as I had been. Cognizant of your favor to me, they have asked me to talk the plan over with you. Some of the more doubtful inquired whether I would hesitate or dislike to do so."

"How did you reply to that?" interrupted Mr. Gridley like a flash.

I replied: "As you are so well aware of what I have done, you surely understand the whole of it."

He continued: "Yes, to some extent; but you did n't say I would go into political work, did you, or agree to any plan of publishing my relation to it for the benefit of the Weed-Seward combination, did you? This, as I regard it, would give Weed the very opportunity to defeat anything I should attempt."

I replied: "No, I made no such pledge for you. I stated only that you had given the subject very close attention, and that you thought the situation was full of pitfalls for us. As I understand it, you are to make your own plan, conduct it to success, publish or not, as you like, exercise your own judgment in the management of it, and call on those

whom you desire for help. The purely political organization will do nothing that will interfere with you, and will
not conflict or approach your work without your consent.
In reply to those who thought I might hesitate about going over this in full with you, I said, 'I have not only neither
hesitation nor doubt in taking it up and explaining it to
you, but I will be glad to do it.' I felt certain you would
use all honorable means in your power and to better purpose than any other man."

After this full discussion, Mr. Gridley seemed pleased,
and said: "Well, Oglesby is the right man to lead the
masses. No one can do it better. When other work becomes necessary, others will be found without measure to
take it up. I feared they might select some one to divide
work with me. I did n't want it that way, and could n't
have it. You have not only done well, but I must say you
have acted discreetly. I want you to buckle on your armor
and keep in politics with me. I will not take you from your
business until it becomes a necessity; but you must keep
ready to go any day for awhile. No man must fail or shirk
his duty. I am not a politician, and do not wish to have
anything to do with the strictly political part of it; but I
am anxious for this, that all possible preparation be made
in season to harmonize and get the delegates or the men
that will come from the three doubtful States you have named
to agree. Mr. Seward can not and should not be nominated
without the consent of two of them. Without their votes
he can not be selected, and should not expect nor desire
the nomination without the best of reasons for believing
that he is the most available man. No man can be so considered with the doubtful States against him.

"This is the key to the political situation, and should
not be neglected. I hope it will not be for one moment.
For myself, much as I desire Mr. Lincoln's nomination, and,
strong as our efforts should be to compass it, I shall be in

favor of dropping the contest if we can not bring at least one of these doubtful States to his support."

At this point I interrupted him to say, "Our folks had assurance that Indiana would be as well united for Lincoln as Illinois."

He resumed: "Then, indeed, there was something more to your meeting than brass horns, rockets, and rainbows. We will stir the cause to its foundation. We must have them turn out their Indiana paraders from the Ohio to the Wabash, and in the north end from Fort Wayne to Toledo, to Michigan City and the lake. Illinois must swarm in on every train, and farm-wagons must be used for sixty miles out. From Cairo and all Egypt, Kaskaskia, Alton, Quincy, and Danville to Galena and the lead-mines, and from every direction, they must assemble their hosts and attend the Convention in uncounted thousands, marching and shouting for victory—such a host, such a gathering, such a singing, and such joy among the people, as has not been seen since Moses assembled the children of Israel on the plains of Goshen in sight of Pharaoh, and hurried them through the Red Sea. Spontaneous outbursts, popular uprisings, and providential happenings are all right and proper, but they should never be depended on to the exclusion of our immediate duty and what we have on hand. Israel Putnam, the farmer hero soldier, replied to a good brother: 'It is well to depend on Providence. I do. But do n't neglect to keep your bullets ready and your powder dry.' This is an undertaking such as none of us have ever gone through with before. It is a contest, and it will be an earnest and absorbing one to the close.

"Mr. Weed is not a bad man; but he is a deep, long-headed, cunning one. He will do very much what shrewd, able leaders like him, who control men in any considerable numbers and the measures to aid or be aided, always do. He will swarm his legions in from every quarter, shout us

down, take us and the town, nominate his man, and Van
Burenize the Administration, if his man is elected. Seward
is, in many respects, such a man as Van Buren—so much
so that I wonder he is not nominating himself; for in all
that concerns the Presidential office he is by far the more
likely man of the two.

"Now, Robert, this is the situation; and we must pull
off our coats and do the most pushing work we have ever
done or seen done in this State. I would be glad if the
most pretentious men, who want the very best places, had
to do the work. I feel, however, that we are honored in
having the very hardest work turned over to us, and the
opportunity of having such a man and such a friend and
such a grand leader to follow. Never before have I felt
the utter want of a corps of supporters, as we do now,
when we are going into the most difficult and uncertain
campaign of all we ever had without our best—yes, incomparable—leader, who is now silent, as our candidate.

"Think for a moment how comfortably easy we would
feel, if he, or some one like him, could manage it in progress and detail; but that could not be. Robert, I tell you,
he is among the greatest men ever seen on this earth. Cromwell and Washington were no better; and comparison ends
there, for there are no others. He can manage any man
I have ever seen him undertake; and he has, in my presence, tackled some men mean enough to beat their wives—
the kind that Satan will accept only in an emergency. I
do not know that it is necessary to apprise him of what
I will try to do; for he is so instinctively informed and conscious of what we are all doing that, the moment he knows
Gridley has jerked off his coat, he will know exactly what
Gridley is doing.

"I have done some things already. There are some
hotels in Chicago that will not be New York headquarters.
Some railroad men have had a little insight, and will have

visions and such traffic as they never suspected or thought possible. There are tons of pork and beans and always wheat and corn in the town to feed a million. The boys are all in for Lincoln; and there is hardly one of them with two or three dollars in his pocket who will not jump at the opportunity to go to the Convention, to march and shout and sing for Lincoln. Let us see that they have the very best chance."

In the manner described the progress and plan for the nomination began and took shape. Everything was delayed, as Mr. Lincoln desired, until the meeting of the State Committee at Springfield, early in February, 1860. When it assembled, there was a full attendance and as many as fifty prominent advisers, men from all parts of the State. The conclusion about Lincoln as a candidate, and that he would be taken up, had passed from man to man all over the State. This attracted an unusual number, so that · there were in attendance the most capable and earnest men then supporting Mr. Lincoln.

The plan was approved without exception. Not one had been heard of who was not heartily in favor of the committee's openly announcing Lincoln as our candidate, as a necessary beginning, knowing the State Convention would carry it earnestly to conclusion. They invited every Republican and friendly-disposed person in the State cordially to co-operate with us in Mr. Lincoln's support, as the most available and acceptable candidate to the people of the doubtful States named. It was found on comparison that the people had a better appreciation of him than the politicians suspected or understood; and unity prevailed in wishing him success without an ambitious clash or jarring sound anywhere.

The matter was very generally discussed, not only by the members of the committee, but by all in attendance. There was no desire to interfere with the movement, nor even to gainsay the propriety or wisdom of the announcement, which all agreed was the duty of the party and the State, to begin with. None were opposed to an ardent and enthusiastic campaign, realizing that our candidate was a man of the people, and that it would be as near an upheaval in the State and many other Western communities as any personal movement in our politics had ever been. However, although all were earnest and desired the wisest interest and enthusiasm, all were considerate and cautious. They were a strong, purposeful assemblage of Western men, to urge that every preparation should be made and that every one's "lamp should be kept trimmed and burning." The best means of getting ready, with the help of the men of our State and the co-operation of outside friends, were all put in active operation. The strong men of the tribes were numbered, and every one of them was held ready for the call to duty.

Mr. Gridley's suggestions for the moving multitudes that should ride and walk into Chicago from all over the land were given and met universal approval. Plans and preparations ahead were agreed to as well as could be in anticipation for a general muster and turnout for all who could walk in line or "work a spell to help Abe Lincoln out on the biggest run he had ever struck." In true Western fashion they determined that "if you are going to have a general hunt, we 'd better all go, and leave the women and children to take care of the farms and the stores and post-offices until we get back."

Mr. Gridley's plan, as far as known, and his personal attention to his own part of it in the city of Chicago, were gone over with the proper executive committee, where they were fully approved under his management. He was to be furnished advisory help and means as he wished and needed. The committee called the State Convention for May 8th at Decatur. It declared Abraham Lincoln our candidate for President. It was agreed that Oglesby, in his robust and persevering way, should lead the canvass in the field before and after Convention, and his ideas prevailed. It was settled that the indispensable way to win was to give widespread notice that the State of Illinois was going to have a general muster and mass-meeting in Chicago. The members and visitors went home rejoicing all the way, telling crowds in every town and at railway stations on the way, as hopeful as they were, that "Honest Abe Lincoln" was our candidate, and that he was going to run.

The work grew day by day, without let or hindrance. The men who led through this remarkable movement to nominate Mr. Lincoln, like the hosts that came afterward, were those who had ability, learning, perseverance, and tact, that up to their time had never been developed nor equaled. As we recall their work, their continuance and character, they pass before us in line, heroes who never knew and never hearkened to what men call defeat. To them it was only a "resting-spell" to lose an election, and later a battle taught them that out of the gloom of disaster or temporary defeat they gained better experience and knowledge of more certain roads to victory.

Lincoln was a leader of such strength, goodness, sense, and high capacity that we are lost in wonder in the inquiry when another such will comfort men again in their peril and distress. While we remember this, let us not forget that he was sustained by those of greater strength, character, and service than the ten thousand Greeks under Xenophon. He was so situated and sustained by thousands of valorous, sacrificing men that he had a right to expect success. Without them there could have been no Lincoln, nor without a similar following could there have been a Douglas.

Oglesby was in the harness for the leader, as he himself had often led. In Springfield there were Milton Hay, James Matheney, Judge Logan, Jackson Grimshaw, Wm. H.

Herndon, and a host of younger men. Near by was Richard Yates, of Morgan County, who declared he could and would open the Mississippi, and, to do it, would have taken the able-bodied men of the State with him. At Bloomington there were Mr. Gridley, the burden-bearer, who had seen so much of fickle fortune and fleeting honors that wisely, through a long and useful life, he declined all public office. In this comparative repose Weed's discoverers passed him by. There was Leonard Swett, eminent among criminal pleaders. He was an alibi and emotional alienist, a psycho-physiological helper, a medico-legal advocate of stricken-minded men everywhere, with no man to contend for a higher place. He was the most scholarly and capable man that learning and high ambition could make.

The people at Bloomington and the bar and of the surrounding county had intelligence and talent in every direction of human effort or endeavor. In the work of education the three Munsells—three Methodist preachers—were starting a university. Dr. Worrell, the strict disciplinarian, and good Dr. Goodfellow, with a lot of ambitious young men then unheard of, were in the work to found a seat of learning as it might come under their persevering industry. Dr. Hovey and a full Faculty of trained and skilled teachers were there in the management of the State Normal School, a professional school for the education and training of teachers as a part of the completed public-school system, with over seven hundred students.

There were Judge Magoon, the two Fells, old Father Brookaw (who still lives), the two Funks, one of whom—Isaac, the State senator—split a desk in the chamber of the Senate with his naked fist to emphasize the fact that "we are going to save the Union"—all these were for Lincoln, with a score of hearty, willing workers, who made success certain, who believed in the busy, beautiful town. There were four of us young men who started out from the town in the '50's, hand in hand, like ambitious boys, all trying to hear or learn or listen, and all for Lincoln. They were William Orme, the bright and scholarly, the oldest, who, after his patriotic career, passed away in the midst of his years, after rising to the rank of a brigadier-general in our country's service. The next was the gallant, the daring, Apollo-formed Colonel Harvey Hogg, who fell at the front at Bolivar, Tenn. The third was Lawrence Weldon, the polite and polished gentleman, the fascinating pleader, and the best listener of all the four. He is now a periwigged justice. He is of sober habits and one of the lovers of Lincoln who stood in the ranks, where he saw and realized the strength of the cause and the greatness of the good man and mighty leader. The writer was the fourth of these four, where there were thousands like us in the great State. He has been, for a lifetime, deeply earnest in the progress and the men and the work that have made the Great West the colossus of production, commerce, and civilization, our great Mississippi Valley. Then there was David Davis.

In the Bloomington of that day they were almost all of one mind, from wherever you began with them—men, women, and children, down to the five-year-olds just beginning in politics and learning and ability to talk, when they were all for Lincoln, and told you so. Colonel C. H. Moore, of Clinton, who still survives, and was so intimately related in business affairs as to be one of the Bloomington bar, was one of the most zealous and intimate friends of the great leader, whose talents and means were always at his service.

In Champaign County there were a dozen or more able and devoted friends of Lincoln, among whom were Judge Cunningham, who was always to be relied on; J. B. McKinley, A. C. Burnham, Captain M. B. Thompson, and B. F. Harris. The first were lawyers, able, good men. Harris, who still lives, was a farmer and stockman, whose resolution and judgment never lacked energy. Colonel Wm. M. Coler, the brave soldier of two wars, was one of the leading members of the Champaign bar. He was a Democrat who liked Lincoln, who went all the way to Washington to tender him the services of a regiment raised a few days after Sumter fell, which the good President accepted. He, with Logan, McClernand, and other heroic Douglas Democrats, gave proof of earnest loyalty in being among the first to enlist in the cause of our country. These, and two thousand who marched under the flag of freedom, made Champaign, with McLean and Vermilion, three of the most cherished of the home counties of Lincoln.

There was, in Vermilion County, James H. Black, who reached well-earned distinction as soldier, statesman, and friend of his comrades in the Pension Office. Ward Lamon, who was associated with Mr. Lincoln in his Vermilion County business, lived there. He was a competent, active, and daring young man, whom Mr. Lincoln took with him on his trip to his inauguration, after which he became marshal of the District, where he remained and was of incalculable benefit to the President. There was Oliver Davis, of Danville, who succeeded Judge David Davis on the bench of the famous Eighth Circuit, in which Mr. Lincoln had none but friends. These, with hundreds of as capable men as could have been found in any one of our commonwealths of that day, were earnest supporters of Mr. Lincoln, whom they had sustained as Whig and Republican leader in succession. Besides these of the middle counties who knew him so well, there were able leaders in every part of the State, who had carefully considered his availability as a candidate from the close of the debate of 1858, and who then came to his support.

Mr. Lincoln was party candidate for United States senator against General Shields about 1852, and in 1854, when

Trumbull was elected, again in 1858 against Judge Douglas. He had also been the choice of our State for Vice-President at the first Republican Convention at Pittsburg in 1856, when Fremont was nominated for President. He would in all probability have received that distinction had it not been considered a prudent necessity to select an Eastern man for the place, seeing that Fremont was a Western one. As political promotion ran, he was in proper line for advancement as a Presidential candidate, all the more distinctly and reasonably because he was starting out with the agreement and support of two doubtful States, necessary ones for the election of any Republican candidate, as then appeared plain enough.

There was nothing unusual in his candidacy, as has often been misrepresented. Of the several gentlemen who were candidates, no one of them had been longer before the people as an able and conspicuous party leader, and no one had rendered such acceptable party service as he had in placing before the public and defending the policy of his party and his principles, as he had in the memorable Douglas-Lincoln debate.

It was one of the well-digested Weed plans to defeat him, to affect surprise and wonder that "a backwoods lawyer" should be pushed forward as a "Presidential possibility." It was the flood of this pestilential stuff that led so many careless and thoughtless people to think that the genius and leader who associated and contended with the eminent and experienced men of his time on equal grounds was not qualified for the high office. Many of these in a darker than any "Western ignorance" were stuffed with this story for many a day.

Of the many able men in our State besides those in the home counties, who earnestly supported him, were Senator O. H. Browning and Governor John Wood, of Quincy; Generals Rinaker and Palmer, of Macoupin; O. M. Hatch,

Jesse Dubois, and several of the Hay family, of Pike County; Kuykendall, of Jonesboro; Judge B. C. Cook, of Ottawa, and General S. A. Hurlbut, of Belvidere. The two most prominent supporters who probably turned hundreds where others turned one to his support were Owen Lovejoy and E. B. Washburn, then prominent and leading members of Congress, where, by skillful and patient management, they prepared the way to make him respected everywhere as a leader and acceptable to many delegates to the Chicago Convention.

In Chicago there were several able Republican leaders who, by February, 1860, were harmoniously and zealously united in his support and in persevering attention to it. There were "Long" John Wentworth, long time Congressman and Democratic leader in the city and all the rest of Northern Illinois; Ebenezer Peck, independent Whig and Republican, with Lincoln from the days of the old Vandalia capital to the removal to Springfield and on, and Isaac N. Arnold, the learned and experienced member of the older Chicago bar, and an able member of Congress, who, besides, wrote one of the most entertaining of all the lives of Lincoln.

Of the newspapers, the *Tribune* and the *Evening Journal* espoused his cause valiantly. Throughout the city energy and spirit prevailed where dull, soggy lassitude had reigned or poked along in politics through the lately passed December, when I first looked through the busy town on this business. N. B. Judd, who had been one of the men who defeated Lincoln in voting for Trumbull had come over to him, with Palmer and Cook, the three who defeated him. Like all new converts, they were zealous; and Judd, the most prominent of them, was member of the State Committee for Chicago. He was zealous and earnest, and appeared to be doing the best he could.

With these leaders and a following of the most enthusiastic men who had ever undertaken political affairs in our State, with hard work on every hand, we kept nearing the eventful Convention. To suppose that so many thousands of well-informed, anxious, earnest men and several hundred capable leaders, only a part of whom have been mentioned, would depend on a "spontaneous uprising" or popular enthusiasm is preposterous. On the contrary, the movement to make him our candidate, in which preliminary work he himself labored six long years in prominent, indefatigable contest, without design for himself, it is true, went on. It was carefully prepared, managed, and conducted as the engineer holds the flying express to track and time.

All details of management were calculated for, determined upon, and carried out, with the best men available for every part of it, selected under leadership that was satisfactory to Mr. Lincoln and the most trusted of experienced advisers about him. Thus the management was everywhere satisfactory and so smoothly and swiftly carried on as to resemble a popular uprising and an unexpected result. It all went on in unexampled progress, with Dick Oglesby in the field, Washburn and Lovejoy in Washington, and Asahel Gridley at the wires at Chicago.

I was in that city again later in February and on in March. As before said, there was a transformation from the previous December. The Tremont House, then by far the largest and most commodious hotel in the city, was announced as Illinois Headquarters, to be for several days before and during all Convention week. The Sherman House, next in size, was not to be hired to any State, but the proprietor, strongly for Lincoln, would furnish free public rooms for State meetings and committees to all his guests and his friends, with the understanding that the more of them there were for Lincoln, the better it would please him.

The necessity for a large separate building for the Convention that would seat as many as six thousand, and in which about twice as many could stand and be squeezed, was urgent; but many of the celebrities, prominent men, notabilities, and others, who were dragged along at first, were then in full accord; and the building was in satisfactory progress, as sure to be ready as Gridley and a lot of Chicago men had the grit to build it.

The general officers of the lake lines, of the railroads, and all transportation companies, boat-line managers and railway superintendents, were busy preparing for excursions, low rates, long and short hauls, such as people had never heard of even in breezy, windswept Chicago. Men were busy everywhere. The method and regularity of every part of the plan was plain and satisfactory proof that the business could not have been more efficiently and carefully conducted. The talk of Lincoln's probable selection had gained so much in the public mind that it was apparent that no end of hard work had been done to change thousands from Seward since December.

It was again about March 1, 1860, that the most important Lincoln meeting outside of the State up to that date was held while we were still in Chicago. The plans had been considered by a few for some weeks. It was, in substance, agreed to before the parties met at a consultation in Washington by the members of Congress of the three doubtful States. Whoever began the work, it was the desire of Mr. Lincoln that the meeting should be held, and, if possible, some plan of action agreed to that would unite these States in the support of a candidate most likely to be acceptable in them.

That this might be done, those from Illinois were authorized to say that Mr. Lincoln would withdraw whenever a more acceptable candidate could be presented and united upon. It was a strong combination from the beginning, increasing in reasonableness and adaptability until the agreement was made. Mr. Washburn was then, and had been a long time, one of the most prominent members of Congress. He had been a Whig, which all the more gave him the opportunity to unite the wavering members of Congress on Mr. Lincoln.

There was not a more capable worker and organizer than he was in the session of 1859-60. To emphasize this point, he and Mr. Lincoln had been close and intimate friends for years. They had held correspondence that was often a letter a day each until the subject was decided. In the progress of this he had the efficient help and assistance of many of the ablest men in Congress in the West at the time. Owen Lovejoy, whom we have frequently referred to, aided Washburn from the beginning. Lovejoy was an experienced and able member of the House, who was especially successful in influencing the most advanced anti-slavery members and their constituents all over the East to the support of Mr. Lincoln, most of whom had been for Seward because of his more pronounced opinion against slavery, as they understood it—Lovejoy being one of the most advanced on the subject by reason of his close relation to so many anti-slavery members and his remarkable persuasive power over men. On purely moral questions he was able to bring thousands of his faction to the support of Lincoln, as no other man could have done. Among them were several prominent men from New England and elsewhere, notably Thaddeus Stevens and Joshua R. Giddings, in themselves two of the chief and ablest leaders in the party.

RICHARD YATES

OLIVER P. MORTON

EDWIN D. MORGAN

CASSIUS M. CLAY

CHAPTER XLIV.

FROM the assembling of Congress, in December, 1859, it became more and more apparent every day that the division in the Democratic party was irreconcilable. This led the wisest and most experienced men in public affairs in all parties to consider the grave situation in the threatened disruption and, next, their most prudent course when it was done. In such an event it was plain enough that the success of the Republican party was probable. There were many of the more conservative in the Middle and border States who feared that Seward was "too ultra" on the slavery disputes, and that many of his supporters and advisers were even more so than himself. Then there were others, to whom Weed was more objectionable than Seward.

Greeley's break with both of them created widespread objection, more distinct and positive against Weed and his Albany management. In this dissolving, where parties were breaking and tearing to pieces on every hand, the Republican party became the beneficiary and received most of the discontented voters.

As the Republican party was forming and gathering its strength from so many breaking-up and discordant factions, it was a matter of the utmost delicacy to unite them in harmonious party accord as to declarations and candidates on such general terms of agreement and conceding spirit, that the bitterness and disputes of the breaking parties would not be carried into the new one. Hence it was common for men to come into the Republican party every day who had been political contestants all their lives. In this topsy-turvy tumbling of parties it was possible for two such influential members of Congress as Washburn and Lovejoy were to do much to advance the interests of Mr. Lincoln, which they accomplished so well and discreetly that there was neither jar nor backset in their well-wrought plans.

That they did all that was accomplished at Washington is not and should not be claimed; but that they did much, and contributed more than any others there to Lincoln's success, is certain. They were in constant communication with him, doing what seemed best to all of them. Seward was on the ground in the same sort of campaigning for himself. Whether others realized the fact or not, neither one of them ever misunderstood that they were the rivals-in-chief for the Republican nomination from the close of the Douglas-Lincoln debates.

A lot of irrelevant and immaterial story-weaving has been done concerning Lincoln's candidacy and nomination, much of it to the effect that both came to him in an unexpected, accidental, or unusual way. If this were true, all we know of him would be to little purpose. He was talked to and written to and of by hundreds, perhaps thousands of zealous friends and correspondents, too many of whom came to believe that in some unusual or may be startling manner they could nominate him. Some of them were even so confident as to state that they were first in the movement. To all of these, kind-hearted and wise man that he was, he could do no less than decline and be friendly and patient with them; for he was sober-minded and so well grounded in common sense that he was not inclined to folly when, of course, he could not be a candidate under any such bringing out.

He was, however, a leader, always a capable and foreseeing one, who, as he grew in strength, capacity, wisdom, and experience, made himself a candidate by making himself capable and worthy the distinction. As one seeking place or office, he was never a candidate; but from 1858 he was as conscious and well-informed as any man that, in approval of his principles and conduct, a growing political force among his fellow-citizens was making him a candidate in the way that fitted the cause and the time. In furtherance of this end he answered and fulfilled the wishes and expectations of wise and influential friends, when he, the growing leader, without a rival, waxed and strengthened with the rising party to a nomination as honorably earned as it was cordially given.

As movements progressed, he had no lack of information about them. His campaign was not managed by one man, as Weed was doing for Seward apparently. There were, as we have seen, several skilled and experienced men at the helm. Who were the men and what they were doing was as familiar and well known to him as to them. He was the people's choice; but under his own advisement and the lead of the best skilled among his friends his nomination came about in care and direction that prepared the way for it.

Among these friends none were more forceful than Frank P. Blair, Jr., of St. Louis, and Henry S. Lane, of Indiana. Blair was young, ambitious, and one of the most capable politicians of the time in his own strength, and stronger by reason of his family's influential career. He was a member of Congress from Missouri, as much Republican as his mixed constituency permitted. The Republicans and some zealous friends were supporting Edward Bates, of that State, as a candidate at Chicago. The younger Blair had grown from childhood under the care, education, and training of his father, F. P. Blair, Sr., who was one of the clearest-headed and most experienced politicians of the land from the time of President Jackson.

The elder Blair established a newspaper in Washington about 1824. He was an ardent adviser and supporter, as

well as a resolute defender, of the hero of New Orleans and
his party through his Administration and for a whole generation. The Blair newspaper and the family became a
power in the land. In 1860, in advanced age, the elder
Blair retired, but his sons—Montgomery, in Baltimore, and
Frank, in St. Louis—were succeeding in political affairs
and business as well under the assistance and counsel of the
experienced father.

The elder Blair predicted Abraham Lincoln the coming
leader from 1858. Long before this he predicted the overthrow of Douglas and the party separation. No man then
living was better qualified to forecast what extremities the
hot-tempered Southern disunionists would venture. He
had sustained Jackson, and was familiar with every political
movement, and knew every party leader from Calhoun's premeditated rebellion in 1831.

The Blairs came to the support of Lincoln in a qualified
sense, it is true, but in a very effective sort of preparation
for the undertaking which passed contingency as the plans
matured. The old man, who had been cognizant of and
participated in political movements for more than thirty
years, and the two vigorous young men entering earnestly
into the cause of our prairie leader, were no small accession.

Henry S. Lane was an able and distinguished man. · He
was the Republican leader in his State of Indiana, and, with
Oliver P. Morton, then a young man of well-known ability,
took charge of the Lincoln movement in their State. This
was a pleasant and in no sense a difficult task; for the
people of that State were as heartily and about as unanimously for him as our own State. The Democratic leaders
of the State—Jesse D. Bright and G. N. Fitch—followed
the South. In doing so they drove thousands of loyal Democrats from their party. In this condition the Republicans
had more than equal chances of carrying the State. Lane
was one of the most prudent leading men of the time.

He was a personal friend and fellow-pleader of Lincoln's for years. No one who supported Lincoln through the getting ready and the real trial of the Convention did so more effectively, if indeed any one did as much, as he in achieving the great success.

Buchanan's puerile and treacherous Administration had alienated a full quarter million of loyal Pennsylvania Democrats—permanently, too; for the Quaker-German people of that colony and State were anti-slavery as well as loyal. The wonder is not that the State had left the Democratic party almost unanimously, but that, in an enlightened age, it had produced and grown to leadership palsied images like Black and Buchanan.

Simon Cameron, clear-headed and canny as any descendant of his clan or kingdom, and John W. Forney, both Democrats, saw these Quakers and Germans, thoroughly disgusted, leaving the disloyal pro-slavery faction in swarms. They prepared to lead these loyal Democrats into the Republican party, whither they were drifting without leadership. Cameron had won distinction much as Lincoln did. He had come up with the people, and knew that they were right. In turn they respected him so much for leaving and denouncing so many faithless leaders that his State of Pennsylvania declared him their candidate for President.

About the first of March the very important meeting of the delegates to the conference from the doubtful States was held in Chicago. There were present Lane, of Indiana, with a friend. Lane was a candidate for governor of Indiana, and elected to that office, and afterwards a United States senator. The following winter, O. P. Morton, who was elected with him, succeeded Lane, and held the office of governor through the war in faithful discharge of every duty. With Lane, who was leader of this movement as far as he saw fit and thought prudent, there were F. P. Blair, of St. Louis, and an accredited representative of

Simon Cameron; John Wentworth, Richard J. Oglesby, and
a representative of Mr. Gridley, as Gridley could only be
there part of the time. The three last were from Illinois
and were, of course, deeply interested in the success of Mr.
Lincoln.

The plans of the coming campaign, as far as they could
be anticipated, were discussed at length by these representative men, some of whom were earnestly in favor of Lincoln's nomination, to start with. The others were so contingently, should it so develop, as they expected, that the
opposition to Seward could be turned for him. The opposition to Seward was not personal. It was sincerely
believed by all present that he could not carry any two
of the three doubtful States there represented; consequently
his selection would be, as they thought, no less than folly
in the angered, excited condition of affairs.

There was no vote made nor asked for to test the
strength of any candidate or plan. None was suggested,
as the conference was held mainly for a full friendly consultation on the men and conditions involved. It was, however, generally expressed that there was urgent necessity
that the three States should act together to the extent of
preventing any nomination unsatisfactory to them. It was
agreed that the strongest candidate, as developed, should
have the support of all in the emergency of preventing an
unacceptable nomination, and that they would recommend
to the delegates from the three States to unite in the support of one of their own citizens.

The results following this conference justified Mr. Gridley's summing up, as soon as it was over, which ran about
as follows: "The nomination of Mr. Lincoln is almost half
won. We have two points in five, and the other appears in
reach. It is time to close in with renewed energy, consummate the plans, and carry them forward with all our
might. We should now take up the third and win, if we

can, or not blame anybody if we lose. Our first was to get possession of this city with all its means and facilities. That is now done. The next was to unite at least two of the three doubtful States. The conference has given us all of them. If we are wise and energetic enough to carry out the plans, Mr. Lincoln will be nominated in a burst of popular enthusiasm. Let us keep our heads level, press forward as we can, and be sure that neither neglect nor folly of ours shall delay or beat us."

Mr. Lincoln was timely informed of all that had been done, and it had his full approval. This was emphasized after his election, in that four of the seven members of his Cabinet were close friends and were fully represented by the members attending the Chicago conference; namely, Bates, of Missouri; Blair, of Maryland; Cameron, of Pennsylvania, and Smith, of Indiana, Oglesby declining a fifth place, that the President might recognize other sections of the country.

It must not be understood these were agreed upon, or that any bargain was made at the meeting. No such subject was spoken of, or, as far as any one present knew, thought of. It was too remote then to be in any one's mind. It is proof beyond doubt, however, of what was achieved before and after the Conference, and Mr. Lincoln's fidelity to his friends, who, as he said, "stood by me when I needed help."

Among his best-remembered observations about such things is something like this: "My obligations to those called the common people, of which I am one, are the greatest. They are not spoken of for effect, or, as one of the taking phrases in politics, but because it is true to the letter that they have always come to my support beyond my own or anybody's expectation. Next to these my obligations are to those who have stood by me through trials and adversities. Many of them decline favors when I have influence.

I intend to stand by them when I can, all those who have been so kind and so faithful to me."

Mr. Lincoln's religious beliefs became one of the topics of consideration and controversy in every political campaign in which he engaged, singularly enough in even those where he was not a candidate. Most men of his time were liberal-minded enough to say no more of it than was known and authorized by his own statements. These were plain and simple enough, it would seem, for any one to understand. His conduct was so strictly upright and moral that no one ever questioned it; yet there were those who were of that form of unbelief themselves who spoke of him as a "skeptic or unbeliever," as inclination led them; but that was about all there ever was, in foundation or fact, in such statements.

The truth is that, whatever may have been the tenets of his faith, no man ever more devoutly reverenced God or more positively and unequivocally stated it than he did. The men who delighted to talk of his "skepticism" could never produce a single word, statement, or act of his in support or corroboration of what was never more than irresponsible assertion. In 1846, Rev. Peter Cartwright, for over fifty years a Methodist preacher and circuit-rider, was his Democratic opponent for Congress. At one of Cartwright's meetings a zealous Democratic brother asked him: "What do you know about Abe's religion? Has he got any?" Cartwright replied quite emphatically: "I am a Democrat, and I am running for Congress against Mr. Lincoln on political grounds, and not on his or my own religious beliefs or opinions. The people are supposed to know what his beliefs are and to be satisfied about them, or they would n't be running either one of us for Congress in this Christian country. The Constitution gives us the liberty of worshiping God as we please, and to exercise our rights free from any kind of interference. I want Democrats to vote for me because I am a Democrat, and not because I am a Methodist. I expect Whigs to vote for Mr. Lincoln because they are Whigs, and not because of his or their religious ideas."

In this Mr. Cartwright was trying to discipline and bring into party lines several hundred Democrats who were then supporting Mr. Lincoln; but he made a fair statement about their religious beliefs in saying that the people were satisfied with them. It is true, further, that most of those pioneer people believed in and attended some church, and, whether right or wrong, if it could have been truthfully stated that he was a "skeptic," or even an irreligious man, no party would have been running him for Congress. Of this no one understood the facts better than Dr. Cartwright, which, plainly stated, were that the people knew him and Mr. Lincoln both to be Christian gentlemen in faith and belief. This of itself should settle Mr. Lincoln's religious standing and character. The Doctor had ample means of knowing what Lincoln was. He wanted to go to Congress, but he was not "skeptic" enough to use a falsehood or a false impression to get there.

Mr. Lincoln was a constant and careful Bible-reader all his days. He was not in any sense a doubter, nor did he read it constantly through motives of curiosity. He was, in all his doings, a serious, earnest man, one who did this because of his settled, unalterable convictions. He read and believed the Scriptures because "in them are the words of eternal life," as well as the foundation of all law and rule and precept for the welfare of Governments instituted by men. No subject, king, leader, or prophet was ever more impressed with God's control and management of everything on the earth or in the universe of worlds down to the most diminutive details. He relied perfectly and complacently on the direct help and intervention of God in all human affairs. Moses, David, Luther, and others followed and trusted the Most High in every day's progress; but no one of them more constantly or faithfully depended on him. With the same faith, and following these devout and faithful leaders in earnest and faithful observance of the same rules, he, too, became God's prophet and leader of his people.

In speaking of Paine's "Age of Reason," he laid it aside, saying: "I have looked through it, carelessly it is true; but there is nothing to such books. God rules this world, and out of seeming contradictions, that all these kind of reasouers seem unable to understand, he will develop and disclose his plan for men's welfare in his inscrutable way. Not all of Paine's nor all the French distempered stuff will make a man better, but worse. They might lay down tons and heaps of their heartless reasonings alongside a few of Christ's sayings and parables, to find that he had said more for the benefit of our race in one of them than there is in all they have written. They might read his Sermon on the Mount to learn that there is more of justice, righteousness, kindness, and mercy in it than in the minds and books of all the ignorant doubters from the beginning of human knowledge."

In one of his addresses in 1858 he said: "My friend [Douglas] has said that I am a poor hand to quote Scripture. I will try it again, however. It is said in one of the admonitions of our Lord, 'As your Father in heaven is perfect, be ye also perfect.' The Savior, I suppose, did not expect any human creature could be as perfect as the Father in heaven; but he said, 'As your Father in heaven is perfect, be ye also perfect.' He set that up as a standard; and he who does most in reaching that standard attains the highest degree of moral perfection. So I say in relation to the principle that all men are created equal, let it be as nearly reached as we can. If we can not give freedom to every creature, let us do nothing that will impose slavery upon any other creature."

In one of his cheeriest moods, one day, I remember, the subject of the many Protestant sects was being considered and talked over. One good old brother, a kind-hearted man and as timid, lamented the number of sects, and hoped that some day a harmonizing spirit would prevail among all Christian believers, and that all of them would unite in one Church organization to serve the Master. Mr. Lincoln said: "My good brother, you are all wrong. The more sects we have, the better. They are all getting somebody in that the others could not; and even with the numerous divisions we are all doing tolerably well.

"It is not a certainty by any means that a quiet time is the best for progress. It is not so by any means in the progress of human liberty or the release of men from superstition and persecution under the forms of religion. The greatest achievements have always come in stirring, fighting times, like those of Luther, Cromwell, and the American Revolution. What we need is not fewer sects or parties, but more freedom and independence for those we have. The sects are all right and will get through all right in the end. God is going to be more merciful to men trying to do right than most people think. He is so much more familiar with human frailties than a little sect in any single organization can be, that there is scarcely room for doubt that He will deal more gently with blundering, sinning humanity than the sects would deal with one another. I would rather there were more than less, if one were to hold all the power.

"Yet sects are right, and should hammer away until they reach the best that is attainable. God intends that men should fight their way to better conditions, and not be lazy or timid, or expect that their passage would be an easy one through the world, or beyond in ignorant idleness. We are often confronted with the fear of too many sects, as so many timid people among them so often dread, and wonder which is right and which is best among them. They are all right, and the Methodists are the best in this country; for they outnumber all others combined. So the weight of public opinion is certainly with them.

"We are Presbyterians, you know, the hardheaded Scotch sect that has done so much for human rights, enlightenment, free institutions, and freedom of speech the world over; so self-reliant and decided in their ways that they would n't yield the oldest opinion they have for a new cut road to heaven. They are as hardheaded in opinion, for illustration, as our hands are in this country when cornshucking is over.

"In our rigid doctrinal way of running things we have turned out more other sects and people than we now have in 'the true orthodox mother Church.' We seldom compromise with our independently-inclined members, but turn them out to found a new sect. In this way we have as many as twenty of them scattered all over the earth, leading people to better living by the hundred thousand, whereas, if we had not quarreled and divided regularly and successfully, we would only have the hardheaded, close-opinioned regular Church, with most of it in Scotland. I tell you, sects are right, as some kinds of old trees grow and do as well when the sprouts are cut and transplanted.

"Think of the sect-drilling so many of us have passed through, mostly to our advantage, as responsible beings. Our people came from the good old Quaker stock, through Pennsylvania, Virginia, and Kentucky. Circumstances took us into the Baptist sect in Indiana, in which several of our people have remained. While there, a good Methodist elder rode forty miles through a winter storm out of his way to preach my mother's funeral sermon at Spencer's Creek. Here in Illinois we are with the Presbyterians, where the Methodists are as thick as bees all about us. They are all good, Brother B——. Do n't concern yourself a moment about the number or their differences. But be sure you do as to the rights you have in any of them, to speak, to believe, and to act independently. Luther, Calvin, Knox, Wesley, and many others, did mankind a worthy and never-ending good when they got independent enough to start new sects in religion, and brave enough to defend them."

In conversation we never tired of him. His manner was so full of interest, so peculiar, so homelike and friendly, and his humor was beyond any one's description of it. As he took up a cause or illustrated a point, all were absorbed in it as he led to conclusions. His entertainments were full of thought, and it was pleasing as well as instructing to follow him through one subject after another as he discussed and plainly laid open all there was of worth or interest in these pleasing reviews. The most difficult thing about them was to sit down and write a description that would make them intelligible.

A dear friend, who was a long-time acquaintance of his, said: "You must not neglect to recognize the deep tenderness and delicacy of feeling in his character. There is an incident related of him which represents these as well as anything I remember.

"In the early pioneer days, when he was a practicing attorney, and 'rode the circuit,' as was the custom at that time, he made one of a party of horsemen, lawyers like himself, who were on their way, one spring morning, from one court town to another. Their course was across prairies and through the timber; and as they passed by a little grove, where the birds were singing merrily, they noticed a little fledgeling which had fallen from the nest, and was fluttering by the roadside. After they had ridden a short distance, Mr. Lincoln stopped, and, wheeling his horse, said, 'Wait for me a moment; I will soon rejoin you;' and as the party halted and watched him, they saw Mr. Lincoln return to the place where the little bird lay helpless on the ground, saw him

tenderly take it up and set it carefully on a limb near the
nest. When he joined his companions, one of them laugh-
ingly said, 'Why, Lincoln, what did you bother yourself and
delay us for with such a trifle as that?' The reply deserves
to be remembered. 'My friend,' said Lincoln, 'I can only
say this, that I feel better for it.' Is there not a world of
suggestion in that rejoinder?" (From Mrs. C. E. Larned,
April, 1898.)

He was one of God's men, said so, and realized the
truth and responsibility of that sacred relation. He "talked
with God all night," and said just before his Inauguration,
"I go to undertake a greater responsibility than Washington, and can only succeed, as he did, by the help of the
God that saves or destroys nations."

I was pleased to find published, some time since, an interesting letter by General James F. Rusling, sustaining
the truth of his direct communings with and reliance on
God. A thousand of such letters no doubt could have been
written, if others had been as observing and considerate as
General Rusling. It reveals anew, in the busiest time of his
highest duty, the foundations of his strength, firmness, and
Divine reliance. His character was so complete that com-
muning and counseling with God was part of his daily observance and progress.

A Protestant minister, who was a schoolmate, related a
conversation with him only a few days before his death.
The young man was kind-hearted and liberal-minded. He
was well acquainted with the President, and had been his
neighbor for years. He was then a chaplain in the army
near Washington. He called to see him about getting some
sick men to their homes. The President took a deep interest in doing all he could, as he always did for the comfort and relief of any soldier or sailor. In this he made
provision at once for these as Chaplain B—— desired.

Afterwards, in a pleasant, homelike way, he said in his talk with his neighbor friend: "You have been a broad-minded Christian man. I have always commended you and have kept you in mind. As this desperate, bloody strife has grown and increased, I have seen and realized the necessity of a broader Christian charity to all men. You remember we grew up without much consideration one way or the other, full of opinions and prejudices against the Roman Catholic Church. Many of them, it is true, originated where there were ample and sufficient causes.

"In the dreadful progress of the war I have learned much and have as steadily moderated old errors and ignorant prejudices that have been kept alive too long. As soon as things are settled and peace returns, I intend to recommend in the most appropriate way I can that the pope appoint Bishop Hughes a cardinal, and so far interfere in the ecclesiastical affairs of the Church. I shall do so because I believe in the man, who I know well deserves the promotion, or more, if his Church has better things to give him. We are, as a people, under lasting obligations to him, the same as we are to thousands of our good men of the pulpit and altar, so well known.

"Bishop Hughes's predilections, like those of many thousands in his Church, were decidedly against us at the beginning. When we laid the conditions properly before him and he understood it was the cause of our country and the integrity of the Union, he took labor on himself in the most rapid and effective way to change unlimited thousands from doubtful and undecided lookers-on to active Unionists all over our country; and he turned sympathy our way more than any other could in Europe. He was so active and energetic about it that thousands of his followers took up our cause as their own, enlisted, and have helped fight our battles. We must be honest and unsectarian enough to accord

them equal standing with all other Christian sects and de-
nominations who have served, suffered, and died for their
home and country.

"To Bishop Hughes we owe the gratitude due a great
leader in his Church, who was true to our country against
his immediate and influential surroundings. Without doubt
there were mercenary men and aliens about him in sufficient numbers, with means and influence, to have increased
and made much more trouble if they could have taken
Hughes with them. It was bad enough as it was. On the
other hand, he became a mountain of strength to us in
the time when our emergencies were greatest, and a grateful people should properly remember him and his."

About a week before the Chicago Convention, on the
10th of May, the Illinois Republican Convention met at Decatur. The town is centrally situated. Every county was
represented with all its strength of delegates and citizens
in anxious, earnest attendance. They were intelligent, robust, and enthusiastic young men, who were eager for the
most stirring and dangerous-looking political contest any of
us had ever been in. The underlying dangers grew stronger;
for somewhere in the South every day some prominent man
or newspaper was being added to the number who declared
that, in the event of the election of a Republican President,
they would secede, and go with their States out of the
Union. The Southern leaders were preparing the way for
the election of a Republican in the division of the Democracy, and as zealous in forcing secession as they were in
their party's ruin. In the progress of this turmoil and
fevered agitation the Illinois Republicans and co-operating
anti-slavery friends assembled, with a full thousand vigorous young men as delegates, alternates, and friendly advisers,
cheering for Lincoln, not only at Decatur, but on every incoming train through all parts of their route. The main
question was no longer whether Lincoln was available, but

how prudently and within reasonable bounds to do the best that was possible for him.

When the Convention assembled, it was a typical enthusiastic gathering of Western men. Oglesby and his colaborers had done all that need be where all the people were mostly of one mind. The fire was kindled, and what was by that time a spontaneous outburst of enthusiasm for Lincoln took possession of the crowds. A shout for "Abe Lincoln" rolled over, sweeping everything before it, lasting over ten minutes, every one standing, waving his hat or flag, with the platform, chairs, aisles, doors, windows, and passage-ways crowded full, all vociferating at the top of their voices.

Oglesby was made chairman of the Convention. At the proper moment a passage was opened. The order of business was stated, "that John Hanks would bring to the platform two walnut rails, of those which he and Abe Lincoln made in the winter of 1830 to inclose Thomas Lincoln's farm." Oglesby's announcement rang out like clarion notes on a swelling breeze. He had a strong voice of marvelous power, and the incident of the rails lighted the flame in every heart for our great leader. He did not say much, and could not, because the crowded assemblage were applauding all at once.

He began what he called "my speech to nominate Abraham Lincoln, which I began in earnest." This was taken up and finished by the whole crowd, all shouting, "Abe Lincoln!" and shaking hands in the general satisfaction, hilarity, and enthusiasm. He began again: "My friends, be sober-minded, and come to order, so we can transact the little business that is necessary to complete our arrangements and pay our tribute to the greatest man in our State. We have a citizen among us whose ability and distinction we know not of." "Yes, we do; Abe Lincoln!" was shouted back by thousands. The chairman continued: "Years ago he followed the occupation of splitting rails. Many of you have done the same—" Then the shouts were renewed: "Abe Lincoln! Yes, he is the man"—then more shouts—"and we are going to nominate him for Pres—" The shouting again continued ten minutes. "Hanks, bring on the rails," Oglesby took opportunity to get in, and so finished his speech, when the shouting ran free, with handshaking and a general jollification for a full half hour.

Hanks finally got on the platform with the two weather-beaten rails; and for another half hour there was a general Lincoln jubilee. Hanks shook hands all around, more generally with the delegates of a State Convention than any other dozen men had ever done in our knowing. The rails, properly inscribed, in Hanks's care, were ordered to be sent along, with the compliments of the Illinois Convention and the people of the State, to the forthcoming National Convention.

Mr. Lincoln was present, and made a handsome and heartfelt acknowledgment in his most pleasing and neighborly way. He fully recognized the gracious and unanimous indorsement of the Convention. He thanked them all personally, and held an hour's conference with them, taking every one by the hand and exchanging congratulations with those who had so faithfully stood by him through all the ups and downs of his political career. All were overjoyed, and parted with the determination of a more vigorous campaign for the rest of it and the resolute feeling "that, somehow or other, Abe Lincoln is going to win."

The men who had done the most in seeing and talking to their neighbors, getting them to the Convention, and going over the details, in the enthusiasm of the hour, neglected to agree on four of the most capable and general favorites as delegates for the State at large, who, in addition to two from each Congressional district, were to represent the State and our candidate at Chicago. Others had been more attentive, and hurried through their "slate" selection of David Davis, O. H. Browning, of Quincy; N. B. Judd, of Chicago; and G. Koerner, of Belleville. The last-named was the most appropriate one selected, because of his German ancestry, in recognizing the necessity of conciliating foreign elements, which policy has had its run in that and many other parties before and since. Personally there was nothing to say against the gentlemen selected, but, in comparison with those who had carried on the campaign, they had done almost nothing, and were not entitled by previous service or experience for the coming contest with prominent Eastern leaders. However, the men who had made Lincoln's candidacy successful concluded to continue in his cause as zealously as ever, regardless of the slight and neglect to send our best men as delegates.

These would have been, if it had been limited to the four most experienced and best-qualified to be our four chief delegates: E. B. Washburn and Owen Lovejoy, then prominent members of Congress; John Wentworth, of Chicago, who had long been a member of Congress, and one of the ablest and best-trained politicians in any party in the country; and "Dick" Oglesby, whom most people believed to have done more than all others, and to have "discovered Mr. Lincoln to his own people as the leader above all others."

This was one of the unpleasant features of the situation, that, while Weed was coming himself, with no restriction on his selection of any of the able Republicans of New York, our best men had to attend as outside advisers; and Governor E. D. Morgan, Wm. M. Evarts, Geo. W. Curtis, Ex-Governor Preston King, and himself, five of the most capable and distinguished men of the land, were to be the leaders of the Seward forces—as able, experienced, and consummate politicians as ever sat in any Convention.

These capable New York leaders were to be there to manage and contend with our four gentlemen; who, however competent, were then almost unknown outside of our State. We should have had Mr. Washburn and others named, who would have had no superiors on the floor of the Convention. Wentworth, by reason of his long acquaintance and his knowledge of men and affairs, should have been included, as among our most experienced and successful party managers. A great many were discouraged over the result, who, though unwilling to do it, felt very much like withdrawing and giving it up.

We had a little meeting in Bloomington and another in Chicago shortly afterwards. There were several long faces until Mr. Gridley got up and said: "Gentlemen, the campaign is in good shape. We have news from all over this State and Indiana. Lane has added the northern half of his State as excursionists to Chicago. They are going to attend the meeting by thousands. Without any personal animadversions, I think we are going to win. At least, every man must pull off his coat and get at work with that determination; for many a good cause has been lost through a little fear, some disappointment, and, worse, indecision. The good Lord often chooses the weak and lowly of the earth to confound the powerful and the mighty. We can not tell just how it is all coming about, but we are tolerably sure to win if we keep our heads clear and our legs going. Washburn, Lovejoy, Wentworth, Oglesby, Peck, Arnold, Swett, and a dozen others, are in to stay, with their harness on up to their shoulders; and they will stay until they win or the whole thing breaks and snaps to pieces. They are sincere and hard in the swirl of the tide, and will pull to the shore, delegates or not, in or out of the Convention. Others might not have been as zealous if they had not been so. These and scores of our truest men will; so we are all right. We are come to the crossing where victory awaits the truly brave and capable, and every man must do his duty."

In addition to Mr. Seward's high qualifications as a statesman of wisdom and ability, he had been governor of his Empire State, and had served almost twelve years in the United States Senate, where he was during the exciting debates of 1850. He was more generally recognized as the chief leader of the Republican party than any of the dozen others who had fought and contended for its restrictive measures against slavery from its beginning. Besides, his capable friend, Weed, had perfected plans for securing the distinguished honor they so fully expected him to receive. Ninety per cent of the Republican newspaper press supported him. More than that proportion of the opposition Democratic press, in both factions, recognized him as the coming Republican candidate. A large majority of the leading and prominent men in his party, and a larger proportion of the voters in it, were in his favor; hence, taking political questions and leaders as they had moved along for the four years following Fremont's defeat in 1856, the opinion ran without much contention that Mr. Seward would, without doubt, be nominated in 1860.

In his support there was no lack of means, numbers, or influence. As these were all in readiness, and as public approval seemed to be going and settling things in advance, there seemed to them scarcely a doubt of his success. His fitness and capacity were generally recognized. His managers were so self-confident that they passed unheeded all the warnings of the Republicans in the doubtful States, fully assured that they could nominate him without their assent or help; and, with their New York means and methods, they would attend to the doubtful States afterward. They were full of these notions, without thought of meeting permanent obstacles in their way, until the assembling at Chicago.

The truth then dawned upon their experienced chief leaders—Morgan, King, Curtis, and Evarts, as well as

Weed—that a combination was forming against them. It appeared to be serious enough, but an undiscoverable plan to them. It became more alarming as they began to un-cover it and see where the difficulty lay. They had been heedless too long, but they were able and resourceful men, who went after obstacles with a will and vigor that was all that men could do.

They looked for a consultation to be held in opposition to them, rather than to one already made. They feared that sentiment was centering on Lincoln, because the city was so demonstrative for him, early as it was, then the day before the meeting. They had provided for their thou-sands who came there on several trains; but these were "nowhere" to compare with the crowds and the noise and the talk for "Abe Lincoln." Late as it was, they under-took repairing the breach. Mr. Evarts, who was always one of the most impressive and earnest men and pleaders, with scarce a rival, with Ex-Governor Preston King and some more of the prominent men of their delegation, vis-ited and pleaded with every other delegation, making as many as sixteen or eighteen twenty-minute addresses each in behalf of Seward on the first afternoon and evening be-fore the Convention.

They persevered in this arduous sort of labor to the end. They well sustained their chief, and most eloquently related his fitness, experience, capacity, and strength; but they could discover neither his weakness and defective po-sition, nor the metes and bounds of the growing coalition against him. They realized that there was one; for no talking, visiting, counting, or checking could raise their list of votes above 190—hardly that, some murmured—when it would take 235 to nominate. Where the sorely-needed 45 were to come from, none of them knew.

They were well trained in such affairs, and understood

full well, that there was a movement against them; but
it was so well managed that many well in it, as far as Horace
Greeley was, did not fully comprehend its force. It was
so well kept in hand that, while it was rapidly maturing,
he wired his paper, the *Tribune,* "No successful combination
can be made against Seward, and he will be nominated."

They saw that the management for Lincoln was superb,
and the city was full of spirit and enthusiasm for him;
but there was no sign of any unfriendly movement against
Seward or any other candidate. The Illinois people—delegates, citizens, everybody—were more cordial to the New
Yorkers than were the followers of any other candidate;
so the Yorkers mingled with the Illinois people by choice,
took kindly to Lincoln, and in sincere good-will said they
would take him for second choice if they could not get
Seward. Thus the well-planned campaign for Lincoln gathered strength and prospered.

The Seward people suspected the Bates movement as the
probable one on which the combination would be made
against them, in which contingency they—Weed, Morgan,
King, and Evarts—all agreed that, rather than vote for
Bates, they would end the contest by going with all their
force to Lincoln. A more delicate task than making Lincoln acceptable to the New Yorkers as their second choice
was seldom, if ever, undertaken. It was not any one man's
doing that took our delegation and Lincoln's friends
through the swarming crowd and earnest contention without serious blunders; for all toiled and persevered, and every
trusted man obeyed. If any one did more than another, it
was Oglesby, who had done so well at Decatur.

The completed plans, the fitting details and assignments,
the swiftly-moving and harmonious progress all over the
city and in the Convention could not, in any apparent way,
have been better. Wentworth said: "Illinois was in a good

humor, every one, down to the four-year-olds, and doing his best. They would do anything you desired, and would be pleased to march all night and anywhere into the surrounding country if it was a Lincoln parade."

They were making the campaign, not on any candidate's defects; for it was conceded that they were all deserving men, and that Seward, their principal contestant, was conspicuously so. They were earnestly in favor of Lincoln, who was strong, capable, available, the friend of men, now contending for the rights of the most lowly, but always with and on the side of the common people.

In the debates of 1850, on what were known as the Compromise Measures, Mr. Seward said: "It is true that the National domain is ours. It is true it was acquired by the arms and with the valor of the whole Nation. But we hold, nevertheless, no arbitrary power over it. We hold no arbitrary power over anything, whether acquired lawfully or seized by usurpation. The Constitution regulates our stewardship. The Constitution devotes the domain to union, to justice, to welfare and liberty. But there is a higher law than the Constitution, which regulates our authority over the domain and devotes it to the same noble purposes. The territory is a part—no inconsiderable part— of the common heritage of mankind, bestowed upon them by the Creator of the universe. We are his stewards, and must so discharge our trust as to secure, in the highest attainable degree, their happiness."

This was sense and statesmanship that would have been commendable in any age, as righteously needed now as when Seward, Greeley, Lincoln, Benton, Chase, Douglas, and Wade, and thousands of followers in all parties, advocated and demanded free homes for a free and enlightened people. They were more anxious that the rights of a free people should be protected than for the forcible subjugation or acquisition of any territory. They believed that God's higher law applies to nations as to men, and that the lower human laws should be raised up and adjusted to the higher Divine law.

At Rochester, New York, Mr. Seward, in 1858, said: "Shall I tell you what this collusion means? They who think that it is accidental, unnecessary, the work of interested or fanatical agitators, and therefore ephemeral, mistake the case altogether. It is an irrepressible conflict between opposing and enduring forces; and it means that the United States must and will, sooner or later, become either entirely a slaveholding Nation or entirely a free-labor Nation."

These wise and wholesome declarations of Mr. Seward were profusely used against him by the faint-hearted in all parties, and prated against him by the slave-leaders, who were then in active conspiracy for our country's ruin. These were no more than any conscientious, moral man found it a duty to say, nor more than the Divine parallel which Mr. Lincoln so forcibly and aptly used against slavery, "A house divided against itself can not stand."

Mr. Seward had been in the contest against them longer and in much more conspicuous public service. Every bitter and slanderous accusation which the half-pro-slavery parties would tolerate was uttered against him, and against Lincoln no less, but not so generally nor so long. Seward's weakness did not lie altogether in his positive declarations; for Lincoln's were stronger when he boldly and unqualifiedly declared the truth spoken by the Master "unconstitutional." But Seward had aroused more enmity and jealousy. In the Central Western States many thousands from the slaveholding States were still deeply tinctured by the influences of a life spent, not so much against slavery, as against "the Abolitionists." These Southern, free-State-seeking emi-

grants, who fled from States having slavery as from a pesti-
lence, would not vote for a candidate such as Mr. Seward
was; for, rightfully or wrongfully, he had long been called
an "Abolitionist." More than this, their prejudice had been
so skillfully wrought upon by their pro-slavery friends,
neighbors, and sometimes kin, that they would not take
kindly to any man in New England or New York. This
strong prejudice had been predominant for more than a
generation, and was one of the real causes behind the more
trivial ones given that, more than all others, defeated Daniel
Webster so often for the Whig nomination.

This prejudice was, in 1860, still strong against the
same people, as much against Mr. Seward as it had been
against Mr. Webster. This would have lost Mr. Seward
several thousand votes in the doubtful States, and proved
the determining weakness which, if there had been no other,
would have been considered sufficient reason for nominating Mr. Lincoln. As a citizen of one of the most doubtful
States, he was as acceptable to the other two important
ones as to his own, and the most available man of all the
three.

There was this about Mr. Weed's management, it was
a compact organization, with complete control as far as it
went, but repugnant and unsuited to the independent men
of the Middle and Western States. It was the rule of the
"boss" before his time out West. Mr. Seward's cause would
have been in much better hands if some prominent and capable member of Congress had been put in charge of it.
There was also a feeling against New York's political methods in the public mind, as shown in and about Washington, where there were still recollections and traditional
stories of DeWitt Clinton's haughty ways and President
Van Buren's courtly aping of the glitter of royalty. The
domineering ways, the gayly-accoutered bands of musicians,
and the stylish dress worn by thousands of the New Yorkers,

provoked the plainer delegates farther West. Had it not been for the earnest work of Evarts, Morgan, King, Curtis, and others, their ostentatious display would have broken the strength of the Seward movement the first day. As it was, their style and conduct started up a strong reaction against them.

CHAPTER XLV.

THE Tremont House, the most commodious and central hostelry in the city of Chicago, was Illinois Headquarters, in which were our several hardworking divisions. There were the delegates and the committee-rooms, all public. There were, in addition, those of Oglesby, Wentworth, Washburn, Lovejoy, and Gridley, all at work, earnest and continuous in what they were doing. They were all co-operating in harmonious progress with service and attention that gave the leaders full information from all over the town every half hour, or as often as required.

The midnight of the day before the Convention brought reports to within thirty minutes from every State delegation. These were condensed to four pages, closely written, for private information. The brief conclusions were "If Lincoln can hold second place to the fifth ballot, his chances are good. To begin with, Pennsylvania will give him six or seven votes. Kentucky and the other border States will give him thirty, perhaps a few more. Illinois, Indiana, and some scattering votes will make over fifty, or something over eighty votes, all told, on the first ballot. This will be double that for any other except Seward, who will have about one hundred and ninety on the first ballot. The directions are that every man is to keep earnestly and vigorously at work in his particular duty. Be prudent and discreet, extend a cordial greeting, and give a generous welcome to all, and antagonize none. Mr. Lincoln is gaining as the second choice of several delegations. Advance his cause in every honorable way, and in this be capable, and do your best."

THE WIGWAM AT CHICAGO IN WHICH LINCOLN WAS NOMINATED

STATE-HOUSE IN WHICH WAS LINCOLN'S OFFICE DURING HIS CAMPAIGN

This was the summary, told where it could be, with a warning to avoid boasting, but urging every one in line and to make every street parade and Lincoln meeting a pronounced success.

A little later, Mr. Gridley wrote a characteristic note to Bloomington, and a copy went also to Springfield, where words were weighed and balanced. "The movement is ours. Town in working order and under control. Long John [Wentworth] never legged out a better plan. Illinois and Indiana delegations half in; will double by noon. We'll have a twelve-mile torchlight procession to-morrow night.

"Lincoln will win if Seward holds his forces through three or four ballots. These will be sure to break; but we want Lincoln well up to two hundred votes before that. He will have about ninety to start with. The Collamer, Chase, McLean, and Bates men will come to us as second choice, if Seward's hold to him and are not thrown to some other than Lincoln in the break-up. We are developing strength, and may get some New Yorkers, if Seward's forces break. We believe Lincoln will be more acceptable to Weed than any other, unless they could concentrate on Dayton, which seems improbable. We can't locate him and his Jersey delegation.

"Both delegations from Ohio are friendly to us. Either one will defeat the other on the first opportunity after the first ballot or two by coming to Lincoln. We could deal with either, but we fear driving the other to Seward. We want both, and will not break their 'harmony' by taking to either. Cameron is doing well with his Pennsylvanians. Six or seven of them will help us to start with, and enough more to keep Lincoln in the second place. Evarts, Morgan, King, and Curtis are persevering and doing well for Seward, but hardly better, if as well as Lane, Oglesby, Arnold, Swett, and others who follow them.

"It is a battle of men, a fine opportunity for the bold

and daring in a field of. timid and doubting ones. Lane's sagacity and oversight have not missed a pin scratch. Frank Blair's performances are wonderful. He ought to be a soldier; for he is a master of action, tactics, and detail. Think of it! He is holding Greeley calm, even hopeful at times, when all the rest of the United States could n't keep the old man quiet one evening. He is holding the Bates movement strong and balanced to a hair. He has the Missouri, Kentucky, and border State delegations of sixty 'to seventy, all for Bates and Lincoln, except a few who, singularly enough, are pronounced for Seward. This latter gets them all in as delegates without protest, I am told.

"In the fullness of time, Blair will swing these border seventy votes for Lincoln. All things are fair in war, they say. Politics does n't differ much from it. What opportunities I have missed! Cheer up 'for Lincoln, and send in the boys. We want to fill the town from Calumet Swamp to Lake Street, ten miles along the lake-shore."

Everything prospered in the interest of our candidate. The Illinois and Indiana management prospered under a full dozen co-operating leaders in and with their delegations. Wherever they were needed, all were busy and faithfully engaged. Old men, young men, and the women of the household put in every word and stroke for the leader whose strength and hope and belief in a higher destiny for our country than a slave empire had lighted the hearts of millions of freemen.

We have given the plans, the hopes and fears, of those nearest, the deepest and most earnestly concerned in the undertaking. We have been careful and particular, because much has been said as to how the nomination was brought about, some believing that it was done almost without preparation. This was largely due to the general and enthusiastic approval that followed. It was however, all that could be done by honest effort and endeavor, and as much a work of persevering and complete qualification for every part of the plan on the part of our people as it was of those of Mr. Seward, lacking nothing but time.

The determining factors in the selection of who should be the chief leader in the cause were not the plans or work of any one man, nor of any hundred men, however faithfully and earnestly they persevered, nor even of the State that seemed full of able men. The people were wrought up as they never had been. They determined that the highest leadership should go to him who could best fill the hope of a patriotic people, the one whom God, in his wisdom, had fitted to save this Nation and the liberties of a free people. Their combined judgment that halted, hesitated, considered, and reconsidered, led the delegates to take up the man of the common people, not the one with the most numerous following, but the one who, in their judgment, had more of the qualities in himself than any other man to lead in the portending strife. Anticipating a little, but showing how Mr. Lincoln grew in the minds of those strong representative men, the chairman, Mr. Ashmun, who was an impartial presiding officer as any whom all parties could agree upon, when chosen, was for Mr. Seward. He believed his selection the most suitable; but as things came and went and turned and tossed in that crucible of discussion and debate, before the balloting was over, he was anxious for Lincoln's success, and glad to be one of those carrying the Convention's authoritative notification to him at his home in Springfield.

From this time Ashmun not only supported him as the wisest possible to be chosen, but always held him afterward as his own true friend. Such action was not exceptional; for many of the most deliberate among these sober-minded men did likewise. The conviction came and grew in marvelous ways, and was strengthened as his character and beliefs became wider and better known. These, when knit together, like the man and his cause, bespoke the truth that, in the unfolding plans of the Master, he, like Luther, William of Orange, and Washington, had laid the foundation and created his own leadership.

The work of the Convention went smoothly on. It was called to meet Wednesday, the 16th of May, 1860. On the Monday before, the 14th, thousands arrived. Tuesday brought more thousands. By Wednesday, the opening day, there were such hosts and multitudes that no estimate was better than a guess. None present put the crowds at less than one hundred thousand visitors. When fifteen thousand were in line of march, there appeared to be no appreciable diminution in the crowd and lookers-on.

The accommodations and preparations for the gathering, the railroad conveyance, the housing and the feeding of these immense multitudes were the best that could be made. There were less than a dozen railways centering in the city, where there are over fifty now. Cars were scarcer in proportion. All kinds were in constant use—passenger, freight, box, open, and stock cars. All of these carried hundreds of the marching "Wide-awake Clubs," and there were other thousands on every road and boat-line. The nights were pleasant. Many carried their blankets, and slept under shelter somewhere, as there was no lack of this.

There was labor as well as duty in the progress which gave them appetites; but there was food, and plenty of it; for Chicago always had the raw material on hand to feed a million. Wide-awake clubs had been organized all over the country. These were made up of the active and vigorous young men of the cities, towns, and farms, who improvised the simple uniform of an oil-cloth cap and cape, to protect their clothing from the dripping of the oil in the torches they carried. The most imposing parade of the kind that had been seen up to that time was the fifteen thou-

sand marchers, who, with some others, filled twelve to fifteen
miles of blazing torchlighted streets every night, from Tuesday to Friday of Convention-week. One of the features
of every night's parade was John Hanks and his companions,
carrying the celebrated walnut rails of the Decatur Convention, covered with banners and inscriptions. They created and stirred up enthusiasm of multiplied thousands.
Everybody took kindly to the rails. It was one of the most
exhilarating displays ever witnessed in this country. There
were thousands marching in blazing lines, crossing and re-
crossing, like a figure 8, opening and countermarching, salut-
ing and cheering Abe Lincoln, the "rail splitter," until the
always marching columns had passed and repassed Hanks
and the rails and each other several times.

The Wigwam, a rough board structure for the occasion
that would seat five thousand besides delegates, and hold as
many more standing in crowded passage-ways, was completed. The railways were bringing in all sorts of trains,
like the lake-boats, swarming with people. The committees
of management kept things flying, as they said. There were
carloads or trainloads of delegations from almost every
county in Illinois south to Belleville and East St. Louis
and east to Charleston, and from Terre Haute, Indianapolis,
Fort Wayne, and all places north in Indiana to the State
line, with some from Michigan and Wisconsin.

Everything prospered in the interest of Mr. Lincoln.
The crowds were there; for very low rates had been secured.
There was no hiring people to go. They knew what was expected, and were anxious to go. The main thing was to
get any kind of a conveyance to the city. They willingly
gave their time, paid their way, and bore patiently whatever there was of discomfort in behalf of the cause to help
nominate a man so nearly one of them and to their liking.
Whatever there was or could be in the effect of hearty and

local indorsement emphasized by a hundred thousand fellow-citizens was given in the unmistakable presence, enthusiasm, and cheering of more people than could be counted.

Several attempts to get up outside demonstrations for Mr. Seward near Chicago were begun, with no interference save overwhelming shouts for Lincoln, when they were generally abandoned. After the Convention some of the disappointed claimed the nomination was forced by the local preparations, enthusiasm, and demonstrations, which were strong and convincing to some, perhaps. But it is not probable that these were the determining causes, for a more deliberate or stronger-minded assemblage of men never gathered in grave and serious council to save a country from its treacherous foes.

Volumes could be written, as they have been, and the theme exhausted in tracing the course and career of the men of that Convention: much more than half of them gave their service, and many of them their lives, to our cause and country. Some of them became able and distinguished leaders in civil and military life, governors, senators, and representatives. They were men of such honor and trustworthiness that, beyond controversy, they could influence the sensible and sober-minded delegates, without counting the effect of fiery parades and local enthusiasm.

Mr. Weed, after his arrival, was astonished and, in the end, confounded at the strength, ease, and symmetry of the movement and its management. He inquired several times: "Who has charge of this fine movement that seems to lack nothing of spirit, elasticity, or detail, that shows the master hand behind it all? From what I have heard, I could attribute it to Mr. Lincoln himself, but surely he is not conducting it. Some one here has caught his tact, the skill, the power, and sagacity, that we have not heard of." He was informed there were several committees, and that all united in effort and purpose, neglecting nothing that could advance the cause of our leader. He replied: "Yes, I have no doubt your committees are working well. That much we know. Do you know who moves the committees? Douglas has had the credit of being a faultless leader, and doubtless he has the talent; but, as I understand, he never moved and led such a body of men as these in any Convention. Surely there is such a man."

Later, when the Convention was over, when he had visited and congratulated Mr. Lincoln, when he had, of his own free will, assured him of support and confidence and co-operation, which he fulfilled and lived up to, he said, in familiar approval: "We can not but concede your leadership after your bouts and campaigns with Douglas and this climax at Chicago; but as we know you could not and did not manage your own campaign, I would like to know who is the undiscovered genius who anticipated us, met us at every turn, and—well—beat us? It was all honorable. There seems to be no need of concealing anything, and as there can be no reason for secrecy now, it would please me to know him."

Mr. Lincoln replied: "Well, I will tell you all I know about it. I have not had much to do with it myself. I have advised with a few friends, it is true, but with those who knew about as well beforehand, as after, all I had to say. Most of this has been published. A lot of our folks have taken a hand and helped along all they could. I do n't know who had charge of things in Chicago. You, being there, with very clear perceptions and good judgment on such affairs, should know better than I do. We have had efficient committees. Where all have worked together so well it is difficult to make distinctions. In the midst of such zealous and general support I have no occasion to speak particularly of what any one of the many friends did for me. It seems no discredit to the many that some have been better able to lead. All appear to have done well, much more for me personally than I feel myself prepared for or entitled to. It is the cause more than anything there can be in me or about me that commanded devotion and labor in such measureless perseverance. Oglesby, Washburn, Wentworth, Lovejoy, Gridley, Arnold, Swett, Peck, Davis, Judd, and others, of this State, with Lane, Blair, and other able helpers outside, have labored incessantly in my behalf."

Mr. Weed replied at once: "I have known all the others and what they did; but what of Mr. Gridley? Is he a politician?"

Mr. Lincoln replied: "No; the reverse of that. He has no desire for public life, and avoids the places about him at home that men generally are pleased to hold. I have no better friend. He has energy, capacity, and decisive character. He risks his judgment and wins most of the time."

"Yes, yes," slowly replied Mr. Weed. "He surely does; and he has been in the political campaign up to his eyes for you, regardless of what he desires. I knew there was a genius behind that splendid management, and so we have discovered him. I want to see him and congratulate him on his clean, close-shearing plans and progress that never missed his purposes a hair's-breadth."

Before returning home, he met and liked Mr. Gridley. He, as many others, urged him to enter the political campaign, where there was no lack of opportunity; but after having sustained his warm friend as skillfully as successfully, he resumed the even tenor of his way, a respected and honored citizen who "would not go into politics."

These—Lincoln and Weed—parted, always remaining true friends, the two strongest men in their party of that day. Some time later Mr. Weed, speaking of the result, said: "Of course, we were much disappointed in the defeat of Mr. Seward, both for himself and our State; but the cause has in no way suffered. Indeed, it stands better, as it is, with our candidate rising so rapidly in the people's confidence and public estimation. The Convention made no mistake in its choice. Nine out of every ten delegates went home satisfied. Mr. Seward has never seemed disappointed or dissatisfied for a moment. He continues in the cause as earnestly as ever, asserting that Lincoln's selection was as good as could have been made, and will prove the best should he carry the doubtful States, which his friends, with apparently good reasons, expect him to do."

The delegates to the Convention were conservative and clear-headed men. They took, first, a careful and deliberate survey of the whole situation. They were confident of success under wise management, if a candidate acceptable to the doubtful States was selected. With that settled in his favor, Mr. Seward could have been nominated on the first ballot. When it was discovered that these three States had united on Mr. Lincoln, it was virtually settled that he would be nominated before any ballot was cast, if our people continued their prudent course without mistakes or blunders.

This was so well considered and determined, as we have seen, that Mr. Weed, the great organizer and leader, soon saw the sense of the settlement and its urgent propriety. Mr. Seward, the founder of the party, if it had any single one, and most prominent leader from its organization, confirmed this view, and, in his unselfish and ungrudging way, gave it earnest and continuous support.

This was triumph indeed for Mr. Lincoln and his faithful friends. It was incontestible proof of his high capacities as a leader, more decisively shown in the wisdom and statesmanship of an Administration whose members were selected in conformity with the party settlement made at Chicago. Seward, Weed, and their followers—leaders and men—gave lasting evidence of their patriotic devotion to our cause when they agreed to Mr. Lincoln's nomination as the best that could have been made, handed him the standards, intrusted him, as the party's hope, and followed in all as well as they had led.

On Wednesday, the 16th of May, the great Convention assembled, with its nine hundred and thirty delegates and alternates, representatives of the people in their rising against the encroachments of the slave-masters. It was the history-making assemblage that marked a great change in our National life. The prayer opened their hearts in the presence of the God of nations. Governor E. D. Morgan, of New York, chairman of the National Committee, announced the purposes of the meeting. In a few appropriate words he nominated David Wilmot, of Pennsylvania, who in the '40's, as a revolting Democrat, was independent enough to leave his party to save his people, for temporary chairman. He was elected in a responsive shout that rolled over the immense audience, to the roof, and out, at every window and opening, passing on for squares in every direction. This was the first shout of thousands in a Convention that was going "to holler for freedom and our man as long as our throats hold out." Such a shouting, huzzaing multitude of people had never been seen nor met anywhere in our country. The spirit of liberty that filled them was abroad in the land, while they were ringing out chorus after chorus of vociferous applause as it pleased them.

The first day, as usual, was devoted to organization, introductions, and making acquaintances, election of officers, the selection of committees, the adoption of rules of order, and the conduct of business. Mr. George Ashmun, of Massachusetts, was made permanent chairman. His familiar and friendly way of dispatching business, and his impartial methods and course, justified the wisdom of his selection. Illinois, under a better management, could easily have had Washburn as chairman; but then Massachusetts was all the better pleased with Mr. Lincoln in that their man presided over the meeting.

GEORGE WILLIAM CURTIS

JOHN A. ANDREW

CHARLES SUMNER

MAJOR-GENERAL FRANK P. BLAIR

GEORGE ASHMUN

The important business of the second day was the report, the discussion, and the adoption of a platform or declaration of principles. This was a task of the Convention about as important as the naming of a candidate. There were many men in the Convention, as there were in the party and the movement, who held all sorts of diverging views, on slavery particularly, as well as on other important public affairs.

Among them were delegates representing all shades of belief on slavery, from Giddings, of Ohio; Curtis, of New York; and Horace Greeley, of the New York *Tribune,* who were pronounced anti-slavery advocates without qualification, commonly known as Abolitionists, to David Davis, O. H. Browning, and others, who had never spoken against it, to F. P. Blair, of Missouri, and several delegates from the slave States, who desired a declaration of non-intervention with slavery in the States where it existed.

To unite these varying opinions, to get a platform that had anything worthy of statesmanship in it, be declarative enough to deserve the support of independent, patriotic people, to say enough against slavery, and not too much, took all there was of skill and ingenuity among them to look up and appoint a committee of word-choppers and phraseologists. In this art of politics, that was an easy task sometimes, the committee labored with downright fatigue, earnestly, for hours, in no playful sort of mood, in almost continuous session, until well into the second day, when some kind of platform report was a conspicuous necessity.

Late on the second day the committee reported resolutions which, in substance, declared for the integrity of the Union of the States, denouncing disunionism in every form; denouncing the Buchanan pro-slavery plan of attempting to force slavery into Kansas, explicitly so the Lecompton Constitution; denouncing the reopening of the African slave-trade; that they were opposed to the Squatter Sovereignty plan and the .Democratic policy of non-intervention with slavery in the Territories; denying the authority of any Administration, Congress, or any Territorial Legislature to establish slavery in any Territory; that they were opposed to any further restrictions on the naturalization of foreign-born citizens. A resolution was reported in favor of increased import duties and for the encouragement of home industries. This was a start in the direction of higher protective tariffs. They reported another in favor of the prompt admission of Kansas under its free- State Constitution; another in favor of river and harbor improvements, as the increase of commerce and navigation required; and another in favor of a special land-grant for the purpose of building a railroad across the continent to the Pacific Ocean. These were all, with a general declaration against slavery and polygamy as twin-relics of barbarism; but there was no outspoken assertion or declaration in favor of the doctrines of the rights of men. Strangest of all strange things was this omission in .a party led by Seward, Lincoln, Sumner, Chase, Giddings, Lovejoy, and hundreds of like belief.

While considering the report, Mr. Giddings, of Ohio, offered an amendment recapitulating the clause of the Declaration of Independence lately defended so courageously by Mr. Lincoln, "that all men are endowed by their Creator with certain inalienable rights, among which are life, liberty, and the pursuit of happiness." Under strong pressure of the Platform Committee, the amendment was voted down. The old Silver Grays had got their conservatism into the platform at last, just as they had managed the appointment of delegates at the Illinois Convention and several other States in like manner. Their explanation in voting this declaration of American liberty down was that they "did not want a long line of generalities to explain."

They were prepared for the immediate adoption of the

report, hoping to shut off debate in so large a body of men for want of time and the impatience to get home, such as occurs in every National Convention. To Giddings's argument the committee replied that, although they believed in the Ten Commandments, they would not want them in a political platform. The event passed carelessly and unnoticed by many in the unavoidable confusion and noise of so many talking or trying to talk at once. Even the quick apprehension of Chairman Ashmun had not caught the deep importance and peril of the proceeding. When Giddings's amendment was so peremptorily voted down, he retired at once. This attracted the chairman's immediate attention, and some heavy raps brought the Convention to order, and stillness, even silence, prevailed some minutes.

When the anti-slavery section, made up of men, many of whom had grown gray in the cause, and who had borne the moral, if not the political, burden for years, had full understanding of the subject, it is a mild description to say that consternation reigned in that Convention for as long as thirty minutes. Full fifty wanted the floor at once. Some were contending for the committee's platform as reported, but ten times as many against it. Chairman Ashmun, in this critical juncture proved the wisdom of his selection, and saved the coming crash. He called a vice-president to the chair, intending to move for a recess, if nothing better could be done to repair the unpatriotic design or blunder, whichever it might be. In all this, however, the committee harangued, and held firmly to their report, making every effort to force its adoption without amendment.

While Ashmun was speaking, a hasty conference was held, in which it was stated that the adoption of the committee's report without amendment would split the Convention wide open. Mr. Curtis, of New York, who was then forcible and well-nigh invincible in speech, was selected to present the amendment again, urge its adoption, or move

for a recess and reconsideration as the last resort before
division. Mr. Ashmun returned hastily to the chair, where
he recognized Mr. Curtis at once. With some vehement
hammering he restored order out of angry dispute and
threatening confusion. In as firm expression and as positive
demeanor he stated the question, that it must be fairly entertained, considered, and disposed of; that amendments
to the platform were in order, and held equal parliamentary
standing with the report of the committee. He stated more
emphatically that, if order was not preserved and free discussion permitted without force, it would be employed.
Recognizing the gentleman from New York, he sat down.

Mr. Curtis was at his best, fully warmed up to the gravity and deep importance of the occasion. He delivered a
righteous protest of indignation and condemnation against
those who would flinch in the cause of human liberty in
such truth, sincere pleading, and pathetic power that it
came to their senses a revelation never to be forgotten.
After presenting Mr. Giddings's amendment, he said, in
substance: "Mr. Chairman, we are face to face with an overwhelming catastrophe. The precipice over which dismembered and disintegrating parties have leaped to destruction
is before us, from which there can be no escape from disaster except in return to a declaration and defense of the
principles upon which our government is founded—the rights
of men. The committee report seems oblivious to the commanding necessity that the party of freedom must declare
it, and that now, in the ill-considered haste that makes no
speed, we are hurrying the action that will leave the party
immolated in the record that rejected the fundamental
truth.

"To those who knowingly desire this we say, Depart in
peace, laying no polluted hand on the immortal principles
declared and sustained by the truly heroic, if not better,
men. If this platform remains without change, with the

foundering blunder in it, which we should yet believe due more to heedless mistake than to deliberate intent, who is there among our worthy and distinguished leaders that will plant themselves upon it for its defense? Surely not Mr. Seward, who declares a higher than human law for the hope of men; nor Mr. Lincoln, whose logic and reasoning have never been clearer than in his defense and broadening interpretation of these immortal principles.

"I have to ask you whether you are prepared to remain on the record in our free country as voting down the leading truths of the Declaration of Independence? Think well, gentlemen, before, upon the free prairies of the West, in this year of 1860, you falter and quail before the men in Philadelphia in 1776."

The patriotic lashing brought instant relief. The Giddings amendment was restored and adopted in a storm, rather than a vote, that swept the Convention in a wave of sentiment and enthusiasm that, for the time, overwhelmed the old-line Silver Grays, but only so; for, in some way or other, they were a returning and continuing burden until Mr. Lincoln rose in the majesty of God's offended law and the rights of a bleeding, exasperated people to strike in one unerring blow the shackles that held a race in bondage.

It is seldom given men the opportunity to castigate the designing ones and mend such thoughtless blunders and the more crafty designs on the part of such conservative leaders; but, being the man for it and prepared, Mr. Curtis did it well and effectively. A hundred were springing to the breach, but it was all over when Curtis sat down. Mr. Giddings returned to the Convention, where he was congratulated by a great many friends. He deserved all of it; for in his long and faithful service in behalf of human liberty he had seldom served the cause so well, if ever. With harmony restored and the platform amended, the second day's session closed with increasing crowds and Seward's men doing well in fine and well-managed parades, but never more than one-fifth approaching the Lincoln demonstrations.

When Mr. Giddings's amendment was rejected, Mr. Lincoln was notified and his advice requested. The dispatch to him read about as follows: "Convention impatient, discussing platform. Over-conservative committee is rushing report. Convention has just voted down the Giddings amendment that all men are created equal, etc. What can we do?" He replied at once. His message was in the hall when Mr. Curtis closed, and, the crisis having passed, it was not read. It was positively distinct: "Party rejecting the truths of the Declaration of Independence will go to pieces. Have a recess; reconsider the Giddings amendment. Time and reflection will restore men's reason and bring better judgment."

The Convention had righted itself, obviating any use of Mr. Lincoln's message. Mr. Seward also had been informed. Owing to the delay, he was later in replying, when the result of the reconsideration had been received. He was equally emphatic in favor of restoration of the Giddings amendment. Nine-tenths of the party held the same way, yet the small faction of reactionaries floundered and almost brought the division, which would have resulted in the election of Judge Douglas as President.

On Thursday evening, the second day of the Convention, the Lincoln leaders sat down for a conference after the hardest day's labor most of them had ever known. The reports were encouraging, but everything seemed hanging and depending on continuous, unremitting perseverance. The closest estimates put Lincoln's vote at about one hundred and Seward's at two hundred. From all sources of information it appeared that Lincoln was the second choice of about all the delegations outside of the Seward following and New Jersey, beyond this that the Jersey delegation was non-committal. From other sources it was conceded to Seward, which completed his two hundred votes.

, It did not appear on information from any reliable source that Seward could get the additional thirty-five votes to nominate him without a break in the Lincoln movement. This did not appear probable; but to these persevering men, where strength and duty well performed were pleasures, they took nothing for granted, and redoubled their energies and increased their forces about the town in the crowds as they increased and the contest was closing in. Politeness, ceaseless energy, constant care, clear heads, and flying feet where there was anything to do or report were the last admonitions from the committee.

Thursday night was the culminating performance. The scene was brilliant, grand, and spectacular, with delegations, companies, clubs, numberless bands of music, and full-toned, vociferous men, no matter whose standard they bore, fifteen thousand torch-bearers in line. It was an inspiring display, those marching thousands of strong-limbed, full-chested, loud-toned, vociferous men, no matter whose standard they bore, nor for whom they cheered. They were free, independent men, full of the same patriotic love of country, the type and mold of the coming invincible American.

On the third day's assembling there was feverish anxiety on every face. The work and worry had set their marks deep in the features of the leaders of fifties and hundreds and thousands. The louder noise of cheering was hushed in the Wigwam, but the murmuring thrill of ten thousand strained and softened human voices was like the subdued roar of some mighty torrent, not silenced, but hushed, held down, until its bellowing fullness rolled over the countless multitude. The opening was cheerful. The prayer was impressive. All other business had been satisfactorily adjusted. There remained the absorbing one of naming the leaders for the contest.

When the current affairs had been disposed of, Mr. Evarts, of New York, nominated Wm. H. Seward, of that State, in the good old way of naming your man and sitting down. He could talk, as everybody knew, and he had been doing so almost incessantly through the week for his friend and colleague. But the graceful naming of his candidate, by an advocate who could easily talk four hours, in less than so many minutes, set the measure for all, and the nominating speeches were no more than naming them in answer to a roll-call of the States, when some one of each delegation named their favorites, as they desired.

Mr. Evarts named Mr. Seward, of New York. When Illinois was called, Mr. Judd nominated Abraham Lincoln. In the same way Bates, of Missouri; Collamer, of Vermont; Cameron, of Pennsylvania; Chase and McLean, of Ohio, and Dayton, of New Jersey, were named by their respective delegations, with no more than ordinary cheering; but when Mr. Lane, of Indiana, seconded the nomination of our candidate, the swelling tide of cheering for Lincoln began.

As this first volley of sound rolled away, Michigan, just across the lake, seconded the nomination of Seward. The New Yorkers rose in a body, a stalwart lot of men, with a thousand auxiliaries to take up the cry. It was a formidable roar, when, with their cohorts in and out of the Wigwam, they overlapped the Illinois and Indiana noise and explosion out and out, and, in thunders of applause that was a grand performance, they felt sure they had the sound of the Convention on their side. Illinois and Indiana had not fallen in this first fray of the conflict of throats and blare of trumpets, horns, and drums. Our folks were more properly getting ready and waiting for the next onset in the struggle. There were few who thought and none who felt sure that the New York-Michigan roar could be approached or equaled.

The movement had reached high tide when the occasion

came for the trial, when a part of the Ohio delegation, with
the concurrence of about two hundred who were coming
in later, seconded Lincoln's nomination. At this Illinois,
Indiana, and the Lincoln delegates in a dozen States and
the crowds squeezing one another up to the rails opened
their throats, spread their chests, and began the rising,
swelling roar for Lincoln, that soon overcame the crowd
and the Convention, and then rolled over their heads, where
it was taken up and swollen, echoed and re-echoed over the
three hundred thousand visitors and citizens for half an
hour in rolling billows of indescribable sound. It was the
concluding encounter of sound and impulse of eighty thousand against twenty thousand. The prairies won. •

It was stoutly asserted at the time, and it seems as
firmly held by many writers since, that on the third day,
just before the balloting began, Seward's forces in the Convention fully expected success. This may have been the
belief of the vigorous Seward crowd in a mass, who were
purposely strong and outspoken; for to have conceded a
weakness anywhere then would have been defeat beforehand; hence to proclaim his certain success was a well-considered part of their plan. But to the Seward managers
defeat must have been a foregone conclusion from the
evening of the first day, when it became known to all of
them that no tally-sheet counted more than two hundred
votes for their man, with New Jersey included. This left
him thirty-three votes short of a nomination, and outside
of these two hundred it was not known where he would get
another vote. If his chief leaders believed in his final
success, it was on the kind of information not trusted by
those in opposition on our side.

The information at our headquarters was not that Lincoln's success was certain, but that, with the support of the
doubtful States, his chances were the best. It was as near
a certainty as could be that the movement against Seward

would win. It was not a combination against Seward further than necessity compelled it to be. It was the deliberate conclusion of the most thoughtful men of that memorable Convention, many of them personal friends of Seward, who were in search of the most available candidate, regardless of personal or sectional preferences, that he was not the man.

To the doubtful-minded delegates, when the whole situation was brought before them, it was all resolved in the single question, which was, Who among these capable men is the most available and can carry the three doubtful States, which are all necessary to elect our candidate? The answer by our people invariably was this: Two of the most doubtful—Illinois and Indiana—are positively for Lincoln without division. Part of Pennsylvania, and all of it, contingently, are for him. Ohio is as heartily for our man as Indiana, when it has complimented its two favorites, neither of whom does it expect to nominate. With these the Bates following will be turned over to Lincoln any moment it will nominate him.

In the hushed stillness of ten thousand men crammed together in the Wigwam, the roll-call of the States for the first ballot was called. When it was over, the result went through the vast crowd, as a full thousand tally-sheets had it. It passed through the multitude in a few minutes, and all over the land as fast as the wires could carry it. The count was short: Seward, 173; Lincoln, 102; all others, 190. It developed the logic and reasonableness of the Lincoln campaign, and it more than foreshadowed Seward's defeat.

The New Yorkers, who had not before then suspected defeat, saw it in the figures of the first talley-sheet. Thousands sympathized with them; for there was no feeling but respect and admiration for their candidate and themselves. If the men alone had been the issue, Seward might have won, even after the first ballot; but in the battle of availability he had fallen twelve votes behind the conceded estimate of two hundred, including New Jersey. The ballot showed that Jersey was in the wind, because three times their vote would not have nominated him.

Lincoln had gained two above our estimate. He was conceded to be the coming man by thousands who had doubted before, and these words, or something to the same effect, passed hurriedly all over the assembly. One tall, stalwart Ohio delegate mounted a chair and called out: "If he gains on the next ballot and gets the break from the complimentary nominees, he's a sure winner. Ohio is going to him next time. Two men in one State for President are one too many; and when one goes to him, all will. Two-thirds of us are for him anyway. Vermont is going for him in a lump in a ballot or so." Another delegate across the aisle, standing near Frank Blair, said: "The Bates vote will go to Lincoln whenever Frank Blair raises his hat on the Missouri standard. We see now that Seward can't get another vote, except from Jersey. It is always shaky when the biggest crowd is on the other side. I think we might as well nominate Lincoln on the next ballot." These and a thousand such expressions ran through the throngs who pushed their way wherever a man could be squeezed in.

With the Lincoln tide rising, the second roll-call of the States began. It would be an endless task to recite the strained interest and the excitement that prevailed. Hundreds wanted to cheer the States voting on their side; but the interest became so intense to see and hear how the vote ran that all noises were suppressed. There were more tally sheets, more counting done than before. Every one who had a pencil and any kind of paper, scrap, or fragment, was checking up the vote. It was a short tally, with only two names to write—Seward and Lincoln—and then make the best mark possible for every State as it voted. As the Lincoln vote increased, it was all that the best-trained could do to keep down the shouts; but eagerness prevailed, and they waited and wrote and punched away at their tallies on envelopes and ragged pieces of paper.

Five minutes more time for the vote would have made the run that came later. As the call reached Ohio, Lincoln gained six, and Pennsylvania came in with forty-four, completing its full vote, and Vermont with its ten, rounding out the second ballot. Seward had 184, a gain of 11, all that Jersey would give in Seward's strongest poll. Lincoln had 181, a gain of 79, with 50 friendly votes of the States passed on the roll before Pennsylvania and Vermont were reached. These were ready to change to Lincoln, but concluded that the best and easiest way was to wait for another ballot rather than precipitate confusion at its close.

The word was passed through the crowd, and went everywhere: "Seward, 184; Lincoln, 181. He is a sure winner next time. Hold your lungs, boys, for a bigger blast than you have ever given." The New Yorkers were gritty, and held their strength in the best discipline ever known in any Convention in those days. If there had been a break in the second ballot, Lincoln would have won on that; for it was about as good as settled by it. To the Lincoln's men's enthusiasm they replied: "Boys, if you win, you've got to fight it out every inch to the end. We believe you have a good man. We know that we have, and we are going on with our next ballot. New York has seventy votes for Seward."

The interest was so intense that the waiting for accurate counting and announcing the regular vote was harassing and painful. Every one knew what it was long before it was over, where a minute was a long time under such tension and anxiety. It seemed that "something would snap" very soon, as one said. Another said: "Jim, can't we let go now and lift the roof?" Jim said: "No; sit quiet. Keep your senses till we win. Those Yorkers would lift the roof and us with it, if we get too previous. Keep your legs under ye, and yer head on top, and we'll take the town after the next ballot."

The call was everywhere in the Convention and outside, "Vote! vote!" It took level heads and determination to prevent a stampede from the Seward forces. Michigan, Wisconsin, and Iowa could barely be held for another vote. When the roll was called through to the bottom, a full thousand tablets, envelopes, and scraps of paper had the result: Seward 180, a loss of four and a half, and Lincoln 231 and a half, technically lacking one and a half votes, but virtually nominated. For a moment everything was still. Then four delegates were asking recognition. Carter, of Ohio, got it, and reported a change of four votes to Lincoln. A thousand tally-keepers shouted, "Lincoln!" almost at once at the top of their voices. Our Illinois people had a cannon on the roof of the Wigwam. A delegate pulled the signal, and the double-loaded gun began the outside noise for Lincoln instantly.

When the roll-call was complete, the chairman announced, "Abraham Lincoln, of Illinois, having received three hundred and sixty-four votes, is declared our candidate for President of the United States." Mr. Evarts then gracefully moved to make the nomination unanimous, which was carried with a shout. The news spread by every means and avenue of communication. The wires were ready, and wherever they went the event so anxiously expected was announced. The mails were full. The papers were soon full of it, and the thousands of visitors began their homeward return, scattering the details of the news to every city, village, and railway station on their route. On that evening a general rejoicing was held all over Illinois and most of Indiana, and in many other places from Maine to California. In a few minutes Senator Hannibal Hamlin, of Maine, was selected as candidate for Vice-President. A bet-

ter man could hardly have been chosen. The appointment
of some committees finished the labors of the Convention.
The management for Lincoln was wisely and well done.
Of the conspicuous leaders, all were prominent men in public affairs, except Mr. Gridley, who had capacities and means
at hand for effective help and co-operation such as no other
person had.

In this situation some one had to take the lead, keep
everything going, and trust to others for remuneration when
it came, if ever. This part of it Mr. Gridley undertook and
carried on to notable success. He was the leading spirit, not
only with his means, but in methods which could not have
been bettered. The plans went regularly and smoothly on.
He had the help of several able and efficient men; but in
the business of what could have been properly called the
Committee of Ways and Means, he was the heart and soul,
and kept everything moving forward.

Chicago was then small for such a gathering. In addition it was before the days of competent general and local
committees. In all his operations there was no useless waste
of money; neither was there a lack of it for any necessary
purpose. Mr. Swett was with him as much as any one
and well informed of his progress. Swett was asked frequently how the business went on. He was always willing
enough to answer those whom he thought it would benefit
and who had the right to know. His estimate was, in the
statements he frequently made: "There was not a dollar
wasted or improperly used that I ever heard of. The work
progressed with such regularity, symmetry, and adaptability
that it was soon established what a master Gridley was in
such operations. You want to know how much he advanced
and about how much he was out in the end? Of the former,
we counted it up and kept the run of it until it was consider-
ably over one hundred thousand dollars. Of the other, that
is, how much he ever got back, he only said that whatever

the amount was that he was out, it went willingly, and he would have doubled it any day when there was necessity. It was never a question of how much, but how best to use the means honestly for Lincoln's success."

The railroads met all the extra expenses of preparing and getting ready for the transportation of the crowds, and made a nice sum out of it. They made the lowest possible rates, and used every kind of cars that the people would ride in. The people themselves, with some occasional help from the towns they lived in, paid their fares and generally for their subsistence. The lowest items of expense were for printing, stationery, music, postage, and clerk hire. The largest were for the building of the Wigwam and the rent of the hotels for the committees and for headquarters. These made an immense sum in the aggregate to take care of Mr. Lincoln's interests in the assembled multitude.

On the adjournment of the Convention, Mr. Ashmun, the president of the Convention, with a committee of delegates, repaired to Springfield, where Mr. Lincoln was, and formally notified him of his nomination. The gentlemen of the committee were generously entertained in the Lincoln household and by the people of Springfield, who heartily appreciated the distinguished honor conferred on their fellow-citizen.

Mr. Lincoln's reply to the committee's address was extemporaneous, and not preserved. His letter of acceptance is as follows:

"SPRINGFIELD, ILL., May 23, 1860.

"Hon. George Ashmun, President of the Republican National Committee:

"SIR,—I accept the nomination tendered me by the Convention over which you presided, of which I am formally apprised in the letter of yourself and others acting as a committee for that purpose.

"The declaration of principles and sentiments which accompanies your letter meets my approval, and it shall be my care not to violate it in any part.

"Imploring the assistance of Divine Providence, and with due regard to the views and feelings of all who were present and represented in the Convention, to the rights of all the States and Territories and people of the Nation, to the inviolability of the Constitution, and the perpetual Union, harmony, and prosperity of all, I am now happy to co-operate for the practical success of the principles declared by the Convention.

"Your obliged friend and fellow-citizen,

"A. LINCOLN."

Mr. Herndon said: "The news of his nomination found him in the office of the Springfield *Journal.* Naturally enough he was nervous, restless, and laboring under more or less suppressed excitement. He had been tossing ball, a pastime frequently indulged in by the lawyers of that day, and had played a few games of billiards to keep down, as another has expressed it, the excitement that possessed him. When the telegram containing the result of the last ballot came in, although calm and apparently unmoved, a close observer could have detected in the compressed lips and serious countenance evidences of deep and unusual emotion. As the balloting progressed, he had gone to the office of the *Journal,* and was sitting there in a large arm-chair when the news of his nomination came. What a line of scenes must have broken in upon his vision as he hurried from the newspaper office to tell a little woman down the street the news! In the evening his friends and neighbors called to congratulate him. He thanked them feelingly, taking each one of them by the hand. A day later the committee from the Convention, with the chairman, called and delivered the formal notice of his nomination."

CHAPTER XLVI.

THUS Abraham Lincoln was nominated for the highest position and office within the gift of the American people at the age of fifty-one years, in the full strength of his manhood. He was well fitted for every public duty— a genius in his intellectual endowment and a Hercules in his physical powers.

It was his formulation of the nature and evils of slavery more than personal considerations that determined his selection. It was his characteristics as a man, leader, and statesman that made him the ideal man of the people. In all the relations of life he gained the confidence of his fellow-men as they knew more and more of him. He had never reached any position by accident, but by the most earnest thought, action, and preparation that was possible. He was kind, considerate, and wise, and in his great-hearted nature knew more of what was in the human heart, its sorrows, and its woes, as it appeared to his friends, than any other living man. He grew to be the hope of all men and of a race of men in bondage. He had never been—no matter how deeply you fathomed him—other than the true and constant friend of his fellow-men. No power could intimidate or dissuade, and no emolument or fortune could tempt him one moment from the defense of his fellow-men who required his help. This was Lincoln. Such he lived, and such he died. It would be a world's victory for freedom to have another like him.

The nomination made little change in his habits or manner of living. If there was difference, he was more friendly and familiar with his neighbors and the hundreds of people who called to see him, to whom he was always accessible and friendly.

The State officers gave him one of the large rooms on the ground floor of the old State-house for an office and reception-room. He and his secretary managed the business of the campaign, as it needed his personal attention. He attended to all sorts of things in his usual friendly way, in and out of season, as they came. People went to see him regularly and at random. No one failed to receive a kind recognition from the great, big-hearted man, whose public service in and for the Presidency began May 18th, the afternoon of the day of the third ballot at Chicago.

After this he conceded the right of the people to his time and attention as a public servant, dealing with them kindly, patiently, and in every way the best he could to make them feel comfortable and at ease. He was confident, and so acted from the beginning. He said that in his mind there was an unaccountable certainty or an intuition that he would be elected. His office in the old capitol was a fit and proper selection. It had old memories about it and strong attachments for many. It was the people's tabernacle during the period of the State's greatest growth and progress for more than a generation.

It was to many, like myself, an object of much interest. To us it recalled the business that brought my father to the State in the '40's, to help complete the ragged-looking pile of stone. It was the place where he so resolutely contended with Judge Douglas on the evil and injustice of slavery, where we first knew him so well and began our pleasant acquaintance with Mr. Lincoln. People of all parties came to congratulate him. Many of his Democratic personal friends asked him, in one form or another, whether he desired their support. His answer generally ran something like this: "You should not vote for me unless you believe that the principles I represent are the best under which our government can be administered. Your vote and mine are our highest privileges. In them we protect or squander our most precious rights. They should always be given and exercised as the result of our most careful and deliberate judgment."

As the months passed, it became more and more probable that he would be elected. The pro-slavery *régime* and Buchanan's Administration, under its baleful control, had struck the Democratic party a deadly blow. Douglas, although strong and determined, was fighting as a leader and a candidate almost alone against thousands, and with the patronage of a slavery-corrupted, slavery-extending Administration against him.

In Maine the Republicans elected a governor and State officers by 18,000 plurality in September. In Pennsylvania, which Buchanan carried by a large majority in 1856, the Republicans elected a governor and State officers by about 32,000 majority in October. Ohio, too, elected a State ticket and Congressmen by majorities ranging from 12,000 to 27,000 in the same month. In Indiana the Republicans won by about ten thousand majority in October.

These State elections almost certainly pointed to Lincoln's success. The Presidential election was held November 6, 1860. The result was as expected by well-informed men in all parties, and to none more clearly than the Southern conspirators. Republican electors were chosen in seventeen free States, with three out of the seven in New Jersey, giving Mr. Lincoln 180 Electoral votes, with popular vote of 1,866,350, and Douglas 12 Electoral votes, with popular vote of 1,375,157. This was approximately the loyal vote, amounting to 3,241,507. The vote of Breckinridge and Lane was 72 Electoral votes, with popular vote of 845,763. The Electoral vote for Bell and Everett was 39 and the popular vote 589,581. These two were mainly the pro-slavery vote, 1,435,344.

This vote of November, 1860, has been variously com-
mented upon, and used, as such events generally are, to
suit the purposes and intent of the reviewers. When the
Presidential Electors voted, and the announcement in Congress was made of the result on the 13th of February, 1861,
it was settled beyond dispute that Lincoln and Hamlin
were duly elected President and Vice-President, according
to lawful and Constitutional form.

It was proof, strong as votes could make it, that 3,241,-
507 of our 4,676,851 legal voters were loyal Unionists and
positively opposed to any form of National dismemberment;
that 1,866,350 were positively opposed to any further extension of slavery, that another loyal 1,375,157 were as firmly
opposed to slavery extension, unless it was done by the
consent of the legal voters of any Territory at a fair. election before or at its admission as a State. Thus the vote
of November, 1860, bore such an emphatic condemnation
of secession or disunion that the slaveholders' conspiracy
had neither promise nor hope of success, except in war
and bloody insurrection.

The Southern revolt was promoted by a triangular sort
of propaganda which had every agency in operation for
the advancement of its purpose a few days after the promulgation of the Presidential vote. This body of insurrectionists was made up, first, of the governors of the slave
States, with the few influential political leaders, sustained
by the county and municipal authorities. This was the
bottom round. The next was made up of their public men
in general in and about Washington, such as senators, representatives, military and naval officers, judges, and prominent citizens in and out of office, and supernumeraries and
legionaries to the number of about five thousand. This
was the second round and one of the strongest and most
noisy parts of their organization. Then there was the chief
cabal of the despots presided over by Jefferson Davis. This

was conducted under absolutism as rigid and irresponsible as Davis and the few he admitted chose to make it. This was the third, or top round of the Confederacy and slave empire conspiracy. Thus, without the vote or concurrence of the voters in any county or State, they had the completed political machinery in actual and progressive control in every slaveholding community, all of which was put in uninterrupted operation as the dictator desired.

The power of the Nation, had it been properly exercised by a loyal and capable President, could have suppressed and dispersed the forces of this rising rebellion as fast as it was organized. It was not because our laws were weak, or for lack of strength to support them; for they had been authoritatively interpreted and firmly enforced by former Presidents. In 1794, what was known as the "Whisky Rebellion" was promptly suppressed with military force by President Washington. There was no question of lack of authority or the wisdom or propriety in the use of the military power of the Government necessary to do so, as recognized by any reputable authority.

Chief-Justice Marshall, sustained by the undivided Supreme Court, decided, asserted, and reasserted, in several decisions, the entirety and inviolability of the Constitution as the fundamental law and bond of National unity. As we have had occasion to relate, President Jackson suppressed a rising insurrection and attempted nullification of the laws of the United States by the people and State of South Carolina in 1830-1. Jackson did this effectually, swiftly, and without loss of life or property by his courageous exercise of the National power. This should have remained a Constitutional bulwark, pointing out the President's unmistakable duty in the face of any threatened insurrection, such as confronted the Buchanan Administration. His guilty Cabinet, however, not only failed to suppress it in its beginnings, but, availing themselves of the bad advice and the cowardly inaction of the President, nursed the murderous rebellion into strength.

Daniel Webster, in addition to the legal precedents against Calhoun and Hayne and the numberless smaller coadjutors, interpreted the Constitution as the unbreakable basis of fundamental law and unity so clearly that all men, however unlearned, knew it could only be broken in the wreck of the Nation by parricidal war.

In the face of all this, with guilty knowledge or as inexcusable ignorance, the Buchanan Administration raised not a hand against the open insurrection of the slaveholders. It was not altogether a suddenly-planned scheme, but, as frequently told in and out of Congress, it had its beginning as far back as Calhoun's project for a Southern slave empire, that was to include the slave States, Mexico, the West Indies, and Central America to the isthmus. This had so successfully progressed in 1845-8 that, in war for the extension of slavery and the eventual empire, more than half of Mexico's territory was taken in a wide, continuous belt to and along the Pacific Ocean.

In 1860 the slaveholders became so bold and imperious in their desires that they successfully disrupted the party which they could no longer control. In furtherance of these long-planned results, waiting then only the event of Lincoln's election, their preparations for separation, war, and destruction went on with treasonable rapidity, such as no respectable nation, one worth keeping alive, ever permitted.

Our slow Constitutional processes of changing policy and Administration gave the insurrectionists four months' start in getting ready for war. In 1856, in the event of Fremont's election, they desperately planned what they came to be carrying out in 1860-1. John M. Mason, then a senator from Virginia, one of the cabal of four or five chief conspirators, wrote about it quite unreservedly, and as fully explained the whole of it to Jefferson Davis, then Sec-

retary of War in the Cabinet of President Pierce. His letter is as follows:

"SELMA, near WINCHESTER, VA., Sept. 30, 1856.

"MY DEAR SIR,—I have a letter from Governor Wise,
of this State, of the 27th, full of spirit. He says the governors of North Carolina, South Carolina, and Louisiana have
already agreed to rendezvous at Raleigh, and others will—
this in your most private ear. He said further, that he
had officially requested you to exchange with Virginia, on
fair terms of difference, percussion for flint-lock muskets.
I do n't know the usage or power of the department in such
cases; but if it can be done, even by liberal construction, I
hope you will accede.

"Was there not an appropriation at the last session for
converting flint-lock into percussion arms? If so, would
it not furnish good reason for extending such facilities to
the States? Virginia probably has more arms than the
other Southern States, and would divide in case of need.
In a letter yesterday to a committee in South Carolina I gave
it as my judgment, in the event of Fremont's election, the
South should not pause, but proceed at once to immediate,
absolute, and eternal separation. So I am a candidate for
the first halter. Wise says his accounts from Philadelphia
are cheering for 'Old Buck' in Pennsylvania. I hope they
may not be delusive.

"Yours,   J. M. MASON."

This was proof of the deplorable condition of public
affairs in 1856. In the four years succeeding, to March,
1861, under Buchanan, disloyalty had grown and fattened
until more than half of the political, civil, and military
offices were filled with men who were actively plotting,
planning, and accelerating the Nation's ruin. In these
high places, thousands of public servants were aiding to the

full extent of their means the establishment of a slave confederacy. How could it have been otherwise when this projected slave nation was near its zenith in organization and the Union appeared to be dissolving, with no power to force the obedience of a State as the President declared?

The great Republic was falling to pieces, as the world-wide story went. This was corroborated by all that the President and his Cabinet, with other treason-spreading officials, did. In this Cabinet three of the seven were active conspirators, while of assistants, subordinates, and other employees, more than half of them, in every department, were known to be up to their eyes in hatching treason. Senator Clingman, of North Carolina, said: "About the middle of December, 1860, I had occasion to see Secretary Jacob Thompson, of the Interior, on some official business. On my entering the room, he said to me: 'Clingman, I am glad you have called; for I intended presently to go up to the Senate and see you. I have been appointed a commissioner by the State of Mississippi to go down and get your State of North Carolina to secede; and I wished to talk with you about your Legislature before I start in the morning to Raleigh, to learn what you think of my chance of success.' I said to him that I did not know he had resigned. He replied, 'O no, I have not resigned.' 'Then,' I replied, 'I suppose you will resign in the morning.' 'No,' he answered, 'I do not intend to resign; for Mr. Buchanan wishes us all to hold on and go out with him on the 4th of March.' 'But,' said I, 'does Mr. Buchanan know for what purpose you are going to North Carolina?' 'Certainly,' he said, 'he knows my object.' Being surprised at this, I told Secretary Thompson that Mr. Buchanan was probably so much perplexed by his situation that he had not fully considered the matter, and that, as he was already involved in difficulty, we ought not to add to his burdens, and then suggested to him that he had better see the President again, an'd, by way of inducing him to think the matter over, mentioned what I had been saying to him. Mr. Thompson said, 'Well, I can do so; but I think he fully understands it.' In the evening I met Secretary Thompson again at a small party, and as soon as I approached him, he said: 'I knew I could not be mistaken. I told Mr. Buchanan all you said, and he told me that he wished me to go and hoped I might succeed.' I could not help exclaiming, 'Was there ever before any potentate who sent out his own Cabinet ministers to excite an insurrection against his Government?' The fact that Mr. Thompson did go on this errand, and had a public reception before the Legislature, and returned to his place in the Cabinet, is known; and this incident seems to emphasize and recall it."

Jefferson Davis, who was then well known, was full in the movement. Clingman was not with them then, but was soon afterwards. He knew of all the happenings, and gave incontestible evidence of the treason-corrupted Administration. In November, 1860, after the result of the Presidential election was known, the governor of Mississippi issued his proclamation convoking a special session of the Legislature to consider the propriety of calling a Convention, and invited the senators and representatives in Congress to meet him for consultation as to the character of the message he should send to the Legislature when assembled. While engaged in this consultation referred to, a message approved by two members of Buchanan's Cabinet was handed Senator Jefferson Davis, urging him to proceed immediately to Washington.

Davis said: "The dispatch was laid before the governor and members of Congress present in conference with him, and it was decided that I should comply with the summons. On my arrival at Washington I found, as had been anticipated, that my presence there was desired on account of the influence which it was supposed I might exercise with

the President—Mr. Buchanan—in relation to his forthcoming message to Congress. On paying my respects to
him, he told me that he had finished the rough draft of his
message, but that it was still open to revision and amendment, and that he would like to read it to me. He did so,
and very kindly accepted the modifications which I suggested. The message was, however, afterward somewhat
changed."

The President, above all others, should be a conservator
of the law. He should obey it and require obedience of
those in executive office with him. In the exercise of his
powers it should be his care to know that peace and civil
order prevail and are sustained, and that the humblest citizen is safe in the protection of every right. It is his duty
to provide that public property of every kind and description is protected and cared for; that commerce and navigation have their proper safeguards and care wherever our
commerce exists under our flag. It is his duty to see that
the postal laws have careful attention, and that the service is the best; that the revenue laws are obeyed; that the
revenues and imposts are collected and disbursed as provided in law; that revolts, insurrections, or unlawful resistance to the laws of the United States, in whatever form
or character, are promptly suppressed. He must repel invasions, and to enforce the statutes he can call the entire
military and naval forces of the Nation. When these are
insufficient, he can call into service the militia forces of
the States.

The President's powers and duties under law are clearly
established. They should have guided President Buchanan
in the rising rebellion, whereas, on the contrary, he flagrantly neglected and disobeyed the laws of our country,
consorted with its enemies and conspirators for its dismemberment, and accepted and abided by interpretations
of law made by disloyal advisers. This anomalous "poten-

tate" was the only one whom Senator Clingman ever heard
of "who associated with conspirators for the overthrow of his
own and his country's Government." Naturally enough, he
wired for the immediate presence of the chief conspirator,
Jefferson Davis, to assist him in the interpretation of law
and recommendations to Congress, when he needed loyal
advice for the execution of the law. He framed his message to Congress as far as Davis's advice and counsel could
shape it, recommending non-action by recognizing and letting the Southern Confederacy alone.

This message of December, 1860, gives concluding proof
of Davis's statement that the President did "read the message to me, and very kindly accepted all the modifications
which I suggested." This was kind, indeed, to accept an
un-heard-of Constitutional interpretation from the chief of
the forming insurrection, and embrace it in a message to
the Congress of the Nation that was to be dismembered under and with the concurrence of its officers and servants!
The principal clause of the message is: "You may be called
on to decide the momentous question whether you possess
the power by force of arms to compel a State to remain in
the Union. The question, fairly stated, is, Has the Constitution delegated to Congress the power to coerce a State
into submission, which is attempting to withdraw, or has
actually withdrawn, from the Confederacy? If answered in
the affirmative, it must be on the principle that the power
has been conferred upon Congress to declare and make war
against a State. After much serious reflection I have arrived at the conclusion that no such power has been delegated to Congress or to any other department of the Federal Government. It may be safely asserted that the power
to make war against a State is at variance with the whole
spirit and intent of the Constitution. But if we possessed
this power, would it be wise to exercise it under any circumstances? Our Union rests upon public opinion, and

can never be cemented by the blood of its citizens shed·in
civil war.   Congress possesses many means of preserving
it by conciliation; but the sword was not put in their
hand to preserve it by force."

This was the pitiful palaver of the weak and neglectful old man, who had little, if any need for a dispute as to
what were and what were not the rights of the States.   His
chief duty at the time was the prompt and vigorous enforcement of the laws of the United States, which were then being defiantly violated in Charleston and vicinity.· He ought
to have assembled a land and naval force there competent
and able to enforce our laws and protect our forts, shipping, and all other public property.

Buchanan and his Administration had so faithfully
served the Southern leaders so many years that not even
the just indignation of an outraged people could bring the
repentance and change of heart necessary to begin the work
of saving the Nation.   The powerful United States stood before its conspiring foes with its "hands down" four months
in the face of rising insurrection and unchecked, rapid
preparation for war, extending from the people of one to
eleven States.

In addition to this deadly inertia and guilty cowardice
on the part of the highest authorities in the land, a money-
panic swept over the country in 1857, and was followed by
a severe industrial depression.   This continued to the time
of the exciting agitation through the winter of 1860-1.
Everything in the land was at its lowest ebb.   The pendulum
of the Nation's life was swinging slow, almost ready to
stop.   At the best the Republic was but sustaining a slug-
gish existence, waiting, almost famishing, for a leader.   Thousands were out of employment.   Acute distress prevailed
everywhere except on the farms.   The gaunt skeleton of
hunger stalked abroad in every community, while the farmer's products were without value.   Industry, like patriot-

ism, was dwindling away under statesmanship that had neither ways nor means to promote the people's progress and welfare.

It was a direful time. The weak, trembling President was bowed down and cowed. He had not intended that the plotting of the slave-leaders should ripen into secession, When he could not prevent it, and rebellion was open and defiant, not being sufficiently grounded in the doctrine that "faith without works is dead," he called on the people to meet and have a day of prayer, to beseech "the Most High for the restoration of peace." Under more righteous conditions this would have been right; but something besides prayer was sorely needed. If Buchanan's faith and works had held together, he would have put forty thousand militia and a fleet of the best ships into Charleston Harbor in the middle of December, 1860. In that case there would have been only a small revolt. As it was, he left Major Anderson in Fort Moultrie with one hundred men, without support, or even subsistence, to hold out as long as he could against twenty thousand.

In calling people to devotion and prayer, he said: "The Union of the States at the present moment is threatened with alarming and immediate danger. Panic and distress of a fearful character prevail throughout the land. Our laboring population are without employment, and consequently deprived of the means of earning their bread; indeed, hope seems to have deserted the minds of men. All classes are in a state of confusion and dismay, and the wisest counsels of our best and purest men are wholly disregarded." He undoubtedly referred to himself and Jefferson Davis.

He continued: "Humbling ourselves before the Most High, . . . let us implore him to remove from our hearts that false pride of opinion which would impel us to persevere in wrong for the sake of consistency rather than yield a just submission to the unforeseen exigencies by which we are now surrounded. An Omnipotent Providence may overrule existing evils for our permanent good. In response to numerous appeals, the 4th day of January proximo is hereby set apart as a day of fasting, humiliation, and prayer."

This bore date December 14, 1860, on which fateful day the first act of establishing a "Southern Confederacy" was accomplished and agreed to by thirty senators and representatives from the States of North and South Carolina, Georgia, Florida, Alabama, Mississippi, Louisiana, Texas, and Arkansas, as follows:

"ADDRESS OF CERTAIN SOUTHERN MEMBERS OF CONGRESS.
"WASHINGTON, December 14, 1860.

"To OUR CONSTITUENTS,—The agreement is exhausted. All hope of relief in the Union through the agency of committees, Congressional legislation, or Constitutional amendments is extinguished, and we trust the South will not be deceived by appearances or the pretense of new guarantees.

"In our judgment, the Republicans are resolute in the purpose to grant nothing that will or ought to satisfy the South. We are satisfied the honor, safety, and independence of the Southern people require the organization of the Southern Confederacy—a result to be obtained only by separate State secession. The primary object of each slaveholding State ought to be its speedy and absolute separation from a Union with hostile States."

Thus the first document of the so-called new nation was agreed to and promulgated, not in an oppressed country seeking any kind of relief, but under the roof and shadow of a National Capital where they had mostly governed, and where all their lawful demands had been conceded. Without giving truthful explanation or reasons for this murderous alternative; without dutiful or honorable appeal to the God of nations or the judgment of honest men, before whom they entered this daring rebellion, they at once plunged into war, or revolution, as they were pleased to call it.

These men did not retire from the service and pay of the United States at once, as brave and honorable men would have done; but they remained in the Cabinet, the Supreme Court, the army and navy, and in the Senate and House of Representatives for varying periods, that they might embarrass and obstruct legislation or the progress of civil or military movements against them as long as they were permitted.

Every statement in their pronunciamento was false, as these Southern Congressmen well knew. Whether true or false, it served them the same purpose. They were ready for the venture, and were going to risk the terrible hazard and consequences of attempted revolution. They counted upon it, and held Buchanan's guilty, consenting Administration from interfering with them for four long months, giving them time for preparation and "firing the Southern heart."

Nothing then had been decided against the South. Nothing was in contemplation against them, save the restrictions of slavery subject to the vote of the people. The truth is, they had long before determined to make the entire United States a slave country, or, in the event of failure, to separate and build an American Confederacy or slave empire. Prepared for it or not, they were ready in mind for the hazard; and the ambition of their leaders was to plunge them irrevocably into it.

The personnel of the Government and Administration in the winter of 1860-1, at the time of the pro-slavery break-up and secession, was: James Buchanan, President, to March 4, 1861; Lewis Cass, of Michigan, Secretary of State to December 12, 1860; J. S. Black, of Pennsylvania, Secretary of State to March 4, 1861; Howell Cobb, of Georgia, Secretary of the Treasury to December 12, 1860; Philip F. Thomas, of Maryland, Secretary of the Treasury to January 11, 1861; John A. Dix, of New York, Secretary of the Treasury to March 4, 1861; John B. Floyd, of Virginia, Secretary of War to December 30, 1860; Joseph Holt, of Kentucky, Secretary of War to March 4, 1861; Isaac Toucey, of Connecticut, Secretary of the Navy to March 4, 1861; Jacob Thompson, of Mississippi, Secretary of the Interior to December 30, 1860; Joseph Holt, of Kentucky, Postmaster-General to February 12, 1861; Horatio King, of Maine, Postmaster-General to March 4, 1861; Jere S. Black, of Pennsylvania, Attorney-General to December 20, 1860; Edwin M. Stanton, of Pennsylvania, Attorney-General to March 4, 1861; J. C. Breckinridge, of Kentucky, Vice-President to March 4, 1861.

The Senate was pro-slavery Democratic until in January, 1861, when several Southern Senators resigned as their States seceded. Wm. Pennington, of New Jersey, was Speaker of the House of Representatives, in which the Republicans had a small plurality, which increased to a large majority after the Southern members, with their States, seceded and joined the Confederacy.

The retirement of Secretary Cass was a stunning blow. He had remained in office longer than he desired, with the hope of bringing the President to a realization of his duty, instead of which he had been controlled by the disloyal members of his Cabinet and the chief conspirators under Davis. These had earnestly wrought and helped through the scheme and plans for dividing and destroying the Democratic party. They had achieved, as they believed, the overthrow of Douglas. Cass, however, did not believe in this. He had done some questionable things for them, but he was the personal friend of Douglas, believed in his integrity and restoration. He had grown tired of their scheming disloyalty, and was positively for the Union and as much opposed to hidden or outspoken disloyalty and disunion. He knew as well as any one that Douglas was the real leader of all that was left of Democracy in the free States, and that Buchanan was following to the logical and inevitable consequences of his four-years' progress of party-destroying policy. Buchanan was still, in December, in collusion with conspiring traitors, neglecting his highest duty to enforce the laws, but in close conference and correspondence with pretentious commissioners, whose avowed object was the treasonable one of the withdrawal of their States from the Union. There was more of General Cass in the juncture, in character, wisdom, experience, and statesmanship than in all that was left of Buchanan's Administration, when all were counted.

Jere Black succeeded General Cass. He was able, learned, and resourceful—a man of the Caleb Cushing order—crafty, scheming, belief-twisting. He could write himself in or out of any party or policy where men could do it; but the old general and long-time party leader went out on the direct issue of re-enforcing the forts, enforcing the laws, and saving the Union by force, if necessary, without respect to States. It made a direct issue, with two sides, that the dodgers could not dodge. It meant that there would not be standing-room in the Democracy of the free States under any other policy, and that political paralysis had stricken the doomed, trembling Administration.

Howell Cobb, of Georgia, Secretary of the Treasury, resigned, with little, if any, disguise about it, to help secession of his State. Floyd, Secretary of War, and Thompson, Secretary of the Interior, remained a few days longer as eavesdroppers and informers for the benefit of their fellow-conspirators, until they were virtually driven out, leaving a malfeasance of one or more millions, taken by one or both of them, in the shape of hypothecated Indian trust funds, which were never accounted for.

On the 20th of December, South Carolina, in Convention assembled, seceded from the Union, and thereby "became a free and independent State." Major Robert Anderson, who was left to his own resources, with only one hundred men for the protection of two forts, wisely abandoned Fort Moultrie, on the land side, and occupied Fort Sumter, which was entirely surrounded by water, in Charleston Harbor, December 26th. This prudent act of Major Anderson, the South Carolinians claimed, was a violation of agreement, pending the demand of Governor Pickens on the President for the surrender of the forts. Anderson had surprised them in a real strategical movement, which should have been supported at once with all the supplies and boats and men that were necessary to relieve him. He was in a water-protected battery fort, with enough supplies for three months. He intended to fight, and these Charleston seceders knew it too well to undertake an assault on equal chances.

In their dilemma, by reason of Anderson's sensible move, they at once sent commissioners to remonstrate with the President against it. Anderson had taken the best possible position for defense, which, too, was a plain enough duty in his weak and unsupported condition. These commissioners proceeded to Washington, when, audacious as it may seem, they demanded the return of Major Anderson and his little force of one hundred men to Fort Moultrie, which was then dismantled and occupied by their recruits, or the surrender of both forts to Governor Pickens. General Cass had left the Cabinet, and had washed his hands from the pollution of consorting with declared enemies. Cobb had gone into secession, and Floyd and Thompson, the President very well knew, should have been removed before this for the best of reasons.

The effect of all this was piling up the ruins about the President. He was deep in consorting and parleying with these treason-bearing commissioners. He felt that it was not right, and he was not going to concede all they were demanding; but, weak beyond description, without the spirit of a leader, the courage of a man or natural common sense for such an occasion, he was in consternation. In his shaking perplexity he received, on the 30th of December, from Jere Black, then Secretary of State, notice that he and Stanton, then Attorney-General, would retire from the Cabinet, following the example of General Cass, if he parleyed with these commissioners. The act had roused enough patriotism and fear in Black to make him dread the responsibility of the treason he had willfully permitted to gain such ascendency.

This brought the President sufficiently to his senses to send for Secretary Black, to whom he at once surrendered all that was left of his power and authority. He virtually resigned the management of the Government for the few weeks of his expiring term to his Cabinet. From that time forward, Black, Stanton, Holt, and Dix did the best possible with the means at hand for the preservation of the Government and its properties. But the available forces, supplies, and munitions of war were as nothing compared with what was being organized and equipped against us.

A plump, plain reply to the South Carolina commissioners "that they would not be received or conferred with" sent them home at once, with notice that the conspirators had been removed from the Cabinet, and that the policy of the Administration was entirely changed, that the forts would be protected and defended.

This reformed Cabinet which, in effect, retired a President with his own consent, did not feel authorized to do what should have been done earlier. The President should have done what President Lincoln did later: call into service a land and naval force competent to suppress the rising rebellion. Their best reason for not doing so was that Congress was then in session, and that it did not, in so many words at the time, authorize this necessary and unavoidable policy. This may have been the proper course; for, as things were going in January, 1861, there was not a leader in the Buchanan Administration fit for the task.

There were several reasons for the procrastination that kept the Nation idle and its people unemployed, which was the worst conduct in the face of organizing Southern armies, separating States, and a dissolving Congress. The indecision, cowardice, and collusion that passed the danger-line, with the forming revolt plain to every one, had its effect on the people. They were in distress; halting doubt and lack of spirit existed everywhere. The pro-slavery merchant class, North and South, took advantage of the depression, and attributed the low condition of things and the prevailing distress to the success of "the Abolitionists," whom they derisively called "black Republicans." Wendell Phillips, the impassioned disciple of anti-slavery, was forced to cancel his engagements for fear of his hurting the business of some Eastern city.

Boston, the cradle of liberty and the tea business, was sternly informed that trade demanded a rest from slavery agitation. George W. Curtis, who had saved the split on the assertion of the truths of the Declaration of Independence at Chicago, was informed that it would not be wise to lecture on some patriotic subject, previously arranged for in Philadelphia, "and that trade matters were in very sensitive condition with our Southern correspondents."

Fernando Wood, the Tammany mayor of New York City, openly advised secession of the city and its attachment to the Confederacy as a State, or in some other satisfactory relation. The New York *Herald* newspaper advised the separation of the city, and union with the South, and kept one of the first

made Rebel flags ready to string across the street, in expectation of the approval of its recommendation. Horace Greeley,
was so thoroughly disgusted with the slow progress of public
affairs, the growing strength of the secession movement, and
the vacillating and cowardly conduct of so many in public
and private life, and in business particularly, that he was
wrought up to publish in the *Tribune,* then the most widely
read newspaper of the time: "Let the South go, in peace,
without war, on the basis of slavery and slave labor, where
they will soon destroy themselves."

It was a winter of doubt, danger, and despondency, when
it took men with strong, resolute hearts to believe in the integrity and unity of the Nation, as against its more active and
outspoken foes and its doubting, half-paralyzed, wavering,
war-dreading supporters. Doubt and uncertainty were so
prevalent and predominant, that the strongest men lamented,
dreaded the future, and prayed that nothing might precipitate
the crash and collapse of all that was left of the weak, falling-
away Administration at Washington, before the inauguration
of Lincoln. There were few, indeed, through that weary
period who believed that Lincoln could have been elected, if
the doubting and fearful spirit of the winter of 1861 had prevailed in the previous November. The people of the free
States had been so often threatened with war by the noisy
men and newspapers of the South, that there were not many
in the North who believed they would venture into such
a conflict.

Perhaps the worst that happened was that it was truthfully told that "Congress had weakened." Some of the strongest Republicans were not demanding legislation to restrict
slavery and prevent its introduction into new territory, which
their platform emphatically declared to be their leading political belief. Instead, they undertook the old, worn-out business of raising committees and conferences, which were expected to get together, harmonize, and with some kind of

concessions to slavery, report a basis for another humiliating compromise.

The much-abused squatter sovereignty doctrine of Douglas was accepted by all the Republicans and Democrats alike, who were left in Congress. They accepted it as the only proper solution attainable of the slavery question in the Territories; not of course by those seceding, but those left of all parties led by Senator Green of Missouri. He had taken Douglas's place as chairman of the Senate Committee on Territories. A similar committee in the Republican House introduced enabling acts for the organization of Nevada and some other Territories on the plan of the famous Kansas-Nebraska Act.

In the stormy debates of the winter, Vice-President Breckinridge left the chair of the Senate to contend "that the South should have some share in the common territory of the Union for the extension of its system of labor, and that they should not be excluded by unfriendly or prohibitory legislation from the national domain, which belongs of right to the people of the free and slave States alike." This became Douglas's opportunity and his time for a rebuke to the seceding conspirators always to be remembered. He rose and stated in reply that "the South had no ground whatever for complaint, and that whatever there was of danger to their slave system in the situation had come upon them as the result of their own deliberate planning and preparation. Except the election of Mr. Lincoln by a plurality of their own making, not an act nor a line of legislation in force or then proposed had in the least changed the relation or condition of their slave labor system. There was not an act or statute or Territorial code that prevented or prohibited any slaveholder from taking a slave into any Territory of the United States.

"When slaves are so taken into the Territory, the laws of the land, as interpreted by the Supreme Court, protects the slaveholder in the ownership and protection of his slaves.

This being the situation, and having a Republican House of Representatives at the other end of the Capitol for two years acquiescing in the present plan of Territorial settlement, there never was a time in the history of the Republic when there was less restriction upon the institution of slavery or less difficulty in the way of its extension into the Territories;—with this condition only, that, in full conformity with all our institutions, slavery could only remain in a State or Territory after its organization, by the consent of the majority of its legal voters, honestly expressed and declared.

"As this is the truthful condition of the much-discussed subject of slavery, it can not be for lack of protection of their property, the continuance of the institution where it exists, or the means for its extension, that this seceding, Union-dissolving movement has been undertaken and is now making such unchecked and furious headway.

"It discloses the truth that some of you conspirators against your country have undertaken the ruin and overthrow of Democracy in the establishment of a purely slaveholding nationality, and that you vainly expect to escape the treasonable consequences of your plunge into the dark, in what you imagine can be a peaceable separation and dissolution of the Union, which, in the light of all history, can have no other than a woeful ending. When such a conflict is forced upon us there will be, and can only be, two parties; one will be for our country, the other will be against it."

Breckinridge made no reply, nor did Jefferson Davis, Benjamin, Mason, or Toombs, of the conspiring senators; nor did Seward, Chase, Fessenden, nor Ben Wade make note or comment or reply to add to or take from the masterly logic of Douglas. He was never more self-possessed, fearless, and outspoken in the cause of our country and against its enemies than on this settling of Breckinridge and his admiring conspirators.

Whatever was true of others, whoever might flinch and

quail in the face of coming disaster, no stain or touch of it could attach to Douglas. He was there, the strongest, the boldest, and the most pronounced leader in that expiring Congress, one-third of which was going out of it into unprovoked rebellion. He was the only leader in Washington in that Congress who could have arrested the revolt against the Union, if he had been called into Buchanan's Cabinet on the retirement of General Cass. Perhaps not even he could have done so when it had gained such furious headway; but surely he would have used force against force with such skill and power that two years of Lincoln would have done more than four as it came, with the uninterrupted Rebellion threatening the Capitol at his inauguration.

This last service of Douglas was skillful, tireless, patriotic, and heroic. He stood in the Senate without a superior, the defender of the Union against any or all its foes. He was the stumbling-block that a pro-slavery Administration could not loosen, the rock on which the apologetic and fiery blast of treason and disunion lashed in vain. Douglas alone, through that desperate winter, successfully met every foe and sustained himself and our country against the swollen and boasting Confederacy and a failing, faltering Administration.

Regardless of conciliating committees, doubting Unionists, and the begging commercial spirit of many weak and cowardly Northern communities, the work of secession and Congressional leavetaking went regularly on. In the winter seven cotton States formally seceded. Succeeding each withdrawal, their senators and representatives in Congress made explanations—the first time in the annals of Government when such acts were tolerated by any National Assembly—of what they alleged were good and sufficient reasons for treasonable separation.

These quittings or retirements were artful, plain or blunt, plausible, smoothly, or insolently and carelessly made, as the manner of the men who made them. Jefferson Davis, who

postured to the last moment as a Union man, fully justified
the course of his State, which he considered the sole arbiter
in the proceedings; but he would have felt himself bound to
retire with his State if his belief had been otherwise. In
short, without any real cause assigned, he proceeded to justify
secession, conceding by the way that Calhoun made a mistake
in attempting to nullify the laws of the Union while remaining a member of it.

The Southern leaders had been making preparation for
separation for years, as we have seen. Their system of a
landed aristocracy, where a few men in each community and
State control public affairs, was not, and could not, be kept
in harmony with the simple form of Democracy and the equal
rights of men. They had no reasons for a dissolution, more
than the grasping desires of greedy men for increased or unlimited power. Senator Toombs, of Georgia, in order to hurry
up action in his State, said bluntly and plainly enough for
any one to understand, that the Southern leaders who had
managed the South would offer no terms of settlement or
compromise acceptable to the people of the Nation as represented by the vote of the followers of Lincoln or those of
Douglas. When about leaving the Senate, he said: "The
first condition would be that slave property should be securely
protected in any Territory of the United States until the
period of the formation of a State Government, when the
people could determine it.

"Second. That property in slaves shall have the same protection from the Government in all its departments everywhere which is extended to other property, provided that there
shall be no interference with the privilege of any State to
prohibit or establish slavery.

"Third. That persons committing crimes or offenses
against slave property shall be surrendered for trial to the
State where the offenses against the laws of the State were
committed.

"Fourth. That fugitive slaves should be returned, under the Act of 1850, without being entitled to writs of habeas corpus, a trial by jury, or any other obstructions in the States to which they fled.

"Fifth. That Congress should pass efficient laws for the punishment of all persons aiding or abetting insurrection or other acts to disturb the tranquillity of the people or government of any other State.

"Sixth. That without these concessions the Union can not be maintained. If any proposition is made, it must be for immediate action. We are as ready to fight now as we shall ever be. I am for equality, or war. In closing, I denounce Lincoln as an enemy to the human race, deserving the execration of all mankind."

The good of this bad proposition was that there was little or no sophistry about it. The settlements demanded would have firmly established a slave Nation, where slavery could not be spoken against, or would have caused separation and war.

CHAPTER XLVII.

THE secession of the Southern States went on, not as the Southern people voted or in any way determined, but under the control of the cabal and its chieftain, Jefferson Davis, at Washington, as follows:

South Carolina	In Convention,	December	20, 1860
Mississippi	"	January	9, 1861
Florida	"	"	10, 1861
Alabama		"	11, 1861
Georgia		"	24, 1861
Louisiana		"	26, 1861
Texas	"	February	23, 1861
North Carolina	"	May	21, 1861
Arkansas	"	"	26, 1861
Virginia	In Legislature,	April	17, 1861
Tennessee	"	June	8, 1861

There was a vote in Texas which was made necessary by the strong opposition of the ·loyal old general and Ex-President of the Republic of Texas, Samuel Houston. It was a formal affair, and the voting was all one way.

A majority of the people of Virginia, North Carolina, and Tennessee were strongly opposed to separation, and so voted whenever an opportunity was given; but the leaders prepared and protracted their schemes with and without all the coercion required, until they forced these States into the movement very much as they recruited the men for their army, taking all into their armies, as the war continued, from fifty years down to boys less than fifteen years of age, by a merciless conscription. In the same way they forced these three States into the merciless fury of war.

Secession and its consequences were truthfully foreshadowed by several of their leaders and thousands of their people. Among others, Alexander H. Stephens, of Georgia, who became their Vice-President, said: "This step, secession, once taken, can never be recalled. All the baleful and withering consequences that must follow will rest on this Convention for all coming time when we and our posterity shall see our lovely South desolated by the demon of war, which this act of yours will inevitably provoke. Our green fields and waving harvests shall be trodden down by a murderous soldiery, and the fiery car of war sweep over our land, our temples of justice laid in ashes, and every horror and desolation upon us.

"Who but this Convention will be held responsible for it, and but him who shall have given his vote for this unwise and ill-timed measure shall be held to a strict account for this suicidal act by the present generation, and be cursed and execrated by posterity in all coming time for the wide and desolating ruin that will immediately follow this act you now propose to perpetrate? Pause, I entreat you, and consider for a moment what reasons you can give that will satisfy yourselves in calmer moments, what reasons you can give to your fellow-sufferers in the calamity that it will bring upon us.

"Now, for you to attempt to overthrow such a Government as this under which we have lived for more than three-quarters of a century, in which we have gained our wealth, our standing as a Nation, our domestic safety, while the elements of peril are around us, with peace and tranquillity, accompanied with unbounded prosperity and our rights unassailed, is the height of madness, folly, and wickedness, to which I will neither lend my sanction nor my vote."

On the 4th of February, 1861, delegates from the seceding States assembled at Montgomery, Alabama. On the 8th a Provisional Constitution was adopted, creating the "Confederate States of America" providing for the organization of a Provisional Government under it. In this new fundamental law nothing of form or importance was changed from the provisions of our Constitution, except that slavery, in place of liberty, was made "the corner-stone."

On the 9th the delegates elected Jefferson Davis President, as had been the foregone conclusion from the beginning. They elected Alexander H. Stephens Vice-President. The latter was qualified on the 10th. Davis followed, and was qualified on the 16th, when the officers were inaugurated and the Confederates States proclaimed a nation. The Cabinet selected was Robert Toombs, of Georgia, Secretary of State; C. G. Memminger, of South Carolina, Secretary of the Treasury; L. P. Walker, of Alabama, Secretary of War; S. R. Mallory, of Florida, Secretary of the Navy; J. H. Reagan, of Texas, Postmaster-General; Judah P. Benjamin, of Louisiana, Attorney-General.

In form, with ample power and the facilities and resources of the seven cotton and sugar States to rely upon, the long-planned insurrectionary Government was organized seventeen days before the inauguration of President Lincoln. Congress was still disputing over plans and compromises, which these revolted States would not even entertain. Doubt and hesitation prevailed everywhere, except among the projectors of this Confederacy and the pro-slavery leaders, in or out of the newly-made slave aristocracy.

The insurrectionists knew beyond peradventure that the movement was an earnest and deadly one; so much so that only one party was left in their jurisdiction. They were never inclined to tolerate divided opinion, so that, after secession, they quickly converted their whole population to their side, as they did Stephens. Like many such really true-hearted men, he came where he could contend with them no longer. While this was true, what folly it was for our people to talk longer of doubt or compromise, and discuss it in Congress!

Nevertheless, from the success that would come from the secession and co-operation of all the slave States, the leaders in Virginia, with their conferees in and about Washington, played a double game for weeks. They held out delusive hopes to sincere-minded senators, representatives, and prominent men who saw and dreaded the coming collision. Their treacherous designs were well and faithfully executed, the purpose of which was to carry the border States into the movement with them.

This talked-of compromise kept the Union leaders for weeks in a cautious, halting, and indecisive condition. Five or ten thousand troops, marched immediately into Richmond, would have aroused enough patriotic Union men, any time before the 1st of March, to have confined the revolt to the cotton States. This false palaver was kept up until Representative John A. Logan and some other brave spirits went to Richmond, handed the pretended loyalists a blank sheet of paper, on which they asked them to write their terms of compromise. They had none to write. The game was over. Logan had cut the cord. A united South had been their design; all else was delusion and deception.

In the last days of January, 1861, the resignation of many of the senators from the seceding States gave the Republicans a majority in the Senate. Thus they gained control of both Houses of Congress. On the 29th the Territory of Kansas was admitted, under what was known as the Wyandot Constitution, as a free State, which had been adopted by the people of the Territory at an election held for that purpose, October 4, 1859. At this election there were 10,421 votes for and 5,530 against it.

This result had been a foregone conclusion for years. The slave-leaders were defeated in every attempt to make it a slave State. After the irrecoverable defeat of the Lecompton Scheme in 1858, they closed up their plan, and proceeded, in more desperate execution, for the destruction of the Democratic party, the dissolution of the Union, and the separate supremacy of their coming empire.

Mr. Lincoln was much distressed by the condition and course of public affairs at Washington and the dread prevailing in our commercial cities. The progress of disunion and the uninterfered-with spread of the insurrection and the seizure of forts, arsenals, and public property went on through the winter after his election. He could do nothing but wait with patience and thoughtful preparation for the terrible consequences, as day by day made more certain what would follow through the neglect of the wickedly-weak Administration. He had the apprehension, the prescience of the coming struggle. Was it superstition, or a partial vision, that would train and subdue his mind to the overburdening sorrow? However and whatever it was, the impression was deep and lasting, as the few to whom he explained it well understood. One feature of it, to which he used himself, as to any daily occurrence, was his oft-repeated belief, "I will not return to Springfield after this is over."

When he parted with Mr. Herndon, his law partner, at the foot of the office stairway, he pointed to the old sign of "Lincoln & Herndon, Lawyers," saying: "Billy, let it hang there. I will not be back, you know; but it will show that I have something to return to when this business of being President is over. I will feel better to remember it hanging in its old place. Good-bye; God bless you!" There was something in this presentiment, or whatever it may have been called, that deeply impressed him, and which he wanted to be freed from; but it always came back to him.

As a notable instance of it, in the fall of 1863 preparations for his attendance for one day at the Sanitary Fair in Chicago had been made. There was to be a run through Illinois, a day or two in the old home at Springfield, and the return through Southern Indiana, the scene of his struggling boyhood days. He was worn and weary with the dull round of duties and the load that never lifted. The change would have been a great relief, even if the people crowded to see him as they never had any other man, and made it a three or four days' trip almost without rest.

He would have talked with them, and they with him, in the way that would have been helpful and assuring to all. He was anxious for the day that promised this partial relief from a week's corroding care. He was to be in Chicago, Bloomington, Decatur, Springfield, Champaign, Danville, and a hundred other places at home, and in his own house, where he would see so many cherished friends, and the little children most of all. Thus he looked forward for the day as a boy does his summer frolic.

But listen: Chickamauga had rolled its reverberating thunder back almost to Washington. Another deluge of American blood had wetted the ridges and the rocks below the Tennessee. A great army that he loved as his soul was in peril in Chattanooga. The overworn President held himself down to his desk, that no single duty might be left undone. The relief trip was put off, and must come another day.

I was in Springfield several times in those anxious months of the winter, and remained some ten days, just before his departure for Washington. Hundreds came to see him every day, and never too many. Some remonstrated, who thought he was giving too much time, merely shaking hands and talking with enthusiastic and overexcited people. He replied: "Let them come; all that want to. If they give up their time and spend their money to come ten, twenty, or a hundred miles or more to see me, I will be the more industrious and kind enough to meet these big-hearted fellows and their wives, every one of whom has something in him that encourages and helps me on. There is something fresh and strong in every face. Not one in a thousand talks about office, or expects to receive an appointment, or to know who will be in the Cabinet."

To his friends he was kind, and as free as ever on the subjects he felt it proper to talk over. He had an amusing way of restraining those who are always bothering public men to know what is not wise and what they do not want to tell. To an overanxious newspaper man, who wanted to know all about his Cabinet, he said: "I would be glad to tell you about the Cabinet if I thought it was the right thing to tell and make public. I believe that the public are entitled to a full knowledge of public affairs, for in our country it is their own business. As soon as the details of our policy and those who are to be in the Cabinet are agreed upon, I desire that the public may be fully informed. The Cabinet is a subject that is being diligently considered. Several gentlemen are talked of and about, and the correspondence about it is progressing as fast as it can well be carried on. If I should give you all the information you desire, some would have the right to say that my talk about them and their relation to it was premature, and they might resent it. Further, I would not feel at liberty to talk to you about that until you have their consent." The newspaper man promptly said, "I can get that easy enough, if you will please tell me who they are." Mr. Lincoln, in a broad smile, replied, "My dear sir, that is just what I am trying to find out myself."

His afternoon talks were pleasant, cheerful, and freely entered into. Hundreds called every week, where all were welcome, and were pleased to meet him. Some of them had been friends for a lifetime; some of them had known him for longer, and some for shorter periods; some had never met him before, and some only once; but all received the same cordial reception. It was a hard task for one, even with his remarkable memory, to remember so many and the circumstances where and when he met and knew them. He did much of this, however, surprising many of his callers in what he remembered at once on meeting them. When there was lapse of memory or doubts about their former meetings, and his friends were perplexed about them, often more than he was, he took up the matter of the slight acquaintance as earnestly as themselves, and often recalled circumstances until it was made as clear as possible. He enjoyed their coming and the recalled events as much as these farmer friends, whom he had seen and talked to perhaps an hour at some one of their homes ten years before.

He talked over the distressing situation, from day to day, just as other people did. He said openly and without reserve that his policy would be conciliatory as long as there was hope of escaping war and preserving the integrity of the Union; that if war came upon us, he would be governed by the Union people, who would willingly risk their lives to save the Nation.

In February he gave up all hope of a restoration of the cotton States without a struggle. The vital point in any policy was to keep the border States from joining in the movement. He believed that, as Buchanan lost the opportunity of suppressing the revolt until the gulf or cotton States were prepared for defense, perhaps the apparently slow and dilatory proceedings at Washington were the best to keep the more considerate and less excitable border State people out of it.

He could not have accomplished much in any other way if he had desired it. The waiting policy had made such headway that he and his Cabinet could not change it in the least until the opening hostilities and fall of Fort Sumter. The sympathizers made an effort to carry Missouri, and called a Convention to secede in formal Convention; but the Convention was loyal, and the secession officers, with Governor Claiborne Jackson and some forty or fifty members and attaches of his disloyal State Government, were compelled to flee from the capital. In addition, there was not such another soldier in position elsewhere at the beginning of the war, where he could have saved the arsenal, as Captain Lyon did at St. Louis, thus keeping Missouri from secession.

While no prudent friend about Lincoln or visiting him had any unusual desire to know or spread information as to his policy or who would be members of his Cabinet, it was well understood that, while he would concede all that was justifiable to preserve peace, no policy recognizing the right of any State to withdraw, or the loss of any Territory, would be agreed to.

To most of those at home and those who visited him during the winter, it became generally known that Seward, Chase, Bates, and some one from Indiana and Pennsylvania, each, would be offered Cabinet positions, which, so far, had been expected from the time of his nomination.

Mr. Lincoln's power over men was so distinct and his insight into human character so penetrating that those about him never told anything to him or his business that he did not wish them to tell. Thus they acted without urging or persuasion. Everything came in the way of honoring and respecting true manhood, so that his friends parted with him, no matter what they had discovered, with stronger reasons than any promise or obligation could have created for not telling what they knew should not be told.

Monday morning, the 11th of February, 1861, the day fixed for his departure from Springfield, came with heavy winter weather, turning to snow. There were as many as two thousand out to hear his last good-bye, stormy as the day continued. For almost an hour the line filed past him, taking him by the hand, with a fervent "God bless you!" parting with the great commoner and coming President as a father. From the platform of the train he said: "Fellow-citizens, friends, and neighbors: No one not in my situation can understand the feeling of sadness that comes over me at this parting. To this community and the never-failing kindness of its people I owe all that I am. Here I have lived and been one of you for a full quarter of a century, and have grown from a young to a much older man. Our children have been born here. One lies yonder, and is [pointing] buried among yours. The time has come. I am leaving this best of homes without knowing when or whether I may ever return, with a heavier load and a greater task than rested upon Washington, the Father of Our Country. Without the assistance of that Divine Being who ever supported and attended him, I can not succeed. With that assistance I will not and can not fail. Trusting in Him who will and can go with me and yet remain with you and be everywhere, in every heart for good, let us confidently hope that all will be well. To His care commending you, as I hope in your prayers you will commend me and beseech His care, I bid you all an affectionate farewell."

Before leaving Springfield he had accepted invitations agreeing to visit a number of cities and make a tour of several days on his way to Washington. Many had to be declined for want of time, among which were Boston and other New England towns. This he sincerely regretted for many reasons, chief among them that he loved to commingle with and be one of the people, who had made him President.

His route selected took him through Indianapolis, Cincinnati, Columbus, Cleveland, Pittsburg, Buffalo, Albany, New York, Trenton, Philadelphia, and Harrisburg. What was done and what was said on the tour would fill a large book, and prove an entertaining one. It was a good man's visit, talking and listening to and associating with several millions of his fellow-citizens, where every day's progress was a feast for thousands.

No better definitions of the foundation principles on which our Government is founded, no higher conception of the strength and spirit of our institutions, no more sincere devotion to the rights of men were ever told in such plain, forcible truth, mingled and fashioned in freedom's forging heat. All of them should be read and pondered by all who believe in men. Here we must be content with some selections from them.

At Indianapolis he said: "Let me say that, for the salvation of the Union, there needs be but one single thing—the hearts of a people like yours. When the people rise in a mass in behalf of the Union and the liberties of this country, truly it may be said, 'The gates of hell can not prevail against them.' In all trying positions in which I shall be placed, and doubtless I shall be placed in many such, my reliance will be upon you and the people of the United States. I wish you to remember, now and forever, that it is your business, not all mine, that if the Union of these States and the liberties of this people shall be lost, it is but little to any man fifty years of age, but a great deal to the thirty millions of people who inhabit these United States, and to their posterity in all coming time. It is liberty for yourselves; for me only as one of you. I appeal to you again to bear constantly in mind that not with politicians, not with Presidents, not with office-seekers, but with you is the question, Shall the Union and shall the liberties of this country be preserved to the latest generations?"

At Columbus, to the Legislature in joint session, he said "It is true, as it has been said by the president of the Senate, that a very great responsibility rests upon me in the position to which the votes of the American people have called me. I am deeply sensible of that weighty responsibility. I can not but know, what you all know, that there has fallen upon me a task such as did not rest upon the Father of Our Country; and so feeling, I can but turn and look for that support without which it will be impossible to perform that great task. I then turn back to the American people and to that God who has never forsaken them. I have not remained silent from any real anxiety. It is a good thing that there is no more anxiety, for there is nothing going wrong. It is a consoling circumstance that, when we look out, there is nothing that really hurts anybody. We entertain different views upon political questions, but nobody is suffering any-thing. This is a most consoling circumstance, and from it we may conclude that all we want is time, patience, and a reliance on that God who has never forsaken our people."

At Steubenville he made the foundation of our liberties a very plain subject: "I feel that the great confidence manifested in my abilities is unfounded. Indeed, I am sure it is. Encompassed with vast difficulties as I am, nothing shall be wanting, on my part, if I am sustained by God and the American people. I believe the devotion to the Constitution is equally great on both sides of the river. It is only the different understanding that causes the difficulty. The only dispute on both sides is what is their rights. If the majority should not rule, who should be the judge? Where is such a judge to be found? We should all be bound by the majority of the American people; if not, then the minority must control. Would that be right? Assuredly not. I reiterate that the majority should rule. If I adopt a wrong policy, the opportunity for condemnation will occur in four years' time. Then I can be turned out, and a better man with better views put in my place."

He said to the Senate at Trenton, New Jersey: "In the Revolutionary struggle few of the States of the old thirteen had more of the battlefields of the country within their limits than New Jersey. May I be pardoned if on this occasion I mention that, away back in my childhood, the earliest days of my being able to read, I got hold of a small book, such a one as few of the younger members had ever seen, Weems's 'Life of Washington.' I remember all the accounts there given of the battlefields and struggles for the liberties of our country. None fixed themselves upon my imagination so deeply as the struggle here at Trenton. The crossing of the river, the contest with the Hessians, the great hardships endured at that time, all fixed themselves on my memory, more than any single Revolutionary event; and you all know, you have all been boys, how these early impressions last longer than others. I recollect thinking then, boy even though I was, that there must have been something more than common that these men struggled for. I am exceedingly anxious that that thing,—that something even more than National independence; that something that held out a great promise to all the people of the world, for all time to come—I am exceedingly anxious that this Union, the Constitution, and the liberties of the people shall be perpetuated in accordance with the original idea for which that struggle was made. I shall be most happy indeed if I shall be a humble instrument in the hand of the Almighty and of this, his almost chosen people, for perpetuating the object of that great struggle.

"You give me this reception, as I understand, without distinction of party. I learn that this body is composed of a majority of gentlemen who, in the exercise of their best judgment in the choice of a Chief Magistrate, did not think I was the right man. I understand, nevertheless, that they came forward here to see me as the Constitutionally-elected President of the United States, to meet the man who, for the time being, is the representative of the majority of the Nation, united for the single purpose to perpetuate the Constitution, the Union, and the liberties of the people. As such I accept this reception more gratefully than I could do did I believe it were tendered to me as an individual."

After this he addressed the representatives as follows: "I shall do all in my power to promote a peaceful settlement of all our difficulties. The man does not live who is more devoted to peace than I am. None would do more to preserve it; but it may be necessary to put the foot down firmly.

[Loud cheering.] If I do my duty and do right, you will sustain me, will you not? [Louder cheering.] Received as I am by the members of a Legislature, the majority of whom do not agree with me in political sentiments, I trust that I may have your assistance in piloting the ship of State through the voyage, surrounded by perils as it is; for if it should suffer wreck now, there will be no pilot ever needed for another voyage."

In old Independence Hall, in Philadelphia, he re-declared and reanimated the Declaration of Independence in burning thoughts and words that will live, without explanation, alongside the greatest charter of human freedom: "I am filled with deep emotion at finding myself standing in this place, where were collected together the wisdom, the patriotism, the devotion to principle from which sprang the institutions under which we live. You have kindly suggested to me that in my hands is the task of restoring peace to our distracted country. I can say in return, sirs, that all the political sentiments I entertain have been drawn, so far as I have been able to draw them, from this hall. I have never had a feeling, politically, that did not spring from the sentiments embodied in the Declaration of Independence. I have often pondered over the dangers which were incurred by the men who assembled here and framed and adopted that Declaration. I have pondered over the toils that were endured by the officers and soldiers of the army who achieved that independence. I have often inquired of myself what great principle or idea it was that kept this Confederacy so long together. It was not the mere matter of the separation of the Colonies from the mother land, but the sentiment in the Declaration of Independence, which gave liberty, not alone to the people of this country, but hope to all the world, for all future time. It was that which gave promise that in due time the weight would be lifted from the shoulders of all men, and that all should have an equal chance.

This is the sentiment embodied in the Declaration of Independence.

"Now, my friends, can this country be saved on that basis? If it can, I will consider myself one of the happiest men in the world if I can help to save it. If it can not be saved upon that principle, it will be truly awful. But if this country can not be saved without giving up that principle, I was about to say I would rather be assassinated on this spot than surrender it. Now, in my view of the present aspect of affairs, there is no need of bloodshed and war. There is no necessity for it. I am not in favor of such a course. I may say in advance that there will be no bloodshed until it be forced upon the Government. The Government will not use force unless force is used against it.

"My friends, this is wholly an unprepared speech. I did not expect to be called on to say a word when I came here. I supposed it was to do something towards raising a flag. I may therefore have said something indiscreet. ["No, no, go on."] But I have said nothing but what I am willing to live by, and, if it be the pleasure, to die by."

At Harrisburg, on the same day, before the Pennsylvania Legislature, among other entertaining subjects, he continued the patriotic one of the morning at Independence Hall: "Allusion has been made to the fact, the interesting fact perhaps we should say, that I for the first time appear at the capital of the great commonwealth of Pennsylvania, upon the birthday of the Father of His Country. In connection with that beloved anniversary in the history of the country, I have already gone through one exceedingly interesting scene this morning in the ceremonies at Philadelphia. Under the control of gentlemen there, I was for the first time allowed the privilege of standing in the old Independence Hall, to have a few words addressed to me there, and opening up to me an opportunity of expressing, with much regret, that I had not more time to say something of my own feelings excited by the occasion,—somewhat to harmonize and give shape to the feelings that had really been the feelings of my whole life. Besides this, our friends there had provided a magnificent flag of our country. They had arranged it so that I was given the honor of raising it. When it went up, I was pleased that it went to its place by the strength of my own feeble arm. When, according to the arrangement, the cord was pulled, and it floated gloriously to the wind, without an accident, in the bright, glowing sunshine of the morning, I could not help hoping that there was, in the entire success of that beautiful ceremony, at least something of an omen of what is to come.

"I could not help feeling then, as I have often felt in the whole proceeding, I was a very feeble instrument. I had not provided the flag; I had not made the arrangements for elevating it to its place; I had applied but a very small portion of my feeble strength in raising it. In the whole transaction I was in the hands of the people who had arranged it, and if I can have the same generous co-operation of the people of the Nation, I think the flag of our country may be kept flying gloriously.

"While I am exceedingly gratified to see the manifestations upon your streets, of your military force here, and as fully satisfied with your promise to use that force upon a proper emergency; while I make these acknowledgments, I desire to repeat, in order to preclude any possible misconstruction, that I do most sincerely hope that we shall have no use for them, that it will never become their duty to shed blood, most especially never to shed fraternal blood. I promise that, so far as I may have wisdom to direct it, so painful a result shall not in any wise be brought about; it shall be through no fault of mine."

On the night of February 22d, Mr. Lincoln, with Mr. W. H. Lamon as his only companion, made the unexpected night ride from Harrisburg, through Baltimore, to Wash-

ington, reaching the Capital early on the morning of the
23d without accident or mishap of any kind. The reasons
given for this sudden change of plans were that Mr. Seward,
General Scott, and others were so fully convinced of the
existence of a plot to assassinate Mr. Lincoln en route that
they urged the change to a night ride upon him as a necessity.

This subject was at once considered by the party, of
whom Mr. N. B. Judd, of Chicago, and Judge David Davis
were members. These coincided with Seward, Scott, and
Chase. Mr. Lincoln made the night ride, but very much
against his own judgment, as it was that of Colonel E. V.
Sumner, his military escort, who did not believe that there
would be any serious interference on their way; but that if
any should be discovered, there were ample forces at hand
at once to disperse it.

Mr. Seward, who had so long been one of the boldest
and most daring advocates against slavery aggression and
the schemes of the slavery conspirators, seemed to stagger
and fail unexpectedly in the face of their culminating plans
for war. He was so timid and fearful as to become almost
cowardly in being a pleader in useless attempts at compromise or settlement. General Scott was then an infirm,
gouty old man, overborne with age and the burden of years,
but who, about fifty years before, at the time of Lundy's
Lane, or later at Cerro Gordo, would have taken a President
openly and alone from Philadelphia, or anywhere else, to
Washington, relying on American patriotism and fair play
for protection.

The example of the night ride was bad. It encouraged
every rowdy, blusterer, and secessionist boaster all over the
land. It wholly misrepresented the courage and character
of Mr. Lincoln, who was brave and had often faced danger,
who in after life always regretted the mistaken night ride.
It was at a time, although there was much excitement, that
Governor Hicks, of Maryland, and the authorities of Balti-

more would have preserved order. If there were well-grounded fears, General Scott had several companies of faithful and well-trained regulars at Washington, who could have been used as an escort, or a whole brigade of those training Pennsylvania volunteers would have made it a grand excursion to have taken the President-elect to Washington. Their bright uniforms and flashing blades might have been soiled, but their glittering, loaded guns and strong, steady arms would have been better persuaders of civil order than peace conventions and night rides in the face of arming rebellion. These only prolonged the dreadful work that came, which piled upon us all the more, because it had been so much neglected.

On Monday, the 4th of March, 1861, Mr. Lincoln was inaugurated without difficulty or obstruction of any kind. Secretary of War Joseph Holt, with the approval of President Buchanan, who got stronger as his term shortened, and good old General Scott, had made some very efficient rifle-ball and buckshot and light artillery preparations to suppress disorder. Having made this good preparation, there was no disorder. As a result, the inauguration went peacefully on, and there was none of the dreaded rioting to suppress. Thus came the succession of Abraham Lincoln as President of the United States, which was as peacefully done and proclaimed as that of any of his predecessors.

"What fools these mortals be," and how men do not learn from experience, was fully shown in the success of the plans for preserving order at the inauguration. At the time Washington was as full of boasting and arming seceders as Richmond. General Scott, with his Lundy's Lane toggery and equipment—better, with his old spirit of getting into rather than getting out of danger—could have taken his Washington force of regulars, with what he could have rapidly assembled, swept into Richmond by railway the same night, and have driven every secessionist out of the State, and reduced the insurrection down to a cotton State conspiracy at once; but his genius for war was gone. He, and all the leaders with him, waited. The people were compelled to wait, for there was then no Lyon nor Grant nor Thomas nor Logan, with any separate command near Washington; hence Richmond became a quasi-competing capital.

Mr. Lincoln's Inaugural Address was kind and friendly; but down deep in its meaning it was firm. This, with Douglas present and aroused to sustain the President, as the leader of the faithful and loyal Democracy, gave promise of more effectual force to save the Union than the three months' peace Conventions, palavering, and Constitutional-dickering amendments of statesmen like Crittenden, John Minor Botts, Tom Corwin, and one weaker, Kellogg, of Illinois, the kind of tender-hearted men to whom Mr. Seward and some other doubting party leaders listened so long that they almost fell into their sleepy, do-nothing plans. This was going on while the revolters of the South were out trooping and ready to fight—men who needed a good licking more than anything else to prepare them for a compromise on slavery that would last. Not then, but in time they got it.

Chief-Justice Taney administered the oath of office to Mr. Lincoln. President Buchanan treated Mr. Lincoln well under the circumstances. He seemed pleased, and even animated a little, to be rid of an office which had brought neither peace nor happiness for him, while the pro-slavery conspirators, by their treason, their open rebellion, and their going made a loyal citizen out of a very poor and weak President.

Senator Edward D. Baker, of Oregon, formerly Lincoln's Springfield neighbor, and his Whig competitor for a nomination to Congress in 1844, where Colonel Hardin defeated both, introduced President Lincoln to the vast assemblage weathering the March storm to see and hear the great leader from Illinois.

Judge Douglas was there to renew his personal friendship; more emphatically, to assure the President of his unqualified support and to break the ice for a closer co-operation than the President might have felt at ease in asking. Douglas stepped to the front conspicuously, and took his position almost by the side of Mr. Lincoln. When the ceremonies began, Lincoln was holding his new silk hat, which was not only his headgear, but the receptacle, as usual, for his memoranda. There were no places to hang hats on the walls or the stone columns of the great, east portico of the Capitol. His hat needed better care, any way. He could n't hold it himself very well, and ceremony prevented his wearing it, as others did theirs, as the President is always expected to stand the inauguration storm and address bareheaded. Several about them were wondering what he was going to do with his hat. Judge Douglas, fully aware of the situation and the contents of the hat, held out his hand, saying, "Mr. President, I will take care of it for you." The President replied at once: "Thank you, Judge; I will be obliged indeed. The pavement is wet, and I do n't see a peg anywhere in any one of these stone pillars. I am obliged."

It was a small incident, but Mr. Lincoln understood and appreciated its full significance at once. In a short time afterward he said to a friend: "Douglas's patriotic course is the very best. He has done well by me ever since I came here. Few men can do what he can to help save the country, if, indeed, any other can do as much. All the other leaders of his party could not overthrow him. He has been cordial, and is willing to give me the benefit of his long acquaintance here and the wisdom of his experience. I am going to be friendly with him, and to be so I will go more than halfway."

His Inaugural Address was short, about as anticipated. It was very much in effect what his addresses en route had foreshadowed. Though friendly, it was heroic in emphasis that the Union must and would be preserved. In the following selection its main features are given

"Fellow-citizens of the United States,—In compliance with a custom as old as the Government itself, I appear before you to address you briefly, and to take, in your presence, the oath prescribed by the Constitution of the United States to be taken by the President before he enters upon the execution of his office.

"Apprehension seems to exist among the people of the Southern States that by the accession of a Republican Administration their property and their peace and personal security are to be endangered. There has never been any reasonable cause for such apprehension. Indeed, the most ample evidence to the contrary has all the while existed and been open to their inspection. It is found in nearly all the public speeches of him who now addresses you. I do but quote from one of those speeches when I declare that I have no purpose, directly or indirectly, to interfere with the institution of slavery in the States where it exists.

"I believe I have no lawful right to do so, and I have no inclination to do so. Those who nominated and elected me did so with full knowledge that I had made this and many similar declarations, and had never recanted them; and more than this, they placed in the platform for my acceptance, and as a law unto themselves and to me, the clear and emphatic resolution which I now read:

" '*Resolved,* That the maintenance inviolate of the rights of the States, and especially the rights of each State to order and control its own domestic institutions according to its own judgment exclusively, is essential to that balance of power on which the protection and endurance of our political fabric depends; and we denounce the lawless invasion, by armed force, of the soil of any State or Territory, no matter under what pretext, as among the gravest of crimes.'

"It is seventy-two years since the first inauguration of a

President under our National Constitution. During that
period fifteen different and greatly distinguished citizens have,
in succession, administered the Executive Branch of the Government. They have conducted it through many perils, and
generally with great success. Yet, with all this scope of
precedence, I now enter upon the same task for the brief
Constitutional term of four years, under great and peculiar
difficulties. A disruption of the Federal Union, heretofore
only menaced, is now formidably attempted.

"I hold that, in contemplation of universal law and the
Constitution, the Union of these States is perpetual. Perpetuity is implied, if not expressed, in the fundamental laws
of all national governments. It is safe to assert that no
government proper ever had a provision in its organic law
for its own destruction. Continue to execute all the expressed provisions of our National Constitution, and the
Union will endure forever, it being impossible to destroy
it by some action not provided for in the instrument itself.
Again, if the United States be not a Government proper,
but an association of States in the nature of contract merely,
can it, as a contract, be peaceably unmade by less than all
the parties who made it? One party to a contract may violate it, break it, so to speak; but does it not require all lawfully to rescind it?

"Descending from these general principles, we find the
proposition that, in legal contemplation, the Union is perpetual, confirmed by the history of the Union itself. The
Union is much older than the Constitution. It was formed,
in fact, by the Articles of Confederation in 1774. It was
matured and continued by the Declaration of Independence
in 1776. It was further matured and the faith of all the
thirteen States expressly plighted and engaged that it should
be perpetual by the Articles of Confederation again in 1778;
and finally, in 1787, one of the declared objects for ordain-

ing and establishing the Constitution was to form a more perfect Union.

"But if destruction of the Union by one, or by part only, of the States be lawfully possible, the Union is less perfect than before the Constitution, having lost the vital element of perpetuity. It follows from these views that no State, upon its own mere motion, can lawfully get out of the Union; that resolves and ordinances to that effect are legally void; and that acts of violence within any State or States against the authority of the United States are insurrectionary or revolutionary, according to circumstances.

"I therefore consider that, in view of the Constitution and the laws, the Union is unbroken; and to the extent of my ability I shall take care, as the Constitution itself expressly enjoins upon me, that the laws of the Union be faithfully executed in all the States. Doing this, I deem it to be only a simple duty on my part, and I shall perform it so far as practicable, unless my rightful masters—the American people—shall withhold the required means or in some authoritative manner direct the contrary. I trust this will not be regarded as a menace, but only as the declared purpose of the Union that it will Constitutionally defend and maintain itself.

"In doing this there needs to be no bloodshed or violence, and there shall be none, unless it be forced upon the National authority. From questions of this class spring all our Constitutional controversies, and we divide upon them into majorities and minorities. If the minority will not acquiesce, the majority must, or the Government will cease. There is no other alternative; for continuing the Government is acquiescence on one side or the other. If a minority in such case will secede rather than acquiesce, they make a precedent which, in turn, will divide and ruin; for a minority will secede from them whenever a majority refuses to be controlled by such minority. For instance, why not any portion of a new Confederacy, a year or two hence, arbitrarily secede again, precisely as portions of the present Union now claim to secede from it? All who cherish disunion sentiments are now being educated to the exact temper of doing this.

"One section of our country believes slavery is right and ought to be extended, while the other believes it is wrong and ought not to be extended. This is the only substantial dispute. . . . While I make no recommendation of amendments, I fully recognize the rightful authority of the people over the whole subject, to be exercised in either of the modes prescribed in the instrument itself; and I should, under existing circumstances, favor, rather than oppose, a fair opportunity being afforded the people to act upon it.

"Why should there not be a patient confidence in the ultimate justice of the people? Is there any better or equal hope in the world? In our present differences, is either party without hope of being in the right? If the Almighty Ruler of nations, with his eternal truth and justice, be on your side of the North, or yours of the South, that truth and that justice will surely prevail by the judgment of this great tribunal of the American people. By the frame of government under which we live, this same people have wisely given their public servants but little power for mischief, and have, with equal wisdom, provided for the return of that little to their own hands at short intervals. While the people retain their virtue and vigilance, no Administration, by any extreme of wickedness or folly, can ever seriously injure the Government in the short space of four years.

"My countrymen, one and all, think calmly and well upon this whole subject. Nothing valuable can be lost by taking time. If there is an object to hurry any of you in hot haste to a step which you would never take deliberately, that object will be frustrated in taking time; but no good object can be frustrated by it. Such of you as are now dissatisfied still have the old Constitution unimpaired and, on the sensitive point, the laws of your own framing under it; while the new Administration will have no immediate opportunity if it would desire to change either.

"If it were admitted that you who are dissatisfied hold the right side in the dispute, there still is no good reason for precipitate action. Intelligence, patriotism, Christianity, and a firm reliance on Him who has never yet forsaken this favored land are still competent to adjust in the best way all our present difficulties.

"In your hands, my dissatisfied fellow-countrymen, and not in mine, is the momentous issue of civil war. The Government will not assail you. You can have no conflict without being yourselves the aggressors. You have no oath registered in heaven to destroy the Government, while I shall have the most solemn one to 'preserve, protect, and defend it.'

"I am loath to close. We are not enemies, but friends. We must not be enemies. Though passion may have strained, it must not break our bonds of affection. The mystic chords of memory, stretching from every battlefield and patriot grave to every living heart and hearthstone all over this broad land, will yet swell the chorus of the Union when again touched, as surely they will be, by the better angels of our nature."

At the close, Chief-Justice Taney, the clerk of the court holding the Bible upon which Mr. Lincoln placed his right hand, administered the oath of office, after which Abraham Lincoln was President of the United States. A swell of satisfied applause rolled over the vast assemblage, which separated with more of confidence than had existed for months that the Presidential succession had been peacefully accomplished.

He was congratulated on all sides and by men in all parties, except those in the forming Confederacy and those in States getting ready to join them. His words of wisdom, his pleadings for calmness and deliberation before resorting to war, and his judicious and fortunate selection of a Cabinet, in which the border States were so fairly represented, had much to do in restraining Maryland, Delaware, Kentucky, and Missouri from following in the revolt.

When completed, the Cabinet was: Wm. H. Seward, of New York, Secretary of State; S. P. Chase, of Ohio, Secretary of the Treasury; Simon Cameron, of Pennsylvania, Secretary of War; Gideon Welles, of Connecticut, Secretary of the Navy; Caleb B. Smith, of Indiana, Secretary of the Interior; Montgomery Blair, of Maryland, Postmaster-General; and Edward Bates, of Missouri, Attorney-General.

Many were dissatisfied, as usual, in the meager division of six or seven prominent places among thirty times as many qualified men in as many hopeful communities in the larger States. The selection of the leading contestant for the nomination for Secretary of State had often been made; but no President, except Lincoln, ever took all of his party contestants into his Cabinet. They were able men, however, and must have represented their localities well, or they would not have been supported for the Presidential nomination.

Thaddeus Stevens, not liking the selection because of lack of more pronounced anti-slavery leaders, said of it: "That Mr. Lincoln made his Cabinet out of an assorted lot of his rivals, greater and less, graded on a guess as to qualification, one stump-speaker, and two of the Blair family." Mr. Stevens at the time perhaps did not know that without the "Blair" family Mr. Lincoln would not have been President. However, he (Stevens) learned it, and, notwithstanding, became one of Mr. Lincoln's most ardent friends.

Some of President Lincoln's Cabinet-making was done

in the way of party organization, but more of it to unite
the people of all parties and factions in support of the
Union, a vigorous war policy when it became a necessity,
and the preservation of the Nation in its entirety. Mr.
Cameron was succeeded in one year by Edwin M. Stanton
as Secretary of War; and Mr. C. B. Smith was succeeded
by Mr. John P. Usher as Secretary of the Interior. With
these changes it continued to the close of his first term.
In continuing care, devotion, and undivided attention to
the conduct of public affairs himself, no business in any
department was neglected.

The Senate convened in special session for the purpose
of confirming the Cabinet and other necessary changes
and appointments. The Administration soon took hold of
the public business in regular and systematic conduct and
methods. The Government was resuscitated. The dilapidated conditions were changed to order, celerity, and energy,
where the processes of government were carried on in skillful and providing management. Order and regularity were
inaugurated with energetic plans of taking care and protecting all that had not been lost, wrecked, squandered, and
plundered by the Southern Confederacy supplying conspirators in Buchanan's guilty Cabinet.

In the spring of 1861, Mr. Douglas had been in Congress almost twenty years. In his tireless and industrious
ways of gathering information he had gained knowledge
and understanding of all the men and the course of public
business in progress and detail, as few men in or about
the Capital. He had contended more vigorously than ever
in that session with the disunion leaders, every one of whom
he knew to their smallest leanings and idiosyncrasies as
well as they knew and dreaded him. He was the fearless,
the last, and the unthroned leader of the loyal Democracy.
He had never been more of a leader or defender of his
country than through that dreadful winter.

He was, regardless of his overwrought mind and perishing body, the one who stood the undaunted, although dying, leader of the unpolluted Democracy of our country. He was a tribune of the people in the forum of last appeal before the sword, when no one, nor all the conspiring senators could meet, answer, or distort his patriotic and irrefutable reasoning, his power and logic, where, like Samuel, he stood firm, and denounced the sin and pointed out the sinners.

It would be pleasant to dwell on the closing weeks in the life of Douglas, if space permitted. Mr. Lincoln went to Washington, comparatively a stranger, to be inaugurated. In this necessity Douglas came to his side in friendly relief that gave him the benefit and knowledge of his acquaintance and experience. Not only so, but he brought to his Administration the dutiful support of the strongest faction in the Nation under a single leadership. He did this graciously and generously in the spirit of patriotic service—not a bit like the Old-line Whigs, the Constitutional Union men, or the breaking fragments of Buchanan's two Cabinets, who, for the support they gave, as Douglas did, expected to be secretaries, judges, ministers, or governors.

Judge Douglas made serious mistakes. Who has not? His opponents said he was artful, crafty, and seeking a nomination for President by concessions to slavery, while the reverse was the truth. He declined nominations on such terms as were readily accepted and sought by Van Buren, Cass, Pierce, and Buchanan, of his own party, and as eagerly by Clay, Webster, Scott, Corwin, Everett, and others, of the Whig party. It was further true that those who most actively accused Douglas of seeking position or office were those who continuously sought and failed of nominations in their own party.

Many have quarreled and disputed over Douglas. Many marked him down; but the reasonable and patriotic,

like Lincoln, Seward, and Greeley, always marked him up.
The Southern leaders knew him best, and disclosed it, not
so much in speech, as in conduct.. They realized that, in
twenty years' contest with Calhoun, the Rhetts, Haynes,
Mason, Toombs, Slidell, Benjamin, Yancey, Jefferson Davis, and Breckinridge against him, floundering and falling
all about him on every side, in pairs, sets, and reliefs, they
could neither master nor unhorse him.

He came to Lincoln's support and the salvation of our
country as no other man could, with all his followers, in
the highest performance of duty, so promptly and cheerfully that it was high patriotic service. Still he had to
come, with deep chagrin to many pro-slavery Democrats
and almost as many Republican leaders, who had often
charged him with disloyalty. There was deeper confound-
ing of many in that, although the Republicans had won,
the doctrine of Squatter Sovereignty had become the practical solution of slavery in the Territories, as recognized
in Congress, under which the new Territories were organized; that, too, without any slavery extension. Thus Squatter Sovereignty, though much abused, became the means
of defeating the Southern leaders. In it there was a more
lurking danger to the slaveholder than anything ever proposed by the Republicans.

The propagandists saw it afar off, and set about the
destruction of Douglas. Its threatening danger was that,
if a Territory could exclude or vote slavery out of it, why
not a State? Sure as this they knew that, with Douglas
President, a man who would sustain the right of a State
or Territory to vote slavery out of it, Missouri would do
so. With that done, Tennessee, and probably Kentucky and
North Carolina, would follow or attempt the example. Hence
Douglas became more formidable as a practical leader
against slavery than any living man.

The bitterness of the slave-leaders and the envy of

small men have long attempted to becloud the virtues and power of Douglas as a leader. They wondered at his power and strength, but did not understand it because of their own lack of his integrity and greater qualities. He had ability of the highest order—better, he was a Democrat who never wasted the people's substance, who returned unsoiled to them all the power they had given him. Those who questioned his ability, statesmanship, or high leadership, should point us to another who ever led one and a half million voting men for twenty years, in victory or defeat, to better or more effectual purpose.

When the blows they had long threatened fell on Sumter, he proclaimed the Union anew, brighter, stronger, and more earnest than ever, to every doubting patriot. With him, party had vanished. Wherever there were people, he pleaded with and encouraged them. In this work he came home to us. In Springfield he had such a greeting and such a meeting as perhaps no leader ever met with in the Union.

There were men present of all parties, leaders from every part of the State. Thousands failed to get into the crowded hall, with its hallways, windows, and doors all open. He spoke over two hours in such earnest devotion to Union, land, and liberty, that there was neither noise nor applause. No one of the crowded throng wanted to miss a single word of his earnest words. He said: "We are come again to a division, where there are only two sides, one for and the other against our country. There can be no deeper crime than this madness, this secession and dis-union that will come with the woeful slaughter of untold thousands of our very best men, where there is nothing but human greed and human ambition to fight for. If the sword must be resorted to after fairly-decided elections, our days as a Republic are ended, and we will be numbered with the rotted and wornout nations of antiquity, or become like

Mexico and the little Central American States, where a revolution follows almost every election."

He wrought magic in calling the people to an undivided support of the President. As we carried him out of the hall, trembling and exhausted with the great effort, we knew that his work was done. His clothing was wet with the sweat so profuse that it ran from his face in streams as he called men "to stand by the Union and risk their lives and all that they had that it may be saved." This himself he did, and gave it a few weeks later. His death was hastened, without doubt, by the severe labor of a weak man in this fervent appeal to his own people, ending with saying, "Cast aside every besetting thought, and save the Union!" This was never forgotten by any one who heard it. Going home from this city, May 10th, he died in Chicago, June 3, 1861.

In his own wisdom, God took Douglas, his work all done, when Lincoln was qualified and came to power with might and genius, tempered to the coming storm as the other Illinois leader lay worn and dying. When Lincoln came into control, he had, by this cordial co-operation and good will of Douglas and his followers, become leader of a great majority of our people. After this men of all parties, creeds, and beliefs recognized him as the great leader, where he held the disposal of our vast resources bestowed upon him in confidence that had not been surpassed in the support of any President. The Nation of that day had many worthy and patriotic men. These were all about him, from every party and all their divisions, including the independent, unclassed factions, who were the studious, cautious, and thoughtful men of the day.

In personal ways he was supported by hosts in every calling—farmers, toilers in every occupation, mechanics, students, and the trained and educated, scholars, teachers, and professional people of every grade—by whom he was encouraged as no President since Washington had been. Among them were hundreds of leaders, distinguished by right of service, wisdom, faithfulness, and experience. Some of them were soldiers of renowned ability, having the knowledge, training, and experience as far as military life in a nation so little engaged in war could fit them.

Among all there was no one like Lincoln, who could have touched so many hearts, drawn them to and about him, and have taken so many other leaders and their followers into his hope and confidence. The Nation's resources and powers, so bountifully and unreservedly confided to him, were so well and so wisely used that no life was purposely squandered and no right of the people was lost or taken from them; but the great cause of the rights of man against tyranny and oppression made several hundred years' progress in our four years of war.

It is one of the strongest features of our Government that it will bear the strain of a weak and faithless President and a weaker, more faithless Cabinet, such as Buchanan's, and live through it. These develop, by contrast, the lasting good of Administrations of statesmen like Washington, Jefferson, Jackson, and Lincoln. They were all true and steadfast in the principles on which the Nation based its existence, not builded in the shops of political craftsmen, where skill and cunning make only imitations, but on God's eternal foundations of justice.

Lincoln was re-elected when men were never more excited, but careful, earnest, and determined, and when sacrifice for our country was never so great. It is true that there was a form of opposition. It dragged along into disloyalty, blundering where patriotism was the plain and unmistakable duty. It was bitter and thoughtless, as might have been expected, when the wiser men declined a nomination, and were well content to have Lincoln re-elected, knowing that the Nation would be at its best under his direc-

tion,. and that its highest interest would be well and honestly
managed. Hence, for the time, by this inaction, the opposition fell into the hands of its most vicious and excitable
leaders, when sober sense was never more urgently required.

Those who did the most and were the most active in
sympathy with the slavery rebellion from the beginning
gained easy control. Their wisdom was that a nomination
was necessary. Knowing that some Union soldier would
be an attraction, if any one would be, they offered the nomination to General George B. McClellan on a platform that
was an awkwardly-stated falsehood, yet an earnest expression of their desires. In this long since repudiated declaration of principles there was a resolution which has shamed
the men who made it and the party, as far as they ever
assented to it, ever since, so much that the campaign and
the General, as their candidate against President Lincoln and
his policy, with victory after victory on a hundred fields,
for the Union, made their screed and clamor pitiful and
painful. They failed in most of the States. This fatal,
taunting resolution, charging Lincoln's Administration with
"four years of failure in war," came flapping back in their
faces like a polar storm, leaving them not only beaten, but
with the stained record of sympathy with their country's
foes.

In full and careful deliberation, when all is said that
can be, it stands to reason and truth that Abraham Lincoln
was the chosen and re-chosen leader of our people, com-
mander-in-chief of our armies and navies on field and sea,
with almost unanimous consent. Our cause was just and
true, measured in the light of God's unerring statutes and
wisdom, in the unifying and healing settlements of time,
and confirmed by the righteous judgment of mankind.

To have accomplished such wonderful achievements, to
have left such lasting advances and benefits and so imperishable a name, he was surely no less than God's prophet

and highest leáder to lift our country, with no partition or fragmentary States in hostile contention, from the sorrows and iniquities of our own time and those darker, left-over burdens of the older barbarisms of our race.

Lincoln's life and work came to us in fulfillment of God's continuing promises and favor. As sure as he has already fulfilled his promises, he will still be faithful and true. In his own good time he will again lighten the hearts of men and bless the world and guard our Nation, with all of liberty unharmed, against the tyrannies and greedy usurpations of men.

CHAPTER XLVIII.

IN 1856, James S. Green succeeded Senator Benton, taking his seat. Through the envy of smaller men and the fury and lack of wisdom of the hot-headed Southern leaders, Benton had no successor, except in name, in the Senate from Missouri. Green, as related, took the seat; still, as far as the indomitable energy and reckless daring of the man and the concurrent scheming and planning of Jefferson Davis and his associates could contrive, Atchison was selected to take up the great leadership of Benton. Although both the seat and position in the party had been filled with seeming regularity, Benton's place remained vacant.

Green was a talented, well-informed lawyer, who became a conspicuous pleader, an aggressive and fearless political leader, when under forty. His audacity was best shown that, among twenty as capable and much more experienced in the State, he was the only one of average capacity who would risk and tackle and, in the vehement madness of the Davis *régime*, stand square in the front for the overthrow of Benton. Under these circumstances, Mr. Green entered the Senate in a sort of triumph. Having served and won, in his small way, as the willing servant of the Davis propaganda, he was overestimated, so much so as to believe that he was there for the overthrow of Douglas.

At the time Douglas was sorely perplexed and taxed to his utmost in the unequal contest by reason of the numbers against him. Benjamin, Mason, Breckinridge, and Toombs, with Davis, from his faction, were leading; and Seward,

Chase, Fessenden, Wade, and others of the free North, were assaulting. He stood almost alone against the ablest and most experienced men of all parties and factions, with abject submission to slavery on one side and against the unanswerable logic of freedom on the other. Standing in the tangled embarrassments of expediency, he was no less than surprised at the ardor and intensity of this self-risen leader from Missouri.

The debate ran through the years of the sectional, three-sided discussion of slavery. From Green's relation and position it was a long and tedious progress; but his participation in it is best remembered in the brief and forcible remarks of Judge Douglas.

In an evening's friendly chat, about the year 1860, he said: "When Mr. Green entered the Senate, I was favorably impressed with him; all the more, perhaps, because Benton had so vigorously opposed the submission of slavery or no slavery in the Territories to the people in them. I still firmly believe this is much better than the endless disputing over it in Congress, where, in my opinion, it never can be settled. The people will have to agree to slavery or freedom, or fight it out to the end, as I hope they may, peacefully under our laws. During the debates I was, for a time, continuously surprised and annoyed by his interference and personal debating way which, entirely new to parliamentary procedure, he had undertaken as a personal duty.

"I understood this very well because, admitting that he had talent and learning of an ambitious young man in his new field, he lacked the preparation in argument, and his manner lacked everything in comparison with the polish, deliberation, and *finesse* of Calhoun, Benjamin, or Davis. It resembled more the coarser diatribes of Toombs, and his remarks were so ill-timed, ill-delivered, and so strongly personal that I was sure he was taking his own course and that he was not guided by the ablest among them, who had

repeatedly presented every argument he did without the
personalities, in their most plausible forms.

"To begin with, he seemed to be determined to create
or enlarge what he was pleased to believe was an angry and
irreconcilable estrangement between Mr. Benton and myself. This seemed a smaller political move, new man as he
was, with his reputed talent, fitness, and aspiration, than
any one would think of engaging in.

"It is true that Mr. Benton disagreed with me as to the
policy of submitting slavery or no slavery to the people in
the Territories and the repeal of the Missouri Restriction.
But it was only a difference of belief as to the expediency
of the procedure; for we had been in the Senate so long
and were so intimately known to each other, as full believers
in the principles of Jefferson and the executive greatness
of Jackson, that no question of policy or personal difference ever interfered with our friendship. Mr. Green seemed
to have started out with a personal malignity against Benton, and to impress others with it. This created an unpleasant feeling; for, whatever else might have been said of him,
Senator Benton had pleasing and agreeable ways. His society was sought, and he enjoyed the respect and confidence
of everybody he met in or out of political parties. I told
him that the difference between Mr. Benton and myself
was not personal, and that we accorded each other the
right.

"I did not want to deal with a double-headed leadership
on the Southern slavery side; and, as Mr. Benjamin was
then their recognized leader in the Senate, I determined
not to be annoyed and nagged by this new, self-asserted
authority from Missouri. He was so vainly elated over his
contest with Benton that I would not submit, unless the
Southern senators made him what he was so eagerly assuming. I inquired of Senator Benjamin whether he was an
authoritative leader on their side. Mr. Benjamin replied in

his superior, dignified way that 'Mr. Green would answer for himself,' from which I very well understood he would be pleased to have Mr. Green continue his unusual course as long as he pleased, but with no authority save his own.

"My contention with Calhoun and the Southern leaders, from the beginning, was that the question of slavery, wherever it was treated, considered, or settled, must be under the Constitution, the laws, and the will of the people, and that these powers within their limits were equally supreme. This is the true relation of Democratic principles to slavery and all other applicable differences or subjects of our civil system.

"Their contention had always been a growing one, but I knew several years before the death of Calhoun that he had brought his faction to the belief that slavery was a settled institution under the Constitution, and the avowal that we, who lived in and under the continuing power of a slave Republic, would keep pace with their power to command obedience; hence my lifelong disagreement and vital difference with them.

"On thinking this over carefully, I considered it best, in the running debate, to make Mr. Green a party under Mr. Benjamin, as the other Southern Senators were and so conducted themselves, which policy of debate avoids a double leadership and is more prudent in many ways. To do this I concluded to ask in open debate which of the two, Mr. Benjamin or Mr. Green, was the authorized leader on their side, or whether both were; but before doing so, I concluded to take him through a little unexpected training. I remembered that, in a conversation with Mr. Benton not long before, he said, 'If the subject is submitted to the people of Missouri and intelligently considered, I am confident that two to one would vote slavery out; and, with free. State people increasing so rapidly by immigration, this will be a living issue in the State before many years.' It happened shortly after my conclusion that I met both Benjamin and Green at a committee-meeting, where the business was soon concluded. I turned suddenly, and, addressing Mr. Green, I said, 'If the question of slavery or no slavery is fairly submitted and discussed in your State, how would your people vote on it?' If I had been able and had struck and thrown him on the floor, he might have been somewhat more astonished, but not much. Recovering himself and assuming an angry manner, he replied: 'That is indeed a surprising question for you, who have, ahead of all, so stoutly declared yourself in favor of non-intervention and non-interference with slavery in both States and Territories. Indeed, I may well ask, or even demand, the purpose of such an interrogatory.'

"I replied: 'You are correct. I firmly believe in non-intervention; but, like Benton, if I was convinced that a majority of the people of your State believed that the subject should be fairly submitted, and so requested me, I would feel that it was right in every way for me to meet them and discuss it; for instance, with yourself and Mr. Atchison for slavery and Mr. Benton and myself to contend for the people's right to discuss slavery and vote to retain it or vote it out, as they desired.' He muttered out something of a growl and hurried away in no pleasant humor; and that ended my trouble with Senator Green."

This is a fair illustration of the tact in detail and the ready means—call it what you will—which Douglas possessed in so high degree for party leadership or management. A great many well-informed people believed, and Mr. Green did nothing to correct the misstatement, that Douglas was sorely embarrassed in the slavery debate in the Senate. The truth about it is that, to sustain himself against so many was a serious undertaking, and that he overstudied and overexerted himself; but that he was hampered or nonplused or beaten in argument, or that he lost his temper and therefore his high place as a debater and leader while in the Senate is no more true in the many contests so common than in the case of Mr. Green, whom he so effectually quieted.

The slave-leaders and their abettors everywhere gave credence and as wide circulation as possible to all the stories of the breaking-down and stranding of Douglas throughout that perilous debate; for of all men then in public life he was most in their way. Besides these, many Republican and anti-slavery newspapers were strongly against him through the first two years of contest.

In looking over it now, at this distance, it seems strange that this single debating and reasoning statesman held his own against the field through six long years in the Senate. While this is true, even so capable a reviewer as Mr. Blaine, and many others, have left the subject with such unfair statements as that Green, Benjamin, Fessenden, and others perhaps, got the better of the debate. The truth is that, if Green had told what he knew so well, he would have said that he had no reason to feel any sort of victory or advantage in his meeting and disputing with Douglas.

This was the time when, in the argument and encounter with Green and Benjamin, the latter instantly saw and seized what it would provoke with Douglas and Benton. They were then about ready to take up slavery and anti-slavery in Missouri, and they had to interpose the Lecompton Constitution, which was purposely forced by Davis before the one getting ready under such headway in Missouri.

On the day of Judge Douglas's remarkable address to the Legislature of our State—April, 1861—at Springfield, a few hours before the meeting, some friends and old acquaintances called on him where we were entertained in friendly conversation. The country was in the strain of threatened, foreboding war. It was a time, developed in succeeding events, when we were at war. Although the Administration of President Lincoln had not struck a blow, the slaveholders' rebellion had violently taken possession of all United States property in the slave States, wherever they had the military forces ready to make the seizures.

On President Lincoln's inauguration the mints, post-offices, custom-houses, forts, and navy yards in the South were all taken and under their control, except Forts Moultrie and Sumter at Charleston; Florida Keys, Florida; the forts and navy-yards at Pensacola, Florida; and the arsenal at St. Louis, Missouri. The arms, military and naval stores and equipments, artillery and ordnance, forts and their armaments, had been so held and disposed through the two slave-serving Administrations of Presidents Pierce and Buchanan as to fall an easy capture to the organizing Confederates as soon as they could muster the men to seize and hold them.

The army and navy had been dispersed and so scattered as to render them almost useless, to give rebellion unopposed opportunity for the success of a well-planned revolt. The Nation which they had so treacherously plundered of the munitions and supplies of war lay helpless for the time, unable to rise, as these treason-plotting servants of the Government at Washington believed. But God reigned in those days, and President Lincoln, who feared not, was peacefully inaugurated. The Nation was not dead, not even sleeping.

Judge Douglas, after having done all in his power to make the inauguration and succession of President Lincoln regular and according to precedent in Constitutional forms, was then in his last days, at home with the people, to arouse them, the greatest power in the land, in the imminent and portending approach of war, to the spirit of patriotic resistance that would meet war for secession and slavery with more terrible war for the Union. The inauguration of Abrahim Lincoln without bloodshed and the consent, if no more, of all parties and factions in the loyal States was in itself

a distinct achievement of law and its supremacy. It gave
the people of the free States renewed strength and confidence in our country, rebuilding the hope that, when the
critical period of change was passed, better means would be
forthcoming against our enemies and for our country's salvation and the preservation of our liberties at whatever cost.

We congratulated Judge Douglas on these and his memorable, tireless service and defense through the darkest
struggle the people and Nation had ever passed. He timed
his talk to his strength, and we listened with profound attention to all he had to say, where all was encouragement
and hope, that, without division or party or factional differences, we would give our whole strength to our country's
cause at a time when it was sure to perish without the most
efficient and united effort. I congratulated him on our harmonious agreement and hopeful promise that he, with President Lincoln and all of our people, would be united as one
man for the Union and against all its foes.

The conversation ran irregularly, differing as the men
who called did in their earnest and anxious inquiries. The
subjects, the men, and the incidents considered were brought
forth and talked over. We listened to all he had to say,
but we were affected and distressed to see that long-contin-
ued conversation was more than he was able for. He talked
with increasing interest to all in his pleasing and capable
way, telling us he realized his weak condition and threatening disease, but that it was his highest duty to say everything and do everything he could, regardless of failing
strength or ailments or personal consequences, to arouse
the people to the rescue and the imminent peril before us.

He said in part: "We have indeed passed a dreadful
winter at Washington. Since it is over, and we enjoy the
civil and orderly inauguration of President Lincoln, and
we have that relief, I realize how exhausting it has been
to me. There were days on days when I felt like giving way

under the strain of mind and anxiety. My physical condition did not concern me as much as it should. I did in that what several older and even more feeble men did: I went to every session I had the strength to attend, and when it was necessary, I stood and talked as long as I could; then I sat or lay down for a rest, and sometimes talked an hour or two from my seat.

"I was more firmly convinced than ever before of the correctness of the underlying principles which have guided me through all this contention, that the people form the most reliable source of power in our democratic system. Parties, factions, and those heretofore relied on as strong have shifted and drifted and gone to pieces like half-manned ships before the wind; but they stand, as I have stood with them through the seven-years' dispute, with the satisfaction of seeing all parties come to the doctrine that the people should settle the slavery subject as they do all others, under the rule of the majority. Some people seem to forget that a law or policy not having the will of a majority to support and enforce it, is an unsettled subject in law or government.

"The Republicans broke down in the face of opportunity with unexpected responsibility. They have abused me as few men have ever been denounced, while they held and declared in their campaigns and platforms that Congress should prohibit slavery in all the Territories. When now they have power and the necessity is upon them, they have organized Nevada and Dakotah under the same re-written provisions of the Kansas-Nebraska Act, with the Southern pro-slavery leaders who are left assenting. These Territories were organized under these acts without opposition.

"This people's settlement is a very distasteful doctrine to the Southern slave faction, one which they never have intended to submit to; but they have been biding their time, opposing and denouncing me more than any Democrat since

Jackson. So many hasty, inconsiderate men have not seen and realized that having slavery in about half our States, under our constitutional system, we can not rid ourselves of it in a lump, or all at once, without the consent of these States; therefore as a measure of public policy as well as principle, the strongest force to contend against slave-labor is free labor.

"Mr. Breckinridge, retiring Vice-President, who is returned a member of this Senate from his State, seemed from his lofty manner to think he would surprise and astonish us with the demand that the South should have their share of the new Territories, where they could take their slaves, free and unmolested under the sanction and protection of law. I immediately replied to him that there never had been a time in our history when all our Territories were open to the introduction of slavery as they are now, nor when their property would have been so well protected.

"He was bewildered by my prompt reply to his well-prepared, written-out argument; but as I stated the facts and referred to the recently-passed acts, he saw at once his unpleasant predicament. He was confounded, but far from being satisfied. He appeared rather to be in the mood that Senator Toombs was, but lacked the candor to confess it. When I told Toombs that they have the right to vote slavery into any of the Territories, he, in his coarse and uncivil way, replied: 'We do n't want any voting about it in either States or Territories; we want to take our niggers, horses, mules, and cattle where we go, and drive out the nigger thieves who want to steal any of them, niggers, horses, or mules, one kind as well as the other, as we have need to protect our property.'

"I replied to Toombs: 'At the headlong gait you are taking now toward secession and disunion it will not be long until you find a turn and meet some able-bodied Americans who will do as much driving as you do, and perhaps more than you care for.' At this he retorted more violently: 'We

have no fear of your hordes of mechanics, they will run like
sheep. We have no fear; if we can't get our rights in the
Union, we have our plans ready, and know how to get them
outside of it.' I again replied, 'The attempt to dissolve the
Union by force of arms will be one of the most desperate
struggles the world has witnessed, and I hope in the interest
of humanity it may not be.'

"As to the relative merits of American soldiers, regulars
and volunteers, I am sure that no well-informed man in his
senses would make any distinction between them, North or
South. You, of course, remember that Jefferson Davis, himself in-command of a regiment in the unequal and bloody contest at Buena Vista, said: 'Having had full opportunity to
know, at Buena Vista and on various other occasions, where
their conduct came under my observation, all were alike brave
and heroic without distinction of States or sections. But
yet, if there were differences among our people in their
bravery or capacity for strength and endurance, those of Tennessee, Kentucky, and the Western States were the most
robust and rugged-limbed men; but no one could distinguish
where all were capable.'

"In my reply to Mr. Breckinridge I was particular in
emphasizing, that if the Southern States or any part of them
went into secession they could not honestly do so on the
ground that there was any restriction to the introduction of
slavery into any of our Territories, or the hostile or even unfriendly acts of either Mr. Buchanan's retiring or Mr. Lincoln's incoming Administrations. President Lincoln and the
Republican party have declared that their institutions should
in no wise be interfered with where it existed in the States;
and as they well knew, all our Territories had been organized
under the plan that the South had agreed to for the admission
of Kansas and Nebraska.

"I have been superseded by this ambitious Senator Green
as chairman of the Committee on Territories, the place I held

for so many years; but with the pro-slavery leaders in full control of the Senate and the Republicans of the House, although I have been so persistently opposed, the plan for the people to settle slavery as they choose, has become so well settled and accepted by the people, that neither party desires to change and make the venture of a new policy. It seems to me like the irony of fate that I am spared and still in the Senate, where I can so fully answer and justify my conduct.

"So far as Breckinridge is concerned, and all those who are preparing to go into the revolt, my argument fell on dull and unresponsive ears. There is certain proof that they are getting ready for war, and I predict that this same Breckinridge will soon be declared a recruit to Jefferson Davis, regardless of what his State may do. I was assailed by the coarse and ungentlemanly Wigfall, of Texas, who, poor fellow, knew no better. He was as much out of place in the Senate, as he would have been anywhere among respectable people, or outside of a brawling town-meeting. His blunted ideas of morality braved every feeling of respect as well as shame and criminality, by remaining in the Senate after he and his State asserted their legal separation from and independence of the Government they were openly attempting to destroy.

"When I had so particularly declared my intention of supporting Mr. Lincoln's Administration, which I did unqualifiedly from the time the authoritative announcement of his election was made, I became more than ever the object of their most determined assaults. It seemed that they set this man Wigfall at me as a tormenter, who wanted to know what I would do in certain emergencies and what would be my policy. I replied: 'If you are truthful enough to be believed, you are now a forsworn enemy of your country; and while sitting here as one of its highest officers, a senator, you have advised and abetted the separation of your State, and as far as you have capacity for it you are a public enemy, and therefore not entitled -to the information—one with whom, for good reasons, I have no desire nor authority to hold counsel, and believe that you should be under indictment by the Attorney-General.'

"In one of Wigfall's blundering and pretentious harangues, Senator Mason of Virginia, who was one of the more discreet secessionists, seeing that Wigfall's braggadocio and swagger were an injury to them and their movement, so far as it had any effect, came to his rescue. Mason was full of his own conceit, and almost defiantly asked me the same questions. I replied firmly, but not discourteously, that he 'had no reason to doubt where I would stand in the emergencies which now threatened our country; that I had made positive and unequivocal declarations that I would do all in my power to sustain the entirety and integrity of the Union. Mason wanted to know what I would do in the pending situation in Charleston Harbor, and whether I believed in coercing a State. I replied that it was no part of my duty to take up administrative details which the people had trusted to other and equally capable hands, but that if he and his associates, pro-slavery Democrats, had done their patriotic duty to hold their party and country intact, and not secede, I might have been situated so as to inform him. But as they had invited the catastrophe, I would refer him to President Lincoln, whom the people had lawfully elected and qualified, and that no man knew better than himself how to get the information he assumed to be so eagerly searching for."

Douglas's resolute fight through that deadly winter of 1860-61 was the leading event in that dissolving Congress and apparently dissolving Nation, where he, in the power of a patriot armed for victory, turned his great talents and ungrudging service to the earnest and honest support of President Lincoln. It was an event of such vital import that it promised the salvation of the country; because in the terrible seven years' contest he held the immovable leadership of more men, and more independent ones, than any other man or leader. He had been defeated for President; but he had won a greater victory. He willingly gave up the Presidency, or the thought of it, and brought the free States undivided to the support of the Government. He prevented the division of the free States, as he defeated the forming slave republic or empire in its deliberate purpose to extend its institutions and make us all slaves.

His relation to parties and men and our country was, that his cordial and ardent support of Lincoln's Administration, when so many thousands were hesitating, was a promise of success. His neglect or lethargy, or an indifferent support, would have been an omen of deadly peril; for there were thousands of men who had lived so long in pandering and giving way to the slave power, that without his dauntless and unflinching leadership the North would have been precipitated into disagreements, angry disputes, and divisions.

After his all-winter contest, where so many had weakened and failed, he had serious fears up to the inauguration, whether the separation could be prevented. The great senatorial Republican leaders were timid and faltering in the face of the crisis. Seward, Chase, and Greeley seemed alarmed, hesitatingly conservative, and full of new compromises. Greeley was badly disgusted, in his uneven temper, to the point of letting the South go.

Many of our best men in Congress did the best work, and that which helped so well, by being patient, firm, and discreet. Mr. Lincoln was at home, where he could do no better than prudently get ready for the greater struggle, while for the time in Congress Douglas was the real leader, in whom the cause of the Union rested. While others were full of compromise and concessions, he stoutly contended for submission to law and a Constitutional inauguration of Mr. Lincoln. He prevailed, and by wonderful perseverance in unsurpassed management won the greatest forensic battle of our country. This will be conceded when the clouding excitements of that peril-laden winter are cleared away. He came home a weary, wornout man, nearer the end of his labors than we realized. It was a wonder, indeed, when we remember that he, on the side of the Union, and Jefferson Davis on the side of the conspiring Rebellion, were the great leaders in the culminating storm. There were hundreds of willing and eager men to do all they could; but none to lead like him.

The contest came and passed, and was a furious passage in the conflict that ran so deep and strong as to require a marvelous man, such as he was, to lead. He seemed to be mysteriously strengthened, held up and kept able for his work. In this God accomplished his plan, and kept Douglas in the perilous front. He alone was the right man through that direful winter, when a serious blunder would likely have wrecked a century of freedom. As the brief calm of the approaching storm quieted the excitement for a little while, he laid down his heavy load at the feet of his own people, when the other coming leader was leaving the same people to take up the same load, with the burden heavier than ever. In this we read again that God had the man ready when the hour came.

In his conversation Douglas continued: "As soon as I am a little rested and feel better by the quiet and invigorating breezes of Lake Michigan, in a few weeks I expect to make a campaign through the border States, where I would rather go now, than to any other section. Especially do I want to go through Missouri and Kentucky, meeting the people not only in the larger towns and cities, but in the country settlements, where we can have two or three meetings a day. I want to meet them by thousands, to talk and reason with them against this madness of secession, murder, war, and destruction. In prompt and effective campaigning like this I feel that I can save many of them who are plunging headlong into this stream of ruin.

"I am much encouraged by my renewed and closer relations to Mr. Lincoln. He has grown and developed to a better manhood and more individual strength of character as the weighty responsibilities have been settling down upon ·him. He bears as well the constant and vexing little things, as to who will get this and that place, and who will not, better than hasty and impatient men. In thinking over it I expect to see him reach the higher and more successful diplomacy, for I know he is training himself to the most patient, careful, and comprehensive attention to public affairs I have ever known.

"In.the last two months at Washington I have enjoyed the closest relations with him, at his desire as well as my own. In my long years at the Capital I have become acquainted with all our public men, and have learned how to know and estimate them. This knowledge I have been anxious to give the President, and he. has been appreciative of it. I made it a part of my duty to see and talk with ·him for an hour or two almost every day when best suited to his convenience. We talked of the Southern leaders and our estimates of them, in which he became very much interested. I have known them all personally for years. He agreed with me that there are a dozen or more of them, who are the best qualified and most experienced men in our public and executive affairs. These are well sustained in the Capital and in the lower slave States, who are among the most capable, daring, and audacious leaders that ever went into any revolt, and Davis is the leader and master, as high above all of them as Calhoun was in his day.

"Besides being a pleasant duty, it was a renewal of our long and varied relations. I made a friendly call on him· very soon after his arrival in Washington, and assured him that I would cordially and sincerely sustain him as the lawfully elected and qualified President of the United States. He was at once the Lincoln of the older days, when we were almost boys together. He welcomed me· in a greeting as warm-hearted and appreciative as I had made my visit and avowal sincere and earnest. From that time we arranged for meetings to suit our convenience, his manifold cares, and my feeble condition. He was anxious to know and measure the extent and strength of the rising revolt, and listened carefully to what I knew of the men, and my opinions concerning them, particularly of the irreconcilable leaders. We had little difference; but he was surprised at my estimate of Davis and my belief that Breckinridge would soon join him. In the latter opinion I sincerely hope I am mistaken.

"Of Davis I said: 'He is an ardent, presevering student, who has an exact and critical knowledge of all our public affairs. He has had unusual opportunity to study them through his long public service of almost a lifetime. He is a soldier of merit and distinction, with acquaintance and varied experience, through the Mexican and Indian Wars, for perhaps fifteen years. He has been a representative, senator, or Cabinet officer ever since the Mexican War. He is a States'-rights advocate; but, above all, the politician and determined leader, whose willful purpose is stronger than any party belief or Constitutional restriction. If his plans to force slavery into Kansas had been successful, he fully expected to succeed Buchanan. He is a close follower of the ideas and plans of Calhoun, whose ambition was to found a slave republic, with Mexico, Central America, and the West Indies included. Davis is a capable, brave, and daring leader, who will be cautious and conservative only, because he has had long experience and training, where defeat has often sobered him. He will be at the head of their rebellion, in both civil and military leadership. He is discreet and reasonable enough to want the appearance of an undivided council about him; but with less suavity, discretion, and pleasing address, he is stronger and more inflexible than was Calhoun, the great secessionist. He will contend to the last hope, and may even retire to Mexico or some lesser State when defeated, to continue his efforts to found a slave nation.'

"President Lincoln asked me how long before I believed they had an actual plan for secession in progress. I replied: 'That from the days of Calhoun, perhaps before the encounter with Jackson, they had fully determined, with him as leader, to make this a slave country, or separate and make as strong a one in numbers and territories to our South. In proof of this, every possible extension of slavery was made southward, and all sorts of contrived obstacles were put in the way of concessions of territory to us, for extensions north and north-westward. With Calhoun and Davis out of the way, what is known as British Columbia would have been ours long since. It is now legitimately ours.

" 'The strength of the slave power is in cotton, sugar, and rice, all of which can be produced in great quantities in the lower slave States, while the more healthy border States raise the Negroes for the Southern States' supply. It is a productive and nation-attempting enterprise, in which the profits are counted by thousands of millions, with the promise of unusual profits and increase. They are no less nor more than greedy men, who will oppress men everywhere, where the profits promise so many millions, unless men rise up to fight and die for their liberties as our fathers did. Money in such quantities as the few in the South make out of its staple products can always be used to corrupt governments and subvert liberties, when used on the ignorant, the idle, and the unemployed.'

"Another day, Mr. Lincoln asked me why I seemed so sure that Breckinridge would join them, for since he presided so fairly and impartially in the counting and announcing the vote for President and Vice-President, he had been more hopeful about him. I replied, 'that he did that service well; but he understood very well that we had otherwise provided for it if he in any way declined or neglected his duty as presiding officer of the Senate. If there had been any appearance or disinclination on his part, we would have passed a resolution at once relieving him, and would have done so. No, that was not significant. At the time they wanted to show fairness. They were not ready for any neglect of duty that would bring a rupture then. The refusal to count the vote would have been a violent one, and the effect would have been strongly against them in the border States, even in Virginia. I believe that if Davis had been presiding, the result would have been the same.

" 'One of their reasons for seceding, as they so loudly declared, was your election; hence according to their avowal their desire was that you should be President, better to show the antagonism, the sectional hatred of the Northern people. Since their failure to introduce slavery into Kansas they have been shaping every movement for separation. They do not believe there will be very strong or continued resistance; and if there is fighting, Washington City will be an easy prey for them; with it in their hands we will soon agree to their terms. Their chief object now is, under one pretense or another, to unite all the slave States in secession.

" 'My reason for putting Breckinridge among their chief leaders is, that he has consorted and associated with them. He is more discreet, and in some other ways a stronger man than Davis. There has been a small cabal of them in the Senate who have counseled in some room or corner of it every day. While Davis has been considered the first or chief in this little knot of senators, Breckinridge or Benjamin has always been present, and as regularly considered the next to Davis.

"They had information in advance before the breakup in Buchanan's Cabinet, and were always ready and together, where they enjoyed the reading of those long-drawn-out State papers of Buchanan's and Black's, who you remember virtually conceded all the secessionists desired; that the States could secede as they elected to go; that we could not use force to restrain them, and that we had no Government, only as the States chose to remain.

" 'I told Black one day in the presence of several in the Senate chamber: "You and President Buchanan have written and determined yourselves out of office. If the States can secede and dissolve the Nation, and no force can be used in restraint in your opinion, the President and all of you who so believe should in all decency go home and leave the offices to more patriotic men. You seem to think and talk, as you have written yourselves, officially out of existence. We need no officers, if we have no laws to enforce. Nations have withered by treason, treachery, and decay; but you are the first officers I ever remember to have heard of, being executors of a Nation's laws, who have ever consented to a Government's overthrow for lack of power to enforce its laws. Indeed, you should retire." Mr. Black retired from this argument in a high state of anger, and so I left him.

" 'Breckinridge was always one of these in counsel. These were the chief leaders among them in about the order I have given them. General Cass, Senators Pugh and Stuart, and full twenty repesentatives agreed that their leaders were classed about as follows: Jefferson Davis, Breckinridge, Benjamin, the chief leaders; then following, Mason, Toombs, Slidell, Hunter, Clingman, Pickens, and Stephens. Then there were outside, roaming around, the Rhetts, Yancey, Letcher, Wise, Jo Brown, Yulee, Mallory, and a full hundred more with varying capacities and abilities for mischief, down to such as Wigfall, in great numbers, who are making themselves leaders as inclination and opportunities offer. Representative Frank Blair, Jr., can tell you much more about Breckinridge and many others also. He knows Breckinridge well, and believes he is as capable a leader as Davis, who besides has a wider influence in the border and Western slave States than any man among them.'

"After this, Mr. Lincoln looked sad and disappointed, saying: 'Your information seems conclusive. I would be glad to believe there is room for mistake; but there is hardly reason to doubt what you say. I am glad to be forewarned, and to know what you have told me about them.' In this way together we went over all their leaders, present and prospective, as far as I knew them.

"When the occasion comes, Breckinridge will take the field, and I believe that, if it becomes necessary, Davis will do so. I am sure he will do so if no distinctly capable and conspicuous soldier appears among them to inspire confidence in his leadership, where Davis, as a military leader, will fight as long as they have men and means.

"Benjamin, Mason, Hunter, Slidell, Clingman, and the leaders who have been most active in bringing on the revolt, will tire of the sameness of military rule and the despotism of it under Davis and the few with whom he shares his power, and will, I think, be getting away to Europe on some errand or other. Stephens is not trusted by them, and is sure to be carefully watched. Toombs would be the most aggressive among them and the greatest blusterer for awhile; but he is so hot-tempered that he is likely to have a dozen angry disputes with them, and will very soon neutralize himself.

"Who will be their prominent military leaders besides those mentioned, as well as our own, is a doubtful matter, to be developed in the future. It is almost fifteen years since the close of the Mexican War, and those of our little army most prominent in that have aged so that their days of field service have gone, or mostly they have passed beyond. Of those left, there are Twiggs, Quitman, Bragg, and Sydney Johnston, who may be expected to take the side of the South as their age permits. There is also General Harney, a strong Southern man, quite old, and of doubtful loyalty. He has had, till lately, the important command at St. Louis. I think a younger and entirely reliable soldier should succeed him at once, which I am sure will be done. Colonel Robert Lee, of General Scott's staff. a Virginian, is very popular in Washington. The old general is said to think well of his military capacities; but he is said to be wavering in his idea of duty, whether it is to his country or his State. When any Southern officer of the army or navy does this, it is safe to count him against us.

"Of the older officers of the rank of General I remember General Wool, and the old commander himself, Winfield Scott, who, if he were no more aged and worn than he was through the Mexican War, would be, by all odds, the most competent leader of our armies to-day; but his time for the campaigns of war has gone. He has been one of the powers of the Government for more than a generation, and is a patriotic man among treacherous swarms, whom a hundred Virginias could not turn against his country. He is man and soldier yet, and, though old and passing to a better reward, is one of the mightiest men in the land, a patriot whose sword, as his name, will never be soiled with a cloud or taint of treason.

"I know General Wool, Colonels Robert Anderson, E. Sumner, and several younger men of our small military force, and a few officers of our smaller, but more widely-scattered navy. These I believe will be a nucleus prepared and ready, around which will grow the strongest, most intelligent, therefore the most reliable, military and naval forces which the world has seen for centuries. The American is among the best-informed, the most daring and venturesome, and the most capable of all the races of men, as I learned from a personal inspection of the armies and navies of Europe only a few years since.

"I know that, under the favor of God, the grandsons of the Revolutionary patriots will not see our country separated or dismembered until they are not only beaten, but destroyed, in war; and I feel as certain that hosts as brave as those honored sires or those who saved liberty under Cromwell, or that perished by thousands around the old

Iron Duke at Waterloo, will not suffer the Union to perish or let a single State be torn or wrested from us, and will gather in thousands from the Atlantic to the Pacific under the old flag.

"If they only knew it, these hot-tempered Southern leaders are preparing for the most terrible killing, loss of life, ruin, and destruction of property the world has known in a thousand years. I have been blamed and denounced almost without limit for making concessions to them, which I have done in the hope that it would lead to a peaceful settlement of our differences. Doing so, I have gone to the verge of danger, where I could go no farther without a sacrifice of the liberties of our people, and where it would be cowardly to go farther.

"We are now, it seems, where nothing but bloody war or ruin will quench their rising fury, where, because I must, I say: 'Come on with your reeking cohorts, and we will meet you with thousands and hundreds of thousands of as brave men as ever lived, who know they have but once to die, that no other death is so welcome as to go down heroically contending for the rights and liberties of men, which our forefathers baptized in their blood and left us as a heritage. Come on; I am ready, and our great State will send legions who will open the great river to the Gulf alone, if necessary.'

"I have great faith in President Lincoln. I have known him a lifetime. While we have disputed, antagonized, and stoutly contended with each other, we have lived in and believed in one country. I have done what I could to avert the coming and threatening struggle. I have been in it to the extent of my ability long before him, when now I am pleased—yes, joyful—that he so sincerely appreciates and understands my real position.

"When I recover a little, as God spares me, I will return to the contest and go into the strife wherever I can do the most service. If personal sacrifice of any kind will aid in saving our country, it shall be freely given. To you personally I am thankful for your and your father's friendship, and so to all—to those who have and those who have not voted for me. We are one body of men for our country now. And, in closing, I am more than thankful to know that I could not have served a better, more intelligent, braver, or more patriotic people. I go with your interest in my heart, as I do with your prayers for my early recovery."

He was with us at Springfield almost two days, during which he saw and counseled with more than a thousand friends and acquaintances. It was a time when the people were in a state of great tension and anxiety. The war had actually begun. The madness was in progress. Fort Sumter had fallen. The flag of freedom had gone down in shocking disaster, humiliated, torn, and dishonored at the hands of some of our own people, turned to parricides and destroyers of their own liberties. All were pleased and overjoyed, not only in our own State, but wherever the Republic had friends, to know of the brave counsel and heroic stand of Douglas, that filled their lives with new hopes for our country.

He stirred up more than a million able-bodied men, able to fight—as brave Americans as ever lived—to a full sense of their duty and the priceless value of our free institutions. As he folded his mantle about him to lay himself down to rest, after his twenty years' continuing contest, he saw these springing to the front lines for the desperate strife, in serried lines, for duty, with Grant, Logan, McClernand, Oglesby, Wyman, Fouke, Morrison, Coler, and a hundred other gallant leaders in our own and other States. To all the parting was sad, mingled with the best hope of the people for his welfare and recovery. To many of us it was as if one of our own household had passed away.

MONTGOMERY BLAIR

SIMON CAMERON

WILLIAM H. SEWARD

SALMON P. CHASE

WILLIAM PITT FESSENDEN

CHAPTER XLIX.

WHEN Mr. Lincoln was inaugurated and his Cabinet approved without mishap or unfriendly demonstration of any kind, it was a great relief to meet and pass the notable events without jar or disturbance. There was no trouble because timely and ample means had been provided to prevent it.

With a Republican President legally installed, with the certain support of the loyal Democracy of the free States, the time and opportunity was at hand for the successful inauguration of the principles and policies of the party which had elected its President and Vice-President. Both branches of Congress were Republican, as they had been from the retirement of the seceders in January and February. It was the almost invariable custom to introduce a new policy on the accession of a new or opposition party. On Mr. Lincoln's inauguration this rule was at once set aside. In place of organizing a party Government, he made it the chief purpose of his Administration to save the Nation from destruction. He did this as a work of high statesmanship, when danger was so imminent and probable from its well-organized foes. To this end he sought the help of all loyal men and party organizations.

President Lincoln's grasp of all there was in any subject was so instant and strong, his patience and attention to everything deserving his care were so tireless, that nothing of what he held or came to him as a duty was ever neglected. In illustration, his mastery of detail, during the Lincoln

555

and Douglas campaign of 1858, he knew the political standing of every State newspaper, daily or weekly, of which there were several hundred in the more than one hundred counties, and he had personal acquaintance with almost every one of their publishers, whom he could call by name, and knew his home and his paper on meeting them. In the summer of 1864, when the movement to nominate Secretary Chase against him for President was at its height, a good friend, in talking it over, said it was strong enough to need his attention, and was likely more than he believed it was. Mr. Lincoln said nothing at the time, but on meeting the friend some two weeks later, said: "I've been looking up Mr. Chase's campaign in his own State. I sent for a copy of every political newspaper published in Ohio. More than half of the Republican papers are for me, a quarter of the others are either careless or silent, and not quite one-fourth of them are for him. Of the Democratic press, several are friendly, and some quite pronounced in saying my re-election is the best thing that can be done. Not one of these favors Chase; but all are against him. Until they get his campaign in better fix at home, I do n't think it will amount to much. It is too small a movement to fight hard, and I really believe that his daughter and the Cincinnati papers are about all there is of it. He surely does not expect success, and I do not intend to treat him as though he did."

When the condition of the country became the subject of so much dread and alarm, from the assembling of Congress in December, 1860, it is true that his situation at Springfield did not give him the facilities and opportunities for counsel and consideration he should have had through that perilous winter. All this he realized, but with the belief that he could do no better than patiently wait. He was a man who employed every resource and always prepared himself for his duties, so as to be ready for every emergency. In this preparation he held correspondence with reliable and well-informed friends at Washington and elsewhere all over the country, including several in the border and more southern States. This correspondence took his time and attention, and gave him an infallible index to the course of public sentiment that was far better than doing nothing. It was light on his part, as he was not writing or giving opinions. His main object was to get into direct communication with those who were to be in his Cabinet and other reliable men who would keep him fully informed of the condition of affairs in their several States and the progress of the revolt. He corresponded freely with those who were to be in office with him and some very good friends in Congress, relying chiefly on E. B. Washburn and Owen Lovejoy, of our State. Besides, he had a long list of newspapers for his inspection every day. These, with his wonderful memory, his strong, discerning, and great reasoning powers, soon made him the best-informed man in public affairs in all the land. With an interest that no man surpassed, he watched and saw how strong men faltered and failed in the face of rising rebellion. One of the most painful aspects was to see how business and moneyed interests floundered and fell flat down in nearly all of our cities and money centers in the East, while Davis, Breckinridge, Benjamin, and their associates were laughing in anticipation of what an easy capture the sordid merchants and cowardly mechanics would prove to the brave and fearless sons of the South. These were confident of a peaceful separation or a war that would soon be over, with all the plunder they desired.

Throughout that dread winter there were several able and competent leaders in Congress against secession. They were men of wisdom and experience, who had risen to distinction and high political position in from ten to thirty years of faithful service; but no one of them displayed the talent and fitness to consolidate the several loyal factions into

one strong party against Davis and his submissive and obedient conspirators.

The Democratic party had gone to pieces, as it was commonly told, leaving no one among the many who had served
and risen to place within its ranks so competent to lead as
Douglas.   Black was left as the leader of Buchanan's
stranded Administration, so full of his own conceit that
he made no effort to help reunite the party under Douglas.
Had the latter lived, he would have been the real leader
of the masses of the party; but Black, full of selfishness
and the spirit of the pro-slavery revolt, left his party to
be the prey of dividing factions and sectional leaders.

With this dissolution going on in the Democratic party,
it was an unusual opportunity for a statesman and strategist
of high power, of which Mr. Lincoln availed himself on his
arrival.   Until he did so, there was no harmony of action
or settled policy agreed on by the leaders of the dissolving Democracy or the incoming Republicans.   The Republican party, although it had elected a President and Vice-
President, and held a majority in both Houses, had no
leader who was recognized by all as such in Congress.   This
feature of the condition of political parties and leaders
through the winter must be briefly related to understand
the prevailing cross-purposes and disorganization, the delicate situation and the difficult and patient attention it
took on the part of Mr. Lincoln to get loyal men of every
shade firmly united on one strong line of policy.

It was the field for the trial of any man's real capacities.   Mr. Lincoln came and took the opportunity.   All
others had failed, except Douglas, and he was in position
to do no more than to hold his faction, which he so ably
did.   If Lincoln failed, the best hope was a peaceful separation and division, with two angry, contending sections
as new nations.   The following letter of Senator Toombs
fairly shows the determination of the conspirators to force

secession before any action of Congress, as the letter was written less than two weeks after it had assembled, when it was not known what measures of compromise or conciliation would be agreed to, if any.

The letter is full of misleading statements, which was characteristic of the means and plans to force the Southern people into rebellion; but it lacks nothing on the main subject of secession. It ran as follows:

"WASHINGTON, December 23, 1860.

"SIR,—I came here to secure your Constitutional rights and to demonstrate that you can get no guarantee for these rights from your Northern Confederates.

"The whole subject was referred to a committee of thirteen in the Senate. I was appointed on that committee and accepted the trust. I submitted propositions which, so far from receiving a decided support from a single member of the Republican party of the committee, were treated with derision and contempt. A vote was taken in the committee on amendments to the Constitution proposed by Hon. J. J. Crittenden; and each and all of them were voted against unanimously by the black Republican members of the committee. In addition to these facts, a majority of the black Republican members of the committee declared that they had no guarantees to offer, which was silently acquiesced in by the other members.

"The black Republican members of the committee are representative men of the party and section, and, to the extent of my information, truly represent them.

"The committee of thirty-three on Friday adjourned for a week, without any vote on all the propositions then before them that day. It is controlled by the black Republicans—your enemies—who only seek to amuse you with delusive hopes until your election, that you may defeat the friends of secession.

"If you are deceived by them, it shall not be my fault. I have put the test fairly and frankly. It is decisive against you now. I tell you, on the faith of a true man, that all further looking to the North for security for your Constitutional rights ought to be instantly abandoned. It is fraught with nothing but ruin to yourselves and to your posterity. Secession by the fourth day of March next should be thundered from the ballot-box by the unanimous voice of Georgia on the second day of January next. Such a voice will be your best guarantee for liberty, tranquillity, and glory.   "R. TOOMBS."

To show the heartless falsity of this letter and similar statements about the want of "security for Constitutional rights" is best shown in the resolutions of Senator Clark, of New Hampshire, which were adopted by the Republican Senate in January, 1861, as follows:

"*Resolved,* That the provisions of the Constitution are ample for the preservation of the Union and the protection of all the material interests of the country; that it needs to be obeyed rather than amended; and that an extrication from our present dangers is to be looked for in the strenuous efforts to preserve the peace, protect the public property, and enforce the laws, rather than in guarantees for peculiar interests, compromises for particular difficulties, or concessions to unreasonable demands.

"*Resolved,* That all attempts to dissolve the present Union or overthrow or abandon the present Constitution, with the hope or expectation of constructing a new one, are dangerous, illusory, and destructive; that, in the opinion of the Senate of the United States, no such reconstruction is practicable; and therefore, to the maintenance and existence of the present Union and Constitution should be all the energies of departments of the Government and the efforts of all good citizens."

These resolutions contained all the patching-up and conciliation that should have been offered to the South, or any
other section, as we had done no more than exercise our
Constitutional rights in the election of a President. We had
quietly submitted to their continuous violation of law under
pro-slavery Presidents for twenty years or more. In place
of a strong, united policy in the spirit of these revolution-
ists, the Republicans seemed stunned, alarmed, and fearful
at their success. Business communities commenced their
palavers for an impossible peace. New York, Philadelphia,
and even staid and sober-minded Boston, were tumbling
over one another, haranguing their people and petitioning
Congress to give more guarantees and privileges to the slaveholders, who were laughing at them while up to their eyes
in the opening insurrection. As Toombs put it, they had
determined on secession as their best "guarantee for liberty,
tranquillity, and glory." They had passed the trimmers'
period of compromises and concessions. To them it was
secession in peace or secession bloody, as the exigencies of
the violent movement might require.

Something of the alarm and dread of war that prevailed, principally in the commercial cities of the East, may
be understood from an article published on November 30th,
shortly after Mr. Lincoln's election, in the Albany *Journal.*
Thurlow Weed, the editor, was supposed to represent Senator Seward and his followers. The *Journal* said, among
other things:

"The suggestions, in a recent number of the *Journal,*
of a basis of settlement of differences between the North
and the South, have, in awakening attention and discussion,
accomplished their purpose. We knew that in no quarter
would these suggestions be more distasteful than with our
most valued friends. We knew that the accession would be regarded as inopportune. We knew also the provocations
in the controversy were with our opponents. Nothing is

easier, certainly, than to demonstrate the rightfulness of the Republican party, a party that was created by the repeal of the Missouri Compromise, and owes its recent trial to the determination of slavery to extend and perpetuate its political dominion, aided by two successive and besotted Federal Administrations.

"But unfortunately the pending issue is to be decided irrespective of its merits. The election of Mr. Lincoln is the pretext for, and not the cause of, disunion. The design originated with Mr. Calhoun, who, when he failed to be chosen President of the whole Union, formed the scheme of dividing it, and devoted the remainder of his life in training the South up to the treason now impending. He had, in McDuffie, Hayne, and other statesmen, eloquent auxiliaries. The contagion extended to other Southern States, when, by diligent activity, discipline, and organization, the whole people of the Gulf States have come to sympathize with their leaders.

"Those leaders know that Mr. Lincoln will administer the Government in strict and impartial obedience to the Constitution and law, seeking only the safety of the whole people through the prosperity and glory of the Union. For this reason they precipitate the conflict, fearing that, if they wait for a provocation, none will be furnished, and that, without fuel, their fires will be extinguished.

"This question, involving the integrity of the Union and the experiment of self-government, we repeat, will be decided irrespective of its merits. Three miserable months of a miserable Administration must drag its slow length along before the Republican Administration can act or be heard. During these three months its baleful influences will be seen and felt in the demoralization of public sentiment. Its functionaries and its journals will continue to malign the North and inflame the South, leaving, on the 4th of March, to their successors an estate as wretchedly incumbered and dilapidated as imbecile or spendthrift ever bequeathed. Mismanaged as that estate has been, and wretched as its present condition is, we regard it as an inestimable, priceless, and precious inheritance, an inheritance which we are unwilling to see wholly squandered before we come into possession.

"To our dissenting friends, who will not question our devotion to freedom, however much they may mistrust our judgment, we submit a few earnest admonitions:

"First. There is imminent danger of the dissolution of the Union.

"Second. The danger originated in the ambition and cupidity of men who desire a Southern despotism and in the fanatical zeal of Northern Abolitionists, who seek the emancipation of slaves regardless of consequences.

"Third. The danger can only be averted by such moderation and forbearance as will draw out, strengthen, and combine the Union sentiment of the whole country.

"The disunion sentiment is paramount at least in seven States, while it divides and distracts as many more. Now, is it wise to deceive ourselves with the impression that the South is not in earnest? It is in earnest; and the sentiment has taken hold of all classes with such blind vehemence as to crush out the Union sentiment. It will be said that we have done nothing wrong and have nothing to offer. This, supposing it true, is precisely the reason why we should both propose and offer whatever may, by possibility, avert the evils of civil war and prevent the destruction of our hitherto unexampled blessings of Union."

This has been given at some length because the Weed and Seward faction of the Republican party was the strongest and largest. The proposed remedy, after thus haranguing and hectoring the party leaders for the effect it would produce in the border slave States, and perhaps to influence Mr. Lincoln, was that all, North and South, should unite in calling and submitting all disputes to a National Constitutional Convention.

The country became impressed to a great extent with that idea of settling our difficulties. All the old set of compromisers, except Davis and his united cotton States, believed that two hundred able and capable leaders of all parties, except the secessionists, in and about Congress, could make another compromise. These united in a sincere effort to have such a Convention called or agree on some Constitutional amendment under the lead of good old Senator Crittenden, of Kentucky, who thrummed along all through that dreary winter to reach such agreement. While they were doing this, with the Albany *Journal's* assistance, it was discovered that such emollient policy was having no effect, and that the seceders did not want, and would not have, either a Convention or the proposed amendment, but that they were in the field on the question, pure and simple, for separation or the abdication of Lincoln, who had been fairly elected.

Although the Eastern cities were full of alarmed traders and dickerers and an unnumbered lot of affrighted and skulking politicians, if such a Convention had been called, the free States would not have made any further concessions to the Southern leaders. That was as definitely settled in the Charleston Convention as anything ever could be, where the free State Democracy openly declared that they had made their last concession to slavery. The people, too, except the timid gentlemen mentioned, were angered more than usual at the steady encroachments and oppressions of the slave-power. They were very tired of the blatant, loud-mouthed braggadocio and defiant manners of the plantation Negro-drivers. As firmly as any great people ever settled anything, they did, that the slave States could live contented under our Constitution, as we did; and, if nothing but war or disunion would satisfy them, as they had so offensively declared and threatened for years, it was only left that they should submit or have all the war they desired.

Our people did not desire war; but their concessions to avoid it had all been given before 1860, and had been held by the South to be given because of our cowardly fears. We had reached the place where war was the lesser of the evils confronting us. Our liberties were of more value than life, and our people were ready to defend them. We have been particular to make this narration, to show the broken-up and divided condition of the Republican, as well as all other parties. The truth is, there were no parties left that could enforce their declared beliefs. The free State people—Democrats or Republicans—were without leaders stronger than Douglas, who led the free State Democracy through the winter to its highest duty; but he was passing away, with his work all done, and Seward, who was leading the Republicans, no man could tell whither.

A new leader, and a great one, was so imperatively demanded by the conditions that, unless he appeared very soon, disunion would be a certainty; and the question ran everywhere: Is President Lincoln the man? Has he the great qualities to be the chief leader in this culminating crisis, who can adopt and pursue a policy to save the Union?

By what we have seen, Mr. Seward—strong, capable, and experienced as he was—had failed and fallen in the face of the rising storm. Weed and Seward stood for concession and compromise when such propositions were derided and provoked ridicule. It was not what they had agreed to do, but that against men armed and equipping for war they would hesitate or stop to make any concessions. They, perhaps, did not intend to make any that were important, as they believed, but to hesitate or make any was considered no more than weakness and cowardice by the arming Southern people.

However, there were a great many Republicans who were willing, with no assurance that it would be accepted, or even pacificatory, to make New Mexico, including Arizona, a slave Territory and eventually two slave States; to fasten the Fugitive-slave Law more firmly upon us; to pay in money for every escaped slave; and to request the free States, as far as possible, to suppress all organizations against slavery. The fear of war had led them to make the concessions to slavery that had destroyed both the Whig and Democratic parties, and had completely overthrown such leaders as Pierce, Buchanan, Cushing, Black, Marcy, and Cass, Democrats; and Clay, Webster, Fillmore, Scott, and Corwin, Whigs, and a hundred lesser ones in either party.

The situation was a perilous one, commencing almost immediately after Mr. Lincoln's election. It was full of the danger that a serious mistake or blunder would provoke and bring a hopeless division of his own party, when it was doubtful to many whether the Union could be saved with all parties of Union men firmly united. He was so situated that he could only counsel patience and forbearance for four tedious, dispute-provoking months. Whatever the Weed-Seward faction, like all others, were to be, he had to conciliate and unite them. He began, not by proposing a policy or contending with them, but in requesting Mr. Seward to be Secretary of State. In this way he opened a friendly correspondence, the basis of union of party effort that fixed Seward's mind more intently on that than concessions. The halting, hesitating condition of the Weed-Seward faction made it apparent that a master leader would need to take hold and bring about a united and harmonious combination of parties before it could ever propose a policy for the conduct of government. The Republicans of the Eastern States were sorely divided, as we have related. In Washington and through the border States, free and slave, the questions discussed all winter were either as to the advisability of holding

GIDEON WELLES

EDWIN M. STANTON

WILLIAM DENNISON

EDWARD BATES

CALEB B. SMITH

a National Constitutional Convention, or whether to agree
to what were known as the Crittenden Resolutions, the purposes of which were to offer to make slavery more secure, as
related.

A great many well-informed Union men were anxious
over the excited discussions these questions aroused, when,
if either plan was adopted, it would not have been acceptable
to those in insurrection; and they feared further division.
To those who talked with him at Springfield respecting these,
Mr. Lincoln said: "Let them proceed. These discussions over
proposed Conventions and amendments will do less harm
than the more angry discussions over whether their States
will secede or not. They are in that kind of discussion and
hotly engaged in it further South. It is better to talk of
unreasonable things inside than any proposition to go outside."

When Mr. Seward had accepted, he invited Mr. S. P.
Chase, then a senator-elect from Ohio, to be another member
of his Cabinet. He had been a senator from Ohio before,
elected in 1849, serving his full term of six years. He was
learned, capable, and one of the most pronounced anti-slavery
members. He vigorously opposed the compromise measures
of 1850, advocated and passed under the leadership of Mr.
Clay, and later opposed as strongly the repeal of the Missouri Compromise in 1854. In 1854 he was elected governor
of Ohio, and re-elected by a larger majority. At that time
Senator Chase was one of the most ambitious and fearless
of all the prominent leaders of the Republican party. He
was the antithesis of Seward and all others who had hope
in further efforts at conciliation. He had the restless disposition and the daring spirit, where, once back in the Senate
in that turbulent upheaval, he would have been at once
the most conspicuous leader of the aggressive element of
the party. This Mr. Lincoln understood, and foreseeing,
made him a part of his Administration, placing him where

his high talents did the best that could have been done for the country, as a great financier and helper in the ways and means for war. This action of Mr. Lincoln probably prevented the most dangerous schism possible, then threatening the party, until he could, in his comprehending, patient way, harmonize and consolidate its organization.

Shortly after the election, Francis P. Blair, Jr., of St. Louis, came to Springfield, where he held a two-days' conference before going to Washington. He was a perceptive and generous-hearted man, trained to public life, who always inspired confidence and energy in everybody about him. This was well shown afterwards in his gallant and well-timed service in saving Missouri, and his brilliant military career, with West Point and "Old Fossilism," in the War Office, against him. Mr. Blair had been one of the principals in the Lincoln movement from the beginning. · The Blairs were a leading power in political affairs from the days of Jackson. They were intelligent, well-informed men from Kentucky, with the ambitious desires that take men to the consideration of public affairs, heroic deeds, and war where great principles are involved. The father and eldest son, Montgomery, were then living in Maryland. In their more than one generation of service they had drawn to them and held hundreds of fast friends in many States, especially in the border States, who, at the opportune moment, did necessary and valiant service in our cause, in the extremity when the Union could not have been saved without it.

Mr. Lincoln trusted Mr. Blair fully, for which he had the best and most patriotic reasons, in recognition of faithful and efficient service. In return, Mr. Blair and all his friends trusted and sustained him with their skill, strength, and energy. Without this he could not have found others capable of doing and managing as they did, just right, in that critical juncture of the crisis. Regardless of what was said of the Blair family and the influences of the people

of the border States, it was one of the most fortunate associations of men in our political affairs, when Mr. Lincoln
wisely made the combination, that proved his wisdom in the
strategy of politics and war.

There was no chance for another such high political
affiliation, in the free and border slave States, then possible,
and it was just like Lincoln to make it; for, without harm to
any one, it was the strongest and best movement within his
grasp to keep several States out of the secession that would
certainly have divided the Republic. Mr. Blair, after this
full and friendly conference, proceeded to Washington, conferred with his father, brother, and their many friends in
and out of Congress and all over the country, without notice
or discussion, about this well-managed combination. This
brought to his support the strongest union of political leaders in the country, thus organizing, as he was holding back
patiently, a force that developed his power and statesmanship.

Another division of the Republicans, or perhaps a subdivision of the Seward-Tweed faction, was that made up
of those like Senator Anthony, a slow-going, yet a reliable
and conservative Republican of Rhode Island. He seemed
ready to give the South anything they wanted if they would
only not go to war; but he came up to the fighting standard
so well that he remained in the Senate until the war was
over, and till his death. While the Crittenden compromise
resolutions were under consideration in the Senate in January,
he said:

"I believe that if the danger that menaces us is to be
avoided at all, it must be by legislation, which is more ready,
more certain, and more likely to be satisfactory than Constitutional amendments. The main difficulty is the Territorial question. The demand of the senators on the other
side of the chamber, and of those whom they represent,
is that the territory south of the line of the Missouri Com-

promise shall be open to their peculiar property. All this territory [then embracing New Mexico and Arizona Territories as now organized], except the Indian Reservation, is within the limits of New Mexico, which, for a part of its northern boundary, runs up two degrees beyond that line. This is now a slave Territory, made so by Territorial legislation, and slavery exists there recognized and protected. Now, I am willing, so soon as Kansas can be admitted, to vote for the admission of New Mexico as a State, with such Constitution as the people may adopt.

"This disposes of all the territory that is adapted to slave-labor, or that is claimed by the South. It ought to settle the whole question. Surely, if we can dispose of all the territory that we have, we ought not to quarrel over that which we have not, and which we have no very honest way of acquiring. Let us settle the difficulties that threaten us now, and not anticipate those which may never come. Let the public mind have time to cool. Let us forget, in the general prosperity, the mutual dependence, and the common glory of our country, that we have ever quarreled over the question that we have put at rest; and perhaps when, in the march of events, the northern provinces of Mexico are brought under our sway, they may come in without a ripple on the political sea, whose tumultuous waves now threaten to ingulf us all in one common ruin.

"In offering to settle this question by the admission of New Mexico, we of the North who assent to it propose a great sacrifice and offer a large concession. We propose to take in a State that is deficient in population, and that possesses but imperfectly many of the elements of a member of the Union, and that will require, in one form or another, even after its admission, the aid of the General Government; but we make the offer in the spirit of compromise and good feeling, which we hope will be reciprocated.

"And now, Mr. President, I appeal to senators on the

other side, when we offer thus to bridge over seven-eighths
of the frightful chasm, will you not build the other eighth?
When, with outstretched arms, we approach you so near
that, by reaching out your hands, you can clasp ours in
the fraternal grasp from which they should never be separated, will you, with folded arms and closed eyes, stand upon
extreme demands, which you know we can not accept, and
for which, if we did, we could not carry our constituents?"

In addition to this, Charles Francis Adams, son of President John Quincy Adams, then a representative in Congress
from Boston, during this woeful winter of squatting and
backing down, in the debates made a proposition that the
Constitution be so amended that "no subsequent amendment thereto, having for its object any interference with
slavery, shall originate with any State that does not recognize
that relation within its own limits, or shall be valid without
the assent of every one of the States composing the Union."
Again, about two weeks later, in the House, addressing the
Southern members particularly, Adams said: "Where do we
stand? We offer to settle the question finally in all of the
present territory that you claim, by giving you every chance
of establishing slavery that you have any right to require
of us. You decline to take the offer because you feel it
will do you no good. Slavery will not go there. Why require protection where you will have nothing to protect?
All you appear to desire is New Mexico. Nothing else is
left; yet you will not accept it alone, because ten years of
experience have proved to you that protection has been of
no use thus far."

In passing this period we should remember that such
prominent leaders, and thousands who assumed, and, as far
as we know, did fairly represent their factions, were those
whom Mr. Lincoln had to unite in making up the strongest
union of Americans in the most perilous crisis of the Nation.

To do this he required, and in God's favor possessed, the

genius and higher statesmanship to lead and combine, sustained by able men and with all the means the people had to give.

In the discussion of the Compromise Measures of 1850, Daniel Webster said: " I look upon it, therefore, as a fixed fact, to use the current expression of the day, that California and New Mexico are both destined to be free, so far as they are to be settled at all; which, I believe, in regard to New Mexico, will be but partially for a great length of time; free by the arrangement of things ordained by the Power above us. I have therefore to say, in this respect, also, that this country is fixed for freedom to as many persons as shall ever live in it, by a less repealable law than which attaches to the holding of slaves in Texas; and I will say further, that if a resolution or a bill were now before us to provide a Territorial Government for New Mexico, I would not vote to put any prohibition into it whatever.

"Such a prohibition would be idle, as it respects any effect it would have upon the Territory, and I would not take pains uselessly to reaffirm an ordinance of nature, nor to re-enact the will of God. I would put in no Wilmot Proviso for the mere purpose of a taunt or a reproach; I would put into it no evidence of the votes of a superior power, exercised for no purpose but to wound the pride, whether a just and rational pride, or an irrational pride, of the citizens of the Southern States. I repeat, therefore, sir, as I do not propose to address the Senate often upon this subject, I repeat it, because I wish it to be distinctly understood that, for the reasons stated, if a proposition were now here to establish a Government for New Mexico, and it was moved to insert a prohibition of slavery, I would not vote for it.

"Sir, wherever there is a substantial good to be done, wherever there is a foot of land to be prevented from becoming slave territory, I am ready to assert the principle of the exclusion of slavery. I am pledged to it from the year 1837; I have been pledged to it again and again; and I will perform those pledges, but I will not do a thing unnecessarily that wounds the feeling of others, or that does discredit to my own understanding."

In the course of the same debate in the Senate in 1850, Henry Clay said: "I am extremely sorry to hear the senator from Mississippi [Jefferson Davis] say that he requires, first, the extension of the Missouri Compromise line to the Pacific; and also, that he is not satisfied with that, but requires, if I understand him correctly, a positive provision for the admission of slavery south of that line. And now, sir, coming from a slave State, as I do, I owe it to truth, I owe it to the subject, to say that no earthly power could induce me to vote for a specific measure for the introduction of slavery where it had not before existed, north or south of that line. Coming, as I do, from a slave State, it is my solemn, deliberate, and well-matured determination that no power, no earthly power, shall compel me to vote for the positive introduction of slavery, either north or south of that line.

"Sir, while you reproach, and justly, too, our British ancestors, for the introduction of this institution upon the Continent of America, I am, for one, unwilling that the posterity of the present inhabitants of California and New Mexico shall reproach us for doing just what we reproach Britain for doing to us. If the citizens of those Territories choose to establish slavery, I am for admitting them with such provisions in their Constitutions; but then it will be their own work, and not ours; and their posterity will have to reproach them, and not us, for forming Constitutions allowing the institution of slavery to exist among them."

As heretofore shown, the above and similar proposals concerning the extension of slavery made by these eminent leaders of the Whig party, with further concession for a more rigid Fugitive-slave-returning Law, were the stumbling-blocks over which these two great leaders fell in their ambitions to be President, and for which offending, as it appeared, with the defeat of General Scott for the same reasons, the Whig party dissolved.

Nevertheless, with an exact and complete knowledge of all the wreckages of men and parties which we have outlined, these later leaders, Weed, Seward, Anthony, Adams, and hundreds who had stoutly disagreed with Clay, Webster, Scott, and the Whig party, were willing, in 1861, to surrender quadruple as much, and to appear cowardly in doing it, to the horrid demands of the slaveholders.

Why, it has often been asked, could those later leaders agree to concede so much to slavery and politically survive? In part reply, the reasons are, the Whig party and its leaders, in good faith, gave slavery what they promised up to 1850; whereas these proposers in 1861 were not permitted to enact or fulfill any of their promises. Further, while some of them were clever and promising men, they were in no important act or movement, nor, as the term is applied, distinct or forceful leaders.

About this time, Horace Greeley published and distributed broadcast, through his New York *Tribune,* his unaccountable breakdown, which was, in reality, no more than a "dare you to do it" to the seceders. He and his followers, at least many of them, were indignant beyond expression with the failing and falling of trusted leaders. Rather than submit longer to the slave-robbing hierarchy, in a great impulse, without judgment, for free principles and free men, he wrote, in November, as soon as it was known that Mr. Lincoln was elected, the following:

"The people of the United States have indicated, according to the forms prescribed by the Constitution, their desire that Abraham Lincoln shall be their next President and Hannibal Hamlin their next Vice-President. A very large plurality of the popular vote has been cast for them, and a decided majority of electors chosen, who will undoubtedly vote for and elect them on the first Wednesday in December next. The electoral votes will be formally sealed up and forwarded to Washington, there to be opened and counted on a given day in February next, in the presence of both Houses of Congress; and it will then be the duty of Mr. John C. Breckinridge, as president of the Senate, to declare Lincoln and Hamlin duly elected President and Vice-President of these United States.

"Some people do not like this, as it is very natural. Dogberry discovered, a good while ago, that when two ride on a horse one must ride behind. That is not generally deemed the preferable seat; but the rule remains unaffected by that circumstance. We know how to sympathize with the defeated, for we remember how we felt when Adams was defeated, and Clay, and Scott, and Fremont. It is decidedly pleasanter to be on the winning side, when, as now, it happens also to be the right side.

"We sympathize with the afflicted; but we can not recommend them to do anything desperate. What is the use? They are beaten now; they may triumph next time; in fact, they have generally had their own way. Had they been subjected to the discipline of adversity so often as we have, they would probably bear it with more philosophy, and deport themselves more befittingly. We live to learn, and one of the most difficult acquirements is that of meeting reverses with graceful fortitude.

"The telegraph informs us that the cotton States are meditating a withdrawal from the Union because of Lincoln's election. Very well; they have a right to meditate, and meditation is a profitable employment of leisure. We have a chronic, invincible disbelief in disunion as a remedy for either Northern or Southern grievances. We can not see any necessary connection between the disease and this ultra-heroic remedy; still, we may say, if any one sees fit to meditate disunion, let him do so unmolested.

"That was a base and hypocritical saw that was once raised, at Southern dictation, about the ears of John Quincy Adams, because he presented the petition for the dissolution of the Union. The petitioner had a right to make the request, as it was the member's right and duty to present it; and now, if the cotton States consider the value of. the Union debatable, we maintain their right to discuss it.

"Nay, we hold, with Jefferson, to the inalienable right of communities to alter or abolish forms of government that have become oppressive or injurious; and if the Cotton States can do better out of the Union than in it, we insist on letting them go in peace. The right to secede may be revolutionary, but it exists, nevertheless; and we do not see how one party can have the right to do what another party has a right to prevent. We must resist the asserted right of any State to remain in the Union, and nullify or defy the laws thereof. To withdraw from the Union is quite another matter, and whenever a considerable section of our Union shall deliberately resolve to go out, we shall resist all coercive measures to keep them in. We hope never to live in a Republic where one section is pinned to the residue by bayonets.

"But while we thus uphold the practical liberty, if not the abstract right, of secession, we must insist that the step be taken, if ever it shall be, with the deliberation and gravity befitting so momentous an issue. Let time be given for reflection. Let the subject be fully canvassed before the people, and let a popular vote be taken in every case before secession is decreed. Let the people be told just why they are asked to break out of the Confederation. Let them have both sides of the question fully presented; let them reflect, deliberate, then vote; and let the act of secession be the echo of an unmistakable fiat. A judgment thus rendered, a demand for separation so backed, would be acquiesced in without the effusion of blood; or those who rushed on carnage, to defy and defeat it, would place themselves clearly in the wrong.

"The measures being inaugurated now in the cotton States, with a view to secession, seem to us destitute of gravity and legitimate force. They are the unmistakable evidence of haste, of passion, of distress of the popular judgment. They seem clearly intended to precipitate the South into rebellion before the baselessness of the clamors which have misled and excited her can be ascertained by the great body of her people. We trust that they will be confronted with calmness, with dignity, and with unwavering trust in the inherent strength of the Union and the loyalty of the American people."

Mr. Greeley, although a very well-informed man, a forcible and entertaining writer, who was conducting the most widely-read and circulated newspaper in the country, was, like thousands of many ordinarily well-balanced people, in a state of feverish excitement and uncertainty. Where organizations of all kinds seemed to be going wrong and giving way to disorder and chaos, when Churches, parties, civil and social, and what little military or naval forces we had, seemed to be going to pieces, he got into a fit of useless consternation, and foolishly replied to the secessionists that they might go if they dared.

President Buchanan, with the concurrence of Black, his Attorney-General, and others of his Cabinet, were about declaring, as Mr. Greeley agreed to above, "that a State could not be coerced." This was, in effect, that we had no Nation to save; for if the highest source of power existed in the State, and it could not be compelled to do anything by the Nation, even to the performance of its former voluntary association and allegiance with the other States to make a Nation, then, indeed, we were no more than an unorganized lot of States, all independent of each other and of the general Government.

The principle provocation to Mr. Greeley's loosely-drawn outbreak of indignation, and his proffer to the South, "Go if you dare," was the taunting arrogance of the South, and thousands of men, North and South, who should have had better sense and certainly more judgment, who boasted "that the North could not exist without the trade, good-will, and favor of the South."

In reply to this flaunting and impudent falsehood, if no more, he, like other independent people, in giving his reasons for writing the "Let-the-Union-slide" declaration, gave perhaps his best reasons about as follows: "The South had been so systematically, so outrageously deluded by demagogues on both sides of the slave-line, with regard to the nature and special importance of the Union to the North, that the Union was habitually represented as an immense boon conferred on the free States by the South, whose withdrawal would overwhelm us all in bankruptcy and ruin; that it might do something toward allaying this Southern inflammation to have it distinctly and plainly set forth that the North had no desire to enforce on the South the maintenance of an abhorred, detested Union."

Accordingly, he wrote his declaration, and slammed in the face of the gathering conspiracy his impulsive blast, daring them to do what they had been preparing to do for years. His paper fusilade, as things turned, led very few astray, if any. It was one that could not be defended on the grounds of law, reason, or expediency, and it was certainly very undignified for a great writer. It was a satisfaction, however, to the organizing South, and increased their belief that the North would not fight, and that there would be little, if any, resistance to their separation.

CHAPTER L.

A S we keep pace with these evidences of dissolving parties, demoralized people, and the general disordered state of affairs, we must bear in mind our main purpose we have for reciting these items here, some of which are referred to a second time. The difficulties were rising mountain high in the front of Mr. Lincoln when he came to Washington to shape a policy and build a party. For four long months he had to be silent, and could do no more than observe and grieve over the threatened divisions and falling of faithless leaders.

About November, 1860, the New York *Herald* said: "If, however, Northern fanaticism should triumph over us, and the Southern States should exercise their undeniable right to secede from the Union, then the city of New York, the river counties, the State of New Jersey, and, very likely, Connecticut, will separate from those New England and Western States where the black man is put upon a pinnacle above the white. New York City is for the Union first, and the gallant and chivalrous South afterward."

In accordance with this connivance and agreement to join the conspiracy of this city and surroundings, a dozen or more Northern papers sluiced their war-breeding presses until a stronger hand took the power of the Nation from the palsied hand of Buchanan's pusillanimous Administration. Quailing before the gaunt skeleton of want, distress, and war, they cowardly shrank back from the bloody work they did so much to provoke, and nothing willingly to repress. Under such outspoken disloyalty, Fernando Wood, then **mayor** of the city of New York, openly declared for weeks that the city and other surrounding towns and States would go with the South. For this he was not only not punished, but elected to Congress shortly afterward. The *Herald*, the New York paper referred to, procured one of the first-made Confederate flags for its use; but it never gained even the treasonable right to swing it to the breeze.

Later in the winter again it published a statement as follows: "For less than this, the election of Lincoln, our fathers seceded from Great Britain, and they left revolution organized in every State, to act whenever it is demanded by public opinion. The Confederation is held together only by public opinion. Each State is organized as a complete Government, holding the purse and wielding the sword, possessing the right to break the tie of the Confederation as a nation might break a treaty, and to repel coercion as a nation might repel invasion. Coercion, if it were possible, is out of the question."

In the preliminaries of New York State's adoption of the Constitution, in a letter to Alexander Hamilton, James Madison said:

"My Dear Sir,—Yours of yesterday is this instant come to hand, and I have but a few minutes to answer.

"I am sorry that your situation obliges you to listen to propositions of the nature you describe. My opinion is that a reservation of a right to withdraw, if amendments be not decided on under the form of the Constitution within a certain time, is conditional ratification; that it does not make New York a member of the new Union, and, consequently, that she could not be received on that plan. The Constitution requires an adoption *in toto* and forever. It has been so adopted by the other States.

"An adoption for a limited time would be as defective as an adoption of some of the articles only. In short, any condition whatever must vitiate the ratification. What the new Congress, by virtue of the power to admit new States, may be able and disposed to do in such a case, I do not imagine, as I suppose that it is not the material point at present. I have not a moment to add more than my fervent wishes for your success and happiness. The idea of a right to withdraw was started at Richmond, and considered as conditional ratification, which was itself abandoned as worse than a rejection. Yours,

"JAMES MADISON, JR."

This was the law of the Constitution as interpreted by one of its most careful and learned framers, as against the modern commercialism of New York, that was anxious to agree to secession, and ready, as their authorities said, to go into it. Senator Reverdy Johnson, of Maryland, who was intimate with and lived for a time in the same house with John C. Calhoun, in a letter to Mr. Everett about June, 1861, wrote as follows:

"Calhoun did me the honor to give me much of his confidence, and frequently his nullification doctrine was the subject of conversation. Time and again have I heard him, and with ever-increased surprise at his wonderful acuteness, defend it on Constitutional grounds, and distinguish it, in that respect, from the doctrine of secession. This last he never, with me, placed on any other ground than that of revolution. This he said was to destroy the Government; and no Constitution, the work of sane men, ever provided for its own destruction. The other was to preserve it, was, practically, but to amend it, and in a Constitutional mode."

In the same line of reasoning, Secretary Howell Cobb, of Georgia, in Buchanan's Cabinet, who was for a generation a leading and well-informed representative and senator from his State, in 1851, when asked particularly as to the right of a State to secede, said: "When asked to concede the right of a State to secede at pleasure from the Union, with or without just cause, we are called upon to admit that the framers of the Constitution did that which was never done by any other people possessed of good sense and intelligence; that is, to provide, in the very organization of the Government, for its own dissolution. It seems to me that such a course would not only have been an anomalous proceeding, but wholly inconsistent with the wisdom and sound judgment which marked the deliberations of those wise and good men who framed our Federal Government. While I freely admit that such an opinion is entertained by many for whose judgment I have the highest respect, I have no hesitation in declaring that the convictions of my own judgment are well settled that no such principle was contemplated in the adoption of our Constitution."

These, and many other opinions, which could be given almost without end, establish the truth that there was a time when no respectable authority would have defended secession as a right; that Calhoun, the founder of the idea of a slave republic, only thought of separation as the right of revolution, if contested. It was the madness of smaller men to assert and defend the suicidal right, if such it might be called, of self-destruction of the Nation; not to enlarge or make better the liberties of men, but to crush them down as slaves or victims of slavery's unpaid labor.

Confining our extracts to a few representative newspapers and speeches of leading men, to show the condition and drift of public sentiment, we take the following statement from the Albany *Argus*, a New York Democratic paper, published shortly after Mr. Lincoln's election:

"We are not at all surprised at the manifestation of feeling at the South. We expected and predicted it, and for so doing were charged by the Republican press with favoring disunionism; while, in fact, we simply correctly appreciated the feeling of that section of the Union. We sympa-

thize with and justify the South as far as this; their rights
have been invaded to the extreme limit possible within the
forms of the Constitution, and, beyond this limit, their
feelings have been insulted and their interests and honor
assailed by almost every possible form of denunciation and
invective; and if we deemed it certain that the real animus
of the Republican party could be carried into the Administration of the Federal Government, and become the permanent
policy of the Nation, we should think that all the instincts
of self-preservation and of manhood rightfully impelled them
to a resort to revolution and a separation from the Union;
and we would applaud them and wish them Godspeed in
the adoption of such a remedy."

In January, 1861, a peace conference was held in Albany.
Some forty Democrats, Old-line Whigs, and others attended,
and made lengthy addresses; some offered resolutions. All
of them ran in the line of "peace at any price," concession—
no coercion—and conciliation, until late, when Judge George
W. Clinton, of Buffalo, son of the old governor, Dewitt
Clinton, virtually broke up the meeting with an earnest,
patriotic speech that had more of loyalty and love of country
in it than they had heard for years, and sent them home.
In time and repentance many of them found the means of
getting on the right side. He said:

"We all agree in detesting the very thought of war. But
is our country gone? Is the Union dissolved? Is there
no Government binding these States in peace and harmony?
Why, the proposition was before you ten minutes ago that
the Union was dissolved, and you voted it down. God grant
it may forever continue! O, let us conciliate our erring
brethren who, under a strange delusion, have, as they say,
seceded from us; but for God's sake, do not let us humble
the glorious Government under which we have been so happy,
which has done, and, if we will by judicious means sustain
it, will yet do, so much for the happiness of mankind.

"Gentlemen, I hate to have a word that would offend my Southern brother, erring as he is; but we have reached a time when, as a man—if you please, as a Democrat—I must use plain terms. There is no such thing as legal secession. There is no such thing, I say, unless it is a secession which is authorized by the original compact; and the Constitution of these United States was intended to form a firm and perpetual Union. There is no warrant for it in the Constitution. Where, then, do you find the warrant for it? It is the unhappy delusion of our Southern brethren, who doubt our love for them and our attachment to the Constitution. Let us remove that illusion. We will try to do it. But, if the secession be not lawful, O, what is it?

"I use the term reluctantly, but truly—it is rebellion. [Voices: "No, no, revolution."] It is rebellion—rebellion against the noblest Government that man ever formed for his own benefit and for the benefit of the world. [A voice: "We are all rebels then."] May be so, sir. Gentlemen, this secession doctrine is not a new thing. The people have passed upon it. In other words, it seems to me, and I know I speak the wishes of my constituents, that while I abhor coercion, in one sense, as war, I wish to preserve the dignity of the Government of the United States as well."

The Bangor (Maine) *Union*, a newspaper, in February, 1861, copied and approved the following from the Cincinnati *Enquirer* of the same date: "The difficulties between the North and the South must be compromised, or the separation shall be peaceable. If the Republican party refused to go the full length of the Crittenden amendments, which is the very best the South can or ought to take, then here in Maine not a Democrat will be found who will raise an arm against his brethren of the South. From one end of the State to the other, let the cry of the Democracy be, Compromise or peaceable separation!"

In February, 1861, the. Detroit *Free Press* published a
mess of treasonable bombast so vile and diabolical, so mean
and pusillanimous that there were only a few newspapers
in the free States like it—the Cincinnati *Enquirer*, Chicago
Times, and the New York *Herald*—that would print such
shameful and venal stuff. It is referred to only to represent
an element in the treasonable conspiracy, but an element
Mr. Lincoln had to contend with until the real leader—Val-
landingham—was overwhelmed, and General McClellan, who
was really something of a patriot and soldier, in spite of the
damaging support and association of the rebel sympathizers,
was left stranded, very much as though he had never been.

The miserable diatribe ran, in part, as follows: "We can
tell the Republican Legislature and the Republican Administration of Michigan, and the Republican party everywhere,
one thing, that, if the refusal to repeal the personal liberty
laws shall be persisted in, and if there shall not be a change
in the present seeming purpose to yield to no accommodation
of the National difficulty, and if troops shall be raised in the
North to march against the people of the South, a fire in
the rear will be opened upon such troops, which will either
stop their march altogether or wonderfully accelerate it.
In other words, if, in the present posture of the Republican
party towards the National difficulties, war shall be waged,
that war will be fought in the North. We warn it that the
conflict which it is precipitating will not be with the South,
but with tens of thousands of people in the North. Civil
war shall come. It will be here in Michigan and here in Detroit and in every Northern State."

This was valiant talk indeed—talk in the rear, which,
if it had been sincere or spoken by brave men, might have
given some trouble at a time when the Union people in all
the free and border States were consolidating and organizing for the great struggle. But when war did come, they
found these pretentious writers and blatherskites, like Fal-

staff and his "sojers," Bardolf, Pistol, and Nym, dangerous only as far as treachery and pretense could harm those with whom, for the time, they served.

In strong contrast with the conduct of these noisy and cowardly men, the course of the old hero soldier, General Lewis Cass, who was then leaving Buchanan's Cabinet, gave hope, encouragement, and strength to the assembling hosts of the Nation's defenders. He and his prudent, patriotic service are well remembered, while the others are so well forgotten that few indeed know who they were, and only the memory of their baseness, as of kindred doings of the Tories of the Revolution, remains.

From the election of Mr. Lincoln until his inauguration, while so many well-intentioned, patriotic men, both in and out of Congress, were making their most zealous efforts for conciliation, all such overtures were useless, vain attempts, and resulted in nothing. The Southern leaders held the entire political machinery and organizations of the slave States under unquestioned and despotic control. Their ultimatum had been laid down by Senator Toombs, and was given again in the exact and more definite terms of their acknowledged leader, Jefferson Davis, in the Senate, December 26, 1860. This was: "*Resolved*, That it shall be declared, by amendment of the Constitution, that property in slaves, recognized as such by the local laws of any of the States of the Union, shall stand on the same footing, in all Constitutional and Federal relations, as any other species of property so recognized; and, like other property, shall not be diverted or impaired by the local laws of any other State, either in escape thereto or by the transit of the owner therein. And in no case whatever shall such property be subject to be diverted or impaired by any legislative act of the United States or any of the Territories thereof."

This amendment would have legalized slaves as property under the Constitution, when, with a little additional friendly legislation and as willing Administrations as those of Pierce and Buchanan, they would have protected the owner of this slave property in his sojourn in any State or Territory. What Toombs had declared, "The time is soon to come when I can call the roll of my slaves in the shadow of Bunker Hill Monument," would thus have come true.

In this way, as we have recounted, slavery was almost fastened upon us in that perilous winter, when apparently some compromise that would have been agreed to would virtually have made us a slave Nation out and out, had it not been that the conspirators fully believed that they could separate and make a more desirable combination of slave States, southern countries, and islands, without the free States than with them. They believed that the North would not fight or coerce them to remain in the Union, as so many weak and timid men and newspapers had said.

So many angry disputes in Congress for at least forty years had been settled without war, when the strife actually began in 1861, almost everybody, North and South, expected it to be tided over again with some kind of compromise. In proof of this, as discerning a statesman as Mr. Seward stated, and no doubt fully believed, after Sumter had fallen and war was in progress, "that the insurrection was not as serious as most people imagined, and that with the vigorous work then going on it would not last ninety days."

While the war was in progress, in the fall of 1863, I found a corroboration of this that is worth relating. A well-educated and informed physician was located in Northern Alabama several years before the war, where he had all he could do. He had a fine plantation, was comfortably fixed, and was taking things at their best. He was born and grew to manhood in Southern Pennsylvania, near the Maryland line, where he lived until he got his schooling and college preparation before going South to practice medicine. He was a Democrat, but nothing of a politician. He had supported

Douglas for President in 1860, at his residence in the vicinity of Jere Clemens, a Democrat, who had long been in Congress, and who remained loyal some time after hostilities began. He lived in what was a loyal community as long as it could be, of two or three counties in that part of the State. When I met this Dr. C—— he was in charge of a large Confederate hospital and convalescent camp, with the best facilities at hand. I found that he was suspected after all that he was doing, and that he was much humiliated at his forced relation. I had a pleasant stay in the neighborhood, and a pleasant acquaintance with him. I helped him to many needed medicines and supplies for his sick as far as we could spare them, thus becoming intimate by sympathy in his work. He had many of our sick, and treated them as well as their own soldiers, where he was doing the best he could for them.

In our talk I asked him why he did not leave the South before the war began. He said: "I sold off my crops and rented my plantation for a period of years, and got ready as well as I could every way to go back among my people, to remain until the difficulty, whatever it should prove, might be settled. I did not wait until 1861, but began my preparations in November after Lincoln's election. I first left my family here to make a trip of observation and inquiry. When I left I fully believed we would have war. Mr. Clemens, our most trusted leader, was then in Washington. I was so much suspected that I could not talk much with safety, except to a few trusted friends.

"When I reached Lancaster, Pa., to my surprise I found that all along the Maryland line and on through Chester County to Philadelphia nobody believed there would be war. About everybody I met, both Republicans and Democrats, confirmed this. Neither they nor any reputable people whom they knew believed in coercion of the Southern States to make them remain in the Union. This was the popular talk everywhere, and from the newspapers which I carefully read

every day, and the general talk among the people, I came
to the conclusion that if the Southern States determined to
secede, the separation would be peaceful and without war.
Fully believing this, I returned home in January.

"On my return I talked freely to the people here, telling
them the result of my observations and inquiries in the
North, and along my way home. I came down the Ohio
River and up the Tennessee. On the route I met hundreds
of people, most of whom believed there would be no serious
war. A great many, I suspected, were talking that way
without much knowledge of the subject. I noticed that the
farther West I came the numbers increased very fast who
were not afraid of war breaking out. Many of them, men
of all parties, said that if the South really intends to secede,
and virtually declares war, it will get all it wants of it; but
the peace-believing men largely prevailed.

"As it was not far, I went to Montgomery, the Confederate Capital, early in February, where with short intervals
of coming home, through the month, while they were organizing their new Government, I saw and talked with all of
them, President Davis, Vice-President Stephens, the members of the Cabinet, and prominent leaders from all over the
South. They talked freely. What secret counsel they had
was confined to a few men, about things which the public
had no apparent anxiety to know or interfere with, more than
the common talk indicated. I was suspected; but as a number of prominent men in our State saw the urgent necessity
of my services in the event of war, I was well treated. On
account of professional necessities in that contingency, I was
better respected and talked to and of, with less suspicion than
here at home.

"The public, or outside, talk from President Davis, running through all classes, was that there would be no serious
trouble or war; that what there was of it would be in the
Northern States and along the border, not farther south than

Washington, Cincinnati, and St. Louis. They believed that
these, except Cincinnati, would soon be in our hands; that
the North would be about equally divided; that the most
courageous of them would take up arms against the Abolitionists; that many of them were factory operatives, mechanics, and laboring men who would not fight, and were in
no way fit for soldiers; that the best of them would never
be able to contend with the more chivalrous Southern people.
Behind this talk I saw that their leaders were making instant
preparation for war, and were mustering militia companies
in every town or village wherever a dozen men could be gathered together, and enlisting them into companies, with or
without their consent.

"In the beginning I tried to disabuse their minds of the
story that Northern men would not fight. I found that I
had to stay, for I had remained so long that it did not seem
possible to get away. I was warned not to talk about what
Northern men would do, and soon ascertained that their
leaders wanted this delusion kept up in order to carry the
South into war with as little dispute and opposition as possible until their armies were enlisted. I was given a com-
mission as surgeon without notice or request; and being then
in no condition to leave, I saw that my best interest would be
served, and that it would be in accordance with the history
and teachings of our profession, to accept it. I accepted and
remained as the best I could do—as a necessity and without
a feeling of disloyalty.

"To shorten the story, the war did come; but thousands
did not feel its dread reality and horrible consequences until
they were brought to their own home as the harvest of battle
and its results. After Donelson, they began to think very
seriously, when an entire army of over twenty thousand was
captured and taken out of existence. But in its terrible
reality, they learned its full calamity when from Shiloh on
they knew that Northern men would fight. In proof of it,

there were dead or wounded in almost every household in the Southwest. I was there, and saw so much of it that I prayed God never to see another battle.

"Our own people told me that when the first carload of dead, wounded, and dying soldiers reached here, which was not over one hundred miles from the battlefield, the awful reality and monstrosity of the war burst on the people. For two days and nights following, as train-loads of the dead and wounded came and passed on and returned their dead and wounded to every community, the pallid faces, the ashen lips, and trembling hands told more than words, that they had seen this war for slavery for the first time in all its horrors, and they knew then beyond controversy how much they had been deluded."

When I parted with the good doctor, who was then over fifty years of age, he said: "I have enjoyed your stay so much. I have been glad to be able to tell to some appreciative one why I have served the Confederacy as other thousands have done in similar ways, and must so continue to the end of its failing cause. While technically an enemy of my country, I have not been a willing one. What can I do when it is all over? I know it will always grieve me to have done what it seemed I could not help doing as it came. Can I remain here, and remain what I desire to be, a respected citizen?"

I replied, saying: "Whatever my opinion may be, or however it be considered, I believe that outside of the few hundreds who planned and precipitated the conflict, the brave and courageous Southern men who have honorably and faithfully served, suffered, and died, and all who survive, that have sincerely believed their cause a just one, will never be harshly treated nor unjustly judged by the men of the Union armies; and you, my good doctor, have unqualified reason to hope for full justification. In the terrible struggle you could not have been situated in the South where you could have done more good, if as much, or where you could have better proved the noble character and purpose of our profession. Thousands have recovered, or been relieved and their sufferings ameliorated, while the pains and distress of the passing have been assuaged. All that science and skill could provide, under your care and watchfulness, has been done. In this humane work you have had no enemies, while the Southern men in gray and our own in blue had the same cots, food, service, and attention. Among them the weakest and the most helpless have had the first care and attention."

Thus we parted, and I was pleased to have met and known one of the bravest, kindest men, whose heart and willing hands were constant and true to his suffering kind.

From the time of Mr. Lincoln's leaving Springfield, and after his inauguration, my relation was changed in so many ways that the altered conditions should be mentioned. I kept myself informed of what the President was doing, and his progress from day to day. I deemed in those passing days, when judgment was hardly formed, his new undertaking to be one of the most perilous and momentous of any man's in modern times. He had just been chosen as the leader of a great and intelligent people in a pending upheaval. It must be understood here that while I write and note the run of events of the man, from this time forward, much of it came in the current news of the day and through good friends. But this means I have been enabled to carry on the thread of my story.

As I have kept along it has been understood that our family relations with Judge Douglas gave me unusual opportunities from the beginning. As I grew to boy and man, these opportunities increased, and afforded me the means to understand, as well as any one could, the course and character of public men and affairs. After his death I felt the great loss we had all borne, and that one of the best and most reliable sources of my information was thus suddenly broken. From this time forward, however, I planned and prepared, that when the time came I could devote myself to his personal justification and as far as possible put it in more enduring form than noted items, dates, and remembrances. This purpose has been held from that time, when now to give what I knew of his life and character, and his relation to the great events through which he lived, comes late in life as a pleasant duty.

As I have related, several years before this, about 1854, when the Republican party was being organized in our State, I made the favorable acquaintance of Mr. Owen Lovejoy, brother of Elijah, who was murdered at Alton. He was then a member of the Illinois Legislature, in the session where Mr. Lincoln retired, and brought about the election of Judge Trumbull. From this time many of Mr. Lincoln's friends, who were not full of prejudices and animosities against Abolitionists, had warm friendship for Owen Lovejoy, who was a fearless man and leader, and one of the faithful and steadfast for Lincoln.

Having been classed as an Abolitionist for years, and living in the same congressional district, we soon drifted together, and became close political friends and associates. This soon grew to mutual confidence, which lasted until Mr. Lovejoy's death. I was in this way again placed in close relation with this well-informed and capable leader, whose knowledge of men and affairs and their daily progress was as accurate and comprehensive as that of any one of his day. After the inauguration of Mr. Lincoln, and the fall of Sumter, in April, and several times in the following months, I was with him frequently at Springfield, when for weeks our chief business was gathering, mustering, and enlisting men, and making every possible preparation we could for war. During much of this he was there, and our acquaintance grew and strengthened, and my line of information was kept open.

When President Lincoln was inaugurated he was on the verge of the crisis, in the battle for the Nation's life, that had been planned and plotted against so many years. He stood in the open before the people, face to face with their foes, the master leader of the hosts of freedom, against the combining legions of greed, aristocracy, force, and slavery in the most momentous combat of the century. Many a stout-hearted man would have faltered and failed for want of support and co-operation in that angry, seething turmoil of men and factions. A hundred had conspicuously done so since the previous November election. There was not a leader left to raise the standard of the Union to certain victory and free Government among men then known, who could unite the factions and contending divisions, if President Lincoln could not.

Political parties had all separated in disputing factions. The Republican party, the one then rising, had neither unity in purpose nor action, though it had elected Mr. Lincoln on a declaration of restriction of slavery to the slave States, and prohibition of it in all our Territories. It had surrendered this, when a sufficient number of its leaders in Congress agreed to guarantee the very worst concessions ever offered to slavery, if Davis and his conspirators had been willing to accept them. It is true that there was an uncorrupted body of leaders and loyal men in the Republican and War Democratic parties, in Congress and throughout the free and border States, who resolutely refused to make any further concessions to slavery. But they as firmly demanded the fair and impartial enforcement of the laws in all the States alike. Among these prominent men who have earned the Nation's gratitude were Abraham Lincoln, Hannibal Hamlin, Thaddeus Stevens, W. P. Fessenden, Arthur Tappan, Daniel Clark, John P. Hale, Lewis Cass, George E. Pugh, Senator Stuart of Michigan, E. B. Washburn of Illinois, and three of his brothers from Maine, Wisconsin, and Minnesota; General James Shields and Colonel Edward D. Baker of Illinois; E. D. Morgan and General Daniel E. Sickles of New York; General B. F. Butler and General N. P. Banks of Massa-

chusetts; Owen Lovejoy, John A. Logan, and full twenty
other Republicans and War Democrats of the House of Representatives; S. P. Chase, Ben Wade, E. M. Stanton, and
Joshua R. Giddings of Ohio; Henry S. Lane, Lyman Trumbull, F. P, Blair, Jr., Governor A. J. Curtin, Governor O. P.
Morton, Governor Richard Yates, Joseph Holt, and Winfield
Scott. These and a full thousand such men, who to the extent of their talents, courage, and conspicuous ability did all
they could, should always be respected and honored by the
land they contributed so much to save and transmit to coming generations.

We have insisted and held that President Lincoln was
distinctly chosen leader, and as emphatically sustained as the
emergencies developed and strengthened him from day to
day in God's own way. He was full in the crisis. He was
patient, slow in judgment, but never too late. While the
best and strongest of our other leaders were underrating or
overrating the magnitude, strength, and duration of the revolt, he did neither, but constantly and incessantly kept at
work.

He was an honest man. He was so as President, as he had
been through life, in personal or public affairs. He was candid and not a bit over-dignified "or stuck up" over his distinction. He had few secrets, none about principles or policies, and was as approachable to the humblest as the most
prominent and influential. Any reputable person could have
his attention and earnest consideration, and none ever sought
him in vain on an errand of mercy, or to bring help and
encouragement in the great struggle.

He was, as we have said, an honest, straightforward, undaunted, regular, and every-day-going sort of man, who patiently, fearlessly, and faithfully rounded up his work as he
deliberately carried it on. He did not believe that God would
let the Great Republic perish. He felt that God had called
him to a great work, as great as that of Washington, or

greater. He believed this is God's Nation, and that the furious struggle against it was at His bidding. He said so, and that God could save or destroy, as the Nation did or failed to do His will.

If this interpretation is true, there can be no doubt that he was God's appointed leader as surely as ever any man was called to be a leader in his service. On the part of Lincoln, as we refer to the corroborative evidences of this high call to duty, we should remember that he was severely exact in his use of words and the construction of his sentences; especially was he so in all that pertained to himself, in his many arguments, speeches, and addresses. In illustration of this, I remember his once saying, "I have been studying the difference, for my purpose, between the words 'imperishable and indestructible.'" At another time he distinguished between fitness and qualification. He went over these with the most scrupulous care, as he did other words and phrases, finally selecting the ones best adapted to his use, after patient investigation of their different shadings and meanings.

He found no party strong enough to enforce a policy. It was better that there was none, for no political organization then existing was equal to the undertaking in that terrible crisis. There being none, he was left free to proceed and make a Union party out of men of all parties. In this line of policy he formed his Cabinet.

HON. E. B. WASHBURN

OWEN LOVEJOY

THURLOW WEED

THOMAS H. BENTON

CHAPTER LI.

THE anomalous party conditions can be best shown, perhaps, by reciting some friendly conversations between the President and Thaddeus Stevens, in which Owen Lovejoy participated. Stevens and Lovejoy had been something alike; both were earnest anti-slavery advocates and practical friends of the poor, the needy, and the oppressed everywhere. Stevens was always prepared, and so full of zeal that thoughtfulness was not so much a part of his character as indomitable energy. He was sanguine and ambitious. He did not possess the spirit and genius, the patience and philosophy of Lincoln, or of Lovejoy. He was uneasy in waiting and ready with stinging rebukes, especially when he saw how the "Republican party had balked and mired down in the winter of 1861."

We have noticed Stevens's remark, "That the Cabinet seemed to be made up of a job-lot of the President's political opponents, a stump speaker from Indiana, and two members of the Blair family." He was in no sense a backward or reticent man or leader. He had the keen and sharpened wit that made him a fearless debater, one whom the freshmen of Congress never tackled but once. He had the grasp of affairs, the knowledge and experience that came from long and useful service in behalf of every burdened man of any race, in the struggle for his rights, his living and welfare. He held high respect for President Lincoln before his election, believing him to be an earnest laborer in the same cause with himself.

He was sorely disappointed and in his wrath at the "alarmed commercialism of the big towns that were going to surrender before a battle; at those traders of the leading cities, and the politicians in and about them, and at the chief gang of rascals and traitors in the nest at the Capital," he was doubting, and felt that the President had unnecessarily backed down in the face of danger. Though willing to wait awhile, he was, nevertheless, preparing to make open and pronounced opposition, in which he expected to be supported by a majority in the House of Representatives. Hence it was a serious situation, and would have been a wrecking disaster to a weaker man; but it gave the President his expected opportunity. He knew that he had to lead or surrender, and as well that he needed the unqualified and earnest support of Stevens, whom he held to be the chief leader in the House, and the equal of any man in Congress.

A few days after the inauguration, Mr. Stevens called to pay his respects to the President. They had a pleasant interview; but on Stevens's part, a reserved touching upon public affairs. He was noticeably affected, seeing that the President was visibly burdened and in serious trouble. In telling of it, he said: "When about leaving the President took my hand, saying, 'Mr. Stevens, I want to have a plain and friendly talk with you for an hour or so, when we shall not be bothered as we are sure to be during these usual calling hours. Will you call some evening at your early convenience, or shall I call to see you?' His manner and cordial expression, that one may enjoy but never describe, and the bare idea that he, our President, asked me if he should call to see me, took all the antagonism out of my mind at once, before I had time to offer a word in reply. As soon as I could choke down my agitation over having too suddenly judged him, I was glad as a boy with his first set of marbles to say, 'Mr. President, I shall enjoy a friendly chat, and will time it to suit your convenience.' He replied: 'Come this evening at eight o'clock. Mr. Lovejoy will be in at nine. He is one of our home folks, and if we talk a little long, he can come again. These Illinois friends have a habit of coming in at the side door; but are never bothered, or out of sorts, when I am busy and can not entertain them.' "

Stevens was glad enough to see the way things were running, and said, "Seeing the way you keep house, I think I shall want to join in and get on the footing of your Illionis friends. If it will suit your pleasure, as I know it will his, I shall be pleased to have you admit Mr. Lovejoy as a party to our talk as soon as he arrives; he is on my side, or perhaps, rather, I am on his."

Mr. Stevens called promptly at eight, when without ceremony he was invited in and sat down for an unrestrained political talk with the President. Mr. Lincoln put him at ease at once, saying: "Mr. Stevens, I entertain a high respect for you, as you no doubt understand, as one of the most honest, capable, and fearless friends of freedom. I know something of your disappointment, and have never thought you were altogether wrong. I want you to feel at home here, for this is the people's house, and I desire you to talk plainly and freely. I would rather bear your strongest rebukes here, than to hear that you are dissatisfied and doing so where I could not so well consider our affairs in a proper and friendly way. This will be the shortest cut to a fair understanding as to the best way to conduct the people's Government. I am here to be counseled; you are interested with me and all of us in the public service, just now, to save the Union."

Stevens replied: "Mr. President, I am obliged for your kind and cordial invitation. I have been an earnest worker in our cause for more than a generation, and have gained something as a man who would contend or fight, if you please, for the right as I understand it. I want to be plain with you. I can not have any personal contention or serious difference with you. Your kind heart and unusual commanding powers prevent it, if I should think of being merely contentious. In your high duty you have fitness and qualifications, all that our weak and surrendering President Buchanan lacked. It is ours to supply you with facilities and equipment for the most momentous conflict of modern times, if these arming conspirators so make it.

"But I have feared that your policy, like that of many able and conscientious Republicans here, all winter, that of conciliation to rebels arming for no better purpose than more thoroughly and more widely to enslave men, will serve no good end, and that they will scornfully reject your well-meant efforts. The contest has now passed the bounds of friendly or legislative mending. These same conspirators, with all whom they force or persuade to join them, are, and have been for months, fully intent on separation and war. They will only submit through defeat and disaster so overwhelming that they can not escape the consequences; for, sure as we live, they are brave and courageous enough to fight as Americans.

"With due respect to and a knowledge of their many possible, and, perhaps, good qualities, I do n't like your Cabinet, a nondescript lot of political wind-shifters, like Welles, so recently discovered; an Indiana stumper in a State having several able men; the Blairs; and other respectable gentlemen, having every shade of belief on slavery, from holding 'niggers' plain and plump, to the nonsense of gradual emancipation. They all seem to be mounted on one unruly horse, his back breaking, with the overload of slavery, in the middle; while the President is in the rear, mounted on a small donkey, his legs dragging the ground, in token of his half-riding, half-walking policy, against well-armed and well-mounted insurgents. In contrast with this, I would like to see you a Republican, leading, not tethered or pulled along, nor veering the whole circle of the political compass to catch the lost chieftains of every party wreck in the last ten years. I want you to be the great leader, with a Cabinet of counselors in full accord with our party's declaration on slavery, which, no matter how men may cloud it, is the real issue, that can not be passed or set aside."

During this delivery Mr. Stevens became somewhat excited and very earnest. He rose to his feet, and, although he walked with a cane because of a lifelong injury and lameness, he got about the room quite lively, touching up his subject in good dramatic style. There was more of it than we have given, but this is the substance. His language, drollery, keen witticisms, and pungent satire no man of his day could approach.

When he had finished, or stopped for a short rest, Mr. Lincoln gave a hearty laugh, walked across the room to him, and, extending his hand, said: "Mr. Stevens, I like your story. I have enjoyed it, and I regret that it is one of the kind that is too good to use. Sit down and let us reason together. This is a time for wise consideration and prudent foresight, when it will not do to take a hasty, awkward, or indiscreet step. Solomon says, wisely, I think, 'There is a time for all things.' Some day you would not acquit me if I should fail to use all our resources and gain the support of these slow-minded, halting, half-on-our-side men. Though they are hesitating, it is something worth the doing to hold the friends we have, and bring in as many more doubters. It is better than to dispute over policies, when we have none on which all, so far, can agree, and in getting these and their followers we surely have done a good work.

"When we get the support of an old conservative Whig like Judge Bates, of Missouri, and that of the other members 'of the Blair family,' we get the good-will and generally the active support of the conservative people. Among them are the farmers, not only of the border slave States, but of your own State, Ohio, Indiana, and Illinois, the great

Middle West, where lie the great elements of our strength in men and supplies to save us.

"I am not displeased with your remarks about what might be called the locomotion of the Cabinet on their rearing, unruly horse. That is perhaps a good simile; but I suggest you change the 'donkey' business, for I am going to do a lot of riding myself. Conservative as you hold me to be, I am not more so now than I should be, and not more than I think you would be in my situation. Our Presidents who have best filled the measure of the people's desire have been patient, attentive, and deliberate. Even President Jackson, who was reputed as the most excitable, restless, uneasy, and impulsive, patiently waited and tarried with Calhoun and his small coterie for some two years before he brought his heavy hand down upon them.

"You must concede that our proffered good-will and friendly plans of settlement are not offered to those with arms in their hands, but to the well-intentioned people who are being deceived and misled. All our difficulties and contentions must be arranged, or rearranged, and settled under the Constitution as it exists; and the changes, if any are made, must be made by those who believe in it and sustain it and the Nation it binds together as one mighty people.

"In this slow-going, patient waiting and deliberation, that is so irksome for earnest men like yourself to endure, we should gather wisdom from experience. I have, during my public lifetime, lived alongside and disputed with one of our generally-known, earnest, and impatient great leaders, who, nevertheless, has never lacked these qualities in the course of high and important duty. I refer to Judge Douglas, who has maintained himself as the leader of a larger party following than any other man in our history. Including Clay and Jackson, he makes three of our greatest leaders whose personal followers never deserted them. These were all ambitious and apparently more or less reckless when contending, but all the more calm and deliberate in action; Douglas most so of the three.

"Douglas was said to be shaping his plans to be President, and, to achieve it, would concede anything the South desired. However, he made no conspicuous effort to do so in 1856, when he was the choice of a majority of his party. This conceding would have given him the nomination, but he declined the conditions, which Buchanan at once accepted, and, under the two-third rule, he was beaten. But he yielded nothing. He waited; and, although held to be even irritable by many, and excitable by all, he patiently bided his time until he could strike again, when, in 1857-58, he struck them very hard indeed, and defeated their scheme to take slavery into Kansas under the Lecompton Constitution. This so-named impatient leader waited again until 1860, when, in truth, he defied the pro-slavery Democracy, doing what no other leader among them could have done. He surrendered all his hopes of being elected President by refusing to do what so many men in all parties had agreed to do. By this he divided his party, and made my election, in the early part of the campaign, a possibility, and, before its close, almost a certainty.

"I have referred to these particulars for two good reasons: First, to show the patient waiting, and, in the end, the terrible execution of purpose of the reputed ambitious and impatient Douglas; second, to remind you that, through this patient waiting and sturdy courage of the leader and his loyal followers, my election was brought about and our party success achieved. Therefore there is good reason and wisdom in recognizing, in 'nondescript Cabinets,' this force of loyal Democrats, who are with us and will be true in helping us to save our liberties.

"You say we should be carrying out the declarations and principles of the Republican party, through which we were elected and came into office. This is true enough as a rule of action, if the time has come and we have the numerical strength to carry it into successful operation. That is, it may be if we can have peace and avoid war; but this will be altogether different, if our worst forebodings prove true, and we are now in the crisis of a war settlement of this long-threatening dispute. If this is upon us, as you believe, and for which there is the strongest presumption, in that contingency we will need the help of every party and man we can get, in Cabinets, courts, councils, and Congress, and, most, pressing of all, in our armies and navies.

"You must remember, too, that we have no Republican party strong enough and so organized as to be able to restrict slavery to the States where it exists and prohibit it in all our Territories. Although our party was in majority in both Houses of Congress, by reason of the seceders' withdrawal, since January last, there were enough Republicans, as it was publicly and several times announced, to vote, not to exclude slavery from the Territories of New Mexico and Arizona, but to extend slavery into them, and prepare them, as well as could be, as slave Territories for the present, with the further agreement to admit them, in the course of time, as slave States. But Jefferson Davis and his conspirators, wiser than the children of light, knew very well that this would not settle the dispute. Being better informed, perhaps, than our weakening Republicans, he knew that the people of the free States would repudiate such an agreement; and, as these Territories were in no way adapted to slavery, he declined.

"With these conditions existing, do n't you believe it is wise to observe Douglas's virtue of patience, and wait until the times are more auspicious before we attempt anything like a party Administration? This does not necessarily require us in any way to relinquish our efforts for the restriction of slavery, but, for the present, it is best that we unite the people of all parties in the single purpose of saving the Union.

"On my arrival here, among the first to call was my life-long opponent, not as a mere formal ceremony, but, fully alive to the exigencies of the greatest crisis of our country's history, sincerely to offer his services.

"In full accord with this spirit, General Lewis Cass, of Michigan; Senator Pugh, of Ohio; John A. Logan, and full twenty Democrats, members of Congress, have called to greet me. I must not omit that John A. Dix, E. M. Stanton, Joseph Holt, and a number of others of the late Administration, being loyal Democrats of their faction, though few in number, have assured me of their cordial support in this perilous time.

"In making the Cabinet, by plain and simple rules, I recognized every part of every party that came to our support. Mr. Seward divided the vote very evenly with me up to the last ballot at Chicago. You say that he and Mr. Weed have been conceding too much all winter. We must persuade them to quit it. Mr. Chase is one of our most learned, gifted, and capable men. He has been governor, elected and re-elected. He is a strong personality, whether you agree with or differ with him, and one of the strongest anti-slavery advocates in our cause. The 'stump-speaker from Indiana,' Mr. Smith, is a competent and deserving man, and the least inclined of all to desire the distinction, being anxious that some one else should be found. His State is entitled to a place, and Senator Lane and our friends there deserve more from me than I shall ever be able to give them.

"Custom has established the rule that New England must have at least one place. I respect Vice-President Hamlin, and intend to avail myself of many of his clear-headed notions, more than has been done in late Administrations, iu consulting with the Vice-President. I asked him to name some eligible member from his own region. He suggested several, when, together, we took Mr. Welles. I have understood that he was a Democrat. How long since I have not inquired. The Vice-President should have the credit of his selection, and, as things are turning now, I hope the war Democrats will accept him as one of their number. If you had been making the selection, you would have taken Welles rather than one of the others, who helped to extend slavery into New Mexico.

"I have known Judge Bates a long time. He is a true representative of a large element of our people, whose sympathy and active co-operation are of the highest importance. They are the men who are what is left of the Whigs of two generations, strong, sturdy, slow, and conservative, who have done as much to preserve our free institutions, in the forming of the Nation, and the work of carrying it through its wars and contentions, as any of our people. If he were not in the Cabinet I would not know a man better fitted for his task, or who, while doing so, would better encourage and strengthen his countrymen.

"Respecting the Blair family, about whom considerable is said these days, they and their friends in the several States, who are inclined in this general way, are influential Jackson Democrats. Their loyalty to the Union, like that of the great Democrat, is one of their commendable beliefs, and makes it worth while, yes, positively demands, that we should have them with us. Their help, with that of Senator Lane, was the strongest, best-timed, and most efficient of all that I had outside of our own State.

"Montgomery Blair is an able and a patriotic man, as fair a representative of the loyal Democrats of the border States as you can find, as fairly so as Judge Bates is of the Whig loyalists in them; and between Frank P. Blair,

Jr., and John A. Logan, of our State, rests the leadership of the loyal Democracy, as it appears to me.

"Respecting the selection of Mr. Cameron, of your State, as Secretary of War, I was led to it by several reasons. His friends co-operated and carried out all their promises in such good faith that Lane, Bates, the Blairs, and others of our friends united in recommending him. And, as you understand better than I do, your State, as represented by the delegates in the Chicago Convention, and your members of Congress, united in his support. I do not believe that he is satisfied in his present place, nor that the duties of the office, with its restrictions, precedents, and formalism, that have grown into it so long, are agreeable to him. He has been an able party leader for a long time, and is firmly set in his ideas, so that he may not succeed as he desires. From all I could learn I found him more to my mind than any one of your prominent men, who have, mostly, been striving and straining all winter to outdo each other in concessions to the South, in order to restore peace to our distracted country, as they put it, when nothing more than the election of President has disturbed it."

In this patient way he went over his work of forming the Cabinet, with Mr. Stevens, who interjected many questions in his sharp and direct way of bringing out the facts. The President, continuing, said: "The time will perhaps come when we can organize a party strong enough to contend against slavery as a direct issue, but we can not do so now. We made our campaign of last year against its extension into new territory; but we know now, regardless of that success, that if all the States were here represented, as they should be, there would be more probability of extension than restriction, by act of Congress. Our manifest duty, and the duty of the hour, resting on you as it does on me and on every one of us, is to combine, consolidate, and unite every element of strength for the preservation of our country. Let us go on, gathering a little at a time when we can proceed no faster; be patient and ready to do more as we grow in strength, knowledge, and experience. But get ready and keep ready; provide for the stolen and squandered equipments; organize; and then strike with the strength that is merciful, because it will destroy the foes of our country and restore it."

This conversation was carried on in more of a dialogue than we have been able to give it, or as Mr. Lovejoy summed it up in relating it. Mr. Stevens was deeply affected before the President was half through. As he closed he was overcome and his manner altogether changed. His feeling and judgment yielded to the strength and spirit of the great leader, who, in more of detail, laid the whole subject before his candid judgment. A new man was revealed to Stevens, who there learned that here was no weak President who would give away the fruits of freedom's hard-won victories. He saw the genius of the prophet-leader in his character, that could first plant and sow, and then watchfully, earnestly wait for the harvest, which, when it came, would find the bold, stalwart reaper, bare-armed and girded with strength, with the first sickle in the field.

Mr. Stevens replied: "Mr. President, I might better agree with you as gracefully as I can; not in the grudging spirit of one who has missed his ambition. I am no marplot in a crisis that rocks the earth under our feet. I have not undersized the long-gathering conspiracy against our free institutions. I have not even words to waste on them; they have long planned for separation, in peace or in war; in peace, if we cowardly submit to division and are willing to be redivided and lorded over by the big and little despotisms of Europe; in war, if we are brave enough to fight as our fathers did. If that does come, I am as willing, for nothing else seems adequate. As it will come, I am as anxious to have it over and done with as they can be; but with every gun rammed and shotted for action.

"I have honored you as a wise man, among the first to see and seize the magnitude and lurking disaster to free government, in the moral obliquity to the rights of the most helpless, as well as against the stronger and better favored of our races. I have only been confused and mistaken for a season as to your being the man to lead and command. In your pleading for peace while organizing for war, which under our conditions is honorable for us all, we feared there was something of yielding to some more wicked concessions, like those that have rung and rattled all about us, until their proposers and defenders are either on the other side, or too cowardly to fight on any field, for the undivided Union and the rights of men.

"I am called stubborn, and I am, perhaps, when I feel sure of being in the right; but I yield no one precedence in confessing error or mistake, more readily or sincerely, when I see the wrong as I do now. You are right, Mr. President. All possible concessions should be made to those who are going with us, and not a grain of advantage or a scratch on liberty's escutcheon to those against us. I confess, like many of those who have fought so long when nothing better than the experience of adversity rewarded us, that, when we had something of victory, we felt more sanguine than we should that the party should line up, not for a compromise, but more zealously to contend for another forward movement.

"We neglected our precautions to fit and prepare us for the movement. We should have been uniting, more firmly intrenching ourselves on the ground that all the allies of freedom in common could hold, and not have spent our time and breath, all the past winter, in haranguing and dividing with each other for the certain benefit of the enemy. I am willing now to follow on the basis that will take with us all who want to go, asking no further pledge of faith than fealty to the Union and death to its foes. In this great work we will take recruits for three months, a year, or for their lives, trusting that the air of liberty and the infusion of its free-born spirit will grow and carry them on in the great cause. Make your Cabinets and councils. I will follow as long as I know you are able to lead."

Mr. Lovejoy arrived early in the conversation, and joined them at once, participating in it, when the friendly talk went on, giving him the opportunity to understand it as it is given. Near the close, Mr. Stevens turned to Mr. Lovejoy, saying: "It is about as you predicted. I have surrendered to the President, your great Western leader, in far less than the 'few days' closer acquaintance' you allowed as necessary. I feel free to say to you that there is no humiliation about it. I feel that I have met a kindred spirit in the same cause, struggling harder and serving in it with more of patience, wisdom, and prudence than I have been able to bring. He is better fitted to lead in the crisis than any other among so many true men, whom to follow and sustain will be an honor to us and our people."

Mr. Lovejoy said, addressing Mr. Stevens: "That the President may understand what I said about him, I repeat that I was sure that, with a few days' better acquaintance, you would cordially agree, and that two such eminent leaders in our common cause, with so many characteristic ideas and methods of work so near alike, would act in harmony. You should not only not misunderstand, but should know and trust and heartily support each other. I have known and trusted Mr. Lincoln so freely, without ever being disappointed, that, in questions of policy and the conduct of government, I would in perfect confidence surrender all this to him, as our leader, in God's providence, whom it becomes our highest duty to follow. Now, Mr. Stevens, not to be boastful, but for the good it promises, let us unite

in this, that we recognize President Lincoln as our chief
leader. I feel that I am in advance as to a policy of dealing with slavery; but in this crisis I can wait God's pleasure,
when, as surely as we stand here, he will deal with it and
smite it before the conflict is over. Others will be more
impatient than I am. The President will be sorely troubled;
but we can wait. I will wait, and as I have not troubled
him, I will not trouble him now with what I could say;
for on this we are all too weak to give advice. But I am
as certain as I live, and that we have served in this cause,
that God will make the President's duty plain to him; that
in that supreme hour of trial the people will not be disappointed in our leader of the common people, who, when
known as well as we know him, will be so, through the conflict, by common consent.

"I am overglad that we have had this meeting, where
we could exchange confidence and enjoy that of the President; to know it has been productive of such present results; that it has opened the way, and promises much of
good in hurrying up organization and widening acquaintance
in the future. You remember how earnestly I have wanted
the President here all winter, not to argue or dispute, but
to know and see the men, many of whom, I was fain to
hope he could have held from their mad attempts at compromising.

"Now that he is here, surrounded by so many difficulties,
more, it seems to me, than ever beset any other leader
in the cause of freedom, let us go to work, as I know you
will, to help him. Let him have the best opportunity for
acquaintance with the representatives of the whole land.
If it is your ambition to be in the Cabinet, where there
will probably be changes soon, no one will sustain you more
than I will."

President Lincoln said: "By your consent, just now
given, all concern where and how you are to serve the pub-

lic is handed over to me, to be, as I hope, discreetly used. I appreciate more than I can express your approval of my well-meant efforts; but, to be plain just now, and candid, as the subject deserves, I very much want your services where our duty calls us to-day. I am not a flatterer; I have never been so; all the more I am certain that capable, efficient, and independent leaders in Congress are scarce. Some, who might grow to be such, from party and other reasons, can not be elected; others will not submit to the hard work and drudgery. With due deference to the gentlemen who are elected, very few reach the success that meets their own approval; hence, in good faith, without further word or remark, I want both of you just where you are, with no reference to, and, of course, no reflections on your fitness or qualifications for Cabinet places or other executive duty.

"I would not appoint either one of you, while members of the House, to a Cabinet position, not if all the places were vacant or unprovided for, and for the good reasons I have given. I can find a full dozen well-qualified gentlemen for Cabinet places in Pennsylvania, but there is not another Thad Stevens, commoner and man of the people, able to stand in the forum, able to defend them, and able to · cut his way through any and all sorts of shams and sophistries to the truth. In a different, but as efficient service, the same may be said of the fearless Illinois 'Abolitionist,' Lovejoy, and of Mr. Washburn, your colleague. Your services, your experience, your qualifications, all of you, are such that we have no other men to fill your places, without time and training. This we do not have and can not wait for in the crisis. You are here in your places, just as I am, in pursuance of high and imperative duty. While I am to be obeyed, and, while we are on the subject, if I had all the authority to do so, I would not remove or change any one of you from your present position, a place of the highest importance, in my estimation, unless I could promote you, which I could not do, in a Cabinet position.

"I understand, you will at once think of the selections of Seward, Chase, and others to the Cabinet; but you must remember the relation they have held is an entirely different one from that of either of you. Their friends made them Presidential candidates. That was done in the midst of the upheaval and the breaking-up of all party associations and the inauguration of a new policy. I have desired, as much as possible, to keep in accord with the sentiment and beliefs of the people; hence, in selecting advisers, I have invited these gentlemen, whom you know. I do not believe that they have gained anything personally by the change, but to them, as to me, their present work came to them as a duty. I appreciate what I think is a real sacrifice for most of them on their part. For myself, it was long a high ambition to be a senator; twice I was near being one; but it was not to be.

"Gentlemen, we have had a pleasant evening, and, in the way of knowing each other better, we have been very much benefited. I want more of these friendly meetings with yourselves and the gentlemen you are to bring here, in form and out of form. This is your house and the people's. We are all here to do the best we can with their Government. I want no hesitation or backwardness about it, and if twenty or more of you, members of Congress and your friends, come at once, make yourselves and all of them at ease. Get into the best places you can find in these rooms, the hallways, the porches, and the grounds, and make this home a friendly gathering-place. We will now go to the kitchen apartments, where we will have a plain country lunch, and refresh ourselves, not with that which would only stimulate with a little false courage and leave us with sore heads in the morning, but with that which will strengthen us · for our labors while it invigorates and sustains us with healthy nourishment."

This was a relation concerning President Lincoln when most himself: The men who went to contend with him, the friendly and able leaders, and everybody, like these eminent Congressmen, came away with all their opposition melted into the strongest friendship. All who went, from whatever motive, if honest and sincere, came away fully impressed with the kind heart and the true greatness of the man.

In corroboration of the estimate Mr. Lincoln placed on these three Congressmen, Major James S. Rollins, who was a Unionist member of Congress from Missouri in 1861-62, corroborated it. Afterwards, in 1871-72, he was a member of the Missouri State Senate, where I served with him in friendly relations. On one occasion, in a running chat, he said: "These Congressmen, Thaddeus Stevens, E. B. Washburn, and Owen Lovejoy, were the three strongest leaders, by reason of capacity, tact, and experience, in that memorable Congress. What they agreed to, passed, and what they disagreed to, stopped. I was not always with them; indeed, I was against them as often as with them; but I believe that three stronger and more capable leaders never sat in one Congress. President Lincoln alone could control them, as his pure heart and sincere patriotism reached everybody who knew him, in some way; but in wordy combat or legislative dispute and procedure, they never failed. If they appeared to yield, it was that their victory might be more complete. They were the second power of the Government. Washburn was the polite, attentive, suave gentleman, easy to the point where he stopped, then the head of the three. 'Old Thad' was master of money and details, almost intolerant, who held the purse of the Nation. Lovejoy was the master of oratory and swelling debate, a force without any equal, one to yield to, or go into hopeless opposition, and defy. The three noble and powerful men were a force for the Union which could not be overthrown."

In his deliberate, steady, and persevering way President Lincoln went about and continued the work of forming useful, agreeable, and, in many instances, friendly acquaintances with members of Congress and their friends all over the country. He encouraged governors and many earnest Union men, widely separated, to visit him, talk over the situation freely, and to give their advice and opinions, which were always kindly received. Best of all, he wanted them to give the facts concerning the mind and temper of the people on the strained and threatening conditions so rife in their States and different localities.

In this way he soon came to know, from his own inquiry and observation, many times better than any other man, the prevailing conditions of affairs among the people, and their sentiment, their devotion, their constant desire that our difficulty should be settled, without war, if possible, on honorable terms; but on nothing less than the integrity of the whole country. He did not hesitate to lay aside the formalism of holding high office, going often to see some timid or wrongly-influenced members of Congress, and others at the Capital, in which he did the good service that no one else could have done, on several occasions. He knew his great power over men, and exercised it with all his strength and skill for the cause.

We have related how he almost took charge of the Illinois Legislature in the outset of his career, on the subject of the removal of the State capital. This was his first experience in the progress of his leadership of men, in deliberative bodies of all kinds in our system, in councils, courts, and Legislatures.

The accumulated experience was of incalculable benefit to him at Washington, with his vastly-increased knowledge and wider opportunities. The results were very much the same. What the young beginner did so well at Vandalia, the ripened statesman, the gifted genius, and God's leader wrought out in stronger purpose and higher achievement in his greatly-widened field of labor. He took congress-men, judges, governors, generals, and the people into his great heart and confidence, until he was as father or elder brother to all. No one who knew the facts wondered at good old Representative Kuykendall, Democrat, of that day, when Lincoln was a Whig, who said: "Why, we moved the capital from Vandalia to Springfield because we wanted to do something for Abe. He'd been such a good friend to all of us."

CHAPTER LII.

THE inauguration of President Lincoln, March 4, 1861, was a turning event in human affairs and the most momentous achievement under the Constitution. The Nation was falling to pieces under the clash of contending systems and ideas. The attitude of one section was clearly defined. In the interest of slavery and the productions of slave-labor, seven cotton States were in defiant revolt; four other adjoining slave States were in the same mad career, dallying and threatening, in deceptive pretenses and policy, not to help save, but more effectually to destroy, all that was left of free government. These had daring, well-trained leaders, who were following a well-defined purpose, when for months our Government was designedly left without either, with no one in authority whom all the loyal parties or citizens could follow.

It was not only this, an epoch weighted down with such responsibility for the welfare of the race, but the open field of world-casting events, where all there was of the man, his fitness in toil, his capacities, his faith in himself, his genius, God leading him, were to be tried to the verge of human endurance and motive. There were few, if any, precedents to guide the humble Lincoln with such a load resting on him. For him to have failed would have been worse, a thousand times, than never to have been. He was in an undertaking so vast and overwhelming that its shadow never lifted from a mind sobered and burdened with the weal and welfare of his fellow-men.

Without invidious comparison or the slightest desire to

cast reflection on eminent and worthy leaders of the time, it is nevertheless true, that we can in no other way so well illustrate what Lincoln was, and what he was to be, than by the plain, truthful story of what these able and deserving men about him could or could not do or be.

President Buchanan had neither aptitude, celerity, nor the comprehension of what was demanded of an Executive in such direful necessity. Lacking all these, he permitted the successful growth of the Rebellion. His reputation, before his election as President, had grown on his ability as a patient and careful legislator and representative in foreign courts, where he was slow enough not to be misled by their ordinary deceits and double-facings, in which duties he would have been better content.

General Lewis Cass, who had been able and prominent through a long and honorable career, was one of the distinguished and capable men who might have been selected if the loyal Democracy had retained power; but it was well known that his day had passed. With good and patriotic motives, he struck the most decisive blow against conspiring treason, with effect to bring the astounding result of changing the treacherous, secession-hatching policy to inoffensive loyalty, of the Administration, when he resigned from Buchanan's Cabinet. His support of Judge Douglas was faithful and sincere, in the face of the opposition of the conspiring plotters and persecution of Buchanan and his wicked counselors. If General Cass had been able for the service, President Lincoln would have made him a member of his Cabinet, as he frequently stated. As it was, in honored retirement, the patriotic Cass, like Douglas, gave the President his help, support, and advice, of uncounted value.

Besides these, in 1861, the Democracy had no leader among them who could so well control and lead its factions as Douglas, as had been repeatedly shown. What might have been, if the fearless Douglas had recovered, can only be conjectured. That he would have been true and faithful in support of President Lincoln's Union-saving policy there can be no doubt; but what of the question, Could he have led, as Lincoln did? It does not appear probable that he could; for he, with Senator Seward, as the chief Republican leader, spent the previous session in tireless labor, with no more than hopeful results in preparation, to frame a policy on which all the friends of the Union could be united. He was the leader of the strongest single force of men in the land; but neither he, nor Seward, nor both of them, could, through the entire session, to the inauguration, consolidate the friends of the Union in one composite movement that grew to unexampled strength, as the President did before the passing summer was over.

Winfield Scott, the heroic and most distinguished soldier after Washington, was in military command at the Capital through the war-foreboding winter. He was, and had been, through the two disastrous Administrations of Pierce and Buchanan, the strongest power and the unavoidable obstacle in the way of the slave-leaders' determination to carry slavery into Kansas, as we have written. He was then aged and infirm, at seventy-five years; but the power and means of a soldier leader were still manifest in the preparations for a peaceful inauguration, where there was peace and orderly succession, because Scott was ready for the conflict, if Southern sympathizers provoked one. There had been a day when General Scott could have been the chief leader of the American people through the conflict of the war for the Union. As it is, much is due the old patriot for what he did, and perhaps as much for what he would not do; but he had filled the measure of his years, and they were full of the honor of his glorious service. His command, his career, high and full of duty, all well done, were passing, when one of the strongest proofs of Lincoln's able leadership, even in the gloomy beginning of

1861, was that this soldier for fifty years and of many battles gave his full confidence, strength, and unqualified support to the President.

John J. Crittenden, colleague of Henry Clay, standard-
bearer with him, and after him to 1863, of the great State
of Kentucky, was one of the distinguished men and statesmen of the Whig party for almost fifty years. He was, in
actual public life, through the period of the brilliant success of his leader and party, as well of the marvelous development of the Republic, where he was still a prominent
party adviser. He was an experienced and capable statesman, as he had shown himself in both houses of Congress
and as governor of his State. This he was when men like
him were measured with Calhoun, Clay, Webster, Benton,
Marcy, Douglas, Breckinridge, and John Bell. Among them
he was credited with high qualities of leadership; but
through the whole winter of 1861, in zealous and continuous labor, he could not reconcile and unite the fragments
of the once powerful Whig party that had elected Presidents and wisely conducted public affairs.

Senator Seward was and had been one of the most prominent and distinguished members of the Senate for two
full terms, through the angry disputes following the Mexican War, the extension of slavery, and the unsettled
though highly certified settlements, the Compromises of
1850. This was a settlement so far only that the contention disclosed the truth that there could be no other, except in war. He was there a great leader, conceded to be,
alike by friends and opponents of all kinds, in all parties
and divisions of them. He was sustained by the most populous and most powerful of the States—New York—whose
people, leaders, and public press were mainly in accord with
him, as they had been through a long career of approved
public service. Without dwelling on his many virtues and
high attainments, a greater opportunity was within his

grasp through that winter, when he and Douglas were for
months the uncontested leaders of the two great political
parties that were to unite and save the Union when it was
to be done.

These able and patriotic men bent all their energies in
the most conciliatory spirit to bring about a harmonious
agreement with the misguided South. Further, when, in
the full tide of the growing revolt, they saw that union of
all who would help save it was high necessity, they labored
to that end with all their great powers, with some progress,
but, much to their disappointment, without the success that
should begin such a noble purpose. In contrast, the Union
of these two loyal parties was soon achieved after Mr. Lincoln's arrival, when he "went more than half way" to meet
the good intentions of his lifetime party antagonist and the
people and party that sustained him.

It took greatness of mind, character, and leadership on
the part of these truly wise and able men. When this union
was made, it was strong, inviolate, and sacred, and it gave
the best promise of the success of a united party combination under the management of the President for the single
and inflexible purpose of saving the Union. In this way he
rose to chief leadership, the one among our best and wisest
men, without a contestant, where he stood the chosen representative of our country against all its foes.

A thousand illustrations would not better confirm his
powers than the apparently easy achievement of cordial
agreement with Douglas, with the resultant co-operation
of these two leading Union forces in voluntary and honorable purpose. If further demonstration of his capacity for
his high duty were needed, it was given from day to day
in his continuing work of uniting the people for peace, and
in peace for war. When he took charge of the Government
of the Republic, it was like a strong ship wallowing in the
billows of an angry sea, when wrathful winds were tearing

the sails from their foremasts and upper rigging. Every breeze was freighted with the desertion of some trusted officials, some new plotting or ripened conspiracy and disaster. We were drifting in stormy seas, near ragged rocks and sunken reefs, with the old pilot stupefied in the poison of treacherous counsel, cowardly advisers, and faithless servants.

The Nation, half broken, was like the fragments of the riven cloth, half destroyed, hanging, loose and ragged, under the swinging loom, when Lincoln, as the weaver, took the parted ends, thread by thread, patiently, uncomplainingly, but earnestly, until it was all mended, and the shuttle flew fast again under the sounding strokes of the weaver's beam; and the fabric, reunited, was as fair and strong as ever. All this he did, and so well that men, for a time, in the haste, hurry, and fast changing events of war, waste, and the striking reform on slavery and reconstruction, forgot the direful condition of the Government in the dismal days of March, 1861. Winfield Scott then held the Capital with less than five companies of soldiers and marines, including part of a company of artillery. Our small forces were scattered, our ships sailing every sea except our own, and our army and marine force was so distant and separated as to be out of reach along the shore from Norfolk, Charleston, Key West, and Pensacola to Texas.

Every arsenal and armory in the free States had been emptied and stripped of its arms, ammunition, and military stores as far as it could be; and the supplies and munitions were hurried, in threatening peril, in no peaceful or defensive movement, into the revolting States. The treasury was bankrupt, and our bonds, when sold, were discounted over twelve per cent at the ruinous rate of eight per cent interest. Parties had been torn to fragments and disputing factions, with no one strong enough to unite a majority of their members, declare or enforce any policy or course of action. The party that elected the President passed the winter without agreeing, and, when left with a majority in both branches of Congress by the desertion of the seceders, could do no better than make hopeless efforts at conciliation and settlement of slavery in the face of conspiring and arming treason.

Seward, who was full in the front of the conflict, was restrained by the metropolis of his State and the Nation in its overpowering commercialism. Weed, the more stalwart of the two, the sponsor and colaborer, stood appalled in the certainty of the coming catastrophe; and Greeley, the valiant and most independent journalist of his time, was so incensed at the faithless desertion of the anti-slavery cause by its professed followers from so many quarters of the free States that he broke down, disappointed and sore, in the zenith of polemical victory, offering to submit to separation as the best possible solution. He was so oblivious in the excitement of the angry disputes as not to see, in the first separation, perhaps twenty others, with dependency on some European court as the inevitable result.

The palsied Administration of President Buchanan was doing well to do nothing, even where there was urgent need for prompt and vigorous action, as there was, to supply and re-enforce our forts and garrisons along the South Atlantic and Gulf coasts. A great victory for the Union was achieved in the forced retirement of the treason-plotting Secretaries and the succession of Dix, Stanton, and Holt, their successors. It was a complete change when every movement did not mean harm and disaster to the Government, as had been the case for months.

This was the condition when the President found the Government without a head, with its departments, offices, forces, and properties running at loose ends in a state of the most hopeless disorganization. Resolves and the anxious desires, with all the authority they could exercise, of our most eminent public men and officers, could not unite and consolidate parties against the mustering of the obedient followers of Jefferson Davis in openly-declared revolt. The disorder, the upsetting entanglements, vicious plannings, and thoughtless concessions to rising insurrection, the want of harmony, the want of recognized authority, and the want of skilled and trained men to use the forces at hand, were existing conditions, planned for and happening as the conspirators had schemed and prepared for. Their *finesse* and ingenuity, for months and years, left the Capital, the archives of the Nation, its properties, valuables, and treasures, in condition to become an easy prey to a brigade of militia under as capable and daring a leader as Jefferson Davis.

This capture and overthrow of the Republic would have been the result to expect had not the President come equipped to take the forward road in the measured tread of the veteran, to duty and victory. In this chaotic disorganization he had the hardest struggle of his Administration. He had to be active, alert, determined, and persevering where all others, or nearly all, were in a high state of excitement, impatient, censorious, or fault-finding, because the President did not do something, avow his policy, act at once in the face of such imminent danger to us all. If sympathizers and concessionists, as thousands were, they would ask why he did not adopt a lenient and sensible policy that would avert the calamity and horrors of civil war. All these, and more, sounded about him in the face of the plain and unequivocal declaration of his policy in his Inaugural Address.

There had been so many derelictions of duty, unfulfilled and violated engagements of great parties and officials, that the import and rugged truth of his declarations went, for a time, unheeded in many places. They were slow to accept and realize that, though he was the most patient and forbearing where there was time and hope of amendment, when his mind was made up and the line of duty was plain, no one was ever more earnest and determined in the use of all his power.

In those dread returning days from the inauguration to the first terrible blow of the conflict, the drift of public sentiment was running against the President, when he could do no better than be silent under the hasty judgment. This, too, was more apparent than real; for the few dissatisfied, as usual, made the most noise and complaint. It was, in general, the effervescence of restless men, who, ever in moments of danger, are noisy in declaring their •half-molded, ill-considered opinions. For awhile these appeared to prevail, but the more thoughtful and sturdy men of the farms and our industries, who were called stubborn-minded, were giving the President the few weeks he needed for acquaintance, examination, and time. In these few weeks his Administration was held and placed where, by default of his predecessors, it was without means. The wise and only prudent course left was to let the arming conspirators strike, as they defiantly declared they would, in proof that nothing short of separation and destruction of the Union would be satisfactory to them. In this period of unsurpassed peril to the Union, while the Preesident was busy day and night, there was promise of a better understanding, even in the short time, in the fruits of his well-directed and as well-considered labor. In this time he united such leaders as Judge Douglas, General Cass, Governor Andrew Curtin, Winfield Scott, General B. F. Butler, Senator Seward, Governor S. P. Chase, Chas. Sumner, Henry Wilson, Hannibal Hamlin, Wm. H. Fessenden, John A. Logan, John A. McClernand, Thaddeus Stevens, Senator Ben F. Wade, Senator Geo. E. Pugh, Joshua R. Giddings, E. B. Washburn, Owen Lovejoy, and a full hundred more—the leading statesmen in all parties, and so held among our people. Their avowed and unqualified support of President Lincoln called a halt in hasty judgment, when sober and considerate people, in as firm and convincing modes, conceded to the President the leadership he had earned.

In the few weeks following, the predominant sentiment in the free States was for peace, even to the point of hitherto unheard-of concessions to slavery, if only the Nation were preserved intact and undivided; but as deep and determined resolution prevailed that it should not be divided. The strength of this latter determination Davis and his confederates were not wise enough to discern, or, if so, were willing to hazard the contest, even against a united North and more than half of the border States. This they thought improbable, and continued to rely on the certainty of a divided North long afterwards, with no better foundation than the promises of their dupes in the North, who served slavery for office and emolument, and who, like all such mercenaries, deserted them when they had neither to give.

For the few weeks President Lincoln stood in the most responsible, trying, and perilous situation held by any President in our history. A mistake would have been his downfall and the Nation's ruin. He had to bear, for the time, the opprobrium of concessionists and sympathizers with the South of every degree. They said that he was going to wage a war of coercion against the South, regardless of aggression or submission on their part, against which they had the right to arm and defend themselves. Besides such false declarations, asserted and reasserted, he had to bear the constant reproof of friends and some weak supporters that he was negligent in the face of arming treason.

In the wisdom that God has given to few men, with skill and fitness to correspond, he rose superior to the emergency, as the purest metal survives the most intense heat of the crucible. He well understood at his inauguration that the time for suppressing the revolt in its incipiency had passed; that any attempt to do so on his part without organization and the means and forces at hand would be supreme folly.

This was the trap Davis had planned, and he waited expectantly for the President to fall into it, when the cry of invasion, coercion, and usurpation would be raised and heralded, printed, published, and announced in plaintive oratory, and fanned on every breeze as "the policy of the Abolition Administration."

The President waited, waited in the face of friendly disapproval, waited until the delay forced the conspirators into the position where Lincoln's unequaled strategy put them. They were crumbling away in disorganization for want of a foe or a hostile act by any armed force in time to resist pretended coercion, and they were compelled to do the hostile act themselves, to fire on the flag of their country. In plain words, with a master hand, and with the genius for his high leadership which many good people have not yet discovered, he held his vantage-ground from the beginning. He forced them to strike the flag, shed the blood of its defenders, and take their true position without shadow of dissembling. He forced them to act as enemies of the Union and in actual war against our country, for its dissolution and ruin.

It is altogether out of the question to lay aside the coverings and soberly to review such excited, fevered conditions, or to disclose the danger and peril that surrounded the President in the first weeks of his Administration. His strongest support, for the time, was that of his life-long opponent, Douglas, who was passing to his rest. We could only render fair judgment or make proper estimate of the peril through which he and the Nation passed in those dark days of March and April by knowing all the facts and circumstances and their relations to each other. The Continental Army at Valley Forge was brave and patriotic, yet it would have broken up and melted away, and the cause would have been lost had it not been for the patient care, presence, and continuous labor of Washington. As well

among many able, patriotic men in Washington City in this
opening rebellion, no one of them, save Abraham Lincoln,
could have united and held the hosts of valiant men in the
broken and separating Nation.

This movement, forcing the conspirators to strike the
flag when defended only by the regular forces of the Government, before any volunteers had been called, resulted, as
he had seen, in the instant condemnation of the act. There
was an immediate obliteration of party lines, and the Union
was sustained by all loyal people on the simple basis of defending it against all its foes.

The exercise of the higher powers of the mind, or the
genius courageously and successfully to conduct, direct, and
manage fleets and armies through campaigns in war and
statecraft, is defined and described in the single word
strategy. It is a gift of God to very few in great emergencies. When the gifted leader uses this Divine power at
its best, in part or in whole, he must set himself about it
in the most diligent and persevering way, to the study of
courses, systems, and facts, gathering all the knowledge in
general and in detail belonging to the subject and his undertaking in its broadest and most comprehensive sense. At
his inauguration, Mr. Lincoln was not without the ordinary
information of men of his acquirements and standing concerning wars, conflicts, military and naval affairs; but he
saw at once the necessity of more and better knowledge
on all these subjects. He grasped the idea for more particular and thorough study that he might understand for himself the proper course and conduct of war. He began his
investigation with the diligence and ambition he had when
he used to walk four miles to the justice's office to read and
study the statutes of Indiana and the attached Declaration
of Independence, the Constitution, and the old Articles of
Confederation.

In the zeal of a beginner he took up the geography,

topography, the water-courses, and other physical features of our country, the boundaries, the States and Territories, the smaller community divisions and their conditions, their relations to each other as well as the relation of our own to other countries. He learned all he could of the independent governments, possessions, and dependencies of our continent, of our rivers, lakes, bays, inlets, and coast-lines on every ocean, gulf, and harbor, their means of defense, or their want of them, including all there was of commerce and navigation, their relation with the shipping and railways then in use.

He took up the subject of products and the means of subsistence, the areas of crops, their kinds and uses, the areas of swamps, infertile, waste, and barren lands, the timber growth, mountains, and ranges, valleys, openings, gaps, and roads through them; our plains, their roads and highways, and especially the physical features of the big river, the Mississippi, its valleys, shore-lines, towns, and people, as he had never before thought necessary. Then he examined the settled regions, population, and the particular character and inclinations of their inhabitants, their industries, their industrial progress, their products and facilities for life and liberty, their prospects, capacities, and needs, and the climatic and hygienic conditions, tendencies, and peculiarities of the people in every section.

He found time amid his never-ceasing and perplexing zeal to carry on this study into the endless fields of nature, the industrial pursuits and the course and progress of our people in them, until he was up to and abreast of the skilled and learned leaders or strategists in their several lines of duty. He entertained intelligently, discussed, and considered any subject, duty, or necessity with Farragut, Dupont, Ericsson, Foote, Worden, Porter, or Winslow, what there was of river, harbor, and sea maneuvering or sailing, defense, and conflict. He did the same with Winfield Scott, the old hero of Canadian, British, and Mexican campaigns; with **McClellan,** Hooker, Pope, Burnside, Butler, and Meade, of what there was of war forces, equipment, and organization, and what there was and what there was not, as it should be, in their own and their armies' conduct in the desperate sacrifice. He held the same relations and inquiries in common consent with all these because of his equal capacity, knowledge, and information at their or his own instance or desire, also with the hero leaders, who led their columns always to victory, F. P. Blair, John A. Logan, P. H. Sheridan, W. S. Hancock, and the one and only General U. S. Grant.

In the same persevering way, as his field of labor and duty widened, when Britain in chief and other meddlers of all sorts in unison scented their prey in our distress and hoped for dismemberment, he plodded on, taking up the more comprehensive subject of nation against nation in conflict, what was and what was not war, and how it was waged, in truth, or in dubious evasion and artful definitions, to evade responsibility for unfriendly acts. In the case of Britain it was a critical juncture, with dreadful and momentous consequences in prospect, which might have resulted in another war with Britain, with Russia probably, friendly to us. The burning question was, How far and how long is it prudent, under the strain and provocations of malicious and half-hidden foes, too cowardly to take the responsibility of their concealed alliance, to bear this clandestine help of the chief ally of the insurrection under deceitful pretenses of neutrality? With the prudent determination that "we must have only one war at one time," President Lincoln held back our aggravated people as no other man or leader could have done.

He pushed forward, when he found it necessary, to learn and unravel the intricacies and deceptions of diplomacy and statecraft, as practiced in all the aristocracies of Europe, to understand the duties and privileges of nations in peace or in war, the same of allies and belligerents of all grades, and of neutrals in their several relations. In short, he took up and learned the systems of international law to as good purpose as he had mastered so many kindred subjects, what there was of protocols, declarations of amity, peace, or war, conferences, alliances, and treaties, until he understood them for use to his needs and liking, and knew of them well enough to administer the Government in the prudence and wisdom that kept us free of a conflict that it would have been folly and madness to provoke at the time.

In all of this he was rising in the progress, success, and management of international polity, dealing as an Executive who, in position, parleying, and conclusion, was never entrapped, deceived, or outwitted by the capable, scheming, and double-faced Administrations of Palmerston, Russell, Gladstone, Northcote, and others of the most successful land-grabbers during four years of British cabinets, nor by the mimic maneuvers of the Pompadour Napoleon. He was an honest American, as clearheaded as he was sincere, fearless, and warm-hearted, a man faithful to freedom, whom the secretly hostile monarchs and Administrations of Europe could neither overthrow nor disconcert. Had he lived, he would have brought Britain to a settlement that is still open for one of his kind in character and strength.

CHAPTER LIII.

WE have seen how true President Lincoln was to the principles of human freedom on the subject of human slavery. So he remained to its final settlement. When other leaders and eminent men were content to dispute or contend and concede, he struck at the root of the evil, declaring on the basis of God's truth "that slavery must perish." He was no less true and faithful to other reforms that are as necessitous, as we now believe, for the emancipation of men from the greed of their fellows of the same character, differing only in degree and relation from slavery, because it steals men's labor without taking possession of their bodies, and is of the evils that go with slavery and its wickedness.

His life was devoted to the labor of helping his people get homes and hold them. In his public, as in his professional career, he was true to one of his lifetime declarations of principles which he constantly maintained, that "the lands belong to the people." In the best faith in the progress of this fundamental idea, he urged it ahead and zealously supported it in the use of the most effectual and well-chosen means amid all the strife, until Congress passed the act known as the Homestead Law of 1862, by which the public lands were set apart for homes of the people. If this first considerable step in land reform had been carried out in good faith, and had not been thwarted nor infringed and almost set at naught by colossal land-grants of a domain of selected lands more than equal to six States as large as

Kansas, we would have been far ahead as in the other reform, that of the abolition of all bonded and mortgaged indebtedness. These reforms he ardently supported, and believed them to be necessary in getting out from under the operation of laws which have burdened us for centuries. This can only be done by their unqualified repeal, in which our condition is that shown in the great historian Buckle's statement that "the first and most efficient methods of reform lie in the repeal of bad laws."

If this land reform had prevailed without evasion, abridgment, or gifts to grinding corporations, not only all our public lands might have been set aside for homesteads, but the principle would have grown until all lands not so occupied would have gradually become the homes of independent, self-sustaining people, and yielded them a support. It might have been ere this a great and beneficent reform that would have found homes for the millions now crowded like animals, often worse, in factory towns and choked-up cities without homes and bereft of the hope of ever getting them.

Mr. Lincoln read his Bible every day. He held it to be his treasure and indisputable authority. In its texts and principles he founded the basis of every argument or declaration he ever used against slavery. He did this, too, in his remarkable progress and high distinction as a lawyer. In the same way he grounded his belief and framed his reasoning on his land and debt reforms in profound respect and obedience to Divine authority. His principal references to the debt subject were Romans xiii, 8: "Owe no man anything but to love one another; for he that loveth another hath fulfilled the law." He referred about as often to Matt. vii, 12: "Therefore all things whatsoever ye would that men should do to you, do ye even so to them; for this is the law and the prophets." He often repeated this as the most distinct definition of Christ's gospel. It is law by the Master's authority, and, if law, it is a fundamental law underlying all human conduct, which must necessarily be directed and controlled by it. In accord with this humane and merciful rule of action, no system of debt can long exist.

He believed that the principal exception for contracting any debt was making one to get a homestead, but that, in doing this, unusual industry and rigid economy should follow in order for its payment. These were, in our country, generally incurred to get Government lands or farms while lands were cheap. To his lasting honor it was often said, in some form, that no settler in debt or distress ever appealed to him without getting all the help he was able to give, and that usually it was all that was needed. He was a man of works and so seldom beaten that many who knew him well did not believe he was ever defeated. Of my own knowledge, running through his practice of more than twelve years, I never knew of his complete defeat in defense of a settler, nor his refusal to take every one's claim where he believed the claim was valid, or his ever appearing in any proceeding against a settler.

He would compromise his cases in court or out, usually getting more time, but always getting the best that was possible for the debt-burdened settler. His work for the people getting homes was always unselfish and persevering, not exceptional; for it must be said, to the credit of the big-hearted lawyers and other strong-willed and capable men, that in almost every county, surely at every United States land office, there was to be found an able lawyer who was ready to take up the cause of the striving and home-building settler, and would stand by him to the end. While Mr. Lincoln was not alone in this good work, he was always a leader in it.

He had a long and grim experience with the burden of debt himself, which he scrupulously paid as he became able. He was compelled to carry it along for years, under high rates of interest, to meet the higher, if not holier obligation of helping support his aged parents. From occasional observations and the few remarks of his trial of lingering debt I came to believe that his personal experience brought a distinct cast of thought and reflection after he was free from it that always inclined him to the help of the poor and distressed; and he usually made their cause his own.

In his arguments with and among friends he was often asked direct questions about his no-debt-contracting policy for public improvements. A common one was, "How could you carry on great enterprises without heavy debts, for a short time at least, as circumstances might require?" His reply was: "The people in any capacity, public or otherwise, can make small or great improvements at much less expense when they are paid for as the work progresses. It is, too, usually better done when there is the responsibility of having to pay for it as it goes on, the people take more interest and give it more attention, enough to see that it is well done. It creates a better feeling concerning public affairs when the people are conducting public works, watching and preventing useless expenditure. Above all, large debts are a bad example; and in the experience of men and nations these always lead to unnecessary extravagance, frequently to corrupt schemes, such as we have had in our attempted improvements, which could have been completed to some useful purpose, for canal or railway, if it had been done under honest management.

"If our money, limited to what we had to spend, had been paid for labor and material for these improvements, we would have had something to show for it; but it was filtered through Boards and Commissions in making enormous loans. Knowing that the money came easy, they squandered it every way, giving large salaries and commissions, making also many insecure and fraudulent contracts. All this left our State with eleven millions of debt and not a mile of completed canal or railroad. If you will study the operations of it, you will agree with me that, State or man, you should pay as you go."

In making up his chain of title in support of his declaration that "the lands belong to the people," he began with Genesis i, 28-31: "And God blessed them, and God said unto them, Be fruitful, and multiply, and replenish the earth and subdue it, and have dominion over the fish of the sea. and over the fowl of the air, and over every living thing that moveth upon the earth. And God said, Behold, I have given you every herb bearing seed, which is upon the face of all the earth, and every tree in which is the fruit of a tree yielding seed; to you it shall be for meat. And to every beast of the earth and to every fowl of the air, and to everything that creepeth upon the earth, wherein there is life, I have given every green herb for meat; and it was so. And God saw everything that he had made, and, behold, it was very good. And the evening and the morning were the sixth day."

As Mr. Lincoln contended, this seems to convey to Adam and his descendants, to all of his who were to be born and to replenish the earth, alike, without distinction, the complete authority of the Creator to subdue, populate, and inhabit the earth, and to have dominion over all it contained, over all things without distinction, whether the seas, animals, fowls, or the air and light, all alike, and to one thing the same as another, and the same over one thing as the other, whether they be lands, seas, water, air, or light. Hence a man's title to the lands of the earth is good, and good only for his equal share of it, the same as that of any other man or woman, descendant of Adam and Eve.

Whoever deprives men or women of lands and a home of their own upon the earth not only dispossesses his fellow-men of their rights, but flies in the face of God's law, and is defying him in puny, though merciless and wicked disobedience. Mr. Lincoln believed that all human government should be founded upon and conducted in accord with the principles of Divine law; hence, in sustaining his beliefs against slavery, his ideas of debt and land reforms, he sought his foundations in the truth as God declared it to man. If he had lived through his second term, he would have had occasion to extend land reform after the close of the war in 1865, not only as to the public lands of the vast region west of the Mississippi, but in favoring, recommending, and helping to extend it elsewhere, so that, under his powerful influence and resourceful management of whatever he earnestly tried to do, it would probably have become the policy of the State Governments as well, in which way, under his leadership, it would have prevailed.

Now that it has been neglected so long, it appears best that the promise for the achievement of this much-needed reform should go on under some strong, honest leader, in taking it up anew as part of the plan for the acquisition of the great Northwest, and the opening it up for homestead settlement, without diverting any of it in land-grants or other squanderings. If this should be carried out in friendly spirit, under capable and efficient administration, it would be extended and become the settled policy of our country.

So far, apart from the recent Spanish cessions, the Indians excepted, we have extended equal citizenship and civil rights to the inhabitants of all our Territorial acquisition, and have in every instance enlarged, and never limited nor circumscribed the rights and privileges of any people. In all acquisitions on the continent the regions have been sparsely inhabited, but opened up very soon afterwards for settlement, pioneering, adventure, and the skilled enterprise and forward movement of our people, with the effect of settling them and extending our civilization over the continent with its beneficent influences and comfortable homes more rapidly and with better improvements and better means of living than any people have done before.

It seems that no' great advance for the general good and betterment of our people or mankind has been made since Lincoln's time. But in the prevalence and prevailing discontent of toilers and producers we are about ready for the inauguration of another real advancing reform that will lighten the load of the millions whose labor creates all there is of property and wealth. There has never been a better or more propitious opportunity than now. There are thousands of brave and capable men ready and eager to follow in such movements where there were only hundreds in Lincoln's day. The reform must be founded on the truth that "all men are created free and equal." Then, too, there must be a true, real statesman and leader of men, with God's image clear and distinct in his spirit and character; for none other can lead. We are ready to follow such a man in the cause of the doctrine, "Owe no man anything" and "The lands belong to the people."

Obedience to God's simple rules of living and justice and charity to our fellow-men would have made our race truly prosperous and happy, and kept them so. If God's edict, "In the sweat of thy face shalt thou eat bread," and "Replenish the earth, and subdue it, and live upon it," had been observed and obeyed, the means of exchanging a hundred pounds of grain for a day's labor would have been simple enough, and, as strangely simple to wranglers and confounders in finance, it would have easily settled the currency and money questions.

Mr. Lincoln held this belief, and frequently said so. As early as 1854 I remember his saying, in substance: "If the people could rest secure in the belief that there would be gradual and certain emancipation of slavery, which Mr. Clay and his best friends so long and faithfully contended for, and as certainly a removal of all bonded and mortgaged indebtedness, with every family owning its own homestead, not subject to any lien, except taxes, then the questions of

banking and currency could soon be definitely and satisfactorily settled. This should not be done without proper safeguards for the people. Four out of five of them, women and
minors, are without voice or power and without protection
against commerce, trade, and banking systems, which usually
degenerate to a game where the keenest, most overreaching
and unscrupulous take all the weaker have. Experience
proves that wealth, power, and luxury, in the hands of a few,
with widespread poverty of the working people, are followed
by certain decay, national as well as individual. Nor is
there much wisdom in seeking new fields for our progress
in interfering with the Russo-Chinese imbroglio or with
the Asiatic islands of the Pacific. There the lands are so
overpopulated, with two hundred to four hundred inhabitants to the square mile, that comfortable living is exceptional and barely possible in the most seasonable years. The
least shortage occasions widespread want and suffering. The
domain is insufficient for their own people, and all the benefits of commercial undertakings would be shared by the rich
and powerful few who control the shipping and commerce
of the world."

To the hardy, supple-limbed, broad-chested, free, and
intelligent Americans, strong in youth, with ambitious designs and desires for a new and world-expanding field for
adventure, there is a region where the opportunity is at
our door, in the almost boundless Northwest. Instead of
contending for existence on Asiatic islands, with from two
hundred to four hundred half-fed and ill-developed Malays
to the square mile, there are great stretches of forests,
mineral lands, and fertile valleys, with more than one square
mile for each inhabitant. This vast, unopened field, which
belongs to us by right, and the inevitable spread of our
industrial, educational, social, and religious institutions,
should be opened to settlement for our people as soon as
the negotiations for its transfer to the United States can

be completed. This should be done without delay, **for it** is certain to be ours at no distant day.

That peace and amity may prevail between our country and Britain, this Northwest Territory should be peacefully given us, after more than a century's wars and waste. Our sacked and burned Capitol, with its valuable archives, and the destruction of the President's residence, remain an open, unsettled account. The driving of our merchantmen from the seas, the privateering and plundering, the clandestine warfare that swept all the navigable waters of the earth, save our own, clean of our shipping, ships, and commerce, to the amount of full two billion dollars' value, have never been compensated for. To quiet settlement of all these, Britain should haste to relinquish her claims, and transfer to us all the territory west of Lake Superior and Hudson Bay, as an earnest of this amicable desire to remunerate us in part for the destruction, the evils, and the damages she has wrought against us.

There are several other important reasons why this should be done. More than half of the population, including Alaska, are our people; as mining adventure attracts more, this ratio will increase. In the ordinary immigration to that region, outside of mining fields and coast towns, it will not probably reach fifty thousand in ten years under British policy; whereas, under the movements so common to us, five millions of people and five American States will be carved out of that wilderness, and be no unreasonable expectation, within a few years.

Another urgent and growing necessity for the early, peaceable, and friendly transfer, is that the grinding and oppressive system of Britain, of all Europe as well, drives to our shores about half a million of their people every year. Unused to comfortable living or self-supporting pursuits, they are flying from an existence that barely allows them to live, with deepening degradation and increasing poverty.

This immense influx, without a proportionate new field for agriculture or industrial occupation, chokes up our cities and easily accessible States with a greater increase of population than can find employment or be readily assimilated. The result is disturbed industrial conditions, reductions of wages, strikes, and distress, bordering on starvation, in a land of plenty. All this comes of the driving here of so many thousands who can find nothing to do.

If we are to take these victims of oppression in such multitudes, we must of necessity have all the open room of seas, gulfs, lakes, and lands on the continent for expansion. If we are to find the means for the relief and support of those who must emigrate or starve, we should determine at once to take the whole region, to the Polar seas and the Pacific Ocean.

There would be in this act of restoration of our own territory no more than the rectification of our frontier to the lines defined and demanded by our ablest statesmen of their time, Clay, Webster, Benton, and Douglas. The boundary was curtailed to its present unsatisfactory limit by the slavery serving and spreading Administrations of Tyler and Polk, when they were doubling slavery's area in the Southwest. In all of this, Britain, true to its record of devouring greed and continuing enmity to our free institutions, contrived and carried out the humiliating theft of our territory that would sustain millions under our systems of labor, sense, and skill. Our people founded and built the commonwealths of New England in a less fertile and resourceful region, with a climate almost as rigorous.

In this adventure, Britain took our territory wantonly, when it had neither subjects nor commerce of consequence in it, where it had neither people to develop or inhabit it, nor the means at hand to subdue and reduce it. It took it "because they could," with the slaveholders' connivance; contending for all of it; much more than they got; contending for what is now the State of Washington, and part of the State of Oregon—all they could take from us without war, in the most prolonged disputing of scheming lords and contriving, arbitrating, monarchy land accumulators. All this was done that they might limit our progress and help to work our injury, rather than for any real good and lasting advantage its occupation could bring to their people.

This vast, unknown, undivided country, with its seas, bays, gulfs, water-sheds, water-basins, two of the largest rivers of the world, and many smaller ones, the immense valleys of the Mackenzie and the Yukon, cover an area, including Alaska, as large as the United States. It is a region with boundaries approximately as follows: Commencing near the west point of Lake Superior at the crossing of the 47th degree, north latitude, and the 95th parallel, west longitude, thence north on the shore of Hudson Bay to Franklin Bay, or Gulf, to the Polar seas, about 1,660 miles; thence west to Alaska, 45 degrees, some 2,500 miles; thence around the coast lines of Alaska over 3,000 miles; thence down the Pacific Coast line to Puget Sound on the 47th degree, north latitude; thence east to Lake Superior to the place of beginning, some 2,000 miles. This irregular, square-shaped body of land and water, subdivided, would make fifty States of an average size of Kansas, each two hundred miles wide by four hundred miles in length, of about 80,000 square miles—512,000,000 acres. This, with twenty people to the square mile, would be 1,600,000 population for each State. This widening domain is larger than our present area in States and Territories, excepting Alaska, which is included in this estimate of areas of this immense Northwest. The area is larger than all of Russia in Europe. It has several chains of inland fresh-water lakes, running up to thousands in number, full of the most desirable food fishes, waterfowl, wild geese, ducks, and smaller birds in flocks of millions.

It is the richest and most extensively-wooded region in the world that has not been invaded by the woodman and his wood-destroying ax. In the abundance of the rivers and fresh-water lakes there are valleys with co-extensive forests, running hundreds of miles in many places, that have never been explored. These are full of deer, elk, moose, and many smaller animals, and some herds of bison on the more open plains. The wide distribution of these fresh-water streams, lakes, and small basins gives the central region an even summer climate and moisture that usually protects it from severe drought. The fertile lands, so far, have only been estimated. A fair average of these estimates would give about two million square miles, which, with the timber and forest areas, make this a field for adventure and development that will be inexhaustible for hundreds of years. Besides, there are extensive fields of coal, iron, zinc, copper, and many clays, stone in endless form and variety, so useful in building and engineering enterprises. The area fit for the production of grains and grasses within reach of its present small farming population, as given in estimates of hunters and trappers, whose observations have been the most extensive, is about one million five hundred thousand square miles. In addition to these there are recently-discovered gold regions of such vast extent and fabulous resources in the inception of their development, that they have spread the feverish ambition of the gold-hunters from the hive of the pure gold-worshipers of Jerusalem to Lombard Street and Wall Street.

With all these advantages this is the coming region of hope, for strong-armed, big-hearted Americans, who never hesitate in the face of obstacles, or shrink from the danger of pioneering adventure, where it promises the opening of a new country and better life and living. There is little need of healthy, well-developed men and women doubting the climate. They can live there in better health, with more of the vigor and strength of robust manhood, in almost any part of it, when acclimated and they get modern conveniences, than in the tropics of America or Asia.

When we come to consider the cold and inclement seasons, there and elsewhere, we may learn that seven or eight States as large as Maine, with better and more fertile lands and a milder climate, can be made on the Southern border. We can learn that all of Denmark, Sweden, and Norway, more than half of Germany, and all of Russia in Europe—five countries, two of them among the strongest of the earth—lie in the same latitude with this great Northwest. By reason of the milder temperature of the big Pacific Ocean, the conformation of the country, its wide forests, and the distribution of fresh water bodies, the American has the milder and more even climate. All of them are north of 50 degrees north latitude.

These countries have population as follows: Denmark, 3,000,000; North Scotland, 1,000,000; Sweden and Norway, 6,000,000; Russia in Europe, 95,000,000; North Germany, 25,000,000; total, 130,000,000.

Great Britain is about all north of fifty degrees, but has a climate greatly modified by the waters of the Gulf stream. All of Scotland north of Aberdeen has a more inhospitable climate than Southern Alaska; nevertheless the sturdy Highlanders of those frozen seas have no superiors among men in physical development or hardihood anywhere on the earth.

CHAPTER LIV.

ON the early morning of April 12, 1861, General Beauregard, with seven thousand Confederates, assaulted Fort Sumter in Charleston Harbor, South Carolina. The fort was occupied by seventy officers and men of the United States army, commanded by Major Robert Anderson. The old work was in no condition for defense, under the fire of several batteries erected at every convenient angle during the five months of unmolested preparation. The officers' quarters were soon burning under the bombardment; the old brick walls crumbled away under the heavy shot of the siege guns. The powder magazine soon became inaccessible by reason of the twisted, heated, and half-unhinged doors, and it was in constant danger of explosion.

With their ammunition almost exhausted, and no hope of holding the antiquated and indefensible structure, it was surrendered next day on honorable terms. On Sunday, the 14th, the garrison, with arms, accouterments, and colors waving, after a salute of fifty guns, evacuated the old fort. Our loss was one man killed and three wounded by an explosion. The Confederates reported no loss.

With this act the long-threatened and unprovoked war to divide the Union was begun. Compromise and our abandonment of the Negro to his fate of slavery had failed. The gun in a bloody hand was come at last to end the long dispute; but the curse of Cain was not more certain than that slavery or the Republic had to perish in the conflict.

On the 9th of January previous, President Buchanan's reorganized Administration made an ineffectual attempt to reprovision the fort with commissary and subsistence supplies with the merchant vessel, *Star of the West*. It was fired upon, an open act of war, and not permitted to enter Charleston Harbor. President Lincoln's Administration fitted out another expedition of several vessels for the same purpose in March, but these did not reach Charleston until after the surrender.

The hostile reduction of the old fort, although it had been expected and dreaded for months, fired the spirit of the half-wakened, half-conscious, peace-loving people. Like a tornado it aroused the patriotism of the fathers, the mothers, the daughters, and the strong and sturdy sons of freedom, the successors to the American heritage of liberty, so dearly bought. Nothing had so stirred the people since the torch that called men to arms in the Old South Church of Boston, and the galloping midnight rider, Paul Revere, on his flying horse summoning the minute-men to the fields of death and deathless fame.

On Monday, April 15th, the woeful story of the captured fort, the torn-down and dishonored flag, was carried over the wires and spread on the wings of the wind. In the same way these carried also the summons of the President on the several States for seventy-five thousand volunteers, as a militia force, in support of the Government and the public defense. These troops were raised, mustered into service, and at and on their way to the Capital within a few days. While the revolting States and several disloyal governors of the border States did not respond to the call, all the free States did in prompt order, and the loyal people of the border States themselves mustered and organized troops, until over one hundred thousand men answered the call.

A short time afterwards the President called an extra session of the Thirty-seventh Congress, to meet on the following Fourth of July. He postponed the date some weeks in order that Kentucky might have representation. The delay,

for this and other reasons, to avoid inconsiderate and precipitate action, and to afford time to mold all the Union-support-
ing parties and factions into one strong, national Union party,
was wise and prudent. When Congress assembled, this loyal
Union organization was complete and potential in all things
affecting the progress of the war and the integrity of the
Union. By his sober and wise management, President Lincoln had risen to uncontested and trusted leadership.

The wisdom of this conservative, or peace, policy of Lincoln's Administration, in the beginning months, has seldom
been fairly recognized. It was vigorously assailed from many
quarters. The ambitious, daring, and enthusiastic objected
to it, because they believed that an immediate assault on the
important assemblings in the South would suppress the insurrection as you would suppress a street fight or a riot.
These had forgotten or had not considered the situation;
that the Southern State Governments were all on the side of
and fostering the revolt; that the National Government was
then without military forces, or the means of speedily providing and equipping them; while the South had been preparing
for war for thirty years or more, and that the cotton States
had then been mustering and drilling a militia force of some
one hundred and fifty thousand for five months.

Sympathizers with the South, of every degree, faced either
way as it seemed best to them, in the clandestine help given
the conspirators. They assailed every preparation to supply
the forts or enforce the laws, unless there were some new
and more binding guarantee to slavery, and the Constitution
were so amended. They denounced the Administration vigorously when it was not provoking hostilities at once as they
secretly desired. They kept pleading for peace and concessions, which the conspirators ardently affected to desire,
while they were the only ones threatening to disturb it. They
wanted to be attacked and oppressed, and have their States
invaded at once, as they asserted and declared so often they

would be; but President Lincoln, with higher statesmanship and strategy, would not allow it just then, and he did wisely better in not doing it. His cautious conduct of affairs kept all the border States from going into the secession movement, except Virginia, which was divided, and about one-third of that State soon became the loyal State of West Virginia. His management gave us the morale and support of the five important States, Delaware, Maryland, West Virginia, Kentucky, and Missouri; thus taking from the forming conspiracy almost half of their expected strength.

These States, which would have been driven into secession without Lincoln's timely and patient leadership, furnished the Union armies 275,000 volunteers or more. This was a truly formidable force, as we would have learned with sorrow if they had been forced into war against us. Missouri enlisted 110,000, while Kentucky with 75,000 kept close in number to the strong Western States of Iowa, Michigan, and Wisconsin. The others on the border stood to their duty in the thick of the strife. This was masterly control, with actual results, in five States saved and accounted for. Besides the President was doing well in other movements and rising to higher planes of achievement. His border State management can be given in a simple proposition, about like this: The thirty years' leadership and control of the South held the slave States, including those of the border, in a compact body, in the interest of slavery, against the ablest leaders of the time, North and South. Jefferson Davis was the strongest leader in action the South ever had. He had conspired successfully, as he and his followers believed; and it appeared probable that they would take all the slave States at once into their conspiracy. Nevertheless, Lincoln with genius, patient labor, and superior skill, took five of the best and strongest of the slave States from them in the first movements of the open insurrection.

When Congress assembled he was master of the situation

on the Union side—master, not only because he had power
and could command the short-lived aspirants all about him,
who were passing in timely and untimely succession; but because the growing multitudes of the common people by the
hundreds of thousands liked him, believed in him, and were
following him, as they would follow no other man in the
crisis.

Congress at the special session, without serious dispute or
difference, sustained him in all that he asked or desired. In
his message the President advocated the policy of an honest
enforcement of the laws of the land, in which the right of
every one, even those in revolt, should be respected, as he had
declared in his Inaugural Address. From this he proceeded
to more emphatic recital of the conspirators' designs and
purposes, a deeper revelation and analysis of the causes in
conflict, advancing to the higher consideration of human
right, manhood, and resolute defense of the Union.

He said: "They have forced upon the country the distinct
issue, immediate dissolution or blood. . . . And this issue
embraces more than the fate of these United States. It presents to the whole family of man the question, whether a
constitutional republic or democracy, a government of the
people by these same people, can or can not maintain its territorial integrity against its own domestic foes. It presents
the question whether discontented individuals, too few in
number to control the Administration, according to organic
law, in any case, can always, in the pretenses made in this
case, or any other pretenses, or arbitrarily without any pretense, break up their Government, and thus practically put
an end to free government on the earth. It forces us to ask,
Is there in all Republics this inherent and fatal weakness?
Must government, of necessity, be too strong for the liberties
of its own people, or too weak to maintain its own existence?

"So viewing the issue, no choice was left but to call out
the war power of the Government; and so, to resist force em-

ployed for its destruction by force employed for its preservation. . . ."

Having reached this solid and unyielding foundation of a united people in law and in government, he determined, as their Executive, to defend and preserve their liberties, and to defend the same liberties in principle for all men. He closed, saying, "And having chosen our course, without guile and pure purpose let us renew our trust in God, and go forward without fear and with manly hearts."

It was found that our little army was scattered and out of reach, in the most inconvenient and remote situations, where it took months to get the small commands to convenient points where they could be supplied, recruited, and reorganized for active service. The same was true of our ships, shipping, and naval forces, which were scattered everywhere. It is a significant truth, and an example of the hold our system has on the minds of the common people, embracing our private soldiers and sailors, that while more than half of their officers, who had been trained and educated at the public expense, went into secession with their States, many of them without even this flimsy pretense, none of the enlisted men of the army or navy did so. All of them remained true and loyal as far as known, to their lasting honor and credit, and to the good name of American soldiers and sailors.

The members were in such accord, and the necessities so present and urgent, that no Congress ever framed by law, in a thirty days' session, so much needful legislation. Acts were passed for the mobilization of an army of 400,000, with several thousand for the navy, which grew into forces of a million men within two years. Other acts provided for supplying, arming, equipping, subsisting, and paying these vast assembling forces; and for gathering and rebuilding what there was of the wandering fleet. Among other pressing duties, they immediately began refashioning, supplying, and making the navy as powerful, destructive, and defensive as modern skill and invention permitted. There were lines on lines of detail, necessary to create and equip armies and vessels, all of which were carefully and patiently gone over and provided for. These acts and provisions of law were enlarged and sustained, both in letter and policy, through the four years of war, waste, and destruction.

When the war came our country had grown to a wonderful prosperity. In the production of all the necessities of life and comfortable living it was far ahead of what it had ever been, or the condition of any other country on the earth. Yet in the midst of this plenitude, one of the most injurious acts of the conspirators was to leave the Government they had attempted to destroy and so nearly ruined, without the means of carrying on its ordinary civil processes in time of peace, without borrowing money. No revenues were provided to pay such loans or accruing interest. Hence the credit of the Nation was down to the bottom, as it had been planned for and designed. However, the Administration and Congress met the unexpected demand as statesmen and patriots. They framed and provided a system of revenue, tariff customs, treasury certificates, and commercial regulations, that produced funds to carry on the war, eventually producing as much as five hundred million dollars annually— a financial victory that sustained the Union among the people, as the army and navy did on the field and sea.

Slavery was the cankering sin of centuries, coming to us through our civilization, our Constitution, our laws and precedents, our institutes of right and justice, our societies, Churches, and political parties. It was the yielding to wrong, in its ruthless, torturing wickedness, as reckless and contumacious in the eyes of justice as a slaver at sea who emptied half his cargo of chained humanity into six fathoms of water to lighten his load for flight, or in closer quarters all of his cargo, corsair-like, to escape just and certain punishment.

More wicked and bloody than all we can tell were the crimes and the multiplying iniquities of this consuming evil against men, and its culminating conspiracy to destroy the Republic, the only hope of free Government on the earth.

President Buchanan, at the close of a twisted and tortured career, fled from the Capital into grateful retirement, not only bereft of the name of faithful and honorable service he had earnestly desired to render his country, but almost robbed of his reason. He was barely rescued, he and the Nation, from slavery's clutch of death by the only power that could loosen its grip, the favor of God and the determined will of the people.

This vile system had stricken every party and leader in their most vulnerable part. It spared none save Satan's elect. It sought every party or man who stood a bar to its progress or control, with promise or threat, which was equivalent in the end to a time when the party or man was useless, or could serve or contend with it no longer. Its support came to be fatal to every party or distinguished leader who accepted anything at its hands, even so much as a pretended compromise.

It came to General Winfield Scott, not only in his age but in his younger manhood, in his brightest years and highest ambition. It was a dead weight of conservatism and lethargy to the gallant soldier who was in the front of the strife wherever his country called him. For over fifty years it was a breaking load he could not rise from under. He was for years held back from where he might have been President, finally defeated, and himself and his party obliterated, because they were conservative on slavery to the point that neither side trusted or believed in them. On this slavery subject alone was he conservative, and hesitated only in face of its besetments.

He was one who in all other works of duty never doubted, nor asked time or lagged one moment in what came to him in ordinary life or his campaigns. These had all been earnestly conducted, without respite, almost without caution, in the face of danger, wherever fearless assault and celerity of movement gave promise of victory. Whether it was across lakes or rivers, in front or in forest obstructions, as against the British in Canada or over an ocean gulf, through and over fortified mountain ranges under the tropical sun of Mexico, in all he was in himself the impersonation of an American soldier, always in the battle, the most intrepid and daring. He was this, but the incubus of conservatism in the face of slavery, at a certain stage in public affairs, held the great soldier down. He had grown up with it and in it. And as its demands had often been settled in compromise, it ran in his mind, as it had with many loyal people like him, that this might be done again, even after it darkened the sky in settled gloom. Apart from this growing up and training in the conservatism of slavery, he showed his loyalty and superiority as a military leader, and his services to his country were gratefully recognized by the people.

He was the one man whom the otherwise powerful conspirators could not shake or remove from his place at the head of the army. Knowing this, President Lincoln understood that the old hero soldier was the strongest, uncorrupted force of the Government left. Though aged and infirm, his was the power that kept it alive through the dreadful months of the preceding winter. He was and had been there, so also he had been the uncounted, the unbidden, yet the insurmountable holding-back power of patriotism, through the time of the treason-hatching conspiracy and the no less faithless Administration of the Government, from the lamentable death of the patriot Taylor to Lincoln.

He had not been necessarily on the side of slavery—never so when its leaders came in conflict with honesty, duty, or his country, as he proved in the long Kansas struggle; but he had been so hedged in and hampered by it, like the statesman of

his time, as often to be helpless against it; for men were infatuated with the belief that compromise would settle it as
had always been done.

He was eminent alike in peace and in war, and in the
critical juncture he was believed in and followed faithfully
by more than half of the officers who were to command and
lead the Union armies. He had also been believed in and
followed more confidingly by almost all who were deserting
to command and lead the other side. From this study of
Scott you can understand how the President counseled with
and confided in him, who had the knowledge, the experience,
and standing of "the old man at the head of the army." With
his little body of a few hundred loyal soldiers he was the
mainstay of the Nation in the peaceful succession of President Lincoln.

When President Lincoln went to the Capital he could do
no better than go to the honored soldier to get his best help
and cordial co-operation. His services were fresh in remembrance and as satisfying to the incoming as they had been
to the retiring President. It was into this fatalism, this
gnawing conservatism of slavery, that he was plunged on his
inauguration, where he was to lead the legions of right in a
battle to death with the Dragon. He knew who the old hero
was, out of what distinct civilization he came, how he was
encompassed round about; and he knew him to be the most
experienced in the fast coming emergencies, the one to rely
on whose system and training-school had made, as far as men
and systems can, what there was of coming military leaders
on both sides.

It was well that it was so; for if the President had been
differently minded, and had taken to other plans and advisers in the beginning, neither he nor our people were in
condition to force the conflict to advantage. Here, again,
Lincoln stood alone. His career had been such, that he had
risen slowly and patiently to the chief leadership in the great

cause, so firmly set against the great wrong that he was almost alone, with no power above him but God, to lead in the
greatest combat of modern times. He was in continuing
relation to his cause, where he had been from its beginnings;
where he had to rise out of the heated disputes and fiery conflicts the real leader, trained in the work, the reasoning, the
onset and the crashing destruction, to final and complete
victory.

He was chosen of God to lead, as event succeeding event
confirmed. After a long voyage down the Mississippi River
to New Orleans, in the marts of commerce and in its slave
pens, when a boy of seventeen he saw horrid slavery in practical progress; and there he answered the Divine inspiration
with his solemn promise that, "As God gives me strength I
will strike it." After a few years' time for reflection he was
there again, where he as solemnly reaffirmed his promise.

Those who consider this no more than an ordinary event
must remember, that as boy or man he was always truthful,
honest, and conscientious, and that if any man was inspired,
he surely was, as it appears when the simple facts are considered. He had nothing of the character to be the subject
of any delusion, but was as firmly held to realities in belief
as to candor and truth. In the strongest verification of this
his whole life and conduct proved him. As God is truth and
hates wrong, and as surely as he has not abandoned good and
righteous men and righteous purposes on the earth, he was
with and led Abraham Lincoln from the cotton and slave
marts of New Orleans to slavery's final overthrow.

Again in the Illinois capital, at Vandalia, with the Executive, the Legislature, the courts, and men of affairs from
all over the State, where over two hundred leaders of all parties were assembled, Abraham Lincoln and Dan Stone, representatives from Sangamon County, were the only two who
"protested" against the prevailing slavery subserviency, and
openly declared "that slavery is wrong." In the beginning

of the contest with Senator Douglas, against the advice of friends, against the declared belief of all parties except the Abolitionists, if they might have been a party, he declared as openly as on former occasions that "a house divided against itself can not stand;" and that "slavery or the Union must perish." So, too, he then determined for himself against his advisers the questions he would ask Douglas.

Thus briefly we have traced him, boy and man in his wonderful development against slavery, to the Presidency, surrounded by a deadly conservatism. He rose out of it with the heaviest load upon him ever borne by mortal man, slow in emerging as the sin had been deep in the minds of indifferent, wicked, and careless men.

When the President sat down to go over the rolls of the officers who should command with the old hero of Cerro Gordo, then seventy-five years old, it appeared that he was scarcely less ripe for decay than the best certified lot of soldier statesmen, who were to lead the hosts of brave men against the Rebellion. The conservatives, who were anxious to lead, but not to lead too far or rashly, were not all, in bodily make-up and physique, so superanuated as the old general; but for ready, unhampered service, effectiveness, and availability they were the most constitutional malady stricken, bandaged, splintered, plastered, patched, and mended assortment of warriors, for movement against the slaveholders' rebellion, that could have been gathered up anywhere in America, and unlike anything that could have been picked up outside of West Point.

Except a very few barely known, who were rising slowly with their commands and were sustained by them, they were all inoculated with the dead conservatism that was the common disorder of the soldiers and the soldier statesmen. In this infectious malady of conservative constitutionalism, every one of them was instantly ready against a "nigger," or any opinion or plans that did not suit them, or that did not include "time for organization, evolution, and movement." Under it a mere tyro in military affairs could set aside at once any law, judgment, or decree against slavery or its protection as being "unconstitutional;" and that was the end of it. It never got any one of these men ready, in due time, for a decisive battle or a campaign. They were thoroughly infatuated and swelled out with the doctrine of "States' rights." They could readily tell you how to hold a "nigger" as a slave in a slave State, and how to take a "nigger" out of a free State or military camp where he had escaped, and "return him as a fugitive," under "the Constitution and laws," to his rebellious master; but you could not find them ready to move a man or an army or a gun into a rebellious State or community until it was certain that it was not to be "an Abolition war to free the niggers," or to infringe their masters' rights, "under the Constitution." With ninety-five slaveholders out of every hundred in open rebellion, or in earnest sympathy with it, it took the old slavery-tinctured West Pointers two years to learn that God and the American people fully understood the relation of that peculiar institution to the Rebellion.

In this sort of beginning, with lack of leaders and opportunity, General Scott could do no better, nor could President Lincoln do otherwise, than to take some of these slavery-chilled soldiers as leaders of our armies. They appeared to be competent, and in appearance seemed satisfactory, before we knew the extent and depth of the slavery curse that poisoned all, or nearly all, the brave men who happened to be trained and educated at West Point under pro-slavery Administrations. The conspiring leaders and their abettors, in whole or in part, South or North, had used their influence to mislead and destroy the prominent officers of our army, by approval or threats, as they had too successfully maneuvered with Clay, Webster, Benton, Cass, and a hundred lesser men.

In the progress of the strife there came an end of this

baneful conservatism. Our Western armies were doing the work unlooked for by the conspirators and slavery apologists everywhere. They were advancing in war and into Southern territory, raising up to higher commands as they went along, in the joined wager and blows of battle leaders like Lyon, Grant, Thomas, Sheridan, Sherman, Rosecrans, Logan, and Blair, who could fight and win battles and force their invincible columns ahead in less than three days after an action, yes, on the next morning; and move forward steady and determined as on the day before, on one or other flank of the enemy, in continuing battles and victories. All these were either cured of or never had this deadly malady of conservative constitutionalism.

All this "out West" was done in disregard of "the art of war" in Europe, and with still more pointed indifference to the tactics and strategy of stupefied West Pointers. Our Eastern armies, too, though in a much slower gait, held back by so much clogging at the top, were training on hard-contested fields, where lives were sacrificed to prove the strength of old-time tactics every day; but the brave men were making records for and pushing forward such leaders as Meade, Hancock, Sykes, Sedgwick, Warren, Reynolds, Sickles, Wright, and Terry.

In the century struggle, in the rising of freedom against slavery, in the opening strokes of the mightiest struggle since Charles Martel's contest with the Saracens at Tours in 732, conservatism under and entangling General Scott prevailed as nothing else could. With his growing to manhood, his fitting for service and war, his Virginia citizenship in its polite, gentlemanly, but fossilized ideas of progress in war, as in enterprise, it had not rotted out his sterling patriotism as it had that of the greater part of two generations among whom he had grown to honored and respected age; but it held him down half chained and half helpless in the face of the rising and spreading insurrection. Although slavery was going in the inevitable crash, it left its poisoned and infected conservatism or do-nothingism against it.

So conservatism remained in the army and in the war office, where it commanded policy and campaigns, until the whole of it was overthrown by the President, by advancing General U. S. Grant and his valiant *confreres.* This was not done to the discredit of General Scott and many able and worthy officers of the army, but because of the utter worn-outness of the system and its infection of disloyalty.

The three great armies of the Union, mobilized at the first and remaining evenly so to the end, were the armies of the Potomac, the Cumberland, and the Tennessee. These were the most powerful bodies of troops that ever tramped the earth, or ever faced the foe in war. Without long lists and muster-rolls, that would mystify, rather than enlighten, these mighty forces took the field for war, under the full sweep and swing of conservatism in 1861-62, under the command of Generals G. B. McClellan, D. C. Buell, and H. W. Halleck respectively.

This is not our story of the war, but a short review and recapitulation of some leading events, to the lowest ebb and passing of the crisis, when the country, under the military mismanagement of this same deadly conservatism, was wasting men and idling away opportunities, worse in procrastination, sickness, and disease than in active war. It seemed to be more concerned for the slaveholder, his abettors and their pretended rights and the rights of revolting States, than for the life and well-being of the Nation. All this God permitted in wisdom beyond our ken, that the humiliated and angered people might be aroused to rise in their power once for all, and write the death-warrant of slavery.

The Republic was indeed in the ashes of despair in the darkened summer and fall of 1862, when only one of our great armies stood holding its own, and that the least sustained. This when conservatism was defending the Capital and the States east of Ohio, with an army on .the north side of the Potomac, and the States west, on·the line of the Ohio River, with an army then defending Louisville and Cincinnati. All were falling··back, except Grant's army of. the Tennessee, which was not defending.

· In this direful flow of the conservative tide, what of President Lincoln? Was he doing anything, or was he, too, going down in the last swirl of soporous stupidity? ·The answer was an emphatic "No, indeed." And it was plain enough for the most witless to understand, if they could have known and interpreted all that his sorrow-laden leader was doing. In January, 1862, he ordered a general advance of all of .the armies of the Union. He wrote it, the order, himself, meaning to say just what he did say, that the rule for the conduct of the war was to advance upon and destroy the armies of the Rebellion. Instead of being sunk in the sleepy drench of the conservatism all about him, he was rising out of it in ·the only way it. could be done; in the strength and heroism of our undefeatable armies.

He was searching for leaders, brave and capable enough to fight battles, and to lead such incomparable armies, trusting that in the general. advance he would find them... This was January, full six months before the darkest August and half of September, 1862—six months ahead, as .far as he could be, but held down. Yet he was moving fast as he could. Grant with one of our three great armies was moving forward, not backward an inch. General W. S. Rosecrans, who held valiantly the front line with him, was a few weeks after leading the second of these three great armies to victory. The grinding· again was slow; but the President in well-earned leadership was rising as God's prophet and the hope of the. Nation. He removed General Halleck from command of the Western armies by "promoting" him, so the rosters read, "to the command of the armies of the United States;" but then, this command was limited "to the War Office at

Washington," where there were many such commanders of our armies. Until Grant rang out the old regime of "Fight and fall back," by the new one of "Fight and move forward by the right or left flank," it was quite difficult to tell just who next under the President and Secretary Stanton had command of the armies of the United States. However, Halleck got to Washington to help Stanton, and remained. Buell, poor, neglected Buell, one of the last remnants of the conservative old school, burned down in his socket and was jarred out forever by the guns of Perryville.

General Halleck was the author of "General Order No. 3" superseding his predecessor General Fremont's slave liberating one. Under this order every camp of the Union army was made the hunting-ground for rebellious slaveholders to search and capture their fugitive slaves, wherever our soldiers could be outraged by such unlawful inquisition. When Halleck went to Washington to "command the armies of the United States," or to be a clerk in the War Office, whichever it was, he did not abandon his position, but declared that he had "no interest in the black man whatever, one way or another; and that my position is a military one without reference to the Negro race."

The army of the Cumberland contained, all told, about one hundred and twenty-five thousand men, the very best of American manhood. It had no occasion in reason to fear meeting any force on the continent, if it had been properly assembled, supplied, and led, which conditions unfortunately were never all fulfilled in due time. Yet through all its War Office planned campaigns and half-made concentrations, it held the middle country of the enemy, from Florence, Alabama, to Chattanooga, Tennessee, and what this line covered, from first to last, as it was taken and occupied. It never fought with half of its effective force present for duty, when at least three-fourths of it should have been. But regardless of this, it fought all the time and never murmured.

It made campaigns that it deplored, especially the one back to Louisville in September, 1862, that it openly repudiated and condemned, but executed as a soldier's sacrifice. Buell was the only man who openly defended it. Through all it never lost a battle; not even Chickamauga, where it met Bragg's fully-recruited and concentrated Western army, reenforced by Longstreet, with the best corps of Lee's army. In place of reaching the Ohio River in a rearward campaign in October, Buell should have occupied Chattanooga by the first of July, 1862, and have held it, where he would have been sustained by the Union people and the .recruits from Kentucky, East Tennessee, and the mountainous region round about. Our army could have held it then, as they did after so many battles; but Buell was not made to fight and win battles. Here he conspicuously failed, when no man had better opportunity for success and a better chance to reach a soldier's highest ambition than he had. When he ought to have been heading directly for Chattanooga, in June, 1862, from Corinth, some rumors that Bragg was advancing into Kentucky where he would break our line of communications and separate us from our base of supplies, the Ohio River, turned him the wrong way. The dread of meeting Bragg's army so fully alarmed him, that he turned our main column northeast to Nashville, where we arrived in a few weeks with our principal force of about fifty thousand men. If they had had a good commander, who trusted to the sense and valor of the men, we could have defeated Bragg's army any day he offered us battle; whereas, we lay idle several weeks until September.

All this went on, while Bragg and his not equally-equipped force of about fifty thousand men, lay in and about Lebanon, some twenty miles east, where we could have met and beaten them, or driven them back and then taken Chattanooga. This could have been done then as well as, or better, than we did after waiting and wasting the health and lives of thousands, and executing over five hundred miles of marching, cowardly looking backward and catching up in campaigning. Chattanooga was taken in September, 1863, when we had all the means to take it, except a leader, in June, 1862. Here again the grinding was slow, but God was disciplining the people in sorrow and sacrifice to the courage that would strike and destroy the cause of the Rebellion, as bravely as they were then striking the thousands of the poor, deceived, and misled, though heroic Southern men, who were falling in legions with arms defending the sin that degraded and 'held them down.

It is difficult to write temperately of such generals as Halleck and Buell. The latter, who had been honored to command such an army, from cowardice or equally bad motive, was, against the judgment of every other man capable of expressing an opinion in that army, willing to abandon Nashville, and came very near doing it, with all that had been achieved in eighteen months of fighting and campaigning. The disgraceful abandonment would have been all he could do, not to save his country in a forward march and perhaps a battle, as was ordered by the President, but to subject it to a deplorable defeat past any reckoning.

This base desertion and abandonment was overruled, in the outspoken indignation of the army, which would not submit, little as they were inclined to insubordination. A conference resulted, which should be remembered, as it was called by many at the time, "the general class meeting of the army of the Cumberland and the loyalists of Tennessee, with Governor Andrew Johnson, Parson W. G. Brownlow, and the Rev. Colonel Granville Moody, class-leaders, and Generals J. M. Palmer and J. S. Negley, doorkeepers and stewards of the congregation." This came about late in August in one of the earnest daily meetings, then often held in the Capitol building at Nashville, in the office of Andrew Johnson, who was then military governor of Tennessee. The first three named, after an earnest meeting sent for General Buell and such officers as he desired. He soon appeared with some members of his staff, when for an hour the dispute was vigorously carried on, until Governor Johnson, in his patriotic wrath, rose, shaking his hand almost over the quailing, drawn-up form of the little general, and denounced him in his round, sonorous, almost thunderous, voice.

The governor said in substance: "General Buell, you shall not evacuate Nashville; not at least without my going ahead of you to denounce the cowardly act, that would surrender one of our strongest military positions. It can be held, even if you retreat, until we are relieved by a soldier worthy of his country's honor. This can be done by Generals Palmer's and Negley's divisions." Both these being present, expressed their ability to do so.

In this strained condition of the conference, Parson Brownlow turned to Colonel Moody, saying: "Brother Moody, this is the time of the Lord, when men are weak. Let us turn to him in agonizing prayer, that he desert us not in these sorrowful days, when there is a dearth in the land of valiant men to lead the hosts of freedom." They prayed earnestly, in humility. Several came in like-minded, among whom were Colonels Jaquith, Allen Buckner, and others, who joined as effectively as they buckled in their belts on the front lines, and the conference prayer or class meeting lasted an hour, to much profit, on that dismal morning. Brother Moody closed with a fervent appeal to God, "Not to forget or abandon us, or leave us to the ignorance or cowardice of those who are unworthy to lead brave men; but to save this Nation, cemented by the blood of our Revolutionary fathers and the patriotism of Washington and his heroes, who courted death, rather than dishonor; not to suffer any one to surrender this city and military position, in gaining which so much of life and treasure and waiting and sorrow had been given and endured." When he arose, Parson Brownlow said, laying his hand on the brave preacher's shoulder, "The Lord has prevailed, and the divisions of Palmer and Negley will remain; · the city and this region will be secure with them until they are re-enforced." General Buell, who had said little during this remarkable meeting, retired, leaving Brownlow's statement undisputed, in pursuance of which the two divisions remained.

In the heat of dispute, General Buell was addressed by Governor Johnson: "Have you any authority to retreat on your base line of the Ohio River?" Buell muttered something about having authority from Washington, "To conduct my campaigns to the best advantage, as my judgment approves," and something more that was not understood. Governor Johnson, continuing said: "This place, with its supplies and what can easily be concentrated here, is a sufficient base for your army. You should be concerned chiefly now about Bragg's base line and break it, and defeat his army, only twenty miles east. The Hermitage, and the spirit of its owner, the old hero, should arouse every Union man to do his best. Bragg's army is neither so large nor so well equipped and supplied as yours. You should be as eager as your powerful Western army is, to meet the enemy, where it is not probable that you will have equal opportunity again. But if you have any uncertainty, you are perhaps not the leader to meet Bragg, who is something in the line of fighting soldiers. In the event of making this useless, and to our minds highly objectionable, movement, you must leave us the two divisions; and with them we will hold Middle Tennessee until we can do better."

The movements went on; six of our nine splendid divisions chased Bragg about two hundred miles on parallel, or converging roads, on a run to Louisville, which place was in command of General Nelson. He had been driven back from Southeast Kentucky by the Confederate General Kirby Smith, with a much superior force; but on reaching Louisville Nelson was strongly re-enforced, until the Union troops were full thirty thousand. A number of them were new recruits, it is true; but they were nevertheless the kind of men who won our battles, and never failed under capable leaders. Notwithstanding all the disasters of conservatism, the new recruits covered every delinquency. With Grant at Shiloh, or Rosecrans and Thomas at Stone River and Chickamauga, thousands of these same new recruits stood and held the firing lines alongside of the veterans of other fields.

CHAPTER LV.

THE army of the Cumberland reached Louisville, September 29, 1862, in such condition for campaigning that it began its return march, following Bragg's Confederate army in two or three days' time, as soon as the situation was understood. The dread of Bragg's army was sincere, and prevailed everywhere, among friends and foes, for the good reasons that it supplied itself wherever it could, wholly indifferent about prices or values, for it paid for nothing, but was energetic and swift in taking the best, and all it could carry away.

When it reached Louisville, most of the command had been on continuous march from below the south line of Tennessee. We had been without any word but rumors, and had no reliable information concerning the progress of the war. We were indignant at our own useless retreat; but more, if possible, to learn that the army of the Potomac, that had neither lack of men and supplies nor want of means for concentration, and supposed to have a brave and capable commander, had been as badly managed, and that its campaigns had been as disastroulsy conducted as our own; worse, indeed, because of its position, greater strength, and responsibility. We learned that after several hotly-contested engagements, and one quite decisive battle at Malvern Hill, while the army was safely and securely holding position on James River, only a few miles from Richmond, McClellan in utter abandonment of his well and hardly-won base, had given it up in anxiety for the "Defense of Washington!" What else of profound military necessity there was for this retreat we heard not;

but learned that our Halleck made a run with Lee, and beat him a little to Washington, saved it, headed him off on the north side of the Potomac in Maryland, where he fought another pretty decisive battle at Antietam, and drove him across and back to his own side of the famous river. All in all, he defeated Lee there as easily as he could have done on James River. He might then have taken Richmond, which that valiant army had need to do later. It would seem that he could have taken it and saved Washington more effectually by doing so. During this flight of armies and Lee's march to capture Washington, as was supposed, and finally to take Maryland and perhaps Pennsylvania, Mc-Clellan fell into the trap to defend Washington at all hazards, when these Southern armies were doing their best in recruiting and plundering raids.

General John Pope, who had won merited distinction in moving forward and taking things in his vigorous Western campaigns, was an Illinois soldier and a personal friend of Governor Yates and President Lincoln. In this flight to a base of supplies and to save Washington, he was placed in command of some emergency-gathered and rapidly-organized forces, called "The Army of Virginia." By the rules of conservatism, this inadequate force was to hold back Lee's advancing army until McClellan could, in easy time, without discomfort, locate Lee's army, and place his own where it could properly "defend Washington," as it should be done.

Lee was one of the chiefs of conservatism, but, not appreciating the delicate situation of the slavery sympathizers at the head of our army, although he was second man in the Confederacy, began fighting Pope in earnest at Manassas in August, regardless of McClellan's ambition to be first man on the Union side, where he could "defend Washington" and make it as little of an "Abolition war" as possible. Lee appeared to be indifferent to the precarious counterpoise of holding up half-made friends on both sides, or at least those not opposed to, but as deeply tinctured as possible with the conservatism of slavery, as the leaders of our army. McClellan apparently believed that, with something of war and fighting, which could not then be avoided, concessions could be made, and a compromise or a treaty would give slavery all it started out to get, which so many of our weak statesmen were ready to give. Lee altogether upset this plan by assaulting Pope in deadly joined battle, and was so furious in his attacks that he made Pope believe he was determined to take Washington. Pope, thinking that the Capital was in real danger, and, being a soldier ready to fight, not only held Lee's army back, but, in two or three days, with blow for blow, repulsed it, with serious and heavy losses. But he was so heavily outnumbered that he had to fall back on the defenses at Washington, as conservatism predicted and desired.

Before doing so, Pope called on Halleck, whom he knew and till then trusted, for the help and re-enforcement he had been promised. Halleck stormed in and about the War Department, and wrote fierce letters to McClellan, Franklin, and others, until it really looked as though a desperate effort was made to support and re-enforce Pope. But the conservative division and corps leaders who had fought and marched and stood the shot and shell and heard every sound afar off, from the Chickahominy to Malvern and half-way down James River, could not hear the thunder of twenty batteries of mixed artillery five miles away, at the second Bull Run. One of them could not read a plain order of Pope's, who was in command, and obey it, until the next day. All this and multiplied insubordination, with no effective support given, as evidenced in piles of orders, letters, records, and testimony, establish the truth that the Achilleses and Ajaxes of conservatism "sulked in their tents," on the roads, in camps, and in hearing of hostile guns. · It was all done that General Pope might be smothered for his presumption in fighting Lee's army with all the men he could gather, as duty led him. As settling this, McClellan wrote, on August 29th, at 3 P. M., when Pope was sorely pressed and falling back for want of one division, or even as much as a fresh brigade: "I am clear that one of two courses should be adopted: first, to concentrate all our available forces to open communication with Pope; second, to leave Pope to get out of his scrape and at once use all our means to make the Capital perfectly safe.".

Two corps leisurely joined Pope the day after his defeat. "Washington was safe;" indeed, it had not been in any real danger. Pope's campaign and defeat were of real benefit to the country, as he bore his sacrifice like a soldier, and returned to the West again in faithful service. Although he was defeated at Bull Run, he and the brave men who fought with him inflicted such severe losses on Lee's army that the army of the Potomac, under McClellan, got the full benefit of this sacrifice, and defeated Lee at Antietam all the more easily on the following 17th of September, only three weeks later. Besides this, the useless retreat from James River, that brought only delay and more waste and campaigning, till the same fighting contest had to be renewed; the maneuvering about the disobedience and the desertion of Pope, all revealed McClellan, the last of the conservative commanders of our armies, to the President and the country as nothing else could have done.

It is an unpleasant task to place these great army leaders, who were not all made up of defects, where they should be; but the truth is, and should be told, that the three, with opportunities that could not have been improved, all failed in the terrible crisis when the Nation was in its death-grapple with slavery. No one of them seemed to realize and understand that the time was come when God would destroy one or the other. They were in the stupor of conservatism, the fatalism of social, economical, moral, religious, and political affairs, that never moved an inch forward for human rights since the world began. It is no exaggeration to say that this fatal conservatism in the war for the Union cost thousands on thousands of brave men's lives and countless treasure, for which, in the nature of things, there can be no restitution or apology. These are gone, and we can only revere the memory of those whose sacrifice brought the Nation to its knees in repentance.

It was nothing to these conservatives and their apologists that so many died or suffered, or would suffer; the sounding braggadocio ran and the more impudent and impertinent in detail it was written, the better; for instance, when they loudly asserted "that there never were such generals as theirs, such organizers, such strategists, such masters of military science, engineering, and equipment, as these heroes of the backward and paralleling retreats or scientific movements." They said "none had organized, and none could organize, brigade, divide, and maneuver such splendid armies, the like of which had never been seen, such that can not be equaled, and that they and their generals had saved every other army and command from disaster and defeat, as no other discipline or organization ever had done or ever would do." Then, too, they could easily prove by the Confederates that all they said of their great generals was true; that they were the greatest and most capable military leaders living, except Lee, Jo Johnston, Longstreet, and Stonewall Jackson. Further, they could prove and establish it as well by the small Counts of Orleans and Paris, and Lord John Russell, the Dukes of Dublin, and another splinter of aristocracy that wanted to be a duke and have Wellington's fame in succession as well as his place at the head of the British army. Besides these there were numerous counts and lords all over Europe who would indorse everything done for the men and the cause of the

Confederacy, to the piratical crews of the vessels built and shipped from the Mersey at Liverpool.

The European estimates and opinions ran about like this, taken from the London *Times:* "The raw American levies are in the field. There can be no doubt that the Northern States, relying on such forces, are destined to certain and inevitable defeat. Their only show of respectable resistance was under the command of a tactician, engineer, and organizer, such as McClellan was proving himself, who, while reaping victory such as they had, has been relieved. In all the fray which the Americans are enthusiastic enough to call war, Lee and Jackson are the only ones who have risen to the mediocrity of leaders of their pioneer mobs that are armies by sufferance."

In this situation, with two strong Confederate armies casting their eyes into and coveting the "flesh-pots" of Pennsylvania and Ohio and Indiana, and only one of our principal armies commanded by a competent fighting soldier, the land was in sore peril; and the load of the President, his anxiety, responsibility, and sympathy for those who could only hope and weep was all that his melancholy spirit could bear. His only relief came in the willing sacrifice of lives sacredly given for liberty. In hope and anguish the Christian people of the land indorsed his course as the safe and prudent one against the false, unfriendly, and severe censure of our military conservatives and their sustainers.

In the settling gloom of those September campaigns we were, through faith like Abraham's, on the true road to victory and a purified Nation. We were in progress, developing leaders who were trained among their men on rugged roads and smoking fields, and bringing them to the front, like Grant, Thomas, Rosecrans, Sheridan, Meade, Warren, Sickles, Sykes, Hancock, Sherman, Logan, Lyon, and Blair—patriots seasoned in the strife, who led our volunteers, making such valiant and puissant legions as the world had not before seen. These, in due time, struck the rebellion to death in synchronous pounding, rising in the cause of freedom. They ratified Lincoln's emancipation policy, and re-established the half-broken Nation by hammering blows that rattled through shaking kingdoms up and down the earth.

Here we must close with some mention of the one great act of the President's life and the passing of the crisis—the emancipation of a race—what there is of the master and this master-stroke of war. The real story is best told as it is known to me through my conferences with Owen Lovejoy, a true man and great leader in the cause of freedom. Mr. Lovejoy was one of the most earnest, sincere, and commanding speakers or leaders ever heard in Congress. He was strong and stalwart of body and limb, never timid or lacking the courage and integrity that faced any danger. He was withal so entertaining in his reasoning, so trained a gentleman, that he drew men of all parties in heartfelt sympathy to the support of our cause in candid and deep emotional pleadings that few men were equal to and none surpassed. His powerful eloquence and the absorbing interest his addresses created may be better understood by knowing that he often spoke out of doors for two hours to twenty thousand people, who remained intent to the outer rim until his last words were spoken. He was no less earnest and engaging in conversation. I am pleased, indeed, to be able to preserve the spirit and enough of his and the President's expressions, hoping to tell the story that it may interest the reader as one of the most important in the reaching and passing of the crisis of the century. This story always fascinated and held in deep attention all who heard Mr. Lovejoy's relation of it. In substance he said:

"In the somber days of 1862, sullen fate seemed leading us the wrong way at a rapid stride. I was not in despair, as many were; for I trusted in our volunteer armies, and believed that, in time, of themselves, they would shake off the slavery incubus, its sympathizers, the blockheads, and blunderers who were leading them; for they were not as well led as they could lead themselves. McClellan was leaving the peninsula, which, if he had good reasons for taking, it was unaccountable why he should abandon it.

"Lee, who was apprised of our movements in advance, took advantage of this blunder, and was ahead of him to Manassas, about thirty miles from Washington. Here he was unexpectedly checked, not by McClellan, but by the hastily-gathered troops under General Pope, who, for lack of support, and with overwhelming forces against him, was stubbornly yielding and falling back on Washington. He did not do this, however, until he had won the equivalent of a victory, unrecognized as it has been. In movement and strategy, as well as in battle, he was able to cope with Lee and hold him back until McClellan had time for his slow concentration and movement in Lee's rear. He moved, it is true, but so slowly as to give support to the jealous leaders who, in their country's humiliation, enjoyed Pope's retreat and discomfiture above all else; that, too, when it seemed less blamable than their retreat from before Richmond.

"Grant and Rosecrans were holding their own and fighting their way, even gaining a little, down the Mississippi. This was consolation and a light in the dark, in the drift of wrecked and half-paralyzed leaders. An example requiring no further illustration of what soldiers in earnest could do was boldly shown by these generals and their armies. The news from this quarter was about all there was of that kind; for the ugly rumors were confirmed that Buell was retreating to the Ohio River in a race with Bragg, with Louisville as their objective point, and that another Confederate force was, in like manner, hovering near and threatening Cincinnati.

"In this sore trouble, when half-hearted men, as well as cowards, were wilting and withering like Jonah's gourds; when honest, patriotic men were anxiously looking into each other's serious faces every day all over the land, with the blunt eloquence of 'What shall we do?' I, with several of the faithful of our Abolition section, was in perplexity, not as to what we thought should be done, but whether the time had come for us to declare ourselves for soldier leaders like Grant and Rosecrans, and that slavery, the whole cause of the war, must be stricken to death. I was in this quandary, full of thought for the most grievously tried man of all, when a request was handed to me, 'that I would call on the President that evening.' Somehow, without another word, my doubts about him were dissipated at once. Anyway there was the place to reason for a decided change in most of what we were doing. The President, in kindness, called me, and I felt at once that I was facing one of the most trying duties I had ever confronted. I had never faltered in the support of the President, but I was in real fear that he was dallying with fatal delay, and that my road was plain, even to an open difference with friend and leader.

"I was prompt in going. At the President's door I met Thaddeus Stevens. He looked anxious and careworn. Grasping my hand warmly, he said: 'I am glad to see you here. The President needs your support and your strongest encouragement. He is in such deep melancholy that, in his high purpose to do his duty and bring hope and as little of his grief as possible to others, he scarcely conceals his own. Be kind, and remain, as needs be. No one could better come. You know how to be firm, but learn better how to help this burdened man.' I asked Mr. Stevens to return with me, but he replied, as he passed, quickly and emphatically: 'No. It is a time when you must talk to him alone.'

"The President received me in his cordial, warm-hearted

way, so common to all who came, but I saw at once an unusual earnestness of expression. The lines were deeper drawn in his careworn face that was always a study and always thoughtful. He said: 'I see you often and have no reason to complain of your lack of interest in what comes to you as your duty, or to me as a public servant, or to the friendship that has never been strained; but I am now, as I believe you are, and as thousands of anxious watchers are, in thought, looking for some forecast that will light up the way to a better knowledge of what is left us to do and the strength that God alone can give us to do it. There is no one in Congress whom I have talked with more freely and without ceremony. Let us have an old, homelike talk, and go over these balky-looking jobs that have turned things the wrong way on our side. I have a hesitancy and perplexity beyond the telling how to rebuke or question soldiers, justly at fault, who are offering, and many of them giving, their lives for our country. I am sincere in saying that I should take the field and stand or fall with the men who are doing so much more than I am. If with them, it would seem reasonable that I should say who shall and who shall not lead our brave men, and more of how they should do it. So far I have been persuaded that it would be something of weakness to our cause; but I assure you that, long before our cause seems hopeless, I shall take the field, that, when I do, you can go along if you desire.'

"To this I replied at once: 'Mr. President, it will not do to think of your doing such a thing in the present condition of public affairs. Our armies would receive you with devotion and rejoicing at once, and, as far as the best and bravest can go, they would be invincible and resistless with you as their leader; but the other side, too, would be stimulated to unexpected resistance. Thousands of our people at home, however, would at once accept it as proof of the Nation's weakness, without cause, as we know. But with this and whatever effect could be produced by our enemies here and abroad, your heroic act would be used and traduced by your enemies, and magnified beyond reason or expectation. I feel, though, that, if our emergencies become desperate enough, that you should do as you say. When it does—which I pray God to avert—I will go with you, whithersoever your interest and duty call, and I can promise you that there are more than a hundred resolute, fearless men, in and about the House of Representatives, who will go out in defense of our country any day, as General Logan did at the first Bull Run, with guns in their hands, or as you send them.

" 'I feel that I have a right to say this; for when our first troops were mustering at Springfield, I went there and remained some weeks. I did all I could in the work of organizing, and offered to go in any capacity I might be selected to fill. Several companies agreed to unite in making me a Colonel, but the current of opinion soon turned against me when my friends and yours decided it would not do. They talked to Governor Yates about it. He agreed with them, telling me that my highest duty was here in Congress, to do all I could, as experience had taught me, for our volunteers and the hard work of sustaining you through the crisis; in effect, he would not agree to my appointment except in a great emergency. It seems to me, however, that other vital things that are uppermost in your mind, as they are in mine, are upon us, and are the turning events that make them the crisis in the Nation's life or death.'

"The President, aroused, walked across the room several times in deep and profound study as we discoursed. The evening was close. We went to a large window, where we sat and talked some time, perhaps half an hour. I was waiting his pleasure, knowing I had said enough, and would have retired with no more, if he had seemed inclined. He fully understood me; for no man ever had keener insight or perceptions. I thought just then that a day or two longer would be better for us both, giving time for reflection; but, looking up, I saw that his face had brightened, and by his manner that he was going to discuss the vital issues, as I then believed them to be. I there resolved that, to the best of my powers, I would help relieve him of the great load that he was making too much his own. In a soft, easy voice, mingled with feeling too pathetic for any description, he proceeded, revealing his thoughts, his anxiety, and the heavy burden that was weighing this great, strong man to the earth.

"He continued about like this: 'You are representing the counties that make up my home and my home people as much as, perhaps more, than any one in the State, with the addition of Sangamon. In these counties and among their people are the strongest and most steadfast people of my life, who have never failed me, who seldom ask anything in recognition, who have never done so when they thought it would in the least embarrass me. You have been faithful with them, and deserve, with them, more than I will ever have to give. You have sustained me without complaint when you were far ahead in respect to the proper management of slavery. I am referring now to the period since the war began. I know how you stand, and, as we have talked freely before, I want you to do so now as my friend. Tell me how you would proceed in my place, with due respect for the thousands of loyal people who differ with you. I have given it thought and concern, the best I could, for many weeks, long before the present situation confronted us.'

"Saying this, he handed me Mr. Greeley's protest. I said: 'Mr. President, as you are aware, I have had differences with you, which I have never hesitated to tell you of and give my reasons for them. I have been pleased that you have always considered them as frankly as I have stated them. I am glad that I am with you to-night, that you have asked me, and that you further desire a free expression on my part. I want to do my very best for you and for the sorely-tried Nation. We fully understand the crisis in all its bearings, and in few words we can reach the vital turning where, I believe, it will be a relief to take it up at once. I am glad that I came and that it came about by your kind invitation. When I received it, I was blaming you and was framing how I would see you and make an open declaration of my objections to your present policy. I came, not as I was intending, but as you kindly desired. I see now that we are not to differ, but that I am to serve and patiently wait with you until you see the right, as I have little doubt you do or soon will. Perhaps even now we stand together, as we should, and as we all must, waiting God's pleasure and the temper of his people as he leads them.

"'I have only to advise now that, in all things, you follow God's warnings as you understand them and as he leads you and his people in what we are pleased to call public sentiment. The unraveling of this tangle is now far beyond what you can do, or all of us. It rests, where you should rest, where I implore you to take it. Lay the great load that hangs so heavy on your shoulders before the Father, and in earnest and sincere submission ask him to lead the way.

"'In the faith of all who have long waited with you, let me inquire, Is not Mr. Greeley right in asking you to promulgate the law known as the Confiscation Act, which you have approved, liberating every slave whose owner is in the rebellion, or who gives it aid and comfort? Again, don't you believe that God is putting us—the great and powerful people that we are, with armies that no other should defeat or overcome—in the grinding humiliation and dust and ashes of defeat, and almost of despair, before half as well-equipped Confederate armies, because we are unfaithful to Him who made us, and are thankless for the bounties

he has given us? You and, through you, all of us are saying, "If I could save the Union without freeing the slaves,
I would do it." As I live and must bear whatever of responsibility may come, I do not believe that God will do it; but
I do believe the contrary, and that he will let this Nation
go to destruction, as he has let hundreds before us for lesser
oppressions of mankind if we do not do it. I as firmly believe, Mr. President, that, if you take this great cause to
the Father in the earnest desire of your willing heart, you
will rise from your knees a free man, armed to strike slavery
to the death in this present opportunity.'

"This was all I could say. I had talked with emotion
in absorbed interest, and was fearing that the President
would feel that my remarks were more of reproof than
the kind interest and advice he needed so much in the crisis;
but his face brightened again, when I saw I was not misunderstood. We were walking the floor then for relaxation
from so much sitting during the full hour I had been with
him, when he resumed: 'Mr. Lovejoy, I am glad you came,
and more pleased that you said what you did in the way
you said it, freely, firmly, and as kindly as such things can
be said. I feel sure now that I understand you, and I credit
you with the friendly, courageous, and unequivocal declaration of your belief. I have been thinking—hesitating a
little, I confess—along the same lines for more than two
months, beginning before McClellan's retreat; but you know
I am only President, and must give every side of this vital
issue a hearing in earnest consideration, then wait, after
my mind is made up, until the time comes to act, especially
so when a change is determined upon.

" 'You are comparatively a free man, representing a district which, to its honor, has acted as one man from the first
mutterings of war. It has sustained you in the same spirit
it has filled its regiments and fought in the cause. You
are here now, fresh from our district, representing men at

home and in their camps, who, with few exceptions, are on one side, while I am the lonesome President of this great people—lonesome because there is much of what is burden-some in such a crisis that I can not share with such friends, nor the home district, until the time comes to act. I am beset and hampered with many hindering concerns for the public good which must be borne in silence. I must hear all sides fairly before I exercise the citizen's right of free speech, to say what I think, or tell what I am going to do.

"'I see the force of Mr. Greeley's demand and your ref-erence to it, that the act best known as the Confiscation Act should be promulgated as law. This brings with it another feature, as to what should be the conduct of the Adminis-tration about slaves and slavery. We have to consider how to deal with the Negroes as slaves and fugitives, and whether to arm them in their own cause and contest for freedom. There is want of uniformity, where the subject in these, as in all its bearings, is deep in my thoughts. I have held back, as every one should know, to preserve the cordial co-opera-tion of the border States that have so honestly and loyally stood with us, and which will continue to do so, as I believe. I have had an earnest hope that some acceptable form of emancipation, with compensation for loyal slaveholders and confiscation for the disloyal ones, as the law stands, could be reached; but its progress has not fulfilled our hopes.

"'In all of it, if the Administration or myself—for which I assume the greater responsibility—has made a mistake about slavery, it has not been from negligence or avoidable delay. On the contrary, it has been uppermost in my mind. I know you do not desire me to say more now than this. But I do want to assure you that it will be settled, so far as I can determine and take it, in the course and judgment upon it that you say is righteous and just—that it is God's conflict; that, as he gives us light, so it shall be. Come to see me as the strife goes on. All you have to say shall be welcome and duly considered. Please talk with Mr. Stevens. I enjoyed his visit—hardly like yours; for yours brings so much of home with it to go over and consider.'

"In prayer, at parting, we laid our cause before God, who made and built the Nation, whom we have trusted so long. I did not know what to expect in every item or movement, but my faith was strengthened, and I knew that Abraham Lincoln was rising, constant and equal to the crisis.

"In a few days after this, our army was gathering in and about Frederick, Maryland, forty miles northwest of Washington City. Lee had crossed the Potomac a few miles below Harper's Ferry. The Union and Confederate armies lay confronting each other, not more than a dozen miles apart, in daily preparation and expectancy of battle. The anxiety was deep and strained. War and its horrors were real and predominant to thousands who had only considered them afar off. These were now present, a threatening danger, and were moving their way, not only on Washington, but Baltimore, Philadelphia, even toward New York and other cities full of what they needed and would take with little ceremony when within their reach. Many careless and indifferently loyal people were truly aroused and alarmed. Although many lagged and others sympathized, none of them wanted to feed so hungry and needy a crowd as Lee's army on the terms they offered for provisions and other supplies and plunder, nor to contribute their money and other light movables to men whose authority to 'raise moneys and revenues' was the open end of an ugly-looking gun in the hands of a Confederate tax-gatherer, custom-purveyor, and exciseman, as well as slave-driver, all in one.

"In time, with these wicked hosts of Confederates, killing the people and reaping their harvest of destruction in the heart of the free States, and further threatening the great cities of trade and traffic, it became as clear as the sun at noonday that slavery was the underlying and moving cause of the war. Lee's and Bragg's armies were heading for the fat lands and the rich spoils of the nearest to hand—of friend, foe, or sympathizer—that the black man might remain a slave and the white man's wages be kept down within 'Constitutional limits.'

"A Pennsylvania farmer said of these invasions: 'This thing of slavery is coming home to the people, and it does n't pay. It is getting worse every day. It was deep enough in our pockets before, but now these fellows on the other side are coming in hungry swarms to take what we have left.' This opening of men's minds through their pockets came so fast that the statesmen and common people who had been surfeited with the cry, 'This is not a war to free the niggers,' in March and April were turning to be Abolitionists, a hundred thousand a day, in September. They saw, in war at their doors, in lost lives, burning cities, and the stern logic of disaster, a clearer light, and they said openly: 'We are as ready now to abolish slavery, while we are about it, and settle the whole of it at once, as we will ever be.' The President had to wait for this ripening of the conscience of the people against slavery; for no leader, President or reformer, can safely go ahead of them without danger or the loss of his cause.

"I kept up my visits to the President, more frequently than usual, not to be obtrusive, but to show my interest when I knew that he was in such sore perplexity. I felt that he was right in what he was doing. I did not want to bother him, but to conduct myself in a way to make him feel that he was constantly in our minds and that he was among friends.

"The day came when the battle was more imminent, when it had begun, as later news informed us. All were in great anxiety and stress of mind, and the greater number were in sore doubt, or predicting defeat. Many were even in alarm, giving way to rumors. Bad as it seemed on our side, a number of us began talking strongly the other way to check the rebel rumor of a 'Union stampede,' which some of Lee's sympathizers were anxious to get started. I went over to the President's, to see how things were going there. He was engaged, but soon found an excuse to retire. When we were alone, I saw that a great change had been wrought. He was comparatively at his ease. His face and features, distinctly, in smoothed-out lines and cheerful manner, disclosed a new-born hope. He was alive again, and, as he grasped my hand firmly, I felt that the faith of God was in the man, and that his soul was full of it. He stood before me, calm, resolute, and determined—the Lincoln of other and brighter days. He said: "I am glad you have dropped in. I wanted to see you just a few minutes out of the rush about us. But things are going all right; we are going to win a victory.'

"The President then led the way to his quiet office. I could not help remarking: 'I saw before we retired that you are relieved and a new man. I have been talking on the side of victory, too, with a few who are standing out against our weaker brethren, some of whom are full of surmises of a victory for Lee—those who are always reminding us of his superior military abilities, and are blurting out their forebodings of disaster to our armies. I will be all the better pleased to hear the good news that so animates and assures you of victory.'

"The President replied: 'I have no news from the front more than you have. The War Department has given out all the dispatches to the public. It is not that to which I referred. God is going to give us a victory, perhaps not a very decisive one, but it will be considerable enough to be a distinct defeat of Lee's army. You seem surprised—only interested, you say, and that you do not doubt my faith, and that you have faith, too. Well, this is encouraging, and cheers me on the way. I took the whole subject and laid it before God in three days' and nights' faithful, incessant prayer. I wrestled with him, talking with him, and pleading, as only a believing, earnest man can plead.

" 'I told him this was his country, that it was great because of his bounteous provisions for all there is in life, subsistence, and his unremitting blessings to us; that it stands to-day the hope of mankind to all the earth, the only great Nation that has the principles in force and the strength and virtue that can prevail against the foes of human liberty. I told him that we were doing all we could, or that those of us in control believed we were; that I felt weaker before him than a broken reed; that if I had erred or made serious mistake, it was from the want of more exact and better knowledge how to serve my country and my fellow-men. I told him that I believed the days of miracles had passed, but that, in my relation to our people and Government, I desired to understand his purposes and will; that I was sorely perplexed to know whether the time had come to destroy slavery and accomplish his will, without which our acts would be as nothing.

" 'All this I laid before our Maker in faith and sincerity and in repentance that was as sincere. I made this covenant with God that, if he would give us the victory in the pending battle, I would make the black men free. I said further, our people were giving their substance and their lives with such devotion and courage that every obstacle to the restoration of peace and the reunion of free people should be removed. When I arose, I was as you see me. Slavery shall be stricken, as I promised him long years ago. He is now in his wrath. I know that he will give us the victory. No event that has passed could be more certain in my mind; but this is only the change. We are to push forward with renewed zeal to greater and final victories, to work and sacrifice that will accomplish all that is possible for the rights of our fellow-men. This has come to me, my friend, almost in your presence. You have truly shared this consolation with me, and felt as much of it as any one. I am satisfied, and a strange feeling comes over me, that, when this job is done, speaking plainly, when peace is restored, my work will be finished.'

"I had long been in the work, and had something of his faith. I said: 'Mr. President, God has wrought a great work. You have had an astonishing vision. You have walked with God, and are his prophet. He is in his wrath, I doubt not, as you feel. We have reached the higher ground where the conflict will rage more desperately and deadly. We must gird ourselves anew, accept the faith, and follow at any sacrifice, go out among his people, stand with them, convince them of their right, and do battle for his cause of human liberty to the end.'

"I watched, as so many did, and saw the great leader often, keeping so close to the wires that there was never an hour that we did not have news from the field of Antietam and our army, until Lee and his defeated army were driven across the Potomac into Virginia. It all came to pass as the President had seen. It was not a great victory, nevertheless it was one, foreshadowing what we could do and expect when cleansed of slavery under God's favor and Lincoln's untrammeled leadership. I had followed in faith, and, although so near him in his great trial and exaltation, I did not know in detail what he would do; but I did know that slavery was doomed. On the next day, promptly, in fulfillment of his high covenant with God, he issued his proclamation of freedom. The Emancipation Act, the charter of the black man's freedom, was thus made law.

"Some faint-hearted thought this work of righteousness set us back; but I have never believed it. On the contrary, I believe it would have been a hundred times worse for us if it had not been done."

CHAPTER LVI.

WHEN President Lincoln issued the great proclamation of freedom, September 22, 1862, to be effective the first day of January following, he had reached, was passing, and finally passed the crisis of the great struggle, the turning event of his distinct career as reformer and President. This was by far the most momentous and far-reaching act of the nineteenth century. By it the strings and chords of slavery and sympathizing evil were cut loose, and the freedom of man as a true and Divine principle spread far and wide over the earth. It cut the bindings that hampered and tied up thousands of our people. It lifted the load of the slave's unpaid labor in competition from all who toiled. It did drive, perhaps, a few more into active sympathy with the Rebellion; but brought few, if any, to them who were brave enough to join their armies because of it.

The business of searching for and apprehending fugitives or "runaway niggers" in military camps, and delivering them to their masters, and the forays of Negro pursuers, hounds and men, in the free States passed like Sennacherib's legions in the breath of the Lord. This warrant of a Nation's freedom spread over mountain, hill, and valley and tented field, from the Potomac to the Suwanee, and Missouri's Meramec to Ponchartrain, swelling in a grand chorus the joy of another people, who had crossed another Red Sea to liberty.

The constitutionalism and conservatism of slavery at the head of our armies got their staggering blow. Later they fell away completely when Grant crossed the Rapidan, and were sorted and packed in limbo, as relics, with the old flint-locks of the Revolution.

The fall elections of 1862 were the only evidence ever offered, that the proclamation was a mistake. This was more imaginary than real. They proved to be no more than opinions, for the next election, closely following, reversed these, and set aside all our enemies had asserted, as well as the fears of faint-hearted loyalists, proving nothing, as elections frequently do. Several free States gave majorities against the Administration, it is true; but it was no benefit whatever to the slaveholders' Rebellion.

Of these State elections, it should be remembered of the million volunteers or more, soldiers and sailors then in service, few of them voted. Our armies were stronger then in our cause than they had ever been. They were in better condition than ever to express themselves concerning slavery, when with opportunity they would have cheerfully voted for and supported the President as they did generally in 1864, when the laws were changed permitting them to vote. Another distinct result was that as trifling with slavery was over with, our campaigns were more vigorously conducted with more of determined spirit and purpose in all our movements afterwards.

From all that could be seen and gathered at the time, those unfriendly State elections would have been more seriously against us if the proclamation had not been issued by reason of the loss of interest of all anti-slavery people. It came in God's own time, when in his wrath he would tolerate the sin and oppression no longer. The time had come in the progress of the war, that whether we met the dead drag of an unfriendly election or conservative paralysis at the head of our armies, we had come to believe them temporary and passing obstacles, to which we paid no attention and marched on.

In the shortest possible time the strongest proof of the President's wisdom and management was the great change and rise of the Negro people. They were so stoutly active for their freedom, and so earnest about it, that no one could be mistaken. All they asked was the opportunity to get into the ranks, fight for it, die for it, and help to win it. The news that President Lincoln "Had done issued de procla- mashun dat freed de brack men" spread over the land, as we have said, to our front and through the lines to the remotest corner of the Confederacy in a few days. It spread in the way that all believed it. It was carried day and night, from man to man in swift and solemn trust, until the toilers caught it in the canebrakes and cottonfields. "In de brilin' sun, 'long on de Gulf ob Mexico an' to de las' point ob de Eber- glades ob Floridee, all heard it an' shouted, 'Glory to de good Lawd dat 's hearn us!' " They got down on their knees in their cabins and in their fields, openly or secretly wherever they could, and as they could but sincerely do everywhere, "thankin' de good Lawd agen fer dis gret blessin' ob free- dum an' prayin' him to bress an' tek keer ob, de very bes' you kin, de great Mas'r Linkum."

They believed in the President, and followed him as faith- fully as, or better than, Israel followed Moses. They had faith, and lived for freedom. By thousands they served, fought, and died for it, in the strength that neither sophistry, deception, persecution, nor death could shake. Soon they were turned, rising up a new and invigorated people. They were seeking labor for wages, as the means of bettered life and living, like their fellow-men of so many colors and dif- ferent kinds of hair.

· Very soon some of them began picking up a gun here and there, and were helping in the scouting, the skirmish, and battle wherever they were let do it. Some companies were organized, and the recruiting of colored American soldiers began. These served and fought well, and the idea of enlist- ing colored troops grew and strengthened. Our soldiers took it up, and agreed that a black man might as well take a gun and fight for his freedom on our side, as to build forts, move army trains, or toil for an army in camp, or dig in the field for its subsistence, only to be a slave on the other side.

The companies grew into regiments, brigades, and divisions. These stood in the front ranks where every skirmish and battle took them. They fulfilled their promise, and fought side by side with us, as they are doing to this day, like men who have earned and are worthy the freedom that came in the low tide of 1862. This direct and straightforward striking the scourge, as the plain and unmistakable cause of the war and all its spreading evils, gave us the unchecked sympathy and prayerful help of the friends of freedom everywhere.

Our friends of liberty in Britain, much to their credit, took up our cause by the hundreds of thousands, that too, where the shortage of cotton because of our war was shutting down hundreds of mills, thereby throwing thousands of our best friends out of employment; often into distress. Still the sturdy yeomanry loved freedom more, and in the practice of more economical living with increased energy in other directions, they stood with us to the end, in word and deed, that should be remembered by the friends of liberty for all time. Many of these mill people of Britain and Ireland came over, where they enlisted with us in the thickest of the strife, as the Germans did in great numbers. In a few weeks afterwards these were transformed into American soldiers, and they and theirs, who left all they had to come over and help us, are with us to-day. These English, Irish, and Scotch common people were so much minded like ourselves, that when they had opportunity they took to Mr. Beecher's great campaign through Britain as our brethren, and in unnumbered thousands day and night for months, with Beecher, John Bright, and human liberty, made one of the greatest and most effective campaigns for the rights of men ever made in any cause or country.

While these better and more noble-minded were truly and honestly on our side, steadfast and faithful in the darkest swing of the storm, the Administrations of Palmerston, Russell, and Gladstone and their associated tyrants of the sea, with the consort of every intriguing court of Europe, from London, Paris, and Vienna, to Mount Carlo, Russia alone excepted, were our clandestine and fast-responding enemies. In England, in the face of its free and friendly people, and as much against its more honorable Queen and her noble-hearted husband, these freedom-hating ministries kept their shipyards open, working day and night to build Confederate vessels for privateering enterprises.

When our Covenant of Freedom was openly proclaimed, it did not enlarge the area or give more strength to the insurrection and its slave-spreading conspiracy; but it did bring those in it face to face with collapse and surrender, or the most stubborn defense of their uncaptured territory. Their armies being brave and trained Americans, there remained no doubt of the desperate conflict ahead. Their conspiring leaders, more unhesitatingly than ever, plunged them deeper in the dreadful progress of carnage that was furrowing the earth with trenches for miles, to bury the heaps of heroes slain.

Little, if anything, was added to the roster of the Confederate armies; but the men in them, first of all, realized that the clogs were all off on the Union side, and that "the chute to the mill-race was wide open," against them henceforward. It was to be a conflict to the death. Before this direful foreboding the seven hundred thousand brave Southern American soldiers buckled their armor more firmly on, and held their guns with stronger grip, knowing well it pointed to the only hope of victory, or to a line of Confederate graves. These brave Southern men fought four long years for their Southern empire, where no nation of Europe could have maintained such a conflict half so long, without

the help and direct intervention of one or more of them on
the field, or the opening of their maritime ports, as Britain
had promised to do for the South. This would have been
done but for the great uprising of the common people of
Britain in our favor. These Southern soldiers passed through
this terrible war with a courage that never failed, with so
much of valor and heroic sacrifice. They fought for their
cause with so much of honor and credit to the American
character, that the few bad examples should be forgiven
for the general good. The lives and health of half a
million Southern soldiers, ninety-eight per cent of whom were
so poor as never to have been able to own a slave, were
one of the last, but very costly, items of payment for the
extinction of slavery. It was a bad system that differed little
from other bad ones left, one that took poor men's lives by
the million to make a few greedy men rich.

When President Lincoln struck slavery its mortal blow,
the armies of the Union sustained him, generally in hearty
response and approval. In Grant's army of the Tennessee
it was received and agreed to in the ordinary way without
comment against it. It had worked up to the conclusion that
slavery was doomed to certain destruction, and its members
conducted themselves accordingly. General Grant and Com-
modore Foote let this idea develop without interference, so
that when freedom was proclaimed, there was nothing to reverse. They had not permitted slave-hunting in their commands. On the contrary, they employed slaves, colored people, by thousands in laborious operations on the rivers, fleets,
camps, and fortifications. These they protected, and surrendered none who were searched for as fugitives; hence what
was a great change some places, was a development of their
policy. This was soon followed by Negro enlistments up and
down the big river.

In Buell's army of the Cumberland it was received and
approved with more or less rejoicing, because the men be-

lieved it was right; further, the removal of Buell appeared
more certain. By this time he was so generally disliked by
the entire army, that his usefulness, whatever it might have
been, had certainly passed. He had been given command to
begin with, not by reason of brave or gallant service, but
because he was selected by and represented the frosted conservatism at the head of the army. Although so favored,
through jealousy or envy on the part of one or both, Buell
had a serious difference with Halleck at the time, when both
were twisted out of joint by the proclamation. Halleck, in
the merciless spirit of envious men and fossilized in lazy
methods of war, could dispute and hate better than agree and
fight the enemy. Hence in his worst distress he deserted
Buell, and helped in his removal, finally his retirement, where
he became one of the soured victims of the slave-worshipers
he had served so long. He had issued slave-hunting orders
like Halleck; but fugitive searching in his army was seldom
tolerated; so Halleck's and Buell's orders burned themselves
out, and went to the Rebellion record of relics, with all that
was left of the slave-catching business, when the "uniformity"
President Lincoln desired was substituted in the conduct of
the war, and suddenly obeyed.

In the army of the Potomac the proclamation was respected and sustained, as all orders of the President were,
willingly or not by its "great soldiers and organizers" at the
very top of it; but this was feeble and formal alongside the
hearty welcome and indorsement it received from the war-
worn and over-tramped veterans, who said, "God bless you,
President Lincoln; and God bless you freedmen; come and
join us, and help win your freedom." Soon afterwards colored brigades filled out the lines, and the lights and shadows
of that mighty, fighting army, their valor and achievements,
are beyond the telling. This was about the first of our armies
to come under the chilling influences of slavery conservatism;
about the last to be entirely relieved of it. But the relief

came when General Grant rose to the certain leadership of a soldier that President Lincoln had reached his statesmanship and the broad strategy of war.

In the fall of 1862 I had a talk with Governor Yates, in which he spoke of a friendly interview he had recently had with President Lincoln about the war, and among other things about what he thought of General Pope's campaign in Virginia. Both of them were friends of Pope, who was an Illinois man. The President regretted Pope's discomfiture all the more because he had selected him and given him command with the hearty indorsement of the governor. He said: "However, General Pope gave us good and valiant service. He hit Lee a terrible blow with half as many men, where twice as many were ready to help. The slow maneuvering that balked us at the top was our chief obstacle, for our soldiers, God bless them! never falter, whether they march and fight with the commander that suits them, or with one whom they could better lead themselves. The soldier who is to lead this strong army of heroic men, with its splendid organization and almost perfect equipment, must rise in it and have the full confidence and cordial support of all its parts; or he must rise to undisputed leadership in some other of our armies, where of himself he can inspire the confidence that leads to victory. My eyes are open for the coming man; but if no better appears in time and the emergency exists, I will go myself and lead."

By his great act of emancipating four million slaves, President Lincoln rose to the broad and wise statesmanship that saved our Nation in its territory and integrity at home, as well in the wider grasp of the world's affairs. It brought us the valuable help of our friends in Britain and elsewhere, against the clandestine war of two or more hostile British administrations, and the smaller plottings and the invasion of Mexico by Europe's sneaking wizard of destruction. Henceforward the issues were made up and declared, to our content and ιο that of mankind. It was no longer to be a war for a slave empire on the one side, and a patched-out slave Republic on the other. The armies of the Union were stripped clean of their conservative hinderments, and marched forward in the greater campaigns of the conflict.

President Lincoln had reached high leadership in as wise statesmanship among the people and our armies ere this. Afterwards it became an undisputed control, grounded on his own and the righteous judgment of our people. He knew and understood that he was master-man and leader, as God made him, and that in his wisdom and conduct the issues of the great conflict depended. He was not in this presumptive, never obtrusive, and never assumed or appeared as dictator. He was always considerate, mild, and yielding to the point where he could yield no more; but in principles and choice of men to lead, when he had reached his determination, he was resolute, firm, and solid as the serf-beaten rock.

Here we rest. Here he stood before all men, as he did with and among the great leaders and statesmen of his Administration and his time, to whom he announced his forthcoming proclamation of freedom as follows: "When the rebel army was at Frederick, I determined, as soon as it should be driven out of Maryland, to issue a proclamation such as I thought most likely to be useful. I said nothing to any one; but I made the promise to myself—and to my Maker. The rebel army is now driven out, and I am going to fulfill that promise. I have got you together to hear what I have written down. I do not wish your advice about the main matter, for that I have determined for myself. This I say without intending anything but respect for any one of you."

He was great and strong, and prevailed. He knew his gifts well. He prepared himself in every way open to his advancement, and forged ahead with the honest zeal of a reformer. He surmounted every obstacle, laid aside every minor and selfish consideration, every temporary or seeming

advantage, that he might the more certainly strike the underlying evil and carry on his work against it with all his
strength. He was so profoundly and devoutly impressed with
his duty, so faithful and persevering in it, and waited so
patiently his declared interpretation and its exact fulfillment, that these proved him to be no less than God's prophet.

He was unswayed by disappointment, defeat, or seeming disaster. He was on the unpopular side, and the under
one, for more than twenty-five years, and was usually defeated with his party. But he took his defeat complacently,
without murmur or a word about being neglected. In God's
time he came to leadership, when he rose steadily in work
that proved him the best friend of men for more than
eighteen centuries. He carried our Nation through the greatest conflict of modern times, sealing it a victory forever,
in his complete triumph over every contention, his patriotic
service, his sacrifice, his exaltation and return to his Maker
when the great labor of his life was done.

Most of the world's great reformers have wrought out
their work through similar conflicts. Christ said, "I came
not to send peace, but a sword." (Matt. x, 34.) By this
he did not mean to declare that his gospel of peace should
be preached, propagated, or carried into the hearts of men
by forcible means; but, knowing well the greedy and murderous spirit of disobedient and despotic men, he knew that
the civil and religious rights of his people would need to
be gained and protected by the strong arm of law and "the
sword."

Luther was protected in his civil rights by the powerful
Elector of Saxony and his allies, a sort of Confederated Germany. In that time, if any one of the German States had
been seriously threatened, all of them would have united,
as they did afterwards against the political aggression of the
popes, the decaying power of Charles V, and his more cruel
son, Philip II. However, Luther endured a long and angry

contest, coming near to war and bloodshed very often, over which he triumphed only by reason of this available power of the sturdy, heroic Germans who so bravely and righteously sustained him.

William of Orange and his brave Netherlanders fought their way to victory against Philip II, the butcher Alva, and the devil, through long years of disaster and death, regardless of losses and the most merciless and bloody despotism ever known in Europe.

Oliver Cromwell hewed out and cut his way against all resistance, in one of the most successful campaigns in the world's progress, with his brave yeomanry of God-fearing men. He overthrew a merciless dynasty. He tried and executed a king who would have expeditiously and heartlessly slain all of them if he had been restored to power. He did this in an era not to be measured by the conditions of to-day, but when, to preserve the limited rights and liberties of the freest and most enlighted people, he could do no better.

Washington and his ragged and barefooted veterans founded this Nation on the well-defined basis of freedom, equality, and popular government—one that before their day had been no more than a dream of mankind.

Lincoln, as devoted a hero as any of these, with the help of millions of co-patriots, took up the mightier work of saving the people's liberties. He, in leadership that stands alone, overthrew the slaveholders' defined limitations of human rights. By the grace of God in repentance and the awakened conscience of the people, he enlarged these to include the black men, who, in the pursuit of life, liberty, and happiness, were made, for all time, equals among the sons of men, bringing them under the benign power of Christ's Golden Rule, "Whatsoever ye would that men should do to you, do even so to them."

President Lincoln encountered force without cause in

beginning his work of saving the Nation. He preferred peace and the amicable settlements of disputes, and to save the Union he would have foregone the amelioration of slavery for the time, to avert civil war. But the conspirators and the enemies of free government everywhere were never more mistaken than when they believed him too weak or timid to use force in his line of duty when he had cause to do so. Although suddenly brought to the use of force, he took up the study of the subject in his usual diligent way, in all its bearings. He persevered until he became the master spirit and strategist in the art of war. When he saw that war was inevitable, actually upon us, he at once set about using the most potent and powerful forces available to keep the Nation from falling to pieces in the onset.

While it is an unexplained mystery, it is still true that our progress, like that of other peoples under great leaders, has always been, and apparently had to be, through struggle and conflict. Either through persevering adventure or war we have reached our high place among nations and our supremacy on the American Continent. Standing as we do to-day, without any hostile rival in the roll of nations, we can not realize the desperate condition our country was in at the time of President Lincoln's inauguration and for a few weeks following. He was so nearly alone in the work of uniting the loyal people that, if he had not succeeded beyond what any other man or leader had done, secession, with its continuing evils, would have been inevitable.

The war went on in campaigns and advancing movements that overcame every obstacle to complete success. It was carried on by leaders and men who had the strength, power, and equipment to win victory at twice its fearful cost, had duty required. They neither faltered nor hesitated, but pressed forward to the waste and bloody sacrifice, all the more brave and determined since they knew they must meet and utterly defeat Americans of our own kind and kindred. It

was a great struggle, as the world measures conflict, won
on fields of carnage that staggered men in wonderment. In
imagination we see our great leaders and our multitudes of
God's heroes on both sides pass before us in grand review.
As they move along the Nation's highway, amid floods of
imperishable light in harmonious fellowship and concord,
there are no conquerors and no slaves, no servants and no
foes. All are equal under the same laws, all bettered alike,
the unshackled slaves, the freed masters, and the free citizens, because the sin that cursed and darkened the whole
land has been purged away and forever obliterated.

President Lincoln was re-elected in 1864; inaugurated
the second time, March 4, 1865. No change in the vigorous policy of conducting the war was made or thought of.
It was continued to the end, in faith and fulfillment, that
the integrity of the Nation and the liberties of the people
should be maintained and strengthened, but never abridged
nor diminished. There was little change in the Cabinet.
The war was in furious progress. Grant was in front of
Richmond, with cannon and belts of artillery, brigades and
divisions of men overlapping in lines of bristling steel, steadily closing down on the fated Rebellion.

In his second Inaugural Address the President closed,
saying: "With malice toward none, with charity for all; with
firmness in the right, as God gives us to see the right,
let us strive on to finish the work we are in; to bind up
the Nation's wounds, to care for him who shall have borne
the battle, and for his widow and his orphan—to do all
which may achieve and cherish a just and a lasting peace
among ourselves and with all nations."

When the work was done, when Lee had surrendered
on April 11th on Grant's generous terms, the great achievement of the prophet-leader was accomplished, and he, too,
passed over, as he predicted. A darker hand than ever shad-
owed the sun on this continent, and a more vicious-tempered

heart than our civilization had produced before this deliberately slew the noble-minded, great-hearted man.

On April 11th, President Lincoln delivered an address counseling harmony and a forgiving spirit in the reconstruction of our war-wasted country.

On Good Friday, April 14, 1865, at eight o'clock P. M., he, with his family and some friends, attended the play of "Our American Cousin" at Ford's Theater in Washington, where he was assassinated by John Wilkes Booth, a player of less than ordinary repute. He shot the President with a pistol, holding it almost against his head. He fell forward unconscious almost at once. He was removed to a dwelling across the street, where he expired, without returning consciousness, the next morning, April 15th, at seven o'clock and twenty-two minutes. Booth was not in or connected with the Confederate cause, which he honored so much by being too cowardly as never to enter the ranks of the rebel army.

President Lincoln thus passed from us in the hour of his triumph, when "his spirit returned to God, who gave it." He left his tribute to the men who saved the Nation and the principles for which they served and died in uncounted thousands, that will endure in the hearts and hopes of mankind as long as they honor themselves.

Address Delivered at the Dedication of the Cemetery at Gettysburg.

Fourscore and seven years ago our fathers brought forth on this continent a new Nation, conceived in liberty and dedicated to the proposition that all men are created equal.

Now we are engaged in a great Civil War, testing whether that Nation, or any nation so conceived and so dedicated, can long endure. We are met on a great battlefield of that war. We have come to dedicate a portion of that field as a final resting-place for those who here gave their lives that that Nation might live. It is altogether fitting and proper that we should do this.

But, in a larger sense, we can not dedicate—we can not consecrate, we can not hallow this ground. The brave men, living and dead, who struggled here have consecrated it far above our poor power to add or detract. The world will little note nor long remember what we say here; but it can never forget what they did here. It is for us, the living, rather, to be dedicated here to the unfinished work which they who fought here have thus far so nobly advanced. It is rather for us to be here dedicated to the great task remaining before us—that from these honored dead we take increased devotion to that cause for which they gave the last full measure of devotion; that we here highly resolve that these dead shall not have died in vain; that this Nation, under God, shall have a new birth of freedom; and that government of the people, by the people, for the people, shall not perish from the earth.

ABRAHAM LINCOLN.

November 19, 1863.

Lightning Source UK Ltd.
Milton Keynes UK
UKHW020304051218
333419UK00008B/414/P